ft

Windows Server 2016
Inside Out

Orin Thomas

Windows Server 2016 Inside Out

Published with the authorization of Microsoft Corporation by:
Pearson Education, Inc.

Copyright © 2017 by Orin Thomas

ISBN-13: 978-1-5093-0248-2
ISBN-10: 1-5093-0248-4

Library of Congress Control Number: 2017937640

1 17

Trademarks

Microsoft and the trademarks listed at https://www.microsoft.com on the "Trademarks" webpage are trademarks of the Microsoft group of companies. All other marks are property of their respective owners.

Warning and Disclaimer

Special Sales

For information about buying this title in bulk quantities, or for special sales opportunities (which may include electronic versions; custom cover designs; and content particular to your business, training goals, marketing focus, or branding interests), please contact our corporate sales department at corpsales@pearsoned.com or (800) 382-3419.

For government sales inquiries, please contact governmentsales@pearsoned.com.

For questions about sales outside the U.S., please contact intlcs@pearson.com.

Editor-in-Chief	Greg Wiegand
Senior Acquisitions Editor	Laura Norman
Development Editor	Troy Mott
Managing Editor	Sandra Schroeder
Senior Project Editor	Tracey Croom
Editorial Production	Backstop Media
Copy Editor	Rachel Jozsa
Indexer	Julie Grady
Proofreader	Christina Rudloff
Technical Editor	Ajay Kakkar
Cover Designer	Twist Creative, Seattle

Contents at a glance

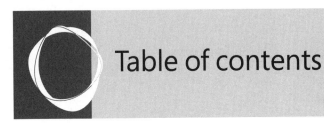

Table of contents

What do you think of this book? We want to hear from you!

Microsoft is interested in hearing your feedback so we can improve our books and learning resources for you. To participate in a brief survey, please visit:

https://aka.ms/tellpress

What do you think of this book? We want to hear from you!

Microsoft is interested in hearing your feedback so we can improve our books and learning resources for you. To participate in a brief survey, please visit:

https://aka.ms/tellpress

Introduction

Windows Server 2016 is more than just another iteration of the Windows Server operating system. Not only does Windows Server 2016 include a raft of new features and an entirely new way of deploying workloads through Windows Server and Hyper-V containers, Windows Server 2016 debuts Nano Server, a scaled down refactored version of Windows Server, which has minimal disk space and RAM requirements.

While Microsoft's focus is firmly on the cloud, the innovations present in Windows Server 2016 demonstrate that the company isn't neglecting customers who wish to maintain on-premises workloads. Not only is Windows Server 2016 able to host traditional on-premises roles including domain controller, DNS server, DHCP server, certificate server, Remote Desktop Server, Web Server, file server and virtualization host, it also functions as a stable and reliable host for workloads including SQL Server, Exchange Server, SharePoint, and the System Center suite.

This book provides you with a comprehensive overview of Windows Server 2016's functionality. You will learn about the current thinking when it comes to how you should deploy and manage Windows Server 2016. You will also learn how to use Server Core in preference to the traditional "full GUI" version, and how to use PowerShell's Just Enough Administration functionality. This is all important to know when maintaining Windows Server 2016, whether you've got it deployed in a server room in your building's basement, at your local datacenter, or as an Infrastructure as a Service VM in the cloud.

Who this book is for

This book is primarily written for IT Professionals who work with Windows Server operating systems on a regular basis. As such, it's likely that Windows Server 2016 isn't the first version of Windows Server that you've been responsible for managing. This is because the majority of Windows Server administrators have been working with some version of the operating system for more than a decade, with a good percentage having experience going back to the days of Windows NT 4. With that in mind, this book doesn't spend a great amount of time on introductory concepts or techniques, and instead aims to provide intermediate to advanced coverage of the most important roles and features available with Windows Server 2016.

This book is also written under the assumption that as an experienced IT Professional, you know how to use a search engine to find relevant technical information. This leads to an obvious question, "why would I buy a book if I can find relevant technical information with a search engine?" The answer is that even though you may be good at tracking down technical information and have experience filtering useful knowledge from wildly inaccurate guesses, you can only search for something if you have an idea about it in the first place.

When presenting at conferences and user groups on Windows Server topics, I regularly encounter IT Professionals who have worked with Windows Server for many years who are unaware of specific functionality or techniques related to the product, even if that functionality or technique has been available for many years. This is because Windows Server 2016 includes so many roles, features and moving parts that you're unlikely to know everything about the operating system. My aim in writing this book is to give you comprehensive coverage so that you'll learn things that you didn't know or simply missed, because when you've been solving a critical problem, you've been focused on the specifics of that problem and haven't had time to exploring every facet of what the Windows Server operating system is capable of.

Book features & conventions

This book uses special text and design conventions to make it easier for you to find the information you need.

Text conventions

- **Abbreviated menu commands.** For your convenience, this book uses abbreviated menu commands. For example, "Click Tools, Track Changes, Highlight Changes" means that you should click the Tools menu, point to Track Changes, and click the Highlight Changes command.

- **Boldface type.** Boldface type is used to indicate text that you enter or type.

- **Initial Capital Letters.** The first letters of the names of menus, dialog boxes, dialog box elements, and commands are capitalized. Example: the Save As dialog box.

- **Italicized type.** Italicized type is used to indicate new terms.

- **Plus sign (+) in text.** Keyboard shortcuts are indicated by a plus sign (+) separating two key names. For example, Ctrl+Alt+Delete means that you press the Ctrl, Alt, and Delete keys at the same time.

Book features

Inside OUT

These are the book's signature tips. In these tips, you'll get the straight scoop on what's going on with the software—inside information about why a feature works the way it does. You'll also find handy workarounds to deal with software problems.

MORE INFO

More Info will often denote a location on the Internet where you can learn more about a specific subject referenced in the text. It will usually be a link to a relevant TechNet article or conference presentation.

➤ Cross-references point you to other locations in the book that offer additional information about the topic being discussed.

Current Book Service

This book is part of our new Current Book Service, which provides content updates for major technology changes and improvements related to Windows Server 2016. As significant updates are made, sections of this book will be updated or new sections will be added to address the changes. The updates will be delivered to you via a free Web Edition of this book, which can be accessed with any Internet connection at *MicrosoftPressStore.com*.

If you've got a suggestion for the next update of the book, email it to the author, Orin Thomas, at *orin.thomas@outlook.com*.

Register this book at *MicrosoftPressStore.com* to receive access to the latest content as an online Web Edition. If you bought this book through *MicrosoftPressStore.com*, you do not need to register; this book and any updates are already in your account.

How to register your book

If you have not registered your book, follow these steps:

1. Go to *www.MicrosoftPressStore.com/register*.

2. Sign in or create a new account.

3. Enter the ISBN found on the copyright page of this book.

4. Answer the questions as proof of purchase.

5. The Web Edition will appear under the Digital Purchases tab on your Account page. Click "Launch" to access your product.

Find out about updates

Sign up for the What's New newsletter at *www.MicrosoftPressStore.com/newsletters* to receive an email alerting you of the changes each time this book's Web Edition has been updated. The email address you use to sign up for the newsletter must be the same email address used for your *MicrosoftPressStore.com* account in order to receive the email alerts. If you choose not to sign up, you can periodically check your account at MicrosoftPressStore.com to find out if updates have been made to the Web Edition.

This book will receive periodic updates to address significant software changes for 12 to 18 months following first publication date. After the update period has ended, no more changes will be made to the book, but the final update to the Web Edition will remain available in your account at *MicrosoftPressStore.com*.

The Web Edition can be used on tablets that use current web browsers. Simply log into your *MicrosoftPressStore.com* account and access the Web Edition from the Digital Purchases tab.

For more information about the Current Book Service, visit www.*MicrosoftPressStore.com/CBS*.

Support & feedback

The following sections provide information on errata, book support, feedback, and contact information.

Errata & support

We've made every effort to ensure the accuracy of this book and its companion content. Any errors that have been reported since this book was published are listed on our Microsoft Press site at:

https://aka.ms/WinServ2016CBS/errata

If you find an error that is not already listed, you can report it to us through the same page.

If you need additional support, email Microsoft Press Book Support at mspinput@microsoft. com.

Please note that product support for Microsoft software is not offered through the addresses above.

We want to hear from you

At Microsoft Press, your satisfaction is our top priority and your feedback our most valuable asset. Please tell us what you think of this book at

https://aka.ms/tellpress

The survey is short, and we read every one of your comments and ideas. Thanks in advance for your input!

Stay in touch

Let's keep the conversation going! We're on Twitter: *http://twitter.com/MicrosoftPress*

Administration Tools

Windows Server 2016 comes with a number of built-in tools that you can use to manage the operating system. Although you can often use multiple tools to perform the same tasks, Microsoft's general systems administration philosophy is that while you can do almost everything with a graphical console such as Active Directory Administrative Center or the Server Manager console, any task that you do repeatedly should be automated using Windows PowerShell.

In this chapter we'll look at why you should perform administration tasks remotely, what to consider when putting together your remote administration toolkit, and the various tools that you can use to remotely administer Windows Server 2016.

Remote not local

Windows Server 2016 is designed to be administered remotely rather than locally. For example, with the Nano Server deployment option, which you'll learn about more in Chapter 2, "Installation Options," you can only perform basic configuration tasks at the console. If you want to do anything more substantial, you need to establish a remote PowerShell or a Remote Server Administration Tool (RSAT) console session.

This "remote first" philosophy shouldn't come as a surprise to experienced administrators. While there are some times that you do need to physically interact with server hardware, today's servers and workloads are increasingly virtualized and containerized. It's rare for servers to be in on-premises server rooms, and more likely that they will be located in remote datacenters or the cloud. As a server administrator, it's increasingly unlikely that you be in physical proximity to the servers you are responsible for managing. Your Windows Server 2016 server administration strategy should be based on the assumption that physically being in front of a server is likely to be the exception rather than the rule. This requires you to be familiar with how to use your tools remotely, rather than signing on to each server individually using Remote Desktop and firing up the console that is relevant to the role or feature that you want to manage.

> ## Inside OUT
>
> ### *Automate where possible*
>
> The role of server administrator increasingly involves creating and deploying automation solutions. When Windows NT4 was released, it wasn't unusual for the average Windows Server administrator to be responsible for managing less than 20 physical servers. Today, because of automation, the average Windows Server administrator is responsible for managing hundreds, if not thousands of servers. You should automate the tasks that you perform where it is possible and makes sense. In the long run this will reduce the amount of time that you spend on tasks that you know how to do, so you can spend more time figuring out how to perform those tasks you don't know how to do.

Privileged Access Workstations

Servers are only as secure as the computers that you use to manage them. Privileged Access Workstations (PAW) are specially configured computers that you use to perform remote administration tasks. The idea of a PAW is that you have a computer with a locked down configuration that you only use to perform server administration tasks. You don't use this computer to read your email or browse the internet, you just use it to perform server administration tasks. An increasing number of security incidents have occurred because a privileged user's computer was infected with malware and that computer was then used to perform server administration tasks.

Consider configuring a PAW in the following way:

- Configure Device Guard to allow only specifically authorized and digitally signed software to run on the computer.

- Configure Credential Guard to protect credentials stored on the computer.

- Use BitLocker to encrypt the computer's storage and protect the boot environment.

- The computer should not be used to browse the internet or to check email. Server administrators should have completely separate computers to perform their other daily job tasks. Block internet browsing on the PAW both locally and on the firewall.

- Block the PAW from accessing the internet. Software updates should be obtained from a dedicated secure update server on the local network.

- Server administrators should not sign on to the PAW using an account that has administrative privileges on the PAW. In Chapter 18, "Security," you'll learn about using secure account forests to improve account security.

- Only specific user accounts used by server administrators should be able to sign on to the PAW. Consider additional restrictions such as sign-on hours. Block privileged accounts from signing into computers that are not PAWs or servers to be managed, such as the IT staff's everyday work computer.

- Configure servers to only accept administrator connections from PAWs.

- Use configuration management tools to monitor the configuration of the PAW. Some organizations rebuild PAWs entirely every 24 hours to ensure that configurations are not altered. Use these tools to restrict local group membership and ensure that the PAW has all appropriate recent software updates applied.

- Ensure that audit logs from PAWs are forwarded to a separate secure location.

- Disable use of unauthorized storage devices. For example, you can configure policies so that only USB storage devices that have a specific BitLocker organizational ID can be used with the computer.

- Block unsolicited inbound network traffic to the PAW using Windows Firewall.

Inside OUT

Jump Servers

Jump servers are another security procedure that can be used in conjunction with privileged access workstations. The idea with jump servers is that you only allow servers to accept administrative connections from specific hosts. For example, you only allow domain controllers to be administered from computers that have a specific IP address and a computer certificate issued by a specific certification authority. You can configure jump servers to only accept connections from PAWs and servers to be administered to only accept connections from jump servers. Some organizations that use jump servers have them rebuilt and redeployed every 24 hours to ensure that their configuration does not drift from the approved configuration.

Remote Server Administration Tools

The Remote Server Administration Tools (RSAT) are a set of consoles that you can install on a computer running Windows 10 that allow you to manage computers running Windows Server 2016. The RSAT consoles can also be installed on a computer running Windows Server 2016. If you want to install every RSAT console, issue the command:

```
Install-WindowsFeature -IncludeAllSubFeature RSAT
```

Installing the RSAT tools on a computer running Windows 10 involves downloading the latest version of the RSAT tools from Microsoft's website. You can determine the location of this download using your favorite search engine.

Inside OUT

Windows 10 for Server 2016

The RSAT tools for Windows 10 can manage Windows Server 2012 R2, Windows Server 2012, and Windows Server 2008 R2. The RSAT tools packages for Windows 8.1 can only be used to manage servers running Windows Server 2012 R2, Windows Server 2012, Windows Server 2008 R2 and Windows Server 2008, and not Windows Server 2016. Similarly the RSAT tools for Windows 7 can only be used to manage servers running Windows Server 2008 R2 and Windows Server 2008 and can't be used to manage Windows Server 2012, Windows Server 2012 R2, and Windows Server 2016. Put another way, only the most recent version of the client operating system gets a version of the RSAT tools to manage the most recent version of the Server operating system.

RSAT consoles

Table 1-1 provides a list of the RSAT tools that are available on Windows Server 2016. Most of these tools are available from the Tools menu of the Server Manager console.

Table 1-1. RSAT consoles

Console	Function
Active Directory Administrative Center	An advanced console for managing Active Directory users, computers, domains, forests, as well as Dynamic Access Control and Authentication policies. It performs most of the functions from the traditional Active Directory management consoles available on earlier versions of the Windows Server operating system
Active Directory Domains and Trust	Console for configuring and managing trust relationships between domains and forests
Active Directory Rights Management Services	Manage and configure Active Directory Rights Management Services
Active Directory Sites and Services	Manage Active Directory Site configuration, including Global Catalog servers and universal group membership caching

ADSI Edit	Active Directory object and attribute editor
Certification Authority	Manage Active Directory Certificate Services
Cluster-Aware Updating	Manage Cluster aware updating
Component Services	Manage component services, view the event log and manage services
Computer Management	The Computer Management console that issimilar to the Computer Management console in Windows Server 2008 R2. Allows you to manage Tasks, Event Viewer, Shared Folders, Local Users and Groups, Performance, Device Manager, Disk Management, and Services
Connection Manager Administration Kit	Allows you to create and deploy remote access connections
Defragment and Optimize Drives	Allows you to manage the defragmentation and optimization of drives
DFS Management	Manage Distributed File System
DHCP	Manage Dynamic Host Configuration Protocol servers
Disk Cleanup	Console that allows you to remove files and folders that are no longer necessary, such as old update and temporary files
DNS	Configure and manage DNS servers
Event Viewer	View and manage event logs
Failover Cluster Manager	Configure and manage failover clusters
Fax Service Manager	Configure and manage the fax service
File Server Resource Manager	Console for managing file servers, including file classification, storage reports, and quotas
Group Policy Management	Console for management of group policies, including running resultant set of policy reports
Hyper-V Manager	Configure and manage Hyper-V virtualization
Internet Information Services (IIS) 6.0 Manager	Configure and manage version 6 of IIS
Internet Information Services (IIS) Manager	Configure and manage version 7 and later of IIS
iSCSI Initiator	Configure iSCSI initiator settings
Local Security Policy	Configure and manage local security policy settings
Network Load Balancing Manager	Configure and manage network load balancing
Network Policy Server	Configure Network Policies

CHAPTER 01

ODBC Data Sources (32-bit)	Manage 32-bit ODBC data sources
ODBC Data Sources (64-bit)	Manage 64-bit ODBC data sources
Online Responder Management	Configure and manage Online Certificate Status Protocol arrays
Performance Monitor	View performance information
Print Management	Configure and manage print servers
Remote Access Management	Configure and manage remote access
Remote Desktop Services	Configure and manage Remote Desktop Services
Resource Monitor	Real time monitoring of RAM, CPU, Disk and Network utilization
Routing and Remote Access	Configure and manage routing and remote access, including DirectAccess
Services	Configure and manage services
Services for Network File System (NFS)	Configure and manage Network File System
Shielding Data File Wizard	Manage Shielded Data files and policies
System Configuration	Manage system configuration
System Information	View system information
Task Scheduler	Configure and manage scheduled tasks
Template Disk Wizard	Configure and manage template virtual hard disks for shielded VMs
Volume Activation Tools	Configure and manage volume licensing
Windows Deployment Services	Configure and manage Windows Deployment Services
Windows Firewall with Advanced Security	Configure and manage Windows Firewall with Advanced Security
Windows Memory Diagnostics	Perform memory diagnostics to check if server memory is corrupted. May require a reboot
Windows Server Backup	Configure and manage Windows Server Backup
Windows Server Update Services	Configure and manage Windows Server Update Services server
WINS	Configure and manage Windows Internet Naming Services server

Server Manager console

Perhaps the most important console that is available in the RSAT tools is the Server Manager console. This console opens automatically on a computer running Server 2016 if you install the Server with Desktop Experience option. A number of roles that had separate consoles in previous versions of Windows Server have that functionality included in the Windows Server 2016

Server Manager console. For example, many storage management tasks and IPAM tasks are completed in Server Manager rather than in individual role related consoles.

When you launch Server Manager console, it will query the servers that you have added to the All Servers group to determine which roles are installed on those servers. It will then provide a list of categories based on the roles detected on the servers. Figure 1-1 shows an All Servers group where the AD CS, AD DS, DHCP, DNS, and IIS roles have been detected on servers DC1 and S1.

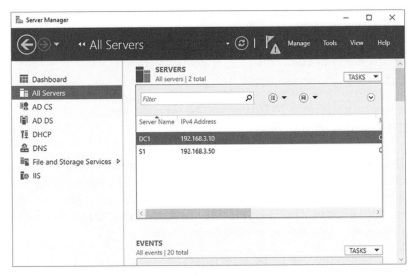

FIGURE 1-1 All Servers list

To add servers to the All Servers, group, right click on the All Servers node of the Server Manager console and click Add Servers. On the Add Servers dialog box, shown in Figure 1-2, select the servers either by querying Active Directory, searching on the basis of DNS name, or importing servers from a list.

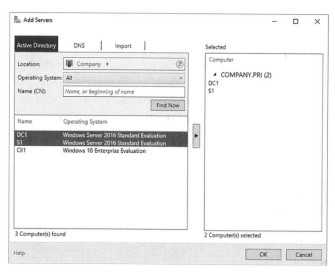

FIGURE 1-2 Add Servers to All Servers

Once you have a list of roles in Server Manager, you can perform role specific administration on each server by right clicking on that server. When you do this, the appropriate RSAT console will be launched with the target server in focus. Figure 1-3 shows DC1 selected in the list of DNS servers, with the option of launching the DNS Manager console. You can also use the context menu, available by right clicking, to (where supported):

- Add roles and features to the target server

- Restart the target server

- Open the Computer Management console

- Open a Remote Desktop Connection session to the target server

- Open a Windows PowerShell session on the target server

- Configure NIC Teaming on the target server

- Manage the server using an alternate set of credentials

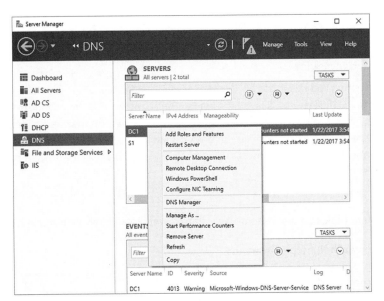

FIGURE 1-3 Server Manager individual server context menu

PowerShell

PowerShell is Microsoft's primary scripting, automation and management tool. It's not hyperbole to suggest that the most important skill for Windows Server administrators going forward is PowerShell. In almost all cases, you can access greater functionality and settings through PowerShell than you can through the RSAT consoles.

PowerShell includes a substantial amount of documentation explaining what each cmdlet can do and how you can do it. In each chapter of this book, you'll learn the names of the PowerShell cmdlets that are relevant to each role. Once you know the name of the command you want to use to perform a task, you can use PowerShell's built in help to teach you the precise details of how to use that cmdlet to perform that task.

Inside OUT

Latest documentation

The first thing you should do on an internet-connected server when you need help with a PowerShell cmdlet is to run the update-help cmdlet. This will pull the most up-to-date PowerShell documentation from Microsoft's servers on the internet down to your local server. This documentation is almost always the same as the cmdlet's documentation available on Microsoft's website, so it saves you a search with your favorite search engine.

Some important basic commands to get you started with PowerShell are listed in Table 1-2.

Table 1-2. PowerShell help commands

Cmdlet or command	Functionality
Update-Help	Update the help documentation for each cmdlet to the most recent version available from Microsoft
Get-Command	List all PowerShell commands available on the computer
Get-Command -Module <ModuleName>	Get all cmdlets in a specific PowerShell module. For example, to view all the DNS server cmdlets, run the command Get-Command -Module DNSServer
Get-Command -Noun <NounName>	Each PowerShell cmdlet is made up of a verb-noun combination. You can use this command to view all cmdlets associated with a particular noun. For example, to view all of the cmdlets associated with the DNSServer noun, run the command Get-command -noun DNSserver
Help <cmdletname>	View the summary help documentation for a specific PowerShell cmdlet
Help -detailed <cmdletname>	View the detailed help documentation for a specific PowerShell cmdlet
Help -examples <cmdletname>	View examples of how to use a specific PowerShell cmdlet to perform tasks

Modules

Modules are collections of PowerShell cmdlets. In older versions of PowerShell you needed to manually load a module each time you wanted to use one of its associated cmdlets. In Windows Server 2016, any module that is installed will load automatically when you try to run an associated cmdlet. Viewing cmdlets by module using the Get-Command -Module <modulename> cmdlet allows you to view just those cmdlets associated with a specific role or feature.

PowerShell Gallery

The PowerShell gallery is a collection of modules published by the community that extend the functionality of PowerShell beyond what is available with a default installation of Windows Server 2016. Table 1-3 lists the commands that you can use to get started with the PowerShell gallery.

Table 1-3. PowerShell Gallery basics

Command	Function
Find-Module -Repository PSGallery | out-host -paging	Will list the available modules in the PowerShell gallery in a paged format. You'll be prompted to install the NugetProvider to interact with the PowerShell gallery
Find-Module -Repository PSGallery -Name <ModuleName>	Will list the modules with a specific name. You can use wildcards. For example, to view all modules that start with the name AzureRM, run the command Find-Module -Repository PSGallery -Name AzureRM*
Install-Module -Repository PSGallery -Name <ModuleName>	Will install the module Modulename. For example, to install the AzureRM module, run the command Install-Module -Repository PSGallery -Name AzureRM
Update-Module	Will update any module that you've installed using Install-Module
Get-InstalledModule	View all modules installed from the PowerShell gallery

Remoting

PowerShell remoting is enabled by default on Windows Server 2016, but by default requires a connection from a private network and an account that is a member of the local Administrators group. A remote session allows you to run commands on a remote computer in a manner similar to how you'd remotely enact commands when connected using an SSH session.

You can enter a remote session to a Windows Server 2016 computer that is a member of the same Active Directory forest by using the command, which will prompt you for the credentials that you will use to connect to the remote computer.

```
$cred = Get-Credential

Enter-PSSession -computername <computername> -Credential $cred
```

You can enable PowerShell remoting using the Enable-PSRemoting cmdlet if it has been disabled. PowerShell remoting relies upon WSMan (Web Server Management). WSMan uses port 5985 and can be configured to support TLS over port 5986.

Remote PowerShell connections are made to a defined, usually the default endpoint. The account used to make a connection to this remote endpoint needs to have local Administrator privileges on the target computer. With Just Enough Administration, which you'll learn about in Chapter 18, you'll learn about creating additional endpoints that allow connections to limited privilege restricted sessions.

To enable PowerShell remoting to computers that are not domain joined, you need to configure the trusted hosts list on the client computer that you want to establish the remote session from. You do this on the client computer using the set-item cmdlet. For example, to trust the computer at IP address 192.168.3.200, you'll need to run the command:

```
Set-Item wsman:\localhost\Client\TrustedHosts -Value 192.168.3.200 -Concatenate
```

Once you've run the command to configure the client, you'll be able to establish a PowerShell remote session using the Enter-PSSession cmdlet. If you want more information about remoting, you can run the following command to bring up help text on the subject:

```
Help about_Remote_faq -ShowWindow
```

One to many remoting

PowerShell allows you to run one command against many machines. This is termed one to many remoting, but is also known as fan out administration. You can use one to many remoting to run the same command against any number of computers. Rather than signing on to each computer to check if a particular service is running, you can use PowerShell remoting to run the same command that checks the status of the service against each computer within the scope of the command.

For example, you can use the following command to read a list of computers from a text file named computers.txt:

```
$Computers = Get-Content c:\Computers.txt
```

You can then use the following command to get the properties of the Windows Update service:

```
Invoke-Command -ScriptBlock { get-service wuauserv } -computername $Computers
```

You can also use the Invoke-Command cmdlet to run a script from the local computer against a number of remote computers. For example, to run the script FixStuff.ps1 against the computers in the file computers.txt, run the following command:

```
$Computers = Get-Content c:\Computers.txt
```

```
Invoke-Command -FilePath c:\FixStuff.ps1
```

PowerShell ISE

PowerShell Integrated Scripting Environment (ISE) is a tool available on computers running Windows 10 and the graphical version of Windows Server 2016 that you can use to create, manage, and run PowerShell scripts and commands.

PowerShell ISE includes a script pane, a command window, and also provides you with the option of a list of available cmdlets sorted by module as shown in Figure 1-4.

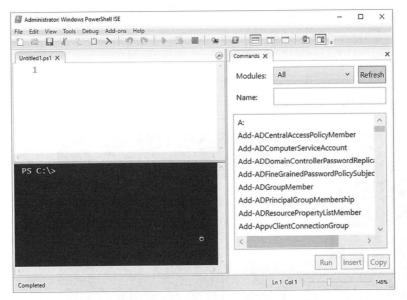

FIGURE 1-4 PowerShell ISE

PowerShell ISE includes the following functionality:

- **IntelliSense**. Provides code completion. Displays possible cmdlets, parameters, parameter values, files and folders. Code completion functionality extends to the command window.

- **Color coding**. PowerShell code is color coded to assist code readability. This color coding extends to the command window.

- **Visual debugging**. Allows you to step through PowerShell code and configure and manage breakpoints.

- **Brace Matching**. Allows you to locate matching braces to ensure that all opened braces are matched by closing ones.

- **Context sensitive help**. Allows you to view information about cmdlets, parameters and values.

- **Run all code or just a selection**. Rather than running all of the PowerShell code in the script pane, you can instead just highlight and run discrete lines of PowerShell code.

Remote tabs

Remote tabs allow you to establish remote PowerShell sessions using PowerShell ISE rather than using the Enter-PSSession PowerShell cmdlet. To initiate a remote session, click on the New Remote PowerShell Tab item on the File menu of PowerShell ISE. You'll be prompted for the address of the computer that you want to connect to as well as the name of the user account with which you want to make the connection as shown in Figure 1-5.

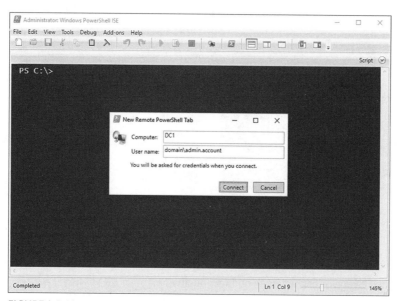

FIGURE 1-5 New remote PowerShell tab

Once a session is established, you can use the PowerShell ISE script pane to run scripts or sections of PowerShell code in the same manner that you would do so if using PowerShell ISE on the local computer.

Snippets

Snippets are commonly used small sections of code that you can insert into your PowerShell scripts. Figure 1-6 shows an If-Else snippet already in the script pane, with the properties of a do-while snipped displayed. You can add snippets to the PowerShell ISE using the New-Snippet cmdlet.

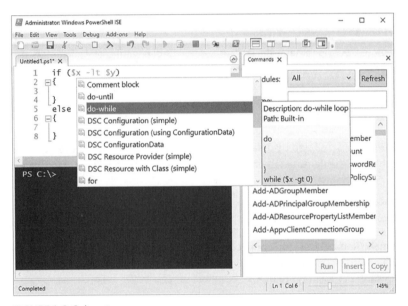

FIGURE 1-6 Snippets

PowerShell Direct

PowerShell direct allows you to create a connection from a virtualization host to a VM running on that host. To use PowerShell Direct, you must have Hyper-V administrator privileges on the Hyper-V host computer and administrator credentials on the virtual machine that you wish to connect to. PowerShell direct can allow you to make a connection to a virtual machine that may not otherwise be configured to support remote connections.

PowerShell direct only works with Hyper-V hosts and guests running Windows Server 2016 and Windows 10. To get a list of the virtual machines on the host Hyper-V server, use the command Get-VM. To connect to the virtual machine using PowerShell direct, use the Enter-PSSession cmdlet with the -VMName parameter.

Remote Desktop

Remote Desktop is the way that many administrators are likely to perform one-off tasks remotely on servers running the GUI version of Windows Server 2016. While best practice is to increasingly use PowerShell for remote administration, sometimes it is quicker to just establish a Remote Desktop session and to perform tasks on the remote server in a manner that appears similar to being directly signed on at the console.

Inside OUT

Remote Desktop and Azure

Remote Desktop remains the default method of connecting to Azure Infrastructure as a Service VMs running the Windows Server 2016 operating system when those virtual machines are deployed from the gallery. You'll learn more about running Windows Server 2016 on Azure in Chapter 17, "Windows Server 2016 and Azure IaaS."

Remote Desktop is disabled by default on computers running Windows Server 2016. You enable it either through the Remote tab of the System Properties dialog box, or by running the following PowerShell command:

```
Set-ItemProperty -Path "HKLM:\System\CurrentControlSet\Control\Terminal Server" -Name
"fDenyTSConnections" -Value 0
```

You can make Remote Desktop connections to computers running the Server Core installation option if Remote Desktop is enabled. Remote Desktop is not available on computers running the Nano Server installation option.

By default, Remote Desktop Connection connects to Remote Desktop services on port 3389. When you enable Remote Desktop using the GUI, a remote desktop related firewall is automatically enabled. If you enable Remote Desktop using PowerShell, you'll also need to manually enable a firewall rule to allow connections. You can do this using the following PowerShell command:

```
Enable-NetFirewallRule -DisplayGroup "Remote Desktop"
```

By default, the Allow connections only from computers running Remote Desktop with Network Level Authentication option is selected, as shown in Figure 1-7. Network Level Authentication requires that a user be authenticated prior to the remote desktop session being established. Network Level Authentication is supported by the Remote Desktop Connection client available on all Windows operating systems, but may not be supported by third party Remote Desktop clients.

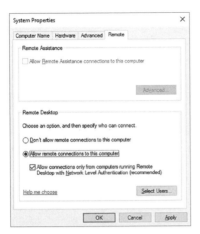

FIGURE 1-7 New remote PowerShell tab

Only users that are members of the local Administrators group and members of the local Remote Desktop Users group are able to make connections via Remote Desktop. If you want to grant someone permission to access the server without granting them full administrative privileges, add them to the local Remote Desktop Users group.

Inside OUT

Just Enough Administration

Just Enough Administration (JEA) allows you to grant access, through a PowerShell endpoint, to only specific PowerShell cmdlets and parameters. This is a more effective way of giving someone limited administrative access than providing them Remote Desktop access to a server. You'll learn more about JEA in Chapter 18.

You can map local volumes to a remote host in an active Remote Desktop Connection session by configuring the Local Resources and Devices setting on the Local Resources tab of the Remote Desktop Connection dialog box as shown in Figure 1-8. While it is less effective over low bandwidth connections, it can provide a simple way to transfer files from your client computer to a remote server instead of setting up FTP or another file transfer method.

FIGURE 1-8 New remote PowerShell tab

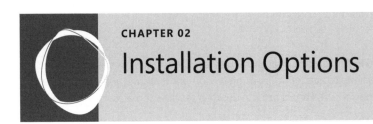

CHAPTER 02

Installation Options

Prior to installing Windows Server 2016 you need to make a number of decisions. The choices that you make will be determined by the role that you want the server to play in hosting your organization's workloads. You'll need to decide which edition of Windows Server to install. You'll also need to decide whether you'll install the Server with Desktop Experience, also known as Server with GUI, Server Core, or Nano Server. In this chapter you'll learn about the different editions and versions of Windows Server 2016. You'll also learn how to configure a Nano Server image for deployment.

Windows Server 2016 editions

There are two primary editions of Windows Server 2016 and several minor editions of Windows Server 2016. The primary editions are:

- **Windows Server 2016 Standard**. An edition of Windows Server 2016 suitable for environments where most servers are deployed physically rather than as virtual machines. It is licensed on a per processor core basis and requires Windows Server Client Access Licenses (CALs).

- **Windows Server 2016 Datacenter**. This edition of Windows Server 2016 is suitable for datacenters that include a high degree of virtualization. They are licensed on a per processor core basis and require Windows Server CALs.

The minor editions of Windows Server 2016 are:

- **Windows Server 2016 Essentials**. This is the edition of Windows Server for small businesses. It supports up to 25 users and 50 devices, and is licensed on a per processor basis. It doesn't require CALs due to the user and device restriction.

- **Windows Server 2016 Multipoint Premium Server**. It's designed for the education market and only available to academic licensing customers. It allows multiple terminals to be connected to a special customized remote desktop services server, and is licensed on a per-processor basis.

- **Windows Storage Server 2016**. It functions as a storage solution and is only available in OEM channels. It contains processor based licensing that does not require a CAL.

- **Microsoft Hyper-V Server 2016**. This is a freely available hypervisor that does not require a license or CALs.

Table 2-1 lists the different limitations between Standard and Enterprise editions of Windows Server 2016.

Table 2-1. Edition limitations

Item	Standard Edition	Datacenter Edition
Maximum users	Determined by available client access licenses	Determined by available client access licenses
Maximum SMB connections	16,777,216	16,777,216
Maximum routing and remote access connections	No limit	No limit
Maximum Internet Authentication Service connections	2,147,483,647	2,147,483,647
Maximum Remote Desktop Services connections	65,535	65,535
Maximum x64 processor sockets	64	64
Maximum RAM	24 TB	24 TB
Included virtualization guest licenses	2 included VM license as well as Hyper-V host	Unlimited VM licenses as well as Hyper-V host
Included Windows container licenses	Unlimited	Unlimited
Included Hyper-V container licenses	2	Unlimited

The primary difference between the two servers is the way that virtual machines are licensed. The Datacenter edition allows you to host unlimited virtual machines, and Standard edition allows you to host two before you'll have to purchase a license for each additional virtual machine. Although you should check the cost yourself, if you're hosting more than half a dozen virtual machines running a Windows Server operating system, or half a dozen Hyper-V containers, you'll be better off purchasing the Datacenter edition.

The only difference in the roles supported between Windows Server 2016 Standard edition and Windows Server 2016 Datacenter edition is that Datacenter edition supports hosting shielded virtual machines, something that cannot be done with the standard edition. Shielded virtual machines are BitLocker encrypted virtual machines that can't be tampered with by a virtualization administrator.

Another difference between the two editions is that Datacenter edition supports inherited activation as a host or guest virtual machine. Standard edition only supports inherited activation when hosted as a guest virtual machine on a Hyper-V host running Datacenter edition. Inherited activation means that activation occurs automatically based on the Windows Server edition. This can save a lot of time if you are hosting a large number of Windows Server 2016 virtual machines, because you don't need to use license keys or KMS servers.

Windows Server servicing branches

Depending on the installation option you choose, Windows Server 2016 supports two separate servicing branches: , the Long Term Servicing Branch (LTSB) and the Current Branch for Business (CBB).

LTSB

LTSB provides five years of mainstream support with five years of extended support. This is similar to the support options provided for previous versions of Windows Server, such as Windows Server 2012 R2. This means that Microsoft will provide software updates for computers that use LTSB until at least 10 years after the release of Windows Server 2016.

LTSB is the only servicing branch that is available to servers installed using the Server Core and Server with GUI installation options.

CBB

A CBB release will be provided with support and software updates from Microsoft until just after the next+1 version of the current branch is released. CBB support will be provided only for two branches at any time. CBB support only applies to computers deployed using the Nano Server installation option. For example, if your organization deploys version CBB#1 of Nano Server, that version of Nano Server will still receive updates and support until just after CBB#3 is released.

LTSB support is not available for Nano Server, and CBB support is not available for servers deployed using the Server Core or Server with GUI installation options. Nano Server is only supported in production to organizations that have a Software Assurance agreement with Microsoft.

Inside OUT

Nano is Short Term

Although the exact timing will depend on when Nano Server CBBs are made available, a Nano Server deployment is likely to have around 18 months support before you need to perform an upgrade to a newer version of Nano Server. Microsoft tends to preference workload migrations to in-place upgrades, so you should avoid deploying long term workloads to host computers running the Nano Server installation option.

Server Core

Server Core is the default installation option for Windows Server 2016. As Server Core has fewer components, it doesn't need to have software updates applied as often as the Server with GUI installation option does. Because components such as the built-in web browser have been removed, Server Core is less vulnerable to malware than the Server with GUI installation option. Additionally, because it doesn't require all of the components, it has a lower resource footprint.

Unlike previous versions of the installation routine, the nature of Server Core is not explicitly called out by the Windows Server 2016 installation wizard shown in Figure 2-1. The version listed as Desktop Experience is the Server with GUI option. The Standard version is Server Core. Unless you are paying attention, it's possible that you'll accidentally deploy Server Core rather than Server with GUI.

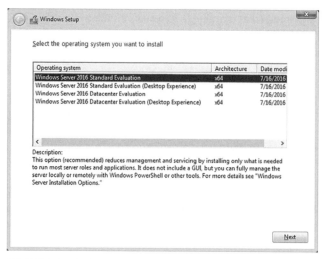

FIGURE 2-1 Windows Server 2016 installation options

Server Core interface

The Server Core interface is a command prompt. Like Figure 2-2 shows, to interact with the command prompt you must sign on using CTRL-ALT-DEL. You can then sign on with a domain based or local administrator account.

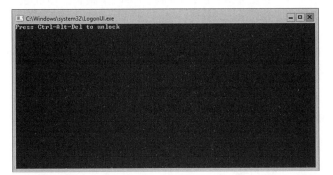

FIGURE 2-2 Server Core Desktop

Once you have signed on, you can enter a local PowerShell session by typing PowerShell.exe. Server Core is primarily a command line environment, but there are some graphical tools that can be launched from the command prompt or Task Manager. These include:

- **Task Manager**. This functions in the same way as Task Manager on Server with GUI or Windows 10. Can use Task Manager to run tasks by selecting the Run New Task item on the File menu.

- **Notepad**. You can launch Notepad.exe to edit and view the contents of text files.

- **MSInfo32.exe**. It allows you to view information about the installation.

- **Regedit.exe and Regedt32.exe**. They allow you to edit the registry on a Server Core computer.

- **TimeDate.cpl**. It opens the Time and Date Control Panel.

- **Intl.cpl**. It opens the regional settings Control Panel.

- **Iscsicpl.exe**. This opens the iSCSI Initiator Properties Control Panel. It allows you to connect to shared storage over iSCSI.

CHAPTER 02

Inside OUT

Oops

If you type Exit at the Server Core command prompt, the command prompt closes. While I've seen some administrators reboot their Server Core computers to get it back, there is an easier way. If you do accidentally close your command prompt, press CTRL-ALT-DEL, select Task Manager, click More Details, click File, click Run New Ttask and then type **cmd.exe**. This will give you back a command prompt without requiring you to log out or restart the computer.

Server Core Roles

Server Core supports the following roles, which you can install using the Add-WindowsFeature PowerShell cmdlet, or by using the Add Roles and Features Wizard. The Server Core Roles are available in the Server Manager console, shown from a remote computer in Figure 2-3.

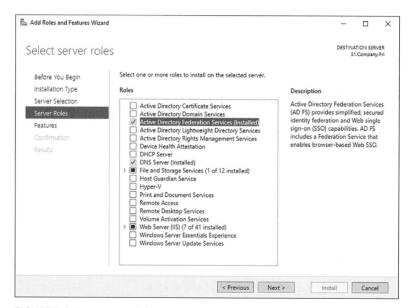

FIGURE 2-3 Server Core Roles

- Active Directory Certificate Services

- Active Directory Domain Services

- Active Directory Federation Services

- Active Directory Lightweight Directory Services (AD LDS)

- Active Directory Rights Management Services

- Device Health Attestation

- DHCP Server

- DNS Server

- File and Storage Services

- Host Guardian Service

- Hyper-V

- Print and Document Services

- Routing and Remote Access Server

- Remote Desktop Services Connection Broker

- Web Server (including parts of ASP.NET)

- Windows Server Essentials Experience

- Windows Server Update Services

Server Core also supports the following features shown in Figure 2-4.

FIGURE 2-4 Server Core Features

- .NET Framework 3.5

- .NET Framework 4.6

- Background Intelligent Transfer Service (BITS)

- BitLocker Drive Encryption

- BranchCache

- Client for NFS

- Containers

- Data Center Bridging

- Enhanced Storage

- Failover Clustering

- Group Policy Management

- I/O Quality of Service

- IIS Hostable Web Core

- IP Address Management (IPAM) Server

- iSNS Server service

- Management OData IIS Extension

- Media Foundation

- Message Queuing

- Multipath I/O

- MultiPoint Connector

- Network Load Balancing

- Peer Name Resolution Protocol

- Quality Windows Audio Video Experience

- Remote Differential Compression

- Remote Server Administration Tools

- RPC over HTTP Proxy

- Setup and Boot Event Collection

- Simple TCP/IP Services

- SMB 1.0/CIFS File Sharing Support

- SMB Bandwidth Limit

- SNMP Service

- Telnet Client

- VM Shielding Tools for Fabric Management

- Windows Defender Features

- Windows Internal Database

- Windows PowerShell

- Windows Process Activation Service

- Windows Server Backup

- Windows Server Migration Tools

- Windows Standards-Based Storage Management

- WinRM IIS Extension

- WINS Server

- WoW64 Support

While it is possible to install and manage these roles using PowerShell, either directly or through a remote PowerShell session, most administrators are likely to deploy and manage these roles and features using remote consoles.

As you learned in the Chapter 1, "Administration Tools," Microsoft encourages organizations to manage all servers remotely. It doesn't matter that Server Core doesn't have a GUI, you'll almost never be logging on directly, but can instead connect using remote administration tools.

Inside OUT

Locked In

Windows Server 2012 and Windows Server 2012 R2 allowed you to switch between the Server Core and Server with GUI installation option. This gave administrators the ability to deploy the Server with GUI and then pare it back to Server Core if they found that they didn't need all of the extra components that Server with GUI included. This gave server administrators who deployed the Server Core option an escape hatch. If they found that they couldn't run a specific application on Server Core, they could always bump it up to Server with GUI. Windows Server 2016 doesn't give you that option. The option you choose at deployment is the one you'll be stuck with. While this makes sense in terms of Microsoft's philosophy around deployment, which is where if you want to make a substantive change you should redeploy from scratch rather than reengineer the existing deployment, it probably means that fewer administrators will deploy Server Core. This will happen because they know that applications will always work on Server with GUI, but that they can't be sure that they might work with Server Core.

When to deploy Server Core

The key to deploying Server Core in your organization is determining whether or not it is suitable to use for a specific workload. Server Core is perfect for infrastructure type roles such as Domain Controller, DNS server, DHCP server and file server. Server Core may be less suitable in hosting applications that have complex dependencies.

If you are thinking about deploying Server Core, you should perform tests to verify that each workload you intend to host on Server Core functions as expected. Even though Server Core is Microsoft's current preferred deployment option, third party server hosted applications often have dependencies that require them to be installed on the Server with GUI installation option.

Server Core can be installed from the Windows Server 2016 installation media, or deployed using a variety of methods from the install.wim file that is located on the installation media. You'll learn more about deployment and configuration in Chapter 3, "Deployment and Configuration."

Inside OUT

Wget

Server administrators often need to download files from a location on the network or a location on the internet to a server computer to perform one task or another. This can get especially complicated if the server is on the perimeter network, because you can't directly copy the file or files that you need from a network share. Both Server Core and Nano Server don't have a browser, so you can't use Internet Explorer to retrieve those files. What you can do is use the PowerShell wget command (which is just an alias to the Invoke-WebRequest cmdlet) to download a file directly from a location on the internet to the filesystem of the computer that you are running the command on.

Server with GUI

Server with GUI, officially known as Server with Desktop Experience, is the version of Windows Server that IT pros who have been using and managing the product since the 1990's and 2000's are likely most familiar with. Server with GUI comes with a full desktop environment, including a web browser. You can also install software on Server with GUI that you would normally install on a computer running the Windows 10 operating system.

You are likely to deploy Server with GUI if you need to host Remote Desktop Session Host servers. Additionally, you'll deploy Server with GUI if you need to host an application that has dependencies that are unavailable on Server Core.

Microsoft's recommendation is that you deploy Windows Server 2016 with the Desktop Experience only in situations where it is impractical to deploy Server Core or Nano Server. While many administrators who have worked with Windows Server for many years will choose the Server with GUI installation option out of habit, deploying this version of Windows Server in the future is likely to be the exception rather than the rule.

Roles and Features

If you're new to Windows Server 2016, you're likely to use the Add Roles and Features Wizard, shown in Figure 2-5, to add and remove roles and features from a computer running the Server with GUI option. While you can use this feature of the Server Manager console locally or remotely, you can only use it to manage roles and features on one server at a time.

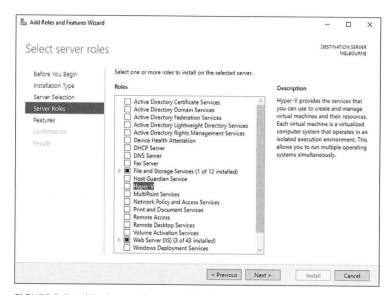

FIGURE 2-5 Add roles and features wizard

PowerShell provides a better set of tools for adding, removing, and querying the status of features with the Add-WindowsFeature, Get-WindowsFeature and Remove-Windows-Feature cmdlets. For example, Figure 2-6 shows the start of a list of all possible features on a computer, with several features, such as Active Directory Certificate Services, Active Directory Domain Services, DHCP Server, DNS Server, and File and Storage Services installed.

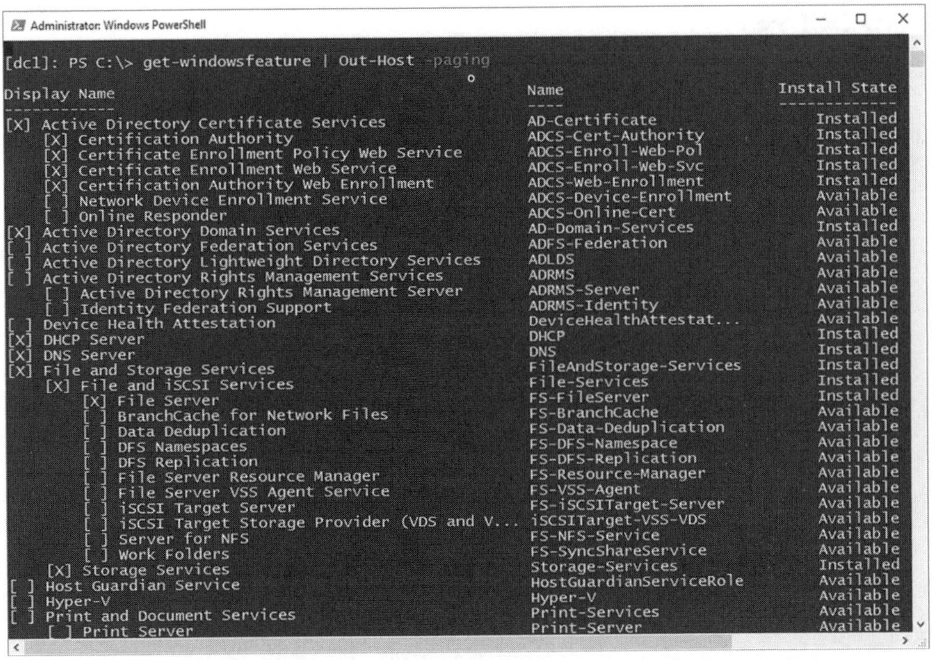

FIGURE 2-6 View installed features with PowerShell

For example, the following commands install the Hyper-V role on all computers listed in the text file virt-servers.txt and then restarts those servers once the role installation is complete:

```
$Computers = Get-Content c:\virt-servers.txt

$Invoke-Command -ScriptBlock { Add-WindowsFeature Hyper-V -Restart } -Computername
$Computers
```

Inside OUT

Desired State

Adding and removing roles and features using Server Manager or PowerShell is a reasonable way to approach small numbers of server modifications. If you need to deploy a large number of servers that have a consistent configuration of roles and features, you're better off using configuration management tools like PowerShell Desired State Configuration, Puppet or Chef. With these tools, you deploy the server, and the configuration management system configures it with roles, features, and settings according to your specifications. You'll learn about using tools such as Desired State Configuration and Chef in Chapter 3.

CHAPTER 02

Nano Server

Nano Server is a very small footprint version of Windows Server 2016 that requires a minimal amount of RAM and disk space. Nano Server accomplishes this by only including what it needs to perform a task. Nano Server can run with a few hundred megabytes of RAM and a few hundred megabytes of disk space. This means that you can host far more Nano Server VMs on a Hyper-V host than you can instances of Windows Server running Server Core or Server with GUI simply because both these options require substantially greater system resources.

With a traditional Windows Server 2016 deployment, you deploy the server and then go in and add roles and features as necessary. This is possible because the files that allow for those roles and features to be deployed are already included with the deployment. Including these files gives you a high degree of flexibility in terms of changing the configuration of a server that has already been deployed, but it comes at a cost of increasing the amount of data that you need to store to enable that flexibility.

Nano Server also differs from other Microsoft server operating systems in that it has a bare bones console that only exists to allow remote access to the server. Rather than signing on locally and being able to perform administrative tasks, Nano Server is designed so that other than during initial configuration or dire troubleshooting scenarios, you perform all administrative tasks remotely rather than directly on the server.

Nano Server Console

As Figure 2-7 shows, the Nano Server console provides you with enough basic tools to configure the Nano Server's network properties, which firewall rules are active, and the WinRM settings. The philosophy behind this interface is that you only use it to set things up so that you can connect to the server using a remote PowerShell session to perform almost all other administrative tasks.

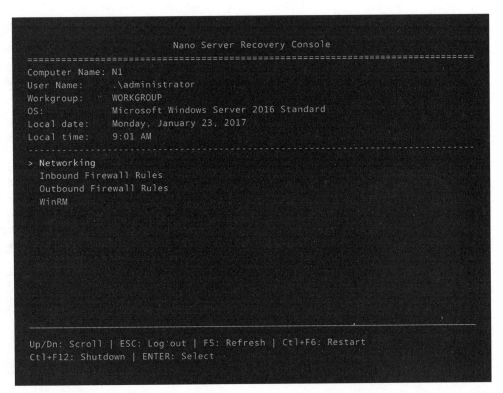

FIGURE 2-7 Nano Server Recovery Interface

You can use the Nano Server Recovery console to reconfigure network options as shown in Figure 2-8. Nano Server supports IP address configuration through DHCP or through manual configuration. You can use the Nano Server Recovery Console to enable or disable WinRM. You can also use the console to configure inbound and outbound firewall rules.

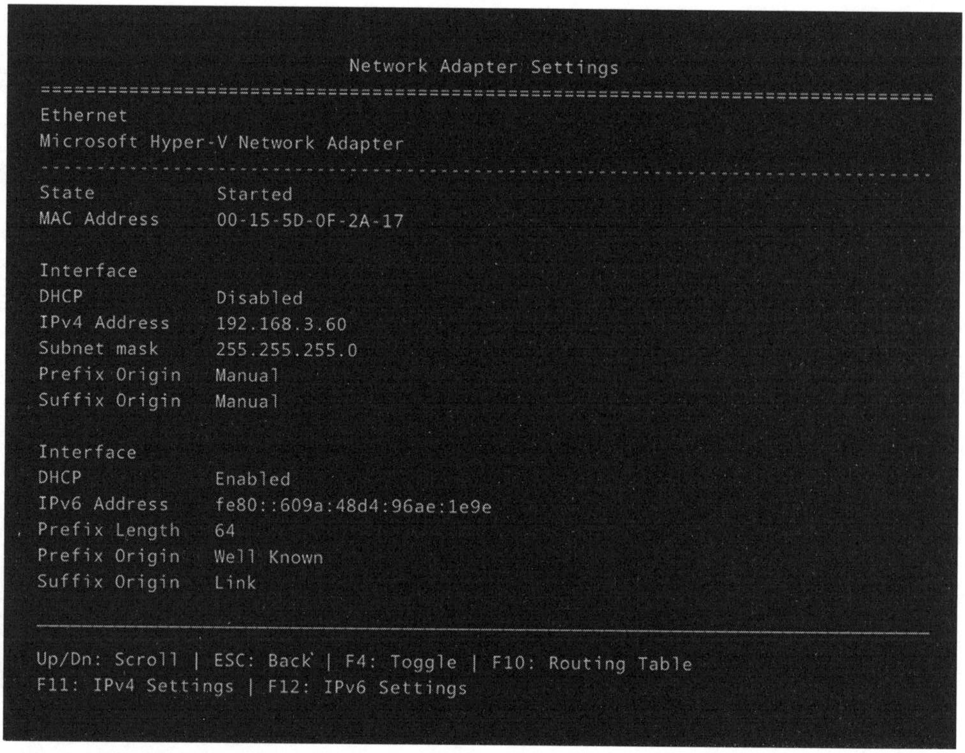

```
                         Network Adapter Settings
================================================================================
Ethernet
Microsoft Hyper-V Network Adapter
--------------------------------------------------------------------------------

State              Started
MAC Address        00-15-5D-0F-2A-17

Interface
DHCP               Disabled
IPv4 Address       192.168.3.60
Subnet mask        255.255.255.0
Prefix Origin      Manual
Suffix Origin      Manual

Interface
DHCP               Enabled
IPv6 Address       fe80::609a:48d4:96ae:1e9e
Prefix Length      64
Prefix Origin      Well Known
Suffix Origin      Link
_____

Up/Dn: Scroll | ESC: Back | F4: Toggle | F10: Routing Table
F11: IPv4 Settings | F12: IPv6 Settings
```

FIGURE 2-8 Nano Server Network Adapter Settings

Supported Roles and Features

One of the reasons that Nano Server uses the CBB support cadence rather than LTSB is that Microsoft intends to regularly add functionality to Nano Server. By limiting the support they offer for a specific branch to 18-24 months, you'll be forced to update to a more capable version of Nano Server on a regular basis.

Nano Server currently supports the following roles:

- Containers

- Data Center Bridging

- DNS Server

- Failover Clustering

- File Server

- Hyper-V

- Web Server (IIS)

Nano Server currently has the following limitations:

- Only supports 64-bit applications, tools, and agents.

- Has no group policy support (although it does support Desired State Configuration).

- Cannot be configured to access the internet through a proxy server.

- PowerShell on Nano Server is the PowerShell Core version, rather than the full Desktop Edition available on Server Core, Server with GUI, and Windows 10.

Inside OUT

Future of Windows Server

Jeffrey Snover, the architect of Nano Server and the instigator of PowerShell has repeatedly said that Nano Server represents the future of Windows Server. Snover expects Server with GUI to be deployed less often as Nano Server becomes more functional. He believes administrators will choose to build lean servers to host very specific workloads rather than to deploy bulky general purpose servers that support having their configuration changed at any time after deployment. While Nano Server might not seem like much in 2017, within a couple of years Microsoft believes it will make up the majority of your organization's Windows Server deployments.

Domain Join

Joining a Nano Server to an Active Directory domain isn't straightforward. You can't use the Add-Computer cmdlet to perform the domain join as you can on computers running Server Core, Server with GUI, or Windows 10.

To join a Nano Server to an Active Directory domain, you need to first create an offline domain join blob on a computer that is already connected to the domain with a user account that has the right do join computers to the domain. For example, to prepare a domain join blob for a computer running Nano Server named NS1 for the domain contoso.internal, run the following command on a domain joined computer:

```
Djoin.exe /provision /domain contoso.internal /machine NS1 /savefile .\odjblob
```

You'll then need to transfer the odjblob file across to NS1. You can do this by running the following commands, which will deposit the file odjblob in the root directory on nano server NS1, where you provide administrative credentials for NS1 after executing the first line.

```
$cred = Get-Credential

$session = New-PSSession -Computername NS1 -Credential $cred

Copy-Item c:odjblob -Destination 'C:' -ToSession $Session
```

You can then use the Enter-PSSession cmdlet to enter a remote PowerShell session onto Nano Server N1.

You'll need to add the address for NS1 into your TrustedHosts list using the cmdlet:

```
Set-Item wsman:\localhost\Client\TrustedHosts -Value NS1 -Concatenate
```

And then connect using the Enter-PSSession cmdlet and the $cred variable:

```
Enter-PSSession -ComputerName NS1 -Credential $cred
```

Once you've established the remote session to NS1, you can enact the following command to join the nano server to the domain:

```
Djoin /requestodj /loadfile c:\odjblob /windowspath c:\windows /localos
```

Then restart the Nano Server to complete the domain join operation. You can do this by issuing the Restart-computer cmdlet.

Creating Nano Server Images

You can't install Nano Server by booting from the Windows Server 2016 installation media. You must instead specially craft an installation image that includes only the roles, features, and drivers that are appropriate for the deployment you are about to make. For example, if you want to deploy a Nano Server instance as a VM that hosted Windows Containers, you'd add the appropriate driver package for Nano Server to function as a virtual machine and Nano Server to function as a container host to the Nano Server image. Part of the philosophy behind Nano Server deployment is that you only include what you need in the image. If you need something extra, you create a new image and include that extra component, rather than trying to add that extra component to your existing deployed image.

Nano Server Image Builder

Nano Server Image Builder is a graphical tool that you can use to build Nano Server images for bare metal and virtualized deployment. When you build an image for bare metal deployment, Nano Server Image Builder will create a bootable USB flash drive that you can use to install Nano Server on physical hardware. You can also use Nano Server Image Builder to create a prepared Nano Server virtual hard disk that you can use as the operating system disk for a Hyper-V virtual machine.

To use Nano Server Image Builder to build a Nano Server Image, you need access to the following:

- Access to the NanoServer folder of the Windows Server 2016 installation media. This can be stored locally or on a network share accessible to the computer on which you are running Nano Server Image Builder.

- Know the names you want to use for each Nano Server computer.

- Have any necessary drivers available if you intend to create an image that will be deployed on bare metal hardware.

You can download Nano Server Image Builder for free from Microsoft's website. Nano Server Image Builder requires the Deployment Tools and Windows Pre-installation Environment (PE) components of Windows ADK as shown in Figure 2-9.

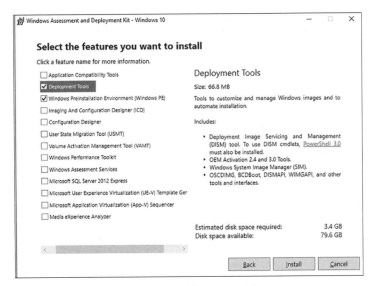

FIGURE 2-9 Nano Server Image Builder prerequisites

To create a Nano Server image using Nano Server Image Builder, perform the following steps:

1. Install and then start the Nano Server Image Builder.

2. On the Select Scenario page, shown in Figure 2-10, click Create a new Nano Server image.

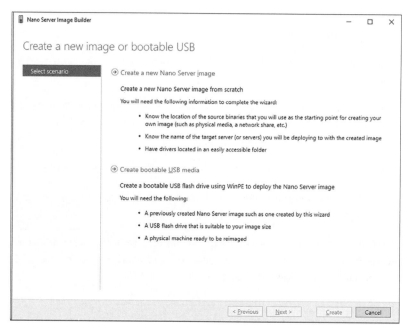

FIGURE 2-10 Select Nano Server Image Builder scenario

3. On the Select Installation Media page, specify the location that hosts the NanoServer folder copied across from the Windows Server 2016 installation media.

4. On the License page, review and agree to the license agreement.

5. On the Deployment Information page, shown in Figure 2-11, specify whether to create a virtual machine image or a physical machine image. If creating a virtual machine image, you can specify here whether you are using a .vhd or .vhdx file simply by specifying the file suffix. This page also allows you to configure the maximum size of the virtual hard disk file and the location to copy the image creation log files.

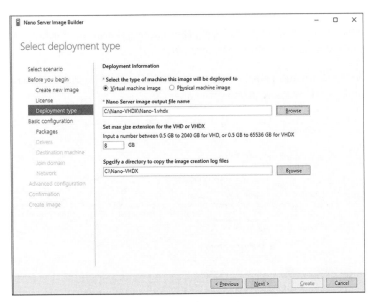

FIGURE 2-11 Configure deployment information

6. On the Packages page, choose whether the image will be for the Datacenter edition of Windows Server 2016 or the Standard edition. You can also select which roles to install. Figure 2-12 shows the Containers and DNS Server role being added to the Nano Server image.

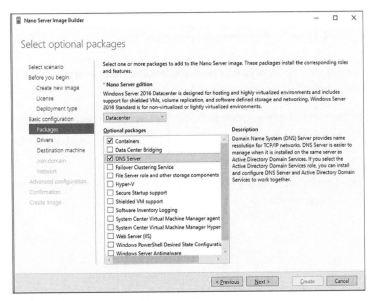

FIGURE 2-12 Select optional packages

CHAPTER 02

7.   On the Drivers page, specify any additional drivers that will be necessary for the Nano
     Server image. If you are deploying Nano Server as a virtual machine, the necessary
     Hyper-V drivers will already be included.

8.   On the Destination machine page, shown in Figure 2-13, specify the computer name,
     administrator password and time zone.

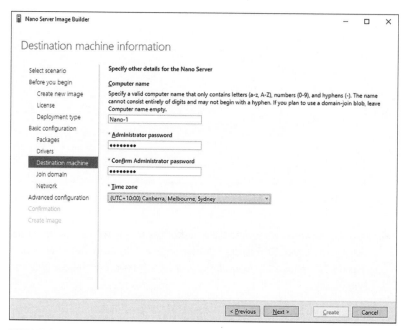

FIGURE 2-13 Destination computer properties

9.   If you've already configured a domain join blob, you can specify it on the join domain
     page.

10. On the Network page, shown in Figure 2-14, you can specify the following settings:

     ▪   Enable WinRM and remote PowerShell connections from all subnets

     ▪   Configure VLAN settings

     ▪   Specify whether the Nano Server's IP address will be obtained from a DHCP server
         or is set manually

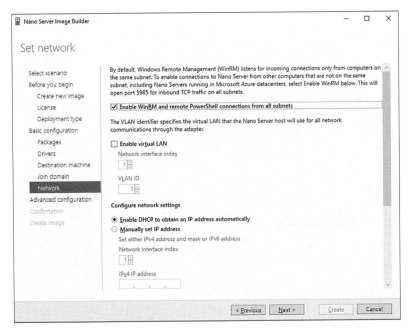

FIGURE 2-14 Network settings

11. On the Advanced configuration page, you can choose whether to create a basic Nano Server image, or you can configure additional options including applying software updates, add scripts, files, or binaries, and configure debugging methods.

12. On the Confirmation page, click Create. As shown in Figure 2-15, the Nano Server Image Builder will also provide you with the PowerShell cmdlet used to generate the Nano Server image.

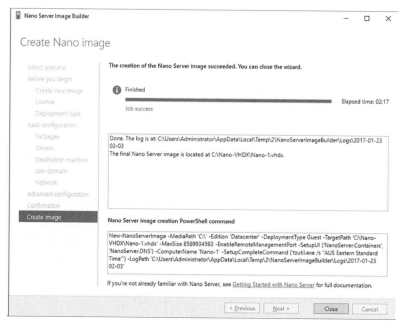

FIGURE 2-15   Create image

Nano Server Image PowerShell Cmdlets

The NanoServer folder of the Windows Server 2016 installation media contains a NanoServerImageGenerator PowerShell module. This module hosts contains the following Nano Server image management cmdlets:

- **New-NanoServerImage**. Use this cmdlet to create a new Nano Server image.

- **Edit-NanoServerImage**. Use this cmdlet to modify an existing Nano Server image.

- **Get-NanoServerPackage**. Use this cmdlet to view available Nano Server packages.

CHAPTER 03

Deployment and configuration

Depending on the size of your organization, you might deploy a couple of servers and then leave them in production for years, or, as we saw when it came to the (ongoing) retirement of Windows Server 2003, well over a decade. Other organizations deploy servers on a more frequent basis. Some even use a process where rather than applying software updates to a production server and incurring downtime as the update is applied and the server rebooted, they find it faster to deploy a newly patched computer, to migrate the existing workload to the new host, and then to decommission the original server.

This type of iterative deployment is possible because the tools around managing the configuration of servers have evolved. Today, deploying and configuring a new server is no more bothersome than deploying an application would have been a decade ago. In this chapter you'll learn about how you can use Windows Server images, Windows Deployment Services, Virtual Machine Manager, Desired State Configuration, Puppet, and Chef to deploy and manage the configuration of computers and virtual machines running the Windows Server 2016 operating system.

Bare metal versus virtualized

Today, almost all new workloads are virtualized. For most organizations, virtualization hosts are the primary remaining physically deployed server, with almost all other workloads running as virtual machines. Unless you have specific reasons not to virtualize a workload, you should run Windows Server 2016 as a VM rather than as a physically deployed server.

The security available with shielded VMs addresses one of the final objections that many organizations have had around deploying servers virtually rather than physically. With shielded VMs, you can provide the same level of security to a workload than you can to a physically deployed server sitting in a locked cage in a datacenter.

At present your best bet with deploying virtualization hosts is to choose the Server Core installation option because this has a smaller installation footprint and a reduced attack surface
compared to the Server With Desktop Experience option. When you deploy a Server Core virtualization host, you manage Hyper-V remotely from a privileged access workstation, or a tool
such as Virtual Machine Manager.

Inside OUT

Nano virtualization host

At some point in the future, more organizations will find the Nano Server installation
option a more appropriate host for virtual workloads. Many organizations are presently
reluctant to deploy Nano Server as a host for infrastructure roles simply because it is only
available in a Current Branch version rather than a Long Term Servicing Branch.

Windows images

With Windows *images*, the entire operating system as well as associated drivers, updates, and
applications is stored within a single file, known as an image file. During installation, this image
is applied to the target volume. Windows images use the Windows Imaging (WIM) file format,
which have the following benefits:

- **Multiple deployment methods.** You can use a variety of ways to deploy Windows
  images. While unusual these days, you can deploy .wim files using a traditional DVD-
  ROM, from a bootable USB drive, from a network share, or through specialized deployment technologies such as Windows Deployment Services (WDS) or System Center
  Virtual Machine Manager. While it is possible to use System Center Configuration Manager to deploy Windows Server, Configuration Manager is primarily used with client
  operating systems rather than server operating systems.

- **Editable.** You can mount an image and edit it, enabling, disabling, or removing operating system roles and features as necessary.

- **Updatable.** You can update an image without having to perform an operating system
  image capture.

The Windows Server 2016 installation media contain two .wim files in the Sources folder: Boot.
wim and Install.wim. The installation media uses Boot.wim to load the preinstallation environment that you use to deploy Windows Server 2016. Install.wim stores one or more operating
system images. For example, as Figure 3-1 shows, the Install.wim file available with the evaluation version of Windows Server 2016 contains four different editions of Windows Server 2016.

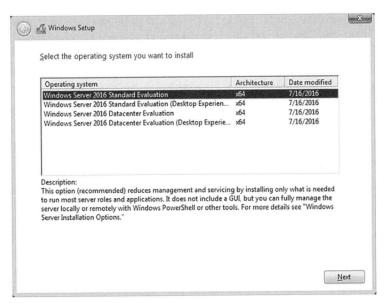

FIGURE 3-1 Windows Server 2016 editions

Modifying Windows images

The Deployment Image Servicing and Management (DISM) tool is a command-line tool that you can use to manage images in an offline state. You can use Dism.exe to perform the following tasks:

- Enable or disable roles and features

- List roles and features

- Add, remove, and list software updates

- Add, remove, and list software drivers

- Add, remove, and list software packages in .appx format to a Windows image

For example, you can take the Install.wim file from the Windows Server installation media and use Dism.exe to mount that image, add new drivers and recent software updates to that image, and save those changes to an image all without having to perform an actual deployment. The advantage is that when you do use this updated image for deployment, the drivers and updates that you added are already applied to the image and you won't have to install them as part of your post-installation configuration routine.

You can use the Microsoft Update Catalog (*https://catalog.update.microsoft.com*) to search for drivers for images that you use with physically deployed servers. This site stores all of the certified hardware drivers, software updates, and hotfixes published by Microsoft. Once you download drivers and software updates, you can add them to your existing installation images by using Dism.exe or the appropriate PowerShell cmdlets in the DISM PowerShell module.

Servicing Windows images

As an IT professional responsible for deploying Windows Server, you need to ensure that your deployment images are kept up to date. The latest software updates should be applied to the image, and any new device drivers for commonly used server hardware should be included.

The main goals of an image servicing strategy are the following:

- Ensure that the latest software updates and hotfixes are applied to the image before the image is deployed to new servers.

- Ensure that the latest drivers are applied to the image before the image is deployed to new servers.

If you don't take these steps, you'll have to wait until after you've deployed the operating system before you can apply updates and drivers. While Windows Server updates are cumulative now and you won't need to spend hours updating an image from RTM, it's quicker to have the most recent update already applied to the image than it is to wait for the server to deploy, retrieve the latest update, and then wait for it to download and then install. Having updates apply after deployment has occured consumes a significant amount of time and also substantively increases network traffic. One of your aims when performing a deployment should be to get the server operational and hosting workloads as quickly as possible.

You can use the DISM (Deployment Image Servicing and Management) utility or the associated PowerShell cmdlets in the DISM PowerShell module to service the current operating system in an online state or perform offline servicing of a Windows image.

Servicing images involves performing the following general steps:

1. Mount the image so that it can be modified.

2. Service the image.

3. Commit or discard the changes made to the image.

Mounting images

By mounting an image, you can make changes to that image. When you mount an image, you link it to a folder. You can use File Explorer, Windows PowerShell, or Cmd.exe to navigate the structure of this folder and interact with it as you would any other folder located on the file system. Once the image is mounted, you can also use Dism.exe or PowerShell to perform servicing tasks, such as adding and removing drivers and updates.

A single WIM file can contain multiple operating system images. Each operating system image is assigned an index number, which you need to know before you can mount the image. You can determine the index number using Dism.exe with the /Get-wiminfo switch. For example, if you have an image named Install.wim located in the C:\Images folder, you can use the following command to get a list of the operating system images it contains.

```
Dism.exe /get-wiminfo /wimfile:c:\images\install.wim
```

Figure 3-2 shows the result of this command and lists the images contained in Windows Server 2016. The Standard Evaluation Edition of Windows Server 2016 with the Server Core installation option is assigned index identity 1, the Standard Evaluation with the desktop experience is assigned index identity 2, the Datacenter evaluation with the Server Core installation option is assigned index identity 3 and the Datacenter evaluation with the desktop experience is assigned index identity 4.

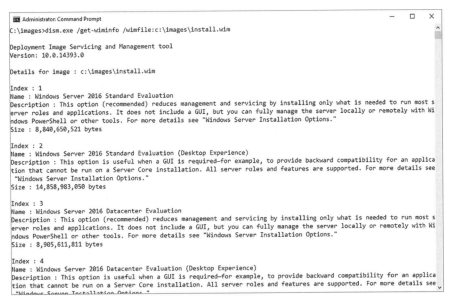

FIGURE 3-2 Details of an operating system image

You can accomplish the same task using the Get-WindowsImage PowerShell cmdlet. For example, to view the contents of the image Install.wim in the C:\Images folder, run the following command shown in Figure 3-3:

```
Get-WindowsImage -ImagePath c:\images\install.wim
```

CHAPTER 03

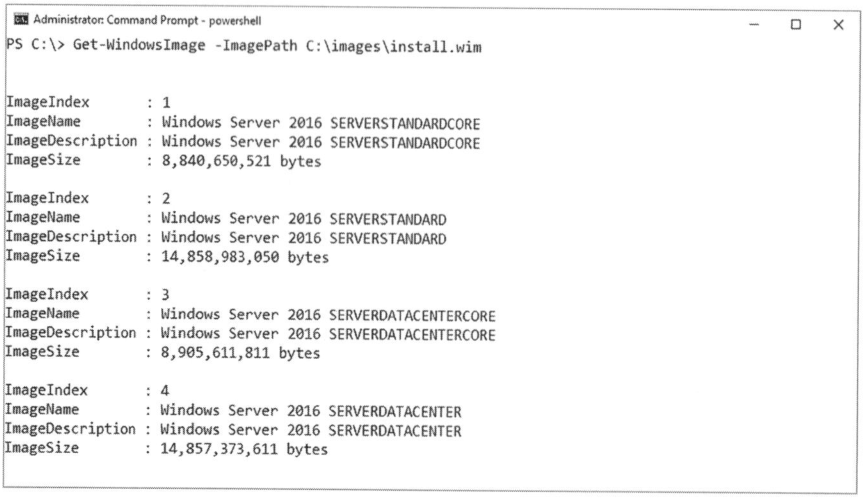

```
Administrator: Command Prompt - powershell                                    —  □  ×
PS C:\> Get-WindowsImage -ImagePath C:\images\install.wim


ImageIndex       : 1
ImageName        : Windows Server 2016 SERVERSTANDARDCORE
ImageDescription : Windows Server 2016 SERVERSTANDARDCORE
ImageSize        : 8,840,650,521 bytes

ImageIndex       : 2
ImageName        : Windows Server 2016 SERVERSTANDARD
ImageDescription : Windows Server 2016 SERVERSTANDARD
ImageSize        : 14,858,983,050 bytes

ImageIndex       : 3
ImageName        : Windows Server 2016 SERVERDATACENTERCORE
ImageDescription : Windows Server 2016 SERVERDATACENTERCORE
ImageSize        : 8,905,611,811 bytes

ImageIndex       : 4
ImageName        : Windows Server 2016 SERVERDATACENTER
ImageDescription : Windows Server 2016 SERVERDATACENTER
ImageSize        : 14,857,373,611 bytes
```

FIGURE 3-3 Windows Image details

Inside OUT

DISM and PowerShell

Coverage is provided of both DISM and PowerShell commands around image management because a large number of IT professionals are used to the former and may still use DISM in scripts. In the long run it's probably a good idea to use PowerShell, but it's also fair to say that DISM is going to be around for some time yet.

Once you have determined which operating system image you want to service, you can use the /Mount-image switch with the Dism.exe command to mount that image. For example, to mount the Standard Edition of Windows Server 2016 from the Install.wim file that is available with the Evaluation Edition in the C:\Mount folder, issue this command.

```
Dism.exe /mount-image /imagefile:c:\images\install.wim /index:2 /mountdir:c:\mount
```

Alternatively, you can accomplish the same goal using the following Mount-WindowsImage command:

```
Mount-WindowsImage -ImagePath c:\images\install.wim -index 2 -path c:\mount
```

Adding drivers and updates to images

Once you have mounted an image, you can start to service that image. When servicing images used to deploy Windows Server, the most common tasks are adding device drivers and software updates to the image. You can use the /Add-Driver switch with the Dism.exe command to add a driver to a mounted image. When using the switch by itself, you need to specify the location of the driver's .inf file. Rather than adding a driver at a time, you can use the /Recurse option to have all drivers located in a folder and its subfolders added to an image. For example, to add all of the drivers located in and under the C:\Drivers folder to the image mounted in the C:\Mount folder, use the following command.

```
Dism.exe /image:c:\mount /Add-Driver /driver:c:\drivers\ /recurse
```

Similarly, you could use the Add-WindowsDriver cmdlet to accomplish the same objective by issuing the command:

```
Add-WindowsDriver -Path c:\mount -Driver c:\drivers -Recurse
```

You can use the /Get-Driver option to list all drivers that have been added to the image and the /Remove-Driver option to remove a driver from an image. In PowerShell, you use the Get-WindowsDriver cmdlet and the Remove-WindowsDriver cmdlets. You can remove only the drivers that you or someone else has added to an image. You can't remove any of the drivers that were present in the image when Microsoft published it. You might choose to remove an existing driver if the driver you added in the past has since been updated.

You can use Dism.exe with the /Add-Package switch to add packages that contain updates or packages in .cab or .msu format. Software updates are available from the Microsoft Update Catalog website in .msu format. For example, if you can download an update from the Microsoft Update Catalog website named Cumulative Update For Windows Server 2016 for x64-based Systems (KB4010672) to the C:\Updates folder on a computer, as shown in Figure 3-4.

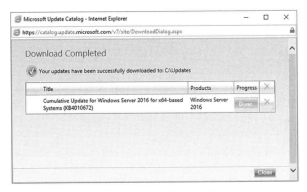

FIGURE 3-4 Downloading cumulative update

If you mounted a WIM image of the Windows Server 2016 operating system in the C:\Mount folder, you could apply the update to the image by using the command shown in Figure 3-5:

```
Dism.exe /image:c:\mount /Add-Package /PackagePath:"c:\updates\AMD64-all-
windows10.0-kb4010672-x64_e12a6da8744518197757d978764b6275f9508692.msu"
```

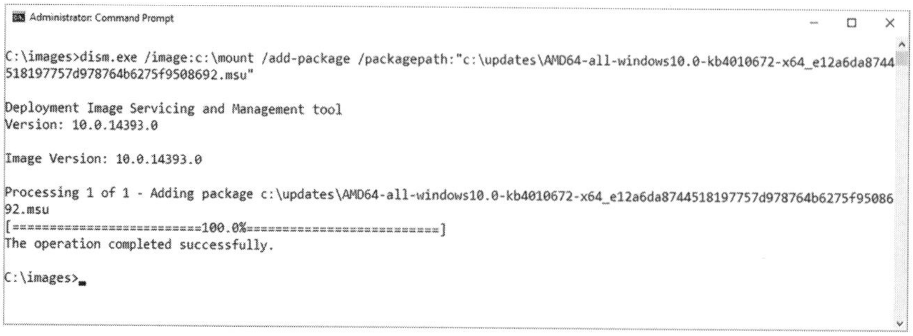

FIGURE 3-5 Applying update to an image

You can accomplish the same thing with the following Add-WindowsPackage command:

```
Add-WindowsPackage -path c:\mount -packagepath "c:\updates\AMD64-all-
windows10.0-kb4010672-x64_e12a6da8744518197757d978764b6275f9508692.msu"
```

Adding roles and features

You can determine which features are available in a mounted operating system image by using the /Get-Features switch. Features include both Windows Server 2016 roles and features. For example, to learn which features are available in the image mounted in the C:\Mount folder, use this command as shown in Figure 3-6.

```
Dism.exe /image:c:\mount /Get-Features
```

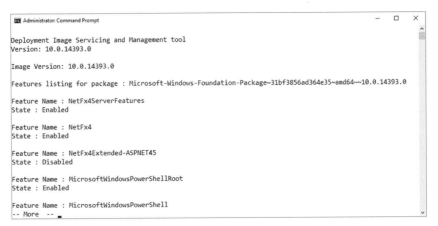

FIGURE 3-6 View features

You can enable or disable a specific feature using the /Enable-Feature switch. For example, to enable the NetFx3ServerFeatures feature, which enables the .NET Framework 3.5 server features in an image, use this command.

```
Dism.exe /image:c:\mount /Enable-Feature /all /FeatureName:NetFx3ServerFeatures
```

Some features in the Windows Server image are in a state in which they are listed as having their payload removed, which means that the installation files for that feature are not included in the image. If you install a feature that had its payload removed when the operating system was deployed, the operating system can download the files from the Microsoft update servers on the Internet. You can also specify the location of the installation files. The installation files for the features that have had their payload removed in Windows Server are located in the \Sources\sxs folder of the volume in which the installation media is located.

You can add these payload-removed features to an image by using Dism.exe and specifying the source directory. For example, to modify an image mounted in the C:\Mount folder so that the Microsoft .NET Framework 3.5 features are installed and available, issue this command when the installation media is located on volume D, as shown in Figure 3-7.

```
Dism.exe /image:c:\mount /Enable-Feature /all /FeatureName:NetFx3 /Source:d:\sources\sxs
```

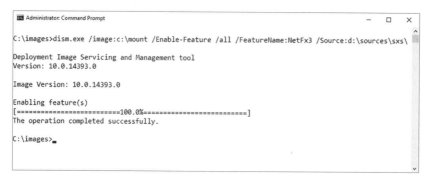

FIGURE 3-7 Enabling a feature

Inside OUT

.NET Framework 3.5

While features like WINS and SMB 1 remain available within Windows Server 2016, .NET Framework 3.5 is not only not installed by default, but has been quarantined off into its own separate installation folder. One might suspect that Microsoft wants it to be difficult to install. The problem is, such a huge variety of software, including relatively new software, depends on .NET Framework 3.5, that installing it is more of a hassle than it needs to be.

Committing an image

When you finish servicing an image, you can save your changes using the /Unmount-Wim switch with the /Commit option. You can discard changes using the /Discard option. For example, to make changes and then commit the image mounted in the C:\Mount folder, use this command.

```
Dism.exe /Unmount-Wim /MountDir:c:\mount /commit
```

You can use the Save-WindowsImage PowerShell cmdlet to save changes to an image without dismounting the image. You use the Dismount-WimImage cmdlet with the Save parameter to save the modifications that you've made to an image and then dismount it. For example, to dismount and save the image mounted in the C:\Mount folder, run the command:

```
Dismount-WimImage -Path c:\mount -Save
```

Once you have committed the changes, the .wim file that you originally mounted is updated with these modifications. You can then import this .wim file into WDS, use it to build a virtual hard disk, or use it with bootable USB installation media to deploy Windows Server 2016, or with these updates and modifications already applied.

Build and capture

When you perform a build and capture, you deploy an operating system; provision that operating system with updates, applications, and drivers; and then capture that operating system for deployment. Build and capture is used less often with server operating systems because they rarely require the same sort of application deployment that is required for client operating systems. If you can just pull a container with an updated application down onto an operating system after deployment, there is little reason to include it in the image. Additionally, with tools such as Desired State Configuration, Chef, and Puppet, many post installation and configuration tasks can be completely automated, reducing the hassle of post installation configuration.

If your deployment strategy does involve the deployment and capture of Windows Server 2016, you need to remember that you'll need to generalize the image prior to capture, removing any configuration information that is specific to the installation. You can perform this task using the Sysprep.exe utility. Sysprep.exe is included with Windows Server 2016 and is located in the C:\Windows\System32\Sysprep folder. When you use Sysprep.exe to prepare the image, you can configure the image to return to the system Out-of-Box Experience (OOBE) as shown in Figure 3-8. This is the same experience you get when Windows Server boots for the first time, though in this case all of the updates, applications, and drivers included in the captured image are included in the newly deployed image.

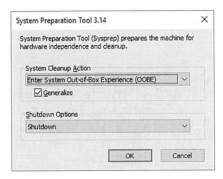

FIGURE 3-8 Sysprep

You can use Dism.exe with the /Capture-Image switch or the New-WindowsImage PowerShell cmdlet to capture an image.

Answer files

Answer files present a traditional method of performing operating system deployment and configuration. While not as comprehensive as newer technologies such as desired state configuration that assist not only in deployment, but ongoing configuration, answer files allow you to automate the process of deploying Windows Server.

Instead of having to manually select specific installation options and perform post–installation configuration actions such as joining a newly deployed server to an AD DS domain, you can automate the process with answer files. During setup, the Windows Server looks for a file on local and attached media named Autounattend.xml. If this file is present, Windows Server automatically uses the settings contained in the file to configure the new server deployment.

As its name suggests, Autounattend.xml uses the XML file format. Although it is certainly possible for you to manually edit this XML file using a text editor such as Notepad, this process is complicated, and you are likely to make errors that cause the file to not work. The Windows System Image Manager (known as Windows SIM) is a GUI-based tool that you can use to create an answer file. When using the tool, you must specify the image for which you want to create an answer file. Windows SIM then creates a catalog file for all the options that you can configure. After you configure all the settings that you want automated during installation and post-installation configuration, you can have the tool output an answer file using correct XML syntax. Windows SIM is included with the Windows Assessment and Deployment Kit (Windows ADK), which you can download from the Microsoft website.

To create an answer file using Windows SIM, perform the following steps:

1. Download and install Windows ADK from the Microsoft website using the installation defaults. You can do this with Chocolatey, covered later in this chapter, by running the following command:

    ```
    Choco install -y windows-adk-all
    ```

2. Copy the file \Sources\install.wim from the Windows Server installation media to a temporary directory on the computer on which you have installed Windows ADK.

3. Open Windows SIM from the Start screen.

4. In the Windows SIM interface, click File, and then click Select Windows Image. Open the file Install.wim.

5. Select an operating system image in the install image for which you wish to create an answer file. For example, Figure 3-9 shows the selection of the Standard edition with Desktop Experience operating system.

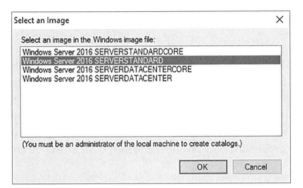

FIGURE 3-9 Select an image

6. When prompted to create a catalog file, click Yes.

7. Click File, and click New Answer File.

8. Use Windows SIM to select each component that you want to configure. Figure 3-10
    shows how you can configure installation to join the contoso.com domain.

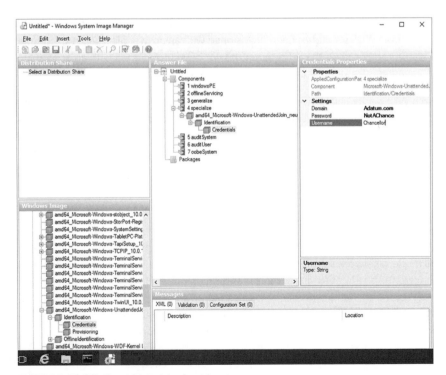

FIGURE 3-10 Windows System Image Manager

Windows Deployment Services

Windows Deployment Services (WDS) is a server role that you can deploy on computers running Windows Server. WDS enables you to deploy operating systems, including Windows 8.1, Windows 10, Windows Server 2012, Windows Server 2012 R2, Windows Server 2016, to computers over the network. WDS sends these operating systems across the network using multicast transmissions, which means that multiple computers receive the same operating system image while minimizing the use of network bandwidth. When you use multicast transmissions, the same amount of traffic crosses the network independently of whether you are deploying an operating system to one computer or 50.

Deploying Windows Server through WDS involves performing the following steps:

1. An operating system deployment transmission is prepared on the WDS server.

2. The media access control (MAC) addresses of Pre-boot Execution Environment (PXE)–compliant network adapters are made available to the WDS server.

3. The computers that are targets of the transmission boot using their PXE–compliant network adapters.

4. These computers locate the WDS server and begin the operating system setup process. If the WDS server has been provisioned with an answer file, the setup completes automatically. If the WDS server has not been provisioned with an answer file, an administrator must enter setup configuration information.

Each WDS server can have only one unattended installation file for each processor architecture. Because unattended installation files differ between server and client, you either need to swap unattended files when you are switching between client and server, or have multiple WDS servers. WDS can be used in conjunction with other technologies such as Desired State Configuration where an answer file only performs basic configuration tasks, with the substantial tasks completed by an advanced configuration technology.

WDS requirements

WDS clients need a PXE–compliant network adapter, which is rarely a problem because almost all modern network adapters are PXE–compliant. You can also use WDS to deploy Windows Server 2012 and later to virtual machines running under Hyper-V. The trick to doing this is to use a legacy rather than a synthetic network adapter when creating the virtual machine as a Generation 1 virtual machine. This isn't necessary when using Generation 2 virtual machines because the Generation 2 virtual machine network adapters support PXE booting.

If you have a computer that does not have a PXE–compliant network adapter, you can configure a special type of boot image known as a discover image. A discover image boots an environment, loading special drivers to enable the network adapter to interact with the WDS server. You create the boot image by adding the appropriate network adapter drivers associated with the computer that can't PXE boot to the Boot.wim file from the Windows Server installation media.

WDS has the following requirements:

- A Windows Server DNS server must be present on the local area network (LAN).

- An authorized Dynamic Host Configuration Protocol (DHCP) server must be present on the network. You can host WDS and DHCP on the same computer as long as you configure the options shown in Figure 3-11.

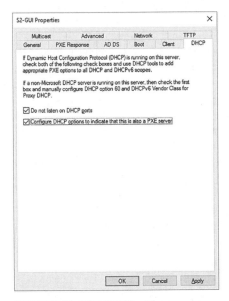

FIGURE 3-11 WDS DHCP settings

If you install WDS from the Add Roles And Features Wizard, you can configure these settings automatically. Although the WDS server does not require a static IP address, it is good practice to ensure that infrastructure roles such as WDS always use a consistent network address. You can install WDS on computers running the Server Core version of Windows Server, but not currently on Nano Server.

When installing WDS on Server Core, you have to specify the location of the source files or ensure that the server has a connection to the Internet, which enables them to be downloaded automatically. Although it is possible to manage WDS from Windows PowerShell, most administrators use the graphical WDS Remote Server Administration Tools (RSAT) from a computer running Windows 10 or Windows Server 2016 with the desktop experience.

Managing images

Images contain either entire operating systems or a version of a special stripped-down operating system known as Windows PE. Windows PE functions as a type of boot disk, enabling a basic environment to be loaded from which more complex maintenance and installation tasks can be performed. WDS uses four image types: boot image, install image, discover image, and capture image.

- **Boot image.** A special image that enables the computer to boot and begin installing the operating system using the install image. A default boot image, named Boot.wim, is located in the sources folder of the Windows Server installation media.

- **Install image.** The main type of image discussed in this chapter. Contains the operating system as well as any other included components, such as software updates and additional applications. A default install image, named Install.wim, is present in the sources folder of the Windows Server installation media. Install images can be in .vhd or .vhdx format, though you can only manage install images using the WDS console in Windows Server 2012 R2 or Windows Server 2016.

- **Discover image.** This special image is for computers that cannot PXE boot to load appropriate network drivers to begin a session with a WDS server.

- **Capture image.** A special image type that enables a prepared computer to be booted so that its operating system state can be captured as an install image. You add capture images as boot images in WDS.

To import an image into WDS, perform the following steps:

1. Open the Windows Deployment Services console.

2. Click Install Images. From the Action menu, click Add Install Image.

3. Choose whether to create a new image group, or to use an existing image group.

4. Specify the location of the image file.

5. In the Available Images page of the Add Image Wizard, select the operating system images that you want to add. When the image or images are added, click Next, and then click Finish.

Configuring WDS

The installation defaults for WDS are suitable when you deploy the role in small environments. If you are deploying WDS in larger environments and do not choose to implement System Center Virtual Machine Manager for server operating system deployments, you might want to configure the options discussed in the following sections, which are available by editing the properties of the WDS server in the Windows Deployment Services console.

PXE response settings

With PXE response settings, you can configure how the WDS server responds to computers. As Figure 3-12 shows, you can configure WDS not to respond to any client computers (this effectively disables WDS), to respond to known client computers, or to respond to all computers but require an administrator to manually approve an unknown computer. Known computers are ones that have prestaged accounts in Active Directory. You can prestage computers if you know the MAC address of the network interface card (NIC) that the computer uses. Vendors often supply a list of MAC addresses associated with computers when you purchase those computers, and you can use this list to prestage computer accounts.

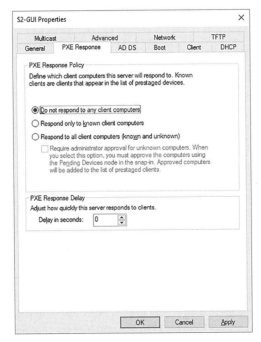

FIGURE 3-12 PXE Response settings

You use the PXE Response Delay setting when you have more than one WDS server in an environment. You can use this setting to ensure that clients receive transmissions from one WDS server over another, with the server configured with the lowest PXE response delay having priority over other WDS servers with higher delay settings.

Client naming policy

The client naming policy enables you to configure how computers installed from WDS are named if you aren't using deployment options that perform the action. You can also use the settings on this tab, shown in Figure 3-13, to configure domain membership and organizational unit (OU) options for the computer account.

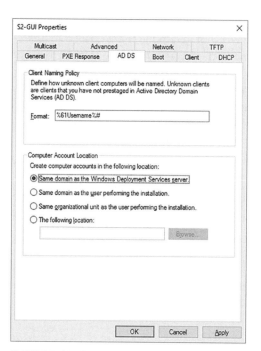

FIGURE 3-13 Client Naming Policy

WDS boot options

In the Boot Options tab of the WDS server's Properties dialog box, shown in Figure 3-14, you can configure how clients that PXE boot interact with the WDS server. You can also configure a default boot image for each architecture supported by WDS. By default, once a client has connected to a WDS server, someone must press the F12 key to continue deploying the operating system. In environments in which you are performing a large number of simultaneous deployments, requiring this level of manual intervention might substantially delay the deployment.

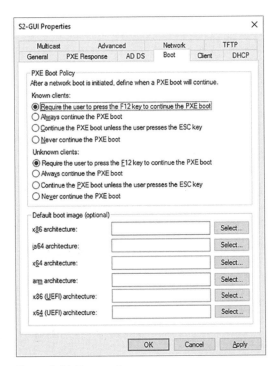

Figure 3-14 Boot options

Multicast options

The default settings of WDS have all computers that join the multicast transmission receiving the installation image at the same speed. If you frequently deploy operating systems, you are aware that sometimes there are one or two computers that have network adapters that slow a transmission that should take only 15 minutes into one that takes half a day. You can configure the transfer settings on the Multicast tab, shown in Figure 3-15, so that clients are partitioned into separate sessions depending on how fast they can consume the multicast transmission. You still have those slow computers taking a long time to receive the image, but the other comput-ers connected to the transmission can complete the deployment quicker.

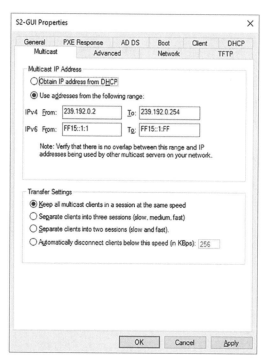

Figure 3-15 WDS multicast options

Other options

Although you are less likely to need them, you can configure other options on the following tabs:

- **Advanced tab**. You can configure WDS to use a specific domain controller and global catalog (GC) server. You can also configure whether WDS is authorized in DHCP. DHCP authorization occurs automatically when you install the WDS role.

- **Network tab.** You can specify a User Datagram Protocol (UDP) port policy to limit when UDP ports are used with transmissions. You can also configure a network profile to specify the speed of the network, minimizing the chance that WDS transmissions slow the network down.

- **TFTP tab.** You can specify maximum block size and Trivial File Transfer Protocol (TFTP) window size.

Configuring transmissions

You use WDS transmissions to set WDS to transfer the operating system image to PXE clients. When configuring a WDS transmission, you need to decide what type of multicast transmission you are going to perform in the Multicast Type page of the Create Multicast Transmission Wizard, as shown in Figure 3-16.

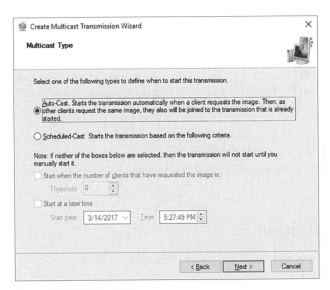

Figure 3-16 Multicast type

The difference between these options is as follows:

- **Auto-Cast.** A transmission starts whenever a client requests the image. If another client requests the same image, the client joins the existing transmission, caching data from the current transfer, and then retrieving data that was transmitted before the client joined the transmission. This is the best option to use when you are performing one-off deployments.

- **Scheduled-Cast.** You choose either to start the transmission when a specified number of clients have joined, or at a particular date and time. This is the best option to use when you are deploying the same operating system image to a large number of computers.

To configure a WDS transmission, perform the following steps:

1. Open the Windows Deployment Services console, expand the WDS server from which you want to perform the deployment, and click Multicast Transmissions. In the Action menu, click Create Multicast Transmission.

2. Provide a name for the multicast transmission.

3. In the Image Selection page, specify which operating system image you want to deploy using the transmission.

4. In the Multicast Type page, specify whether you use Auto-Cast or Scheduled-Cast. If you choose Scheduled-Cast, select the number of clients, or the transmission start time.

Driver groups and packages

You can stage device drivers on a WDS server by importing the device driver as a package. A driver package contains the extracted driver files. You can import the driver package into WDS by locating the driver's .inf file. When using the WDS console, you can either import individual driver packages, or all of the drivers in a set of folders.

In the WDS console, you can organize drivers into driver groups. A driver package can be a member of more than one group, and deleting a driver group does not delete the associated driver packages. You can use driver groups with filters to limit which driver packages are available to WDS clients.

Virtual Machine Manager

For most organizations, the majority of their server deployments involve virtual machines rather than deploying to bare metal physical hardware. While tools such as the Hyper-V console and WDS are adequate for smaller environments, if you need to deploy hundreds or thousands of virtual machines each year, you need a more comprehensive set of tools than those that are included with the Windows Server operating system.

System Center Virtual Machine Manager is one tool that you can use to manage your organization's entire virtualization infrastructure, from virtualization hosts, clusters and VMs, through to managing the entire networking and storage stack. In this section, you'll learn about VMM templates, storage, networking, and host groups.

Virtual machine templates

A Virtual Machine Manager VM template allows you to rapidly deploy virtual machines with a consistent set of settings. A VMM VM template is an XML object that is stored with a VMM library, and includes one or more of the following components:

- **Guest Operating System Profile**. A guest operating system profile that includes operating system settings.

- **Hardware Profile**. A hardware profile that includes VM hardware settings.

- **Virtual Hard Disk**. This can be a blank hard disk, or a virtual hard disk that hosts a specially prepared, sysprepped in the case of Windows based operating systems, version of an operating system.

You can create VM templates based on existing virtual machines deployed on a virtualization host managed by VMM, based on virtual hard disks stored in a VMM library, or by using an existing VM template.

VM templates have the following limitations:

- A VM template allows you to customize IP address settings, but you can only configure a static IP address for a specific VM when deploying that VM from the template.

- Application and SQL Server deployment are only used when you deploy a VM as part of a service.

- When creating a template from an existing VM, ensure that the VM is a member of a workgroup and is not joined to a domain.

- You should create a separate local administrator account on a VM before using it as the basis of a template. Using the built-in administrator account causes the sysprep operation to fail.

MORE INFO VIRTUAL MACHINE TEMPLATES

You can learn more about virtual machine templates at *https://technet.microsoft.com/ en-us/system-center-docs/vmm/manage/manage-vm-template*.

VMM storage

VMM can use local and remote storage, with local storage being storage devices that are directly attached to the server and remote storage being storage available through a storage area network. VMM can use:

- **File storage**. VMM can use file shares that support the SMB 3.0 protocol. This protocol is supported by file shares on computers running Windows Server 2012 and later. SMB 3.0 is also supported by third-party vendors of network-attached storage (NAS) devices.

- **Block storage**. VMM can use block-level storage devices that host LUNs (Logical Unit Numbers) for storage using either the iSCSI, Serial Attached SCSI (SAS), or Fibre Channel protocols.

VMM supports automatically discovering local and remote storage. This includes automatic discovery of the following.

- Storage arrays

- Storage pools

- Storage volumes

- LUNs

- Disks

- Virtual disks

Using VMM, you can create new storage from capacity discovered by VMM and assign that storage to a Hyper-V virtualization host or host cluster. You can use VMM to provision storage to Hyper-V virtualization hosts or host clusters using the following methods:

- **From available capacity**. Allows you to create storage volumes or LUNs from an existing storage pool.

- **From writable snapshot of a virtual disk**. VMM supports creating storage from writable snapshots of existing virtual disks.

- **From a clone of a virtual disk**. You can provision storage by creating a copy of a virtual disk. This uses storage space less efficiently than creating storage from snapshots.

- **From SMB 3.0 file shares**. You can provision storage from SMB 3.0 file shares.

VMM supports the creation of a thin provisioned logical unit on a storage pool. This allows you to allocate a greater amount of capacity than is currently available in the pool and is only possible when:

- The storage array supports thin provisioning

- The storage administrator has enabled thin provisioning for the storage pool

MORE INFO STORAGE IN VMM

You can learn more about storage in VMM at *https://technet.microsoft.com/en-us/ system-center-docs/vmm/manage/manage-storage-overview.*

Inside OUT

Storage classifications

Storage classifications allow you to assign a metadata label to a type of storage. For example, you might name a classification used with a storage pool that consists of high speed solid state disks as Alpha, a classification used with Fibre Channel RAID 5 SAS storage as Beta, and iSCSI SATA RAID 5 as Gamma. The labels that you use should be appropriate to your environment.

VMM networking

A VMM logical network is a collection of network sites, VLAN information, and IP subnet information. A VMM deployment needs to have at least one logical network before you can use it to deploy VMs or services. When you add a Hyper-V based virtualization host to VMM, one of the following happens:

- If the physical adapter is associated with an existing logical network, it remains associated with that network once added to VMM.

- If the physical adapter is not already associated with a logical network, VMM creates a new logical network, associating it with the physical adapter's DNS suffix.

You can create logical networks with the following properties:

- One connected network. Choose this option when network sites that comprise this network can route traffic to each other and you can use this logical network as a single connected network. You have the additional option of allowing VM networks created on this logical network to use network virtualization. You can also select the option of having VMM automatically create

- VLAN-based independent networks. The sites in this logical network are independent networks. The network sites that comprise this network can, but do not require, the ability to route traffic to each other.

- Private VLAN (PVLAN) networks. Choose this option when you want network sites within the logical network to be isolated independent networks.

You create network sites after you have created a VMM logical network. You use network sites to associate IP subnets, VLANs, and PVLANs with a VMM logical network.

MORE INFO   VMM LOGICAL NETWORK

You can learn more about VMM logical networks at *http://technet.microsoft.com/en-us/library/jj721568.aspx.*

Logical switches

VMM logical switches store network adapter configuration settings for use with VMM managed virtualization hosts. You configure the properties of one or more virtualization host's network adapters by applying the logical switch configuration information.

You should perform the following tasks before creating a logical switch:

- Create logical networks and define network sites.

- Install the providers for any Hyper-V extensible virtual switch extensions.

- Create any required native port profiles for virtual adapters that you use to define port settings for the native Hyper-V virtual switch.

When you configure a VMM logical switch, you configure the following:

- Extensions

- Uplinks

- Virtual Ports

Extensions

You use logical switch extensions to configure how the logical switch interacts with network traffic. VMM includes the following switch extensions:

- **Monitoring.** Allows the logical switch to monitor, but not modify, network traffic.

- **Capturing.** Allows the logical switch to inspect, but not modify, network traffic.

- **Filtering.** Allows the logical switch to modify, defragment, or block packets.

- **Forwarding.** Allows the logical switch to alter the destination of network traffic based on the properties of that traffic.

Uplink port profiles

Uplink port profiles specify which set of logical networks should be associated with physical network adapters. In the event that there are multiple network adapters on a virtualization host, an uplink port profile specifies whether and how those adapters should participate in teaming.

Teaming allows network adapters to aggregate bandwidth and provide redundancy for network connections.

Virtual port profiles

You use port classifications to apply configurations based on functionality. The following port profiles are available:

- **SR-IOV.** Allows a virtual network adapter to use SR-IOV (Single Root Input Output Virtualization).

- **Host management.** For network adapters used to manage the virtualization host using RDP, PowerShell, or another management technology.

- **Network load balancing.** To be used with network adapters that participate in Microsoft Network Load Balancing.

- **Guest dynamic IP.** Used with network adapters that require guest dynamic IP addresses such as those provided by DHCP.

- **Live migration workload.** Used with network adapters that support VM live migration workloads between virtualization hosts.

- **Medium bandwidth.** Assign to network adapters that need to support medium bandwidth workloads.

- **Host cluster workload.** Assign to network adapters that are used to support host clusters.

- **Low bandwidth.** Assign to network adapters that need to support low bandwidth workloads.

- **High bandwidth.** Assign to network adapters that are used to support high bandwidth workloads.

- **iSCSI workload.** Assign to network adapters that are used to connect to SAN resources using the iSCSI protocol.

MORE INFO PORT PROFILES AND LOGICAL SWITCHES

You can learn more about port profiles and logical switches at *https://technet.microsoft.com/en-us/system-center-docs/vmm/manage/manage-network-port-profiles*.

Virtual machine networks

In VMM, virtual machines connect to a VMM logical network through a VMM virtual machine network. You connect a virtual machine's network adapter to the virtual machine network rather than the logical network. You can have VMM automatically create an associated virtual machine network when you create a logical network. If you have configured a logical network to support network virtualization, you can connect multiple VM networks to the logical network and they will be isolated from each other.

You can use network virtualization to configure logical networks in such a manner that different VM tenants can utilize the same IP address space on the same virtualization host without collisions occurring. For example, tenant alpha and tenant beta use the 172.16.10.x address space when their workloads are hosted on the same virtualization host cluster. Even though tenant alpha and tenant beta have virtual machines that use the same IPv4 address, network virtualization ensures that conflicts do not occur.

When you configure network virtualization, each network adapter is assigned two IP addresses:

- **Customer IP address**. This IP address is the one used by the customer. The customer IP address is the address visible within the VM when you run a command such as ipconfig or Get-NetIPConfiguration.

- **Provider IP address**. This IP address is used by, and is visible to, VMM. It is not visible within the VM operating system.

MORE INFO   VIRTUAL MACHINE NETWORKS

You can learn more about virtual machine networks at *https://technet.microsoft.com/ en-us/system-center-docs/vmm/manage/manage-network-vm-networks*.

MAC address pools

A MAC address pool gives you a pool of MAC addresses that can be assigned to virtual machine network adapters across a group of virtualization hosts. Without MAC address pools, virtual machines are assigned MAC addresses on a per-virtualization host basis. While unlikely, it is possible that in environments with a very large number of virtualization hosts, that the same MAC address may be assigned by separate virtualization hosts. Using a central MAC address pool ensures that doesn't happen. When creating a MAC address pool, you specify a starting and an ending MAC address range.

MORE INFO   MAC ADDRESS POOLS

You can learn more about MAC address pools at *https://technet.microsoft.com/en-us/ system-center-docs/vmm/manage/manage-network-mac-address-pools*.

Static IP address pools

An IP address pool is a collection of IP addresses that, through an IP subnet, is associated with a network site. VMM can assign IP addresses from the static IP address pool to virtual machines running Windows operating systems if those virtual machines use the logical network associated with the pool. Static IP address pools can contain default gateway, DNS server, and WINS server information. Static IP address pools aren't necessary because VMs can be assigned IP address information from DHCP servers running on the network.

> #### MORE INFO IP ADDRESS POOLS
>
> **You can learn more about IP address pools at *https://technet.microsoft.com/en-us/ system-center-docs/vmm/manage/manage-network-static-address-pools*.**

Private VLANS

VLANs segment network traffic by adding tags to packets. A VLAN ID is a 12-bit number, allowing you to configure VLAN IDS between the numbers 1 and 4095. While this is more than adequate for the majority of on premises deployments, large hosting providers often have more than 5,000 clients, so have to use an alternate method to segment network traffic. A PVLAN is an extension to VLANS that uses a secondary VLAN ID with the original VLAN ID to segment a VLAN into isolated sub networks.

You can implement VLANs and PVLANs in VMM by creating a logical network of the Private VLAN type. When you create a logical network of this type you have the option, when adding a network site, of specifying the VLAN and/or PVLAN ID, as well as the IPv4 or IPv6 network.

Adding a WDS to VMM

In a scalable environment, you'll need to add additional Hyper-V host servers on a frequent basis as either a standalone server or as part of a failover cluster to increase your capacity. While it's possible to use another technology to deploy new Hyper-V host servers to bare metal, the advantage of integrating virtualization host deployment with VMM is that you can fully automate the process. The process works in the following general manner:

1. Discovery of the chassis occurs. This may be through providing the MAC address of the chassis network adapter to VMM.

2. The chassis performs a PXE boot and locates the Windows Deployment Services (WDS) server that you have integrated with VMM as a managed server role. When you integrate WDS with VMM, the WDS server hosts a VMM provider that handles PXE traffic from bare metal chassis started using the VMM provisioning tool.

3. The VMM provider on the WDS server queries the VMM server to verify that the bare metal chassis is an authorized target for managed virtualization host deployment. In the event that the bare metal chassis isn't authorized, WDS attempts to deploy another operating system to the chassis. If that isn't possible, PXE deployment fails.

4. If the bare metal chassis is authorized, a special Windows PE (Preinstallation Environment) image is transmitted to the bare metal chassis. This special Windows PE image includes a VMM agent that manages the operating system deployment process.

5. Depending on how you configure it, the VMM agent in the Windows PE image can run scripts to update firmware on the bare metal chassis, configure RAID volumes, and prepare local storage.

6. A specially prepared virtual hard disk (in either .vhdx or .vhd format) containing the virtualization host operating system is copied to the bare metal chassis from a VMM library server.

7. The VMM agent in the Windows PE image configures the bare metal chassis to boot from the newly placed virtual hard disk.

8. The bare metal chassis boots into the virtual hard disk. If necessary, the newly deployed operating system can obtain additional drivers not included in the virtual hard disk from a VMM library server.

9. Post deployment customization of the newly deployed operating system occurs. This includes setting a name for the new host and joining an Active Directory Domain Services domain.

10. The Hyper-V server role is deployed and the newly deployed virtualization host is connected to VMM and placed in a host group.

The PXE server needs to provide the PXE service through Windows Deployment Services. When you add the VMM agent to an existing Windows Deployment Services server, VMM only manages the deployment process if the computer making the request is designated as a new virtualization host by VMM.

To integrate the WDS server with VMM to function as the VMM PXE server, you need to use an account on the VMM server that is a member of the local Administrators group on the WDS server. PXE servers need to be on the same subnet as the bare metal chassis to which they deploy the virtualization host operating system.

VMM host groups

Host groups allow you to simplify the management of virtualization hosts by allowing you to apply the same settings across multiple hosts. VMM includes the All Hosts group by default.

You can create additional host groups as required in a hierarchical structure. Child host groups inherit settings from the parent host group. However, if you move a child host group to a new host group, the child host group retains its original settings with the exception of any PRO configuration. When you configure changes to a parent host group, VMM provides a dialog box asking if you would like to apply the changed settings to child host groups.

You can assign host groups network and storage. Host group networks are the networks that are assigned to the host group. These resources include IP address pools, load balances, logical networks, and MAC address pools. Host group storage allows you to allocate logical units or storage pools that are accessible to the VMM server for a specific host group.

MORE INFO   VMM HOST GROUPS

You can learn more about VMM host groups at *https://technet.microsoft.com/en-us/ system-center-docs/vmm/manage/manage-compute-host-groups*.

VMM virtualization host requirements

To be able to configure a bare metal hardware chassis so that it can function as a VMM managed Hyper-V virtualization host, the hardware chassis needs to meet the following requirements:

- **X64 processor**. This needs to support hardware assisted virtualization and hardware-enforced Data Execution Prevention (DEP). In some cases, it may be necessary to enable this support in BIOS.

- **PXE boot support**. The hardware chassis must be able to PXE boot off a PXE enabled network adapter. The PXE enabled network adapter needs to be configured as a boot device.

- **Out of band (OOB) management support**. System Center VMM is able to discover and manage the power states of hardware chassis that support BMC (Baseboard Management Controller). VMM supports the following protocols:

  - SMASH (Systems Management Architecture for Server Hardware) version 1 over WS-Management

  - DCMI (Datacenter Management Interface) version 1.0

  - IPMI (Microsoft Intelligent Platform Management Interface) version 1.5 or version 2.0

Placement rules

Placement rules allow you to configure how VMM identifies a suitable host for a VM deployment. Usually this is based on the available resources on the virtualization host or the host cluster. By configuring host group placement rules, you can create rules that dictate the conditions under which a new VM can be placed on a virtualization host in the host group.

To add a placement rule, edit the properties of the host group and on the placement tab click Add. You then specify a custom property and one of the following requirements:

- Virtual Machine Must Match Host

- Virtual Machine Should Match Host

- Virtual Machine Must Not Match Host

- Virtual Machine Should Not Match Host

Host reserves

Host reserves allow you to configure the resources that VMM should set aside for the host operating system. When VMM is going to place a new VM on a host, that host must be able to meet the VM's resource requirements without exceeding the configured host reserves. You can configure host reserves for:

- CPU

- Memory

- Disk I/O

- Disk Space

- Network I/O

Dynamic optimization

Dynamic optimization allows virtualization host clusters to balance workloads by transferring VMs between nodes according to the settings configured at the host group level. Whether or not the transfer occurs depends on whether the hardware resources on a node in the virtualization host cluster fall below the configured settings. Dynamic optimization only applies to clustered virtualization hosts and does not apply hosts that are not members of a cluster.

> ### MORE INFO   VIRTUAL MACHINE MANAGER
>
> You can learn more about Virtual Machine Manager at *https://technet.microsoft.com/en-us/system-center-docs/vmm/vmm*.

Infrastructure configuration as code

As infrastructure, including servers, storage, and networks, has increasingly become virtualized, configuration of that infrastructure has increasingly become defined by code. This means that, rather than having to build out a template image, it's increasingly possible to define the properties of a server and the workload it hosts through a template written in a format such as JavaScript Object Notation (JSON), Ruby, or XML.

For example, with Azure it's possible to load a JSON template that defines not only the properties of a virtual machine workload, but the network and storage settings associated with that workload. It also becomes increasingly possible to alter the properties of a running workload by modifying and reapplying the template rather than going through the workload's management interface and applying changes manually.

Other advantages of infrastructure configuration as code include:

- You can version that code, rolling back changes by simply applying an earlier version of a set of templates in the event that a set of changes wind up causing unforeseen problems.

- You can test the infrastructure code in a development environment before deploying it in a production environment. For example, you can test that the infrastructure code to build your production VM workloads functions as expected on a test Hyper-V server before deploying the same code onto your production Hyper-V failover cluster.

The Lability PowerShell module, hosted on GitHub at *https://github.com/VirtualEngine/Lability* provides a set of PowerShell tools that allow for the automatic creation of entire Hyper-V based testing labs by running a set of scripts that do the following:

- Create updated base operating system virtual machine hard disk images by:
  - Automatically downloading required operating system evaluation software from the Internet.
  - Using the WIM images stored on those evaluation versions of Windows operating systems, create sysprepped virtual machine parent disks.
  - Applying the most recent software updates to ensure that the base operating system virtual machine hard disks are up to date.

- Creating Hyper-V internal and external networks.

- Creating fully functional virtual machines including:
  - Creating new virtual machines from the base operating system virtual hard disks.
  - Connecting these newly created virtual machines to appropriate Hyper-V internal and external networks.

- Injecting Desired State Configuration resources into the VMs from the host machine.

- Injecting Unattend.xml files into the newly created VMs.

- Invoking the DSC Local Configuration Manager to trigger application of the DSC resources.

In Virtual Machine Manager you can deploy a multi-tier virtual machine service by creating, configuring, and deploying the appropriate VM and service templates. Tools such as Lability demonstrate that it's possible to deploy entire environments quickly from scratch just with scripts, tools such as DSC, and base operating system's installation media.

Inside OUT

Infrastructure Developer

Infrastructure Developer provides an alternative way of describing some of the descriptions that are associated with DevOps. Many of us that came up through IT operations are suspicious of any new approach, simply because most of us have been in the industry some time and we've seen different fads come and go. Many IT professionals staff actually work in environments that don't have a single developer. That means the idea of adopting "a DevOps" mindset seems irrelevant to the way that they actually do their job on a day-to-day basis because deployments of brand new software happen infrequently rather than every day. However, because configuration is increasingly defined through code it's not unreasonable for IT Operations staff whom work with configuration code to be termed "Infrastructure Developers." Rather than creating and modifying application code, what we'll be doing is creating and modifying the code that defines our organization's infrastructure. For the most part, we're doing the same sort of things we were doing when we got into the industry in the 90s, it's just that now we're using a new set of code-based tools.

Desired State Configuration

Desired State Configuration (DSC) is a configuration management technology that's built into Windows Server 2016 through PowerShell version 5 and higher. At a high level, a DSC configuration file describes how a computer should be configured rather than just a script that configures a computer. A component of DSC, called the Local Configuration Manager, takes a configuration file that describes how the server should be configured and ensures that the server is configured in that way.

Almost all of the tools required to use DSC are built into Windows Server 2016. You can also use DSC in a homogeneous Windows environment without the need to deploy a third-party operating system. A current disadvantage of DSC is that it can be challenging and complicated to configure and that it isn't as developed as other third-party configuration tools where the tool forms the basis of an organization's business model. The PowerShell team is currently in the process of extending DSC and PowerShell to work with computers running Linux, though this effort is very much in its preliminary stages.

Not only does DSC perform initial configuration of a server, but it can also enforce that configuration. You can configure DSC so that any changes that might be made to the server's configuration that aren't made through DSC will automatically roll back the next time DSC runs. This makes DSC an excellent tool for ensuring that servers in your organization retain configurations that meet compliance requirements. If you manage configuration entirely through DSC, you perform configuration changes by modifying DSC configurations rather than signing onto a server and modifying the configuration manually.

DSC can also work in audit mode. When using DSC in audit mode, you can generate log data describing how a computer's configuration deviates from that specified in a configuration file. This can be useful in determining how a computer's configuration may have drifted from a baseline, and can also be used to determine what updates need to be made to a DSC configuration file when modifications are made to a server that you wish to retain.

Inside OUT

Idempotency

An important concept when using tools including Desired State Configuration, Chef, and Puppet is idempotency. Idempotency allows the same technique to be applied multiple times to something, always producing the same result. This is important for these tools because they apply a specific configuration to a system on a periodic basis. In the case of configuration, applying the configuration tool should either bring the existing configuration into line with the desired configuration or, if the desired configuration is already set, should not alter that configuration further.

DSC configuration files

DSC configuration files describe how a computer should be configured. Configuration files require at least one node and require at least one configuration item per node. A configuration file can have multiple nodes, with different configuration items in each node. Generally you create one configuration for each different computer type in your organization. For example, one for computers that host the DHCP server role, another for computers that function as file servers.

The following hypothetical configuration would ensure that the WINS and Windows Server Backup features were present on a computer.

```
Configuration TestDscConfiguration {

    Node "TEST-SVR" {

        WindowsFeature InstallWINS {

            Ensure = "Present"

            Name = "WINS"

        }

        WindowsFeature InstallBackup {

            Ensure = "Present"

            Name = "Windows-Server-Backup"

        }

    }

}

TestDscConfiguration
```

When you run a DSC configuration script, it generates a MOF file. The MOF file is what the LCM uses when determining which configuration to apply to a computer. You compile a configuration script by dot sourcing it. For example, if you saved the above script as TestConfiguration.ps1 in the c:\DSCTEST folder and .sourced it, it would create a new folder named TestDscConfiguration and in that folder place a new file named TEST-SVR.mof.

MOF files contain the configuration data that you want to apply to the Windows Server node. MOF files are created by running DSC configuration files. You can deploy MOF files to the LCM on a Windows Server node by using the Push method to inject a file into a running computer, or configure a pull server from where nodes can retrieve MOF files and DSC resources.

MORE INFO   DSC CONFIGURATION

You can learn more about DSC configuration files at *https://msdn.microsoft.com/en-us/powershell/dsc/configurations*.

Local Configuration Manager

The Local Configuration Manager (LCM) is present on each computer that uses DSC. The LCM is the component that takes a MOF file and DSC resources and uses it to enact a DSC configuration. You can view the current settings of the LCM using the Get-DscLocalConfigurationManager cmdlet, as shown in Figure 3-17.

Figure 3-17 LCM settings

DSC resources

DSC resources are used by the LCM. They can be PowerShell scripts, or an item compiled into a DLL. Resources are stored in resource modules, which are distributed to the LCM to allow it to carry out the configuration instructions stored in the MOF. DSC resource modules must be present on any computer where they are used to create or apply a configuration script.

The PowerShell Gallery hosts a wealth of DSC resources that can form the basis of your DSC configuration scripts and configurations. DSC clients can obtain resources directly from DSC pull servers. If you are using another method of deploying configurations, such as the push method or copying method, you'll need to ensure that the appropriate DSC resources are stored on the computer you want to configure using DSC.

DSC push model

You can push a MOF file to a target computer using the Start-DscConfiguration cmdlet and a PowerShell remoting connection. This is effective in smaller and test environments and can be used to push MOF files to target computers. For example, you might use this to push a MOF file to a test virtual machine running under client Hyper-V on your Windows 10 computer. The DSC push model requires that PowerShell remoting be enabled on each computer that is to be the target of a DSC push action. This is less of an issue with Windows Server 2016 because PowerShell remoting is enabled by default on this operating system.

Each time you use Start-DscConfiguration to push a new configuration to a node, the push action overwrites any existing configuration on the target node. Once you push the new configuration, the LCM on the target node begins immediately processing the MOF file. This makes the DSC push model a great way of testing configurations because you don't have to wait for the DSC cycle to restart to process the update, something that is necessary when using DSC pull servers.

A substantial drawback to using DSC push is that any resources that are to be used by the MOF file must already be present on the node you are configuring through push. Should you wish to use new resources for a configuration, you'll need to transfer them to the target node prior to pushing the new configuration.

DSC pull server

DSC pull servers are computers running Windows Server 2012 or later that function as central DSC repositories. Rather than push DSC configurations to each node, each node can be configured to poll a DSC pull server, downloading new MOF files and resources as they become available. DSC pull servers are almost always configured as web servers. It's possible to use a standard file server as a pull server, but file servers lack some of the functionality of IIS-based pull servers, such as the ability to function as a compliance server. Compliance servers allow you to view a central repository of information about each node's compliance with DSC configuration settings.

When you deploy a pull server, you specify a location to store MOF files and a location to store DSC resource files in zipped format. MOF files stored on a pull server use a Globally Unique Identifier (GUID) for identification. Each MOF file and DSC resource module zip file must be stored with an associated checksum file. You can generate checksum files using the New-DSC-Checksum cmdlet.

MORE INFO   DSC

You can learn more about DSC at *https://msdn.microsoft.com/en-us/powershell/dsc/overview or by consulting The DSC Book which is available through PowerShell.org*.

Chef

Chef is a third-party configuration management solution. Unlike DSC, where you have to build most of the infrastructure out yourself and you're generally reliant upon a community to build resources for you unless you can build them yourself, Chef provides you with software and resources that you can use to manage the configuration of computers running a variety of operating systems. Chef allows you to manage servers running both Windows and Linux based operating systems.

Inside OUT

Chef in Azure

While you can spin up your own Linux instance in Azure and install Chef on that IaaS VM, there is also a fully preconfigured Linux IaaS VM in the Azure gallery.

Chef servers

Chef uses a client/server architecture. You manage the configurations that you want to deploy on a server as cookbooks, and the clients of those servers apply those cookbooks and recipes to Chef nodes to meet your configuration objectives. When deploying Chef, you have two primary options, Hosted Chef and a Chef Server that you are responsible for managing.

Hosted Chef

Hosted Chef is an instance of Chef Server hosted in the cloud by the Chef organization. The big benefit of Hosted Chef is that like any software as a service solution, the Chef organization takes care of the entire infrastructure. Hosted Chef requires that clients have a connection to the Internet so that they can communicate with the server. This makes it great for workloads running on Internet connected networks, but problematic for organizations who need configuration management on isolated networks.

Installing Chef Server

You can deploy Chef Server on-premises on a server running a Linux operating system. At present, you can't deploy Chef Server on a computer running Windows Server 2016, though you can manage a Chef Server from any computer with a browser.

Chef Server is supported on the following operating systems:

- Red Hat Enterprise Linux 7, 6, and 5

- SUSE Linux Enterprise Server 12 and 11

- Ubuntu 16.04, 14.05, and 12.04

To install Chef Server on Linux, perform the following tasks:

1. Obtain the appropriate Chef Server package for the Linux server that you are going to use to host Chef Server from *https://downloads.chef.io/chef-server* and store it in a temporary directory on the Linux server that you want to function as the Chef server. In the following example, the package for Ubuntu LTS 16.04 is used.

2. Install the package. On a Linux server running Ubuntu, you would do this with a command similar to the following:

   ```
   Sudo dpkg -i ./chef-server-core_12.13.0-1_amd64.deb
   ```

3. Once the package has installed, run the following command to begin configuration, which takes a moderate amount of time:

   ```
   Sudo chef-server-ctl reconfigure
   ```

4. Once configuration has completed, create a new user. For example, to create a new user named melbournevictoria and to store the certificate associated with that user in the ~/certs folder of the account used to deploy Chef server, run the following command (note that the username is in lower case and the password does need to be passed to the console):

   ```
   Sudo chef-server-ctl user-create sydneymelbourne Sydney Melbourne sydney@company.
   pri P@ssw0rd --filename ~/certs/sydneymelbourne.pem
   ```

5. You can create an organization and associate the user that you created with that organization using the following command, where the organization name in this case is Contoso (ensure that you enter the organization name in lower case):

   ```
   Sudo chef-server-ctl org-create contoso "Contoso-Chef" --association_user syd-
   neymelbourne --filename ~/certs/contoso.pem
   ```

6. To install the web-based management console, run the following command:

   ```
   Sudo chef-server-ctl install chef-manage
   ```

7. Then use the following commands to configure the console:

   ```
   Sudo check-server-ctl reconfigure
   ```

   ```
   Sudo chef-manage-ctl reconfigure --accept-license
   ```

8. You can then verify that the server is functioning by using a standards compliant web browser to navigate to the FQDN of the Chef server, as shown in Figure 3-18. You should sign in with the account created in step 4.

CHAPTER 03

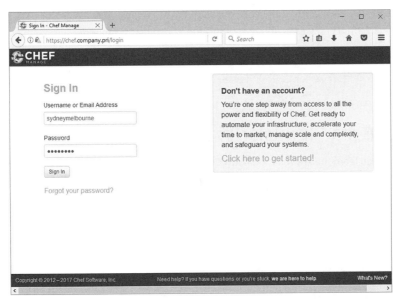

Figure 3-18 Chef console

9. If you navigate to the Administration node, you'll be able to view the organization that you created and the users that are members of that organization, as shown in Figure 3-19.

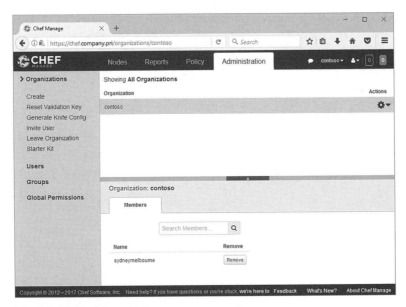

Figure 3-19 Chef Organization

10. Once you have verified the configuration of the console, you can install and configure Chef's reporting capability by running the following commands:

```
Sudo chef-server-ctl install opscode-reporting

Sudo chef-server-ctl reconfigure

Sudo opscode-reporting-ctl reconfigure --accept-license
```

MORE INFO   INSTALLING CHEF SERVER

You can learn more about installing Chef Server at *https://docs.chef.io/install_server.html*.

Chef Development Kit

You use the Chef Development Kit (ChefDK) to author recipes, cookbooks, and policies. You can install the Chef Development Kit by downloading the relevant files from Chef's website, or, if you have Chocolatey configured, as described later in this chapter, by running the following command from an elevated command prompt:

```
Choco install -y chefdk
```

Performing this installation gives you access to the ChefDK PowerShell prompt, which allows you to use PowerShell to interact with ChefDK.

Starter Kit

The Starter Kit is a package that you can download from your Chef server that contains all of the information and files needed to connect to an organization hosted on your Chef server. You can find this package by clicking Starter Kit in the sidebar menu when you have the organization selected in the Administration tab, as shown in Figure 3-20.

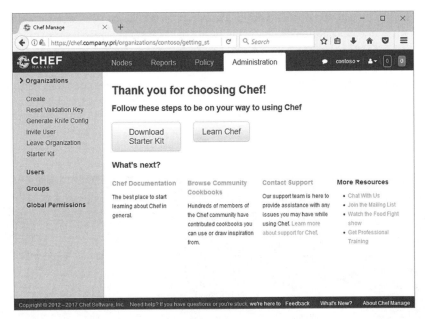

Figure 3-20 Starter Kit

The Starter Kit is a zipped file that has the basic structure of a Git repository. You can add this file structure to a Git repository if you want to implement source control. The file knife.rb, shown opened in Visual Studio Code in Figure 3-21, contains the settings of the organization on the Chef Server.

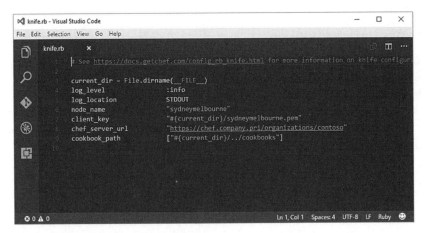

Figure 3-21 Chef organization settings

To use ChefDK with the Chef Server, you need to have the TLS certificates assigned to the server present on the workstation on which you have ChefDK installed. Even if your computer trusts the TLS certificate, you'll still need a local copy of the public certificate to use the Knife utility in the ChefDK to interact with your organization's Chef server. You can retrieve the TLS certificate that is assigned to the Chef server by running the following command in the chef-repo folder from the Chef Development Kit shell that becomes available when you install the ChefDK. The certificate is added to the trusted certificates area of the Chef Git repository folder structure that was created when you unzipped the Starter Kit, as shown in Figure 3-22.

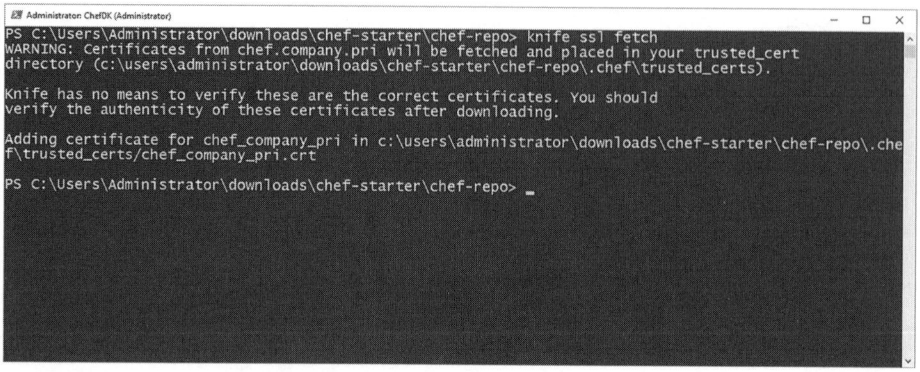

Figure 3-22 Acquire Chef certificate

You can verify that the certificate has installed correctly by running the following command from the chef-repo folder using the ChefDK PowerShell prompt:

```
Knife SSL check
```

Recipes and cookbooks

You use a chef recipe to specify what configuration a Chef node should have. You bundle recipes into cookbooks and deploy cookbooks against Chef clients. A default Windows cookbook is available from the Chef website. You can download the current example Windows cookbook from Chef and the ohai cookbook that is a dependency of the Windows cookbook by running the following command from the chef-repo\cookbooks folder using the ChefDK PowerShell prompt:

```
Knife cookbook site download windows
```

```
Knife cookbook site download ohai
```

This downloads both the Windows cookbook and the ohai cookbook in tar and zip format. You can use a utility such as 7-zip to extract the cookbooks. Once extracted, place the cookbooks in the cookbooks folder, as shown in Figure 3-23.

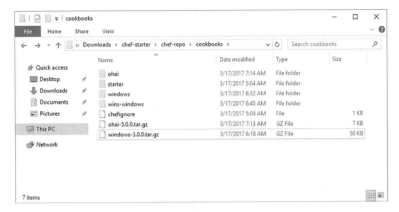

Figure 3-23 Cookbooks

You can use the Windows cookbook as a base cookbook on which you can create additional specific cookbooks. For example, to create a cookbook named wins-windows that installs the WINS server feature on a Windows Server computer, perform the following steps:

1. In the Chef-repo\Cookbooks folder, run the following ChefDK PowerShell command:

```
Chef generate cookbook wins-windows
```

2. Open the file Chef-repo\cookbooks\wins-windows\recipes\default.rb in Visual Studio Code and add the following lines, as shown in Figure 3-24:

```
windows_feature "WINSRuntime" do

    action :install

end
```

Figure 3-24 Default.rb

3. To configure the new cookbook's dependency on the existing example Windows cookbook, open the file Chef-repo\cookbooks\wins-windows\metadata.rb and add the following line, as shown in Figure 3-25:

```
depends 'windows'
```

Figure 3-25 Configure dependencies

4. In the Chef-repo\Roles folder, create a new file named wins-windows.rb and enter the following text shown in Figure 3-26:

```
name "wins-windows"

description "test WINS install"

run_list "recipe[wins-windows]"
```

Figure 3-26 wins-windows.rb

5. From the Chef-repo\Cookbooks folder, run the following command to push all current cookbooks from the computer that hosts ChefDK to the Chef server:

```
Knife cookbook upload --all
```

6. Next change into the Chef-repo\Roles folder and run the following command to create the relevant role:

```
Knife role from file .\wins-windows.rb
```

7. You can verify that cookbooks are present on the Chef Server on the Policy tab of the Chef console, as shown in Figure 3-27.

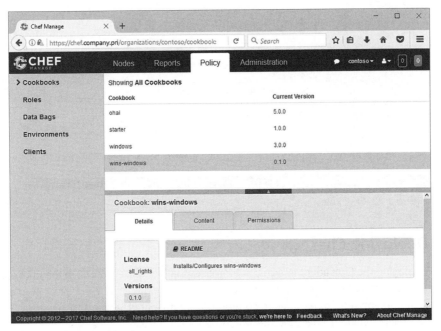

Figure 3-27 All Cookbooks

8. You can verify that the roles have uploaded correctly by checking the Roles section when the Policy tab is selected, as shown in Figure 3-28.

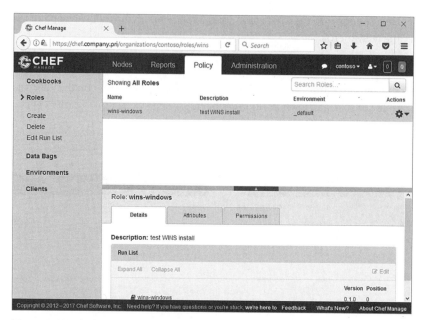

Figure 3-28 Chef Roles

Deploying Chef agents

Deploying the Chef agent to a computer makes that computer a node in the Chef organization. The most reliable method of ensuring that a Chef node has all of the relevant certificates and configuration settings required to communicate with a Chef Server is to perform a knife bootstrap deployment from a computer with ChefDK installed.

Prior to performing this deployment, you should update tools to ensure that you have the latest versions of the deployment tools available. To do this, run the following command from the ChefDK prompt in the Chef-repo folder:

```
Gem update knife-windows
```

To deploy an agent to a Windows Server, you need to ensure that WinRM is configured on both the source and the target computer, and run the following command (where prodserver is the name of the target computer):

```
Knife bootstrap windows winrm prodserver.company.pri --winrm-user Administrator --winrm-password P@ssw0rd --node-name prodserver
```

You can verify that the client is installed on a node and registered with the Chef server by checking the Nodes tab in the management console, as shown in Figure 3-29.

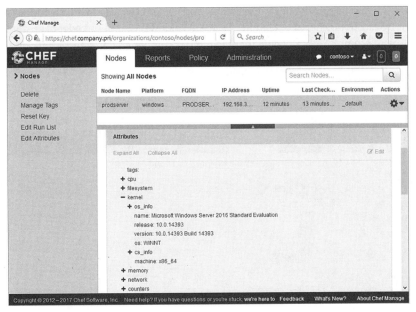

Figure 3-29 Chef node details

Deploying Chef cookbooks and recipes

By applying a role to a node, you deploy the contents of that role, including cookbooks, and their associated recipe. You can apply a role or recipe directly to a Chef node using the console by selecting the node in the console, editing the node's Run List, and then assigning a Recipe or a Run List, as shown in Figure 3-30.

Figure 3-30 Edit Node Run List

The Run List will apply the next time the run applies. You can also manually trigger a run on the client by executing chef-client.bat from the C:\Windows\System32 folder of an administrative command prompt. You can verify that the run has completed correctly by checking the Reports tab of the Chef console, as shown in Figure 3-31.

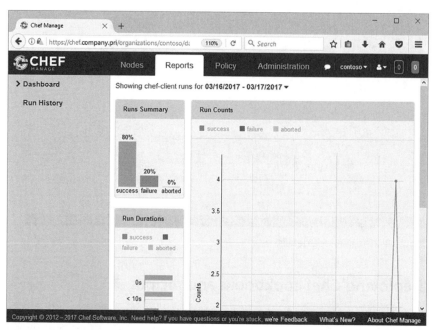

Figure 3-31 Chef Reports

> **MORE INFO   CHEF**
>
> You can learn more about Chef at *https://www.chef.io*.

Puppet

Puppet is suitable for heterogeneous environments where you need to manage the configuration of both Linux and Windows Servers. Puppet uses an architecture where a server, named a "Puppet master," provides a central management point to computers that have the Puppet agent installed.

> **MORE INFO   PUPPET**
>
> You can learn more about Puppet at *https://puppet.com/*.

Puppet master server

The Puppet master server is only currently supported on hosts running a Linux or UNIX based operating systems. If you are responsible for an environment that just has Windows servers, Puppet may not be a good fit because the "Puppet master" server can only be deployed on computers running the following operating systems:

- RedHat Enterprise Linux, CentOS, Scientific Linux, Oracle Linux Version 7 and 6 (x86_64)

- Ubuntu version 16.04, 14.04, and 12.04 (amd64)

- SLES 12 and 11 (x86_64)

Inside OUT

Linux distro selection

Chef and Puppet can be run on a variety of Linux distributions. Most heterogeneous environments have standardized on a single distribution of Linux, so your first choice for a Chef or Puppet host is likely to be the distribution you are already using. If you don't have Linux servers deployed in your environment and do want to use Chef or Puppet, you might consider one of the Ubuntu LTS options as a host, simply because a version of Ubuntu is now available in Windows 10 and there are likely to be more synergies involved in running Ubuntu as part of Windows Subsystem for Linux, and running Ubuntu as the host server for Puppet or Chef.

The Puppet master server stores configuration for all Puppet clients on the network. The Puppet master server requires at least 6GB of RAM, four cores, a hostname that is accessible to other computers on the network, and accessibility on port 3000. You likely need to configure the firewall to be open on the appropriate port manually. The administrator of the Puppet master server needs to have root user, or have sudo privileges on the host server.

To install the Linux computer as a Puppet server, first connect to the server with an account that has the ability to elevate privileges and verify the computer's hostname. Then perform the following steps:

1. You'll need to download a tarball specific to your Linux distribution from the Puppet website to the Linux computer. Extract the tarball downloaded from the Puppet website using the following command:

   ```
   Tar -xvf puppet-enterprise*
   ```

2.   This extracts the puppet installation files. Change to the directory that was created when you extracted the tarball and start the installation script by typing the following command:

```
Sudo ./puppet-enterprise-installer
```

3.   When prompted, select the guided installation. Once the installation is complete, you'll need to open a browser and navigate to port 3000 on the address of the newly deployed puppet server. You'll need to ignore any certificate errors and click Let's Get Started, as shown in Figure 3-32.

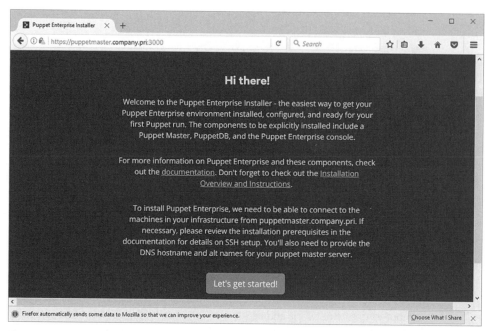

Figure 3-32 Puppet server configuration

4.   On the Puppet Master Component page, provide

- The FQDN of the puppet master server

- Any alias that are going to be used by Puppet clients

- Choose whether to install a PostgreSQL instance for the PuppetDB, and provide a console admin user password, as shown in Figure 3-33.

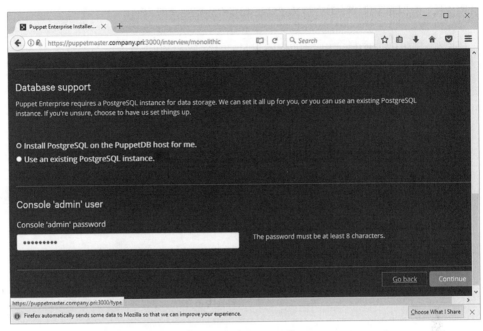

Figure 3-33 Install database and configure admin password

5. After the validation occurs, click Deploy Now. Puppet Enterprise is deployed on the Linux
    server.

You can now connect to the web-based administration interface using the username "admin"
and the password provided in step 4. The Inventory node, shown in Figure 3-34, lists all computers that are currently being managed by the Puppet server.

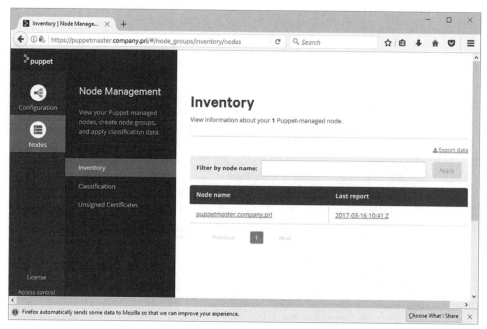

Figure 3-34 Inventory

MORE INFO   DEPLOYING A PUPPET SERVER

You can learn more about deploying Puppet servers at *https://docs.puppet.com/pe/latest/windows_installing.html.*

Deploying Puppet agent to Windows Server

The first step in deploying a Puppet agent to a computer running Windows Server 2016 is to configure the Puppet master server so that it has the correct agent installation software for an x64 version of Windows. You can do this by taking the following steps:

1. In the Puppet administration console, click Classification under the Nodes menu, and in the PE Infrastructure section shown, click PE Master.

2. On the Classes tab, in the Add New Class text box, type **Windows**, and then click pe_repo::platform::windows_x86_x64, as shown in Figure 3-35. Click Add Class, and then click Commit Changes. Unless you run the Puppet agent -t command on the Puppet master server, you'll need to wait up to 30 minutes for the Puppet agent to wake up.

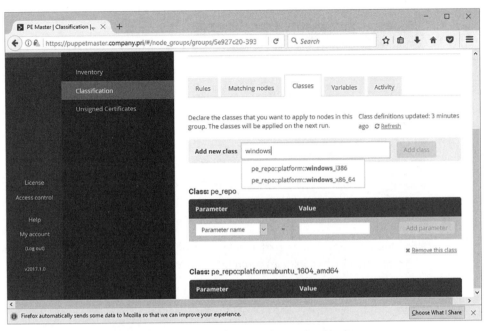

Figure 3-35 Configure Windows as a class

3. On your Windows Server, open a browser and navigate to https://<YOUR PUPPET MASTER HOSTNAME>:8140/packages/current/windows-x86_64/puppet-agent-x64.msi.

4. Run the downloaded installer. On the Welcome page click Next, and then accept the terms of the license agreement.

5. On the Configuration page, ensure that the FQDN of the Puppet server matches the address of your Puppet server, as shown in Figure 3-36, and click Install. Click Finish when the installation completes.

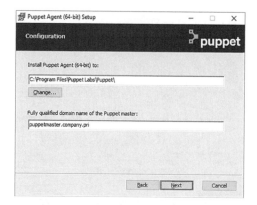

Figure 3-36 Puppet Agent Setup

6. Restart the computer, start an administrative PowerShell session, and run the following command, which initiates communication with the Puppet master server, allowing you to then trigger:

```
puppet agent -t
```

7. You'll then need to return to the Puppet console, navigate to the Unsigned Certificates tab under Nodes, and then sign the unsigned node of the newly detected certificate of your new Windows Server Puppet client, as shown in Figure 3-37.

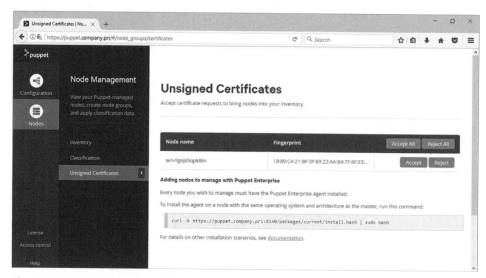

Figure 3-37 Sign unsigned certificates

Managing Windows Server Configuration

Puppet manifest files describe a desired state of a managed server in terms of a list of resources and a set of attributes. You can use any text editor to write a manifest, though you might want to use a tool like Visual Studio Code because it supports syntax highlighting for Puppet syntax. Puppet manifests use the .pp extension.

You can use the Puppet master web-based console to specify which manifests apply to particular Puppet clients, also termed nodes. Once Puppet is installed on a client, you can run Puppet commands from an elevated PowerShell session. Generally, you'll build and test manifests on a development node using the command line tools. Then you can configure the manifests to be distributed and enforced by the Puppet master server.

You can perform the following tasks from an elevated PowerShell prompt on a computer that has the Puppet agent installed:

- You can validate the syntax on a manifest using the "Puppet parser validate" command. For example, run the following command to check the syntax of a manifest file named services.pp:

```
Puppet parser validate c:\test_manifests\services.pp
```

- Manifests are applied using the "Puppet apply" command. You can simulate a Puppet cycle using the --noop option, which runs Puppet in non-enforcement mode. For example, to simulate a Puppet cycle against the services.pp manifest, run the command:

```
Puppet apply c:\test_manifests\services.pp --noop
```

- Once you've checked a manifest in non-enforcement mode, you can enforce the configuration using Puppet Apply.

- Puppet agent allows you to retrieve compiled catalogs from a Puppet master. By default this cycle runs every 30 minutes.

MORE INFO   BASIC WINDOWS CONFIGURATION

You can learn more about basic Windows Server configuration using Puppet at *https://docs.puppet.com/pe/latest/windows_basic_tasks.html*.

Puppet Windows module pack

Puppet Forge is an online community for modules that are submitted by people in the Puppet community, as well as people that work for the organization. Because an extensive community exists around Puppet, it's likely that someone has already written a module to perform a configuration task that you want to perform. You can take their hard work and use it to help configure the systems in your organization.

The Windows module pack is a collection of Puppet modules that you can use to perform common administrative tasks. To install the Windows Module Pack, open an administrative Power-Shell prompt on a computer with the Puppet Agent installed, and run the following command, as shown in Figure 3-38:

```
Puppet module install puppetlabs/windows
```

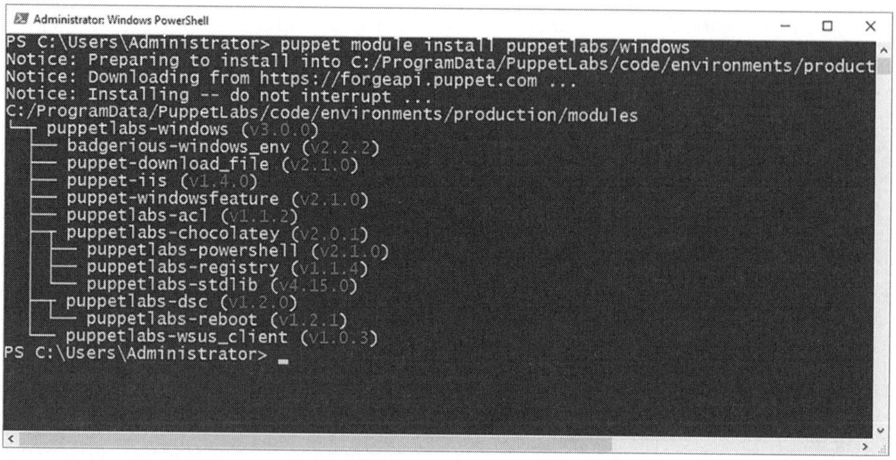

Figure 3-38 Install Windows modules

The Puppet Windows Module pack includes tools that allow you to use Puppet to manage the following:

- Read, create, and write registry keys with the "registry" module.

- Remotely manage the execution of PowerShell scripts with the "powershell" module.

- Manage PowerShell DNS resources using the "dsc" module.

- Configure fine-grained access control permissions using the "acl" module.

- Manage WSUS client configuration using the "wsus_client" module.

- Configure which roles and features are installed using the "windowsfeature" module.

- Download files from various locations using the "download_file" module.

- Build and manage IIS sites and virtual applications using the "iis" module.

- Manage the deployment of software packages using the "chocolatey" module.

- Configure environment variables using the "windows_env" module.

While not comprehensive, you should now have a foundation level understanding of the functionality of what you can do with Puppet, and whether it is worthy of further investigation in terms of inclusion as a part of your Windows Server administration toolkit.

MORE INFO   WINDOWS MODULE PACK

You can learn more about the Windows Module Pack for Puppet at *https://docs.puppet. com/pe/latest/windows_modules.html*.

Inside OUT

DSC, Puppet, or Chef?

There is no right answer to the question "DSC, Puppet, or Chef." If your organization's infrastructure is almost exclusively based on Microsoft products, you might want to consider DSC as a first option to see if it does what you need it to do. The intention of Microsoft is for DSC to be a fully supported way of configuring their products in the future, though it is early days yet. Puppet and Chef have longer pedigrees in the Open Source world and if you already use one of these products, it makes sense to use it to manage Windows Server 2016. Microsoft certainly intends for DSC to work with Linux in the future, but it's also definitely playing catch up in this area compared to Puppet and Chef. What's important to understand though is that Microsoft is working with both of these companies, rather than against them, with the attitude that if all of these technologies provide you with an excellent toolset to manage the configuration of Windows Server 2016, you'll be much more likely to choose Windows Server 2016 than if you could only do configuration management through Microsoft's in-house solution.

Package management utilities

Configuration of servers and applications through tools like DSC, Puppet, and Chef provide an example of one way that the process of Windows server administration has changed in the last decade. Another way that things have changed is through the use of package management utilities. Rather than the traditional process of downloading the current version of software from a vendor's website, vendors are increasingly publishing their software in centralized repositories that you can access through package management utilities. The benefit of package management utilities is that they provide a central location for obtaining software, updating, and removing software applications.

If you've used a Debian derived flavor of Linux, you'll be familiar with the Apt-get utility. Apt-get allows you to install any package prepared for Debian. It also allows you to update packages and the operating system. You can even use Apt-get to perform an entire operating system upgrade.

While not yet as advanced as Apt-get, package management on Windows follows the paradigm that's been available in the Open Source world for several decades. Windows Server both directly and indirectly now supports package management, either directly through cmdlets in the PackageManagement Windows PowerShell module, or indirectly through package providers such as Chocolatey.

Windows Server 2016 includes native support for the installation of a variety of different package management providers through PowerShell. Some providers make available PowerShell resources, others make available pre-packaged software that you would otherwise download and install from the Internet manually. You can view which package providers are accessible by default to a Windows Server 2016 installation by using the Find-PackageProvider cmdlet, shown in Figure 3-39. In this chapter you'll learn about the PowerShell Gallery, NanoServerPackage, and Chocolatey. In later chapters, you'll learn about specific providers, such as the DockerMsft-Provider, which contains the tools used to manage Windows Server and Hyper-V containers, in Chapter 10, including the ability to download containers that run full containerized isolated versions of Microsoft server applications including SQL Server 2016 community edition.

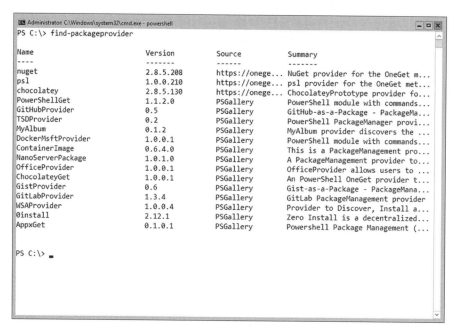

FIGURE 3-39 Package providers

PowerShell Gallery

PowerShell Gallery is a provider that functions as a clearinghouse for PowerShell-related tools and content. The PowerShell team publishes content to the gallery, as do other PowerShell enthusiasts and MVPs. This means that it's fairly likely that if there is a script, cmdlet, or a module that does something you think quite a few people would need to do, someone has probably already created it and published it to the PowerShell gallery. You can interact with PowerShell Gallery with the PowerShellGet module. You can use this module to access cmdlets that do the following:

- Use Find-Module and Find-Script to find items in the gallery

- Use Save-Module and Save-Script to save items from the gallery

- Use Install-Module and Install-Script to install items from the gallery

- Use Publish-Module and Publish-Script to publish items to the gallery

- Add a custom repository to the gallery using Register-PSRepository

Inside OUT

PowerShell community

Sites such as PowerShell.org are run and managed by the PowerShell community contain a wealth of knowledge and advice on how you can best leverage PowerShell to accomplish your goals.

MORE INFO   POWERSHELL GALLERY

You can learn more about PowerShell Gallery at *https://www.powershellgallery.com/*.

Nano Server package provider

The Nano Server package provider provides an online repository to install software packages for the Nano Server installation option of Windows Server 2016. As mentioned in Chapter 2, prior to deploying a Nano Server instance, you decide on its roles and functionality. The Nano Server package provider gives you the ability to add roles to a running instance, rather than having to redeploy the instance from scratch. This is especially useful for Nano Server instances in Azure where you are provided with a basic image and needs to add specific roles or features not included in that image.

To install additional packages on a deployed instance of Nano Server using the Nano Server Package Provider, establish a remote PowerShell session to the Nano Server, and run the following commands:

```
Install-Package NanoServerPackage -SkipPublisherCheck -Force
```

```
Install-PackageProvider NanoServerPackage
```

```
Set-ExecutionPolicy RemoteSigned -Scope Process
```

```
Import-PackageProvider NanoServerPackage
```

Inside OUT

Remote Nano sessions

If you encounter an error in establishing a remote PowerShell session to a Nano Server instance, remember you might need to configure WSMan to allow connections to that host. You can do this with the command
Set-Item WSMan:\localhost\Client\TrustedHosts -Value "Name or IP"

Once you've run these commands, you can view which Nano Server packages can be installed on a running computer:

```
Find-NanoServerPackage | Select Name
```

You can install a Nano Server package using the Install-NanoServerPackage cmdlet. For example, to install the IIS package, run the command:

```
Install-NanoServerPackage -Name Microsoft-NanoServer-IIS-Package
```

Chocolatey

Chocolatey is perhaps the most well-known package provider available for Windows operating systems. It has a very extensive collection of software packages, with anything from commonly used applications such as 7-Zip and Visual Studio Code, through to administration platforms such as Windows ADK. Chocolatey can also be integrated with Puppet, Chef, and DSC.

Chocolatey also runs very well on the Server Core installation option of Windows Server 2016, as well as within Windows Server and Hyper-V containers. It can be substantially quicker to use Chocolatey to retrieve and install a package, for example to install the Windows ADK with all options in the default location on a computer running the Server with Desktop Experience option, run the following command:

```
Choco install -y windows-adk-all
```

This requires substantially less time than searching the Microsoft website, downloading all of the necessary pre-requisites, and running the installation routine.

To install Chocolatey, you'll need to set the PowerShell execution policy to unrestricted using the following command:

```
Set-ExecutionPolicy Unrestricted
```

Then you'll need to run the following PowerShell command:

```
iwr https://chocolatey.org/install.ps1 -UseBasicParsing | iex
```

This installs Chocolatey and all of its dependencies on the local computer.

Inside OUT

Packages at your own risk

In a secure environment, you would not set your execution policy to unrestricted, and you certainly wouldn't download and install packages from a public repository no matter how reputable it may seem. In the long run, you don't know anything about the people building the packages, and while they are most likely simply helpful people trying to make your life easier by packaging software, they could also be a part of the great galactic space lizard malware conspiracy and simply finding a new vector to get malware deployed on your server. Before using a package in production, make sure you test it. When it comes to building secure servers, you'll need to validate the integrity of all software that you deploy, which means that the shortcuts provided by package providers are probably not an option.

Chocolatey has the following advantages when it comes to software deployment on servers:

- Makes the deployment of software extremely simple. Once Chocolatey is installed, further packages can be installed with one line of code.

- Packages are downloaded and installed with one command. You don't need to download a file, unzip it, run the installer, and answer the questions of an inquisitive wizard.

- Package dependencies are automatically installed when you attempt to install a package.

- Maintainers often regularly update packages. This means that you can update all software installed via Chocolatey on a system by running the following command:

```
Chocolatey update all
```

Chocolatey has the following disadvantages:

- Usually requires that the computer you are deploying software on be connected to the Internet. You can configure internal repositories, but you'll have to manage and maintain them yourself, including validating the quality of the software found in those repositories.

- Packages are usually installed in default locations with default settings. You don't get the installation customization options that you get when you install software manually.

- The provenance of the software isn't clear. While it's reasonable to assume that the software is safe, even large vendor app stores have apps that are infected with malware.

Using a simple script, you can install Chocolatey and then use it to download and install a common set of packages. You can also set up your own Chocolatey repository of packages that hosts only packages that you trust. You can then point a local Chocolatey instance at that repository and use it to quickly install software on newly deployed computers running a Windows operating system.

Inside OUT

Great for clients also

Chocolatey is really great for clients and has far more packages designed for computers running the Windows client operating system than it does for servers. It's far simpler to run two lines of code to install Chocolatey, and then download a utility such as 7-zip than it is to open a browser, navigate to the appropriate website, locate the appropriate file, download the appropriate file, and install the appropriate file.

MORE INFO   CHOCOLATEY

You can learn more about Chocolatey at *https://chocolatey.org/*. You can learn more about integrating Chocolatey with Puppet, Chef, and DSC at *https://chocolatey.org/docs/features-infrastructure-automation*.

Active Directory

Active Directory, the identity glue that binds on-premises Microsoft networks together, is at the center of almost all on-premises networks. Although each computer can have its own unique individual user and service accounts, Active Directory provides a central user, a computer, and a service account store.

But Active Directory is more than an identity store; it can also be used to store data for Active Directory-aware applications. One example of this is Microsoft Exchange Server, which stores server configuration information in Active Directory. Other applications, such as System Center Configuration Manager, are also highly dependent on Active Directory.

Active Directory is a topic so vast that completely covering it would require a multi-volume set. In this chapter we look at managing Active Directory. We also cover deploying domain controllers, forests, domains, service accounts, and group policy, as well as examining how to restore deleted items.

Managing Active Directory

Domain Controllers are one of, if not the, highest value target for attackers on your network. An attacker that is able to take control of a domain controller has control over every domain joined computer in the organization. Having control of a domain controller means having control of all authentication and authorization processes in the domain.

As we discuss more in the chapter on security, one strategy for increasing server security is to reduce the attack surface. As mentioned in Chapter 2, where possible you should deploy roles on computers installed in the Server Core configuration, because this configuration has a smaller attack surface than a server that includes desktop components. Server Core is a great option for domain controller deployment, because it provides a reduced attack surface, which strengthens the security of the installation.

Remote rather than local administration

You should perform Active Directory management tasks remotely using consoles or PowerShell rather than signing on to the domain controller directly using RDP. If you're doing all of your administrative tasks remotely using consoles or PowerShell, it won't make any difference to you that you've deployed the domain controller in the server core configuration. Using remote consoles also reduces the chance of malware being introduced to the domain controller. There are countless stories of organizations having their security compromised because an administrator signed on to a server using Remote Desktop, went to download a utility from the Internet using the built in web browser, and ended up with more than they bargained for in terms of malware because they weren't careful about their browsing destination.

A general rule about consoles is that if you need to perform a task a couple of times, you should use a console. If you are new to a task, you're less likely to mess it up if you use a console. This is because a console holds your hand and assists you through the task. If you have to repeatedly perform the same task and it's a task that you are familiar with, you should automate it using tools such as PowerShell. You'll learn about the Active Directory related PowerShell cmdlets later in this chapter.

There are a number of consoles that you can use to perform Active Directory administrative tasks. These include the following:

- Active Directory Administrative Center
- Active Directory Users and Computers
- Active Directory Sites and Services
- Active Directory Domains and Trusts

Active Directory Administrative Center

Active Directory Administrative Center (ADAC) allows you to manage users, computers, and service accounts, to perform tasks with the Active Directory such as Recycle Bin, and to manage functionality such as Dynamic Access Control. Microsoft recommends that you use Active Directory Administrative Center to interact with Active Directory.

Active Directory Administrative Center is a newer console that has better search functionality than the other consoles listed in this chapter, which haven't substantively changed since the release of Windows 2000.

You can use Active Directory Administrative Center to manage the following:

- User, computer, and service accounts

- Domain and Forest functional level

- Fine grained password policies

- Active Directory Recycle Bin GUI

- Authentication Policies

- Dynamic Access Control

ADAC is built on PowerShell, meaning that it provides a graphical interface to build and enact PowerShell cmdlets. You can use the PowerShell History Viewer, shown in Figure 4-1, to see which cmdlets were used to carry out a task that you configured in the GUI. This simplifies the process of automating tasks because you can copy code straight out of the PowerShell history and then paste it into tools such as PowerShell ISE.

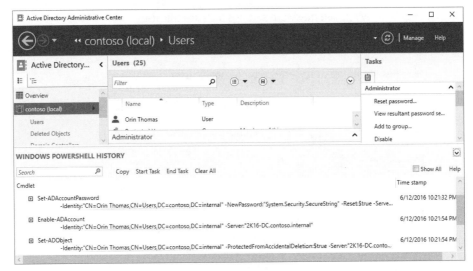

Figure 4-1 Active Directory Administrative Center

One of the most useful elements of Active Directory Administrative Center is the search functionality. You can use this functionality to locate accounts that might require further attention, such as users that haven't signed on for a certain period of time, users configured with passwords that never expire, or users with locked accounts. Using the Add Criteria option in the global search node of the Active Directory Administrative Center, you can search based on the following criteria:

- Users with disabled/enabled accounts

- Users with an expired password

- Users whose password has an expiration date/no expiration date

- Users with enabled but locked accounts

- Users with enabled accounts who have not signed on for more than a given number of days

- Users with a password expiring in a given number of days

- Computers running as a given domain controller type

- Last modified between given dates

- Object type is a user/inetOrgPerson/computer/group/organizational unit

- Directly applied password settings for a specific user

- Directly applied password settings for a specific global security group

- Resultant password settings for a specific user

- Objects with a given last known parent

- Resource property lists containing a given resource property

- Name

- Description

- City

- Department

- Employee ID

- First name

- Job Title

- Last Name

- SamAccountName

- State/Province

- Telephone number

- UPN

- Zip/Postal Code

- Phonetic company name

- Phonetic department

- Phonetic display name

- Phonetic first name

- Phonetic last name

While it should be your first port of call for managing Active Directory, there are several tasks that you can't yet do with Active Directory Administrative Center or with PowerShell, such as running the delegation of Control Wizard. Generally speaking when managing Active Directory using a console on Windows Server 2016, you should use Active Directory Administrative Center as your first option, and fall back to Active Directory Users and Computers if you can't accomplish what you need to in ADAC. Although no explicit date has been given, at some point Active Directory Users and Computers will be deprecated by Microsoft and Active Directory Administrative Center will be the only built in Active Directory administration option available other than PowerShell.

Active Directory Users and Computers

The Active Directory Users and Computers console is the one that many system administrators use to perform basic AD related tasks. They use this console primarily out of habit, because almost all functionality present in this console is also present in Active Directory Administrative Center. Active Directory Users and Computers has been around since the days of Windows 2000 Server.

Active Directory Users and Computers allows you to perform tasks including:

- Running the delegation of control wizard

- Administering different domains within the forest

- Selecting which Domain Controller or LDAP port the tool connects to

- Finding objects within the domain

- Raising the domain functional level

- Managing the RID Master, PDC Emulator, and Infrastructure Master FSMO role locations
- Creating and Editing the properties of:
    - Computer accounts
    - User accounts
    - Contacts
    - Groups
    - InetOrgPerson
    - msDS-ShadowPrincipalContainers
    - msImaging-PSPs
    - MSMQ Queue Alias
    - Organizational Unit
    - Printers
    - Shared Folder
- Resultant Set of Policy Planning

The view advanced features function allows you to see more details of the Active Directory environment. You enable this from the View menu of Active Directory Users and Computers. Enabling this view allows you to see containers that aren't visible in the standard view. If you've ever read a set of instructions that tell you to locate a specific object using Active Directory Users and Computers, and haven't been able to find that object, chances are that you haven't enabled the View Advanced Features option.

The Delegation of Control Wizard is only available in Active Directory Users and Computers. This wizard allows you to delegate control over the domain and Organizational Units (OU). For example, you use this wizard to delegate the ability for a specific group to reset user passwords in an OU. This wizard is useful when you want to delegate some privileges to a group of IT Ops staff, but don't want to grant them all the privileges that they'd inherit if you made them a member of the Domain Admins group. You'll learn more about delegating permissions in Chapter 18.

Active Directory Sites and Services

You use the Active Directory Sites and Services console to manage Active Directory Sites, which indirectly allows you to control a number of things, including replication traffic and which server a client connects to when using products such as Exchange Server. Sites are configured for the forest, with each domain in the forest sharing the same set of sites.

An Active Directory Site is a collection of TCP/IP subnets. Sites allow you to define geographic locations for Active Directory on the basis of TCP/IP subnets. You can have multiple TCP/IP subnets in a site. You should put subnets together in a site where the hosts in that site have a high bandwidth connection to each other. Usually this means being in the same building, but it could also be multiple buildings with very low latency gigabit links between them.

For example, imagine that your organization has its head office in Melbourne and a branch office in Sydney. You can set up two sites: one site for Melbourne and the other for Sydney. This ensures that computers in the Melbourne location interact as much as possible with resources located in Melbourne, and that computers in the Sydney location interact as much as possible with resources located in Sydney.

You associate the TCP/IP subnets in the head office with the Melbourne site and the TCP/IP subnets in the branch office with the Sydney site. After you do this, functionality such as replication topology is automatically configured.

The default name for the site you installed the first domain controller in is Default-First-Site-Name. You should change this as appropriate prior to adding subnets. When you add a subnet, you need to specify its associated site, so add sites first and then add subnets after your sites are present.

To add a new Active Directory Site, right-click on the Sites node in the Active Directory Sites and Services console and click New Site. Specify the site name and choose and select a site link object. A site link object represents a connection between two sites. The default site link object is named DEFAULTIPSITELINK. You can change the site link object later. Figure 4-2 shows the creation of a site named Sydney.

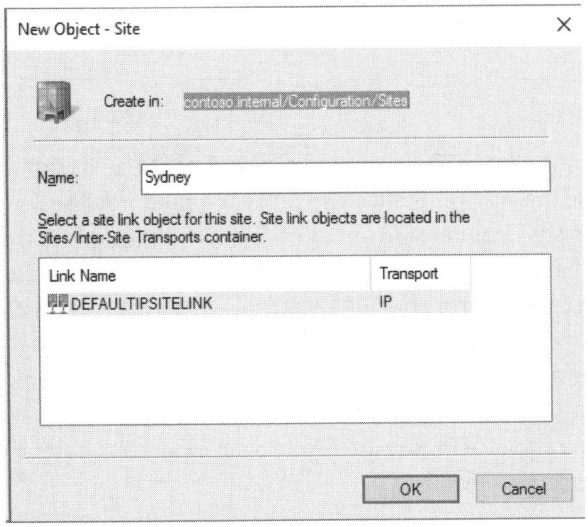

Figure 4-2 Create a new site

To add a subnet, right-click on the Subnets node in Active Directory Sites and Services and then click New Subnet. You can specify the new subnet in IPv4 or IPv6 format. After you've specified the subnet, you need to specify which site the subnet is associated with. Figure 4-3 shows the 10.10.10.0/24 subnet associated with the Melbourne site.

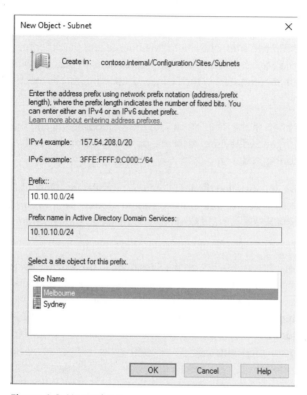

Figure 4-3 New subnet

Site links represent connections between sites. You can create IP or SMTP site links. You almost always use IP site links because these are authenticated and encrypted. You use SMTP site links when the connection between sites is unreliable. When configuring a site link, you can config-ure replication interval, with the default being once every 180 minutes. You can also configure the hours in which replication can occur, the default being 24 hours a day, 7 days a week. You create a site link by right-clicking on the IP node under Inter-Site-Transports in the Active Direc-tory Sites and Services console and by clicking New Site Link. And you specify two or more sites that are connected by the link. After the link is created, you can modify the replication schedule, cost, and the hours replication can occur in. Site links with lower replication costs are preferred over site links with higher replication costs.

A site link bridge is a collection of site links, but you only need to use them when your IP network is not fully routed. For example, you might create a site link bridge to connect the Sydney-Melbourne and Melbourne-Perth site links as a way of ensuring that replication traffic between Sydney and Perth passes through the Melbourne site.

After you've provided information about sites, subnets, site links, and site-link bridges, an Active Directory component called the Knowledge Consistency Checker automatically creates a replication topology using a least-cost spanning tree design.

Domain controllers automatically associate with the site that they are deployed in. If you didn't set up sites and subnets prior to deploying domain controllers in separate locations, right-click on the domain controller that you want to move within Active Directory Sites and Services, click Move, and then specify the destination site.

Active Directory Domains and Trusts

You use the Active Directory Domains and Trusts console to configure and manage trust relationships. By default, all domains in a forest trust each other. Your primary use of this console is to create trust relationships between:

- Domains in separate forests

- Separate forests

- Kerberos V5 realms

When creating a trust, you can choose between the following types:

- **One-Way: Incoming.** In this trust relationship, your local domain or forest is trusted by a remote domain or forest.

- **One-Way: Outgoing.** In this trust relationship, your local domain or forest trusts a remote domain or forest.

- **Two-way.** In this trust relationship, your local domain or forest trusts and is trusted by a remote domain or forest.

When configuring a trust, you can determine whether you want to configure selective authentication. By default, the trust works for all users in the source or destination forest or domain. When you configure selective authentication, you can limit which security principals are allowed access and which resources they are able to access. You do this by configuring those users with the Allowed to Authenticate Permission on each resource computer in the trusting domain or forest.

Domain Controllers

Domain Controllers (DCs) are the heart of Active Directory. Their primary role is to host the Active Directory database, stored in the ntds.dit file. By default, only members of the Domain Admins group can sign on to a DC, because DCs are the only servers that do not have a local Administrators group.

Inside OUT

Always two there should be

Ensure that you have at least two domain controllers in each domain and make sure you take regular backups. In the event that one domain controller fails, the other one is still there to perform all necessary functionality. If you only have one domain controller and you don't have a backup if it fails, you're going to need to rebuild your domain from scratch.

Deployment

Although the wizard for deploying a domain controller has been updated from what it looked like back in Windows Server 2008 R2, the process is still functionally the same. You choose whether you want to:

- Add a domain controller to an existing domain

- Add a new domain to an existing forest

- Add a new forest

If you are adding a domain controller to an existing domain, have the computer domain joined before promoting it. When you add a new domain to an existing forest, choose between adding a child domain or a tree domain. When you add a tree domain, you create a new namespace within an existing forest. For example, you can create the Adatum.com domain in the existing contoso.com forest. Contoso.com remains the root domain of the forest.

Microsoft's recommendation is that you use a registered root domain name, such as Contoso.com for the domain name, rather than a non-externally resolvable domain name like contoso.internal. Windows Server 2016 supports split DNS, which means that you can configure zones so that a subset of records are resolvable for clients on external networks. Many organizations still use non-resolvable domain names and you should only take Microsoft's advice into account if you are deploying a new forest.

When you add a new child domain to an existing forest, you specify the parent domain. For example, you could add the australia.contoso.com child domain to the contoso.com domain. After you've done that, you can add the victoria.australia.contoso.com child domain to the australia.contoso.com parent domain. Adding a child domain requires Enterprise Administrator credentials in the forest.

Domain controllers can also host the DNS service and function as global catalog servers. In Windows Server environments, DNS is almost always hosted on domain controllers. You'll learn more about DNS configuration and options in Chapter 5, "Network Infrastructure." Global Catalog servers are covered later in this chapter.

When deploying a domain controller in an environment with multiple sites configured, you can select which site you want the domain controller to belong to. You can change this after deployment using the Active Directory Sites and Services console.

Directory Services Restore Mode passwords

Directory Services Restore Mode (DSRM) allows you to perform an authoritative restore of deleted objects from the Active Directory database. You have to perform an authoritative restore of deleted items because if you don't, the restored item is deleted the next time the AD database synchronizes with other domain controllers where the item is marked as deleted. Authoritative restores are covered later in this chapter. You configure the Directory Services Restore Mode password on the Domain Controller Options page of the Active Directory Domain Services Configuration Wizard as shown in Figure 4-4.

CHAPTER 04

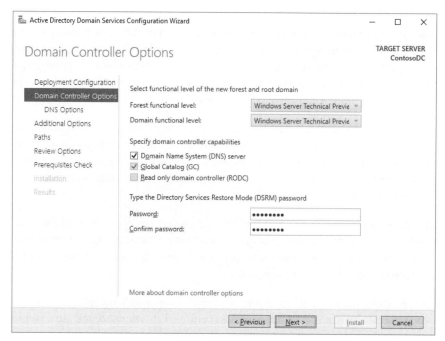

Figure 4-4 Configuring Domain Controller Options

In the event that you forget the DSRM password, which in theory should be unique for each domain controller in your organization, you can reset it by running ntdsutil.exe from an elevated command prompt and entering the following command at the ntdsutil.exe prompt, at which point you are prompted to enter a new DSRM password.

```
Reset password on server null
```

Advanced installation options

One of the advanced installation options for domain controllers is to install from media. Install from media gives you the option of pre-populating the AD DS database for a new DC from a backup of an existing DC's AD DS database, rather than having that database populated through synchronization from other domain controllers in your organization. This is very useful when you need to deploy a DC at a remote location that has limited WAN connectivity and you don't want to flood the WAN link with AD DS database synchronization traffic during domain controller deployment. Instead, you ship a backup of the AD DS database to the remote site and that backup is used to perform initial AD DS database population. After the newly installed DC connects to other domain controllers, it performs a synchronization, bringing the database up to date with a much smaller synchronization than what would be required when synchronizing from scratch.

Server Core

As the reduced attack surface area of server core deployments makes it more secure, domain controllers, which don't have a GUI dependency, are one of several perfect workloads for Server Core deployments. Microsoft recommends deploying domain controllers using the server core deployment option and managing those servers remotely.

Inside OUT

AD DS on Nano Server

Nano Server doesn't support hosting the Domain Controller role yet, but it's likely to be supported at some stage in the future. At that point in time you should consider a Nano server deployment as your primary AD DS deployment option.

To configure a computer running Server Core as a domain controller, you can:

1. Remotely connect to the server using the Server Manager console.

2. Run the Add Roles And Features Wizard to remotely install the Active Directory binaries on the server.

3. Run the Active Directory Domain Services Configuration Wizard to promote the computer to Domain Controller.

You can run the following PowerShell commands either locally or remotely to install the AD DS binaries and promote the server to the domain controller:

```
Install-WindowsFeature AD-Domain-Services -IncludeManagementTools
```

```
Install-ADDSDomainController -DomainName contoso.internal -InstallDNS:$True
-credential (Get-Credential)
```

In addition to running this set of commands, you also need to specify a Directory Service Restore Mode password before the computer running server core completes the domain controller promotion process. You'll need to use the Install-ADDSForest cmdlet if installing the first domain in a new forest. For example,

```
Install-ADDSForest -DomainName contoso.internal -InstallDNS
```

CHAPTER 04

Virtualized domain controllers

Domain controllers can be run on supported virtualization platforms, including the latest version of VMware and Hyper-V. With the production checkpoints feature available in Windows Server 2016 Hyper-V, domain controllers can now be restored from a checkpoint without causing problems. Microsoft recommends that you run virtualized domain controllers on a shielded fabric. You can learn more about production checkpoints and shielded fabrics in Chapter 6, "Hyper-V."

Global catalog servers

Global catalog servers host a full copy of all objects stored in its host directory and a partial, read-only copy of all other objects in other domains in the same forest. They are used when it's necessary to perform a check of other objects in the forest, such as when a check is performed of a universal group's membership, which could contain members from other domains in the forest.

You can use the Active Directory Sites and Services console to configure a server to function as a global catalog server by right clicking on the NTDS settings of the server. Alternatively, you can run the Set-ADObject cmdlet. For example, to configure the DC MEL-DC1 in the Melbourne-Site site as a global catalog server, run the following command:

```
Set-ADObject "CN=NTDS Settings,CN=MEL-DC1,CN=Servers,CN=Melbourne-Site,CN=Sites,CN=Confi
guration,DC=Contoso,DC=Internal" -Replace @{options='1'}
```

Read Only Domain Controllers

Read Only Domain Controllers (RODC) are a special type of DC. They host a read only copy of the AD DS database. Rather than storing the passwords for all users in the domain, RODCs only store the passwords of a specific set of accounts that you configure. The first domain controller in a new domain or forest cannot be a RODC.

The justification for RODCs is that sometimes DCs need to be located in places where servers have poor physical security and might be stolen. For example, many organizations had branch offices where servers were located under someone's desk. A good rule of thumb is that you should consider a location insecure if it is accessible to anyone other than IT. If a janitor can pull out a computer's power cord to power a vacuum cleaner, the computer isn't in a secure location.

If a server that hosts a domain controller is stolen, the best practice is to reset the account passwords that might have been compromised because it's possible, with the correct tools, to extract passwords from the AD DS database if you have direct access to it. If an ordinary DC is stolen, you would in theory need to reset the passwords of every account in the domain because you can never be sure that someone hasn't gained access to the Active Directory database and found a way to extract the passwords of people in your organization.

With shielded VMs and shielded fabrics, it's possible to run a DC in a manner where the VM itself is protected by encryption. In the event that the host server is stolen, the AD DS database cannot be recovered because the contents of the virtualization server's storage is encrypted using BitLocker.

Inside OUT

RODC and Writeable DC Deployment

Since the primary reason to deploy an RODC is because you have concerns about the physical security of a DC, it is extremely unlikely that you would have both an RODC and a writable DC at the same site. RODCs are for sites where in the past, the domain controller was placed in a location that wasn't secure.

RODC Password Replication

One of the most important steps in configuring an RODC is limiting which passwords can be replicated down to the server from a writable domain controller. The default configuration of an RODC has it store almost everything from Active Directory, except for user and computer account passwords. In the event that a user or computer account needs to be authenticated against Active Directory, the RODC acts as a proxy for a writable Windows Server DC. The authentication occurs, but it depends on the WAN link to be functional because if you can host a writable DC locally, you don't need the RODC.

Although you can configure an RODC to not cache any passwords locally, you can configure an RODC to cache the passwords of select staff working at a branch office to speed their logon. Caching passwords also allows branch office users to log on in the event that the WAN link fails. If the WAN link fails and the user's credentials are not cached, the user is simply unable to log on to the domain.

You configure which accounts are able to authenticate using the RODC by using the Password Replication Policy as shown in Figure 4-5. By default, only members of the Allowed RODC Password Replication group can use the RODC to authenticate. This is only the case if the user account is not a member of the Account Operators, Administrators, Backup Operators, Server Operators, or Denied RODC Password Replication Group groups.

CHAPTER 04

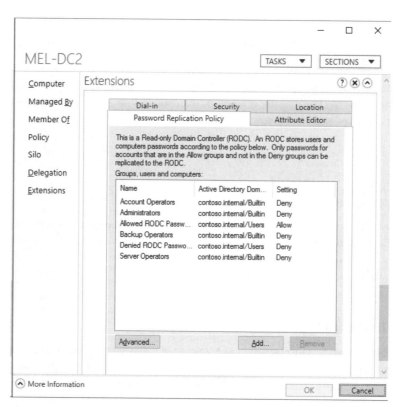

Figure 4-5 Password replication policy

RODC Local Administrators

Because you deploy RODCs as a security measure, they are almost always placed at branch office sites. As resources at branch office sites are often sparse, it is also likely that you'll co-locate other services on the server hosting the RODC role. For example, a server that functions as an RODC can also function as a file server, DNS server, DHCP server, and local intranet server.

If the computer hosting the RODC role also needs to host other roles, you might need to allow a user who works at the branch office, but who is not a member of your organization's usual IT staff, administrator access in case your normal remote administration techniques don't work. RODCs differ from normal domain controllers in that you can grant local administrator access without having to make the user a member of the Domain Admins group.

To configure a user to function as a local administrator on the computer that hosts the RODC role, edit the properties of the RODC's computer account and configure a security group for the Managed By setting.

In Chapter 18, you'll learn about Just Enough Administration, a technology that you can use to allow a user to perform remote administrative tasks on an RODC without being made an RODC local administrator.

Decommissioning an RODC

If you suspect that an RODC has been compromised, you can delete the RODC's account from the Domain Controllers container in Active Directory Users and Computers. When you do this, you get the option of resetting all passwords for user and computer accounts that were cached on the RODC, as well as the option of exporting a list of all potentially compromised accounts.

Virtual domain controller cloning

Windows Server 2012, Windows Server 2012 R2, and Windows Server 2016 support virtual domain controller cloning. Rather than redeploying domain controllers from scratch each time you need one, domain controller cloning allows you to take an existing virtual machine, make a copy of it, and deploy that copy.

Virtual domain controller cloning has the following prerequisites:

- Hypervisor must support VM-GenerationID. The version of Hyper-V included with Windows Server 2012 and later supports this technology, as does the most recent versions of VMware.

- The source domain controller needs to be running Windows Server 2012 or later.

- The domain controller that hosts the PDC Emulator role must be online and contactable by the cloned DC. The computer that hosts the PDC Emulator role must also be running Windows Server 2012 or later.

- The source DC must be a member of the Cloneable Domain Controllers group.

You also need to create the DCCloneConfig.xml file. You can do this by using the New-ADDCCloneConfig cmdlet in PowerShell. When running this cmdlet, you need to specify the cloned DC's IPv4 address information and the site the cloned DC is deployed into. For example, to create the clone configuration file for a clone DC that has the IP address 10.10.10.42 with the subnet mask 255.255.255.0, default gateway of 10.10.10.1, DNS server address of 10.10.10.10, and site name MEL-SITE, issue the command:

```
New-ADDCCloneConfigFile –IPv4Address 10.10.10.402 –IPv4DefaultGateway 10.10.10.1
–IPv4SubnetMask 255.255.255.0 –IPv4DNSResolver 10.10.10.10 –Static –SiteName MEL-SITE
```

After the clone configuration file is created, you import the VM using this file and specify a copy of the source DC's exported virtual hard disk.

CHAPTER 04

AD DS Structure

Active Directory is made up of forests and domains. A forest is a collection of Active Directory domains that share a schema and some security principals. The vast majority of organizations in the world have a single forest domain. Multiple domain forests are generally used by larger geographically dispersed organizations.

Domains

For the vast majority of organizations in the world, a single domain would be sufficient. There are two general reasons for having multiple domains in a forest. The first is that your organization is geographically dispersed and there are issues around domain replication traffic. The second is that your organization is very large. A single domain can hold a staggering number of objects. Unless your organization has tens of thousands of users, a single domain is usually more than enough.

A domain tree is a collection of domains that share a namespace in a parent-child relationship. For example, the domains australia.contoso.com and tonga.contoso.com would be child domains of the contoso.com domain.

You should always deploy at least two domain controllers per domain for redundancy purposes. Make sure that if you have a multi-domain forest, that you are taking regular backups of the domain controllers in the root domain. There has been more than one organization with a multi-domain forest who has had the root domain controllers fail irreparably, making it necessary to redeploy the entire forest from scratch.

Domain functional levels

The domain functional level determines which Active Directory features are available and which operating systems can participate as domain controllers within the domain. The domain functional level determines the minimum domain controller operating system. For example, if the domain functional level is set to Windows Server 2012, domain controllers must run the Windows Server 2012 or later operating system. This rule does not apply to member servers. You can have a domain running at the Windows Server 2016 functional level that still has servers running the Windows Server 2008 R2 operating system.

Inside OUT

Run DC at highest OS level

As domain controllers are so important to your network, Microsoft recommends that, from a security perspective, you always run domain controllers with the most recent operating system. Microsoft's argument is that the most recent operating system is the most secure and that you should pay special attention to the security of your organization's domain controllers.

Windows Server 2016 DCs support the following functional levels:

- Windows Server 2008

- Windows Server 2008 R2

- Windows Server 2012

- Windows Server 2012 R2

- Windows Server 2016

You can introduce a DC running Windows Server 2016 to a domain at the Windows Server 2008 functional level as long as all the appropriate updates are installed. You can raise the functional level after you've retired existing domain controllers running older versions of the Windows Server operating system. If all your domain controllers are running Windows Server 2016, you should update your domain functional level to the Windows Server 2016 functional level.

Inside OUT

2003 no longer necessary

Windows Server 2003 reached end of life more than a year before the release of Windows Server 2016. While all diligent organizations phased out Windows Server 2003 long before this deadline occurred, there are still a small number where Windows Server 2003 DCs are still present. Even when Windows Server 2003 DCs have long been removed, it's not unusual for people to have forgotten to elevate the functional level from Windows Server 2003. As you get greater functionality by raising functional levels and there is no downside to doing so beyond not being able to introduce a domain controller running an operating system below that of the functional level, you should raise functional levels as high as possible

Forests

A forest is a collection of domains that share a schema. There are automatic trust relationships between all domains in a forest. Accounts in one domain in a forest can be granted rights to resources in other domains. As mentioned earlier in the chapter, forests don't need to have a contiguous namespace. A forest can contain both the contoso.com and Adatum.com domains.

There are several reasons why an organization might have multiple forests, with trust relationships configured between those forests. The most common is that one organization has acquired another and multiple forests exist until such a time that the users and resources hosted in the forest of the acquired organization are moved to the forest of the acquiring organization. A less common one is that an organization is splitting off a part of itself and users need to be migrated out of the existing forest and into a new forest prior to the split occurring.

Forest functional levels are determined by the minimum domain functional level in the forest. After you've raised the domain functional levels in the forest, you can raise the forest functional level. Unlike in previous versions of Active Directory, it is possible to lower both the forest and domain functional levels after they have been raised. An important caveat with this is that the forest functional level must be lowered so that it is never higher than the lowest intended domain functional level.

Account and resource forests

Organizations are increasingly deploying what are known as Enhanced Security Administrative Environment (ESAE) forests. In an ESAE forest design, all of the accounts used for administrative tasks in the production forest are hosted in a second forest known as the ESAE, bastion, or administrative forest. The ESAE forest is configured with one-way trust relationships with the production forest.

In their native administrative forest, the accounts used for administrative tasks in the production forest are traditional unprivileged user accounts. These accounts and the groups that they are members of in the administrative forest are delegated privileges in the production forest.

The advantage of this approach is that should one of these accounts become compromised, it can't be used to alter any permissions or settings in the administrative forest because the account only has privileges in the production forest.

Organizational Units

The benefit of a comprehensive OU structure is that it simplifies the delegation of permissions over objects and allows you to apply GPOs closer to the accounts that they influence. While it's possible to filter GPOs based on security groups or WMI queries, it's important to remember that each GPO within a computer and user account's scope must be checked to see if it applies. If you have all of your GPOs applied at the domain level and filtered on the basis of security group or WMI query, your group policy processing time at startup and sign-on is going to be substantially longer than if you apply GPOs as close to the accounts they influence as possible.

Better privilege delegation targeting is also a great reason to have a good OU structure. When delegating privileges, you want to ensure that you only delegate privileges over an appropriate set of objects. For example, imagine that you want to allow each department's administrative assistant to have the ability to reset passwords for users within their respective department. If all the user accounts for your organization are located in one OU, you won't be able to do this because at best you'll provide each administrative assistant with the ability to reset every user's password in the organization. If user accounts are located in department specific OUs, you can then delegate the ability to reset passwords on a per-OU basis. This way the administrative assistant for the Marketing department can be granted the ability to change passwords for user accounts located in the Marketing OU without granting them the ability to change passwords for user accounts located in the Accounting OU.

Inside OUT

OU structures don't always relate to organizational structure

Many organizations have had an AD deployment for more than a decade and a half. A big problem for many is that while the company goes through regular reorganizations, the OU structure doesn't go through a similar reorganization. This might mean that the OU structures don't in any way represent the organizational structure. You should periodically review your organization's OU structure to ensure that it maps in a sensible way to the organizational structure. While you might not implement GPOs at the OU level or delegate privileges, it doesn't mean that you won't do so at some point in the future.

When you create OUs in Windows Server 2016, the OUs are automatically configured so that accidental deletion protection is enabled.

Flexible Single Master Operations (FSMO) roles

The Flexible Single Master Operations (FSMO) roles are five special roles present on domain controllers. Two of these roles, the schema master and the domain naming master, are unique within each forest. The other three roles, PDC Emulator, infrastructure master, and RID master, must be present within each domain in the forest. For example, in a three domain forest there is only one schema master and domain naming master, but each domain in the forest has its own PDC emulator, infrastructure master, and RID master.

By default, FSMO roles are allocated to the first domain controller in a domain. After you have more than one domain controller in each domain, you should manually start to move FSMO roles to other domain controllers. This protects you from a situation where the first domain controller deployed in each domain goes offline and all FSMO roles become unavailable. When you do need to take a domain controller offline for an extended period of time, ensure that you transition any FSMO roles that it hosts to another domain controller in the same domain.

Schema master

The schema master is the single server in the forest that is able to process updates to the Active Directory schema. The Active Directory schema defines the functionality of Active Directory. For example, by modifying the schema, you can increase the available attributes for existing objects as well as enable Active Directory to store new objects. Products including Exchange Server and Configuration Manager require that the default Active Directory schema be extended prior to product installation so that each product can store important data in Active Directory.

The domain controllers that host the schema master role should be located in the root domain of the forest. If you need to extend the schema prior to installing products such as Exchange Server, do so either on the computer that hosts the schema master role or on a computer in the same site. The account used to extend the schema needs to be a member of the Schema Admins security group.

You can determine which computer hosts the schema master role by running the following PowerShell command:

```
Get-ADForest contoso.internal | FT SchemaMaster
```

Domain naming master

The domain naming master is a forest level role that is responsible for managing the addition and removal of domains from the forest. The domain naming master also manages references to domains in trusted forests. In a multi-domain environment, the domain controller that hosts this forest level role should be deployed in the root forest.

You can determine which server hosts the domain naming master role by running the following PowerShell command:

```
Get-ADForest contoso.internal | FT DomainNamingMaster
```

PDC emulator

The PDC emulator role is a domain level FSMO role that is responsible for handling both changes to account passwords as well as domain time synchronization. PDC emulators in child domains synchronize time against the PDC emulator in the forest root domain. You should ensure that the PDC emulator in the forest root domain synchronizes against a reliable external time source.

To determine which domain controller in a specific domain hosts the PDC emulator role, run the following PowerShell command:

```
Get-ADDomain contoso.internal | FT PDCEmulator
```

Infrastructure master

The computer that hosts the infrastructure master role keeps track of changes that occur in other domains in the forest as they apply to objects in the local domain. You should avoid having the infrastructure master role co-located with a domain controller that hosts the global catalog server role unless all domain controllers in the domain are configured as global catalog servers. You can determine which computer in a domain hosts the infrastructure master role by running the following PowerShell command:

```
Get-ADDomain contoso.internal | FT InfrastructureMaster
```

RID master

The RID master processes relative ID requests from domain controllers in a specific domain. Relative IDs and domain Security IDs are combined to create a unique Security ID (SID) for the object. There is a RID master in each domain in the forest. You can use the following PowerShell command to determine which computer hosts the RID Master role:

```
Get-ADDomain contoso.internal | FT RidMaster
```

Seizing FSMO roles

In some cases, a domain controller hosting a FSMO role fails and you need to seize the FSMO role to move it to another domain controller. For example, to move the RID Master, Infrastructure Master, and Domain Naming Master roles to a domain controller named MEL-DC2, run the following command:

```
Move-ADDirectoryServerOperationMasterRole -Identity MEL-DC2 -OperationMasterRole RIDMaster,InfrastructureMaster,DomainNamingMaster -Force
```

Accounts

Accounts represent the identities of security principals in an Active Directory environment. The most common type of account is a user account, which represents a person as he interacts with Windows environment. IT Ops personnel also need to regularly deal with computer accounts, group accounts, and service accounts.

CHAPTER 04

User accounts

User accounts almost always represent real people in an Active Directory environment, with the caveat that some user accounts are used for services rather than a traditional user signing into her desktop computer.

In many organizations, a user account is nothing more than a username, a password, and a collection of group memberships. User accounts can contain substantial additional information including:

- First name
- Last name
- Middle initial
- Full name
- Office information
- Email address
- Web page
- Job title
- Department
- Company
- Manager
- Phone numbers (main, home, mobile, fax, pager, IP phone)
- Address
- User profile location
- Log on script
- Home folder
- Remote desktop service profile
- Dial-in permissions
- Published certificates
- Remote Desktop Sessions settings

- Remote Control settings

You should configure important accounts to be protected from deletion by enabling the Protect from accidental deletion option, as shown in Figure 4-6. Unless this option is removed, the account cannot be deleted. It doesn't stop an account from being removed deliberately, but it does stop the account from being deleted accidentally.

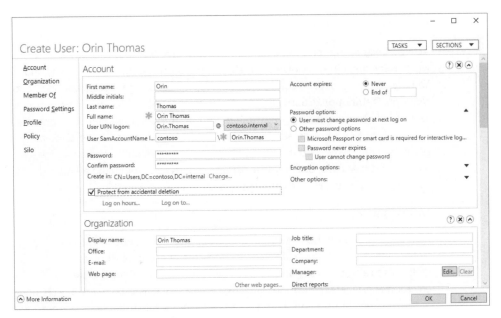

Figure 4-6 User account properties

You learn about securing accounts with log on restrictions, password policies, and authentication silos in Chapter 18.

Computer accounts

Computer accounts represent the computer within Active Directory. You often move computer accounts to specific OUs and then apply group policies to those OUs as a way of configuring the computer. When you join a computer to the domain, the computer account is automatically placed in the default Computers container.

If a computer account becomes desynchronized from the domain it is a member of and loses its trust relationship, you can repair the relationship by signing on with the local Administrator account and running the following PowerShell command:

```
Test-ComputerSecureChannel -Credential Domain\<AdminAccount> -Repair
```

If you don't know the local Administrator account password, but suspect that cached domain administrator credentials might be present, disconnect the computer from the network, either by physically removing the ethernet connection or disconnecting the virtual network adapter, sign in using those credentials, and then run the PowerShell command previously mentioned. Local Administrator Password Solution, which ensures that you don't forget the local Administrator account password, is covered in Chapter 18.

Group accounts

Active Directory supports three different types of group account scopes: Domain local, Global, which is the default, and Universal. It also supports two group types: Security and Distribution. You use security groups to control access to resources, delegate permissions, and for email distribution. Distribution groups can only be used for email distribution. If your organization uses Exchange Server, you manage distribution groups through Exchange. Best practice is to place users within global groups, add those global groups to domain local groups, and assign permissions and rights directly to the domain local groups. By default, members of the Account Operators, Domain Admins, or Enterprise Admins groups can modify the membership of groups. You can also delegate the right to manage groups, which is covered in Chapter 18.

Universal

A universal group can hold accounts and groups from the same forest. Universal groups are stored in the global catalog. If you change the membership of a universal group, this change replicates to all global catalog servers in the forest. Universal groups are great in single forest environments where replication traffic isn't an issue or where there are few changes to universal group membership. Universal groups can be nested within other universal groups, or added to domain local groups.

Global

Global groups can contain user accounts from its home domain. Global groups can also contain other global groups from its home domain. Global groups can be members of universal groups and domain local groups.

Domain local

Domain local groups can have universal groups, global groups, and domain local groups as members. Domain local groups can host accounts from any domain in the forest and accounts from domains in trusted forests. Domain local groups can only be added to domain local groups within its own domain. A domain local group can only be assigned rights and permissions within its own domain. Domain local groups cannot be added to global or universal groups.

Default groups

The groups listed in Table 4-1 are included in a Windows Server 2016 domain by default.

Table 4-1. Important groups

Group	Function
Access Control Assistance Operators	Members can query authorization attributes and permissions for resources on the computer
Account Operators	Members can manage domain user and group accounts
Administrators	Built in administrators group. On a DC this provides unlimited access to the computer and domain
Allowed RODC Password Replication Group	Members can have their passwords replicated to RODCs
Backup Operators	Members can override security restrictions to back up or restore files
Cert Publishers	Members can publish certificates to AD DS
Certificate Services DCOM Access	Members can connect to Certification Authorities
Cloneable Domain Controllers	Domain controllers that can be cloned
Cryptographic Operators	Are able to perform cryptographic operations
Denied RODC Password Replication Group	Members cannot have their passwords replicated to RODCs
Distributed COM Users	Able to launch, activate, and use Distributed COM objects
DNSAdmins	DNS administrators group
DNSUpdateProxy	Group for DNS clients who are able to perform dynamic updates on behalf of services such as DHCP servers
Domain Admins	Members can administer the domain. Automatically members of the local Administrators group on every computer in the domain. Default owner of all objects created in Active Directory
Domain Computers	All computers that are members of the domain
Domain Controllers	All domain controllers in the domain
Domain Guests	Hosts the built in domain Guest account
Domain Users	Hosts all user accounts in the domain
Enterprise Admins	Only present in the root domain of a forest. Can make forest wide changes, such as raising forest functional level or adding domains

Enterprise Key Admins	Members can perform administrative tasks on key objects at the forest level
Enterprise Read-only Domain Controllers	Group for enterprise read only domain controllers
Event Log Readers	Are able to view the contents of event logs on the computer
Group Policy Creator Owners	Members are able to create and modify GPOs
Hyper-V Administrators	Are able to manage Hyper-V on the local machine
IIS_IUSRS	Internet Information Services built in group
Incoming Forest Trust Builders	Members can create incoming, one-way trusts to the forest
Key Admins	Members can perform administrative tasks on key objects at the domain level
Network Configuration Operators	Members can configure networking features
Performance Log Users	Members can schedule logging of performance counters and collect event traces
Performance Monitor Users	Members can access performance counter data locally and remotely
Pre-Windows 2000 Compatible Access	A group that exists for backwards compatibility
Print Operators	Members can manage printers deployed on domain controllers
Protected Users	Members of this group have stricter security controls applied to their accounts
RAS and IAS Servers	Members in this group are able to access the remote access settings of user accounts
RDS Endpoint Servers	Servers in this group host VMs used with RemoteApp programs and personal virtual desktops
RDS Management Servers	Servers in this group can perform administrative actions on other servers running the Remote Desktop Services role
RDS Remote Access Servers	Servers in this group enable users of RemoteApp programs and personal virtual desktop to access resources
Read-only Domain Controllers	Read only domain controllers in the domain
Remote Desktop Users	Granted the right to sign on using remote desktop
Remote Management Users	Members can access WMI resources over management protocols
Replicator	Group supporting file replication at the domain level
Schema Admins	Root domain group. Members are authorized to make changes to Active Directory Schema

Server Operators	Members can administer domain member servers
Storage Replica Administrators	Members can manage storage replica
Terminal Server License Servers	Members are able to update Active Directory information about terminal services licensing
Users	Built in Users group
Windows Authorization Access Group	Have access to computed tokenGroupGlobalAndUniversal attribute on User objects

Service accounts

Service accounts are functionally user accounts used by services to interact with the operating system and resources on the network. By assigning rights to the service account, you can limit what the service can or cannot do.

In Chapter 18 on security you'll learn how to lock down service accounts. One of the key things to remember about a service account is that it should not have the right to log on locally to a computer, but should have the log on as a service right. This is important because administrators in many organizations have bad habits where they grant service accounts unnecessary rights and even go as far as to give all service accounts the same non-expiring password. Sophisticated attackers know this and use this to compromise service accounts and use them as a way to gain privileged access.

Local System

The Local System (NT AUTHORITY\SYSTEM) account is a built in account. It has privileges equivalent to a local administrator account on the local computer. It acts with the computer account's credentials when interacting on the network. This is the most powerful service account and generally you should be reluctant to assign this service account manually to a service given its extensive privileges.

Local Service

The Local Service (NT AUTHORITY\LocalService) account has the same level of privilege as user accounts that are members of the local Users group on a computer. This account has fewer local privileges than the Local System account. Any services assigned to this account access network resources as a null session without credentials. Use this account when the service doesn't require network access or can access network resources as an anonymous user and requires only minimal privileges on the computer it is being used on.

Network Service

The Network Service (NT AUTHORITY\NetworkService) is similar to the Local Service account in that it has privileges on the local computer equivalent to those assigned to a member of the local Users group. The primary difference is that this account interacts with the computer account's credentials with resources on the network.

GMSA

A group managed service account (GMSA) is a service account that is managed by the domain. This means that rather than having to update the service account's password manually, Active Directory updates the password in line with the domain password policy. Many organizations that use regular user accounts as service accounts tend to set a static password for these accounts, which is often simple rather than complex.

Group Managed Service Accounts require the forest functional level to be Windows Server 2012 or higher. Forests at the Windows Server 2008 level support a version of a GMSA called a MSA, but this is more limited than a GMSA with each MSA only being able to be installed on a single machine.

You manage GMSAs using Windows PowerShell. To create a GMSA, specify the name of the account, a DNS hostname associated with the account, and the name of the security principals that are allowed to use the account. For example, to create a GMSA named MEL-SQL-GMSA for the contoso.internal domain that can be used by servers in the MEL-SQL-Servers security group, enact the following command:

```
New-ADServiceAccount MEL-SQL-GMSA -DNSHostname MEL-SQL-GMSA.contso.internal
-PrincipalsAllowedToRetrieveManagedPassword MEL-SQL-Servers
```

To install the account on a specific server so that you can use it, run the Install-ADServiceAccount cmdlet. For example, to install the MEL-SQL-GMSA account on a server so that you can assign the account to services, enact the command:

```
Install-ADServiceAccount MEL-SQL-GMSA
```

When assigning the account to a service, you should clear the password and confirm password textbox. Windows Server 2016 recognizes that the account is a GMSA and manages the password settings.

Virtual account

A virtual account is the local equivalent of a group managed service account. Virtual accounts are supported by products such as SQL Server 2012 as an alternative to the default built in accounts. You can create virtual service accounts by editing the property of a service and setting the account name to **NT Service\<ServiceName>.**

Group policy

Group policy provides a central way of managing user and computer configuration. You can use group policy to configure everything from password and auditing policies to software deployment, desktop background settings, and mappings between file extensions and default applications.

Inside OUT

Not the only configuration management option

It's fair to say that group policy is really starting to show its age. On the server side, Microsoft is pushing Desired State Configuration as the primary method of managing server configuration. On the client side, you often get a better result using tools such as Configuration Manager for on-premises deployments and Intune for clients that aren't domain joined.

GPO Management

The Group Policy Management console is the primary method that the Group Policy is managed through in a standard Windows Server environment. This tool allows you to view Group Policy items from the forest level down. It provides information on which GPOs are linked at the domain, site, and OU level. You can see a list of all GPOs in a domain under the Group Policy Objects node. There is also a WMI Filters node that contains all WMI filters configured for the domain, a Starter GPOs node that contains all starter GPOs, a Group Policy Modeling node, and a Group Policy Results node. By right-clicking on a GPO and selecting Edit, you can edit a GPO in the Group Policy Management Editor. You can output information about a GPO, including which settings are configured and where the GPO is linked, to a file in HTML format using the Get-GPOReport cmdlet.

Advanced Group Policy Management

Advanced Group Policy Management (AGPM) is available to Software Assurance customers through the Microsoft Desktop Optimization Pack. AGPM integrates with the existing Group Policy Management console, extending its functionality. AGPM has several benefits over the standard Group Policy Management console.

The biggest advantage of AGPM is that it enables you to apply a workflow to the management of GPOs, allowing you to use versioning and offline editing. This is an advantage over the standard Group Policy Management console where any changes made to an active Group Policy are automatically propagated to clients that are influenced by that policy. Having offline functionality for editing GPOs allows for GPOs that are already active to be more extensively tested during the revision process than might be the case in a traditional GPO deployment.

AGPM offers a more advanced model for editing GPOs, as it allows administrators to track precisely which person in an organization made a specific change to a GPO. In a traditional Windows Server deployment, even though it is possible to control who has the permissions required to edit and apply a GPO, if multiple people have these permissions, it can be almost impossible

CHAPTER 04

to determine who made a specific change to an existing GPO. Being able to track the changes made to a GPO is very important in a high-security environment.

AGPM uses the following roles in its delegation architecture:

- **AGPM Administrator**. Users assigned this role are able to perform all tasks in AGPM. This includes configuring domain-wide options as well as delegating permissions.

- **Approver**. Users assigned this role are able to deploy GPOs into the domain. Approvers are also able to approve or reject requests from users assigned the Editor role. Users assigned this role are also able to created and delete GPOs, but cannot edit GPOs unless assigned the Editor role.

- **Reviewer.** Users assigned the Reviewer role are able to view the contents of GPOs and compare the contents of GPOs, but they do not have the ability to modify or deploy GPOs. The Reviewer role is designed to review and audit GPO management.

- **Editor.** Users assigned this role are able to view and compare GPOs as Reviewers can. They are also able to check GPOs out of the archive, edit them offline, and then check those GPOs back into the archive. They are unable to deploy GPOs but can request GPO deployment.

Backup and restore

In any environment where you make a change, you need to have the option to roll back that change. Even if you have the AGPM, it is a good idea to regularly back up Group Policy Objects. While GPOs are backed up when you perform a system state backup, they can be troublesome to restore if you delete or modify them in an unintended way. Using a tool like AGPM can reduce the chance that you can't roll back to a previous configuration, but if you don't have AGPM, you should make a backup of a GPO prior to making substantial, or even insubstantial, policy modifications.

Backing up a GPO is straightforward. In the Group Policy Management console, right-click the policy and then click Back Up. On the Back Up Group Policy Object dialog box, enter the folder that you are backing the GPO up to and provide a description. You can back up all GPOs in your organization by right-clicking the Group Policy Objects node within the Group Policy Management console and clicking Back Up All.

You can manage the backups that you have taken of Group Policy Objects by right-clicking the Group Policy Objects node and then clicking Manage Backups. This opens the Manage Backups dialog box. Using this dialog box, you can restore a backed up GPO, verify what settings are applied in a backup GPO, view where the GPO was linked and how it was filtered, the delegation settings on the GPO, and, if necessary, you can delete a specific GPO backup. You can also restore an individual GPO by right-clicking the GPO and then clicking Restore from Backup. When you do this, you have the option of restoring from any backup you've taken of that GPO.

Inside OUT

Restoring GPO doesn't restore links

Note that restoring a GPO does not restore where the GPO was linked. You can, however, configure that prior to restoring the GPO by viewing information about the backed up GPO.

You can use the Import Settings Wizard to import settings from a backed up GPO into an existing GPO. You can use this technique to quickly duplicate GPOs by backing one up, creating a new "blank" GPO, and then importing the settings into the new GPO. To run the Import Settings Wizard, right-click a GPO under the Group Policy Objects of the Group Policy Management console and then click Import Settings. Importing settings into a GPO overwrites all current settings in the GPO, effectively replacing the current GPO with the backed up GPO. You do get the option to back up the GPO that you are going to overwrite when running the wizard and, even if you are completely sure of what you are doing, this is a good option to take.

Policy processing

Group policy is processed in the following order, with subsequent policies overriding previously applied policies where conflicts exist:

- Local

- Site

- Domain

- Organizational Unit

For example, if one policy configures a setting at the AD Site level and another policy configures the same setting at the Organizational Unit level, the policy that configures the setting at the Organization Unit level is applied.

The exception to this is when you configure one of the following settings:

- **Block Inheritance**. The Block Inheritance option allows you block upstream policies from applying. You can configure this option at the Domain or OU level. It blocks all upstream settings except those configured through a policy that has the No Override setting.

- **No Override**. You use the No Override setting to stop the Block setting. Use this on policies that you need to have enforced.

Resultant Set of Policy

The Resultant Set of Policy tool allows you to generate a model of Group Policy application, allowing you to figure out which policies apply to particular objects within the domain. Resultant Set of Policy allows you to figure out why Group Policy application isn't behaving in the way that you expect and allows you to resolve Group Policy conflicts.

There are two ways you can calculate Resultant Set of Policy. The first is to use Group Policy Modeling. The second is to use Group Policy Results. The difference between these is as follows:

- Group Policy Modeling allows you to view the impact of altering site membership, security group membership, filtering, slow links, loopback processing, and the movement of accounts to new OUs on the application of policy.

- Group Policy Results allows you to troubleshoot the application of policy by telling you which settings apply to a specific user or computer account.

By default, members of the Domain Admins and Enterprise Admins can generate Group Policy Modeling or Group Policy Results information. You can delegate permissions so that users can perform these tasks at the OU or domain level.

Inside OUT

Policy in multi-domain forests

Policies linked at the site level in multi-domain forests are stored in the root domain. This can cause challenges with group policy application in scenarios where a site linked policy applies but where no DC with a root domain membership is present in the local site.

Filtering

GPO filtering allows you to determine whether or not a linked GPO applies based on group membership or the results of a WMI query. For example, you could write a WMI query that performs a check so that a GPO only applies if the computer has more than 4 GB of RAM. If the computer has more than 4 GB of RAM, the policy applies normally. If the computer has less than 4 GB of RAM, the GPO does not apply.

Inside OUT

Site linked GPOs

If group policy processing takes too long because of site linked GPOs, the simplest solution is to not link polices at the site level and instead apply them at the domain level and use group policy filtering through a WMI query to ensure that location specific GPOs are applied. An alternative is to place domain controllers that have root domain membership at each site, although this is likely to be more expensive than the policy filtering option.

Group Policy Preferences

Group Policy Preferences work around the idea of eliminating, or at least substantially reducing, the need for traditional startup and logon scripts. Logon scripts have a way of becoming convoluted over time. Group Policy Preferences allow simplification of common logon and startup script tasks such as drive mappings and setting environment variables.

By reducing or eliminating some of the complexity of logon scripts, you can use Group Policy Preferences to reduce configuration errors. You can use Group Policy Preferences to configure the following:

- Applications

- Drive mappings

- Environment variables

- File updates

- Folders

- Ini files

- Registry settings

- Shortcuts

- Data sources

- Devices

- Folder options

CHAPTER 04

- Internet settings

- Local users and groups

- Network options

- Power options

- Printer settings

- Regional options

- Scheduled tasks

- Start menu settings

Some of these items can also be configured using traditional Group Policy. In the event that an item is configured in the same GPO using both policy and preferences, the traditional setting takes precedence. The difference between a Group Policy Preference and a normal Group Policy setting is that a user is able to change a Group Policy Preference if they have the appropriate permissions. For example, users can un-map a mapped network drive. The drive would remain unmapped until the user logged in again, at which point it would be remapped. Generally, if you want to enforce a setting, use a standard Group Policy. If you want to apply the setting and allow users to change it, use a Group Policy Preference. The closest you can come to enforcing a Group Policy Preference is by disabling the Apply Once and Do Not Reapply setting in the policy item's configuration. This way the preference is applied each time group policy refreshes.

You can target Group Policy Preferences so that different preferences can apply to the same item types within a single GPO. You can use the following items to restrict how a Group Policy Preference applies:

- The computer has a battery

- The computer has a specific name

- The computer has a specific CPU speed

- Date

- The computer has a certain amount of disk space

- The computer is a member of a domain

- The computer has a particular environment variable set

- A certain file is present on the computer

- The computer is within a particular IP address range

- The computer uses specific language settings

- Meets the requirements of an LDAP query

- The computer has a MAC address within a specific range

- Meets the requirements of an MSI query

- The computer uses a specific type of network connection

- The computer is running a specific operating system

- The computer is a member of a specific OU

- The computer has PCMCIA present

- The computer is portable

- The computer uses a specific processing mode

- The computer has a certain amount of RAM

- The computer has a certain registry entry

- User or computer is a member of a specific security group

- The computer is in a specific Active Directory site

- Remote Desktop Setting

- Within a specific time range

- The user has a specific name

- Meets the requirements of a WMI query

Administrative templates

Group Policy Administrative Templates allow you to extend Group Policy beyond the settings available in GPOs. Common software packages, such as Microsoft Office, often include Administrative Templates that you can import to manage software-specific settings. In early versions of Windows Server, Administrative Templates were available as files in ADM format. Since the release of Windows Server 2008, Administrative Templates are available in a standards-based XML file format called ADMX.

To be able to use an Administrative Template, you can import it directly into a GPO using the Add/Remove Templates option when you right-click the Administrative Templates node. A second option is to copy the Administrative Template files to the Central Store, located in the c:\Windows\Sysvol\sysvol\<domainname>\Policies\PolicyDefinitions folder on any domain controller. You might need to create this folder if it does not already exist. After the folder is present, it is then replicated to all domain controllers, and you are able to access the newly imported Administrative Templates through the Administrative Templates node of a GPO.

Restoring deleted items

Sometimes an Active Directory account, such as a user account or even an entire OU, is accidentally, or on occasion maliciously, deleted. Rather than go through the process of recreating the deleted item or items, it's possible to restore the items. Deleted items are retained within the AD DS database for a period up to the value of what is termed the tombstone lifetime. You can recover a deleted item without having to restore the item from a backup of Active Directory as long as the item was deleted within the tombstone lifetime window.

The default tombstone lifetime for an Active Directory environment at the Windows Server 2008 forest functional level or higher is 180 days. You can check the value of the tombstone lifetime by issuing the following command from an elevated command prompt, (substituting dc=Contoso,dc=Internal for the suffix of your organization's forest root domain):

```
Dsquery * "cn=Directory Service,cn=Windows NT,cn=Services,cn=Configuration,dc=Contoso,dc
=Internal" -scope base -attr tombstonelifetime
```

For most organizations the 180 day default is fine, but some administrators might want to increase or decrease this value to give them a greater or lesser window for easily restoring deleted items. You can change the default tombstone lifetime by performing the following steps:

1. From an elevated command prompt or PowerShell session, type ADSIEdit.msc.

2. From the Action menu, click Connect to. On the Connection Settings dialog box, click Configuration as shown in Figure 4-7 and then click OK.

Figure 4-7 Connection settings

3. Right-click on the CN=Services, CN=Windows NT, CN=Directory Service node and click Properties.

4. In the list of attributes, select tombstoneLifetime as shown in Figure 4-8 and click Edit.

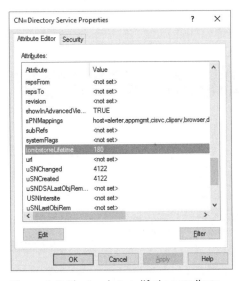

Figure 4-8 The tombstonelifetime attribute

5. On the Integer Attribute Editor dialog box, enter the new value for the tombstone lifetime and click OK twice and then close the ADSI Edit console.

Active Directory Recycle Bin

Active Directory Recycle Bin allows you to restore items that have been deleted from Active Directory, but are still present within the database because the tombstone lifetime has not been exceeded. Active Directory Recycle Bin requires that the domain functional level be set to Windows Server 2008 R2 or higher.

Inside OUT

Enable AD Recycle Bin first

You can't use Active Directory Recycle Bin to restore items that were deleted before you enabled Active Directory Recycle Bin.

Once activated, you can't deactivate Active Directory Recycle Bin. There isn't any great reason to want to deactivate AD Recycle Bin once it is activated. You don't have to use it to restore deleted items should you still prefer to go through the authoritative restore process.

To activate Active Directory Recycle Bin, perform the following steps:

1.   Open Active Directory Administrative Center and select the domain that you want to enable.

2.   In the Tasks pane, click Enable Recycle Bin as shown in Figure 4-9.

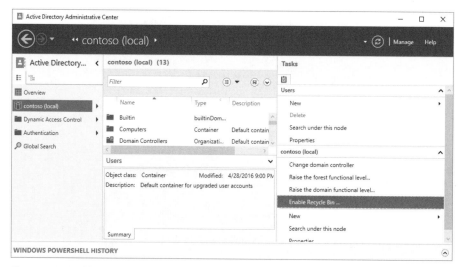

Figure 4-9 Enable Recycle Bin

After you have enabled the AD Recycle Bin, you can restore an object from the newly available Deleted Objects container. This is, of course, assuming that the object was deleted after the Recycle Bin was enabled and assuming that the tombstone lifetime value has not been exceeded. To recover the object, select the object in the deleted items container and then click Restore or Restore To. Figure 4-10 shows Restore being selected, which restores the object to its original location. The Restore To option allows you to restore the object to another available location, such as another OU.

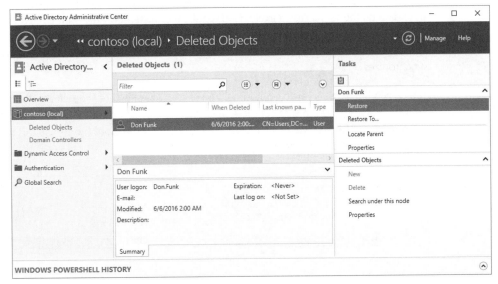

Figure 4-10 The Active Directory Administrative Center Description

Authoritative restore

An authoritative restore is performed when you want the items you are recovering to overwrite items that are in the current Active Directory database. If you don't perform an authoritative restore, Active Directory assumes that the restored data is simply out-of-date and overwrites it when it is synchronized from another domain controller. If you perform a normal restore on an item that was backed up last Tuesday when it was deleted the following Thursday, the item is deleted the next time the Active Directory database is synchronized. You do not need to perform an authoritative restore if you only have one domain controller in your organization because there is no other domain controller that can overwrite the changes.

Authoritative Restore is useful in the following scenarios:

- You haven't enabled the Active Directory Recycle Bin.

- You have enabled the Active Directory Recycle Bin, but the object you want to restore was deleted before you enabled Active Directory Recycle Bin.

- You need to restore items that are older than the tombstone lifetime of the AD DS database.

To perform an authoritative restore, you need to reboot a DC into Directory Services Restore Mode. If you want to restore an item that is older than the tombstone lifetime of the AD DS database, you also need to restore the AD DS database. You can do this by restoring the system state data on the server. You'll likely need to take the DC temporarily off the network to perform this operation simply because if you restore a computer with old system state data and the DC synchronizes, all of the data that you wish to recover will be deleted when the domain controller synchronizes.

You can configure a server to boot into Directory Services Restore Mode from the System Configuration utility. To do this, select the Active Directory repair option on the Boot tab as shown in Figure 4-11. After you've finished with Directory Services Restore Mode, use this same utility to restore normal boot functionality.

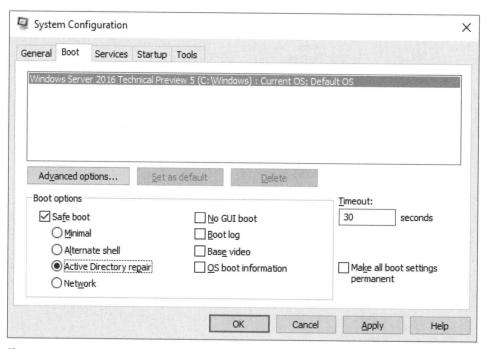

Figure 4-11 System Configuration

To enter Directory Services Restore Mode, you need to enter the Directory Services Restore Mode password. To perform an authoritative restore, perform the following general steps:

1. Choose a computer that functions as a global catalog server. This DC functions as your restore server.

2. Locate the most recent system state backup that contains the objects that you want to restore.

3. Restart the restore server in DSRM mode. Enter the DSRM password.

4. Restore the system state data.

5. Use the following command to restore items:

```
Ntdsutil "authoritative restore" "restore object cn=Mercury,ou=Planets,dc=contoso,dc=-
com" q q
```

Where "Mercury" is the object name, "Planets" is the OU that it is contained in, and "contoso. com" is the host domain.

1. If an entire OU is deleted, you can use the Restore Subtree option. For example, if you deleted the Planets OU and all the accounts that it held in the contoso.com domain, you could use the following command to restore it and all the items it contained:

```
Ntdsutil "authoritative restore" "restore subtree OU=Planets,
DC=contoso,DC=com" q q
```

Active Directory snapshots

You can use the Active Directory database mounting tool, dsamain.exe, to mount the contents of the AD DS database as it exists in snapshots or in backups so that you can interact with it using the Active Directory Users and Computers console. This provides you with a quick way of checking the state of a snapshot or backup without actually having to restore it to a production or development environment. For example, you might do this if you want to check what the AD DS database looked like at a specific point in time to determine the state of particular accounts or organizational units.

If you restored the AD DS database file ntds.dit to the location c:\restore, you can mount this file using the dsamain.exe utility on port 51389 by entering the following command:

```
Dsamain.exe /dbpath C:\restore\ntds.dit /ldapport 51389
```

You can then use Active Directory Users and Computers to connect to the specified port, in this case port 51389, to view the mounted version of the AD DS database.

You can also create snapshots of the AD DS database that you can interact with without having to take a backup. A snapshot is a copy of the AD DS database as it exists at a specific point in time. You create a snapshot of the AD DS database by running the following command from an elevated command prompt on a domain controller:

```
Ntdsutil "Activate Instance NTDS" snapshot create quit quit
```

You can list all current snapshots of the AD DS database on a domain controller by running the following command:

```
Ntdsutil snapshot "list all" quit quit
```

Each snapshot has an odd number associated with it next to the date the snapshot was taken. To select and mount a snapshot, use the command:

```
Ntdsutil snapshot "list all" "mount 1" quit quit
```

This mounts snapshot 1. Make a note of the path the snapshot is mounted on. You can then use the dsadmin.exe command to mount the snapshot so that it is accessible as an LDAP server. For example, to make the snapshot at path C:\$SNAP_201606100306_VOLUMEC$\ accessible on port 51389, use the command:

```
Dsamain.exe /dbpath C:\$SNAP_201606100306_VOLUMEC$\WINDOWS\NTDS\ntds.dit /ldapport 51389
```

You can then use Active Directory Users And Computers to connect to the specified port to view the mounted snapshot. Only members of the Domain Admins and Enterprise Admins groups can view snapshots. While you can't directly copy objects from a snapshot to the production version of the AD DS database, you can use utilities such as CSVDE and LDIFDE to export information from a snapshot and then later import it into the production AD DS database.

Managing AD DS with PowerShell

Many Active Directory administrative tasks are repetitive. If you're likely to perform a task regularly more than once, it's better to script it in PowerShell than work your way through the appropriate wizard multiple times.

There are three PowerShell modules related to Active Directory. The Active Directory PowerShell module (Table 4-2) is the one you're likely to use on a regular basis when managing Active Directory. The GroupPolicy module (Table 4-3) allows you to manage Group Policy from PowerShell. You use the ADDSDeployment (Table 4-4) module when performing deployment tasks.

Active Directory module

Table 4-2. Active Directory module cmdlets

Noun	VerbS	Function
ADAccount	Unlock, Search, Enable, Disable	Allows you to find, unlock, enable, or disable a user, computer, or service account
ADAccountAuthentication-PolicySilo	Set	Allows you to configure the authentication policy or authentication policy silo of an account
ADAccountAuthorization-Group	Get	Gets the security groups for a specified user, computer, or service account based on its token. Uses the global catalog to determine this information
ADAccountControl	Set	Modifies the user account control values of an Active Directory user or computer account
ADAccountExpiration	Set, Clear	Configure account expiration
ADAccountPassword	Set	Configure the password of a user, computer, or service account
ADAccountResultantPass-wordReplicationPolicy	Get	Gets the password replication policy for a user, computer, or service account on a specific RODC
ADAuthenticationPolicy	Set, Remove, New, Get	Manipulate the properties of the AD DS authentication policy
ADAuthenticationPolicyEx-pression	Show	Displays Edit Access Control Conditions windows update or SSDL security descriptors
ADAuthenticationPolicySilo	New, Remove, Get, Set	Manipulate Active Directory Domain Services authentication policy silos
ADAuthenticationPolicySi-loAccess	Revoke, Grant	Manage membership of authentication policy silos
ADCentralAccessPolicy	Remove, Get, Set, New	Manage central access rules and policies
ADCentralAccessPoli-cyMember	Remove, Add	Add and remove rules from a central access policy
ADCentralAccessRule	New, Set, Remove, Get	Manage central access rules
ADClaimTransformLink	Set, Clear, Remove	Manage claims transforms from being applied to one or more cross-forest trust relationships
ADClaimTransformPolicy	New, Set, Get	Manage claim transformation policy objects from Active Directory

ADClaimType	New, Get, Remove, Set	Manage Active Directory claim types
ADComputer	Remove, New, Set, Get	Manage Active Directory computer accounts
ADComputerServiceAccount	Remove, Add, Get	Add service accounts from Active Directory to a local computer
ADDCCloneConfigFile	New	Generates a clone configuration file for a domain controller
ADDCCloningExcludedApplicationList	Get	Manage which Active Directory applications are excluded when cloning the configuration of a domain controller
ADDefaultDomainPasswordPolicy	Set, Get	Manage the default password policy for a domain
ADDirectoryServer	Move	Use this cmdlet to move a DC to another AD site
ADDirectoryServerOperationMasterRole	Move	Move an operations master role to another computer
ADDomain	Set, Get	View and manage the properties of a domain
ADDomainController	Get	View the properties of a domain controller
ADDomainControllerPasswordReplicationPolicy	Remove, Get, Add	Manage which accounts can be replicated to an RODC
ADDomainMode	Set	Set the domain functional level
ADFineGrainedPasswordPolicy	Remove, Get, Set, New	Manage AD fine grained password policy
ADFineGrainedPasswordPolicySubject	Get, Remove, Add	Manage the application of fine grained password policies
ADForest	Set, Get	Manage forest properties
ADForestMode	Set	Configure forest functional level
ADGroup	Get, Set, Remove, New	Manage AD groups
ADGroupMember	Get, Remove, Add	Manage AD group membership
ADObject	Get, Restore, Rename, Set, Move, Remove, Sync, New	Manage AD objects
ADOptionalFeature	Disable, Get, Enable	Configure AD optional features
ADOrganizationalUnit	Set, Get, New, Remove	Manage AD OUs

ADPrincipalGroupMem- bership	Remove, Add, Get	Manage group membership on the basis of user account
ADReplicationAttribute- Metadata	Get	View replication metadata for AD object attributes
ADReplicationConnection	Get, Set	Manage the properties of an AD replication connection
ADReplicationFailure	Get	View information about AD replication failure
ADReplicationPartner- Metadata	Get	View information about AD replication partners
ADReplicationQueueOp- eration	Get	View all operations in the AD replication queue
ADReplicationSite	Set, Get, Remove, New	Manage AD replication sites
ADReplicationSiteLink	Set, New, Get, Remove	Manage AD replication site links
ADReplicationSiteLink- Bridge	Get, Remove, New, Set	Manage AD replication site link bridges
ADReplicationSubnet	New, Get, Set, Remove	Manage AD replication subnets
ADReplicationUpToDate- nessVectorTable	Get	Displays Update Sequence Numbers (USNs) for domain controllers
ADResourceProperty	Set, New, Remove, Get	Manage Active Directory resource properties
ADResourcePropertyList	Remove, Set, New, Get	Manage Active Directory resource property list
ADResourcePropertyList- Member	Remove, Add	Add and remove resource properties from an Active Directory resource property list
ADResourcePropertyValu- eType	Get	View a resource property value type
ADRootDSE	Get	View the root of a Directory Server informa- tion tree
ADServiceAccount	Get, Test, Set, Install, New, Remove, Uninstall	Manage AD Managed Service Account
ADServiceAccountPassword	Reset	Reset AD Managed Service Account password
ADTrust	Get	View the properties of an AD Trust
ADUser	New, Set, Get, Remove	Manage an Active Directory user

CHAPTER 04

ADUserResultantPassword-Policy	Get	Use this cmdlet to determine the resultant password policy for an account that has multiple fine grained password policies applied to it

Group Policy module

Table 4-3. Group Policy module cmdlets

Noun	VerbS	Function
GPInheritance	Get, Set	View and manage which GPOs are applied and whether inheritance is blocked
GPLink	Remove, New, Set	Manage whether a GPO is linked
GPO	Restore, Import, New, Remove, Rename, Backup, Get, Copy	Manage GPOs, including backup restore and copy
GPOReport	Get	Generate a report on a GPO
GPPermission	Set, Get	Manage permissions on policies
GPPrefRegistryValue	Remove, Set, Get,	Manage registry based policy preference settings. Microsoft maintains spreadsheets that map group policy settings to registry settings. To use this cmdlet to set registry settings, you need to consult the spreadsheet
GPRegistryValue	Remove, Get, Set,	Manage registry based policy settings
GPResultantSetOfPolicy	Get	View the resultant set of policy information
GPStarterGPO	New, Get	Manage starter GPO
GPUpdate	Invoke	Triggers a group policy update

ADDSDeployment module

Table 4-4. Active Directory module cmdlets

Noun	VerbS	Function
ADDSDomain	Install	Installs a new Active Directory Domain Services domain
ADDSDomainController	Install, Uninstall	Use to add or remove a domain controller
ADDSDomainControllerInstallation	Test	Runs a prerequisite check prior to installing a domain controller
ADDSDomainControllerUninstallation	Test	Runs a prerequisite check prior to removing a domain controller
ADDSDomainInstallation	Test	Checks the prerequisites for a new Active Directory Domain services domain
ADDSForest	Install	Allows you to install a new Active Directory Forest configuration
ADDSForestInstallation	Test	Allows you to perform a pre-requisite check prior to performing an Active Directory forest installation
ADDSReadOnlyDomainControllerAccount	Add	Use this cmdlet to create a RODC account in the AD DS database
ADDSReadOnlyDomainControllerAc-countCreation	Test	Allows you to check that the necessary prerequisites are in place before you create an RODC account

CHAPTER 04

DNS, DNS and IPAM

DNS and DHCP servers are a part of all networks' core infrastructure. It doesn't matter if your organization has hosts running on Windows, Linux, Mac OS, or on Internet of Things (IoT) devices because DHCP and DNS are likely managing the name and address information for those hosts. While new features have been introduced with each successive server operating system, the core functionality of Windows Server's DHCP and DNS server services hasn't changed much since the release of Windows 2000.

What did change with the release of Windows Server 2012, however, was the inclusion of the IPAM feature. IPAM allows you to centrally manage all of the DNS and DHCP infrastructure. Instead of managing scopes and zones on individual DHCP and DNS servers, after you deploy IPAM, you can manage all of your organization's zones and scopes from a single console.

DNS

At the most basic level, DNS servers translate host names to IP addresses and IP addresses to host names. By querying special records on DNS servers, it's possible to locate mail servers, name servers, verify domain ownership, and locate servers such as domain controllers. While DNS servers are usually deployed on a domain controller on a Windows Server network, it's also possible to deploy them on stand-alone computers and the DNS role is one of the few supported on the nano server deployment option when Windows Server 2016 was released.

DNS zone types

Zones store DNS resource record information. The DNS Server service in Windows Server 2016 supports several zone types, each of which is appropriate for a different set of circumstances. These zone types include primary, secondary, stub, and GlobalNames zones. You can integrate zones into Active Directory or you can use the traditional primary or secondary architecture.

Active Directory integrated zones

Active Directory integrated zones can be replicated to all domain controllers in a domain, all domain controllers in a forest, or all domain controllers enrolled in a specific Active Directory partition. You can create an Active Directory integrated zone only on a writable domain controller, but you can also configure primary and stub zones as Active Directory integrated zones. Domain controllers with DNS servers that host Active Directory integrated zones can process updates to those zones.

When you choose to make a zone Active Directory integrated, you have the option to configure a replication scope. You can configure the zone to be replicated so that it is present on all domain controllers in the domain, in the forest, or within the scope of a custom Active Directory partition. When determining the appropriate replication scope, consider which clients need regular, direct access to the zone and which clients only require occasional, indirect access.

You can use custom directory partitions to replicate a zone to some, but not all, domain controllers. You can only select this option if there is an existing custom DNS application directory partition. You can use the Add-DNSServerDirectoryPartition cmdlet to create a directory partition. For example, to create a DNS Server directory partition called Tasmania on a subset of your organization's domain controllers, execute this command:

```
Add-DNSServerDirectoryPartition -Name Tasmania
```

Active Directory integrated zones use multi-master replication, meaning any domain controller that hosts the DNS zone can process updates to the zone. When creating a DNS zone, you must specify whether the zone supports dynamic updates, which allow clients to update DNS records. This is useful in environments where clients change IP addresses on a regular basis. When a client gets a new IP address, it can update the record associated with its host name in the appropriate DNS zone. There are three dynamic update configuration options:

- **Allow only secure dynamic updates.** You can use this option only with Active Directory integrated zones. Only authenticated clients can update DNS records.

- **Allow both non-secure and secure dynamic updates.** With this option, any client can update a record. Although this option is convenient, it is also insecure because any client can update the DNS zone, which could potentially redirect clients that trust the quality of the information stored on the DNS server.

- **Do not allow dynamic updates.** When you choose this option, all DNS updates must be performed manually. This option is very secure, but it is also labor-intensive.

An Active Directory integrated zone can replicate to a read-only domain controller (RODC). A few things to keep in mind with this configuration are that the RODC hosted zone is read-only and that the RODC cannot process updates to the zone, which is also the case with a traditional writable domain controller. When you replicate an Active Directory integrated zone to an RODC, the RODC forwards any zone update traffic directed at it to a writable domain controller.

You can create an Active Directory integrated primary zone by using the Add-DnsServerPrimaryZone cmdlet with the ReplicationScope parameter. For example, to create the Active Directory integrated zone cpandl.com so that it replicates to all domain controllers in the forest, issue this command:

```
Add-DnsServerPrimaryZone -Name cpandl.com -ReplicationScope Forest
```

When you first install Active Directory, the installation process ensures that the DNS zone associated with the root domain is automatically configured as an Active Directory integrated zone. This root domain zone is automatically replicated to all domain controllers in the forest.

Primary and secondary zones

In traditional DNS implementations, a single server hosts a primary zone, which processes all zone updates, and a collection of secondary servers replicate zone data from the primary zone. One drawback to this model is that if the primary server fails, no zone updates can occur until the primary zone is restored.

Windows Server 2016 supports two types of primary zones: Active Directory integrated zones and standard primary zones. Active Directory integrated zones can only be hosted on computers that also function as domain controllers. Computers running Windows Server 2016 that do not function as domain controllers however, can host standard primary zones. When you create a primary zone on a computer that is not a domain controller, the wizard does not enable you to specify a replication scope for the zone.

Inside OUT

All zone types on a domain controller

The DNS server service on a domain controller supports all zone types. This means that you can choose to deploy a standard or Active Directory integrated primary zone, a stub zone, a reverse lookup zone, or a secondary zone on a domain controller.

A secondary zone is a read-only copy of a primary zone. Secondary zones cannot process updates and can only retrieve updates from a primary zone. Also, secondary zones cannot be Active Directory integrated zones, but you can configure a secondary zone for an Active Directory integrated primary zone. Prior to configuring a secondary zone, you need to configure the primary zone that you want it to replicate from to enable transfers to that zone. You can do this on the Zone Transfers tab of the Zone Properties dialog box. Secondary zones work best when the primary zone that they replicate from does not update frequently. If the primary zone does update frequently, it is possible that the secondary zone might have out-of-date records.

Use the Add-DNSServerSecondaryZone cmdlet to create a secondary zone. For example, to create a secondary zone for the australia.contoso.com zone, where a DNS server hosting the primary zone is located at 192.168.15.100, issue the following command:

```
Add-DnsServerSecondaryZone -Name "australia.contoso.com" -ZoneFile "australia.con-
toso.com.dns" -MasterServers 192.168.15.100
```

Reverse lookup zones

Reverse lookup zones translate IP addresses into FQDNs. You can create IPv4 or IPv6 reverse lookup zones and you can also configure reverse lookup zones as Active Directory integrated zones, standard primary zones, secondary zones, or stub zones. The domain controller promotion process automatically creates a reverse lookup zone based on the IP address of the first domain controller promoted in the organization.

Reverse lookup zones are dependent on the network ID of the IP address range that they represent. IPv4 reverse lookup zones can only represent /8, /16, or /24 networks, which are the old Class A, Class B, and Class C networks. You can't create a single reverse lookup zone for IP subnets that doesn't fit into one of these categories, and the smallest reverse lookup zone you can create is for subnet mask /24, or 255.255.255.0.

Use the Add-DNSPrimaryZone cmdlet and the NetworkID parameter to create a reverse lookup zone. For example, to create an Active Directory integrated reverse lookup zone for the 192.168.15.0/24 subnet, issue the following command:

```
Add-DnsServerPrimaryZone -NetworkID "192.168.15.0/24" -ReplicationScope "Forest"
```

Inside OUT

Reverse lookup zones

Few applications actually require that you configure reverse lookup zones. In most organizations, the only reverse lookup zone is the one that is automatically created when Active Directory is installed. One of the few times where reverse lookup zones seem necessary is when you configure Simple Mail Transfer Protocol (SMTP) gateways because some anti-SPAM checks perform a reverse IP address lookup to verify the identity of the SMTP gateway. The difficulty is that often the SMTP gateway's IP address, being a public address, belongs to the ISP, which means that creating the reverse lookup zone entry is often beyond your direct control as a systems administrator.

Zone delegation

Zone delegations function as pointers to the next subordinate DNS layer in the DNS hierarchy. For example, if your organization uses the contoso.com DNS zone and you want to create a separate australia.contoso.com DNS zone, you can perform a zone delegation so that the DNS servers for the contoso.com DNS zone point to the DNS servers for the australia.contoso.com DNS zone. When you create a new child domain in an Active Directory forest, zone delegation occurs automatically. When you are performing a manual delegation, create the delegated zone on the target DNS server prior to performing the delegation from the parent zone.

Although you can delegate several levels, remember that the maximum length of a FQDN is 255 bytes and the maximum length of a FQDN for an Active Directory Domain Services domain controller is 155 bytes.

Use the Add-DnsServerZoneDelegation cmdlet to add a delegation. For example, to add a delegation for the australia.contoso.com zone to the contoso.com zone pointing at the name server ausdns.australia.contoso.com which has the IP address 192.168.15.100, use the following command:

```
Add-DnsServerZoneDelegation -Name "contoso.com" -ChildZoneName "australia" -NameServer
"ausdns.australia.contoso.com" -IPAddress 192.168.15.100 -PassThru
-Verbose
```

Forwarders and conditional forwarders

Forwarders and conditional forwarders enable your DNS server to forward traffic to specific DNS servers when a lookup request cannot be handled locally. For example, you might configure a conditional forwarder to forward all traffic for resource records the tailspintoys.com zone to a DNS server at a specific IP address. If you don't configure a forwarder, or if a configured forwarder can't be contacted, the DNS Server service forwards the request to a DNS root server and the request is resolved normally.

Forwarders

You are likely to use a DNS forwarder, rather than have your DNS server just use the root server, when you want to have a specific DNS server on the Internet handle your organization's DNS resolution traffic. Most organizations configure their ISP's DNS server as a forwarder. When you do this, the ISP's DNS server performs all the query work, returning the result to your organization's DNS server. Your organization's DNS server then returns the result of the query back to the original requesting client.

You configure forwarders on a per-DNS server level. You can configure a forwarder using the DNS Manager. You can do this by editing the properties of the DNS server and then configuring the list of forwarders on the Forwarders tab.

You can create a DNS forwarder by using the Add-DnsServerForwarder cmdlet. For example, to create a DNS forwarder for a DNS server with 10.10.10.111 as the IP address, issue this command:

```
Add-DnsServerForwarder 10.10.10.111
```

You can't create a forwarder on one DNS server and then have it replicate to all other DNS servers in the forest or the domain, although this is possible with conditional forwarders and stub zones.

Conditional forwarders

Conditional forwarders only forward address requests from specific domains rather than forwarding all requests that can't be resolved by the DNS server. When configured, a conditional forwarder takes precedence over a forwarder. Conditional forwarders are useful when your organization has a trust relationship or partnership with another organization. You can configure a conditional forwarder that directs all traffic to host names within that organization instead of having to resolve those host names through the standard DNS-resolution process.

You can create conditional forwarders using the Add-DnsServerConditionalForwarderZone PowerShell cmdlet. For example, to create a conditional forwarder for the DNS domain tailspintoys.com that forwards DNS queries to the server at IP address 10.10.10.102 and to also replicate that conditional forwarder to all DNS servers within the Active Directory forest, issue this command:

```
Add-DnsServerConditionalForwarderZone –MasterServers 10.10.10.102 –Name tailspintoys.com
–ReplicationScope Forest
```

Stub zones

A stub zone is a special zone that stores authoritative name server records for a target zone. Stub zones have an advantage over forwarders when the address of a target zone's authoritative DNS server changes on a regular basis. Stub zones are often used to host the records for authoritative DNS servers in delegated zones. Using stub zones in this way ensures that delegated zone information is up to date. If you create the stub zone on a writable domain controller, it can be stored with Active Directory and replicated to other domain controllers in the domain or forest.

You can add a stub zone using the Add-DnsServerStubZone cmdlet. For example, to add a DNS stub zone for the fabrikam.com zone using the DNS server at 10.10.10.222 and to also replicate that stub zone to all DNS servers in the forest, execute this command:

```
Add-DnsServerStubZone –MasterServers 10.10.10.222 –Name fabrikam.com –ReplicationScope
Forest –LoadExisting
```

GlobalNames zones

GlobalNames zones are a single-label name resolution replacement for WINS that can utilize existing DNS infrastructure. Deploying GlobalNames zones enabling organizations to retire their existing WINS servers. You can use GlobalNames zones as long as your organization's DNS servers are running Windows Server 2008 or later.

Your organization should consider deploying GlobalNames zones instead of WINS in the following situations:

1. Your organization is transitioning to IPv6. WINS does not support IPv6 and you need to support single-label name resolution.

2. Single-label name resolution is limited to a small number of hosts that rarely change. GlobalNames zones must be updated manually.

3. You have a large number of suffix search lists because of a complex naming strategy or disjoined namespace.

Entries in the GlobalNames zones must be populated manually. GlobalNames zone entries are alias (CNAME) records to existing DNS A or AAAA records. The existing DNS A and AAAA records can be dynamically updated, with these updates flowing on to records in the GlobalNames zone.

To deploy a GlobalNames zone in a forest, perform the following steps:

1. On a domain controller that is configured as a DNS server, create a new Active Directory integrated forward lookup zone and configure it to replicate to every domain controller in the forest using the New Zone Wizard.

2. On the Zone Name page, enter **GlobalNames** as the zone name. You can also accomplish the same task by running the following Windows PowerShell command:

    ```
    Add-DnsServerPrimaryZone -Name GlobalNames -ReplicationScope Forest
    ```

3. Next, activate the GlobalNames zone on each authoritative DNS server hosted on a domain controller in the forest. To do this, execute the following Windows PowerShell command. (where DNSServerName is the name of the domain controller hosting DNS)

    ```
    Set-DnsServerGlobalNameZone -ComputerName DNSServerName -Enable $True
    ```

To populate the GlobalNames zone, create alias (CNAME) records in the GlobalNames zone that point to A or AAAA records in existing zones.

Peer Name Resolution Protocol

Peer Name Resolution Protocol (PNRP) provides IPv6 with a peer-to-peer name resolution method. Devices that are connected to the Internet and that are assigned an IPv6 address can publish their peer name/address combination and provide it to peers. These name combinations include both FQDN and single-label names. Other devices query peers to learn IPv6 addressing information. For example, imagine that there are computers named Sydney, Melbourne, Canberra, Adelaide, Brisbane, Hobart, and Perth. Computer Sydney needs to know the IPv6 address of Perth. Sydney is near Canberra, Melbourne, and Brisbane. Sydney queries Canberra, Melbourne, and Brisbane, one after the other, to determine whether any of them knows Perth's IPv6 address. Rather than using a central server, such as DNS or WINS, PNRP uses the information that each individual computer knows about all the other computers to determine address information. PNRP has the following properties:

- Does not require a centralized infrastructure. Servers are required only for bootstrapping.

- Can scale to billions of names and is fault-tolerant. Multiple computers can host copies of the same PNRP record.

- Names are updated in real time and PNRP is designed to not return stale addresses.

- Can be used to name services rather than just computers.

- Names can be published in a secure or insecure manner. When published in a secure manner, PNRP uses public key cryptography to validate records.

- Installed as a feature.

PNRP peer groups are termed *clouds*. When installed, PNRP can use the following clouds:

- **Global cloud.** Uses the global IPv6 address scope and represents all computers and devices connected to the Internet. There is a single global cloud.

- **Link-local cloud.** Uses all addresses in the link-local IPv6 address scope. It roughly corresponds to the local subnet. An organization can have multiple link-local clouds.

Resource records

DNS supports a large number of resource records. The most basic resource record maps an FQDN to an IP address. More complex resource records provide information about the location of services, such as SMTP servers and domain controllers.

Host records

Host records are the most common form of record and can be used to map FQDNs to IP addresses. There are two types of host records: the A record, which is used to map FQDNs to IPv4 addresses, and AAAA records, which are used to map FQDNs to IPv6 addresses. You can add a new host record to a zone by right-clicking the zone in DNS Manager and then by clicking New Host (A or AAAA). You also have the option of creating a pointer (PTR) record in the appropriate reverse lookup zone, if one exists. You can add host records with the Add-DnsServerResourceRecordA cmdlet and AAAA records with the Add-DnsServerResourceRecordAAAA cmdlet.

Alias (CNAME)

An alias, or CNAME, record enables you to provide an alternate name when there is an existing host record. You can create as many aliases for a particular record as you need. To create a new alias in a zone, right-click the zone in DNS Manager and then click New Alias (CNAME). When you create an alias, you must point the alias to an existing host record. You can use the Browse button to navigate to the target host record or enter it manually. You can also add an alias record to a zone from Windows PowerShell by using the Add-DnsServerResourceRecordCName cmdlet.

Mail exchanger

Mail exchanger (MX) records are used to locate mail gateways. For example, when a remote mail gateway wants to forward an email message to an email address associated with your organization's DNS zone, it performs an MX lookup to determine the location of the mail gateway. After that determination has been made, the remote mail gateway contacts the local gateway and transmits the message. MX records must map to existing host records. To create an MX record right-click the zone in DNS Manager, click New Mail Exchanger (MX), and enter information in the New Resource Record dialog box. The Mail Server Priority field is available to allow for the existence of more than one MX record in a zone and is often used when organizations have multiple mail gateways. This is done so that if an organization's primary mail gateway fails, remote mail servers can forward message traffic to other mail gateways. You can add MX records using the Add-DnsServerResourceRecordMX PowerShell cmdlet.

Pointer record

Pointer (PTR) records enable you to connect IP addresses to FQDNs and are hosted in reverse lookup zones. When you create a host record, a PTR record is automatically created by default, if an appropriate reverse lookup zone exists. To create a PTR record, right-click the reverse lookup zone in DNS Manager, click New Pointer (PTR), and enter the PTR record information in the New Resource Record dialog box. You can create a PTR record from Windows PowerShell by using the Add-DnsServerResourceRecordPtr cmdlet.

> ## Inside OUT
>
> *Unknown Records*
>
> Windows Server 2016 DNS supports "unknown records," which are resource records whose RDATA format is unknown to the DNS server. "Unknown records" are defined in RFC 3597 and can be added to Windows Server DNS zones when they are hosted on computers running the Windows Server 2016 operating system.

Zone aging and scavenging

Aging and scavenging provide a technique to reduce the incidence of stale resource records in a primary DNS zone. Stale records are records that are out of date or no longer relevant. If your organization has zones that relate to users with portable computers, such as laptops and tablets, those zones might end up accumulating stale resource records. This can lead to the following problems:

- DNS queries return stale rather than relevant results.

- Large zones can cause DNS server performance problems.

- Stale records might prevent DNS names being reassigned to different devices.

To resolve these problems, you can configure the DNS Server service to do the following:

- Time stamp resource records that are dynamically added to primary zones. This occurs when you enable aging and scavenging.

- Age resource records based on a refresh time period.

- Scavenge resource records that are still present beyond the refresh period.

After you configure the DNS Server service, aging and scavenging occurs automatically. It is also possible to trigger scavenging by right-clicking the DNS server in DNS Manager and then by clicking Scavenge Stale Resource Records. You can also configure aging and scavenging using the Set-DnsServerScavenging cmdlet. For example, to enable stale resource record scavenging on all zones of a DNS server and to set the No-Refresh and Refresh Intervals to 10 days, issue this command:

```
Set-DnsServerScavenging -ApplyOnAllZones -RefreshInterval 10.0:0:0 -ScavengingInterval
10.0:0:0 -ScavengingState $True
```

DNSSEC

Domain Name System Security Extensions (DNSSEC) add security to DNS by enabling DNS servers to validate the responses given by other DNS servers. DNSSEC enables digital signatures to be used with DNS zones. When the DNS resolver issues a query for a record in a signed zone, the authoritative DNS server provides both the record and a digital signature, enabling validation of that record.

To configure DNSSEC, perform the following steps:

1.   Right-click the zone in DNS manager, click DNSSEC, and then click Sign the Zone.

2.   On the Signing Options page, select Use Default Settings To Sign The Zone.

When you configure DNSSEC, three new resource records are availble

These records have the following properties:

- **Resource Record Signature (RRSIG) record.** This record is stored within the zone, and each is associated with a different zone record. When the DNS server is queried for a zone record, it returns the record and the associated RRSIG record.

- **DNSKEY.** This is a public key resource record that enables the validation of RRSIG records.

- **Next Secure (NSEC/NSEC3) record.** This record is used as proof that a record does not exist. For example, the contoso.com zone is configured with DNSSEC. A client issues a query for the host record tasmania.contoso.comand if there is no record for tasmania. contoso.com, the NSEC record returns, which informs the host making the query that no such record exists.

In addition to the special resource records, a DNSSEC implementation has the following components:

- **Trust anchor.** This is a special public key associated with a zone. Trust anchors enable a DNS server to validate DNSKEY resource records. If you deploy DNSSEC on a DNS server hosted on a domain controller, the trust anchors can be stored in the Active Directory forest directory partition. This replicates the trust anchor to all DNS servers hosted on domain controllers in the forest.

- **DNSSEC Key Master.** This is a special DNS server that you use to generate and manage signing keys for a DNSSEC-protected zone. Any computer running Windows Server 2012 or later that hosts a primary zone, whether standard or integrated, can function as a DNSSEC Key Master. A single computer can function as a DNSSEC Key Master for multiple zones. The DNSSEC Key Master role can also be transferred to another DNS server that hosts the primary zone.

- **Key Signing Key (KSK).** You use the KSK to sign all DNSKEY records at the zone root. You create the KSK by using the DNSSEC Key Master.

- **Zone Signing Key (ZSK).** You use the ZSK to sign zone data, such as individual records hosted in the zone. You create the ZSK by using the DNSSEC Key Master.

You can configure group policy to ensure that clients only accept records from a DNS server for a specific zone if those records have been signed using DNSSEC. You do this by configuring the Name Resolution Policy Table, which is located in the Computer Configuration\Policies\ Windows Settings\Name Resolution Policy node of a GPO. You create entries in the table; for example, requiring that all queries against a specific zone require DNSSEC validation. You can configure the NRPT by using Group Policy or through Windows PowerShell.

DNSSEC is appropriate for high security environments, such as those where IPSec and authenticating switches are in use. DNSSEC protects against attacks where clients are fed false DNS information. In many small to medium sized environments, the likelihood of such an attack is minimal, however in high security environments, enabling DNSSEC is a prudent precaution.

DNS event logs

The DNS server log is located in the Applications and Services Logs folder in Event Viewer. Depending on how you configure event logging on the Event Logging tab of the DNS server's properties, this event log can record information including:

- Changes to the DNS service, such as when the DNS server service is stopped or started.

- Zone loading and signing events.

- Modifications to the DNS server configuration.

- DNS warning and error events.

By default, the DNS server records all of these events. It's also possible to configure the DNS server to only log errors, or errors and warning events. The key with any type of logging is that you should only enable logging for information that you might need to review at some point in time. Many administrators log everything "just in case," even though they are only ever interested in a specific type of event.

In the event that you need to debug how a DNS server performance, you can enable Debug logging on the Debug logging tab of the DNS server's properties. Debug logging is resource intensive and you should only use it when you have a specific problem related to the functionality of the DNS server. You can configure debug logging to use a filter so that only traffic from specific hosts is recorded, instead of recording traffic from all hosts that interact with the DNS server.

DNS options

In high security environments, there are a number of steps that you can take to make a DNS server more secure from attackers who attempt to spoof it. Spoofing can cause the server to provide records that redirect clients to malicious sites. While DNSSEC provides security for zones hosted on the server, most DNS server traffic involves retrieving information from remote DNS servers and passing that information on to clients. In this section, you learn about settings that you can configure to ensure that the information relayed to clients retains its integrity in the event that a nefarious third party attempts to spoof your organization's DNS servers.

DNS socket pool

DNS socket pool is a technology that makes cache-tampering and spoofing attacks more difficult by using source port randomization when issuing DNS queries to remote DNS servers. To spoof the DNS server with an incorrect record, the attacker needs to guess which randomized port was used as well as the randomized transaction ID that was issued with the query. A DNS server running on Windows Server 2012 uses a socket pool of 2,500 by default. You can use the dnscmd command line tool to change the socket pool size to a value between 0 and 10,000. For example, to set the socket pool size to 4000, issue the following command:

```
Dnscmd /config /socketpoolsize 4000
```

You must restart the DNS service before you can use the reconfigured socket pool size.

DNS Cache Locking

DNS Cache Locking provides you with control over when information stored in the DNS server's cache can be overwritten. For example, when a recursive DNS server responds to a query for a record that is hosted on another DNS server, it caches the results of that query so that it doesn't have to contact the remote DNS server if the same record is queried again within the Time to Live (TTL) value of the resource record. DNS Cache Locking prevents record data in a DNS server's cache from being overwritten until a configured percentage of the TTL value has expired. By default, the cache locking value is set to 100 percent, but you can reset it by using the Set-DNSServerCache cmdlet with the LockingPercent option. For example, to set the cache locking value to 80 percent, issue the following command and then restart the DNS server service:

```
Set-DNSServerCache -LockingPercent 80
```

DNS recursion

DNS servers on Windows Server 2012 perform recursive queries on behalf of clients by default. This means that when the client asks the DNS server to find a record that isn't stored in a zone hosted by the DNS server, the DNS server then goes out and finds the result of that query and passes it back to the client. It's possible however, for nefarious third parties to use recursion as a denial-of-service attack vector, which could slow a DNS server to the point where it becomes unresponsive. You can disable recursion on the Advanced Tab of the DNS server's properties or you can configure it by using the Set-DNSServerRecursion cmdlet. For example, to configure the recursion retry interval to 3 seconds, use the following command:

```
Set-DNSServerRecursion -RetryInterval 3 -PassThru
```

Netmask ordering

Netmask ordering ensures that the DNS server returns the host record on the requesting client's subnet, if such a record exists. For example, imagine that the following host records exist on a network that uses 24 bit subnet masks:

10.10.10.105 wsus.contoso.com

10.10.20.105 wsus.contoso.com

10.10.30.105 wsus.contoso.com

If netmask ordering is enabled and a client with the IP address 10.10.20.50 performs a lookup of wsus.contoso.com, the lookup always returns the record 10.10.20.105 because this record is on the same subnet as the client. If netmask ordering is not enabled, the DNS server returns records in a round robin fashion. If the requesting client is not on the same network as any of the host records, the DNS server also returns records in a round robin fashion. Netmask ordering is useful for services, such as WSUS, that you might have at each branch office. When you use netmask ordering, the DNS server redirects the client in the branch office to a resource on the local subnet when one exists.

Netmask ordering is enabled by default on Windows Server 2012 DNS servers. You can verify that netmask ordering is enabled by viewing the advanced properties of the DNS server.

Response rate limiting

Distributed denial-of-service attacks against DNS servers are becoming increasingly common. One method of ameliorating such attacks is by configuring response rate limiting settings, which is a feature that is new to Windows Server 2016 and determines how a DNS server responds to clients sending an unusually high number of DNS queries. You can configure the following response rate limiting settings:

- **Responses per second.** Determines the maximum number of times an identical response can be returned to a client per second.

- **Errors per second.** Determines the maximum number of error responses returned to a client per second.

- **Window.** The timeout period for any client that exceeds the maximum request threshold.

- **Leak rate.** Determines how often the DNS server responds to queries if a client is in the suspension window. The leak rate is the number of queries it takes before a response is sent. A leak rate of 42 means that the DNS server only responds to one query out of every 42 when a client is in the suspension window period.

- **TC rate.** Tells the client to try connecting with TCP when the client is in the suspension window. The TC rate should be below the leak rate to give the client the option of attempting a TCP connection before a leak response is sent.

- **Maximum responses.** The maximum number of responses that a DNS server issues to a client during the timeout period.

- **White list domains.** Domains that are excluded from response rate limiting settings.

- **White list subnets.** Subnets that are excluded from response rate limiting settings.

- **White list server interfaces.** DNS server interfaces that are excluded from response rate limiting settings.

DANE

DNS-based Authentication of Named Entities (DANE) allows you to configure records that use Transport Layer Security Authentication (TLSA) to inform DNS clients of which certificate authorities they should accept certificates from for your organization's domain name DNS zone. DANE blocks attackers from using attacks where a certificate is issued from a rogue CA and is used to provide validation for a rogue website when a DNS server is compromised. When DANE is implemented, a client requesting a TLS connection to a website, such as www.tailspintoys.com, knows that it should only accept a TLS certificate from a specific CA. If the TLS certificate for www.tailspintoys.com is from a different CA, the client knows that the website that appears to be at www.tailspintoys.com might have been compromised or that the client might have been redirected by an attacker corrupting a DNS cache.

DNS policies

You use DNS policies, which are new to Windows Server 2016, to control how DNS servers respond to queries based on the properties of that query. You can configure DNS policies to achieve the following:

- **Application high availability**. The DNS server returns the address of the healthiest endpoint for an application. This differs from DNS round robin where the client would be provided with an address independent of whether the host at that address was online.

- **Traffic management.** The DNS server provides a response to the client that directs them to the datacenter closest to them. For example, clients making DNS requests from

Australia are redirected to an application endpoint in Australia and clients making DNS requests from Canada are redirected to an application endpoint in Canada.

- **Split Brain DNS.** DNS records can be segmented into zone scopes.Records can be placed in different scopes. This allows external clients to query the DNS zone and be only able to access a specific number of DNS records that are members of a scope designed for external clients. Internal clients have access to a more comprehensive internal scope.

- **Filtering.** Allows you to block DNS queries from specific IP addresses, IP address ranges, or FQDNs.

- **Forensics.** Redirects malicious clients to a sink hole host rather than to the host they are trying to reach. For example, if clients appear to be attempting a denial-of-service attack, redirect them to a static page rather than the site they are attempting to attack.

- **Time of day based redirection.** Allows you to configure a policy where clients are redirected to specific hosts based on the time of day when the query is received.

Delegated administration

In some larger environments, you might want to separate out administrative privileges so that the people responsible for managing your organization's DNS servers don't have other permissions, such as the ability to create user accounts or reset passwords. By default, members of the Domain Admins group are able to perform all DNS administration tasks on DNS servers within a domain. Members of the Enterprise Admins group are able to perform all DNS administration tasks on any DNS server in the forest.

You can use the DNSAdmins domain local group to grant users the ability to view and modify DNS data, as well as view and modify server configurations of DNS servers within a domain. Add users to this group when you want to allow them to perform DNS administration tasks without giving them additional permissions. You can assign permissions that allow users or security groups to manage a specific DNS server on the Security tab of the server's properties.

You can also configure permissions at the zone level. To do this, assign security principal permissions on the security tab of the zone's properties. You might do this when you want to allow a specific person to manage host records without assigning them any other permissions. Today most organizations allow DNS records to be updated dynamically. This means that the only zones where you might need to configure special permissions to allow manual management are special ones, such as those that are accessible to clients on the Internet.

Managing DNS with PowerShell

You can manage almost all aspects of DNS server operations using the DNSServer module of Windows PowerShell. Table 5-1 lists the DNS server PowerShell cmdlets.

Table 5-1. DNS PowerShell cmdlets

Noun	VerbS	Function
DnsServer	Set, Get, Test	View and manage DNS server configuration
DnsServerCache	Get, Set, Show, Clear	Manage DHS server cache configuration
DnsServerClientSubnet	Set, Get, Add, Remove	Manage DHS server client subnets for use in DNS policies
DnsServerConditionalForwarderZone	Set, Add	Manage conditional forwarders
DnsServerDiagnostics	Set, Get	View DNS event log information
DnsServerDirectoryPartition	Unregister, Remove, Get, Register, Add	Manage DNS server directory partitions
DnsServerDnsSecPublicKey	Export	Export the DS and DNSKEY data for a DNSSEC signed zone
DnsServerDnsSecZoneSetting	Get, Set, Test	Configure DNSSEC settings for a zone
DnsServerDsSetting	Set, Get	Configure Active Directory server settings
DnsServerEDns	Get, Set	Manage CacheTimeout, EnableProbes, and EnableReception settings
DnsServerForwarder	Add, Set, Get, Remove	Manage DNS server forwarders
DnsServerGlobalNameZone	Set, Get	Manage the global names zone
DnsServerGlobalQueryBlockList	Get, Set	Manage the global query block list
DnsServerKeyStorageProvider	Show	View key storage provider information
DnsServerPolicy	Disable, Enable	Enable or disable DNS server policies
DnsServerPrimaryZone	Restore, Set, Add, CovertTo	Manage DNS server primary zones
DnsServerQueryResolutionPolicy	Add, Get, Remove, Set	Configure DNS server query resolution policy
DnsServerRecursion	Set, Get	Manage DNS server recursion settings
DnsServerRecursionScope	Remove, Set, Get, Add	Configure DNS server recursion scopes

DnsServerResourceRecord	Add, Set, Remove, Get	Manage DNS server resource records
DnsServerResourceRecordA	Add	Add a IPv4 host record
DnsServerResourceRecordAAAA	Add	Add an IPv6 host record
DnsServerResourceRecordAging	Set	Configure resource record aging
DnsServerResourceRecordCName	Add	Add a CNAME record
DnsServerResourceRecordDnsKey	Add	Add a DNSKey resource record
DnsServerResourceRecordDS	Import, Add	Manage delegation signer (DS) resource records
DnsServerResourceRecordMX	Add	Add a mail exchanger (MX) resource record
DnsServerResourceRecordPtr	Add	Add a pointer (PTR) resource record
DnsServerResponseRateLimiting	Get, Set	Configure response rate limiting
DnsServerResponseRateLimitingExceptionlist	Add, Remove, Get, Set	Configure response rate limit exceptions
DnsServerRootHint	Remove, Get, Add, Set, Import	Manage DNS server root hints
DnsServerScavenging	Start, Set, Get	Manage DNS server scavenging setting
DnsServerSecondaryZone	Add, Restore, ConvertTo, Set	Manage DNS server secondary zones
DnsServerSetting	Get, Set	Configure DNS server settings
DnsServerSigningKey	Get, Add, Set, Remove	Manage DNS Server signing keys
DnsServerSigningKeyRollover	Invoke, Enable, Step, Disable	Configure signing key rollover
DnsServerStatistics	Clear, Get	Manage DNS server statistics
DnsServerStubZone	Set, Add	Configure stub zones
DnsServerTrustAnchor	Get, Import, Remove, Add	Configure DNSSEC trust anchor
DnsServerTrustPoint	Get, Update	Configure DNSSET trust point
DnsServerVirtualizationInstance	Remove, Get, Set, Add	Manage virtualization instances
DnsServerZone	Get, Export, Sync, Suspend, Remove, Resume	Manage zones, including export and import
DnsServerZoneAging	Set, Get	Configure zone record aging
DnsServerZoneDelegation	Remove, Add, Get, Set	Configure zone delegation

DnsServerZoneKeyMasterRole	Reset	Transfers key master role for a DNS zone
DnsServerZoneScope	Remove, Get, Add	Manage zone scopes
DnsServerZoneSign	Invoke	Sign a DNS zone (DNSSEC)
DnsServerZoneTransfer	Start	Manage zone transfers
DnsServerZoneTransferPolicy	Add, Get, Set, Remove	Configure zone transfer policies
DnsServerZoneUnsign	Invoke,	Unsign a DNS zone (DNSSEC)

DHCP

DHCP is a network service that most administrators barely pay attention to after they've configured it. The main concern that most administrators have with DHCP is that, up until the release of Windows Server 2012, it has been difficult to configure as a highly available service. While DNS became highly available through its ability to be hosted on any domain controller, the problem with making DHCP highly available was ensuring that when multiple DHCP servers were in play, that duplicate addresses were not being assigned to separate clients. Windows Server 2012 introduced highly available DHCP servers, allowing two servers to share a scope, rather than having to split them according to the old 80/20 rule.

Scopes

A DHCP scope is a collection of IP address settings that a client uses to determine its IP address configuration. You configure a DHCP scope for every separate IPv4 subnet that you want the DHCP servers to provide IP address configuration information to. When configuring an IPv4 scope, specify the following information:

- **Scope name.** The name of the scope. The name should be descriptive enough that you recognize which hosts the scope applies to. For example, Level 2, Old Arts Building.

- **IP address range.** This is the range of IP addresses encompassed by the scope. Should be a logical subnet.

- **IP address exclusions.** This includes which IP addresses within the IP address range you do not want the DHCP server to lease. For example, you could configure exclusions for several computers that have statically assigned IP addresses.

- **Delay.** This setting determines how long the DHCP server waits before offering an address. This provides you with a method of DHCP server redundancy, with one DHCP server offering addresses immediately, and another only offering addresses after a certain period of time has elapsed.

- **Lease duration.** The lease duration determines how long a client has an IP address before the address returns to the lease pool.

- **DHCP options.** There are 61 standard options that you can configure. These include settings, such as DNS server address and default gateway address, that apply to leases in the scope.

You can add a DHCP server scope using the Add-DHCPServer4Scope or Add-DHCPServer-6Scope PowerShell cmdlets. For example, to create a new scope for the 192.168.10.0/24 network named MelbourneNet, enact the following PowerShell command:

```
Add-DHCPServerv4Scope -Name "MelbourneNet" -StartRange 192.168.10.1 -Endrange
192.168.10.254 -SubnetMask 255.255.255.0
```

Inside OUT

IPv6 DHCP

Most organizations are still using IPv4 with their DHCP server. For the sake of brevity, all PowerShell examples are for IPv4, with the cmdlets for managing IPv6 DHCP scopes listed later in the chapter.

Server and scope options

DHCP options include additional configuration settings, such as the address of a network's default gateway or the addresses of DNS servers. You can configure DHCP options at two levels: the scope level and the server level. Options configured at the scope level override options configured at the server level.

Common scope options include:

- **003 Router.** The address of the default gateway for the subnet.

- **005 DNS Servers.** The address of DNS servers that the client should use for name resolution.

- **015 DNS Domain Name.** This is the DNS suffix assigned to the client.

- **058 Renewal time.** This determines how long after the lease is initially acquired that the client waits before it attempts to renew the lease.

You can configure IPv4 scope options using the Set-DHCPServer4OptionValue cmdlet. For example, to configure the scope with ID 192.168.10.0 on DHCP server dhcp.contoso.com with the value for the DNS server set to 192.168.0.100, issue the following command:

```
Set-DHcpServerv4OptionValue -Computername dhcp.contoso.com -ScopeID 192.168.10.0
-DNSServer 192.168.0.100
```

Reservations

Reservations allow you to ensure that a particular computer always receives a specific IP address. You can use reservations to allow servers to always have the same address, even when they are configured to retrieve that address through DHCP. If you don't configure a reservation for a computer, it can be assigned any available address from the pool. Although you can configure DHCP to update DNS to ensure that other hosts can connect using the client's hostname, it is generally a good idea to ensure that a server retains the same IP address.

There are two ways to configure a DHCP reservation. The simplest way is to locate an existing IP address lease in the DHCP console, right-click it, and then select Add to Reservation. This then ties that specific network adapter address to that IP address. The only drawback of this method is that the reservation is for the assigned IP address, and you aren't able to customize it.

If you know the network adapter address of the computer that you want to configure a reservation for, you can right-click the Reservations node under the scope that you want to configure the reservation under, and then click New Reservation. In the New Reservation dialog box enter the reservation name, IP address, and network adapter address, and then click Add to create the reservation. You can also configure a reservation using the Add-DhcpServerv4Reservation cmdlet. For example, to configure a reservation, issue the following command:

```
Add-DhcpServerv4Reservation -ScopeId 192.168.10.0 -IPAddress 192.168.10.8 -ClientId
A0-FE-C1-7A-00-E5 -Description "A4 Printer"
```

DHCP filtering

You can configure DHCP filtering on the Filters tab of the IPv4 Properties dialog box in the DHCP console. DHCP filtering is used in high-security environments to restrict the network adapter addresses that are able to utilize DHCP. For example, you can have a list of all network adapter addresses in your organization and use the Enable Allow List option to lease only IP addresses to this list of authorized adapters. This method of security is not entirely effective because it is possible for unauthorized people to fake an authorized adapter address as a way of gaining network access. You can add a specific network adapter to the allowed list of MAC addresses using the Add-DHCPServerv4Filter cmdlet. For example, to allow a laptop with the MAC address D1-F2-7C-00-5E-F0 to the authorized list of adapters, issue the command:

```
Add-DhcpServerv4Filter -List Allow -MacAddress D1-F2-7C-00-5E-F0 Description "Rooslan's
Laptop"
```

Superscopes

A superscope is a collection of individual DHCP scopes. You might create a superscope when you want to bind existing scopes together for administrative reasons. For example, imagine that you have a subnet in a building that is close to fully allocated. You can add a second subnet to the building and then bind them together into a superscope. The process of binding several separate logical subnets together on the same physical network is known as multinetting.

There needs to be at least one existing scope present on the DHCP server before you can create a superscope. After you have created a superscope, you can add new subnets or remove sub-nets from that scope. It's also possible to deactivate some subnets within a scope while keeping others active. You might use this technique when migrating clients from one IP address range to another. For example, you could have both the source and destination scopes as part of the same superscope and activate the new scope and deactivate the original scope as necessary when performing the migration. You can create superscopes using the Add-DHCPServerv-4Superscope cmdlet. For example, to add the scopes with ID 192.168.10.0 and 192.168.11.0 to a superscope named MelbourneCBD, run the following command:

```
Add-DhcpServerv4Superscope -SuperscopeName "MelbourneCBD" -ScopeId 192.168.10.0,
192.168.11.0
```

Multicast scopes

A multicast address is an address that allows one-to-many communications on a network. When you use multicast, multiple hosts on a network listen for traffic on a single multicast IP address. Multicast addresses are in the IPv4 range of 224.0.0.0 through to 239.255.255.255. Multicast scopes are collections of multicast addresses. You can configure a Windows Server 2016 DHCP server to host multicast scopes. Multicast scopes are also known as Multicast Address Dynamic Client Allocation Protocol (MADCAP) scopes because applications that require access to multi-cast addresses support the MADCAP API.

The most common use for multicast addresses using the default Windows Server 2016 roles is for Windows Deployment Services. You can however, configure the WDS server with its own set of multicast addresses and you don't need to configure a special multicast scope in DHCP to support this role.

Split scopes

A split scope is one method of providing fault tolerance for a DHCP scope. The idea behind a split scope is that you host one part of the scope on one DHCP server and a second, smaller part of the scope on a second DHCP server. Usually this split has 80 percent of the addresses on the first DHCP server and 20 percent of the addresses on the second server. In this scenario, the DHCP server that hosts the 20 percent portion of the address space is usually located on a remote subnet. In the split scope scenario you also use a DHCP relay agent configured with a delay so that the majority of addresses are leased from the DHCP server that hosts 80 percent of the address space. Split scopes are most likely to be used in scenarios where your DHCP serv-ers aren't running on Windows Server 2012 or later operating systems. If you want to provide fault tolerance for scopes hosted on servers running Windows Server 2016, you should instead implement DHCP failover.

Name protection

DHCP name protection is a feature that allows you to ensure that the hostnames a DHCP server registers with a DNS server are not overwritten in the event that a non-Windows operating system has the same name. DHCP name protection also protects names from being overwritten by hosts that use static addresses that conflict with DHCP assigned addresses.

For example, imagine that in the contoso.com domain there is a computer running the Windows 10 operating system that has the name Auckland and receives its IP address information from a Windows Server 2016 DHCP server. The DHCP server registers this name in DNS and creates a record in the contoso.com DNS zone that associates the name Auckland.contoso.com with the IP address assigned to the computer running Windows 10. A newly installed computer running a distribution of Linux is also assigned the name Auckland. Because name protection has been enabled, this new computer is unable to overwrite the existing record with a new record that associates the name Auckland.contoso.com with the Linux computer's IP address. If name protection had not been enabled, it is possible that the record would have been overwritten.

You can enable name protection on a scope by clicking Configure on the DNS tab of the IPv4 or IPv6 Properties dialog box. You can also do this by using the Set-DhcpServerv4DnsSetting or the Set-DhcpServerv6DnsSetting cmdlet. For example, to configure the DHCP server on computer MEL-DC so that name protection is enabled on all IPv4 scopes, issue the following command:

```
Set-DhcpServerv4DnsSetting –Computer MEL-DC –NameProtection $true
```

DHCP failover

DHCP failover allows you to configure DHCP to be highly available without using split scopes. You have two options when configuring DHCP failover:

- **Hot Standby mode.** This relationship is a traditional failover relationship. When you configure this relationship, the primary server handles all DHCP traffic unless it becomes unavailable. You can configure DHCP servers to be in multiple separate relationships, so it's possible that a DHCP server can be the primary server in one relationship and a hot standby server in another relationship. When configuring this relationship, you specify a percentage of the address ranges to be reserved on the standby server. The default value is 5 percent. These 5 percent of addresses are instantly available after the primary server becomes unavailable. The hot standby server takes control of the entire address range when the figure specified by the state switchover interval is reached. The default value for this interval is 60 minutes.

- **Load Sharing mode.** This is the default mode when you create a DHCP failover relationship. In this mode, both servers provide IP addresses to clients according to the ratio defined by the load balance percentage figure. The default is for each server to share 50 percent of the load. The maximum client lead time figure enables one of the partners to take control of the entire scope in the event that the other partner is not available for the specified time.

Prior to configuring DHCP failover, you need to remove any split scopes between the potential partners. You can also choose a shared secret to authenticate replication traffic, but you don't have to enter this secret on the partner DHCP server.

Administration

DHCP servers need to be authorized in Active Directory before they start leasing addresses. DHCP servers on Microsoft operating systems must always be authorized before they start working simply because this reduces the chance that a rogue DHCP server might start leasing IP addresses. Domain Admins group members, or users who have the ability to add, modify, or delete new objects of the DHCP class type on the NetServices folder in Active Directory, are able to authorize DHCP servers.

When you deploy the DHCP server role, the following local groups are created. You can use membership of these groups to delegate DHCP server management permissions to users or groups:

- **DHCP Administrators.** Members of this group can view or modify any DHCP server settings, including configuring DHCP options, failover, and scopes.

- **DHCP Users.** Members of this group only have read-only access to the DHCP server. They can view, but not modify, DHCP server settings, including scope information and data.

Inside OUT

Server 2016 DHCP

The main change regarding DHCP server in Windows Server 2016 is that DHCP no longer supports Network Access Protection (NAP). Other than the lack of support for NAP, the DHCP server in Windows Server 2016 has essentially the same functionality as the DHCP server in Windows Server 2012 R2.

Managing DHCP with PowerShell

You can manage the DHCP role by using the PowerShell cmdlets listed in Table 5-2.

Table 5-2. DHCP PowerShell cmdlets

Noun	VerbS	Function
DhcpServer	Restore, Export, Backup, Import	Backup, recover, export, and import DHCP server configuration
DhcpServerAuditLog	Get, Set	Manage the DHCP server audit log
DhcpServerDatabase	Get, Set	Manage the DHCP server database
DhcpServerDnsCredential	Get, Remove, Set	Configure account that DHCP server uses to manage DHS server records
DhcpServerInDC	Add, Get, Remove	Manage DHCP server authorization in Active Directory
DhcpServerSecurityGroup	Add	Add security groups to a DHCP server
DhcpServerSetting	Set, Get	Manage the DHCP server database configuration parameters
DhcpServerv4Binding	Get, Set	Manage which network interfaces the DHCP server services are bound to
DhcpServerv4Class	Add, Remove, Get, Set	Manage IPv4 vendor or user classes for the DHCP server service
DhcpServerv4DnsSetting	Set, Get	Configure DNS settings at the scope, reservation, or server level
DhcpServerv4ExclusionRange	Add, Get, Remove	Manage IPv4 exclusion ranges
DhcpServerv4Failover	Set, Add, Remove, Get	Configure IPv4 failover relationships
DhcpServerv4FailoverReplication	Invoke	Replicate scope configuration between failover partners
DhcpServerv4FailoverScope	Add, Remove	Configure DHCP IPv4 failover scopes
DhcpServerv4Filter	Remove, Add, Get	Manage DHCP IPv4 MAC address filters
DhcpServerv4FilterList	Set, Get	Manage the filter list status
DhcpServerv4FreeIPAddress	Get	Find free IP addresses in a scope
DhcpServerv4IPRecord	Repair	Reconcile inconsistent records in the DHCP database
DhcpServerv4Lease	Add, Remove, Get	Manage IPv4 DHCP leases
DhcpServerv4MulticastExclusionRange	Get, Remove, Add	Manage multicast exclusions
DhcpServerv4MulticastLease	Get, Remove	Manage IPv4 multicast lease

CHAPTER 05

DhcpServerv4MulticastScope	Remove, Get, Add, Set	Manage IPv4 multicast scopes
DhcpServerv4MulticastScopeStatistics	Get	View IPv4 multicast scope statistics
DhcpServerv4OptionDefinition	Add, Set, Remove, Get	Manage IPv4 option definitions
DhcpServerv4OptionValue	Get, Remove, Set	Configure IPv4 option values
DhcpServerv4Policy	Add, Remove, Get, Set	Manage IPv4 policies
DhcpServerv4PolicyIPRange	Get, Add, Remove	Manage bindings between IP ranges and policies
DhcpServerv4Reservation	Add, Set, Get, Remove	Configure IPv4 reservations
DhcpServerv4Scope	Get, Remove, Set, Add	Manage IPv4 DHCP scopes
DhcpServerv4ScopeStatistics	Get	View IPv4 DHCP scope statistics
DhcpServerv4Statistics	Get	View IPv4 DHCP statistics
DhcpServerv4Superscope	Remove, Rename, Get, Add	Manage IPv4 DHCP superscopes
DhcpServerv4SuperscopeStatistics	Get	View IPv4 DHCP superscope statistics
DhcpServerv6Binding	Set, Get	Manage binding of DHCP server to IPv6 interfaces
DhcpServerv6Class	Remove, Set, Get, Add	Manage IPv6 vendor or user classes
DhcpServerv6DnsSetting	Get, Set	Configure IPv6 DNS settings at the scope, reservation, or server
DhcpServerv6ExclusionRange	Get, Add, Remove	Manage IPv6 exclusions
DhcpServerv6FreeIPAddress	Get	Locate free IPv6 addresses
DhcpServerv6Lease	Add, Remove, Get	Manage IPv6 leases
DhcpServerv6OptionDefinition	Add, Remove, Get, Set	Manage IPv6 option definitions
DhcpServerv6OptionValue	Set, Remove, Get	Manage IPv6 option values
DhcpServerv6Reservation	Remove, Add, Get, Set	Manage IPv6 DHCP reservations
DhcpServerv6Scope	Remove, Add, Get, Set	Manage IPv6 scope
DhcpServerv6ScopeStatistics	Get	View IPv6 scope statistics

DhcpServerv6StatelessStatistics	Get	View IPv6 stateless statistics
DhcpServerv6StatelessStore	Set, Get	Manage the properties of the stateless store
DhcpServerv6Statistics	Get	View IPv6 server statistics
DhcpServerVersion	Get	View DHCP server version information

IPAM

IPAM allows you to centralize the management of DHCP and DNS servers. Rather than manage each server separately, you can use IPAM to manage them from a single console. You can use a single IPAM server to manage up to 150 separate DHCP servers and up to 500 individual DNS servers. It is also able to manage 6,000 separate DHCP scopes and 150 separate DNS zones. You can perform tasks such as creating address scopes, configuring address reservations, and managing DHCP and DNS options globally, instead of having to perform these tasks on a server-by-server basis. IPAM in Windows Server 2016 supports both Active Directory and file based DNS zones.

Deploy IPAM

You can only install the IPAM feature on a computer that is a member of an Active Directory domain. You can have multiple IPAM servers within a single Active Directory forest. You are likely to do this if your organization is geographically dispersed. It's important to note that IPAM cannot manage a DHCP or DNS server if the role is installed on the same computer that hosts IPAM. For this reason, you should install the IPAM feature on a server that doesn't host the DNS or DHCP roles. IPAM is also not supported on computers that host the Domain Controller server role. Additionally, if you want to use the IPAM server to manage IPv6 address ranges, you need to ensure that IPv6 is enabled on the computer hosting the IPAM server.

Configure server discovery

Server discovery is the process where the IPAM server checks with Active Directory to locate Domain Controllers, DNS servers, and DHCP servers. You select which domains to discover on the Configure Server Discovery dialog box. After you've completed server discovery, you need to run a special PowerShell cmdlet that creates and provisions group policy objects that allow these servers to be managed by the IPAM server. When you set up the IPAM server, you choose a GPO name prefix. Use this prefix when executing the Invoke-IpamGpoProvisioning Windows PowerShell cmdlet that creates the appropriate GPOS.

If you use the GPO prefix IPAM, the three GPOS are named:

- IPAM_DC_NPS

- IPAM_DHCP

- IPAM_DNS

Until these GPOs apply to the discovered servers, these servers are listed as having an IPAM Access status of blocked. After the GPOs are applied to the discovered servers, the IPAM Access status is set to Unblocked. After the discovered service has an IPAM Access Status set to Unblocked, you can edit the properties of the server and set it to Managed. After you do this, you are able to use IPAM to manage the selected services on the server.

IPAM in Windows Server 2016 supports managing DNS and DHCP servers in forests where a two-way trust relationship has been configured. You perform DHCP and DNS server discovery in a trusted forest on a per-domain basis.

IPAM administration

You can delegate administrative permissions by adding user accounts to one of five local security groups on the IPAM server. By default, members of the Domain Admins and Enterprise Admins groups are able to perform all tasks on the IPAM server. The five following local security groups are present on the IPAM server after you deploy the role allow you to delegate the following permissions:

- **DNS Record Administrator.** Members of this role are able to manage DNS resource records.

- **IP Address Record Administrator.** Members of this role are able to manage IP addresses, but not address spaces, ranges, subnets, or blocks.

- **IPAM Administrators.** Members of this role are able to perform all tasks on the IPAM server, including viewing IP Address tracking information.

- **IPAM ASM Administrators.** ASM stands for Address Space Administrator. Users added to this group are able to perform all tasks that can be performed by members of the IPAM Users group, but are also able to manage the IP address space. They cannot perform monitoring tasks and are unable to perform IP address tracking tasks.

- **IPAM DHCP Administrator.** Members of this role are able to manage DHCP servers using IPAM.

- **IPAM DHCP Reservations Administrator.** Members of this role are able to manage DHCP reservations using IPAM.

- **IPAM DHCP Scope Administrator.** Members of this role are able to manage DHCP scopes.

- **IPAM MSM Administrators**. MSM stands for Multi-Server-Management. Members of this role are able to manage all DNS and DHCP servers managed by IPAM.

- **IPAM DNS Administrator.** Members of this role are able to manage DHCP servers using IPAM.

Managing the IP address space

The benefit of IPAM is that it allows you to manage all of the IP addresses in your organization. IPAM supports the management of IPv4 public and private addresses whether they are statically or dynamically assigned. IPAM allows you to detect if there are overlapping IP address ranges defined in DHCP scopes on different servers, determine IP address utilization and whether there are free IP addresses in a specific range, create DHCP reservations centrally without having to configure them on individual DHCP servers, and create DNS records based on IP address lease information.

IPAM separates the IP address space into blocks, ranges, and individual addresses. An IP address block is a large collection of IP addresses that you use to organize the address space that your organization uses at the highest level. An organization might only have one or two address blocks, one for its entire internal network and another smaller block that represents the public IP address space used by the organization. An IP address range is part of an IP address block. An IP address range cannot map to multiple IP address blocks. Generally, an IP address range corresponds to a DHCP scope. An individual IP address maps to a single IP address range. IPAM stores the following information with an IP address:

- Any associated MAC address

- How the address is assigned (static/DHCP)

- Assignment date

- Assignment expiration

- Which service manages the IP address

- DNS records associated with the IP address

IP address tracking

One of the most important features of IPAM is its ability to track IP addresses by correlating DHCP leases with user and computer authentication events on managed domain controllers and NPS servers. IP address tracking allows you to figure out which user was associated with a specific IP address at a particular point in time, which can be important when trying to determine the cause of unauthorized activity on the organizational network.

You can search for IP address records using one of the following four parameters:

- **Track by IP address.** You can track by IPv4 address, but IPAM does not support tracking by IPv6 address.

- **Track by client ID.** You can track by client ID in IPAM, which allows you to track IP address activity by MAC address.

- **Track by host name.** You can track by the computer's name as registered in DNS.

- **Track by user name.** You can track a user name, but to do this you must also provide a host name.

Naturally, you can only track data that has been recorded since IPAM has been deployed. So while it is possible to store several years of data in the Windows Internal Database that IPAM uses, you are limited to only being able to retrieve events recorded after IPAM was configured.

Microsoft estimates that the Windows Internal Database IPAM uses is able to store 3 years of IP address utilization data for an organization that has 100,000 users before data must be purged.

You can use IPAM to locate free subnets and free IP address ranges in your existing IP address scheme. For example, if you need 50 consecutive free IP addresses for a project, you can use the Find-IpamFreeRange PowerShell cmdlet to determine whether such a range is present in your current environment.

Managing IPAM with PowerShell

You can manage IPAM with Windows PowerShell cmdlets that are contained in the IPAMServer module. Table 5-3 outlines the functionality of these cmdlets.

Table 5-3. IPAM PowerShell cmdlets

Noun	VerbS	Function
IpamAccessScope	Set	Configure an IPAM access scope
IpamAddress	Export, Remove, Get, Import, Add, Set	Use this set of cmdlets to manage IPAM addresses
IpamAddressSpace	Set, Remove, Get, Add	Use this set of cmdlets to manage an IPAM address space
IpamAddressUtilizationThreshold	Set, Get	Configure the IPAM address utilization thresholds

IpamBlock	Remove, Get, Add, Set	Manage IPAM address blocks
IpamCapability	Disable, Get, Enable	Manage optional IPAM capabilities
IpamConfiguration	Set, Get	Manage the configuration of the IPAM server
IpamConfigurationEvent	Get, Remove	View IPAM configuration events stored in the IPAM database
IpamCustomField	Rename, Add, Remove, Get	Manage IPAM custom fields
IpamCustomFieldAssociation	Remove, Add, Set, Get	Configure association between custom field values
IpamCustomValue	Remove, Add, Rename	Manage values assigned to custom fields in IPAM
IpamDatabase	Move, Get, Set	Manage the IPAM database
IpamDhcpConfigurationEvent	Remove, Get	Manage DHCP configuration events stored in the IPAM database
IpamDhcpScope	Get	View IPAM DHCP scope information
IpamDhcpServer	Get	View IPAM DHCP server information
IpamDhcpSuperscope	Get	View IPAM DHCP superscope information
IpamDiscoveryDomain	Set, Remove, Add, Get	Configure IPAM discovery domains
IpamDnsConditionalForwarder	Get	View information about IPAM DNS conditional forwarders
IpamDnsResourceRecord	Get	View information about IPAM DNS resource records
IpamDnsServer	Get	View information about IPAM DNS servers
IpamDnsZone	Get	View information about IPAM DNS zones
IpamFreeAddress	Find	Locate available IP addresses from the IPAM database
IpamFreeRange	Find	Locate ranges of free IP addresses from the IPAM database
IpamFreeSubnet	Find	Locate free subnets in the IPAM database
IpamGpoProvisioning	Invoke	Configures GPOs necessary to prepare DNS and DHCP servers managed by the IPAM server

IpamIpAddressAuditEvent	Remove, Get	Manage IPAM audit events in the IPAM database
IpamRange	Export, Import, Add, Get, Remove, Set	Manage IPAM IP address ranges
IpamServer	Update	Updates an IPAM server after you update the host server's operating system
IpamServerInventory	Remove, Add, Get, Set	Manage the properties of an infrastructure server stored in the IPAM server inventory
IpamServerProvisioning	Invoke	Use this cmdlet to automate the provisioning of an IPAM server
IpamSubnet	Add, Get, Set, Import, Export, Remove	Manage an IP subnet stored in the IPAM server database
IpamUtilizationData	Remove	Remove existing IPAM IP address utilization information

Hyper-V

Dynamic Memory

You have two options when assigning RAM to VMs—you can assign a static amount of memory or configure dynamic memory. When you assign a static amount of memory, the amount of RAM assigned to the VM remains the same, whether the VM is starting up, running, or in the process of shutting down.

When you configure dynamic memory, you can configure the following values:

- **Startup RAM**. This is the amount of RAM allocated to the VM during startup. This can be the same as the minimum amount of RAM, or a figure up to the maximum amount of RAM allocated. Once the VM has started, it will use the amount of RAM configured as the Minimum RAM.

- **Minimum RAM**. This is the minimum amount of RAM that the VM will be assigned by the virtualization host. When multiple VMs are demanding memory, Hyper-V may reallocate RAM away from the VM until this Minimum RAM value is met. You can reduce the Minimum RAM setting while the VM is running, but you cannot increase it while the VM is running.

- **Maximum RAM**. This is the maximum amount of RAM that the VM will be allocated by the virtualization host. You can increase the Maximum RAM setting while the VM is running, but you cannot decrease it while the VM is running.

- **Memory buffer**. This is the percentage of memory that Hyper-V allocates to the VM as a buffer.

- **Memory weight**. This allows you to configure how memory should be allocated to this particular VM compared to other VMs running on the same virtualization host.

Generally, when you configure dynamic memory, the amount of RAM used by a VM will fluctuate between the Minimum and Maximum RAM values. You should monitor VM RAM utilization and tune these values so that they accurately represent the VM's actual requirements. If you allocate a Minimum RAM value below what the VM actually needs to run, it is likely at some point that a shortage of RAM might cause the virtualization host to reduce the amount of memory allocated to this minimum value, causing the VM to stop running.

Smart paging

Smart paging is a special technology in Hyper-V that functions in certain conditions when a VM is restarting. Smart paging uses a file on the disk to simulate memory to meet Startup RAM requirements when the Startup RAM setting exceeds the Minimum RAM setting. Startup RAM is the amount of RAM allocated to the VM when it starts, but not when it is in a running state. For example, you can set Startup RAM to 2048 MB and the Minimum RAM to 512 MB for a specific virtual machine. In a scenario where 1024 MB of free RAM is available on the virtualization host, smart paging allows the VM to access the 2048 MB required.

Because it uses disk to simulate memory, smart paging is only active if the following three conditions occur at the same time:

- The VM is being restarted

- There is not enough memory on the virtualization host to meet the Startup RAM setting

- Memory cannot be reclaimed from other VMs running on the same host

Smart paging doesn't allow a VM to perform a "cold start" if the required amount of Startup RAM is not available, but the Minimum RAM amount is. Smart paging is only used when a VM that was already running restarts and the conditions outlined earlier have been met.

You can configure the location of the smart paging file on a per-VM basis. By default, smart paging files are written to the virtual machine's folder under C:\ProgramData\Microsoft\ Windows\Hyper-V folder. The smart paging file is created only when needed and is deleted within 10 minutes of the VM restarting.

Resource metering

Resource metering allows you to track the consumption of processor, disk, memory, and network resources by individual VMs. To enable resource metering, use the Enable-VMResourceMetering Windows PowerShell cmdlet. You can view metering data using the Measure-VM Windows PowerShell cmdlet. Resource metering allows you to record the following information:

- Average CPU use

- Average memory use

- Minimum memory use

- Maximum memory use

- Maximum disk allocation

- Incoming network traffic

- Outgoing network traffic

Average CPU use is measured in megahertz (MHz). All other metrics are measured in megabytes. Although you can extract data using the Measure-VM cmdlet, you need to use another solution to output this data into a visual form like a graph.

Guest integration services

Integration services allow the virtualization host to extract information and perform operations on a hosted VM. It is usually necessary to install Hyper-V integration services on a VM, though Windows Server 2016, Windows Server 2012 R2, Windows 10 and Windows 8.1 include Hyper-V integration services by default. Integration services installation files are available for all operating systems that are supported on Hyper-V. You can enable the following integration services:

- **Operating system shutdown**. This integration service allows you to shut down the VM from the virtualization host, rather than from within the VM's operating system.

- **Time synchronization**. This synchronizes the virtualization host's clock with the VM's clock. It ensures that the VM clock doesn't drift when the VM is started, stopped or reverted to a checkpoint.

- **Data Exchange**. Allows the virtualization host to read and modify specific VM registry values.

- **Heartbeat**. This allows the virtualization host to verify that the VM operating system is still functioning and responding to requests.

- **Backup (volume checkpoint)**. For VMs that support Volume Shadow Copy, this service synchronizes with the virtualization host, allowing backups of the VM while the VM is in operation.

- **Guest services**. They allow you to copy files from the virtualization host to the VM using the Copy-VMFile Windows PowerShell cmdlet.

Generation 2 VMs

Generation 2 VMs are a special type of VM that differ in configuration from the VMs that are now termed generation 1 VMs, which could be created on Hyper-V virtualization hosts running the Windows Server 2008, Windows Server 2008 R2 and Windows Server 2012 operating systems. Generation 2 VMs are supported on Windows Server 2016 and Windows Server 2012 R2.

Generation 2 VMs provide the following functionality:

- Can boot from a SCSI virtual hard disk

- Can boot from a SCSI virtual DVD

- Supports UEFI firmware on the VM

- Supports VM Secure Boot

- Supports PXE boot using standard network adapter

There are no legacy network adapters with generation 2 VMs and the majority of legacy devices, such as COM ports and the Diskette Drive, are no longer present. Generation 2 VMs are "virtual first" and are not designed to simulate hardware for computers that have undergone physical to virtual (P2V) conversion. If you need to deploy a VM that requires an emulated component such as a COM port, you'll need to deploy a generation 1 VM.

You configure the generation of a VM during VM creation. Once a VM is created, Hyper-V doesn't allow you to modify the VM's generation. Windows Server 2016 supports running both generation 1 and generation 2 VMs.

Generation 2 VMs boot more quickly and allow the installation of operating systems more quickly than generation 1 VMs. Generation 2 VMs have the following limitations:

- You can only use generation 2 VMs if the guest operating system is running an x64 version of Windows 10, Windows 8.1, Windows 8, Windows Server 2016, Windows Server 2012 R2 or Windows Server 2012.

- Generation 2 VMs only support virtual hard disks in VHDX format.

Enhanced Session Mode

Enhanced Session Mode allows you to perform actions including cutting and pasting, audio redirection, volume and device mapping when using Virtual Machine Connection windows. You can also sign on to a VM with a smart card through Enhanced Session Mode. You enable the Enhanced Session Mode on the Hyper-V server by selecting the checkbox for Allow Enhanced Session Mode on the Enhanced Session Mode Policy section of the Hyper-V server's properties.

You can only use Enhanced Session Mode with guest VMs running the Windows Server 2016, Windows Server 2012 R2, Windows 10 and Windows 8.1 operating systems. To use Enhanced Session Mode, you must have permission to connect to the VM using Remote Desktop through the account you use to sign on to the guest VM. You can gain permission by adding the user to the Remote Desktop Users group. A user who is a member of the local Administrators group also has this permission. The Remote Desktop Services service must be running on the guest VM.

RemoteFX

RemoteFX provides a 3D virtual adapter and USB redirection support for VMs. You can only use RemoteFX if the virtualization host has a compatible GPU. RemoteFX allows one or more compatible graphics adapters to perform graphics processing tasks for multiple VMs. RemoteFX is often used to provide support for graphically intensive applications, such as CAD, in VDI scenarios.

Nested virtualization

Hyper-V on Windows Server 2016, and the version on the Windows 10 client OS, support nested virtualization. Nested virtualization allows you to enable Hyper-V and host virtual machines in a virtual machine running under Hyper-V as long as that VM is running Windows Server 2016 or

Windows 10. Nested virtualization can be enabled on a per-VM basis by running the following PowerShell command:

```
Set-VMProcessor -VMName NameOfVM -ExposeVirtualiationExtensions $true
```

Nested virtualization dynamic memory

Once you've run this command, you'll be able to enable Hyper-V on the VM. You won't be able to adjust the memory of a virtual machine that is enabled for nested virtualization while that virtual machine is running. While it is possible to enable dynamic memory, the amount of memory allocated to a virtual machine configured for nested virtualization will not fluctuate while it is powered on.

Nested virtualization networking

To route network packets through the multiple virtual switches required during nested virtualization, you can either enable MAC address spoofing or configure network address translation (NAT).

You can enable MAC address spoofing on the virtual machine that you have configured for nested virtualization. You can do this with the following PowerShell command:

```
Get-VMNetworkAdapter -VMName NameOfVM | Set-VMNEtworkAdapter -MacAddressSpoofing On
```

To enable NAT, create a virtual NAT switch in the VM enabled for nested virtualization using the following PowerShell commands:

```
New-VMSwitch -name VMNAT -SwitchTypeInternal

New-NetNAT -Name LocalNAT -InternalIPInterfaceAddressPrefix "192.168.15.0/24"

Get-NetAdapter "vEthernet (VmNat)" | New-NetIPAddress -IPAddress 192.168.15.1
-AddressFamily IPv4 -PrefixLength 24
```

Once you've done this, you'll need to manually assign IP addresses to VMs running under the VM enabled for nested virtualization, using the default gateway of 192.168.15.1. You can use a separate internal addressing scheme other than 192.168.15.0/24 by altering the appropriate PowerShell commands in the NAT example.

PowerShell Direct

PowerShell Direct allows you to create a remote PowerShell session directly from a Hyper-V host to a virtual machine hosted on that Hyper-V host without requiring the virtual machine be configured with a network connection. PowerShell Direct requires that both the Hyper-V host and the VM be running Windows Server 2016 or Windows 10 and is not supported for earlier versions of the Windows Server or Windows Client operating systems.

To use PowerShell Direct, you must be signed on locally to the Hyper-V host with Hyper-V Administrator privileges. You also must have access to valid credentials for the virtual machine. If you do not have credentials for the virtual machine, you will not be able to establish a Power-Shell Direct connection.

To establish a PowerShell Direct connection, use the command:

```
Enter-PSSession -vmname NameOfVM
```

You exit the PowerShell Direct session by using the Exit-PSSession cmdlet.

Virtual hard disks

Hyper-V supports two separate virtual hard disk formats. Virtual hard disk files in .vhd format are limited to 2040 GB. Virtual hard disks in this format can be used on all supported versions of Hyper-V. Other than the size limitation, the important thing to remember is that you cannot use virtual hard disk files in .vhd format with generation 2 VMs.

Virtual hard disk files in .vhdx format are an improvement over virtual hard disks in .vhd format. The main limitation of virtual hard disks in .vhdx format is that they cannot be used with Hyper-V on Windows Server 2008 or Windows Server 2008 R2. Virtual hard disks in .vhdx format have the following benefits:

- Can be up to 64 TB in size

- Have larger block size for dynamic and differential disks

- Provide 4-KB logical sector virtual disks

- Have an internal log that reduces chance of corruption

- Support trim to reclaim unused space

You can convert hard disks between .vhd and .vhdx format. You can create virtual hard disks at the time you create the VM, use the New Virtual Hard Disk Wizard, or the New-VHD Windows PowerShell cmdlet.

Fixed sized disks

Virtual hard disks can either be dynamic, differencing or fixed. When you create a fixed-size disk, all space used by the disk is allocated on the hosting volume at the time of creation. Fixed disks increase performance if the physical storage medium does not support Windows Offloaded Data Transfer. Improvements in Windows Server reduce the performance benefit of fixed-size disks when the storage medium does support Windows Offloaded Data Transfer. The

CHAPTER 6

space to be allocated to the disk must be present on the host volume when you create the disk. For example, you can't create a 3-TB fixed disk on a volume that only has 2 TB of space.

Dynamically expanding disks

Dynamically expanding disks use an initial small file and then grow as the VM allocates data to the virtual hard disk. This means you can create a 3-TB dynamic virtual hard disk on a 2-TB volume because the entire 3 TB will not be allocated at disk creation. However, in this scenario you need to ensure that you extend the size of the 2-TB volume before the dynamic virtual disk outgrows the available storage space.

Differencing disks

Differencing disks are a special type of virtual hard disk that is in a child relationship with a parent hard disk. Parent disks can be fixed size or dynamic virtual hard disks, but the differencing disk must be the same type as the parent disk. For example, you can create a differencing disk in .vhdx format for a parent disk that uses .vhdx format, but you cannot create a differencing disk in .vhd format for a parent disk in .vhdx format.

Differencing disks record the changes that would otherwise be made to the parent hard disk by the VM. For example, differencing disks are used to record Hyper-V VM checkpoints. A single parent virtual hard disk can have multiple differencing disks associated with it.

For example, you can create a specially prepared parent virtual hard disk by installing Windows Server 2016 on a VM, running the sysprep utility within the VM and then shutting the VM down. You can use the virtual hard disk created by this process as a parent virtual hard disk. In this scenario, when creating new Windows Server 2016 VMs, you can configure the VMs to use a new differencing disk that uses the sysprepped virtual hard disk as a parent. When you run the new VM, the VM will write any changes that it would make normally to the full virtual hard disk to the differencing disk. In this scenario, deploying new Windows Server 2016 VMs becomes simply a matter of creating new VMs that use a differencing disk that uses the sysprepped Windows Server 2016 virtual hard disk as a parent.

Differencing drives

Differencing disks are a special type of hard disk that is in a child relationship with a parent hard disk. Parent disks can be fixed size or dynamic virtual hard disks, but the differencing disk must be the same type as the parent disk. For example, you can create a differencing disk in .vhdx format for a parent disk that uses .vhdx format, but you cannot create a differencing disk in .vhd format for a parent disk in .vhdx format.

Differencing disks record the changes that would otherwise be made to the parent hard disk by the VM. For example, differencing disks are used to record Hyper-V VM checkpoints. A single parent virtual hard disk can have multiple differencing disks associated with it.

For example, you can create a specially prepared parent virtual hard disk by installing Windows Server 2012 R2 on a VM, running the sysprep utility within the VM, and then shutting the VM down. You can use the virtual hard disk created by this process as a parent virtual hard disk. In this scenario, when creating new Windows Server 2012 R2 VMs, you can configure the VMs to use a new differencing disk that uses the sysprepped virtual hard disk as a parent. When you run the new VM, the VM will write any changes that it would make normally to the full virtual hard disk to the differencing disk. In this scenario, deploying new Windows Server 2012 R2 VMs becomes simply a matter of creating new VMs that use a differencing disk that uses the sysprepped Windows Server 2012 R2 virtual hard disk as a parent.

You can create differencing hard disks using the New-VHD Windows PowerShell cmdlet. You can create differencing hard disks using the New Virtual Hard Disk Wizard or the New-VHD Windows PowerShell cmdlet. You need to specify the parent disk the during creation process.

The key to using differencing disks is to ensure that you don't make changes to the parent disk as this will invalidate the relationship with any child disks. Differencing disks can provide storage efficiencies, because the only changes are recorded on child disks. For example, rather than storing 10 different instances of Windows Server 2016 in its entirety, you can create one parent disk and have 10 much smaller differencing disks to accomplish the same objective. If you store VM virtual hard disks on a volume that has been deduplicated, these efficiencies are reduced.

Modifying virtual hard disks

You can perform the following tasks to modify existing virtual hard disks:

- Convert a virtual hard disk in .vhd format to .vhdx format

- Convert a virtual hard disk in .vhdx format to .vhd format

- Change the disk from fixed size to dynamically expanding, or from dynamically expanding to fixed size

- Shrink or enlarge the virtual hard disk

You convert virtual hard disk type (.vhd to .vhdx, .vhdx to .vhdx, dynamic to fixed, and fixed to dynamic) either using the Edit Virtual Hard Disk Wizard or by using the Convert-VHD Windows PowerShell cmdlet. When converting from .vhdx to .vhd, remember that virtual hard disks in .vhd format cannot exceed 2040 GB in size. So, while it is possible to convert virtual hard disks in .vhdx format that are smaller than 2040 GB to .vhd format, you will not be able to convert virtual hard disks that are larger than this.

You can only perform conversions from one format to another and from one type to another while the VM is powered off. You must shrink the virtual hard disk using disk manager in the VM operating system prior to shrinking the virtual hard disk using the Edit Virtual Hard Disk Wizard or Resize-VHD cmdlet. You can resize a virtual hard disk while the VM is running under the following conditions:

- The virtualization host is running Windows Server 2016 or Windows Server 2012 R2.

- The virtual hard disk is in .vhdx format .

- The virtual hard disk is attached to a virtual SCSI controller.

- The virtual hard disk must have shrunk. You must shrink the virtual hard disk using disk manager in the host operating system prior to shrinking the virtual hard disk using the Edit Virtual Hard Disk Wizard or Resize-VHD cmdlet.

Pass through disks

Pass-through disks, also known as directly attached disks, allow a VM direct access to underlying storage rather than a virtual hard disk that resides on that storage. For example, normally with Hyper-V you will connect a VM to a virtual hard disk file hosted on a volume formatted with NTFS or ReFS. With pass-through disks, the VM instead accesses the disk directly and there is no virtual hard disk file.

Pass-through disks allow VMs to access larger volumes than are possible when using virtual hard disks in .vhd format. In earlier versions of Hyper-V, such as the version available with Windows Server 2008, pass-through disks provided performance advantages over virtual hard disks. The need for pass-through disks has diminished with the availability of virtual hard disks in .vhdx format, because .vhdx format allows you to create much larger volumes.

Pass-through disks can be directly attached to the virtualization host or can be Fibre Channel or iSCSI disks. When adding a pass-through disk, you will need to ensure that the disk is offline. You can use the disk management console or the diskpart.exe utility on the virtualization host to set a disk to be offline.

To add a pass-through disk using Windows PowerShell, first get the properties of the disk that you want to add as a pass-through disk using the Get-Disk cmdlet, and then pipe the result to the Add-VMHardDiskDrive cmdlet. For example, to add physical disk 3 to the VM named Alpha-Test, execute the following command:

```
Get-Disk 3 | Add-VMHardDiskDrive –VMName Alpha-Test
```

A VM that uses pass-through disks will not support VM checkpoints. Pass-through disks also cannot be backed up using any backup program that uses the Hyper-V VSS writer.

Managing checkpoints

Checkpoints represent the state of a VM at a particular point in time. You can create checkpoints when the VM is running or when the VM is shut down. When you create a checkpoint of a running VM, the running VM's memory state is also stored in the checkpoint. Restoring a checkpoint taken of a running VM returns the running VM to a restored state. Creating a checkpoint creates either an .avhd or .avhdx file (depending on whether the VM is using virtual hard disks in the VHD or VHDx format).

Windows Server 2016 supports two types of checkpoints:

- **Standard checkpoints**. These function the same way as checkpoints have in previous versions of Hyper-V. They capture the state, date, and hardware configuration of a virtual machine. They are designed for development and test scenarios.

- **Production checkpoints**. New to Windows Server 2016, they use backup technology inside the guest as opposed to the saved state technology used in standard checkpoints. Production checkpoints are fully supported by Microsoft and can be used with production workloads, something that was not supported with the standard version of checkpoints available in previous versions of Hyper-V.

You can switch between standard and production checkpoints on a per-virtual machine basis by editing the properties of the virtual machine and under the management section, choosing between production and standard checkpoints.

You can create checkpoints from Windows PowerShell with the Checkpoint-VM cmdlet. The other checkpoint-related Windows PowerShell cmdlets in Windows Server 2016 actually use the VMSnapshot noun, though on Windows 10 they confusingly have aliases for the VMCheckPoint noun.

The Windows Server 2016 checkpoint related cmdlets are as follows:

- **Restore-VMSnapshot**. This restores an existing VM checkpoint.

- **Export-VMSnapshot**. It allows you to export the state of a VM as it exists when a particular checkpoint was taken. For example, if you take a checkpoint at 2 p.m. and 3 p.m., you can choose to export the checkpoint taken at 2 p.m., and then import the VM in the state that it was in at 2 p.m. on another Hyper-V host.

- **Get-VMSnapshot**. This cmdlet lists the current checkpoints.

- **Rename-VMSnapshot**. Allows you to rename an existing VM checkpoint.

- **Remove-VMSnapshot**. It deletes a VM checkpoint. If the VM checkpoint is part of the chain, but not the final link, changes are merged with the successive checkpoint so that it

CHAPTER 6

remains a representation of the VM at the point in time when the snapshot was taken. For example, if checkpoints are taken at 1 p.m., 2 p.m., and 3 p.m., and you delete the 2 p.m. checkpoint, the avhd/avhdx files associated with the 2 p.m. snapshot are merged with the avhd/avhdx files associated with the 3 p.m. snapshot so that the 3 p.m. snapshot retains its integrity.

Checkpoints do not replace backups. Checkpoints are almost always stored on the same volume as the original VM hard disks, so a failure of that volume will result in all VM storage files, both original disks and checkpoint disks, being lost. If a disk in a checkpoint chain becomes corrupted, then that checkpoint and all subsequent checkpoints will be lost. Disks earlier in the checkpoint chain will remain unaffected. Hyper-V supports a maximum of 50 checkpoints per VM.

Virtual Fibre Channel adapters

Virtual Fibre Channel allows you to make direct connections from VMs running on Hyper-V to Fibre Channel storage. Virtual Fibre Channel is supported on Windows Server 2016 if the following requirements are met:

- The computer functioning as the Hyper-V virtualization host must have a Fibre Channel host bus adapter (HBA) that has a driver that supports a virtual Fibre Channel.

- SAN must be NPIV (N_Port ID) enabled.

- The VM must be running a supported version as the guest operating system.

- Virtual Fibre Channel LUNs cannot be used to boot Hyper-V VMs.

VMs running on Hyper-V support up to four virtual Fibre Channel adapters, each of which can be associated with a separate Storage Area Network (SAN).

Before you can use a virtual Fibre Channel adapter, you will need to create at least one virtual SAN on the Hyper-V virtualization host. A virtual SAN is a group of physical Fibre Channel ports that connect to the same SAN.

VM live migration and VM failover clusters are supported; however, virtual Fibre Channel does not support VM checkpoints, host-based backup, or live migration of SAN data.

Storage QoS

Storage Quality of Service (QoS) allows you to limit the maximum number of IOPS (Input/Output operations per second) for virtual hard disks. IOPS are measured in 8-KB increments. If you specify a maximum IOPS value, the virtual hard disk will be unable to exceed this value. You use Storage QoS to ensure that no one single workload on a Hyper-V virtualization host consumes a disproportionate amount of storage resources.

It's also possible to specify a minimum IOPS value for each virtual hard disk. You would do this if you wanted to be notified that a specific virtual hard disk's IOPS has fallen below a threshold value. When the number of IOPS falls below the specified minimum, an event is written to the event log. You configure Storage QoS on a per-virtual hard disk basis.

Hyper-V storage optimization

Several technologies built into Windows Server 2016 allow you to optimize the performance and data storage requirements for files associated with VMs.

Deduplication

NTFS volumes support deduplication. Deduplication is a process by which duplicate instances of data are removed from a volume and replaced with pointers to the original instance. Deduplication is especially effective when used with volumes that host virtual hard disk files as many of these files contain duplicate copies of data, such as the VM's operating system and program files.

Once installed, you can enable deduplication through the Volumes node of the File and Storage Services section of the Server Manager Console. When enabling deduplication, you specify whether you want to use a general file server data deduplication scheme or a virtual desktop infrastructure scheme. For volumes that host VM files, the VDI scheme is appropriate. You can't enable deduplication on the operating system volume, only on data volumes.

Storage tiering

Storage tiering is a technology that allows you to mix fast storage, such as solid state disk (SSD), with traditional spinning magnetic disks to optimize both storage performance and capacity. Storage tiering works on the premise that a minority of the data stored on a volume is responsible for the majority of read and write operations. Rather than creating a large volume that consists entirely of SSDs, storage tiering, which can be enabled through storage spaces functionality, allows you to create a volume comprised of both solid state and spinning magnetic disks. In this configuration, frequently accessed data is moved to the parts of the volume hosted on the SSDs and less frequently accessed data is moved to the parts of the volume hosted on the slower spinning magnetic disks. This configuration allows much of the performance benefits of an SSD-only volume to be realized without the cost of using SSD-only storage.

When used in conjunction with deduplication, frequently accessed deduplicated data is moved to the faster storage, allowing both the benefit of reducing storage requirements while improving performance over what would be possible if the volume hosting VM files were comprised only of spinning magnetic disks. You also have the option of pinning specific files to the faster storage, which overrides the algorithms that move data according to accumulated utilization statistics. You configure storage tiering using Windows PowerShell.

Hyper-V virtual switches

Hyper-V virtual switches, termed Hyper-V virtual networks in previous versions of Hyper-V, represent network connections to which the Hyper-V virtual network adapters can connect. You can configure three types of Hyper-V virtual switches.

External switches

An external switch connects to a physical or wireless network adapter. Only one virtual switch can be mapped to a specific physical or wireless network adapter or NIC team. For example, if a virtualization host had four physical network adapters configured as two separate NIC teams, you can configure two external virtual switches. If a virtualization host has three physical network adapters that do not participate in any NIC teams, you can configure three external virtual switches. Any VMs connected to the same external switch can communicate with each other as well as any external host connected to the network that the network adapter mapped to the external switch is connected to. For example, if an external switch is connected to a network adapter that is connected to a network that can route traffic to the internet, a VM connected to that external virtual switch will also be able to connect to hosts on the internet. When you create an external switch, a virtual network adapter that maps to this switch is created on the virtualization host unless you clear the option that allows the management operating system to share the network adapter. If you clear this option, the virtualization host will not be able to communicate through the network adapter associated with the external switch.

Internal switches

An internal switch allows communication between the VM and the virtualization host. All VMs connected to the same internal switch are able to communicate with each other and the virtualization host. For example, you can successfully initiate an RDP connection from the virtualization host to an appropriately configured VM or use the Test-NetConnection Windows PowerShell cmdlet from a Windows PowerShell prompt on the virtualization host to get a response from a VM connected to an internal network connection. VMs connected to an internal switch are unable to use that virtual switch to communicate with hosts on a separate virtualization host that are connected to an internal switch with the same name.

Private switches

VMs connected to the same private switch on a VM host are able to communicate with one another, but are unable to communicate directly with the virtualization host. Private switches only allow communication between VMs on the same virtualization host. For example, VM alpha and beta are connected to private switch p_switch_a on virtualization host h_v_one. VM gamma is connected to private switch p_switch_a on virtualization host h_v_ two. VMs alpha and beta will be able to communicate with each other, but will be unable to communicate with h_v_one or VM gamma.

Virtual machine network adapters

Generation 1 VMs support two types of network adapters: synthetic network adapters and legacy network adapters. A synthetic network adapter uses drivers that are provided when you install integration services in the VM operating system. If a VM operating system doesn't have these drivers, or if integration services is not available for this operating system, then the network adapter will not function. Synthetic network adapters are unavailable until a VM operating system that supports them is running. This means that you can't perform a PXE boot off a synthetic network adapter if you have configured a generation 1 VM.

Legacy network adapters emulate a physical network adapter, similar to a multiport DEC/Intel 21140 10/100TX 100 MB card. Many operating systems, including those that do not support virtual machine integration services, support this network adapter. This means that if you want to run an operating system in a VM that doesn't have virtual machine integration services support, such as a version of Linux or BSD that isn't officially supported for Hyper-V. So, you'll need to use a legacy network adapter, because this is likely to be recognized by the guest VM operating system.

Legacy network adapters on generation 1 VMs also function before the VM guest operating system is loaded. This means that if you want to PXE boot a generation 1 VM—for example, if you wanted to use WDS to deploy an operating system to the VM—you'd need to configure the VM with a legacy network adapter.

Generation 2 VMs don't separate synthetic and legacy network adapters and only have a single network adapter type. Generation 2 VMs support PXE booting off this single network adapter type. It is important to remember that only recent Windows client and server operating systems are supported as generation 2 VMs.

Optimizing network performance

You can optimize network performance for VMs hosted on Hyper-V in a number of ways. For example, you can configure the virtualization host with separate network adapters connected to separate subnets. You do this to separate network traffic related to the management of the Hyper-V virtualization host from network traffic associated with hosted VMs. You can also use NIC teaming on the Hyper-V virtualization host to provide increased and fault-tolerant network connectivity. You'll learn more about NIC teaming later in the chapter.

Bandwidth management

An additional method of optimizing network performance is to configure bandwidth management at the virtual network adapter level. Bandwidth management allows you to specify a minimum and a maximum traffic throughput figure for a virtual network adapter. The minimum bandwidth allocation is an amount that Hyper-V will reserve for the network adapter.

For example, if you set the minimum bandwidth allocation to 10 Mbps for each VM, Hyper-V ensures that when other VMs need more, they are able to increase their bandwidth utilization until they reach a limit defined by the combined minimum bandwidth allocation of all VMs hosted on the server. Maximum bandwidth allocations specify an upper limit for bandwidth utilization. By default, no minimum or maximum limits are set on virtual network adapters.

You configure bandwidth management by selecting the Enable bandwidth management option on a virtual network adapter and specifying a minimum and maximum bandwidth allocation in megabits per seconds (Mbps).

SR-IOV

SR-IOV (Single Root I/O Virtualization) increases network throughput by bypassing a virtual switch and sending network traffic straight to the VM. When you configure SR-IOV, the physical network adapter is mapped directly to the VM. As such, SR-IOV requires that the VM's operating system include a driver for the physical network adapter. You can only use SR-IOV if the physical network adapter and the network adapter drivers used with the virtualization host support the functionality. You can only configure SR-IOV for a virtual switch during switch creation. Once you have an SR-IOV-enabled virtual switch, you can then enable SR-IOV on the virtual network adapter that connects to that switch.

Dynamic Virtual Machine Queue

Dynamic Virtual Machine Queue is an additional technology that you can use to optimize network performance. When a VM is connected through a virtual switch to a network adapter that supports a Virtual Machine Queue, and a Virtual Machine Queue is enabled on the virtual network adapter's properties, the physical network adapter is able to use Direct Memory Access (DMA) to forward traffic directly to the VM. With a Virtual Machine Queue, network traffic is processed by the CPU assigned to the VM rather than by the physical network adapter used by the Hyper-V virtualization host. Dynamic Virtual Machine Queue automatically adjusts the number of CPU cores used to process network traffic. A Dynamic Virtual Machine Queue is automatically enabled on a virtual switch when you enable a Virtual Machine Queue on the virtual network adapter.

Virtual machine NIC teaming

NIC teaming allows you to aggregate bandwidth across multiple network adapters while also providing a redundant network connection in the event that one of the adapters in the team fails. NIC teaming allows you to consolidate up to 32 network adapters and to use them as a single network interface. You can configure NIC teams using adapters that are from different manufacturers and that run at different speeds (though it's generally a good idea to use the same adapter make and model in production environments).

You can configure NIC teaming at the virtualization host level if the virtualization host has multiple network adapters. The drawback is that you can't configure NIC teaming at the host level if the network adapters are configured to use SR-IOV. If you want to use SR-IOV and NIC teaming, create the NIC team instead in the VM. You can configure NIC teaming within VMs by adding adapters to a new team using the Server Manager console or the New-NetLbfoTeam PowerShell cmdlet.

When configuring NIC teaming in a VM, ensure that each virtual network adapter that will participate in the team has MAC address spoofing enabled.

Virtual Machine MAC addresses

By default, VMs running on Hyper-V hosts use dynamic MAC addresses. Each time a VM is powered on, it will be assigned a MAC address from a MAC address pool. You can configure the properties of the MAC address pool through the MAC Address Range settings available through Virtual Switch Manager.

When you deploy operating systems on physical hardware, you can use two methods to ensure that the computer is always assigned the same IP address configuration. The first method is to assign a static IP address from within the virtualized operating system. The second is to configure a DHCP reservation that always assigns the same IP address configuration to the MAC address associated with the physical computer's network adapter.

This won't work with Hyper-V VMs in their default configuration because the MAC address may change if you power the VM off and then on. Rather than configure a static IP address using the VM's operating system, you can instead configure a static MAC address on a per-virtual network adapter basis. This will ensure that a VM's virtual network adapter retains the same MAC address whether the VM is restarted or even if the VM is migrated to another virtualization host.

To configure a static MAC address on a per-network adapter basis, edit the network adapter's advanced features. When entering a static MAC address, you will need to select a MAC address manually. You shouldn't use one from the existing MAC address pool as there is no way for the current virtualization hosts, or other virtualization hosts on the same subnet, to check whether a MAC address that is to be assigned dynamically has already been assigned statically.

Network isolation

Hyper-V supports VLAN (Virtual Local Area Network) tagging at both the network adapter and virtual switch level. VLAN tags allow the isolation of traffic for hosts connected to the same network by creating separate broadcast domains. Enterprise hardware switches also support VLANs as a way of partitioning network traffic. To use VLANs with Hyper-V, the virtualization hosts' network adapter must support VLANs. A VLAN ID has 12 bits, which means you can configure 4,094 VLAN IDs.

You configure VLAN tags at the virtual network adapter level by selecting the Enable virtual LAN identification checkbox in the virtual network adapter properties. VLAN tags applied at the virtual switch level override VLAN tags applied at the virtual network adapter level. To configure VLAN tags at the virtual switch level, select the Enable virtual LAN identification for management operating system option and specify the VLAN identifier.

Hyper-V Replica

Hyper-V replica provides a replica of a VM running on one Hyper-V host that can be stored and updated on another Hyper-V host. For example, you could configure a VM hosted on a Hyper-V failover cluster in Melbourne to be replicated through Hyper-V replica to a Hyper-V failover cluster in Sydney. Hyper-V replication allows for replication across site boundaries and does not require access to shared storage in the way that failover clustering does.

Hyper-V replication is asynchronous. While the replica copy is consistent, it is a lagged copy with changes sent only as frequently as once every 30 seconds. Hyper-V replication supports multiple recovery points, with a recovery snapshot taken every hour (this incurs a resource penalty, so is off by default). This means that when activating the replica, you can choose to activate the most up-to-date copy or a lagged copy. You can choose to activate a lagged copy in the event that some form of corruption or change made the up-to-date copy problematic.

When you perform a planned failover from the primary host to the replica, you need to switch off the primary. This ensures that the replica is in an up-to-date consistent state. This is a drawback compared to failover or live migration, where the VM will remain available during the process. A series of checks are completed before performing planned failover to ensure that the VM is off, that a reverse replication is allowed back to the original primary Hyper-V host, and that the state of the VM on the current replica is consistent with the state of the VM on the current primary. Performing a planned failover will start the replicated VM on the original replica, which will now become the new primary server.

Hyper-V replica also supports unplanned failover. You perform an unplanned failover in the event that the original Hyper-V host has failed or the site that hosts the primary replica has become unavailable. When performing unplanned failover, you can either choose the most recent recovery point or choose a previous recovery point. Performing unplanned failover will start the VM on the original replica, which will now become the new primary server.

Hyper-V extended replication allows you to create a second replica of the existing replica server. For example, you can configure Hyper-V replication between a Hyper-V virtualization host in Melbourne and Sydney, with Sydney hosting the replica. You cab configure an extended replica in Brisbane using the Sydney replica.

Configuring Hyper-V replica servers

To configure Hyper-V replication, you need to configure the Replication Configuration settings. The first step is to select the checkbox for Enable This Computer As A Replica server. Next, select the authentication method you are going to use. If the computers are part of the same Active Directory environment, you can use Kerberos. When you use Kerberos, Hyper-V replication data isn't encrypted when transmitted across the network. If you are concerned about encrypting network data, you can configure IPsec. Another option if you are concerned about encrypting replication traffic, which is useful if you are transmitting data across the public internet without using an encrypted VPN tunnel, is to use certificate-based authentication. When using certificate-based authentication, you'll need to import and select a public certificate issued to the partner server using this dialog.

The final step when configuring Hyper-V replica is to select the servers from which the Hyper-V virtualization host will accept incoming replicated VM data. One option is to choose for the Hyper-V virtualization host to accept replicated VMs from any authenticated Hyper-V virtualization host, using a single default location to store replica data. The other option is to configure VM replica storage on a per server basis. For example, if you wanted to store VM replicas from one server on one volume and VM replicas from another server on a different volume, you'd use the second option.

Once replication is configured on the source and destination servers, you'll also need to enable the pre-defined firewall rules to allow the incoming replication traffic. There are two rules: one for replication using Kerberos (HTTP) on port 80 and the other for using certificate-based authentication on port 443.

Configuring VM replicas

Once you have configured the source and destination replica servers, you need to configure replication on a per VM basis. You do this by running the Enable Replication wizard, which you can trigger by clicking Enable Replication when the VM is selected in Hyper-V Manager. To configure VM replicas, you must perform the following steps:

- Select Replica Server. Select the replica server name. If you are replicating to a Hyper-V failover cluster, you'll need to specify the name of the Hyper-V replica broker. You'll learn more about the Hyper-V replica broker later in this chapter.

- Choose Connection Parameters. Specify the connection parameters. The options will depend on the configuration of the replica servers. On this page, depending on the existing configuration, you can choose the authentication type and whether replication data will be compressed when transmitted over the network.

CHAPTER 6

- Select Replication VHDs. When configuring replication, you have the option of not replicating some of a VM's virtual hard disks. In most scenarios, you should replicate all of a VM's hard disk drives. One reason not to replicate a VM's virtual hard disk is if the virtual hard disk only stores frequently changing temporary data that isn't required when recovering the VM.

- Replication Frequency. Use this to specify the frequency with which changes are sent to the replica server. You can choose between intervals of 30 seconds, 5 minutes and 15 minutes.

- Additional Recovery Points. You can choose to create additional hourly recovery points. Doing this gives you the option of starting the replica from a previous point in time rather than the most recent point in time. The advantage is that you can roll back to a previous version of the VM in the event that data corruption occurs and has replicated to the most recent recovery point. The replica server can store a maximum of 24 recovery points.

- Initial Replication. The last step in configuring Hyper-V replica is choosing how to seed the initial replica. Replication works by sending changed blocks of data, so the initial replica, which sends the entire VM, will be the largest transfer. You can perform an offline transfer with external media, use an existing VM on the replica server as the initial copy (the VM for which you are configuring a replica must have been exported and then imported on the replica server), or transfer all VM data across the network. You can perform replication immediately or at a specific time in the future, such as 2 a.m., when network utilization is likely to be lower.

Replica failover

You perform planned replica failover when you want to run the VM on the replica server rather than on the primary host. Planned failover involves shutting down the VM, which ensures that the replica will be up to date. Contrast this with Hyper-V live migration, which you perform while the VM is running. When performing planned failover, you can configure the VM on the replica server to automatically start once the process completes and to configure reverse replication, so that the current replica server becomes the new primary and the current primary becomes the new replica server.

In the event that the primary server becomes unavailable, you can trigger an unplanned failover. You then perform the unplanned failover on the replica server (as the primary is not available). When performing an unplanned failover, you can select any of the up to 24 previously stored recovery points.

Hyper-V replica broker

You need to configure and deploy a Hyper-V replica broker if your Hyper-V replica configuration includes a Hyper-V failover cluster as a source or destination. You don't need to configure and deploy Hyper-V replica broker if both the source and destination servers are not participating in a Hyper-V failover cluster. You install the Hyper-V Replica Broker role using Failover Cluster manager after you've enabled the Hyper-V role on cluster nodes.

Hyper-V failover clusters

One of the most common uses for failover clustering is to host Hyper-V virtual machine. The Hyper-V and failover clustering roles are even supported in a Nano Server, which allows organizations to deploy failover clustering capable virtualization hosts that have a minimal operating system footprint.

Hyper-V host cluster storage

When deployed on Hyper-V host clusters, the configuration and virtual hard disk files for highly available VMs are hosted on shared storage. This shared storage can be one of the following:

- **Serial Attached SCSI (SAS).** This is suitable for two-node failover clusters where the cluster nodes are in close proximity to each other.

- **iSCSI storage.** It is suitable for failover clusters with two or more nodes. Windows Server includes iSCSI Target Software, allowing it to host iSCSI targets that can be used as shared storage by Windows failover clusters.

- **Fibre Channel.** The Fibre Channel/Fibre Channel over Ethernet storage requires special network hardware. While generally providing better performance than iSCSI, Fibre Channel components tend to be more expensive.

- **SMB 3.0 file shares configured as continuously available storage.** This special type of file share is highly available, with multiple cluster nodes able to maintain access to the file share. This configuration requires multiple clusters. One cluster hosts the highly available storage used by the VMs, and the other cluster hosts the highly available VMs.

- **Cluster Shared Volumes (CSVs).** CSVs can also be used for VM storage in Hyper-V failover clusters. As with continuously available file shares, multiple nodes in the cluster have access to the files stored on CSVs, ensuring that failover occurs with minimal disruption. As with SMB 3.0 file shares, multiple clusters are required, with one cluster hosting the CSVs and the other cluster hosting the VMs.

When considering storage for a Hyper-V failover cluster, remember the following:

- Ensure volumes used for disk witnesses are formatted as either NTFS or ReFS.

- Avoid allowing nodes from separate failover clusters to access the same shared storage by using LUN masking or zoning.

- Where possible, use storage spaces to host volumes presented as shared storage.

Cluster quorum

Hyper-V failover clusters remain functional until they do not have enough active votes to retain quorum. Votes can consist of nodes that participate in the cluster as well as disk or file share witnesses. The calculation on whether the cluster maintains quorum is dependent on the cluster quorum mode. When you deploy a Windows Server failover cluster, one of the following modes will automatically be selected, depending on the current cluster configuration:

- Node Majority

- Node and Disk Majority

- Node and File Share Majority

- No Majority: Disk Only

You can change the cluster mode manually or, with Dynamic Quorum in Windows Server 2016, the cluster mode will change automatically when you add or remove nodes, or a witness disk, or a witness share.

Node Majority

The Node Majority cluster quorum mode is chosen automatically during setup if a cluster has an odd number of nodes. When this cluster quorum mode is used, a file share or disk witness is not used. A failover cluster will retain quorum as long as the number of available nodes is more than the number of failed nodes that retain cluster membership. For example, if you deploy a nine-node failover cluster, the cluster will retain quorum as long as five cluster nodes are able to communicate with each other.

Node and Disk Majority

The Node and Disk Majority model is chosen automatically during setup if the cluster has an even number of nodes and shared storage is available to function as a disk witness. In this con-figuration, cluster nodes and the disk witness each have a vote when calculating quorum. As with the Node Majority model, the cluster will retain quorum as long as the number of votes that remain in communication exceeds the number of votes that cannot be contacted. For example, if you deployed a six-node cluster and a witness disk, there is a total of seven votes. As long as four of those votes remain in communication with each other, the failover cluster retains quorum.

Node and File Share Majority

The Node and File Share Majority model is used when a file share is configured as a witness. Each node and the file share have a vote when it comes to determining if quorum is retained. As with other models, a majority of the votes must be present for the cluster to retain quorum. Node and File Share Majority is suitable for organizations that are deploying multi-site clusters; for example, placing half the cluster nodes in one site, half the cluster nodes in another site and the file share witness in a third site. If one site fails, the other site is able to retain communication with the site that hosts the file share witness, in which case quorum is retained.

No Majority: Disk Only

The No Majority: Disk Only model must be configured manually and used only in testing environments because the only vote that counts toward quorum is that of the disk witness on shared storage. The cluster will retain quorum as long as the witness is available, even if every node but one fails. Similarly, the cluster will be in a failed state if all the nodes are available, but the shared storage hosting the disk witness goes offline.

Cluster node weight

Rather than every node in the cluster having an equal vote when determining quorum, you can configure which cluster nodes are able to vote to determine quorum by running the Configure Cluster Quorum Wizard. Configuring node weight is useful if you are deploying a multi-site cluster, and you want to control which site retains quorum in the event that communication between the sites is lost. You can determine which nodes in a cluster are currently assigned votes by selecting Nodes in the Failover Cluster Manager.

Dynamic quorum

Dynamic quorum allows a cluster quorum to be recalculated automatically each time a node is removed from or added to a cluster. Dynamic quorum is enabled by default on Windows Server 2016 clusters. Dynamic quorum works in the following manner:

- The vote of the witness is automatically adjusted based on the number of voting nodes in the cluster. If the cluster has an even number of nodes, the witness has a vote. If a cluster has an even number of nodes and a node is added or removed, the witness loses its vote.

- In the event of a 50 percent node split, dynamic quorum can adjust the vote of a node. This is useful in avoiding "split brain" syndrome during site splits with multi-site failover clusters.

An advantage of dynamic quorum is that as long as nodes are evicted in a graceful manner, the cluster will reconfigure quorum appropriately. This means that you can change a nine-node cluster so that it is a five- node cluster by evicting nodes, and the new quorum model is automatically recalculated assuming that the cluster only has five nodes. With a dynamic quorum, it is a good idea to specify a witness even if the initial cluster configuration has an odd number of nodes, because that way a witness vote will automatically be included in the event that an administrator adds or removes a node from the cluster.

Cluster networking

In lab and development environments, it's reasonable to have failover cluster nodes that are configured with a single network adapter. In production environments with mission-critical workloads, you should configure cluster nodes with multiple network adapters, institute adapter teaming, and leverage separate networks. Separate networks should include:

- A network dedicated for connecting cluster nodes to shared storage

- A network dedicated for internal cluster communication

- The network that clients use to access services deployed on the cluster

When configuring IPv4 or IPv6 addressing for failover cluster nodes, ensure that addresses are assigned either statically or dynamically to cluster node network adapters. Avoid using a mixture of statically and dynamically assigned addresses because this will cause an error with the cluster validation wizard. Also ensure that cluster network adapters are configured with a default gateway. While the cluster validation wizard will not provide an error if a default gateway is not present for the network adapters of each potential cluster node, you will be unable to create a failover cluster unless a default gateway is present.

Force Quorum Resiliency

Imagine you have a five-node multi-site cluster in Melbourne and Sydney, with three nodes in Sydney. Imagine also that internet connectivity to the Sydney site is lost. Within the Sydney site itself, the cluster will remain running because with three nodes it has retained quorum. But if external connectivity to the Sydney site is not available, you may instead need to forcibly start the cluster in the Melbourne site (which will be in a failed state because only two nodes are present) using the /fq (forced quorum) switch to provide services to clients.

In the past, when connectivity was restored, this would have led to a "split brain" or partitioned cluster, because both sides of the cluster are configured to be authoritative. To resolve this with failover clusters running Windows Server 2012 or earlier, you need to manually restart the nodes that are not part of the forced quorum set using the /pq (prevent quorum) switch. Windows Server 2016 provides a feature known as Force Quorum Resiliency that automatically restarts the nodes that are not part of the forced quorum set so that the cluster does not remain in a partitioned state.

Cluster Shared Volumes

Cluster Shared Volumes (CSVs) are a high-availability storage technology that allows multiple cluster nodes in a failover cluster to have read-write access to the same LUN. This has the following advantages for Hyper-V failover clusters:

- VMs stored on the same LUN can be run on different cluster nodes. This reduces the number of LUNs required to host VMs because the VMs stored on a CSV aren't tied to one specific Hyper-V failover cluster node, but instead can be spread across multiple Hyper-V failover cluster nodes.

- Switch-over between nodes is almost instantaneous in the event of failover because the new host node doesn't have to go through the process of seizing the LUN from the failed node.

CSVs are hosted off servers running the Windows Server 2012, or later operating systems allow multiple nodes in a cluster to access the same NTFS or ReFS formatted file system. CSVs support BitLocker, with each node performing decryption of encrypted content using cluster computer account. CSVs also integrate with SMB (Server Message Block) Multichannel and SMB Direct, allowing traffic to be sent through multiple networks and to leverage network cards that include Remote Direct Memory Access (RDMA) technology. CSVs can also automatically scan and repair volumes without requiring storage to be taken offline. You can convert cluster storage to a CSV using the Disks node of the Failover Cluster Manager.

Active Directory detached clusters

Active Directory detached clusters, also termed "clusters without network names," are a feature of Windows Server 2016 and Windows Server 2012 R2. Detached clusters have their names stored in DNS, but do not require the creation of a computer account within Active Directory. The benefit of detached clusters is that it is possible to create them without requiring that a computer object be created in Active Directory to represent the cluster, or that the account used to create the cluster has permissions to create computer objects in Active Directory. Although the account used to create a detached cluster does not need permission to create computer objects in Active Directory, the nodes that will participate in the detached cluster must themselves still be domain joined.

Preferred owner and failover settings

Cluster role preferences settings allow you to configure a preferred owner for a cluster role. When you do this, the role will be hosted on the node listed as the preferred owner. You can specify multiple preferred owners and configure the order in which a role will attempt to return to a specific cluster node.

Failover settings allow you to configure how many times a service will attempt to restart or fail over in a specific period. By default, a cluster service can fail over twice in a six-hour period before the failover cluster will leave the cluster role in a failed state. The failback setting allows you to configure the amount of time a clustered role that has fallen, over to a node that is not its preferred owner, and will wait before falling back to the preferred owner.

Hyper-V guest clusters

A guest cluster is a failover cluster that consists of two or more VMs as cluster nodes. You can run a guest cluster on a Hyper-V failover cluster, or you can run guest clusters with nodes on separate Hyper-V failover clusters. While deploying a guest cluster on Hyper-V failover clusters may seem as though it is taking redundancy to an extreme, there are good reasons to deploy guest clusters and Hyper-V failover clusters together.

Failover clusters monitor the health of clustered roles to ensure that they are functioning. This means that a guest failover cluster can detect when the failure of a clustered role occurs and c an take steps to recover the role. For example, you deploy a SQL Server 2016 failover cluster as a guest cluster on a Hyper-V failover cluster. One of the SQL Server 2016 instances that participates in the guest cluster suffers a failure. In this scenario, failover occurs within the guest cluster and another instance of SQL Server 2016 hosted on the other guest cluster node continues to service client requests.

Deploying guest and Hyper-V failover clusters together allows you to move applications to other guest cluster nodes while you are performing servicing tasks. For example, you may need to apply software updates that require a restart to the operating system that hosts a SQL Server 2016 instance. If this SQL Server 2016 instance is participating in a Hyper-V guest cluster, you can move the clustered role to another node, apply software updates to the original node, perform the restart, and then move the clustered SQL Server role back to the original node.

Deploying guest and Hyper-V failover clusters together allows you to live migrate guest cluster VMs from one host cluster to another host cluster while ensuring clients retain connectivity to clustered applications. For example, a two-node guest cluster hosting SQL Server 2016 is hosted on one Hyper-V failover cluster in your organization's data center. You want to move the guest cluster from its current host Hyper-V failover cluster to a new Hyper-V failover cluster. By migrating one guest cluster node at a time from the original Hyper-V failover cluster to the new Hyper-V failover cluster, you'll be able to continue to service client requests without interruption. You can then fail over SQL Server 2016 to the guest node on the new Hyper-V failover cluster after the first node completes its migration before migrating the second node across.

Hyper-V guest cluster storage

Just as you can configure a Hyper-V failover cluster where multiple Hyper-V hosts function as failover cluster nodes, you can configure failover clusters within VMs, where each failover cluster node is a VM. Even though failover cluster nodes must be members of the same Active Directory domain, there is no requirement that they be hosted on the same cluster. For example, you can configure a multi-site failover cluster where the cluster nodes are hosted as highly available VMs, each hosted on its own Hyper-V failover clusters in each site.

When considering how to deploy a VM guest cluster, you need to choose how to provision the shared storage that is accessible to each cluster node. The options for configuring shared storage for VM guest clusters include:

- iSCSI

- Virtual Fibre Channel

- Cluster Shared Volumes

- Continuously Available File Shares

- Shared virtual hard disks

The conditions for using iSCSI, Virtual Fibre Channel, Cluster Shared Volumes and Continuously Available File Shares with VM guest clusters are essentially the same for VMs as they are when configuring traditional physically hosted failover cluster nodes.

Shared virtual hard disk

Shared virtual hard disks are a special type of shared storage only available to VM guest clusters. With shared virtual hard disks, each guest cluster node can be configured to access the same shared virtual hard disk. Each VM cluster node's operating system will recognize the shared virtual hard disk as shared storage when building the VM guest failover cluster.

Shared virtual hard disks have the following requirements:

- Can be used with generation 1 and generation 2 VMs.

- Can only be used with guest operating systems running Windows Server 2016, Windows Server 2012 R2 or Windows Server 2012. If the guest operating systems are running Windows Server 2012, they must be updated to use the Windows Server 2012 R2 integration services components.

- Can only be used if virtualization hosts are running the Windows Server 2016 or 2012 R2 version of Hyper-V.

- Must be configured to use the .vhdx virtual hard disk format.

- Must be connected to a virtual SCSI controller.

- When deployed on a failover cluster, the shared virtual hard disk itself should be located on shared storage, such as a Continuously Available File Share or Cluster Shared Volume. This is not necessary when configuring a guest failover cluster on a single Hyper-V server that is not part of a Hyper-V failover cluster.

- VMs can only use shared virtual hard disks to store data. You can't boot a VM from a shared virtual hard disk.

The configuration of shared virtual hard disks differs from the traditional configuration of VM guest failover clusters, because you configure the connection to shared storage by editing the VM properties rather than connecting to the shared storage from within the VM. Windows Server 2016 supports shared virtual hard disks being resized and used with Hyper-V replica.

Live migration

Live migration is the process of moving an operational VM from one physical virtualization host to another with no interruption to VM clients or users. Live migration is supported between cluster nodes that share storage, between separate Hyper-V virtualization hosts that are not participating in a failover cluster using a SMB 3.0 file share as storage, and even between separate Hyper-V hosts that are not participating in a failover cluster using a process termed "shared nothing live migration."

Live migration has the following prerequisites:

- There must be two or more servers running Hyper-V that use processors from the same manufacturer; for example, all Hyper-V virtualization hosts configured with Intel processors or all Hyper-V virtualization hosts configured with AMD processors.

- Hyper-V virtualization hosts need to be members of the same domain, or must be members of domains that have a trust relationship with each other.

- VMs must be configured to use virtual hard disks or virtual Fibre Channel disks (no pass-through disks).

It is possible to perform live migration with VMs configured with pass-through disks under the following conditions:

- VMs are hosted on a Windows Server Hyper-V failover cluster.

- Live migration is going to be within nodes that participate in the same Hyper-V failover cluster.

CHAPTER 6

- VM configuration files are stored on a Cluster Shared Volume.

- The physical disk used as a pass-through disk is configured as a storage disk resource that is controlled by the failover cluster. This disk must be configured as a dependent resource for the highly available VM.

If performing a live migration using shared storage, the following conditions must be met:

- The SMB 3.0 share needs to be configured so that source and destination virtualization host's computer accounts have read and write permissions.

- All VM files (virtual hard disks, configuration and snapshot files) must be located on the SMB 3.0 share. You can use storage migration to move VM files to an SMB 3.0 share while the VM is running prior to performing a live migration using this method.

- You must configure the source and destination Hyper-V virtualization hosts to support live migrations by enabling live migrations in Hyper-V settings. When you do this, you specify the maximum number of simultaneous live migrations and the networks that you will use for live migration. Microsoft recommends using an isolated network for live migration traffic, although this is not a requirement.

- The next step in configuring live migration is choosing which authentication protocol and live migration performance options to use. You select these in the Advanced Features area of the Live Migrations settings. The default authentication protocol is Credential Security Support Provider (CredSSP). CredSSP requires local sign-on to both source and destination Hyper-V virtualization host to perform live migration. Kerberos allows you to trigger live migration remotely. To use Kerberos, you must configure the computer accounts for each Hyper-V virtualization host with constrained delegation for the cifs and Microsoft Virtual System Migration Service services, granting permissions to the virtualization hosts that will participate in the live migration partnership. The performance options allow you to speed up live migration. Compression increases processor utilization. SMB will use SMB Direct if both the network adapters used for the live migration process support Remote Direct Memory Access (RDMA) and RDMA capabilities are enabled.

Storage migration

With storage migration, you can move a VM's virtual hard disk files, checkpoint files, smart paging files, and configuration files from one location to another. You can perform storage migration while the VM is running or while the VM is powered off. You can move data to any location that is accessible to the Hyper-V host. This allows you to move data from one volume to another, from one folder to another, or even to an SMB 3.0 file share on another computer. When performing storage migration, choose the Move the VM's storage option.

For example, you can use storage migration to move VM files from one Cluster Share Volume to another on a Hyper-V failover cluster without interrupting the VM's operation. You have the option of moving all data to a single location, moving VM data to separate locations or moving only the VM's virtual hard disk. To move the VM's data to different locations, select the items you want to move and the destination locations.

Exporting, importing and copying VMs

A VM export creates a duplicate of a VM that you can import on the same, or a different Hyper-V virtualization host. When performing an export, you can choose to export the VM, which includes all its VM checkpoints, or just a single VM checkpoint. Windows Server 2016 and Windows Server 2012 R2 support exporting a running VM. With Hyper-V in Windows Server 2012, Windows Server 2008 R2 and Windows Server 2008, it is necessary to shut down the VM before performing an export.

Exporting a VM with all of its checkpoints will create multiple differencing disks. When you import a VM that was exported with checkpoints, these checkpoints will also be imported. If you import a VM that was running at the time of export, the VM is placed in a saved state. You can resume from this saved state, rather than having to restart the VM.

When importing a VM, you can choose from the following options:

- Register the virtual machine in place (use the existing ID). Use this option when you want to import the VM while keeping the VM files their current location. As this method uses the existing VM ID, you can only use it if the original VM on which the export was created is not present on the host to which you wish to import the VM.

- Restore the virtual machine (use the existing unique ID). Use this option when you want to import the VM while moving the files to a new location; for example, if you are importing a VM that was exported to a network share. As this method also uses the existing VM ID, you can only use it if the original VM on which the export was created is not present on the host to which you wish to import the VM.

- Copy the virtual machine (create a new unique ID). Use this method if you want to create a separate clone of the exported VM. The exported files will be copied to a new location, leaving the original exported files unaltered. A new VM ID is created, meaning that the cloned VM can run concurrently on the same virtualization host as the original progenitor VM. When importing a cloned VM onto the same virtualization host as the original progenitor VM, ensure that you rename the newly imported VM, otherwise you may confuse them.

VM Network Health Detection

VM Network Health Detection is a feature for VMs that are deployed on Hyper-V host clusters. With VM Network Health Detection, you configure a VM's network adapter settings and mark certain networks as being protected. You do this on the Advanced Features section of the network adapter.

In the event that a VM is running on a cluster node where the network marked as protected becomes unavailable, the cluster will automatically live migrate the VM to a node where the protected network is available. For example, you have a four-node Hyper-V failover cluster. Each node has multiple network adapters and a virtual switch named Alpha maps as an external virtual switch to a physical network adapter on each node. A VM, configured as highly available and hosted on the first cluster node is connected to virtual switch Alpha. The network adapter on this VM is configured with the protected network option. After the VM has been switched on and has been running for some time, a fault occurs causing the physical network adapter mapped to virtual switch Alpha on the first cluster node to fail. When this happens, the VM will automatically be live migrated to another cluster node where virtual switch Alpha is working.

VM drain on shutdown

VM drain on shutdown is a feature that will automatically live migrate all running VMs off a node if you shut down that node without putting it into maintenance mode. If you are following best practice, you'll be putting nodes into maintenance mode and live migrating running workloads away from nodes that you will restart or intend to shut down anyway. The main benefit of VM drain on shutdown is that, in the event that you are having a bad day and forget to put a cluster node into maintenance mode before shutting it down or restarting it, any running VMs will be live migrated away without requiring your direct intervention.

Domain controller cloning

Windows Server 2016 supports creating copies of domain controllers that are running as VMs as long as certain conditions are met. Cloned domain controllers have the following prerequisites:

- The virtualization host supports VM-GenerationID, a 128-bit random integer that identifies each VM checkpoint. The version of Hyper-V available with Windows Server 2012 and later, as well as some third-party hypervisors, support VM-GenerationID.

- The domain controller must be running Windows Server 2012 or later as its operating system.

- The server that hosts PDC emulator Flexible Single Master Operations Role (FSMO) must be able to be contacted. This server must be running Windows Server 2012 or later as its operating system.

- The computer account of the domain controller that will serve as the template for cloning must be added to the Cloneable Domain Controllers security group.

Once you have met these conditions, you'll need to create an XML configuration file named DCCloneConfig.xml using the New-ADDCCloneConfig Windows PowerShell cmdlet. Once created, you'll need to edit this file and specify settings such as computer name, network settings and Active Directory site information. You should also check the template DC using the Get-ADDCCloningExcludedApplicationsList cmdlet to determine if any services that will cause problems with the cloning, such as the DHCP server service, are present on the template DC.

Shielded virtual machines

Shielded virtual machines are a special type of virtual machine that has a virtual Trusted Platform Module (TPM) chip, is encrypted using BitLocker, and can only run on specific approved host that support what is known as a guarded fabric. Shielded VMs allow sensitive data and workloads to be run on virtualization hosts without the concern that an attacker, or the administrator of the virtualization host, might export the virtual machine to gain access to the sensitive data stored there.

Managing Hyper-V using PowerShell

The Hyper-V PowerShell module contains a large number of cmdlets that you can use to manage all aspects of Hyper-V and virtual machines on Windows Server 2016. These cmdlets are described in Table 6-1.

Table 16-1. Remote Access PowerShell cmdlets

Noun	Verbs	Function
VFD	New	Create a new virtual floppy disk
VHD	Convert, Merge, Resize, Optimize, Dismount, New, Mount, Set, Get, Test	Manage virtual hard disks
VHDSet	Optimize, Get	Manage virtual hard disk set files, an update to the VHDX files from previous versions of Hyper-V
VHDSnapshot	Get, Remove	Used to manage snapshots with VHDSets

VM	Wait, Move, Get, Export, Debug, Measure, Import, Save, Resume, Restart, Set, Suspend, Stop, Start, Repair, Checkpoint, Remove, New, Compare, Rename	Use to manage virtual machines
VMAssignableDevice	Add, Get, Remove	Manage VM assignable devices
VMBios	Set, Get	Manage VM BIOS settings
VMComPort	Set, Get	Manage VM COM Port settings
VMConnectAccess	Grant, Revoke, Get	Manage which users can connect to specific VMs
VMConsoleSupport	Enable, Disable	Manage HID device support for virtual machines
VMDvdDrive	Add, Set, Get, Remove	Manage VM DVD drive settings
VMEventing	Disable, Enable	Enable or disable VM eventing
VMFailover	Complete, Stop, Start	Manage VM failover
VMFibreChannelHba	Set, Get, Remove, Add	Manage VM fibre channel HBA settings
VMFile	Copy	Copy a file from the virtualization host to a location within the virtual machine
VMFirmware	Set, Get	Manage VM virtual firmware settings
VMGpuPartitionAdapter	Set, Add, Remove, Get	Manage VM GPU settings
VMGroup	New, Get, Remove, Rename	Allows you to manage VM Groups, which you use to manage groups of machines that might make up a multi-tier application
VMGroupMember	Remove, Add	Add and remove VMs from a specific group
VMHardDiskDrive	Set, Add, Remove, Get	Manage VM hard disk drive settings
VMHost	Set, Get	Configure VM host settings
VMHostAssignableDevice	Add, Mount, Get, Remove, Dismount	Manage VM host assignable devices
VMHostCluster	Get, Set	Configure VM host cluster settings

CHAPTER 6

VMHostNumaNode	Get	View VM host Numa node information
VMHostNumaNodeStatus	Get	View VM host Numa node status
VMHostSupportedVersion	Get	View VM host supported information data
VMIdeController	Get	Manage VM IDE controller settings
VMInitialReplication	Import, Start, Stop	Configure initial VM replication settings
VMIntegrationService	Enable, Disable, Get	Manage VM integration services
VMKeyProtector	Get, Set	Manage VM key protector settings
VMKeyStorageDrive	Set, Remove, Get, Add	Manage VM key storage drive settings
VMMemory	Set, Get	Manage VM memory
VMMigration	Enable, Disable	Manage VM Migration
VMMigrationNetwork	Add, Remove, Get, Set	Configure VM migration network settings
VMNetworkAdapter	Disconnect, Connect, Remove, Test, Add, Set, Rename, Get	Configure VM network adapters
VMNetworkAdapterAcl	Remove, Add, Get	Manage VM network adapter ACLs
VMNetworkAdapterExtendedAcl	Remove, Add, Get	Manage VM Network adapter extended ACL settings
VMNetworkAdapterFailoverConfiguration	Get, Set	Manage VM network adapter failover settings
VMNetworkAdapterIsolation	Set, Get	Manage VM network adapter isolation settings
VMNetworkAdapterRdma	Set	Manage virtual network adapter RDMA settings
VMNetworkAdapterRoutingDomainMapping	Set, Get, Remove, Add	Configure virtual network adapter routing domains
VMNetworkAdapterTeamMapping	Remove, Get, Set	Configure virtual network adapter team mapping
VMNetworkAdapterVlan	Get, Set	Manage VM network adapter VLAN settings
VMPartitionableGpu	Get, Set	Manage VM GPU settings
VMProcessor	Get, Set	Configure VM Processor settings

VMRemoteFx3dVideoAdapter	Remove, Set, Get, Add	Manage RemoteFX3d video adapters
VMRemoteFXPhysical VideoAdapter	Disable, Get, Enable	Manage RemoteFX physical adapters
VMReplication	Get, Stop, Suspend, Remove, Measure, Enable, Resume, Set	Manage VM replication
VMReplication dAuthorizationEntry	Set, Remove, New, Get	Manage VM replication authorization entries
VMReplicationConnection	Test	Check VM replication
VMReplicationServer	Get, Set	Configure VM replication server settings
VMReplicationStatistics	Reset	Reset VM replication statistics
VMResourceMetering	Reset, Disable, Enable	Configure VM resource metering
VMResourcePool	Set, Rename, Get, Measure, New, Remove	Manage VM resource pool settings
VMSan	Remove, Disconnect, Connect, New, Set, Rename, Get	Manage VM SAN settings
VMSavedState	Remove	Remove saved state data
VMScsiController	Remove, Add, Get	Manage VM scsi controller
VMSecurity	Get, Set	Manage VM security information
VMSecurityPolicy	Set	Configure VM security policies
VMSnapshot	Rename, Restore, Export, Get, Remove	Manage VM checkpoints
VMStorage	Move	Move VM storage
VMStoragePath	Get, Remove, Add	Configure VM storage path
VMSwitch	Set, Get, Rename, Remove, Add, New	Manage virtual switches
VMSwitchExtension	Enable, Disable, Get	Manage extensions on a virtual switch
VMSwitchExtensionPortData	Get	View port extensions on a virtual switch
VMSwitchExtensionPortFeature	Set, Add, Remove, Get	Manage switch port features
VMSwitchExtensionSwitchData	Get	View switch port data
VMSwitchExtensionSwitchFeature	Add, Get, Set, Remove	Manage switch features
VMSwitchTeam	Set, Get	Manage switch teams

CHAPTER 6

VMSwitchTeamMember	Add, Remove	Manage switch team membership
VMSystemSwitchExtension	Get	View switch extensions installed on VM host
VMSystemSwitchExtensionPort-Feature	Get	View port level features supported by switch extensions on VM host
VMSystemSwitchExtension-SwitchFeature	Get	View switch-level features supported by virtual switch extensions on VM host
VMTPM	Disable, Enable	Manage virtual TPM settings
VMTrace	Stop, Start	Manage trace settings for VM debugging
VMVersion	Update	Update the version of the VM
VMVideo	Get, Set	Configure video settings for virtual machines

Windows Server 2016 provides a number of software defined storage solutions that allow you to have complex storage configurations managed by the Windows Server operating system, rather than having to manage storage solutions using storage hardware specific vendor management tools. Many of the storage service solutions available in Windows Server 2016 are used by Microsoft in their Azure datacenters where storage provisioning, performance, resiliency and redundancy are all managed through software rather than specific hardware devices.

Storage spaces and storage pools

Storage spaces and storage pools were first introduced to Windows Server with the release of Windows Server 2012. A *storage pool* is a collection of storage devices that you can use to aggregate storage. You expand the capacity of a storage pool by adding storage devices to the pool. A storage space is a virtual disk that you create from the free space that is available in a storage pool. Depending on how you configure it, a storage space can be resilient to failure and have improved performance through storage tiering.

You manage storage spaces and storage pools either through PowerShell or Server Manager.

Storage pools

A storage pool is a collection of storage devices, usually disks, but can also include items such as virtual hard disks, from which you can create one or more storage spaces. A storage space is a special type of virtual disk that has the following features:

- **Resilient storage.** Configure to use disk mirroring or parity in the structure of the underlying storage if available. Resilience is discussed later in the chapter.

- **Tiering.** Configure to leverage a combination of SSD and HDD disks to achieve maximum performance. Tiering is discussed later in the chapter.

- **Continuous availability.** Storage spaces integrate with failover clustering and you can cluster pools across separate nodes within a single failover cluster.

- **Write-back cache.** If a storage space includes SSDs, a write-back cache can be configured in the pool to buffer small random writes. These random writes are then later offloaded to SSDs or HDDs that make up the virtual disk in the pool.

- **Multitenancy.** You can configure Access Control Lists on each storage pool. This allows you to configure isolation in multi-tenant scenarios.

To add storage to a storage pool, perform the following general steps:

1. In Server Manager, navigate to the Storage Pools node under the Volumes node of the File and Storage Services workspace. In this workspace you will see available storage that hasn't been allocated in the Primordial pool as shown in Figure 7-1.

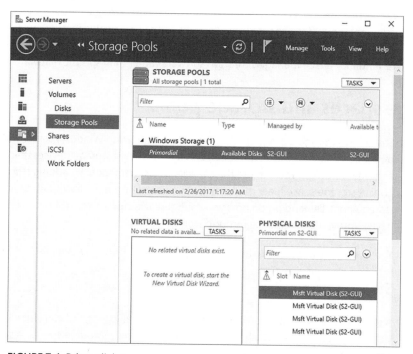

FIGURE 7-1 Primordial storage

2. On the Tasks menu, click New Storage Pool. You can also use the Tasks menu to rescan storage. You might need to use that option if you can't see the storage in the Primordial pool that you want to add to a potential storage pool.

3. On the Storage Pool Name page of the New Storage Pool Wizard, specify a name for the storage pool and select which group of available disks you want to allocate to the storage pool. By default, this will be the disks in the Primordial pool.

4. On the Physical Disks page, specify which available disks you want to add to the new pool. Figure 7-2 shows three disks being allocated using the Automatic allocation type and one disk being allocated as a Hot Spare type. Hot Spares will be swapped in if the existing disk in the storage pool fails.

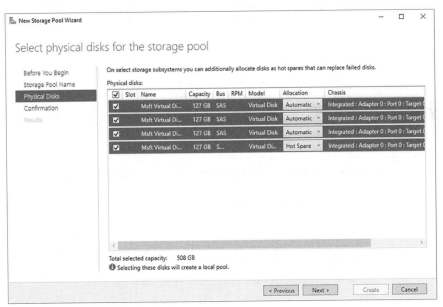

FIGURE 7-2 Adding disks

5. On the confirmation page, review your settings and click Create. When the pool is created, click Close.

You can add and remove disks from an existing storage pool. To add disks to an existing storage pool, perform the following steps:

1. In the Storage Pools node, verify that the disks that you want to add to the pool are available in the Primordial pool.

2. Right-click the storage pool where you wish to add the additional disks, and click Add Physical Disk.

3. On the Add Physical Disk dialog box, select the disks from the primordial pool that you wish to add to the existing storage pool and specify which allocation type they will use. You can choose between Automatic, Hot Spare, and Manual. Figure 7-3 shows two disks being added using the Automatic allocation type.

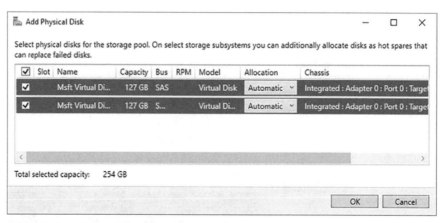

FIGURE 7-3 Adding disks to existing pool

To remove a disk from an existing storage pool, perform the following steps:

1. In the Storage Pools node, select the storage pool from which you want to remove the disk.

2. In the list of physical disks, select the disk that you want to remove. You can right-click on the disk within the pool and select the Toggle Drive Light option, shown in Figure 7-4, as a way of ensuring that you are removing the correct disk.

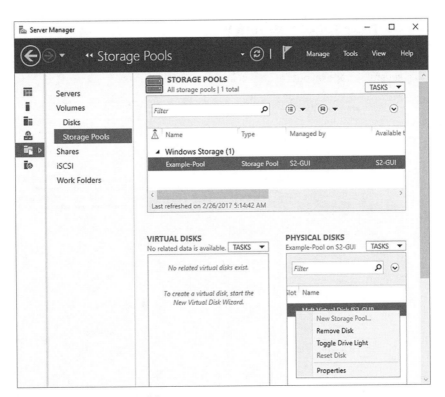

FIGURE 7-4 Toggle Drive Light

3. Once you are ready to remove the appropriate disk from the pool, right-click on the disk and then select the Remove Disk option.

4. You will be presented with a warning message that informs you that the operating system will attempt to rebuild any virtual disks that store data on the disk that you are removing from the pool. This can only happen if there are enough disks remaining in the pool to store the data that is currently stored on the physical disk removed from the pool.

MORE INFO   STORAGE SPACES

To learn more about storage spaces, consult the following link that deals with Windows Server 2012 R2, but is relevant to Windows Server 2016: *https://technet.microsoft.com/ en-us/library/hh831739(v=ws.11).aspx*

Storage space resiliency

When creating a virtual disk on a storage pool that has enough disks, you can choose between several storage layouts as shown in Figure 7-5.

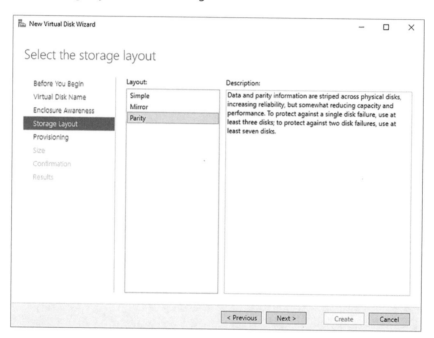

FIGURE 7-5 Storage layout

These options provide the following benefits:

- **Mirror.** Multiple copies of data are written across separate disks in the pool. This protects the virtual disk from failure of physical disks that constitute the storage pool. Mirroring can be used with storage tiering. Depending on the number of disks in the pool, Storage Spaces on Windows Server 2016 provides two way or three way mirroring. Two way mirroring writes two copies of data, and three way mirroring writes three copies of data. Three way mirroring provides better redundancy, but it also consumes more disk space.

- **Parity.** Similar to RAID 5, parity data is stored on disks in the array that is separate from where data is stored. It provides greater capacity than using the mirror option, but it has the drawback of slower write performance. Windows Server 2016 provides two types of parity: single parity and dual parity. Single parity provides protection against one failure at a time. Dual parity provides protection against two failures at a time.

- **Simple.** This option provides no resiliency for the storage, which means that if one of the disks in the storage pool fails, the data on any virtual hard disks built from that pool will also be lost.

If you configure disks in the storage pool that use the hot spare option, storage spaces will be able to automatically repair virtual disks that use the mirror or parity resiliency options. It's also possible for automatic repairs to occur if spare unallocated capacity exists within the pool.

Storage space tiering

Storage space tiering allows you to create a special type of virtual disk from pool of storage out of a combination of SSD and traditional HDD disks. Storage tiering provides the virtual disk with performance similar to that of an array built out of SSD disks, but without the cost of building a large capacity array out of SSD disks. It accomplishes this by moving frequently accessed files to faster physical disks within the pool, thus moving less frequently accessed files to slower storage media.

You can only configure storage tiers when creating a virtual disk if there is a mixture of physical disks with the HDD and the SSD disk type in the pool upon which you want to create the disk. You cannot undo storage tiering from a virtual disk once the disk is created. You configure storage tiering for a virtual disk by selecting the Create Storage tiers on this virtual disk option during virtual disk creation as shown in Figure 7-6.

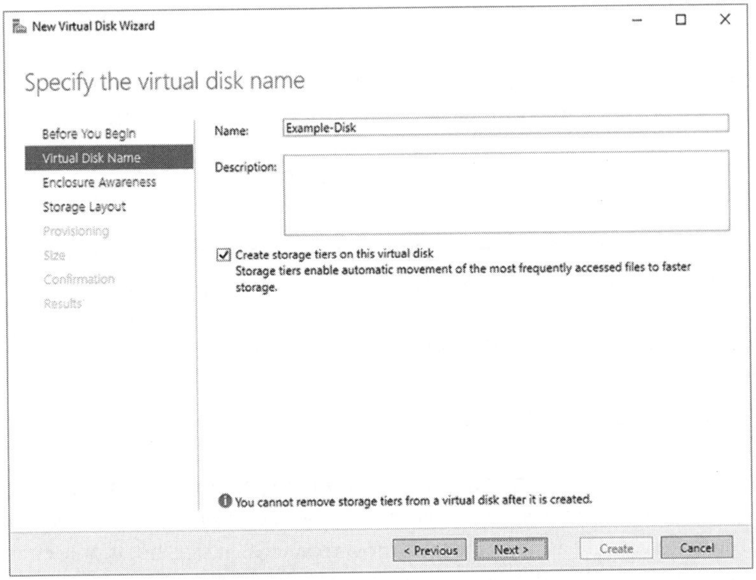

FIGURE 7-6 Enable storage tiering

One challenge when configuring storage tiering is ensuring that you have media market as SSD and HDD in the pool. While media will usually be recognized correctly, in some cases you must specify that a disk is of the SSD type, allowing storage tiering to be configured.

You can specify the disk media type using the following PowerShell procedure:

1. First determine the storage using the Get-StoragePool cmdlet.

2. To view whether physical disks are configured as SSD or HDD, use the Get-StoragePool cmdlet and then pipe that cmdlet to the Get-PhysicalDisk cmdlet as shown in Figure 7-7.

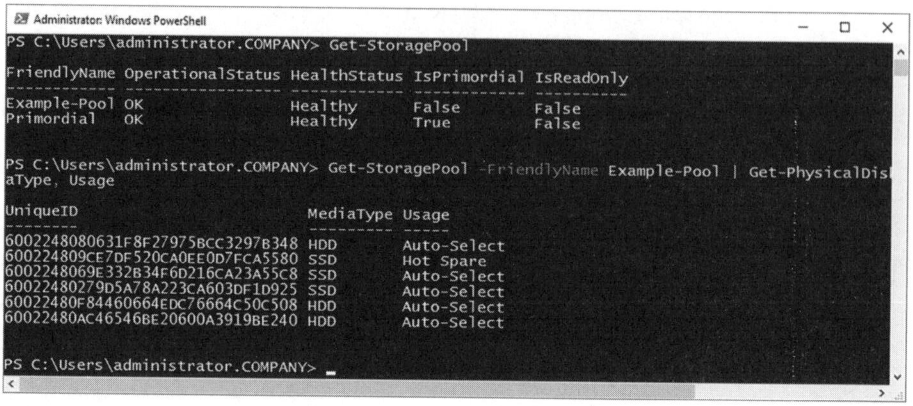

```
Administrator: Windows PowerShell                                          —   □   ×
PS C:\Users\administrator.COMPANY> Get-StoragePool

FriendlyName OperationalStatus HealthStatus IsPrimordial IsReadOnly
------------ ----------------- ------------ ------------ ----------
Example-Pool OK                Healthy      False        False
Primordial   OK                Healthy      True         False

PS C:\Users\administrator.COMPANY> Get-StoragePool -FriendlyName Example-Pool | Get-PhysicalDis
aType, Usage

UniqueID                         MediaType Usage
--------                         --------- -----
6002248080631F8F27975BCC3297B348 HDD       Auto-Select
600224809CE7DF520CA0EE0D7FCA5580 SSD       Hot Spare
60022480069E332B34F6D216CA23A55C8 SSD      Auto-Select
60022480279D5A78A223CA603DF1D925 SSD       Auto-Select
60022480F84460664EDC76664C50C508 HDD       Auto-Select
60022480AC46546BE20600A3919BE240 HDD       Auto-Select

PS C:\Users\administrator.COMPANY> _
```

FIGURE 7-7 View disk media types

3. For example, to view the identity and media type of physical disks in the storage pool, Example-Pool, issue the command:

```
Get-StoragePool -FriendlyName ExamplePool | Get-PhysicalDisk | Select UniqueID, Medi-
aType, Usage
```

4. Once you have determined the UniqueIDs of the disks that you want to configure as the SSD type, you can configure a disk to have the SSD type using the Set-PhysicalDisk cmdlet with the UniqueID parameter and the MediaType parameter set to SSD. Similarly, you can change the type back to HDD by setting the MediaType parameter to HDD.

Thin Provisioning and Trim

Thin Provisioning allows you to create virtual disks where you specify a total size for the disk, but only the space that is actually used will be allocated. For example, with thin provisioning you might create a virtual hard disk that can grow to 500 GB in size, but is only currently 10 GB in size, because only 10 GB of data is currently stored on the volumes hosted on the disk. Figure 7-8 shows where you select the provisioning type on the New Virtual Disk Wizard.

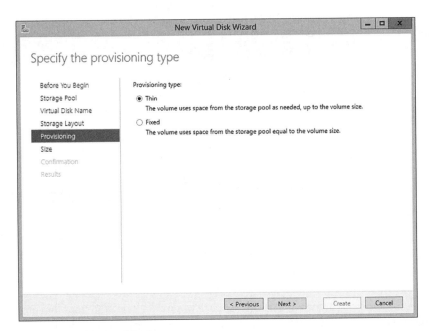

FIGURE 7-8 Thin Provisioning

You can view the amount of space that has been allocated to a thin provisioned virtual disk, as well as the total capacity in the Virtual Disks area when the Storage Pools node is selected in the Server Manager console, as shown in Figure 7-9. When you create a virtual disk, the maximum disk size available is determined by the amount of free space on the physical disks that make up the storage pool rather than the maximum capacity of the existing thin provisioned disks. For example, if you have a storage pool with two physical disks of 10 TB capacity, you can create more than two thin provisioned disks that have a maximum size of 10 TB. You can create thin provisioned disks 10 TB in size as long as the actual allocated space on the storage pool doesn't exceed 10 out of the 20 available TB. It is possible to create thin provisioned disks in such a way that the total thin provisioned disk capacity exceeds the storage capacity of the underlying storage pool. If you do over allocate space, you'll need to monitor how much of the underlying storage pool capacity is consumed and add disks to the storage pool, because that capacity is exhausted.

FIGURE 7-9 Capacity and allocation

Trim is an automatic process that reclaims space when data is deleted from thin provisioned disks. For example, if you have a 10 TB thin provisioned virtual disk that stores 8 TB of data, 8 TB will be allocated from the storage pool that hosts that virtual disk. If you delete 2 TB of data from that thin provisioned virtual disk, Trim ensures that the storage pool that hosts that virtual disk will be able to reclaim that unused space. The 10 TB thin provisioned virtual disk will appear to be 10 TB in size, but after the trim process is complete, it will only consume 6 TB of space on the underlying storage pool. Trim is enabled by default.

> **MORE INFO**   **THIN PROVISIONING AND TRIM STORAGE**
>
> To learn more about thin provisioning and trim storage consult the following link: *http://technet.microsoft.com/en-us/library/hh831391.aspx.*

Creating virtual disks

A storage space virtual disk is comprised from capacity available in the storage pool. As long as there is available capacity, you can create multiple virtual disks from a single storage pool. To create a new virtual disk using an existing storage pool, perform the following steps:

1. In Server Manager, navigate to the Storage Pools node under the Volumes node of the File and Storage Services workspace. In the Tasks menu of the Virtual Disks area, select New Virtual Disk.

2. On the list of available storage pools, shown in Figure 7-10, select an available storage pool upon which to create a new virtual disk and click OK.

FIGURE 7-10 Select storage pool

3. On the Enclosure Awareness page, select whether or not you want to enable enclosure awareness. Doing so will mean that copies of data are stored across separate storage enclosures. For enclosure awareness to work, you'll need multiple enclosures to host the disks that make up the storage pool.

4. On the Storage Layout page you will be presented with the available layout options. Depending on the type and number of disks, you can choose between Simple, Mirror, and Parity.

5. On the Provisioning Type page, you can choose between thin and fixed provisioning.

6. On the Size page, shown in Figure 7-11, you can choose a size for the disk. If you choose the thin provisioning option, the maximum amount of space in the storage pool is not listed. If you choose the fixed option, the total amount of storage currently available in the pool is listed.

CHAPTER 07

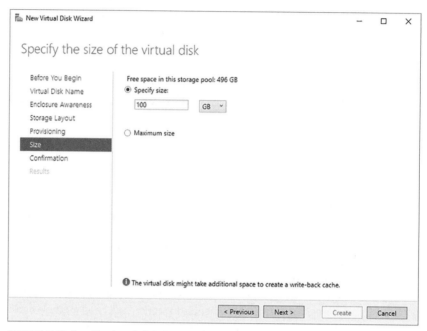

FIGURE 7-11 Specify virtual disk size

7. On the Confirmation page verify that the settings match what you intend and click Create.

Storage Spaces Direct

Storage Spaces Direct provides a form of distributed, software-defined shared-nothing storage that has similar characteristics to RAID in terms of performance and redundancy. It allows you to create volumes from a storage pool of physical drives that are attached to multiple nodes that participate in a Windows Server 2016 failover cluster.

Storage Spaces Direct has the following properties:

- You can scale out by adding additional nodes to the cluster.

- When you add a node to a cluster configured for Storage Spaces Direct, all eligible drives on the cluster node will be added to the Storage Spaces Direct pool.

- You can have between 2 nodes and 16 nodes in a Storage Spaces Direct failover cluster.

- It requires each node to have at least 2 solid state drives and at least 4 additional drives.

- A cluster can have over 400 drives and can support over 3 petabytes of storage.

- Storage spaces direct works with locally attached SATA, SAS, or NVMe drives.

- Cache is automatically built from SSD media. All writes up to 256KB, and all reads up to 64KB, will be cached. Writes are then de-staged to HDD storage in optimal order.

- Storage Spaces Direct volumes can be part mirror and part parity. To have a three-way mirror with dual parity, it is necessary to have four nodes in the Windows Server 2016 failover cluster that hosts Storage Spaces Direct.

- If a disk fails, the plug-and-play replacement will automatically be added to the storage spaces pool when connected to the original cluster node.

- A storage spaces direct cluster can be configured with rack and chassis awareness as a way of further ensuring fault tolerance.

Storage Spaces Direct is designed to function as a replacement for expensive large scale hardware storage arrays. Storage Spaces Direct is related to the technology used in Azure data centers. Azure uses software defined storage rather than vendor specific high performance storage solutions.

MORE INFO   STORAGE SPACES DIRECT

To learn more about storage spaces direct, consult the following link: *https:// technet.microsoft.com/en-us/windows-server-docs/storage/storage-spaces/ storage-spaces-direct-overview.*

Storage Replica

Storage Replica allows you to replicate volumes between servers, including clusters, for the purposes of disaster recovery. You can also use storage replica to configure asynchronous replication to provision failover clusters that span two geographically disparate sites, while all nodes remain synchronized.

You can configure Storage Replica to support the following types of replication:

- **Synchronous replication.** Use this when you want to mirror data and you have very low latency between source and destination. This allows you to create crash-consistent volumes. Synchronous replication ensures zero data loss at the file system level should a failure occur.

- **Asynchronous replication.** Asynchronous storage replica is suitable when you want to replicate storage across sites where you are experiencing higher latencies.

Storage Replica is available only in Windows Server 2016 datacenter edition and is not available in the standard edition of the operating system. Participant servers must be members of the same Active Directory Domain Services Forest.

Storage Replica operates at the partition layer. This means that it replicates all VSS snapshots created by the Windows Server operating system or by backup software that leverages VSS snapshot functionality. Storage Replica may work as a solution for organizations that are currently using DFS Replication as a disaster recovery solution to move data offsite.

Storage replica has the following features:

- **Zero data loss, block-level replication.** When used with synchronous replication, there is no data loss. By leveraging block-level replication, even files that are locked will be replicated at the block level.

- **Guest and host.** Storage Replica works when Windows Server 2016 datacenter edition is a virtualized guest or when it functions as a host operating system. It is possible to replicate from third party virtualization solutions to IaaS virtual machines hosted in the public cloud as long as Windows Server 2016 functions as the source and target operating system.

- **Supports manual failover with zero data loss.** You can perform manual failover when both source and destination are online, or have failover occur automatically if the source storage fails.

- **Leverage SMB3.** This allows Storage Replica to use multichannel, SMB direct support on RoCE, iWARP, and InfiniBand RDMA network cards.

- **Encryption and authentication support.** Storage Replica supports packet signing, AES-128-GCM full data encryption, support for Intel AES-NI encryption acceleration, and Kerberos AES 256 authentication.

- **Initial seeding.** You can perform initial seeding by transferring data using a method other than storage replica between source and destination. This is especially useful when transferring large amounts of data between disparate sites where it may make more sense to use a courier to transport a high capacity hard disk drive than it does to transmit data across a WAN link. The initial replication will then only copy any blocks that have been changed since the replica data was exported from source to destination.

- **Consistency groups.** Consistency groups implement write ordering guarantees. This ensures that applications such as Microsoft SQL Server, which may write data to multiple replicated volumes, will have that data replicated in such a way so that it remains replicated sequentially in consistent way.

Supported configurations

Storage replica is supported in the following configurations:

- **Server to Server.** In this configuration, storage replica supports both synchronous and asynchronous replication between two standalone services. Local drives, storage spaces with shared SAS storage, SAN, and iSCSI-attached LUNs can be replicated. You can manage this configuration either using Server Manager or PowerShell. Failover can only be performed manually.

- **Cluster to Cluster.** In this configuration, replication occurs between two separate clusters. The first cluster might use Storage Spaces Direct, Storage Spaces with shared SAS storage, SAN, and iSCSI-attached LUNs. You manage this configuration using PowerShell and Azure Site Recovery. Failover must be performed manually.

- **Stretch Cluster.** A single cluster where nodes are located in geographically disparate sites. Some nodes share on set of asymmetric storage and other nodes share another set of asymmetric storage. Storage is replicated either synchronously or asynchronously depending on bandwidth considerations. This scenario supports Storage Spaces with shared SAS storage, SAN and iSCSI-attached LUNs. You manage this configuration using PowerShell and the Failover Cluster Manager GUI tool. This scenario allows for automated failover.

The following configurations are not supported on Windows Server 2016, though they may be supported at some point in future:

- Storage Replica only supports one-to-one replication in Windows Server 2016. You cannot configure Storage Replica to support one-to-many replication or transitive replication. Transitive replication is where there is a replica of the replica server.

- Storage Replica on Windows Server 2016 does not support bringing a replicated volume online for read-only access.

- Deploying Scale-out File Servers on stretch clusters participating in Storage Replica is not a supported configuration.

- Deploying Storage Spaces Direct in a stretch cluster with storage replica is not supported.

Configuring replication

To configure replication between two servers running Windows Server 2016 Datacenter edition that are members of the same domain, perform the following steps:

1. Ensure that each server meets the following requirements:

●   Has two volumes, one volume hosts the data that you want to replicate, the other that hosts the replication logs.

●   Ensure that both log and data disks are formatted as GPT and not MBR.

●   Data volume on source and destination server must be the same size and use the same sector sizes.

●   Log volume on source and destination volume should be the same size and use the same sector sizes. The log volume should be a minimum of 9 GB in size.

●   Ensure that the data volume does not contain the system volume, page file, or dump files.

●   Install the File Server role service and Storage Replica feature on each server as shown in Figure 7-12. Installing these features requires that you restart the computer.

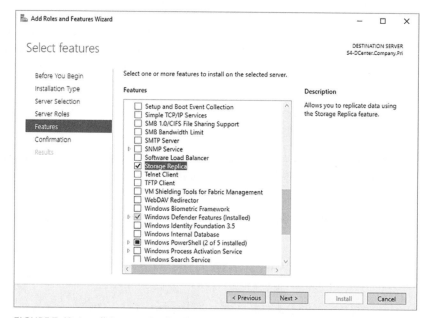

FIGURE 7-12 Install Storage Replica feature

2. Use the Test-SRTopology cmdlet to verify that all Storage Replica requirements have been met. To do this, perform the following steps:

●   Create a temp directory on the source server that will store the Storage Replica Topology Report.

- Make a note of the drive letters of the source storage and log volumes and destination storage and log volumes.

- The following command will test Storage Topology for a source computer named S3-DCenter with the source volume of E: and the log volume of F: to a destination computer named S4-DCenter with the destination volume of E: and destination log volume of F: for 15 minutes, writing the results to the c:\temp folder.

```
Test-SRTopology -SourceComputerName  S3-DCenter -SourceVolumeName e: -SourceLogVolu-
meName f: -DestinationComputerName S4-DCenter -DestinationVolumeName e: -Destination-
LogVolumeName f: -DurationInMinutes 15 -ResultPath c:\temp
```

When the test completes, view the TestSrTopologyReport.html file to verify that your configuration meets Storage Replica requirements. Once you have verified that the configuration does meet requirements, as shown in Figure 7-13, you can use the New-SRPartnerShip cmdlet to create a storage replica partnership.

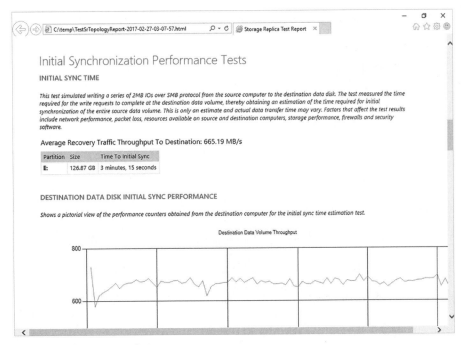

FIGURE 7-13 Storage replica test

For example, the following command will configure Storage Replica group named SR71 for a source computer named S3-DCenter with the source volume of E: and the log volume of F: to a destination computer named S4-DCenter with the destination volume of E: and destination log volume of F:

```
New-SRPartnerShip -SourceRGName SR71 -DestinationRGName SR72 -SourceComputerName
S3-DCenter -SourceVolumeName e: -SourceLogVolumeName f: -DestinationComputerName
S4-DCenter -DestinationVolumeName e: -DestinationLogVolumeName f:
```

You can check the status of Storage Replica replication by running the Get-SRGroup, Get-SRPartnership, and (Get-SRGroup).replicas cmdlets. Once Storage Replica is active, you won't be able to access the replica storage device on the destination computer unless you reverse replication or remove replication.

To switch direction, use the Set-SRPartnerShip cmdlet. For example, to reverse the replication direction of the Storage Replica partnership configured above, use the following command:

```
Set-SRPartnerShip -NewSourceComputerName S4-DCenter -SourceRGName SR72
-DestinationComputerName S3-DCenter -DestinationRGName SR71
```

When you run this command, you will receive a warning that data loss may occur and whether or not you want to complete the operation.

To remove replication, run the following commands on the source node:

```
Get-SRPartnership | Remove-SRPartnership
```

```
Get-SRGroup | Remove-SRGroup
```

Then run the following command on the destination node:

```
Get-SRGroup | Remove-SRGroup
```

By default, all replication when Storage Replica is configured is synchronous. You can switch between synchronous and asynchronous replication using the Set-SRPartnership cmdlet with the ReplicationMode parameter.

Storage Replica uses the following ports:

- **445.** Used for SMB, which is the replication transport protocol.

- **5895.** Used for WSManHTTP. This is the management protocol for WMI/CIM/PowerShell.

- **5445.** iWARP SMB. This port is only required if using iWARP RDMA networking.

MORE INFO   STORAGE REPLICA

To learn more about storage replica, consult the following link: *https://technet.microsoft.com/en-us/windows-server-docs/storage/storage-replica/storage-replica-overview.*

SMB 3.1.1

Windows Server 2016 uses SMB (Server Message Block) 3.1.1. SMB 3.1.1 contains substantial security and performance improvements over previous versions of the SMB protocol. You can determine which version of SMB a server is using by running the Get-SmbConnection cmdlet, as shown in Figure 7-14.

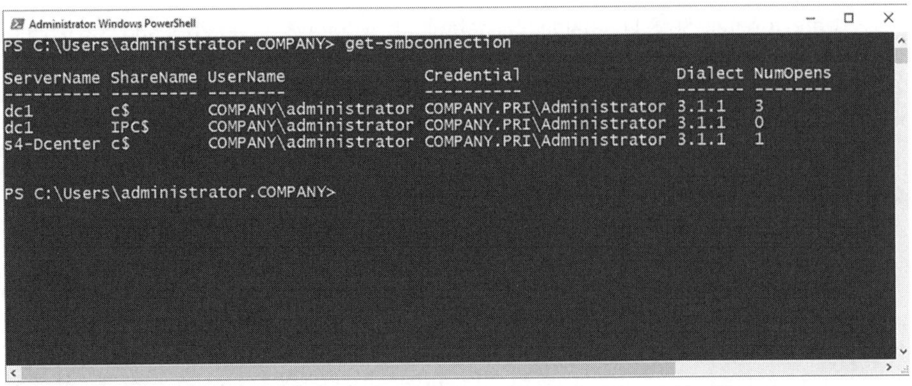

FIGURE 7-14 Storage replica test

The version of SMB that is used depends on the operating system of the client. As newer versions of SMB perform much better and are much more secure than older versions, updating clients and server operating systems to the most recent version ensures that you are running the fastest and most Table 7-1 lists which version of SMB is used when clients or servers communicate with one another.

Table 7-1. Protocol negotiation

OS	Win 10 / WS 2016	Win 8.1 / WS 2012 R2	Win 8 / WS 2012	Win 7 / WS 2008 R2	Win Vista / WS 2008	Older versions
Win 10 / WS 2016	SMB 3.1.1	SMB 3.0.2	SMB 3.0	SMB 2.1	SMB 2.0.2	SMB 1.x
Win 8.1 / WS 2012 R2	SMB 3.0.2	SMB 3.0.2	SMB 3.0	SMB 2.1	SMB 2.0.2	SMB 1.x
Win 8 / WS 2012	SMB 3.0	SMB 3.0	SMB 3.0	SMB 2.1	SMB 2.0.2	SMB 1.x
Win 7 / WS 2008 R2	SMB 2.1	SMB 2.1	SMB 2.1	SMB 2.1	SMB 2.0.2	SMB 1.x
Win Vista / WS 2008	SMB 2.0.2	SMB 2.0.2	SMB 2.0.2	SMB 2.0.2	SMB 2.0.2	SMB 1.x
Older versions	SMB 1.x	SMB 1.x	SMB 1.x	SMB 1.x	SMB 1.x	SMB 1.x

SMB 1 is an old protocol that doesn't include key protections available in later versions of SMB, including pre-authentication integrity, secure dialect negotiation, encryption, insecure guest authentication blocking, and improved message signing. SMB1 is less efficient than version SMB 3 or later, with SMB 3 supporting larger read and writes, peer caching of folder and file properties, durable handles, client oplock leasing model, SMB direct, and directory leasing. SMB 1 is only necessary if your organization is running Windows XP or Windows Server 2003, which at the time of writing, are older than kids that are currently half way through high school.

Unfortunately SMB 1 is enabled by default on Windows Server 2016 and you'll need to configure the operating system so that it is not present. If you are worried that you do have applications on the network that use SMB 1, you can audit SMB 1 utilization by running the command on any file server that has SMB 1 enabled and check the SMBServer\Audit event log:

```
Set-SmbServerConfiguration -AuditSmb1Access $true
```

To remove SMB 1 from a computer running Windows Server 2016, run the following command:

```
Remove-WindowsFeature -Name FS-SMB1
```

MORE INFO   DON'T USE SMB 1

To learn more about why you shouldn't use SMB 1, consult the following link: *https://blogs.technet.microsoft.com/filecab/2016/09/16/stop-using-smb1/.*

iSCSI

iSCSI allows access to storage devices across a TCP/IP network. The iSCSI initiator is a special software component that allows connections to iSCSI targets, which is a storage device that an iSCSI initiator connects to over the network. When you install the iSCSI Target Server role service on a computer running the Windows Server 2016 operating system, you can configure virtual hard disk as iSCSI targets. When an iSCSI initiator connects to this virtual hard disk, it appears on the client as a local disk. While you can use iSCSI targets as local storage, you can also use an iSCSI connected disk as shared storage in failover clusters.

The iSCSI Initiator component is installed by default on all computers running Windows Vista and later client operating systems, Windows Server 2008, and later server operating systems. When you select the iSCSI Initiator for the first time in the Tools menu of the Server Manager console, it will prompt you to have the service start and to have the service be configured to start automatically in the future. Once the service is started, you can configure the iSCSI initiator on the iSCSI Initiator Properties dialog box, which is available when you select the iSCSI Initiator in the Tools menu of the Server Manager console. In most cases the configuration involves entering the FQDN of the server that hosts the iSCSI target in the Target text box and clicking Quick Connect. The iSCSI Initiator Properties dialog box is shown in Figure 7-15.

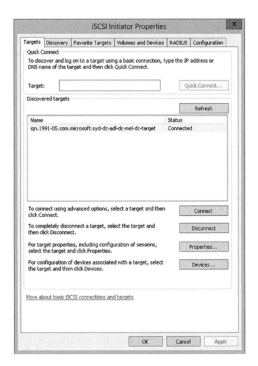

FIGURE 7-15 iSCSI Initiator Properties

You can only connect to an iSCSI target that has been configured to accept connections from the iSCSI initiator you are attempting to connect with. When creating an iSCSI target, you specify which iSCSI initiators can access the target, as shown in Figure 7-16. You can specify initiators on the basis of IQN, DNS Name, IP Address or MAC address.

CHAPTER 07

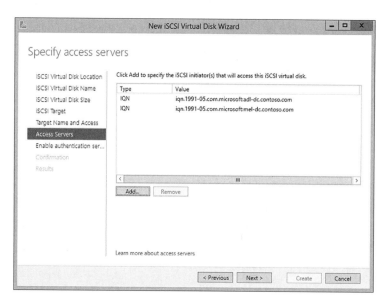

FIGURE 7-16 Configuring access servers

If the initiator is running on a domain joined computer that has the Windows 8, Windows Server 2012, or later operating systems, you can query Active Directory to determine the initiator ID as shown in Figure 7-17. When configuring an initiator ID for a client running a Microsoft operating system, the format is iqn.1991-05.com.microsoft:FQDN. For example, if specifying the initiator ID of cbr.contoso.com, you would use iqn.199-05.com.microsoft:cbr.contoso.com.

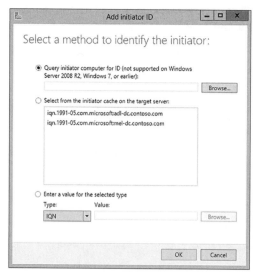

FIGURE 7-17 Identify the initiator

You can create a new iSCSI virtual disk using the New-IscsiVirtualDisk cmdlet. For example, to create a new 10GB iSCSI virtual disk that has the path E:\Disks\Disk1.vhd, you can use the command:

```
New-IscsiVirtualDisk -Path "e:\disks\disk1.vhd" -Size 10GB
```

MORE INFO   ISCSI TARGET

To learn more about iSCSI Target consult the following link: *http://technet.microsoft. com/en-us/library/hh848272.aspx.*

You can use the New-IscsiServerTarget cmdlet to create an iSCSI server target. For example, to configure an iSCSI target that allows computers syd-a.contoso.com and syd-b.contoso.com to access an iSCSI virtual disk, you can use the command:

```
New-IscsiServerTarget -Targetname "Syd-A-Syd-B-Target" -InitiatorIDs DNSName:Syd-a.con-
toso.com,DNSName:syd-b.contoso.com
```

iSNS Server

The iSNS Server role allows you to centralize the discovery of iSCSI initiators and targets. Rather than having to enter the address of a server that hosts an iSCSI target when configuring the iSCSI initiator, the iSNS server provides a list of available targets. You can use the iSNS server with both Microsoft and 3rd party iSCSI initiators and targets. Figure 7-18 shows the iSNS Server Properties dialog box and the addresses of two initiators that have registered with iSNS. Discovery domains allow you to partition initiators and targets into more manageable groups and are useful if your organization uses iSCSI extensively.

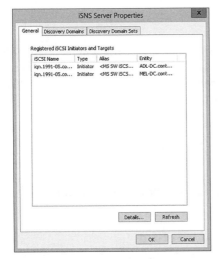

FIGURE 7-18 List of initiators

You can register an iSCSI Initiator running on Windows Server 2012 with an iSNS server through the Discovery tab of the iSCSI Initiators Properties dialog box, shown in Figure 7-19. Using an iSNS server to locate initiators is useful when you have iSCSI initiators running on Windows 7 or Windows Server 2008 R2 and operating systems. With clients running Windows 8 and Windows Server 2012 and later operating systems, you can locate iSCSI IDs through Active Directory.

FIGURE 7-19 Configure iSNS server

Windows Server 2016 does not support registering iSCSI targets through the GUI. You can register an iSCSI Targets associated with a virtual disk with an iSNS server using Windows PowerShell. To register all the iSCSI targets hosted on a computer running Windows Server 2016 with an iSNS server, use the following command:

```
Set-WmiInstance -Namespace root\wmi -Class WT_iSNSServer -Arguments @
{ServerName="ISNSservername"}
```

MORE INFO   ISNS SERVER

To learn more about the iSNS server role consult the following link: *http://technet.micro-soft.com/en-us/library/cc772568.aspx*

Scale Out File Servers

A Scale-Out File Server (SoFS) allows you to share a single folder from multiple nodes of the same cluster. You can use SoFS to deploy file shares that are continuously available for file-based server application storage. This storage is suitable for hosting Hyper-V virtual machine files or Microsoft SQL Server databases with a level of reliability, availability, manageability and performance that equates to what is possible with a storage area network.

Benefits of an SoFS deployment include:

- **Active-Active file share topology.** SoFS allows the same folder to be accessed from multiple nodes of the same cluster. An SoFS file share remains online should one or more cluster nodes fail or be taken down for planned maintenance.

- **Scalable bandwidth.** You can respond to a requirement for increased bandwidth by adding nodes.

- **Automatic rebalancing of clients.** SMB client connects are tracked on a per file share basis, with clients being redirected to the cluster node that has the best access to the storage device used by the file share.

You should consider SoFS file shares for the following scenarios:

- Use SoFS to store shared IIS configuration data.

- Store Hyper-V configuration and live virtual disks.

- Store live SQL Server database files.

While SoFS is suitable for workloads such as Hyper-V VMs and SQL Server Databases, it is not suitable for workloads that generate substantial number of metadata operations. Metadata operations involve opening files, closing files, creating new files, or renaming existing files. So while the name Scale Out File Server does include the words File Server, you wouldn't actually deploy this technology as a traditional departmental file server.

SoFS has the following requirements:

- Storage configuration must be explicitly supported by failover clustering. This means that you must be able to successfully run the Cluster Validation Wizard prior to adding a SoFS.

- SoFS requires Cluster Shared Volumes.

- SoFS does not support ReFS.

MORE INFO   SOFS

To learn more about SoFS consult the following link: *https://technet.microsoft.com/ en-us/library/hh831349(v=ws.11).aspx.*

NFS

Server for NFS Data Store allows clients that use the Network File System (NFS) protocol to access data stored on computers running Windows Server 2016. NFS is primarily used by UNIX and Linux clients, but it is also used by some third party hypervisors. You can configure Server for NFS to leverage Windows-to-UNIX user mappings from Active Directory Domain Services, User Name Mapping, or Both. Identity Management for UNIX can also be deployed to update the Active Directory schema to support UNIX user account data.

Server for NFS Data Store supports continuous availability when deployed on a Windows Server 2016 failover cluster. Once installed, you configure Server for NFS, by editing the properties of the Server For NFS node of the Services For Network File System tool. This dialog box is shown in Figure 7-20.

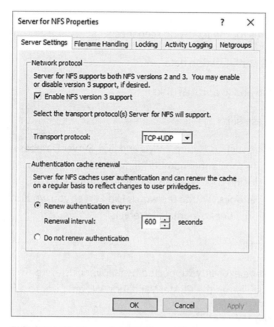

FIGURE 7-20 Server for NFS Properties

You can use this dialog box to configure the following:

- Support for NFS version 3

- Transport protocol (TCP/UPD, TCP, or UDP)

- Authentication cache renewal

- Filename translation (for file characters supported by NFS but NTFS does not)

- File locking wait period

- Activity Logging

- Netgroups for managing access to NFS shares

Even though the Server for NFS dialog box mentions NSF versions 2 and 3, Server for NFS in Windows Server 2016 also includes support for NFS version 4.1. There is also support in the NFS server implementation of Windows Server 2016 for Pseudo file system, sessions and session trunking, and compound RPCs.

MORE INFO   SERVER FOR NFS DATA STORE

To learn more about Server for NFS Data Store consult the following link: *https://technet. microsoft.com/en-us/library/jj592688(v=ws.11).aspx.*

Deduplication

A chunk is a collection of storage blocks. Deduplication works by analyzing files, locating the unique chunks of data that make up those files, and only storing one copy of each unique data chunk on the volume. Deduplication is able to reduce the amount of storage consumed on the volume because when analyzed, it turns out that a substantial number of data chunks stored on a volume are identical. Rather than store multiple copies of the same identical chunk, deduplication ensures that one copy of the chunk is stored with placeholders in other locations pointing at the single copy of the chunk, rather than storing the chunk itself.

Before you can enable deduplication, you need to install the Data Deduplication role service as shown in Figure 7-21.

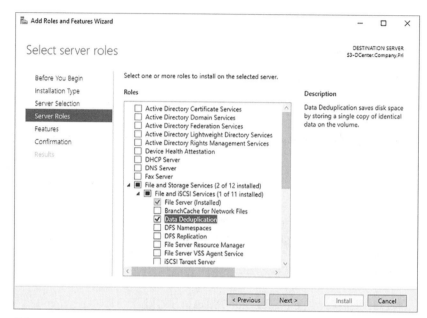

FIGURE 7-21 Enable deduplication

When you configure deduplication, you choose from one of the following usage types as shown in Figure 7-22:

- **General Purpose File Server.** Appropriate for general purpose file servers, optimization is performed on the background on any file that is older than 3 days. Files that are in use are not optimized and neither are partial files.

- **Virtual Desktop Infrastructure (VDI) server.** Appropriate for VDI servers, optimization is performed in the background on any file that is older than 3 days, but files that are in use and partial files will also be optimized.

- **Virtualized Backup Server.** Suitable for backup applications such as System Center Data Protection Manager. Performs priority optimization on files of any age. Will optimize in-use files, but will not optimize partial files.

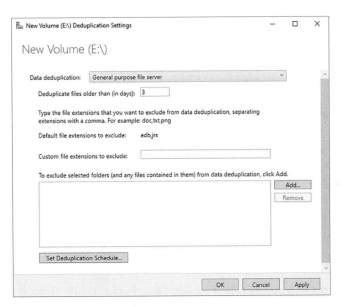

FIGURE 7-22 Deduplication settings

When configuring deduplication settings, you can configure files to be excluded on the basis of file extension or exclude entire folders from data deduplication. Deduplication involves running a series of jobs outlined in Table 7-2.

Table 7-2. Deduplication jobs

Name	Description	Schedule
Optimization	Deduplicates and optimizes the volume	Once per hour
Garbage collection	Reclaims disk space by removing unnecessary chunks. You may want to run this job manually after deleting a substantial amount of data in an attempt to reclaim space by using the Start-DedupeJob cmdlet with the Type parameter set to GarbageCollection	Every Saturday at 2:35 AM
Integrity scrubbing	Identifies corruption in the chunk store and uses volume features where possible to repair and reconstruct corrupted data	Every Saturday at 3.35 AM
Unoptimization	A special job that you run manually when you want to disable deduplication for a volume	Run manually

MORE INFO   DEDUPLICATION

To learn more about Deduplication consult the following link: *https://technet.microsoft. com/en-us/windows-server-docs/storage/data-deduplication/overview.*

Storage Quality of Service

Storage Quality of Service (QoS) allows you to centrally manage and monitor the performance of storage used for virtual machines that leverage the Scale-Out File Server and Hyper-V roles. The Storage QoS feature will automatically ensure that access to storage resources is distributed equitably between virtual machines that use the same file server cluster. It allows you to configure minimum and maximum performance settings as policies in units of IOPS.

Storage QoS allows you to accomplish the following goals:

- **Reduce the impact of noisy neighbor VMs.** A noisy neighbor VM is a virtual machine that is consuming a disproportionate amount of storage resources. Storage QoS allows you to limit the extent to which such a VM can consume storage bandwidth.

- **Monitor storage performance.** When you deploy a virtual machine to a scale-out file server, you can review storage performance from a central location.

- **Allocate minimum and maximum available resources.** Through Storage QoS policies, you can specify a minimum and maximum resources available. This allows you to ensure that each VM has the minimum storage performance it requires to run reserved for it.

There are two types of Storage QoS policy:

- **Aggregated.** An aggregated policy applies maximum and minimum values for a combined set of virtual hard disk files and virtual machines. For example, creating an aggregated policy with a minimum of 150 IOPS and a maximum of 250 IOPS and applying it to three virtual hard disk files, you can ensure that the three virtual hard disk files will have a minimum of 150 IOPS between them when the system was under load and would consume a maximum of 250 IOPs when the virtual machines associated with those hard disks were heavily using storage.

- **Dedicated.** A dedicated policy applies a minimum and maximum value to each individual virtual hard disk. For example, if you apply a dedicated policy to each of three virtual hard disks that specify a minimum of 150 IOPS and a maximum of 250 IOPS, each virtual hard disk will individually be able to use up to 250 IOPS while having a minimum of 150 IOPS reserved for use if the system was under pressure.

You create policies with the New-StorageQosPolicy cmdlet, specifying using the Policy-Type parameter if the policy is Dedicated or Aggregated, what the minimum IOPS are, and what the maximum IOPS are. For example, to create a new policy called Alpha of the dedicated type that has a minimum of 150 IOPS and a maximum of 250 IOPS, run this command:

```
New-StorageQosPolicy -Name Alpha -PolicyType Dedicated -MinimumIops 150 -MaximumIops 250
```

Once you've created a policy, you can apply it to a virtual hard disk using the Set-VMHardDisk-Drive cmdlet.

MORE INFO   STORAGE QUALITY OF SERVICE

To learn more about Storage QoS consult the following link: *https://technet.microsoft.com/en-us/windows-server-docs/storage/storage-qos/storage-qos-overview Storage Replica.*

ReFS

ReFS (Resilient File System) is a new file system that is available in Windows Server 2012, Windows Server 2012 R2, and Windows Server 2016. ReFS is appropriate for very large workloads where you need to maximize data availability and integrity and ensure that the file system is resilient to corruption.

The ReFS file system is suitable for hosting specific types of workloads such as virtual machines and SQL Server data, because it includes the following features that improve upon NTFS:

- **Integrity.** ReFS uses checksums for both metadata and file data. This means that ReFS can detect data corruption.

- **Storage space integration.** When integrated with storage spaces that are configured with mirror or parity options, ReFS has the ability to automatically detect and repair corruption using a secondary or tertiary copy of data stored by Storage Spaces. Repair occurs without downtime.

- **Proactive error correction.** ReFS includes a data integrity scanner that scans the volume to identify latent corruption and proactively repair corrupt data.

- **Scalability.** ReFS is specifically designed to support data sets in the millions of terabytes range.

- **Advanced VM operations.** ReFS includes functionality specifically to support virtual machine operations. Block cloning accelerates copy operations, which accelerate VM checkpoint merges. Sparse VDL allows ReFS to substantially reduce the amount of time required to create very large fixed sized virtual hard disks.

It is important to note that ReFS is suitable only for hosting specific types of workloads. It isn't suitable for many workloads used in small and medium enterprises that aren't hosting large VMs or huge SQL Server databases. You won't choose to deploy ReFS for a file server because it doesn't support functionality such as File Server Resource Manager, file compression, file encryption, extended attributes, deduplication, and quotas.

You configure ReFS as an option when formatting or creating a volume as shown in Figure 7-23.

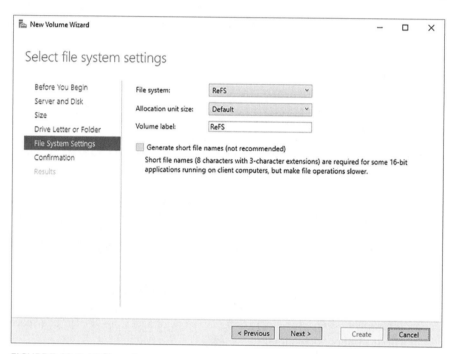

FIGURE 7-23 ReFS file system

MORE INFO   RESILIENT FILE SYSTEM

To learn more about ReFS consult the following link: *https://technet.microsoft.com/ en-us/windows-server-docs/storage/refs/refs-overview.*

Storage related PowerShell cmdlets

There are a number of different modules that contain cmdlets that are relevant to storage services. These are listed over the coming pages.

Deduplication

Table 7-3 lists the PowerShell cmdlets in the deduplication module.

Table 7-3. Deduplication module cmdlets

Noun	Verbs	Function
Dedupfile	Expand	Expand a deduplicated file or directory
DedupFileMetadata	Measure	View file deduplication information
DedupJob	Stop, Get, Start	Manage deduplication jobs
DedupMetadata	Get	View deduplication metadata
DedupSchedule	New, Remove, Get, Set	Configure deduplication schedule
DedupStatus	Update, Get	View deduplication status
DedupVolume	Disable, Enable, Get, Set	Configure deduplication for a volume

iSCSI

Table 7-4 lists the PowerShell cmdlets in the iSCSI module.

Table 7-4. iSCSI module cmdlets

Noun	Verbs	Function
iSCSIChapSecret	Set	Configure iSCSI secret
iSCSIConnection	Get	View iSCSI connection
iSCSISession	Unregister, Register, Get	Configure iSCSI session
iSCSITarget	Connect, Update, Disconnect, Get	Manage iSCSI Target
iSCSITargetPortal	Update, Get, New, Remove	Configure iSCSI Target Portal

iSCSITarget

Table 7-5 lists the PowerShell cmdlets in the iSCSI Target module.

CHAPTER 07

Table 7-5. iSCSI Target module cmdlets

Noun	Verbs	Function
iSCSIServerTarget	Get, Remove, New, Set	Manage iSCSI Server Target
iSCSITargetServerConfiguration	Import, Export	Backup and recover iSCSI target server configuration
iSCSITargetServerSetting	Set, Get	View and manage iSCSI target server setting
iSCSIVirtualDisk	Import, New, Remove, Restore, Convert, Check-point, Set, Get, Resize	Manate iSCSI virtual disks
iSCSIVirtualDiskOperation	Stop	Stop iSCSI virtual disk operation
iSCSIVirtualDiskSnapshot	Set, Export, Dismount, Mount, Get, Remove	Configure iSCSI virtual disk snapshots
iSCSIVirtualDiskTargetMapping	Add, Remove, Expand	Manage iSCSI virtual disk target mapping

NFS

Table 7-6 lists the PowerShell cmdlets in the NFS module.

Table 7-6. NFS module cmdlets

Noun	Verbs	Function
NFSClientConfiguration	Get, Set	View and configure NFS client settings
NFSClientGroup	Remove, Rename, Set, Get, New	Manage NFS client groups
NFSClientLock	Get, Remove	Manage NFS client locks
NFSMappedIdentity	Set, Test, Remove, New, Get, Resolve	Configure NFS mapped identities
NfsMappingStore	Revoke, Get	Configure NFS mapping store
NfsNetgroup	Remove, Get, Set, New	Configure NFS net groups
NfsNetgroupStore	Set, Get	Configure NFS net group store
NfsOpenFile	Revoke, Get	Manage NDF open files
NfsServerConfiguration	Get, Set	Manage NFS server configuration
NfsSession	Get, Disconnect	Manage NFS sessions
NfsShare	Remove, Get, Set, New	Configure NFS shares
NfsSharePermission	Get, Revoke, Grant	Manage NFS share permissions
NfsStatistics	Reset, Get	View and reset NFS statistics

Storage

Table 7-7 lists the PowerShell cmdlets in the X module.

Table 7-7. Storage module cmdlets

Noun	Verbs	Function
DedupProperties	Get	View deduplication properties
Disk	Clear, Initialize, Get, Set, Update	Configure disk
DiskImage	Mount, Get, Dismount	Mount, dismount, and view disk image
DiskStorageNodeView	Get	View disk storage node view
FileIntegrity	Set, Repair, Get	Manage file integrity
FileShare	Get, Remove, Debug, Set, New	Manage file shares
FileShareAccess	Revoke, Grant, Block, Unblock	Manage file share access
FileShareAccessControlEntry	Get	View file share access control entries
FileStorageTier	Clear, Set, Get	Configure and view file storage tiers
HostStorageCache	Update	Update host storage cache
InitiatorID	Remove, Get	View and remove initiator ID
InitiatorIdFromMaskingSet	Remove	Remove initiator ID from masking set
InitiatorIDToMaskingSet	Add	Add initiator ID to masking set
InitiatorPort	Set, Get	View and configure initiator port
MaskingSet	Get, Remove, New, Rename	Manage masking set
OffloadDataTransferSetting	Get	View offload data transfer setting
Partition	Resize, New, Get, Remove, Set	Manage partitions
PartitionAccessPath	Remove, Add	Manage partition access paths
PartitionSupportSize	Get	View partition support size

CHAPTER 07

PhysicalDisk	Add, Set, Remove, Reset, Get	Manage physical disks
PhysicalDiskIdentification	Enable, Disable	Enable or disable physical disk identification
PhysicalDiskStorageNodeView	Get	View physical disk storage node view data
PhysicalExtent	Get	View physical extent information
PhysicalExtentAssociation	Get	View physical extent association
ResiliencySetting	Get, Set	View and configure resiliency setting
StorageAdvancedProperty	Get	View storage advanced properties
StorageDiagnosticInfo	Clear, Get	View and reset setorage diagnostic information
StorageDiagnosticLog	Start, Stop	Start and stop diagnostic logs
StorageEnclosure	Get	View storage enclosure information
StorageEnclosureIdentification	Disable, Enable	Enable or disable storage enclosure identification
StorageEnclosureStorageNo-deView	Get	View storage enclosure storage node view information
StorageEnclosureVendorData	Get	View storage enclosure vendor data
StorageFaultDomain	Get	View storage fault domain information
StorageFileServer	Remove, Get, New, Set	Configure storage file server
StorageFirmware	Update	Update storage firmware
StorageFirmwareInformation	Get	View storage firmware information
StorageHealthAction	Get	View storage health action
StorageHealthReport	Get	View storage health report
StorageHealthSetting	Get, Set, Remove	Configure and manage storage health setting
StorageHighAvailability	Disable, Enable	Enable or disable storage high availability
StorageJob	Stop, Get	Stop or view storage job

StorageMaintenanceMode	Enable, Disable	Enable or disable storage maintenance mode
StoargeNode	Get	View storage node information
StoragePool	Optimize, Set, Update, Remove, New, Get	Manage storage pool
StorageProvider	Set, Get	View and configure storage provider
StorageProviderCache	Update	Update storage provider cache
StorageReliabilityCounter	Get, Reset	Manage storage reliability counter
StorageSetting	Set, Get	View and configure storage setting
StorageSubSystem	Get, Unregister, Set, Register, Debug	Manage storage subsystem
StorageSubsystemVirtualDisk	New	New storage subsystem virtual disk
StorageTier	Get, Remove, New, Resize, Set	Manage storage tiers
StorageTierSupportedSize	Get	View storage tier supported size
SupportedClusterSizes	Get	View supported cluster sizes
SupportedFileSystems	Get	View supported file system information
TargetPort	Get	View target port information
TargetPortal	Get	View target portal information
TargetPortFromMaskingSet	Remove	Remove target port from a masking set
VirtualDisk	Show, New, Get, Hide, Resize, Remove, Repair, Set, Disconnect, Connect	Manage virtual disk
VirtualDiskClone	New	Create a new virtual disk clone
VirtualDiskFromMaskingSet	Remove	Remove a virtual disk from a masking set
VirtualDiskSnapshot	New	Create a virtual disk snapshot
VirtualDiskSupportedSize	Get	View virtual disk supported size

CHAPTER 07

VirtualDiskToMaskingSet	Add	Add virtual disk to masking set
Volume	Optimize, Set, Repair, Format, Get, Debug, New	Manage volumes
VolumeCache	Write	Flushes the volume cache to storage
VolumeCorruptionCount	Get	View volume corruption data
VolumeScrubPolicy	Get, Set	View and configure volume scrub policy

StorageReplica

Table 7-8 lists the PowerShell cmdlets in the storage replica module.

Table 7-8. Storage Replica module cmdlets

Noun	Verbs	Function
SRAccess	Get, Grant, Revoke	Manage storage replica access
SRConfiguration	Export	Backup existing storage replica configuration
SRDelegation	Grant, Revoke, Get	Configure storage replica delegation
SRGroup	Suspend, Sync, Remove, Set, Get, New	Manage storage replica groups
SRMetadata	Clear	Clear storage replica metadata
SRNetworkConstraint	Get, Set, Remove	Manage storage replica network constraints
SRPartnership	Set, Get, New, Remove	Configure storage replica partnerships
SRTopology	Test	Verify storage replica topology

File servers

Traditionally, the most common use for Windows servers has been as a file server. No matter how advanced technology gets, people that work in an organization need a way to share files with each other that is less chaotic than emailing them or handing them over on USB drives. Even with cloud storage options such as SharePoint Online and OneDrive for Business, many organizations still make use of the humble file server as a way of storing and sharing documents. Shared folders also provide a central location that can be backed up on a regular basis, something that gives them utility beyond just being a central location to store documents.

In this chapter you'll learn about how to get more out of your Windows Server 2016 file server by taking advantage of the functionality of File Server Resource Manager, Dynamic Access Control, Distributed File System, and BranchCache.

Inside OUT

Enable deduplication

We talked about deduplication in detail in Chapter 7 "Storage Services." As mentioned there, deduplication is a really useful technology to use with file servers. This is because a surprising number of files stored on file servers are duplicates of one another. Some organizations who have implemented deduplication on file servers found that they reduced storage utilization by up to 80 percent. Remember, to enable deduplication you need to have all of the file shares on a separate volume to the OS volume. Also remember that you can't use deduplication with ReFS volumes, so you have to stick to NTFS if you want to take advantage of this technology with your Server 2016 file servers.

Shared folder permissions

The basic idea with shared folders is that you create a folder, assign permissions to a group, such as a department within your organization, and the people in that group use that space on the file server to store files to be shared with the group.

For example, you create a shared folder on a file server named FS1 called Managers. Next, you set share permissions on the shared folder and file system permissions on the files and folders within the shared folder. Permissions allow you to control who can access the shared folder and what users can do with that access. For example, permissions determine whether they are limited to just read-only access or whether they can create and edit new and existing files.

When you set share permissions and file system permissions for a shared folder, the most restrictive permissions apply. For example, if you configure the Share permission so that the Everyone group has Full Control and then configure the file permission so that the Domain Users group has read access, a user who is a member of the Domain Users group accessing the file over the network has read access.

Where things get a little more complicated is when a user is a member of multiple groups, in which case the most restrictive cumulative permission applies. For example, in a file where the Domain Users group has read access, but the Managers group has Full Control, a user who is a member of both Domain Users and Managers who accesses the file over the network has Full Control permission. This is great for a certification exam question, but can be needlessly complex when you're trying to untangle permissions to resolve a service desk ticket.

Inside OUT

We need to talk about permissions

If you've ever studied for a Microsoft certification and come across file servers, you'll have learned about the difference between shared folder and file system permissions. The general problem with these permissions is that they tend to confuse people, which is why permissions are often incorrectly applied manually and why service desks are inundated with calls about the wrong people having access to a file while the right people can't open it. There are several solutions to the permissions problem. The first is to have permissions set automatically using Dynamic Access Control, where access is determined by rules around the nature of the file and the user trying to access the file. You'll learn about Dynamic Access Control and how you can use it to solve the permissions problem in this chapter. The next solution is AD RMS and WIP, covered in Chapter 14, "Active Directory Rights Management Services," which ensures that permissions stay with the file even when the file is moved away from the file share.

Using File Explorer

You can create shared folders in a variety of ways. The way that many administrators do it, often out of habit, is by using the built-in functionality of File Explorer. You have two general options when it comes to permissions, and also if you are using File Explorer to share folders:

- **Simple share permissions**. When you use the simple share permissions option, you specify whether a user or group account has Read or Read/Write permissions to a shared folder. Figure 8-1 shows this for the Managers group. When you use simple permissions, both the share and file and folder level permissions are configured at the same time. It is important to note that any files and folders in the shared folder path have their permissions reset to match those configured through the File Sharing dialog box. This, however, doesn't happen with other forms of share permission configurations.

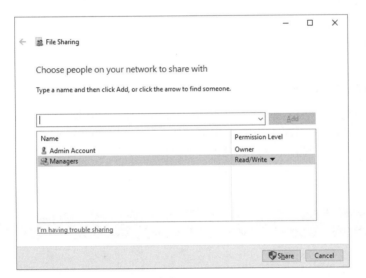

Figure 8-1 Simple share permissions

- **Advanced share permissions**. Advanced share permissions are what administrators who have been managing Windows file servers since the days of Windows NT 4 are likely to be more familiar with. With advanced permissions you configure share permissions separately from file system permissions. You configure advanced permissions through the Advanced Sharing button on the Sharing tab of a folder's properties. Figure 8-2 shows how you configure advanced sharing permissions. When you configure advanced share permissions, permissions are only set on the share and are not reset on the files and folders within the share. If you are using advanced share permissions, you set the file system permissions separately.

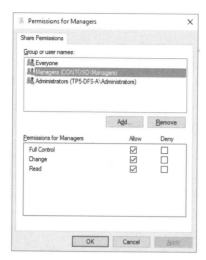

Figure 8-2 Share permissions

Server Manager

You can manage shares centrally through the Shares area of the Server Manager console, as shown in Figure 8-3. The advantage of the Server Manager console is that you can use it to connect to manage shares on remote servers, including servers running the Nano or Server Core installation options.

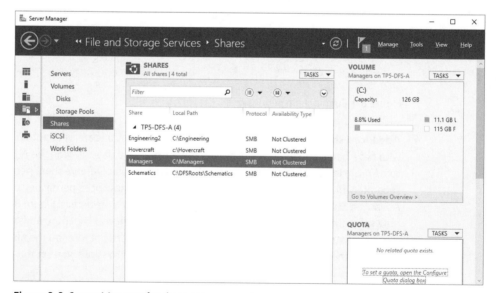

Figure 8-3 Server Manager for share management

When you edit the properties of a share through Server Manager, you can also edit the permissions, as shown in Figure 8-4. This functions in the same way as editing advanced share permissions through File Explorer in that it won't reset the permissions on the file system itself, only on the share.

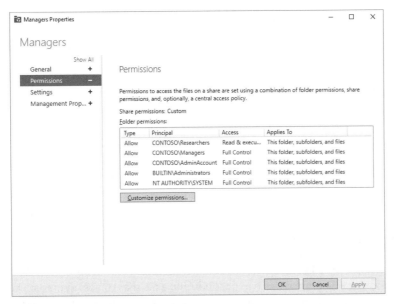

Figure 8-4 Server Manager permissions management

You can also use the Server Manager's share properties interface to edit the following settings:

- **Enable access-based enumeration.** Enabled by default, this setting ensures that users are only able to see files and folders they have access to.

- **Allow caching and BranchCache.** Allows files to be used offline. Also allows the use of BranchCache if the appropriate group policies are applied. You'll learn more about BranchCache later in this chapter.

- **Encrypt data access**. When you enable this option, traffic to and from the shared folder is encrypted if the client supports SMB 3.0 (Windows 8 and later).

- **Specify folder owner email address**. Setting the folder owner's email address can be useful when resolving access denied assistance requests.

- **Configure folder usage properties**. Folder usage properties allow you to apply metadata to the folder that specifies the nature of the files stored there. You can choose between User Files, Group Files, Application Files, and Backup and Archival files. You can use folder usage properties with data classification rules.

File Server Resource Manager

File Server Resource Manager (FSRM) is a tool that allows you to perform advanced file server management. You can use FSRM to configure the following:

- Quotas at the folder level

- File screens

- Storage reports

- File classification

- File management tasks

- Access denied assistance

Folder level quotas

Quotas are important. If you don't use them, file shares tend to end up consuming all available storage. Some users dump as much as possible onto a file share unless quotas are in place and unless you are monitoring storage, the first you'll hear about it is when the service desk gets calls about people being unable to add new files to the file share.

NTFS has had rudimentary quota functionality since the Windows NT days. The reason that most Windows server administrators don't bother with it is that you can only apply it to individual user accounts that are only applicable at the volume level. Needless to say if you have 500 users that you want to configure quotas for, you don't want to have to configure a quota for each one individually. Even with command line utilities, you still need to create an entry for each user.

Luckily, FSRM provides far more substantial quota functionality that makes quotas more practical to implement as a way of managing storage utilization on Windows file servers.

Quotas in FSRM can be applied on a per-folder basis and are not cumulative across a volume. You can also configure quotas in FSRM so that users are sent warning emails should they exceed a specific quota threshold, but before they are blocked from writing files to the file server. You manage quotas using FSRM by creating a quota template and then applying that quota template to a path.

Creating a quota template involves setting a limit, specifying a quota type, and then configuring notification thresholds. You can choose between the following quota types:

- **Hard quota**. A hard quota blocks users from writing data to the file share after the quota value is exceeded.

- **Soft quota**. A soft quota allows you to monitor when users exceed a specific storage utilization value, but doesn't block users from writing data to the file share after the quota value is exceeded.

Notification thresholds allow you to configure actions to be taken after a certain percentage of the assigned quotas are reached. As shown in Figure 8-5, you can configure notifications via email, get an item written to an event log, run a command, or have a report generated.

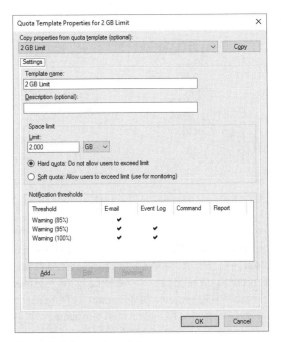

Figure 8-5 Quota template

After you have the quota template created, you apply it to a folder. To do this, select the Quotas node under Quota Management, and from the Action menu, click Create Quota. In the Create Quota dialog box, shown in Figure 8-6, select the path the quota applies to and the quota template to apply. You then choose between applying the quota to the whole path or setting up an auto-apply template. Auto-apply templates allow separate quotas to be applied to any new and existing quota path sub folders. For example, if you applied a quota to the C:\Example path using the 2 GB template, the quota would apply cumulatively for all folders in that path. If you chose an auto-apply template, a separate 2 GB quota would be configured for each new and existing folder under C:\Example.

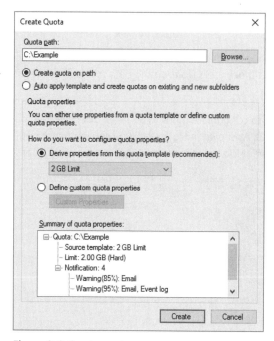

Figure 8-6 Create quota

File screens

File screens allow you to block users from writing files to file shares based on file name extension. For example, you can use a file screen to stop people from storing video or audio files on file shares. File screens are implemented based on file name. Usually this just means by file extension, but you can configure file screens based on a pattern match of any part of a file name. You implement file screens using file groups and file screen templates.

Inside OUT

Doesn't block what is already there

A file screen doesn't block files that are already there, it just stops new files from being written to the share. File screens also only work based on file name. If you have users that are especially cunning, they might figure out that it's possible to get around a file screen by renaming files so they don't get blocked by the screen.

File groups

A file group is a pre-configured collection of file extensions related to a specific type of file. For example, the Image Files file group includes file name extensions related to image files, such as .jpg, .png, and .gif. While file groups are usually fairly comprehensive in their coverage, they aren't always complete. Should you need to, you can modify the list to add new file extensions.

The file groups included with FSRM are shown in Figure 8-7 and include:

- **Audio and Video Files.** Blocks file extensions related to audio and video files, such as .avi and .mp3.

- **Backup Files.** Blocks file extensions related to backups, including .bak and .old files.

- **Compressed Files.** Blocks file extensions related to compressed files, such as .zip and .cab.

- **E-mail Files.** Blocks file extensions related to email storage, including .pst and .mbx files.

- **Executable Files.** Blocks file extensions related to executable files and scripts, such as.exe or .ps1 extensions.

- **Image Files.** Blocks file extensions related to images, such as .jpg or .png extensions.

- **Office Files.** Blocks file extensions related to Microsoft Office files, such as .docx and .pptx files.

- **System Files.** Blocks file extensions related to system files, including .dll and .sys files.

- **Temporary Files.** Blocks file extensions related to temporary files, such as .tmp. Also blocks files starting with the "~" character.

- **Text Files.** Blocks file extensions related to text files, including .txt and .asc files.

- **Web Page Files.** Blocks file extensions related to web page files, including .html and .htm files.

CHAPTER 08

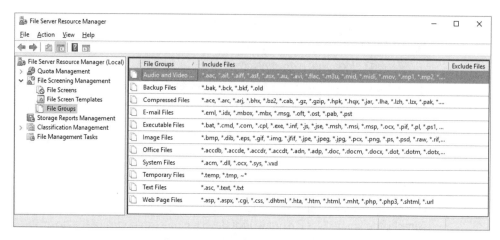

Figure 8-7 File Groups

To edit the list of files in a file group, right-click the file group and click Edit File Group Properties. Using this dialog box, shown in Figure 8-8, you can modify the list of files to include and the
list of files to exclude based on file name pattern. For example, you can do a simple exclusion or
inclusion based on file name suffix, such as *.bak. You also have the option of creating a more
complex exclusion or inclusion based on file name, such as backup*.*, which would exclude all
files with the word backup at the start of any extension.

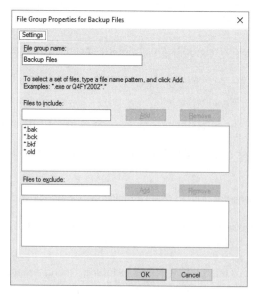

Figure 8-8 File group properties

Exclusions allow you to add exceptions to an existing block rule. For example, you configure a file screen to block all files that have the extension .vhdx. You might then create an exception for the name server2016.vhdx. When implemented, all files that had a .vhdx extension would be blocked from being written to the share except for files with the name server2016.vhdx.

Inside OUT

Not case sensitive

While the NTFS and ReFS file systems are case sensitive, file screens are not case sensitive.

To create a new file group, right-click the File Groups node in the File Server Resource Manager console and click Create File Group. Provide the following information:

- **File group name.** The name for the file group.

- **Files to include.** Provide patterns that match the names of files you want to block from being written to the file server.

- **Files to exclude.** Provide patterns that match the names of files you want to exclude from the block.

File screen templates

File screen templates are made up of a screening type, a collection of file groups, and a set of actions to perform when a match is found. File screen templates support the following screening types:

- **Active screening.** An active screen blocks users from writing files to the file share that have names that match those patterns listed in the file group.

- **Passive screening.** A passive screen doesn't block users from writing files to the file share that have names that match patterns listed in the file group. Instead you use a passive screen to monitor such activity.

The actions you can configure include sending an email, writing a message to the event log, running a command, or generating a report. Figure 8-9 shows the Create File Screen Template dialog box.

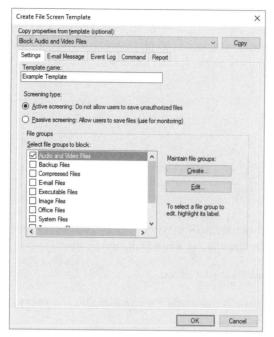

Figure 8-9 Creating a template

After you have configured the appropriate file screen template, create the file screen by apply-ing the template to a specific path. You can also create file screen exceptions, which exempt specific folders from an existing file screen. For example, you might apply a file screen at the root of a shared folder that blocks audio and video files from being written to the share. If you wanted to allow users to write audio and video files to one folder in the share, you could config-ure a file screen exception and apply it to that folder.

Storage reports

The Storage Reports functionality of FSRM allows you to generate information about the files that are being stored on a particular file server. You can use FSRM to create the following stor-age reports:

- **Duplicate Files.** This report locates multiple copies of the same file. If you've enabled deduplication on the volume hosting these files, these additional copies do not consume additional disk space as they are deduplicated.

- **File Screening Audit.** This report allows you to view which users or applications are trig-gering file screens. For example, which users have tried to save music or video files to a shared folder.

- **Files by File Group.** This report allows you to view files sorted by file group. You can view files by all file groups or you can search for specific files. For example, a report on .zip files stored on a shared folder.

- **Files by Owner.** This report allows you to view files by owner. You can search for files by all owners or run a report that provides information on files by one or more specific users.

- **Files by Property.** Use this report to find out about files based on a classification. For example, if you have a classification named "Top_Secret," you can generate a report about all files with that classification on the file server.

- **Large Files.** This report allows you to find large files on the file server. By default, it finds files larger than 5 MB, but you can edit this to locate all files that are larger than a certain size.

- **Least Recently Accessed Files.** This report allows you to identify files that have not been accessed for a certain number of days. By default, this report identifies files that have not been accessed in the last 90 days, but you can configure this to any number that is appropriate for your organization.

- **Most Recently Accessed Files.** Use this report to determine which files have been accessed most recently. The default version of this report finds files that have been accessed in the last seven days.

- **Quota Usage.** Use this report to view how a user's storage usage compares against the assigned quota. For example, you could run a report to determine which users have exceeded 90 percent of their quota.

You can configure storage reports to run and be stored locally on file servers. You also have the option of configuring storage reports to be emailed to one or more email addresses. You can generate storage reports in DHTML, HTML, XML, CSV, and text formats.

To run a storage report, perform the following steps:

1. In the File Server Resource Manager console, select the Storage Reports Management node and then on the Action menu, click Generate Reports Now.

2. On the Settings page of the Storage Reports Task Properties dialog box, shown in Figure 8-10, select the reports you want to run. You can click Edit Parameters to modify the properties of the report.

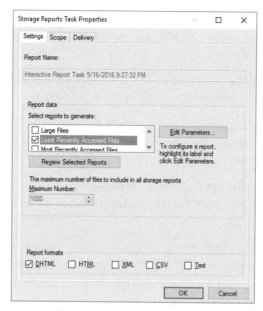

Figure 8-10 Storage reports

3. On the Scope tab of the Storage Reports Tasks Properties dialog box, you can configure which folders the report runs on.

4. On the Delivery tab of the Storage Reports Task Properties dialog box, you can configure the location where reports are saved and the email addresses the reports are sent to.

File classification

File classification allows you to apply metadata to files based on file properties. For example, you can apply the tag "Top_Secret" to a file that has specific properties, such as who authored it or whether a particular string of characters appeared in the file.

The first step to take when configuring file classification is to configure classification properties. After you've done this, you can create a classification rule to assign the classification property to a file. You can also allow users to manually assign classification properties to a file. By specifying the values allowed, you limit which classification properties the user can assign.

Classification properties

You can configure the following file classification properties:

- **Yes/No.** Provide a Boolean value

- **Date-Time.** Provide a date and time

- **Number.** Provide an integer value

- **Multiple Choice List.** Allow multiple values to be assigned from a list

- **Ordered List.** Provide values in a specific order

- **Single Choice.** Select one of a selection of options

- **String.** Provide a text based value

- **Multi-string.** Assign multiple text based values

To configure a classification property, perform the following steps:

1. In the File Server Resource Manager console, navigate to the Classification Properties node under the Classification Management node.

2. On the Action menu, click Create Local Property.

3. In the Create Local Classification Property window, provide a name, select a property type, and configure properties. Figure 8-11 shows a classification property named Sensitivity that gives a Single Choice property type and has the available values Top_Secret and Not_Sensitive. Click OK to save the new classification.

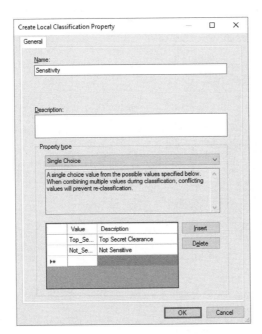

Figure 8-11 Create classification property

Classification rules

Classification rules allow you to assign classifications to files based on the properties of a file. You can use configure three separate methods to classify a file:

- **Content Classifier.** When you choose this method of classification, you configure a regular expression to scan the contents of a file for a specific string or text pattern. For example, you could use the content classifier to automatically assign the Top_Secret classification to any file that contained the text Project_X.

- **Folder Classifier.** When you choose this method of classification, all files in a particular path are assigned the designated classification.

- **Windows PowerShell Classifier.** When you choose this method of classification, a PowerShell script is run to determine whether or not a file is assigned a particular classification.

You can configure classification rules to run against specific folders. When configuring a classification rule, you can also choose to recheck files each time the rule is run. This allows you to change a file's classification in the event that the properties that triggered the initial classification change. When configuring reevaluation, you can also choose to remove user assigned classifications in case there is a conflict. Figure 8-12 shows the Evaluation Type tab of the Create Classification Rule dialog box, which allows you to configure these settings:

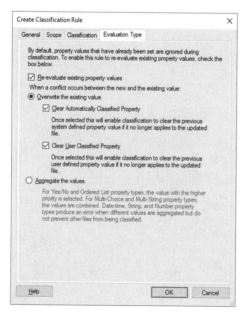

Figure 8-12 Evaluation type

File management tasks

File management tasks are automated tasks that FSRM performs on files according to a schedule. FSRM supports three types of file management tasks. These are:

- **File expiration.** This moves all files that match the conditions to a specific directory. The most common usage of a file expiration task is to move files that haven't been accessed by anyone for a specific period, for example 365 days, to a specific directory.

- **Custom.** Allows you to run a specific executable against a file. You can specify which executable is to be run, any special arguments to be used when running the executable, and the service account permissions, which can be Local Service, Network Service, or Local System.

- **RMS Encryption.** Allows you to apply an RMS template or a set of file permissions to a file based on conditions. For example, you might want to automatically apply a specific set of file permissions to a file that has the Top_Secret classification, or apply a specific RMS template to a file that has the Ultra_Secret classification.

When configuring a file management task, you also need to provide the following information:

- **Scope.** The path where the task is run.

- **Notification.** Any notification settings that you want to configure, such as sending an email, running a command, or writing an event to an event log. With file expiration, you can configure an email to be sent to each user who has files that are subject to the expiration task.

- **Report.** Generating a report each time that the task is run. A notification is sent to the user who owns the file, reports are sent to administrators.

- **Schedule.** When you want the file management task to be run.

- **Condition.** The condition that triggers the management task. For example, Figure 8-13 shows a task that is triggered when the Sensitivity classification property is set to Top_Secret.

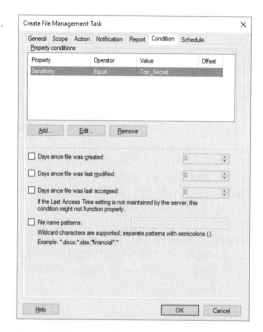

Figure 8-13   Create file management task.

Inside OUT

Cleaning up file servers

Most files become stale after a few months. If a file hasn't been accessed for a year, there's a very good chance that it might never be accessed again. If you are responsible for managing file servers, you should come up with a way of identifying and removing these files on a periodic basis. Storage reports can help you identify them and FSRM file management tasks allow you to move them off the file server in an automated way. Just remember that you might need to keep some files around for a certain amount of time to meet your organization's compliance obligations.

Distributed File System

Distributed File System (DFS) has two advantages over a traditional file share. The first is that DFS automatically replicates to create copies of the file share and its content on one or more other servers. The second is that clients connect to a single UNC address, with the client directed to the closest server and redirected to the next closest server in the event that a server hosting a DFS replica fails.

Using DFS, you can push a single shared folder structure out across an organization that has multiple branch offices. Changes made to files on one file share replica propagate across to the other file share replicas, with a robust built-in conflict management system present to ensure that problems do not occur when users are editing the same file at the same time.

DFS namespace

A DFS namespace is a collection of DFS shared folders. It uses the same UNC pathname structure, except instead of \\ServerName\FileShareName with DFS, it is \\domainname with all DFS shared folders located under this DFS root. For example, instead of:

```
\\FS-1\Engineering
```

```
\\FS-2\Accounting
```

```
\\FS-3\Documents
```

You can have:

```
\\Contoso.com\Engineering
```

```
\\Contoso.com\Accounting
```

```
\\Contoso.com\Documents
```

In this scenario, the Engineering, Accounting, and Documents folders can all be hosted on separate file servers and you can use a single namespace to locate those shared folders, instead of needing to know the identity of the file server that hosts them.

As shown in Figure 8-14, DFS supports the following types of namespaces:

- **Domain-based namespace.** Domain-based namespaces store configuration data in Active Directory. You deploy a domain-based namespace when you want to ensure that the namespace remains available even if one or more of the servers hosting the namespace goes offline.

- **Stand-alone namespace.** Stand-alone namespaces have namespace data stored in the registry of a single server and not in Active Directory as is the case with domain-based namespaces. You can only have a single namespace server with a stand-alone namespace. Should the server that hosts the namespace fail, the entire namespace is unavailable even if servers that host individual folder targets remain online.

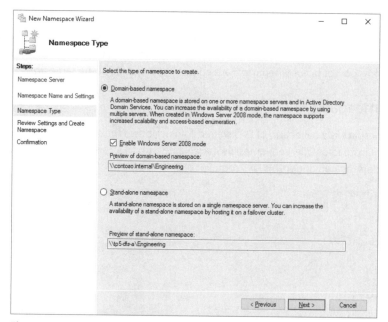

Figure 8-14 Namespace type

Inside OUT

Windows Server 2008 mode

From the perspective of deploying Windows Server 2016, Windows Server 2008 mode might sound like an option that you'd use for backwards compatibility. It's actually the opposite because if you don't select Windows Server 2008 mode, DFS uses Windows 2000 mode. Windows Server 2008 mode supports 50,000 folder targets and access based enumeration, which means that users can only see files and folders that they have access to. The requirements for Windows Server 2008 mode is that you have a domain functional level of Windows Server 2008 or higher, which should be easy given that Windows Server 2003 is no longer supported by Microsoft.

To create a DFS namespace, perform the following steps:

1. In the DFS console, click the Namespaces node. In the Action menu, click New Namespace.

2. On the Namespace Server page, select a server that has the DFS Namespaces feature installed. You can install this feature with the following PowerShell cmdlet:

```
Install-WindowsFeature FS-DFS-Namespace
```

3. On the Namespace Name and Settings page, provide a meaningful name for the namespace. This is located under the domain name. For example, if you added the name Schematics and you were installing DFS in the contoso.internal domain, the namespace would end up as \\contoso.internal\Schematics. By default, a shared folder is created on the namespace server, although you can edit settings on this page of the wizard and specify a separate location for the shared folder that hosts content you want to replicate.

4. On the Namespace Type page, you should generally select domain-based namespace as this gives you the greatest flexibility and provides you with the option of adding additional namespace servers later on for redundancy.

To add an additional namespace server to an existing namespace, ensure that the DFS Namespace role feature is installed on the server you want to add, and then perform the following steps:

1. In the DFS Console, select the namespace that you want to add the additional namespace server to and on the Action menu, click Add Namespace Server.

2. On the Add Namespace Server page, specify the name of the namespace server, or browse and query active directory to verify that the name is correct, and then click OK. This creates a shared folder on the new namespace server with the name of the namespace.

DFS replication

A replica is a copy of a DFS folder. Replication is the process that ensures each replica is kept up to date. DFS uses block-level replication, which means that only blocks in a file that have changed are transmitted to other replicas during the replication process.

You install the DFS replication feature by running the following PowerShell command:

```
Install-WindowsFeature FS-DFS-Replication
```

In the event that the same file is being edited by different users on different replicas, DFS uses a "last writer wins" conflict resolution model. In the unlikely event that two separate users create files with the same name in the same location on different replicas at approximately the same time, conflict resolution uses "earliest creator wins." When conflicts occur, files and folders that "lose" the conflict are moved to the Conflict and Deleted folder, located under the local path of the replicated folder in the DfsrPrivate\ConflictandDeleted directory.

Replicated folders and targets

One of the big advantages of DFS is that you can create copies of folders across multiple servers that are automatically updated. Each copy of that replica is called a folder target.

Only computers that have the DFS replication role feature installed can host folder targets. A replicated folder can have multiple folder targets. For example, you might have a replicated folder named \\contoso.com\Engineering that you have configured targets for in Sydney on \\SYD-FS1\Engineering, Melbourne on \\MEL-FS1\Engineering, and Auckland on \\AKL-FS1\Engineering.

To create a new folder to replicate, perform the following steps:

1. In the DFS console, select the namespace you want to add the folder to.

2. On the Action menu, click New Folder. In the New Folder dialog box, provide a folder name and click Add.

3. If you've already created a shared folder to host the target, enter that address in the Add Folder Target dialog box. Otherwise click Browse, select the server you want to host the folder, and click New Shared Folder.

4. On the Create Share dialog box, shown in Figure 8-15, provide a share name, a local path, and the permissions that you want to apply. The advantage of using the DFS console to create the share is that it ensures all the appropriate folders are created and permissions are applied. You need an account that has local Administrator access on the server that hosts the share to perform these actions. Click OK until all dialog boxes are dismissed to create the new folder.

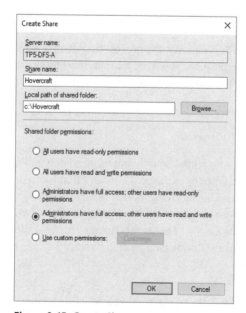

Figure 8-15 Create Share

To add a folder target to an existing folder, perform the following steps:

1. In the DFS console, select the folder under the namespace that you want to add a folder target to.

2. On the Action menu, click Add Folder Target.

3. If you've already created the share, enter the address of the shared folder. Otherwise click Browse.

4. On the Browse for Shared Folders dialog box, click Browse again and use Active Directory to query for the address of the server that you want to have host the folder target. Remember that this server must have the DFS Replication role service installed on it.

5. Click New Shared Folder. In the Create Share dialog box provide a share name, a local path, and the permissions that you want to apply. These should be the same as the permissions you've chosen for other replicas.

6. You need an account that has local Administrator access on the server that hosts the share to perform these actions. Click OK until all dialog boxes are dismissed to create the new folder target.

If this is the first additional target that you've created, you need to configure a replication topology and a replication group.

Replication topology

A replication group is a collection of servers that host copies of a replicated folder. When configuring replication for a replication group, you choose a topology and a primary member. The topology dictates how data replicates between the folders that each server hosts. The primary member is the seed from where file and folder data is replicated.

When creating a replication group, you can specify the following topologies as shown in Figure 8-16:

- **Hub and spoke.** This topology has hub members where data originates and spoke members where data gets replicated out to. This topology also requires at least three members of the replication group. Choose this if you have a hub and spoke topology for your organizational WAN.

- **Full mesh.** In this topology, each member of the replication group can replicate with other members. This is the simplest form of replication group and is suitable when each member is able to directly communicate with the other.

- **No topology.** When you select this option, you can create a custom topology where you specify how each member replicates with others.

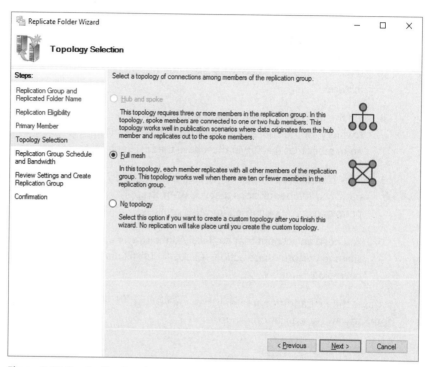

Figure 8-16 Replication topology

Replication schedules

You use replication schedules to determine how replication partners communicate with each other. You use a replication schedule to specify when replication partners communicate and whether replication traffic is throttled so as to not flood the network.

You can configure replication to occur continuously and specify bandwidth utilization, with a minimum value of 16 Kbps and an upper value of 256 Mbps, with the option of setting it to unlimited. If necessary, you can also set different bandwidth limitations for different periods of the day. Figure 8-17 shows where during work hours the cap is set to 512 Kbps and after hours the cap is set at 64 Mbps.

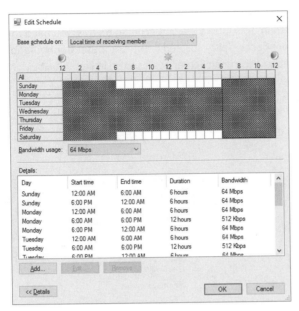

Figure 8-17 Replication schedule

BranchCache

BranchCache speeds up access to files stored on shared folders that are accessed across medium to high latency WAN links. For example, several users in a company's Auckland, New Zealand branch office need to regularly access several files stored on a file server in the Sydney, Australia head office. The connection between the Auckland and Sydney office is low bandwidth and high latency. The files are also fairly large and need to be stored on the Sydney file server. Additionally, the Auckland branch office is too small for a DFS replica to make sense. In a scenario such as this, you would implement BranchCache.

What BranchCache does is creates a locally cached copy of files from remote file servers that other computers on the local network can access, assuming that the file hasn't been updated at the source. In the example scenario, after one person in the Auckland office accesses the file, the next person to access the same file in the Auckland office accesses a copy that is cached locally, rather than retrieving it from the Sydney file server. The BranchCache process performs a check to verify that the cached version is up to date. If it isn't, the updated file is retrieved and stored in the Auckland network's BranchCache.

You add BranchCache to a file server by using the following PowerShell command:

```
Install-WindowsFeature FS-BranchCache
```

After installing BranchCache, you need to configure group policies that apply to file servers in your organization that allow them to support BranchCache. To do this, you need to configure the Hash Publication for BranchCache policy, located in the Computer Configuration\Policies\Administrative Templates\Network\Lanman Server node shown in Figure 8-18.

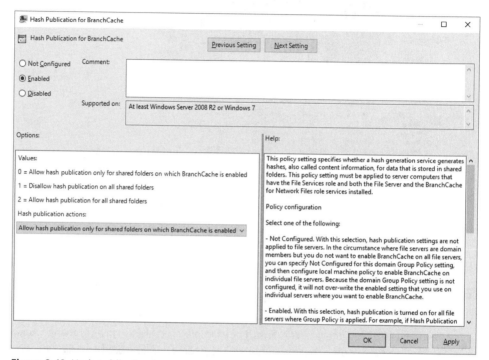

Figure 8-18 Hash publication

You have three options, shown in Figure 8-18, when configuring this policy:

- **Allow hash publication only for shared folders on which BranchCache is enabled.** This option allows you to selectively enable BranchCache.

- **Disallow hash publication on all shared folders.** Use this option when you want to disable BranchCache.

- **Allow hash publication for all shared folders.** Use this option if you want to enable BranchCache on all shared folders.

Generally, there's rarely a great reason not to enable BranchCache on all shared folders, but should you want to be selective, you do have that option. Should you choose to be selective and only enable BranchCache on some shares, you need to edit the properties of the share and enable BranchCache, available through Offline Settings in the Advanced Sharing option, as shown in Figure 8-19.

Figure 8-19 Enable BranchCache

After you've configured your file server to support BranchCache, you need to configure client computers to support branch cache. You do this through configuring group policy in the Computer Configuration\Policies\Administrative Templates\Network\BranchCache node of a GPO. Which policies you configure depends on how you want BranchCache to work at each branch office. You can choose between the following options:

- **Distributed Cache mode.** When client computers are configured for Distributed Cache mode, each Windows 7 or later computer hosts part of the cache.

- **Hosted Cache mode.** When you configure Hosted Cache mode, a server at the branch office hosts the cache in its entirety. Any server running Windows Server 2008 R2 or later can function as a hosted cache mode server.

To configure a branch office server to function as a hosted cache mode server, run the following PowerShell commands:

```
Install-WindowsFeature BranchCache
```

```
Start-Service BranchCache
```

```
Enable-BCHostedServer
```

PowerShell commands

While you can remotely manage file servers using the Remote Server Administration Tools, if you need to manage a large number of servers it is more efficient to use PowerShell. In the next few pages, you'll learn which PowerShell cmdlets are available for managing Windows Server 2016 file servers.

Shared Folder cmdlets

Shared folder cmdlets are in the SmbShare PowerShell module. This is because traditional file shares use the SMB protocol. Sometimes the documentation refers to SMB servers, which is another way of saying file servers. Table 8-1 lists the shared folder related cmdlets available in Windows Server 2016.

Table 8-1. Shared Folder cmdlets

Noun	Verbs	Functionality
SMBBandwidthLimit	Get, Remove, Set	Manage shared folder bandwidth caps
SMBClientConfiguration	Get, Set	View client SMB configuration
SMBClientNetworkInterface	Get	View network interfaces used by client
SMBConnection	Get	View connections from client to shared folders
SMBDelegation	Disable, Enable, Get	Manage constrained delegation authorization for SMB clients
SMBMapping	Get, New, Remove	Manage SMB mappings
SMBMultiChannelConnection	Get, Update	Manage multi-channel connections to SMB shares
SMBMultichannelConstraint	Get, New, Remove	Manages SMB multichannel constrains on shared folders
SMBOpenFile	Get, Close	Manage files that are open from shared folders
SMBPathAcl	Set	Configure the ACL for the file system folder to match the ACL of the shared folder
SMBServerConfiguration	Get, Set	Manage SMB server configuration
SMBServerNetworkInterface	Get	View network interfaces used by SMB server
SMBSession	Get, Close	View and terminate SMB sessions
SMBShare	Get, New, Remove, Set	Manage shared folders
SMBShareAccess	Block, Get, Grant, Revoke, Unblock	Manage permissions on shared folders

File Server Resource Manager cmdlets

One of the challenges with FSRM is that you need to configure it on a per-server basis. When you have complex FSRM configurations, this can make it challenging to deploy the same configuration across multiple servers. One way of simplifying the process of deploying FSRM across multiple file servers is to use PowerShell. By creating and running a PowerShell script, or by using DSC, you are able to apply the same FSRM settings across multiple file servers.

Table 8-2 lists the FSRM related cmdlets on the basis of PowerShell Noun, available verbs, and functionality.

Table 8-2. FSRM cmdlets

Noun	Verbs	Functionality
FSRMAction	New	Create a new action, such as sending an email, creating an event log entry, running a command, or generating a report
FsrmAdrSetting	Get, Set	Manage access denied remediation settings, which display information for users when they are denied access to a file
FSRMAutoQuota	Get, New, Remove, Set, Update	Manage auto apply quotas. Auto apply quotas are quota templates that you can apply at the volume or folder level
FSRMClassification	Get, Set, Start, Stop, Wait	Manage classification processes, such as starting and stopping them
FSRMClassificationPropertyDefinition	Get, New, Remove, Set, Update	Manage classification property definitions
FSRMClassificationPropertyValue	New	Manage classification property values
FSRMClassificationRule	Get, New, Remove, Set	Manage classification property rules
FSRMEffectiveNamespace	Get,	Provides a list of paths that match FSRM namespaces
FSRMFileGroup	Get, New, Remove, Set	Manage FSRM file groups for file screens
FSRMFileManagementJob	Get, New, Remove, Set, Start, Stop, Wait	Manage FSRM file management jobs

CHAPTER 08

FSRMFileScreen	Get, New, Remove, Reset, Set	Manage FSRM file screens
FSRMFileScreenException	Get, New, Remove, Set	Manage FSRM file screen exceptions
FSRMFileScreenTemplate	Get, New, Remove, Set	Manage FSRM file screen templates
FSRMFmjAction	New	Create file management job actions
FSRMFmjCondition	New	Create file management job conditions
FSRMFmjNotification	New	Create file management job notifications
FSRMFmjNotificationAction	New	Create file management notification actions
FSRMMacro	Get,	Lists FSRM macros
FSRMMgmtProperty	Get, Remove, Set	Manage FSRM management properties
FSRMQuota	Get, New, Remove, Reset, Set, Update	Manage FSRM quotas
FSRMQuotaTemplate	Get, New, Remove, Set	Manage FSRM quota templates
FSRMQuotaThreshold	New	Manage FSRM quota thresholds
FSRMRmsTemplate	Get,	View available RMS templates that you can apply using FSRM
FSRMScheduledTask	New	Create an FSRM Scheduled Task
FSRMSetting	Get, Set	Manage FSRM settings
FSRMStorageReport	Get, Remove, New, Set, Start, Stop, Wait	Manage FSRM storage reports
FSRMTestEmail	Send	Send a test alert email using FSRM settings

BranchCache Cmdlets

You can use the BranchCache cmdlets, available when you install the BranchCache feature, to configure and manage BranchCache on both file servers and clients. These cmdlets are listed in Table 8-3.

Table 8-3. BranchCache cmdlets

Noun	Verb	Function
BC	Disable, Reset	Disable or reset BranchCache
BCAuthentication	Set	Configure BranchCache Computer Authentication mode
BCCache	Clear, Set	Manage cache files
BCCachePackage	Export, Import	Export and import cache packages
BCClientConfiguration	Get	View client computer settings
BCContentServerConfiguration	Get	View content server configuration
BCDataCache	Get	Get information about the data cache
BCDataCacheEntryMaxAge	Set	Manage the amount of time data can be stored in the cache
BCDataCacheExtension	Add, Get	Manage cache storage space
BCDistributed	Enable	Configure a computer to operate in distributed cache mode
BCDowngrading	Enable, Disable	Manage whether computers can use Windows 7 BranchCache mode
BCFileContent	Publish	Creates hashes for files on file server that has BranchCache enabled
BCHashCache	Get	View the BranchCache hash cache
BCHostedCacheServer Configuration	Get	View hosted cache server settings
BCHostedClient	Enable	Configure BranchCache to function in hosted cache client mode
BCHostedServer	Enable	Configure BranchCache to function in hosted cache server mode
BCLocal	Enable	Enable BranchCache service to function in local caching mode
BCMinSMBLatency	Set	Configure minimum latency requirement for activation of BranchCache functionality
BCNetworkConfiguration	Get	View BranchCache network settings
BCSecretKey	Export, Import, Set	Manage cryptographic key used for generation of BranchCache segment secrets
BCServeOnBattery	Disable, Enable	Configure whether content discovery requests are responded to depending on whether a computer is running in battery
BCStatus	Get	View BranchCache status and configuration information
BCWebContent	Publish	Creates hashes for web content

DFS Cmdlets

DFS cmdlets are available across two separate PowerShell modules. You use the first set of cmdlets, listed in Table 8-4, to manage DFS namespaces and namespace servers. You use the second set of cmdlets, listed in Table 8-5 to manage DFS replication and folder targets.

Table 8-4. DFS namespace cmdlets

Noun	Verb	Function
DfsnAccess	Get, Grant, Remove, Revoke	Manage permissions for DFS namespace folders
DfsnFolder	Get, Move, New, Remove, Set	Manage DFS namespace folder settings
DfsnFolderTarget	Get, New, Remove, Set	Manage DFS namespace folder target settings
DfsnRoot	Get, New, Remove, Set	Manage settings for DFS roots
DfsnRootTarget	Get, New, Remove, Set	Manage settings for DFS root targets
DfsnServerConfiguration	Get, Set	Manage DFS namespace settings for DFSN root server

Table 8-5. DFS Replication cmdlets

Noun	Verb	Function
DfsrBacklog	Get	Provides list of pending file updates between replication partners
DfsrClone	Export, Get, Import, Reset	Manage a cloned DFS replication database
DfsrConfigurationFromAD	Update	Updates the DFS Replication service by checking Active Directory database
DfsrConnection	Add, Get, Remove, Set	Manage connections between members of a replication group
DfsrConnectionSchedule	Get, Set	Manage connection schedule between members of a replication group
DfsrDelegation	Get, Grant, Revoke	Manage replication group permissions
DfsReplicatedFolder	Get, New, Remove, Set	Manage replicated folders in a replication group
DfsReplicationGroup	Get, New, Remove, Set, Suspend, Sync	Manage replication groups
DfsrFileHash	Get	View a file hash

DfsrGroupSchedule	Get, Set	Manage replication group schedules
DfsrGuid	ConvertFrom	Translates GUIDs to friendly names for a specific replication group
DfsrHealthReport	Write	Generates a replication health report that you can use for diagnostic purposes
DfsrIdRecord	Get	View ID records for replicated files or folders from the DFS replication database
DfsrMember	Add, Get, Set	Manage computer members of DFS replication group
DfsrMembership	Get, Set	View and configure replication group membership settings
DfsrPreservedFiles	Get, Restore	Manage preserved files and folders. Preserved files are ones where there has been a conflict or where files have been deleted
DfsrPropagationReport	Write	Create reports based on the propagation of test files
DfsrPropagationTest	Remove, Start	Manage propagation test files
DfsrServiceConfiguration	Get, Set	Manage DFS Replication service settings
DfsrState	Get	View the DFS Replication state for a member

Dynamic Access Control cmdlets

You can use the cmdlets listed in table 8-6 to manage Dynamic Access Control.

Table 8-6. Dynamic Access Control cmdlets

Noun	Verb	Function
ADCentralAccessPolicy	Get, New, Remove, Set	Manage central access policies
ADCentralAccessPolicyMember	Add. Remove	Add and remove central access rules to a central access policy in AD DS
ADCentralAccessRule	Get, New, Remove, Set	Manages central access rules
ADClaimType	Get, New, Remove, Set	Manage claim types
ADResourceProperty	Get, New, Remove, Set	Manage resource properties
ADResourcePropertyList	Get, New, Remove, Set	Manage resource property lists
ADResourcePropertyListMember	Add, Remove	Manage resource properties in a resource property list
ADResourcePropertyValueType	Get	View resource property value type

CHAPTER 08

Internet Information Services

Many organizations use Internet Information Services (IIS) to host both their public facing website as well as internal intranet services. IIS also supports many different roles, from Outlook Web Access in Exchange Server deployments through to SharePoint, Windows Server Update Services, and Certificate Services Web enrollment.

In this chapter, you learn about how to perform Web server administration tasks, from basic tasks, such as configuring new websites and virtual directories, to more advanced topics such as configuring application pool recycling settings, setting FTP sessions to require TLS, and delegating administrative privileges.

Managing sites

You perform website management in IIS through the IIS Manager console. The key to understanding the IIS Manager console, shown in Figure 9-1, is the Details pane that allows you to configure items depending on the configuration node selected. You are presented with the Details pane when selecting a particular node in the Connections pane, such as the Web server itself, the Applications Pool node, or individual websites. For example, if you open the Authentication node at the Server level, it configures authentication options for the server. If you have a specific website selected, opening the same Authentication item configures authentication for only that website. If you want to configure an item and the item isn't present, you need to verify that the relevant role service is installed.

Figure 9-1 IIS Manager

Inside OUT

Missing items

Specific configuration items are only present within IIS manager when the appropriate role service is installed. IIS installs in a minimal configuration. If you can't find a specific option that you need to configure for a web application that you are hosting, check that the appropriate role service is installed.

Adding websites

The only practical limit for the number of websites that a server running IIS can host is hardware-related. Although you can probably run 10,000 different sites off the same computer or virtual machine, the hardware resources needed to support that number of sites in order to run in a fast and responsive manner is prohibitively expensive.

To run more than one site on IIS, the sites need to be different in one of the following ways:

- **Unique IP address**. You can configure a different site for each IP address associated with the server. Although this isn't useful when you use one of the limited supply of IPv4 addresses, it is useful when it comes to the more plentiful IPv6 addresses. You can use IP address differentiation to ensure that website traffic uses a specific network adapter.

- **Hostname**. If your server has only one IP address, you can still run multiple sites. You just need to ensure that each site uses a unique hostname. IIS parses the hostname in the HTTP request and directs the client to the appropriate site.

- **Port number**. You can also configure different sites that use the same IP address and hostname by assigning them different port addresses. The port address is a less popular way of differentiating websites, because, although it is an effective technique, most people have difficulty remembering to add a separate port address to a URL.

To add a website to an existing server, perform the following steps:

1. Open the IIS Manager console from the Tools menu of the Server Manager console.

2. Right-click the Server node, and then click Add Web Site.

3. On the Add Web Site dialog box, shown in Figure 9-2, enter the following information:

   - **Site name**. The name that represents the site on the server.
   - **Application pool**. The application pool with which the site is associated. The default settings create a new application pool for each new site. You can click the Select button to select a different application pool.
   - **Physical path**. This is where the website files are stored. You can configure site files to be stored on a remote network share. When you do this, you need to specify the authentication credentials used to connect to the network share or the file system. The default credentials use the web user's identity, so you'll need to configure authentication settings if you aren't using a specific account
   - **Type**. Allows you to specify whether the site uses HTTP or HTTPS.
   - **IP address**. Determines whether the site uses all unassigned IP addresses or a specific IP address assigned to the server.
   - **Port**. Determines whether the site uses the default port 80 or 443 for HTTPS sites.
   - **Host name**. The hostname associated with the site.
   - **SSL certificate**. Allows you to select the TLS certificate associated with the site. This option is only available if you select HTTPS at the time. Certificates can be imported if necessary.

CHAPTER 9

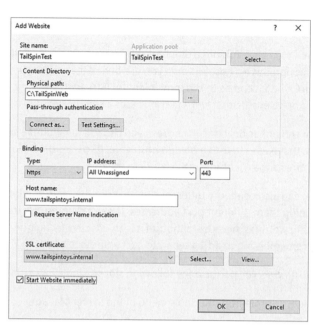

Figure 9-2 Add Website

Inside OUT

Test certificates

You can create a self signed TLS certificate using the New-SelfSignedCertificate cmdlet.

Although you are more likely to use PowerShell to manage IIS on Windows Server 2016, long time IIS administrators often have scripts that call the appcmd.exe utility, which was available in several previous versions of Windows Server and is located in the c:\Windows\syswow64\inetsrv folder, to perform administrative tasks. For example, you can use appcmd.exe to create a new website on port 80 associated with the hostname www.contoso.internal and using the c:\contoso folder using the following command:

```
Appcmd.exe add site /name:contoso /physicalPath:c:\contoso /bindings:http/*:80:www.contoso.internal
```

You can view a list of sites running on a server using the command:

```
Appcmd.exe list sites
```

Virtual directories

You use virtual directories when you want to create a directory on the website that does not map to a corresponding folder in the existing website folder structure. For example, the site www.fabrikam.com might map to the c:\fabrikam folder on a computer running IIS. If you create the folder c:\fabrikam\products, people can access that folder by navigating to the URL *www.fabrikam.com/products*. Instead, if you put the Products folder on another volume, you can use a virtual directory to map the URL *www.fabrikam.com/products* to that alternate location.

To add a virtual directory using the IIS Manager console, perform the following steps:

1. Open the IIS Manager console and navigate to the site for which you wish to add the virtual directory.

2. Right-click the site, and then click Add Virtual Directory.

3. In the Add Virtual Directory dialog box, shown in Figure 9-3, enter the alias for the virtual directory and the path to the virtual directory. If specifying a remote network share, you can configure which account is used to connect to that share.

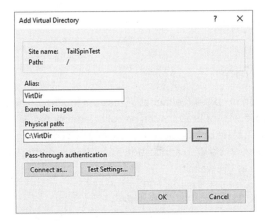

Figure 9-3 Add Website

After you create a website, you can change the settings of the site by viewing its advanced settings, as shown in Figure 9-4. This can be done by clicking on the site in the IIS Manager console and then clicking the Advanced Settings item in the Actions pane.

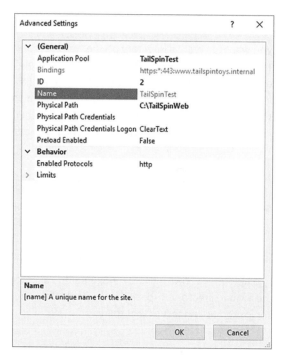

Figure 9-4 Website properties

Adding web applications

A Web application is a collection of content, either at a website's top level or in a separate folder under the website's top level. Applications can be collected together in application pools. Application pools allow you to isolate one or more applications in a collection. When you create a website, it automatically creates a Web application associated with that website. This Web application has the same name as the website.

To create a Web application, perform the following steps:

1.   Open the IIS Manager console and navigate to the site for which you want to create a Web application.

2.   Right-click on the site, and then click on Add Application.

3.   In the Add Application dialog, shown in Figure 9-5, enter the alias of the application, choose which application pool the application is a member of, and specify the path to the application on the server.

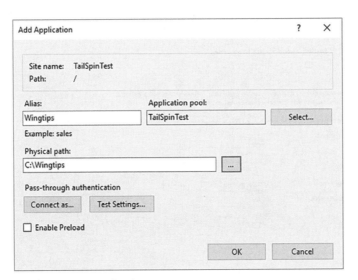

Figure 9-5 Add Application

Configuring TLS certificates

TLS certificates, often inaccurately referred to as SSL certificates because TLS is the successor protocol to SSL, allow clients to encrypt their session with the web server, minimizing the chance that communication between the client and the server can be intercepted, and serve as an identity verification mechanism. You can configure TLS to be required at the server, site, web application, virtual directory, folder, and file level.

The first step you need to take prior to requiring TLS on a particular site is to request and then install a certificate. To do this, perform the following steps:

1.   Open the IIS Manager console, select the Server node, and then double-click the Server Certificates item in the Details pane.

2.   Click the Create Certificate Request item. In the Request Certificate dialog box, shown in Figure 9-6, enter the name for the certificate and your organization's details.

CHAPTER 9

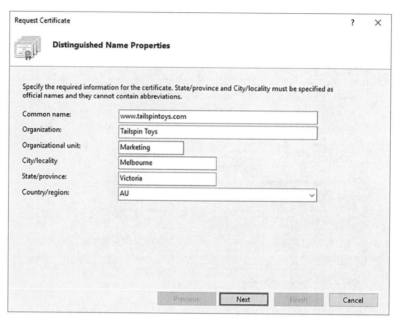

Figure 9-6 Request Certificate

3. On the Cryptographic Service Provider Properties page, enter the cryptographic service provider and the key length that you wish to use for the TLS certificate, and then click Next.

4. Enter a name for the certificate request file. After the certificate request file is created, forward it to a CA.

5. After the certificate has been issued, open the Server Certificates item, and then click Complete Certificate Request.

6. On the Specify Certificate Authority Response page of the Complete Certificate Request Wizard, specify the location of the certificate issued by the CA and a friendly name with which to identify the certificate, and then click OK. This installs the certificate.

After the certificate is installed, you can configure the site, virtual directory, folder, or file to request or require HTTPS. To accomplish this goal, perform the following steps:

1. In IIS Manager, select the site on which you wish to configure TLS.

2. Click Edit Bindings, and then click Add. In the Add Site Binding dialog box, ensure that HTTPs is selected on the Type drop-down menu, and the TLS certificate that you installed is selected on the SSL certificate drop-down menu, as shown in Figure 9-7.

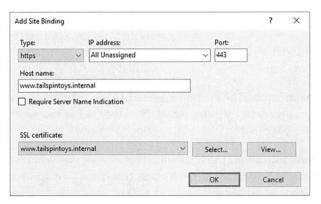

Figure 9-7 Request certificate

3. Select the site, virtual directory, folder, or file on which you wish to enforce TLS settings.

4. Double-click the SSL Settings item in the Details pane. This should be TLS settings, but SSL remains the commonly used term.

5. On the SSL Settings page, ensure that Require SSL is selected, and then click Apply.

Site authentication

Authentication methods determine how a user authenticates with a server or a website. You can configure authentication at the server level or at the site level. If there is a conflict between the authentication methods configured at the server and the site level, the site-level authentication settings have precedence.

- **Active Directory Client Certificate**. This form of authentication works by checking client certificates. These are almost always issued by an internal certificate authority.

- **Anonymous Authentication**. This is the most typical form of authentication for a Web server. Clients can access the web page without entering credentials.

- **ASP.NET Impersonation**. Use ASP.NET impersonation when it is necessary to execute an ASP.NET application under a different security context.

- **Basic Authentication**. Basic authentication works with all web browsers, but has the drawback of transmitting unencrypted base64-encoded passwords across the network. If you use Basic Authentication, you should also configure the site to require an encrypted TLS connection.

CHAPTER 9

- **Digest Authentication**. Digest authentication occurs against a Domain Controller and is used when you want to authenticate clients that may be accessing content through a proxy, something that can be problematic for clients if you configure a server to use Windows authentication.

- **Forms Authentication**. This method is used when you redirect users to a custom web page on which they enter their credentials. Once they've been authenticated, they are returned to the page that they were attempting to browse.

- **Windows Authentication**. Use this method for Intranet sites when you want clients to authenticate using Kerberos or NTLM. It works best when client computers are members of the same forest as the computer hosting the Web server role.

Inside OUT

Authentication methods

Authentication options are only available if you have installed them. If you can't find the method that you want to enable, ensure that you have installed it.

Remember that you need to disable Anonymous authentication if you want to force clients to use a different authentication method. Web browsers always request content from a server anonymously the first time you attempt to access content. If Anonymous authentication is enabled, other forms of authentication are ignored. To enable a specific form of authentication for a website, perform the following steps:

1. Open the IIS Manager console from the Administrative Tools menu.

2. Click the Web Server node. In the Content pane, scroll down, and then double-click the Authentication item.

3. On the list of available authentication technologies, shown in Figure 9-8, click the authentication technology that you want to enable, and then click Enable in the Actions pane.

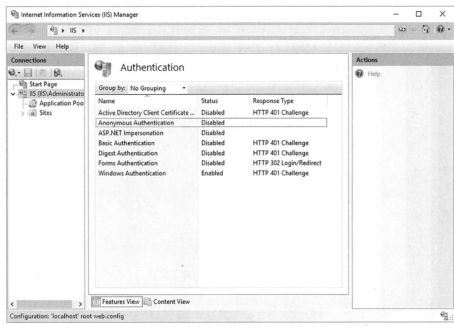

Figure 9-8 Configure authentication

Modifying custom error response

Many sites customize their error responses so that users are provided with something more meaningful than a simple error message. Although the default error messages are perfectly serviceable, many organizations feel that they lack character and like to customize the most popular error messages, such as the 404 error message displayed by the web server when a page is not found.

To modify custom error message settings, perform the following steps:

1. Open the IIS Manager console and select the Server node.

2. Scroll down the Details pane and double-click the Error Pages item.

3. On the Error Pages pane, select the error code that you want to modify, and then click Edit.

4. In the Edit Custom Error Page dialog, shown in Figure 9-9, choose forwarding clients to a static page based on file location, to a URL on the server, or an absolute URL, which can be a page on another website.

CHAPTER 9

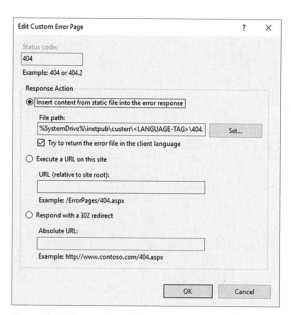

Figure 9-9 Custom Error Page

Adding or disabling the default document

The default document is the document that loads when a client navigates to a web page but doesn't specify which page to load. The Default Documents role service is installed in a default installation of IIS, though this can be removed if you so choose. On servers running IIS, the following default documents are used:

- default.htm

- default.asp

- index.htm

- index.html

- default.aspx

If more than one of these documents is present in the same folder, the document that is higher on the list overrides the documents that are lower on the list. You can add, reorder, or disable default documents using the IIS Manager console by double-clicking on the Default Document item either at the server or the website level as shown in Figure 9-10.

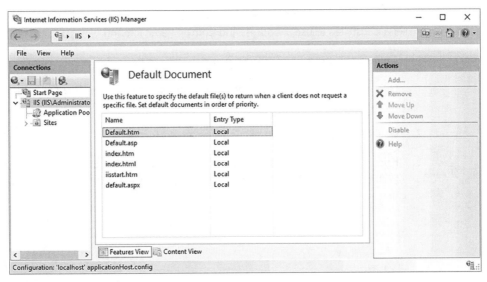

Figure 9-10 Default documents

Directory browsing

Directory browsing allows clients to view the files that are stored in a folder. Directory browsing works only if the default document is not present or has been disabled. To enable directory
browsing, the Directory Browsing role service must be installed. To configure directory browsing, perform the following steps:

1. Open the IIS Manager console and select the site on which you want to enable directory
    browsing.

2. Scroll down in the Details pane and double-click the Directory Browsing item.

3. When Directory Browsing is shown in the Details pane, click Enable, and select the
    items that you want to allow to be displayed when the client is browsing. By default, the
    filename, time, size, extension, and date information are displayed.

IP address and domain name filtering

IP address and domain name restrictions allow you to block or allow access to a site based on
a client's address. You can configure two types of rules: allow rules and block rules. When you
configure an allow rule, only hosts that are on the Allow List are able to access your website.
When you configure a block rule, hosts with an address on your Block List are blocked from
accessing your site. You can configure allow and block rules at the server, site, application,

virtual directory, folder, and file level in IIS. You need to have the IP And Domain Restrictions role service installed to use IP address and domain name filtering.

To configure an IP address and domain name restriction, perform the following steps:

1. Open the IIS Manager console and select the site on which you want to implement an Allow List.

2. Double-click on the IP Address and Domain Restrictions item.

3. If you want to configure an Allow List entry, click Add Allow Entry, and on the Add Allow Restriction Rule dialog box, shown in Figure 9-11, enter the IP address range or IP address that you want to allow.

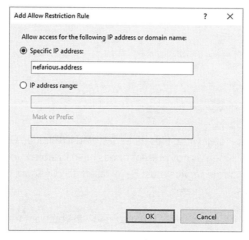

Figure 9-11 Restriction rules

4. If you want to configure a Deny entry, click Add Deny Entry and on the Add Deny Restriction Rule dialog box, and enter the IP address range or IP address that you want to block.

Dynamic IP restriction settings allow you to configure IIS to automatically block traffic based on suspicious request behavior, such as what can occur during a denial of service attack. As Figure 9-12 shows, you can choose to block based on a maximum number of concurrent requests, or a maximum number of requests over a specific period of time.

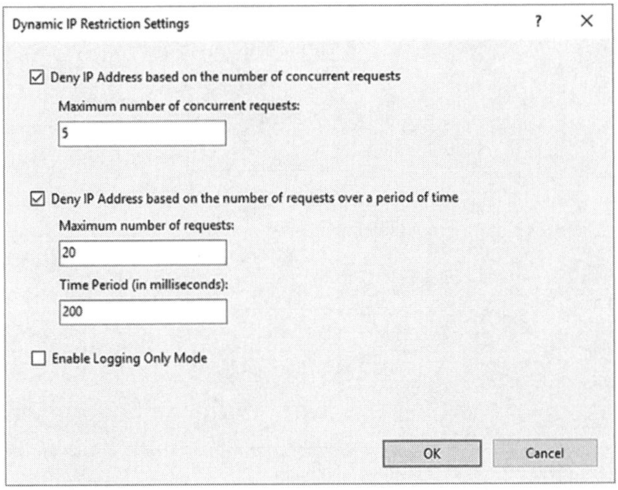

Figure 9-12 Dynamic IP Restriction

URL authorization rules

URL authorization rules allow you to grant or deny access to specific computers, groups of computers, or domain access to sites, web applications, folders, or specific files. For example, you can use URL authorization rules to block everyone except the Managers group from accessing specific pages on the organization's Intranet server. You can also configure URL authorization rules to apply only when the client attempts to use specific HTTP verbs, such as GET or POST. To use URL authorization rules, you need to ensure that the URL Authorization role service is installed on the server. There are two types of authorization rules: Allow rules and Deny rules.

To create an authorization rule, perform the following steps:

1. Open IIS Manager and navigate to the site, virtual directory, folder, or file on which you want to create the authorization rule.

2. Double-click the Authorization Rules item in the Details pane.

3. Click Add Allow Rule or Add Deny Rule depending on the type of authorization rule that you wish to create.

4. On the Add Allow Authorization Rule or Add Deny Authorization Rule dialog box, specify the users or groups you wish to configure the rule for, and any specific HTTP verbs that you wish to trigger the rule. Figure 13-13 shows the Add Allow Authorization Rule dialog box.

Figure 9-13 Authorization rules

If you want to block access to everyone except a specific group of users, remove the default All Users Allow rule and replace it with the rule that grants specific access to the security principals in question.

Request filters

Request filters allow you to block clients from making certain types of requests of your web server. Request filters allow you to block a common form of attack against web applications, one where the attacker enters a specially formatted HTTP request in order to elicit an unplanned response from the web application. SQL injection attacks are one such kind of specially formatted HTTP request. There are several different types of request filters you can configure using the Request Filtering item. Request filters can be configured at the server, site, and file level. To use request filtering, you need to ensure that you install the Request Filtering role service on the server.

You can configure the following types of request filters:

- **File Name Extensions**. This type of filter allows you to specify which type of files clients are not allowed to request from the Web server on the basis of a file extension. The default request filtering settings block 43 different file extensions, and it is relatively easy to add additional extensions by clicking Deny File Name Extension on the File Name Extensions tab of the Request Filtering item.

- **Rules**. This allows you to configure specific rules that check either the URL, query string, or both. If a match occurs, the request is blocked.

- **Hidden Segments**. They allow you to set a list of URL segments that will be blocked to requesting clients. A URL segment is the section of a URL path that lies between slash (/) characters.

- **URL**. They allow you to specify a set of URL sequences (such as setup/config.xml) that the Request Filtering role service blocks to clients. All instances of the URL sequence are blocked within the scope of the filter.

- **HTTP Verbs**. They allow you to restrict which HTTP verbs can be used in requests by clients. For example, you might block clients from using the PUT verb in requests.

- **Headers**. They allow you to specify a maximum URL size for a specific HTTP request header.

You can modify the general request filtering settings, as shown in Figure 9-14, by clicking Edit Feature Settings in the Actions pane. Using this dialog, you can configure the following options:

- **Allow Unlisted File Name Extensions**. If this box is not checked, file extensions that are not explicitly allowed cannot be requested by clients.

- **Allow Unlisted Verbs**. If this box is not checked, HTTP verbs that are not explicitly allowed are blocked.

- **Allow High-Bit Characters**. If this box is not checked, unusual non-ASCII characters are blocked.

- **Allow Double Escaping**. If this box is not checked, URLs can contain double escape characters.

- **Maximum Allowed Content Length**. This text box specifies the maximum size of content that a request can process. Keep this figure small if you do not allow HTTP uploads to your site.

- **Maximum URL Length**. This allows you to restrict the maximum size of a URL request sent to your site.

- **Maximum Query String**. This allows you to restrict the maximum query string size in a URL request sent to your site.

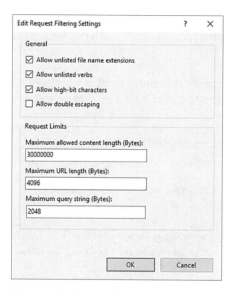

Figure 9-14 Request filtering settings

Application pools

Application pools are collections of web applications that are served by a worker process or a group of worker processes. When you create a new website in IIS, IIS automatically creates an associated application pool. One of the ideas behind application pools is that by separating web applications into their own pools, the failure of one web application does not impact the functioning of other web applications. Application pools allow you to do the following:

- Collect sites and applications that use the same configuration settings.

- Improve security by allowing the use of a custom security account to run an application.

- Silo resources in such a way that one web application cannot address or influence resources in another web application.

Creating application pools

Although new application pools are created each time you create a new site, there are reasons why you want to configure a new application pool. Prior to creating a new application pool, you need to know what pipeline mode you want to use to process requests for managed code. Managed pipeline mode determines how IIS processes requests for managed code. The difference between the two managed pipeline modes is as follows:

- **Integrated**. This mode allows the request-processing pipelines of IIS and ASP.NET to process the request. Most web applications are likely to use this mode.

- **Classic**. This mode forwards requests for managed code through aspnet_isapi .dll. This is the same method used for processing requests on servers running older versions of IIS. Use this mode if an older web application that you have migrated to IIS on Windows Server 2016 does not function well in integrated mode.

To create a new application pool, perform the following steps:

1. Open the IIS Manager console, and then click the Application Pools node.

2. Click Add Application Pool in the Actions menu. This opens the Add Application Pool dialog box shown in Figure 9-15.

Figure 9-15 Add application pool

3. In this dialog box, provide a name for the application pool, select the .NET CLR version for the application pool, and choose the managed pipeline mode.

Configuring application pool recycling settings

Not all developers write code that functions correctly over an extended period of time. If you find that a web application that you need to host on a computer running Windows Server 2016 starts to develop problems after it has run for a lengthy amount of time, you can deal with this by configuring application pool recycling settings to recycle the processes related to the application on a regular basis. You configure application pool recycling settings on the Edit Application Pool Recycling Settings dialog box shown in Figure 9-16. You can configure an application pool to be recycled when the following thresholds are met:

- After a certain amount of time has elapsed. By default all application pools automatically recycle every 1,740 minutes.

- After an application pool has processed a certain number of requests.

- At specific times of the day.

- After an application pool exceeds a certain virtual memory threshold.

- After an application pool exceeds a specific private memory threshold.

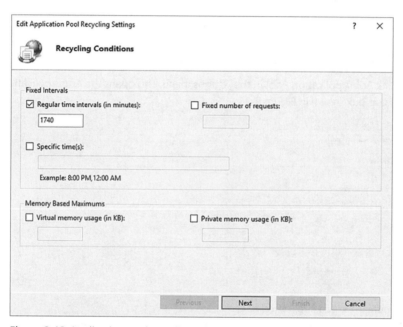

Figure 9-16 Application pool recycling settings

Through the Advanced Settings dialog box, shown in Figure 9-17, you can configure basic set-tings such as the pipeline mode and recycling settings. You can also configure settings includ-ing processor affinity, CPU limits, process orphaning, request limits, and rapid fail protection settings.

Figure 9-17 Application pool advanced settings

IIS users and delegation

IIS allows you to delegate the management of specific websites and web applications. This means that you can allow a specific user to manage a website without giving him logon privileges to the server or control over any other site or web application hosted by IIS.

When you install IIS, it is configured so that it does not allow remote management using the IIS Manager console. You configure IIS to allow remote management using the Management Service item at the server level in the IIS Manager console. This involves installing the Management Service role service and ensuring that the service is configured to start automatically. Using the Management Service item, shown in Figure 9-18, you can configure the following remote management properties:

- **Enable Remote Connections**. This item must be enabled for remote administration connections using IIS Manager Console to work.

- **Identity Credentials**. This allows you to specify whether administrators can connect using Windows credentials or IIS Manager credentials. The default setting only allows Windows user accounts.

- **Connections**. This allows you to specify whether remote management connections can occur on any IP address interface, or whether they are limited to a specific IP address interface. You can also specify which SSL certificate will be used to protect remote administration sessions.

- **IP Address Restrictions**. They allow you to specify which IP addresses or networks are allowed to successfully connect using IIS Administrator.

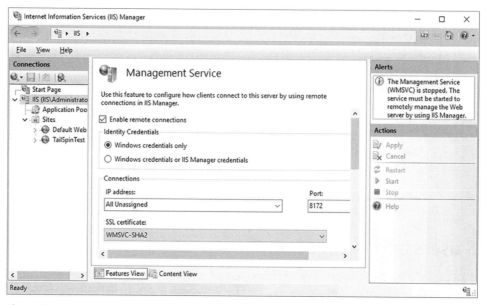

Figure 9-18 Management Service configuration

IIS user accounts

IIS allows you to create user accounts that exist only in IIS. These user accounts do not have any privileges outside IIS, and cannot be used to log on locally to the server. This allows you to assign administrative permissions to users without having to create a corresponding machine local or domain user account.

To create an IIS Manager user, perform the following steps:

1. Open the IIS Manager console and double-click the IIS Manager Users item when the Server level is selected in the IIS Manager console.

2. Click Add User in the Actions pane. This opens the Add User dialog box shown. Enter the user name and password for the IIS user.

Delegating administrative permissions

After you have enabled remote management and, if you choose to create IIS users, configured the appropriate IIS user accounts, you can delegate management permissions on a site or web application through the IIS Manager Permissions item. You can check precisely which permissions users have been delegated by viewing the Feature Delegation item at the server level. You can also modify which configuration items are delegated using the Feature Delegation item.

To delegate administrative permissions over a site, perform the following steps:

1. Open the IIS Manager console and select the website for which you want to delegate administrative permissions.

2. Double-click the IIS Manager Permissions item in the Details pane.

3. In the Actions pane, click Allow User. On the Allow User dialog box select the Windows or IIS Manager User, and then click OK. Figure 9-20 shows user Rooslan delegated permissions over the TailSpinTest site.

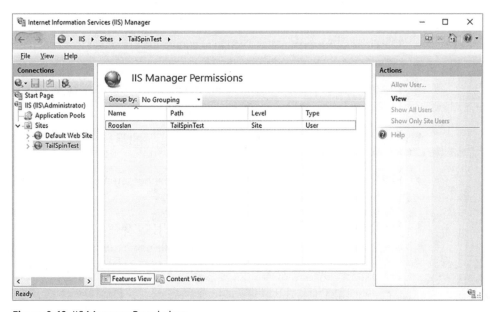

Figure 9-19 IIS Manager Permissions

Managing FTP

Although FTP is a protocol that is almost as old as the Internet itself, and newer ways of transfer-ring files are becoming more popular, many organizations still use FTP as their primary method of uploading data to web servers such as IIS.

The FTP server in Windows Server 2016 supports TLS connections and is fully managed from the IIS Manager console.

From the IIS Management console you can configure the following:

- **FTP Authentication**. This allows you to enable or disable Anonymous or Basic authenti-cation. The default settings have both forms of authentication disabled.

- **FTP Authorization**. It allows you to specify which users or groups are allowed to connect to the FTP server, and whether they have read and write permissions when using FTP.

- **FTP Directory Browsing**. It allows you to specify whether MS-DOS or UNIX-style direc-tory listings are provided. It also allows you to specify if virtual directory, available bytes, and four-digit years information are displayed.

- **FTP Firewall Support**. Allows you to configure the FTP server to accept passive connec-tions from a perimeter network firewall.

- **FTP IPv4 Address and Domain Name Restrictions**. This allows you to block or allow FTP clients based on IPv4 address or client domain name.

- **FTP Logging**. It allows you to configure the FTP logging settings, including how often log files are rotated.

- **FTP Messages**: It allows you to configure FTP banner settings. This is the informational text that is presented to new FTP sessions.

- **FTP Request Filtering**. Using this item, you can configure the following:
    - Configure FTP to allow or block specific file name extensions from transfers.
    - Block segments, such as sensitive folders, from being accessible in FTP.
    - Block particular FTP URLs.
    - Block specific FTP commands from being used during a session.

- **FTP SSL Settings**. This allows you to specify which server certificate is used for TLS though still called SSL) sessions. It also allows you to force the use of TLS as well as enforce 128-bit encryption on FTP SSL sessions.

- **FTP User Isolation**. It allows you to limit which folders an FTP user can navigate. You can configure a user to start in the FTP root directory or a specific user name-related directory.

To add a new FTP site, perform the following steps:

1. Open the IIS Manager console, right-click the Sites node, and then click Add FTP Site.

2. On the Site Information page, enter a name for the site and the directory path that is used to host the site's files.

3. On the Binding And SSL Settings page, shown in Figure 9-20, specify which IP addresses the FTP site listens on, whether the FTP site uses a virtual host name, whether the site starts automatically, whether SSL/TLS is allowed or required, and which server certificate is used in conjunction with the FTP site.

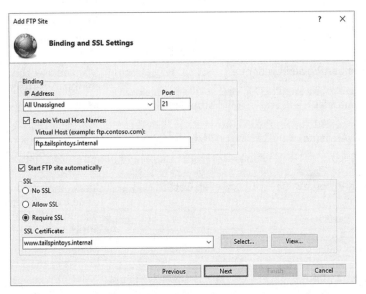

Figure 9-20 FTP site bindings and SSL settings

4. On the Authentication And Authorization Information page, specify whether you'll allow Anonymous and/or Basic authentication. On the Authorization drop-down menu, specify whether you want to allow access for the following:

  - All users

  - Anonymous users

  - Specified roles or user groups

  - Specified users

If you choose to allow access only to specified roles or user groups, you need to specify which roles, users, or user groups you want to grant access.

Managing IIS using PowerShell

You can use cmdlets from two separate PowerShell modules to manage IIS and websites running on Windows Server 2016. The IIS Administration PowerShell module contains a large number of cmdlets that you can use to manage IIS on Windows Server 2016. These cmdlets are described in Table 9-1. The WebAdministration PowerShell module contains a large number of cmdlets that you can use to manage web and FTP sits running on Windows Server 2016. These cmdlets are described in table 9-2.

Table 9-1. IIS PowerShell cmdlets

Noun	Verbs	Function
IISAppPool	Get	View App Pool information
IISCentralCertProvider	Clear, Get, Set, Enable, Disable	Manage the IIS central certificate store
IISCentralCertProviderCredential	Set	Manage user account credentials for the IIS certificate store
IISCommitDelay	Stop, Start	Manage delay of commitment of changes
IISConfigAttribute	Remove	Remove configuration attribute from IIS configuration section or configuration element attribute
IISConfigAttributeValue	Set, Get	Manage configuration attribute value for an IIS configuration section or configuration element attribute
IISConfigCollection	Get, Clear	Manage configuration element objects in an IIS configuration collection
IISConfigCollectionElement	New, Remove, Get	Manage configuration element objects
IISConfigElement	Remove, Get	Manage configuration elements
IISConfigSection	Get	View configuration section object
IISConfiguration	Export	Export IIS configuration
IISServerManager	Reset, Get	Manage IIS Server Manager
IISSharedConfig	Disable, Enable, Get	Manage IIS shared config
IISSite	Stop, Start, New, Get, Remove	Manage IIS Site

Table 9-2. Web Administration PowerShell cmdlets

Noun	Verbs	Function
WebAppDomain	Get	View application domains in which the IIS worker process is running
WebApplication	New, Convert, Remove, Get	Manage web applications in IIS websites
WebAppPool	Start, New, Restart, Remove, Stop	Manage application pools
WebAppPoolState	Get	View application pool states
WebBinding	New, Set, Remove, Get	Configure web bindings
WebCentralCertProvider	Clear, Get, Enable, Set, Disable	Manage configuration settings for central certificate provider
WebCentralCertProviderCredential	Set	Configure user account credentials for central certificate provider
WebCommitDelay	Start, Stop	Manage delay of commitment of changes
WebConfigFile	Get	View file system path of web.config file
WebConfiguration	Backup, Add, Select, Set, Restore, Clear, Get	Manage IIS configuration elements
WebConfigurationBackup	Get, Remove	Manage IIS configuration backups
WebConfigurationLocation	Remove, Get, Rename	Manage location of configuration settings
WebConfigurationLock	Add, Get, Remove	Manage lock status of IIS configuration
WebConfigurationProperty	Set, Add, Remove, Get	Manage configuration properties
WebFilePath	Get	View path to location of specific IIS module
WebFtpSite	New	Create a new FTP site
WebGlobalModule	Disable, New, Get, Remove, Enable, Set	Manage IIS global modules
WebHandler	Get, New, Remove, Set	Manage IIS request handlers
WebItem	Restart, Start, Stop	Manage application pools or websites
WebItemState	Get	View state of application pool or website

WebManagedModule	Get, Set, New, Remove	Manage IIS managed modules
WebRequest	Get	View IIS requests currently being run
WebRequestTracing	Disable, Enable	Manage request tracing for a website
WebRequestTracingSetting	Clear	Clears request tracing configuration
WebRequestTracingSettings	Clear	Clears request tracing configuration as well (not a duplicate)
Website	Start, Get, Stop, Remove, New	Manage websites
WebsiteState	Get	View the state of a website
WebURL	Get	View a website URL
WebVirtualDirectory	Remove, Get, New	Manage web virtual directories

Containers

A container is a portable isolated application execution environment. Containers have been around on Linux for some time, but are new to Windows with Windows Server 2016 and Windows 10. Containers allow developers to bundle an application and its dependencies in a single image. This image can easily be exported, imported, and deployed on different container hosts, from Nano Server on bare metal hardware right through to being hosted and run on Azure. Because dependencies are bundled with applications within a container, IT operations can deploy a container as soon as it is handed off without worrying if an appropriate prerequisite software package has been installed or if a necessary setting has been configured. Because a container provides an isolated environment, a failure that occurs within one container will only impact that container and will not impact other containerized applications running on the container host.

Container concepts

Containers can be a little challenging to conceptualize when you first encounter them. To understand how containers work, you first need to understand some of the terminology involving containers. While these concepts will be fleshed out more completely later in the chapter, at a high level you should understand the following terms:

- **Container image.** A container image is a template from which a container is generated. There are two general types of container images, a base OS image and a specific image, which are usually created for a workload. The difference between these containers on Windows Server 2016 is as follows:

  - **Container base OS image.** This is an image of the Windows Server operating system upon which other container images are built. It comes in either Server Core or Nano Server versions, which represent either the Server Core or Nano Server Platforms. Microsoft publishes container base OS images online in an official container registry. You can download a container base OS image from the container registry to a container host. Microsoft also updates container base OS images as software updates are released.

- **Container Image.** A container image stores changes made to a running container-base OS image or another container image. For example, you can start a new container from a container base OS image, make modifications such as installing Java or a Windows feature, and then save those modifications as a new container image. The new container image only stores the changes you make, and therefore is much smaller than the parent container base OS image. You can then create an additional container image that stores modifications made to the container image that has an installed Java and Windows feature. Each container image only stores the changes made to the image it was run from.

- **Sandbox.** The sandbox is the environment in which you can make modifications to an existing container image before you commit the changes to create a new container image. If you don't commit those changes to a new image, those changes will be lost when the container is removed.

- **Image dependency.** A new container image has the container image off which it was created as a dependency. For example, if you create a container image named Web-Server-1.0 that has the IIS role installed off the Server Core base OS image, then the Server Core base OS image is a dependency for the WebServer-1.0 image. This dependency is very specific, and you can't use an updated version of the Server Core base OS image as a replacement for the version that you used when creating the WebServer-1.0 image. You can then export this container image that only records the changes made to another container host. You can start the image as long as the dependency Container OS base image is present on that container host. You can have multiple images in a dependency chain.

- **Container Host.** A container host is a computer, either virtual, physical, or even a cloud based Platform as a Service (PaaS) solution, that runs containers.

- **Container registries.** Container registries are central storehouses of container images. While it's possible to transfer containers or copy them to file shares using tools like FTP, common practice is to use a container registry as a repository for container images. Public container registries, such as the one that hosts Microsoft's base OS images, also stores previous versions of the container base OS images. This allows you to retrieve earlier versions of the container base OS image that other images may depend upon. DockerHub is the primary public container registry. Container registries can be public or private. You can use a private container registry on your organization's internal network to distribute containers.

> ## Inside OUT
> ### *Data and Containers*
>
> Containers offer a non-persistent isolated application execution environment. An application should run in the container, but shouldn't store application data in a container. Application data should be stored in location separate from the container, such as in a backend database server, Azure storage blob, or other persistent alternative. Containers are good at serving in stateless roles such as load balanced front end web servers, especially because you can start new containers quickly to handle additional load as required.

Container types

Windows Server supports two container types: the Windows Server container and Hyper-V containers. Windows 10 supports only Hyper-V containers. Windows Server 2016 supports Windows Server containers and Hyper-V containers.

Windows Server Containers

Windows Server Containers provide an isolated application execution environment. This is accomplished through process and namespace isolation. Windows Server containers share a kernel with all other containers running on the container host. Windows Server containers also share a kernel with the container host. This is why you can't run Windows Server containers directly on Windows 10.

Hyper-V Containers

A Hyper-V container is a highly optimized virtual machine that also provides an isolated application execution environment. Hyper-V containers don't share the kernel with the container host, nor other containers on the same container host. Hyper-V containers require that the Hyper-V role be installed on the container host. If the container host is a Hyper-V virtual machine, you will need to enable nested virtualization. By default, a container will start as a Windows Server container. You can start a container as a Hyper-V container by using the --isolation=hyperv option.

For example, to create a Hyper-V container from the microsoft/windowsservercore image, issue the command:

```
Docker run -it --isolation=hyperv microsoft/windowsservercore cmd
```

MORE INFO   HYPER-V CONTAINERS

You can learn more about Hyper-V containers at: *https://docs.microsoft.com/en-us/ virtualization/windowscontainers/manage-containers/hyperv-container*.

Inside OUT

Nano Server versus Hyper-V Containers

Both Nano Server and Hyper-V containers provide you with the ability to run applications in an isolated environment where the kernel is not shared with other applications. Hyper-V containers have lower system requirements and faster startup times than Nano Server instances. Nano Server instances can function as hosts for both stateful and stateless applications, whereas the general rule is that you should avoid storing data in containers as containers.

Most organizations will deploy Nano Server in concert with Hyper-V containers, with Nano Server functioning as the container host and the Hyper-V containers storing stateless applications.

Server Core and Nano images

Windows Server containers come in two varieties: Server Core and Nano Server. Containers do not have a GUI element, so all management of containers must be through the command line. The differences between these two container types are as follows:

- Nano Server containers run a containerized version of the Nano Server installation option. Applications that run on Nano Server should run on a container created from the Nano Server container image. Nano Server container images have a lower memory and storage foot print than Server Core installation images have.

- Server Core containers run a containerized version of the Server Core installation option. Applications that run on the Server Core version of Windows Server 2016 should run on a container created from the Server Core container image.

Managing Containers with Docker

Containers on Windows Server 2016 are managed using the Docker engine. The advantage here is that the command syntax of Docker on Windows is almost identical to the command line tools of Docker on Linux. The drawback is that while there is a community maintained PowerShell module for managing Containers on Windows Server 2016 available on GitHub,

PowerShell is not the primary tool for Windows Server container management. Containers are unusual on Windows Server 2016 in that they are a major new operating system feature that doesn't include built-in PowerShell management support.

For Windows Server administrators unfamiliar with Docker syntax, the commands include extensive help support. Typing Docker at the command prompt will provide an overview of all high level Docker functionality, and you can learn more about specific commands by using the --help command parameter. For example, the following command will provide information about the Docker Image command:

```
docker image --help
```

> **MORE INFO   DOCKER ENGINE ON WINDOWS**
>
> **You can learn more about Docker Engine on Windows at:** *https://docs.microsoft.com/en-us/virtualization/windowscontainers/manage-docker/configure-docker-daemon.*

Installing Docker

Docker is not included with the Windows Server installation media. Instead, you need to install Docker from the PowerShell gallery. Installing in this manner ensures that you have the latest version of Docker because it is updated on a frequent basis.

The simplest way to install Docker is to ensure that your Windows Server 2016 computer has internet connectivity. You then run the following command from an elevated PowerShell prompt as shown in Figure 10-1 to install the Docker Microsoft Provider:

```
Install-Module -Name DockerMsftProvider -Repository PSGallery -Force
```

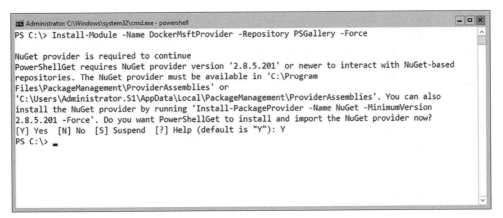

FIGURE 10-1 Install DockerMsftProvider

CHAPTER 10

The next step to take is to install the most recent version of Docker. You do this by executing the following command as shown in Figure 10-2, ensuring that you answer Yes when prompted to install software from a source not marked as trusted.

```
Install-Package –Name docker –ProviderName DockerMsftProvider
```

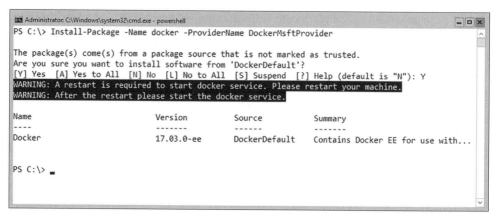

FIGURE 10-2 Install Docker

You'll then need to restart the computer that will function as the container host to complete the installation of Docker. You can update the version of Docker when a new one becomes available by rerunning the following command:

```
Install-Package –Name docker –ProviderName DockerMsftProvider
```

Inside OUT

Docker, Windows and Linux

While you can use the same Docker commands on Windows Server 2016 and your favorite Linux distribution, you can only use the Server Core and Nano Server images on Windows hosts, and you can't directly run Linux containers on Windows computers. You can run them indirectly, however, by hosting a virtual machine on the Windows computer.

Demon.json

If you want to change the default Docker engine settings, such as whether to create a default NAT network, you need to create and configure the Docker engine configuration file. This doesn't exist by default. When it is present, the settings in the file override the Docker engine default settings.

You should create this file in the c:\ProgramData\Docker\config folder. Before editing the Demon.json file, you'll need to stop the docker service using the following command:

```
Stop-Service docker
```

You only need to add settings that you want to change to the configuration file. For example, if you only want to configure the Docker Engine to accept incoming connections on port 2701, you add the following lines to demon.json:

```
{

    "hosts": ["tcp://0.0.0.0:2375"]

}
```

The Windows Docker engine doesn't support all possible Docker configuration file options. The ones that you can configure are shown in the below example:

```
{

    "authorization-plugins": [],

    "dns": [],

    "dns-opts": [],

    "dns-search": [],

    "exec-opts": [],

    "storage-driver": "",

    "storage-opts": [],

    "labels": [],

    "log-driver": "",

    "mtu": 0,

    "pidfile": "",

    "graph": "",

    "cluster-store": "",

    "cluster-advertise": "",

    "debug": true,
```

```
    "hosts": [],

    "log-level": "",

    "tlsverify": true,

    "tlscacert": "",

    "tlscert": "",

    "tlskey": "",

    "group": "",

    "default-ulimits": {},

    "bridge": "",

    "fixed-cidr": "",

    "raw-logs": false,

    "registry-mirrors": [],

    "insecure-registries": [],

    "disable-legacy-registry": false

}
```

These options allow you to do the following:

- **authorization-plugins.** Which authorization plugins to load

- **dns.** Which DNS server to use for containers by default

- **dns-opts.** Which DNS options to use

- **dns-search.** Which DNS search domains to use

- **exec-opts.** Which runtime execution options to use

- **storage-driver.** Specify storage driver

- **storage-opts.** Specify storage driver options

- **labels.** Docker engine labels

- **log-driver.** Default driver for container logs

- **Mtu.** Container network MTU

- **pidfile.** Path to use for daemon PID file

- **graph.** Docker runtime root location

- **Group.** Specify the local security group that has permissions to run Docker commands

- **cluster-store.** Cluster store options

- **cluster-advertise.** Cluster address to advertise

- **Debug.** Enable debug mode

- **hosts.** Daemon sockets to connect to

- **log-level.** Logging detail

- **Tlsverify.** Use TLS and perform verification

- **tlscacert.** Specify which Certificate Authorities to trust

- **tlscert.** Location of TLS certificate file

- **tlskey.** Location of TLS key file

- **group.** UNIX socket group

- **default-ulimits.** Default ulimits for containers

- **bridge.** Attach containers to network bridge

- **fixed-cidr.** IPv4 subnet for static IP address

- **raw-logs.** Log format

- **registry-mirrors.** Preferred registry mirror

- **insecure-registries.** Allow insecure registry communication

- **disable-legacy-registry.** Block contacting legacy registries

Once you have made the necessary modifications to the demon.json file, you should start the Docker service by running the PowerShell command:

```
Start-Service docker
```

Retrieving Container OS image

You can retrieve the latest version of the Server Core base OS container image by running the following command as shown in Figure 10-3:

```
docker pull microsoft/windowsservercore
```

```
Administrator: C:\Windows\system32\cmd.exe - powershell
PS C:\> docker pull microsoft/windowsservercore
Using default tag: latest
latest: Pulling from microsoft/windowsservercore
3889bb8d808b: Pull complete
3430754e4d17: Pull complete
Digest: sha256:34a0199e1f8c4c978d08e5a4e67af961752e41212b7bde9c1ea570ee29dcff2c
Status: Downloaded newer image for microsoft/windowsservercore:latest
PS C:\> _
```

FIGURE 10-3 Pull OS image

You can retrieve the latest version of the Nano Server base OS container image by running the command:

```
docker pull microsoft/nanoserver
```

The latest version of the server core image is updated frequently. Because of dependency issues when working with older containers, you may need an earlier version of the base OS image. To retrieve all versions of the WindowsServerCore image from the public registry, run the command:

```
docker pull -a microsoft/windowsservercore
```

To retrieve all versions of the Nano Server image as shown in Figure 10-4, run the command:

```
Docker pull -a microsoft/nanoserver
```

CHAPTER 10

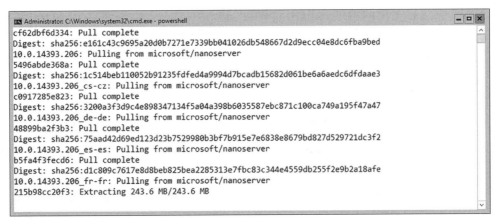

FIGURE 10-4 Pulling all versions of an OS image

Container registries and images

Container registries are repositories for the distribution of container images. The main container registry that will be of interest to Windows Server administrators will be the DockerHub public repository. Microsoft posts container images on the DockerHub registry. This includes not only the base OS images, but images that include evaluation editions of SQL Server as well as technologies such as the latest builds of ASP.NET on containers and Azure CLI.

From the DockerHub registry, you can get the following Microsoft published container images:

- **microsoft/oms.** Includes an OMS agent for Linux containers. Only the Windows based container operating system images will run on Windows Server 2016.

- **microsoft/dotnet.** Includes .NET core for both Linux and Windows Server Core container operating systems. Only the Windows based container operating system images will run on Windows Server 2016.

- **microsoft/vsts-agent.** Includes Visual Studio Team Services agent for Linux based container operating systems. Only the Windows based container operating system images will run on Windows Server 2016.

- **microsoft/aspnet.** Includes IIS 10, .NET Framework, and .NET Extensibility for IIS that allow ASP.NET applications to run on Windows Server Core container operating system.

- **microsoft/iis.** Includes Internet Information Services on Windows Server Core container operating system.

CHAPTER 10

- **microsoft/mssql-server-linux.** This container image contains Microsoft SQL Server on Linux and will only run on Linux container hosts, rather than on Windows Server container hosts.

- **microsoft/azure-cli.** Includes Azure CLI on the Windows Server Core container operating system.

- **microsoft/nanoserver.** Base image for the Nano Server container operating system.

- **microsoft/windowsservercore.** Base image for the Windows Server Core container operating system.

- **microsoft/aspnetcore.** Includes ASP.NET Core on the Windows Server Core container operating system.

- **microsoft/dotnet-nightly.** Includes .NET nightly builds on the Windows Server Core container operating system.

- **microsoft/aspnetcore-build.** Includes images that are used to compile/publish ASP.NET Core applications inside a Windows Server Core container operating system. Differs from aspnetcore image, which allows adding compiled ASP.NET core applications to an image.

- **microsoft/dotnet-samples.** Includes .NET core Docker samples on the Windows Server Core container operating system.

- **microsoft/sample-nginx.** Includes Nginx on both Nano Server and Windows Server Core container operating systems.

- **microsoft/applicationinsights.** Includes Application Insights for Docker on Windows Server Core container operating systems.

- **microsoft/mssql-server-windows-express.** Includes MS SQL Server Express edition on the Windows Server Core container operating system.

- **microsoft/mssql-server-windows.** Includes 180 day preview version of SQL Server for containers on the Windows Server Core container operating system.

- **microsoft/dotnet-framework.** Includes .NET Framework on the Windows Server Core container operating system.

- **microsoft/powershell.** Includes PowerShell on cross-platform container images. Only the Windows based container operating system images will run on Windows Server 2016.

- **microsoft/aspnetcore-build-nightly.** Includes a nightly build of ASP.NET core for the Windows Server Core container operating system.

- **microsoft/sample-httpd.** Includes Apache httpd on the Nano Server and Windows Server Core container operating systems.

- **microsoft/cntk.** Includes a sample of the Microsoft Cognitive Toolkit on a Linux container operating system. Only the Windows based container operating system images will run on Windows Server 2016.

- **microsoft/powershell-nightly.** Includes nightly builds of PowerShell Core on a variety of container operating systems including Windows Server Core and Linux. Only the Windows based container operating system images will run on Windows Server 2016.

- **microsoft/sample-python.** Includes Python on both Windows Server Core and Nano Server container operating systems.

- **microsoft/sample-mysql.** Includes MySQL on both the Windows Server Core and Nano Server container operating systems.

- **microsoft/sample-node.** Includes Node on a Nano Server container operating system.

- **microsoft/dotnet-buildtools-prereqs.** Includes images for building components of dotnet on the Windows Server Core container operating system.

- **microsoft/sample-golang.** Includes the Go programming language on Windows Server Core and Nano Server container operating systems.

- **microsoft/sample-redis.** Includes Redis on both the Windows Server Core and Nano Server container operating systems.

- **microsoft/sqlite.** Includes SQLite on the Windows Server Core container operating system.

- **microsoft/sample-ruby.** Includes Ruby on the Windows Server Core container operating system.

- **microsoft/mssql-server-windows-developer.** Includes MS SQL Server Developer edition on Windows Server Core container operating system.

- **microsoft/sample-rails.** Includes Ruby and Rails samples on both the Windows Server Core or Nano Server based container operating systems.

- **microsoft/sample-django.** Includes a Django installation on Windows Server Core container operating system.

- **microsoft/sample-mongodb.** Includes a mongodb sample on Windows Server Core container operating system.

- **microsoft/dotnet-framework-samples.** Includes samples that allow you to demonstrate a variety of .NET Framework Docker configurations on the Windows Server Core container operating system.

- **microsoft/pbxt.** This container image is only used for the Power BI Data Curation team.

In cases where both a Windows Server Core and Nano Server image exist, you can use the -a option with the docker pull command to retrieve all images. This can be helpful if you don't know the image ID of the specific image that you wish to retrieve. For example, when pulling the microsoft/sample-mysql container image, which includes both Windows Server Core and Nano Server images, use the command *docker pull -a Microsoft/sample-mysql*.

When you pull an image from a registry, the action will also download any dependency images that are required. For example, if you pull an image that was built on a specific version of the Windows Server Core base image and you don't have that image on the container host, that image will also be downloaded from the registry.

MORE INFO   OFFICIAL MICROSOFT CONTAINER IMAGES

You can see which container images Microsoft has made available at: *https://hub.docker. com/u/microsoft/*.

Managing containers

You use Docker to perform all container management tasks on computers running Windows 10. At present, there is no graphical utility for container management available within the operating system, although there are some open source third party tools available.

Starting a container

You create a new container by specifying the container image that you wish to create the container from. You can start a container and run an interactive session either by specifying cmd. exe or PowerShell.exe by using the *-it* option with *docker run*. Interactive sessions allow you to directly interact with the container through the command line from the moment the container starts. Detached mode starts a container, but doesn't start an interactive session with that container.

For example, to start a container from the Microsoft/windowsservercore image and to enter an interactive PowerShell session within that container once it is started, use the command:

```
Docker run -it microsoft/windowsservercore powershell.exe
```

Something else that's important to understand from early stages is that by default, containers use network address translation. This means that if you are running an application or service on the container that you want to expose to the network, you'll need to configure port mapping between the container host's network interface and the container. For example, if you had downloaded the Microsoft/iis container image and you wanted to start a container in detached mode, mapping port 8080 on the container host to port 80 on the container, you would run the following command, shown in Figure 10-5.

```
Docker run -d -p 8080:80 microsoft/iis
```

FIGURE 10-5 Port mapping

This is only the very basic sort of information you'd need to get started with a container and you will learn more about container networking later in this chapter.

You can verify which containers are running using the docker ps command shown in Figure 10-6. The problem with this option is that this will only show you the running containers and won't show you any that are in a stopped state. You can see which containers are on a container host, including containers that aren't currently running, by using the *docker ps -a* command.

```
C:\>docker ps
CONTAINER ID      IMAGE            COMMAND              CREATED        STATUS
      PORTS                NAMES
2064401b1e37      microsoft/iis    "C:\\ServiceMonitor..."  4 minutes ago  Up 4 minutes
      0.0.0.0:8080->80/tcp    elegant_spence

C:\>
```

FIGURE 10-6 List containers

One thing that you'll notice about containers is that they appear to be assigned fairly random names such as sarcastic_hedgehog, dyspeptic_hamster, and sententious_muppet. The reason that Docker assigns random names rather than asking you for one, is that containers are a more ephemeral type of application host than a VM, and as they are likely to only have a short lifespan, it isn't worth assigning any name that you'd need to remember to them. The reason for the structure of the random names is that they are easy to remember in the short term, which makes containers that you have to interact with on a short term basis easier to address than when using hexadecimal container IDs. Figure 10-7 shows the output of the *docker ps -a* command and shows the names of three containers: elegant_spence, happy_wozniak, and romantic_newton.

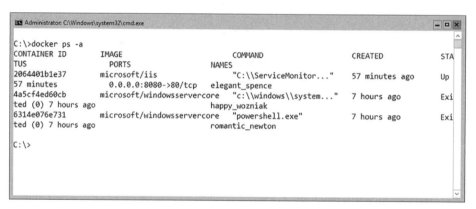

FIGURE 10-7 List all images

Earlier in the chapter you learned that it was possible to start a container in detached mode. If you want to start an interactive session on a container that you started in detached mode, use the command *docker exec -i <containername> powershell.exe*. Figure 10-8 shows entering an interactive session on a container started in detached mode. The hostname command displays the container's ID.

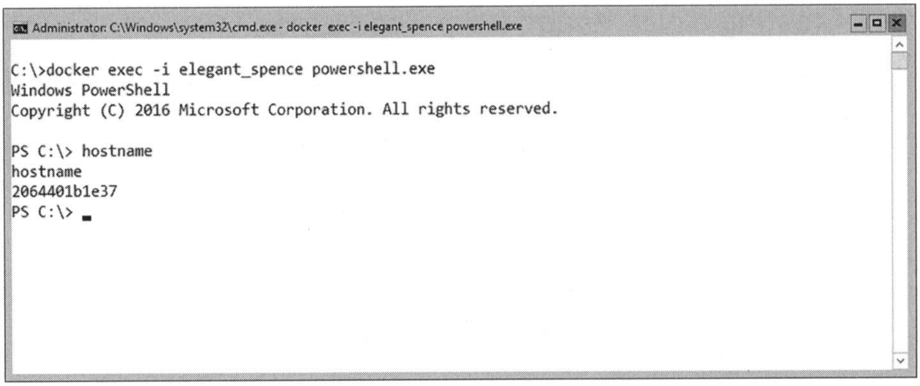

FIGURE 10-8 Start interactive session

In some cases it will be necessary to start a stopped container. You can start a stopped container using the *Docker start <containername>* command.

Modifying a running container

Once you have a container running, you can enter the container and make the modifications that you want to make to ensure that the application the container hosts will run correctly. This might involve creating directories, using the dism.exe command to add roles, or using the *wget* PowerShell alias to download and install binaries such as Java. For example, the following code, when run from inside a container, downloads and installs the most current version of Java into a container based off the Server Core base OS container:

```
wget -Uri «http://javadl.sun.com/webapps/download/AutoDL?BundleId=107944» -outfile
javaInstall.exe -UseBasicParsing

REG ADD HKLM\Software\Policies\Microsoft\Windows\Installer /v DisableRollback /t REG_
DWORD /d 1 | Out-Null

./javaInstall.exe /s INSTALLDIR=C:\Java REBOOT=Disable | Out-Null
```

Once you are finished modifying the container, you can type *Exit* to exit the container. A container must be in a shut down state before you can capture it as a container image. You use the docker stop <containername> cmdlet to shut a container down.

Creating a new image from a container

Once the container is in the state that you want it in and shut down, you can capture the container to a new container image. You do this using the *docker commit <container_name> <new_image_name>* command. Figure 10-9 shows committing a modified container to a new container image named new_iis_java, and verifying the properties of the image using the *docker images* command.

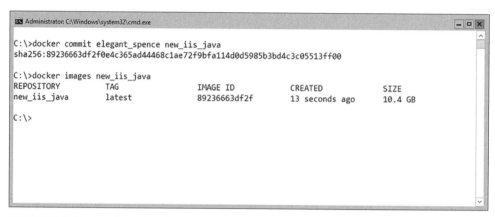

FIGURE 10-9 Docker commit

Once you have committed a container to a container image, you can remove the container using the *docker rm* command. For example, to remove the elegant_spence container, issue the command:

```
Docker rm elegant_spence
```

Using dockerfiles

Dockerfiles are text files that allow you to automate the process of creating new container images. You use a dockerfile with the *docker build* command to automate container creation, something that is very useful when you need to create new container images off regularly updated base OS container images.

Dockerfiles have the elements shown in Table 10-1.

Table 10-1. Dockerfile element

Instruction	Description
FROM	Specifies the container image used in creating the new image creation. For example: `FROM microsoft/windowsservercore`
RUN	Specifies commands to be run and captures into the new container image. For example: `RUN wget -Uri "http://javadl.sun.com/webapps/download/ AutoDL?BundleId=107944" -outfile javaInstall.exe -UseBa- sicParsing` `RUN REG ADD HKLM\Software\Policies\Microsoft\Windows\ Installer /v DisableRollback /t REG_DWORD /d 1	Out- Null`  `RUN ./javaInstall.exe /s INSTALLDIR=C:\Java REBOOT=Disable	Out-Null`
COPY	Copies files and directories from the container host filesystem to the filesystem of the container. For windows containers, the destination format must use forward slashes. For example: `COPY example1.txt c:/temp/`
ADD	Can be used to add files from a remote source, such as a URL. For example: `ADD https://www.python.org/ftp/python/3.5.1/python- 3.5.1.exe /temp/python-3.5.1.exe`
WORKDIR	Specifies a working directory for the RUN and CMD instructions
CMD	A command to be run when deploying an instance of the container image

For example, the following Dockerfile will create a new container from the Microsoft/windowsservercore image, create a directory named ExampleDirectory and then will install the iis-webserver feature.

```
FROM microsoft/windowsservercore

RUN mkdir ExampleDirectory

RUN dism.exe /online /enable-feature /all /featurename:iis-webserver /NoRestart
```

To create a container image named example_image, change into the directory that hosts the file Dockerfile (no extension) and run the following command:

```
Docker build -t example_image .
```

CHAPTER 10

> **MORE INFO   DOCKERFILE ON WINDOWS**
>
> You can learn more about Dockerfile on Windows at: *https://docs.microsoft.com/en-us/virtualization/windowscontainers/manage-docker/manage-windows-dockerfile*.

Managing container images

To save a Docker image for transfer to another computer, use the *docker save* command. When you save a Docker image, you save it in .tar format. Figure 10-10 shows exporting the new_iis_java image to the c:\archive\new_iis_java.tar file.

```
Administrator: C:\Windows\system32\cmd.exe

C:\>docker save new_iis_java -o c:\archive\new_iis_java.tar

C:\>dir c:\archive
 Volume in drive C has no label.
 Volume Serial Number is 8801-D760

 Directory of c:\archive

03/06/2017  01:08 AM    <DIR>          .
03/06/2017  01:08 AM    <DIR>          ..
03/06/2017  01:08 AM    10,628,078,592 new_iis_java.tar
               1 File(s) 10,628,078,592 bytes
               2 Dir(s)  76,931,993,600 bytes free

C:\>
```

FIGURE 10-10 Docker save

You can load a Docker image from a saved image using the *docker load* command. For example, Figure 10-11 shows loading a container image from the c:\archive\new_iis_java.tar file created earlier and when the container image itself had been deleted from the container host.

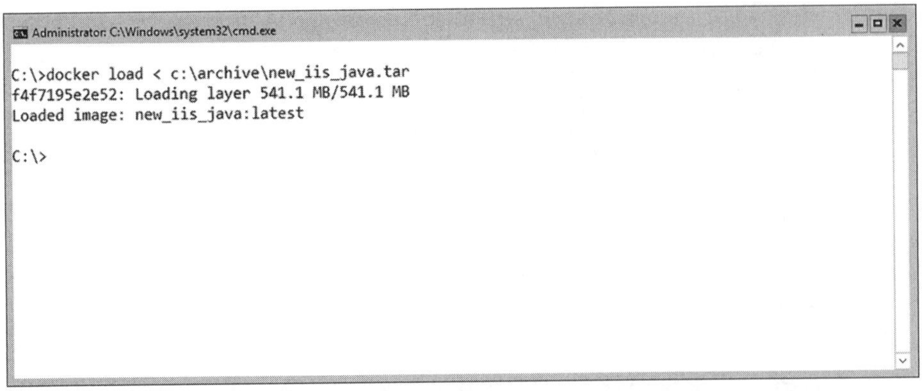

```
Administrator: C:\Windows\system32\cmd.exe

C:\>docker load < c:\archive\new_iis_java.tar
f4f7195e2e52: Loading layer 541.1 MB/541.1 MB
Loaded image: new_iis_java:latest

C:\>
```

FIGURE 10-11 Load archived image

When you have multiple container images that have the same name, you can remove an image by using the image ID. You can determine the image ID by running the command Docker Images as shown in Figure 10-12. You can't remove a container image until the last container created from that image either directly or indirectly has been deleted.

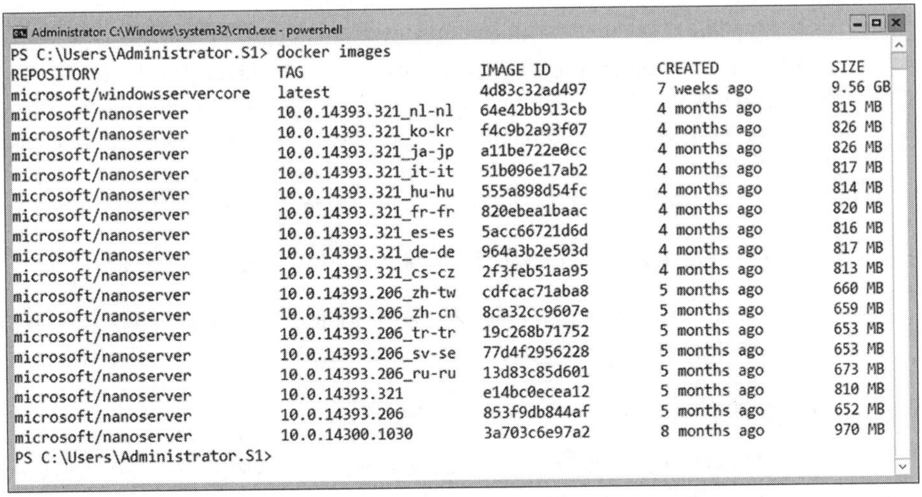

```
Administrator: C:\Windows\system32\cmd.exe - powershell
PS C:\Users\Administrator.S1> docker images
REPOSITORY                        TAG                        IMAGE ID            CREATED             SIZE
microsoft/windowsservercore       latest                     4d83c32ad497        7 weeks ago         9.56 GB
microsoft/nanoserver              10.0.14393.321_nl-nl       64e42bb913cb        4 months ago        815 MB
microsoft/nanoserver              10.0.14393.321_ko-kr       f4c9b2a93f07        4 months ago        826 MB
microsoft/nanoserver              10.0.14393.321_ja-jp       a11be722e0cc        4 months ago        826 MB
microsoft/nanoserver              10.0.14393.321_it-it       51b096e17ab2        4 months ago        817 MB
microsoft/nanoserver              10.0.14393.321_hu-hu       555a898d54fc        4 months ago        814 MB
microsoft/nanoserver              10.0.14393.321_fr-fr       820ebea1baac        4 months ago        820 MB
microsoft/nanoserver              10.0.14393.321_es-es       5acc66721d6d        4 months ago        816 MB
microsoft/nanoserver              10.0.14393.321_de-de       964a3b2e503d        4 months ago        817 MB
microsoft/nanoserver              10.0.14393.321_cs-cz       2f3feb51aa95        4 months ago        813 MB
microsoft/nanoserver              10.0.14393.206_zh-tw       cdfcac71aba8        5 months ago        660 MB
microsoft/nanoserver              10.0.14393.206_zh-cn       8ca32cc9607e        5 months ago        659 MB
microsoft/nanoserver              10.0.14393.206_tr-tr       19c268b71752        5 months ago        653 MB
microsoft/nanoserver              10.0.14393.206_sv-se       77d4f2956228        5 months ago        653 MB
microsoft/nanoserver              10.0.14393.206_ru-ru       13d83c85d601        5 months ago        673 MB
microsoft/nanoserver              10.0.14393.321             e14bc0ecea12        5 months ago        810 MB
microsoft/nanoserver              10.0.14393.206             853f9db844af        5 months ago        652 MB
microsoft/nanoserver              10.0.14300.1030            3a703c6e97a2        8 months ago        970 MB
PS C:\Users\Administrator.S1>
```

FIGURE 10-12 Image list

You then remove the image by using the command Docker rmi with the image ID. For example, Figure 10-13 shows the removal of the image with the ID a896e5590871 using the command:

```
docker rmi a896e5590871
```

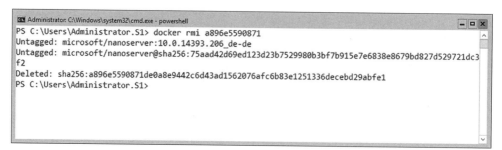

FIGURE 10-13 Remove image

Service accounts for Windows containers

Although containers based on the Server Core and Nano Server operating systems have most of the same characteristics as a virtual machine or bare metal deployment of the Server Core or Nano Server versions of Windows Server 2016, one thing that you can't do with containers is to join them to a domain. This is because containers are supposed to be temporary rather than permanent and domain joining them would clog up Active Directory with unnecessary computer accounts.

While containers can't be domain joined, it is possible to use a group managed service account (gMSA) to provide one or more containers with a domain identity similar to that used by a device that is realm-joined. Performing this task requires downloading the Windows Server Container Tools and ensuring that the container host is a member of the domain that hosts the gMSA. When you perform this procedure, the container's LocalSystem and Network Service accounts use the gMSA. This gives the container the identity represented by the gMSA.

To configure gMSA association with a container, perform the following steps:

1. Download the Windows Server Container Tools from *https://github.com/Microsoft/Virtualization-Documentation/tree/live/windows-server-container-tools*.

2. Ensure that the container host is domain joined.

3. Add the container host to a specially created domain security group. This domain security group can have any name.

4. Create a gMSA and grant the specially created domain security group that the container host is a member of permission to the gMSA.

5. Install the gMSA on the container host.

6. Use the New-CredentialSpec cmdlet on the container host to generate the gMSA credentials in a file in JSON format. This cmdlet is located in the CredentialSpec PowerShell module available from the Windows Server Container tools. For example, if you created a gMSA named MelbourneAlpha, you would run the following command:

```
New-CredentialSpace -Name MelbourneAlpha -AccountName MelbourneAlpha
```

7. You can verify that the credentials have been saved in JSON format by running the Get-CredentialSpec cmdlet. By default, credentials are stored in the c:\ProgramData\Docker\CredentialSpecs\ folder.

8. Start the container using the option *--security-opt "credentialspec="* and specify the JSON file containing the credentials associated with the gMSA.

Once you've configured the container to indirectly use the gMSA for its Local System and Network Service accounts, you can provide the container with permissions to access domain resources by providing access to the gMSA. For example, if you wanted to provide the container with access to the contents of a file share hosted on a domain member, you can configure permissions so that the gMSA has access to the file share.

MORE INFO   ACTIVE DIRECTORY CONTAINER SERVICE ACCOUNTS

You can learn more about Active Directory Container Service Accounts at: *https://docs.microsoft.com/en-us/virtualization/windowscontainers/manage-containers/manage-serviceaccounts.*

CHAPTER 10

Applying updates

One of the concepts that many IT operations personnel find challenging is that you don't update a container that is deployed in production. Instead, what you do is create a new updated version of the container image that the container that is deployed in production is based on. You then remove the container in production and deploy a new container to production that is based on the newly updated image.

For example, you have a container that hosts a web app deployed from a container image named WebApp1 deployed in production. The developers in your organization release an update to WebApp1 that involves changing some existing settings. Rather than modifying the container in production, you start another container off the WebApp1 image, modify the settings, and then create a new container image named WebApp2. You then deploy a new container into production off the WebApp2 container image and remove the original unupdated container.

While you can manually update your Container base OS images by applying software updates, Microsoft releases updated versions of the container base images each time a new software update is released. Once a new container OS base image is released, you, or your organization's developers, should update existing images that are dependent on the container OS base image. Regularly updated container base OS images provide an excellent reason why you should eventually move towards using Dockerfiles to automate the build of containers. If you have a Dockerfile configured for each container image used in your organization, updating when a new Container base OS image is released is a quick and painless automated process.

Inside OUT

Keep old OS images

You'll need to keep your old Container OS base images around until all of the container images that are dependent on that old container OS base image have been replaced by newly updated container images.

Container networking

Each container has a virtual network adapter. This virtual network adapter connects to a virtual switch, through which inbound and outbound traffic is sent. Networking modes determine how network adapters function in terms of IP addressing, whether they use NAT or are connected to the same network that the container host is.

Windows Containers support the following networking modes:

- **NAT.** Each container is assigned an IP address from the private 172.16.0.0 /12 address range. When using NAT, you can configure port forwarding from the container host to the container endpoint. If you create a container without specifying a network, the container will use the default NAT network.

- **Transparent.** Each container endpoint connects to the physical network. The containers can have IP addresses assigned statically or through DHCP.

- **Overlay.** Use this mode when you have configured the docker engine to run in swarm mode. Overlay mode allows container endpoints to be connected across multiple container hosts.

- **L2 Bridge.** Container endpoints are on the same IP subnet used by the container host. IP addresses must be assigned statically. All containers on the container host have the same MAC address.

- **L2 Tunnel.** This mode is only used when you deploy containers in Azure.

You can list available networks using the following command as shown in Figure 10-14:

```
Docker network ls
```

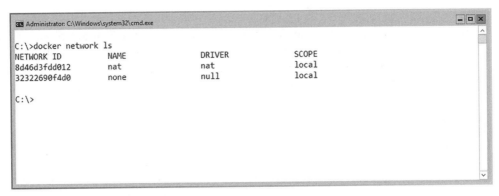

FIGURE 10-14 Network list

To view which containers are connected to a specific network, run the command:

```
Docker network inspect <network name>
```

You can create multiple container networks on a container host, but you need to keep in mind the following limitations:

- If you are creating multiple networks of the transparent or L2 bridge type, you need to ensure that each network has its own separate network adapter.

- If you create multiple NAT networks on a container host, additional NAT networks prefix will be partitioned from the container host's NAT network's address space (by default this is 172.16.0.0/12). For example, 172.16.1.0/24, 172.16.2.0/24 and so on.

NAT

NAT allows each container to be assigned an address in a private address space while connecting to the container host's network use the container host's IP address. The default NAT address range for containers is 172.16.0.0 /12. In the event that the container hosts IP address is in the 172.16.0.0 /12 range, you need to alter the NAT IP prefix. You can do this by performing the following steps:

1. Stop the docker service.

2. Remove any existing NAT networks using the following command:

    ```
    Get-ContainerNetwork | Remove-ContainerNetwork
    ```

3.   Perform one of the following actions:

●   Edit the daemon.json file and configure the *"fixed-cidr":"< IP Prefix > /Mask"* option to the desired network address prefix.

●   Edit the daemon.json file and sett the *"bridge": "none"* option and then use the *docker network create -d* command to create a network. For example, to create a network that uses the 192.168.15.0/24 range, the default gateway 192.168.15.1 that has the name CustomNat, issue this command:

```
Docker network create -d nat --subnet=192.168.15.0/24 --gateway=192.168.15.1
CustomNat
```

4.   Start the docker service.

You can also allow for connections to custom NAT networks when a container is run by allowing use of the --Network parameter and specifying the custom NAT network name. To do this, you need to have the *"bridge: none"* option specified in the daemon.json file. The command to run a container and join it to the CustomNat network created earlier is:

```
Docker run -it --network=CustomNat <ContainerImage> <cmd>
```

Port mappings allow ports on the container host to be mapped to ports on the container. For example, to map port 8080 on the container host to port 80 on a new container created off the windowsservercore image, and running powershell.exe interactively on the container, create the container using the following command:

```
Docker run -it -p 8080:80 microsoft/windowsservercore powershell.exe
```

Port mappings must be specified when the container is created or in a stopped state. You can specify them using the *-p* parameter or the *EXPOSE* command in a Dockerfile when using the *-P* parameter. If you do not specify a port on the container host, but do specify one on the container itself, a random port will be assigned. For example, run the command:

```
Docker run -itd -p 80 microsoft/windowsservercore powershell.exe
```

A random port on the container host can be mapped through to port 80 on the container. You can determine which port is randomly assigned using the *docker ps* command. Figure 10-15 shows a container that has had the port 19175 on the container host assigned to port 80 on the container.

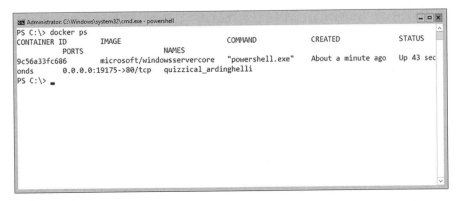

FIGURE 10-15 docker ps

When you configure port mapping, firewall rules on the container host will be created automatically to allow traffic through.

Transparent

Transparent networks allow each container endpoint to connect to the same network as the container host. You can use the Transparent networking mode by creating a container network that has the driver name transparent. The driver name is specified with the *-d* option. You can do this with the command:

```
docker network create -d transparent TransparentNetworkName
```

If the container host is a virtual machine running on a Hyper-V host and you want to use DHCP for IP address assignment, it's necessary to enable MACAddressSpoofing on the VM network adapter as shown in Figure 10-16. The transparent network mode supports IPv6. If you are using the transparent network mode, you can use a DHCPv6 server to assign IPv6 addresses to containers.

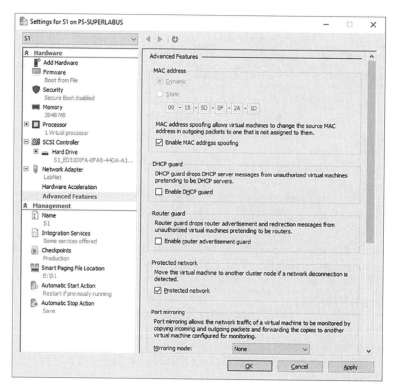

FIGURE 10-16 Enable MAC address spoofing

If you want to assign IP addresses to containers manually, it is necessary, when you create the transparent network, to specify the subnet and gateway parameters. These network properties need to match the network settings of the network to which the container host is connected.

For example, your container host is connected to a network that uses the 192.168.30.0/24 network and uses 192.168.30.1 as the default gateway. To create a transparent network that will allow static address assignment for containers on this network called TransNet, run the command:

```
Docker network create -d transparent --subnet=192.168.30.0/24 --gateway=192.168.30.1
TransNet
```

Once the transparent network is created with the appropriate settings, you can specify an IP address for a container using the --*ip* option. For example, to start a new container from the microsoft/windowsservercore image, enter the command prompt within the container, and to assign it the IP address 192.168.30.101 on the TransNet network, run the command:

```
Docker run -it --network:TransNet --ip 192.168.30.101 microsoft/windowsservercore cmd.
exe
```

As, when you use transparent network, containers are connected directly to the container host's network, you don't need to configure port mapping into the container.

Overlay

You can only use overlay networking mode if the Docker host is running in swarm mode as a manager node. Each overlay network that you create on a swarm cluster has its own IP subnet defined by an IP address prefix in the private address space. You create an overlay network by specifying overlay as the driver. For example, you can create an overlay network for the subnet 192.168.50.0/24 with the name OverlayNet by running the following command from a swarm manager node:

```
docker network create --driver=overlay –subnet=192.168.50.0/24 OverlayNet
```

Layer 2 Bridge

Layer 2 Bridge (L2 Bridge) networks are similar to transparent networks in that they allow containers to have IP addresses on the same subnets as the container host. They differ in that IP addresses must be assigned statically. This is because all containers on the container host that use an L2 bridge network have the same MAC address.

When creating an L2 Bridge network, you must specify the network type as l2bridge. You must also specify subnet and default gateway settings that matches the subnet and default gateway settings of the container host. For example, to create a L2 Bridge network named L2BridgeNet for the IP address range 192.168.88.0/24 with the default gateway address 192.168.88.1 use the following command:

```
Docker network create -d l2bridge –subnet=192.168.88.0/24 --gateway=192.168.88.1
L2BridgeNet
```

> ### MORE INFO   CONTAINER NETWORKING
>
> **You can learn more about networking of containers at: *https://docs.microsoft.com/ en-us/virtualization/windowscontainers/manage-containers/container-networking*.**

Swarm mode

Swarm mode provides container orchestration. This includes native clustering of container hosts and scheduling of container workloads. You can configure a collection of container hosts to form a swarm cluster. To do this, you need to configure the Docker engine on the container hosts to run together in swarm mode.

Swarms include two types of container hosts:

- **Manager nodes.** Swarms are initialized from manager nodes. All Docker commands for the control and management of the swarm must be run from a manager node. A swarm must have at least one manager node, but it's possible for a swarm to have multiple manager nodes. Manager nodes ensure that the state of the swarm matches the intended state. They keep track of services running on the swarm.

- **Worker nodes.** Manager nodes assign worker nodes tasks that the worker nodes execute. Worker nodes use a join token, generated during swarm initialization, to join a swarm.

Swarm mode has the following requirements:

- Docker Engine v1.13.0 or later

- TCP port 2377 for cluster management communication open on each node

- TCP and UDP port 7946 for intra-node communication

- TCP and UDP port 4789 for overlay network traffic

Creating swarm clusters

On the container host that will function as a manager node, run the following command, specifying the IP address of the container host:

```
Docker swarm init --advertise-addr <container_host_ip> --listen-addr
<container_host_ip>:2377
```

The container host will now function as the first manager node in a new Docker swarm. Running the Docker swarm init command will also generate a join-token that you will use to add other nodes to the swarm. You can retrieve the worker node join token at any point in the future from the manager node by running the following command:

```
Docker swarm join-token worker -q
```

Joining additional manager nodes requires the manager node join token. You can retrieve the manager node join token at any point by running the following command on the manager node.

```
Docker swarm join-token manager -q
```

You can add container hosts to the swarm as worker nodes by running the following command:

```
Docker swarm join --token <worker-join-token> <manager_container_host_ip>
```

You can add container hosts as additional manager nodes to the swarm by running the following command:

```
Docker swarm join --token <manager-join-token> <manager_container_host_ip>
```

You can view which nodes are members of a swarm by running the command:

```
Docker node ls
```

Creating overlay networks

Overlay mode allows container endpoints to be connected across multiple container hosts. In a multi-node environment, VXLAN (Virtual Extensible LAN) encapsulation occurs in VFP (Virtual Filtering Platform) forwarding extensions included in the Hyper-V virtual switch. Inter-host communications directly reference IP Endpoints. In single-node environments, intra-host communication occurs through a bridged connection on the Hyper-V virtual switch.

You can create an overlay network by running the following command from a management node, where 10.0.10.0/24 defines the overlay network address space:

```
Docker network create --driver=overlay --subnet=10.0.10.0/24 <OverlayNetworkName>
```

Deploying and scaling swarm services

A swarm service consists of a specific container image that you want to run as multiple instances across nodes in the swarm cluster. Docker swarm allows you to scale the service as required. For example, if you had a container image that allowed you to deploy a frontend web server for a multi-tier application, you can deploy that container image as a swarm service. As requirements dictate, you can increase the number of container instances by scaling the swarm service. Traffic can be automatically load balanced across the swarm service using DNS round robin. This is substantially simpler than starting new container instances across separate container hosts and manually configuring load balancing to take account of the new container instances.

To create a swarm service, you use the Docker service create command to specify the service name, network name, container image name, and set the endpoint mode to DNS round robin. For example, to create a service named SWARMFRONT using the WEBFRONTEND container image and the OverNet overlay network, issue the command:

```
Docker service create –name=SWARMFRONT --endpoint-mode=dnsrr --network=OverNet
WEBFRONTEND
```

Once the service is created, you can scale it using the Docker service scale command, specifying the number of container instances. For example, to scale the SWARMFRONT service to 10 instances, run the command:

```
Docker service scale SWARMFRONT=10
```

You can have more than one service present on a Docker swarm. You can view which services are present by running the following command on a manager node:

```
Docker service ls
```

You can view which container instances make up a service, including which swarm nodes individual containers are running on, by running the following command:

```
Docker service ps <servicename>
```

Inside OUT

Docker Swarm Preview

Swarm mode is not included in version 10.0.14393 of Windows Server 2016 and will be included in a later servicing branch of the operating system.

MORE INFO   SWARM MODE

You can learn more about Swarm Mode at: *https://docs.microsoft.com/en-us/ virtualization/windowscontainers/manage-containers/swarm-mode*.

CHAPTER 11

Clustering and High Availability

The primary high availability technology available in Windows Server 2016 is failover clustering. Clustering allows you to ensure that your workloads remain available if server hardware or even a site fails. Windows Server 2016 also includes network load balancing functionality, which allows you to scale out non-stateful workloads such as web server front ends.

Failover clustering

Failover clustering is a stateful high availability solution that allows an application or service to remain available to clients if a host server fails. You can use failover clustering to provide high availability to applications such as SQL Server, scale out file servers, and virtual machines.

Failover clustering is supported in both the Standard and Datacenter editions of Windows Server 2016. In some earlier versions of the Windows Server operating system, you only gained access to failover clustering if you used the Enterprise edition of the operating system.

Generally, all servers in a cluster should run either a similar hardware configuration or should be similarly provisioned virtual machines. You should also use the same edition and the same installation option. For example, you should aim to have cluster nodes that either run the nano, full, or server core versions of Windows Server, but you should avoid having cluster nodes that have a mix of computers running server core and the full GUI version. Avoiding this mix ensures that you use a similar update routine. A similar update routine is more difficult to maintain when you use different versions of Windows Server.

You should use the Datacenter edition of Windows Server when building clusters that host Hyper-V virtual machines, because the virtual machine licensing scheme available with this edition provides the most VM licenses.

To be fully supported by Microsoft, cluster hardware should meet the Certified for Windows Server logo requirement. You can use Serial attached SCSI (SAS), iSCSI, Fibre Channel, or Fibre Channel over Ethernet (FcoE) to host shared storage for a Windows Server failover cluster. Failover clustering only supports IPv4 and IPv6 based protocols. You install failover clustering by installing the Failover Clustering feature and installing the Failover Clustering Remote Server Administration Tools (RSAT) allows you to manage other failover clusters in your environment.

Inside OUT

The future of clustering

In the past, you likely clustered workloads such as Exchange and SQL to ensure that they were highly available. Today, both products come with technologies that allow you to have a highly available solution without deploying on a failover cluster. These technologies are AlwaysOn Availability Groups and Database Availability Groups. Today, you're more likely to deploy these workloads on virtual machines and to ensure that the virtual machine host is configured in a failover cluster than you are than to directly make the workloads highly available by installing them on a failover cluster.

Cluster quorum modes

Cluster Quorum Mode determines how many nodes and witnesses must fail before the cluster is in a failed state. Nodes are servers that participate in the cluster. Witnesses can be stored on shared storage or even on file shares, although shared storage is the preferred method. This recommendation might eventually change however as continuously available file shares are more widely adopted. Recommended cluster quorum modes involve an odd number of total votes spread across member nodes and the witness.

There are four cluster quorum modes:

- **Node majority.** This cluster quorum mode is recommended for clusters that have an odd number of nodes. When this quorum type is set, the cluster retains quorum when the number of available nodes exceeds the number of failed nodes. For example, if a cluster has five nodes and three are available, quorum is retained.

- **Node and disk majority.** This cluster quorum node is recommended when the cluster has an even number of nodes. A disk witness hosted on a shared storage disk, for example iSCSI or Fibre Channel, that is accessible to cluster nodes has a vote when determining quorum as do the quorum nodes. The cluster retains quorum as long as the majority of voting entities remain online. For example, if you have a four node cluster and a witness disk, a combination of three of those entities needs to remain online for the cluster to retain quorum. The cluster retains quorum if three nodes are online or if two nodes and the witness disk are online.

- **Node and file share majority.** This configuration is similar to the node and disk majority configuration, but the quorum is stored on a network share rather than a shared storage disk. It is suitable for similar configurations to node and disk majority. This method is not as reliable as node and disk majority as file shares are generally do not have the redundancy features of shared storage.

- **No Majority: Disk Only.** This model can be used with clusters that have an odd number of nodes. It is only recommended for testing environments because the disk hosting the witness functions as a single point of failure. When you choose this model, as long as the disk hosting the witness and one node remain available, the cluster retains quorum. If the disk hosting the witness fails, quorum is lost even if all the other nodes are available.

When you create a cluster, the cluster quorum is automatically configured for you. You might want to alter the quorum mode however if you change the number of nodes in your cluster, for example if you change from a four node to a five node cluster. When you change the cluster quorum configuration, the Failover Cluster Manager provides you with a recommended configuration, but you can choose to override that configuration if you want.

You can also perform advanced quorum configuration to specify what nodes can participate in the quorum vote, which you can set on the Select Voting Configuration page of the Configure Cluster Quorum Wizard. When you do this, only the selected nodes' votes are used to calculate quorum and it's possible that fewer nodes would need to fail to cause a cluster to fail than would otherwise be the case if all nodes participated in the quorum vote. This can be useful when configuring how multi-site clusters calculate quorum when the connection between sites fails.

Cluster Storage and Cluster Shared Volumes

Almost all failover cluster scenarios require access to some form of shared storage. Windows Server failover clusters can use SAS, iSCSI, or Fibre Channel for Shared Storage. With the inclusion of the iSCSI Target software in Windows Server, iSCSI is one of the simplest and cheapest of these technologies to implement.

You should configure disks used for failover clustering as follows:

- Volumes should be formatted using NTFS or ReFS.

- Use Master Boot Record (MBR) or GUID Partition Table (GPT).

- Avoid allowing different clusters access to the same storage device. This can be accomplished through LUN masking or zoning.

- Any multipath solution must be based on Microsoft Multipath I/O (MPIO).

Cluster Shared Volumes (CSV) is a technology that was introduced in Windows Server 2008 R2 that allows multiple cluster nodes to have concurrent access to a single Logical Unit Number (LUN). Prior to Windows Server 2008 R2, only the active node had access to shared storage. CSV allows you to have virtual machines on the same LUN run on different cluster nodes. CSV also has the following benefits:

- Support for scale-out file servers

- Support for BitLocker volume encryption

- SMB 3.0 support

- Integration with Storage Spaces

- Online volume scan and repair

You can enable CSV only after you create a failover cluster and then provided storage that will be available to the CSV.

Cluster Networks

While you can create failover clusters with nodes that have a single network adapter, best practice is to have separate networks and network adapters for the following:

- A connection for cluster nodes to shared storage

- A private network for internal cluster communication

- A public network that clients use to access services hosted on the cluster

In scenarios where high availability is critical, you might have multiple redundant networks connected through several separate switches. If you have a cluster where everything is connected through one piece of network hardware, you can almost guarantee that piece of network hardware is the first thing that fails.

You can either use IPv4 or IPv6 addresses that are dynamically or statically assigned, but you should not use a mix of dynamically and statically assigned IP addresses for nodes that are members of the same cluster. If you use a mixture of dynamically and statically assigned IP addresses, the Validate A Configuration Wizard generates an error.

Inside OUT

Default gateways

Even if the cluster validation wizard only gives you warnings when you perform the test, you aren't able to create a failover cluster unless each node is configured with a default gateway. The default gateway doesn't have to be a host that exists, but if you're having trouble in your virtual machine lab with creating a failover cluster, go back and check whether you've configured a default gateway for each node.

Cluster Aware Updating

Cluster Aware Updating (CAU) is a feature included with Windows Server that allows you to automate the process of applying software updates to failover clusters. Cluster Aware Updating integrates with Windows Update, Windows Server Update Services (WSUS), System Center Configuration Manager, and other software update management applications.

CAU uses the following process:

1. Obtains the update files from the source location.

2. Puts the first node into maintenance mode.

3. Moves any cluster roles off the node to other nodes in the cluster.

4. Installs software updates.

5. Restarts the cluster node, if necessary.

6. Checks for additional updates. If updates are found, it performs Steps 4 through 6 until all updates are applied.

7. Brings the node out of maintenance mode.

8. Reacquires clustered roles that were moved to other nodes.

9. Puts the next node into maintenance mode and repeats the cycle starting at Step 3 until all nodes have been updated.

The main benefit of CAU is that it updates a process that in the past you had to perform manually. You can configure CAU to automatically apply updates to cluster nodes when they are approved through WSUS or System Center Configuration Manager, or you can trigger CAU manually as needed.

You can configure the CAU options so that the updates are rolled back across the cluster if after a specified number of attempts an update fails to install on a node. You can also configure Advanced Options, such as requiring scripts to run before and after the update process has occurred, if services hosted on the cluster require special shutdown or startup configurations.

Failover and Preference Settings

Cluster preference settings allow you to configure the preferred owner for a specific cluster role and you can also configure different preferred owners for different cluster roles. Where possible, the role is hosted on the preferred owner. You can configure a list of preferred owners so that if the most preferred owner isn't available, the next preferred owner hosts the role and so on. You configure a role preferred owner on the role Properties dialog box.

You configure whether the clustered role fails back to the preferred owner on the Failover tab of the cluster role's Properties dialog box. When configuring failback, you need to determine whether you want to prevent failback, to have failback occur automatically as soon as the preferred owner is in a healthy state, or configure failback to occur within a certain number of hours of the preferred owner returning to a healthy state.

Node quarantine settings allow you to configure a node so that it is unable to rejoin the cluster if the node fails a certain number of times within a certain period. Configuring node quarantine blocks workloads from being placed back on a quarantined node until the reason for the repeated failure can be dealt with by a server administrator.

A fault domain is a collection of hardware components that share a common point of failure. Windows Server 2016 allows you to configure fault domains at the site, rack, chassis, and node levels. You can use Storage Spaces and Storage Spaces Direct with fault domains to ensure that copies of data are kept in separate fault domains. For example, if you defined fault domains at the site level, you can configure storage spaces so that redundant data resides in separate sites rather than just on separate cluster nodes.

Multi-site clusters and Cloud Witness

Failover clusters can span multiple sites. When configuring a cluster that spans two sites, you should consider the following:

- Ensure that there are an equal number of nodes in each site.

- Allow each node to have a vote.

- Enable dynamic quorum. Dynamic quorum allows quorum to be recalculated when individual nodes leave the cluster one at a time. Dynamic quorum is enabled by default on Windows Server 2016 failover clusters.

- Use a file share witness. You should host the file share witness in a third site that has separate connectivity to the two sites that host the cluster nodes, as shown in Figure 11-1. When configured in this manner, the cluster retains quorum if one of the sites is lost. An alternative to file share witness is Cloud Witness.

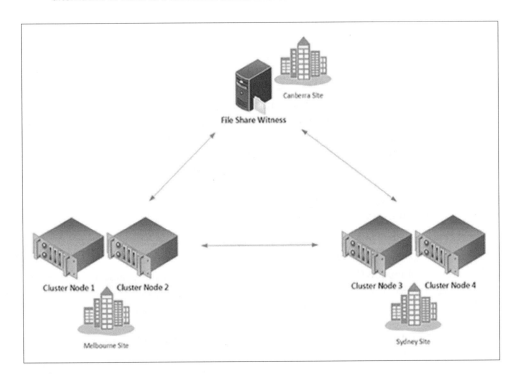

FIGURE 11-1 Multi-site cluster

If you only have two sites and are unable to place a file share witness in an independent third site, you can edit the cluster configuration manually to reassign votes so that the cluster recalculates quorum.

Manually reassigning votes is also useful to avoid split brain scenarios. Split brain scenarios occur when a failure occurs in a multi-site cluster and where both sides of the cluster believe they have quorum. Split brain scenarios cause challenges when connectivity is restored and make it necessary to restart servers on one side of the multi-site cluster to resolve the issue. You can manually reassign votes so that one side always retains quorum if inter-site connectivity is lost. For example by setting the Melbourne site with 2 votes and the Sydney site with 1, the Melbourne site always retains quorum if inter-site connectivity is lost.

Windows Server 2016 also supports cloud witness. Cloud witness has the cluster witness role hosted in Azure rather than at a third site. Cloud witness is suitable for multi-site clusters. To configure a cloud witness, create a storage account in Azure, copy the storage access keys, note the endpoint URL links, and then use these with the Configure Cluster Quorum Settings Wizard and specify a cloud witness.

Virtual Machine Failover Clustering

One of the most common uses for failover clusters is hosting virtual machines. By deploying a workload, such as SQL Server or Exchange on a highly available virtual machine, you can achieve high availability without the need for the application to be aware that it is now highly available. The virtual machine functions normally, provides services to clients on the network, and can switch between cluster nodes as necessary in the event that the individual cluster node hosting it requires maintenance or experiences some sort of failure. Building a Hyper-V failover cluster first involves creating a failover cluster and then adding the Hyper-V role to each node of the cluster.

Virtual machine storage

You should use cluster shared volumes to store virtual machines on a Hyper-V cluster because cluster shared volumes allow multiple cluster nodes to manage a single shared storage device. This allows you to put multiple virtual machines on the same shared storage device, but have those virtual machines hosted by different nodes in the failover cluster. Cluster shared volumes are mapped under the C:\ClusterStorage folder on cluster nodes.

When creating a new virtual machine on a failover cluster, first select which cluster node hosts the virtual machine.

When creating a highly available virtual machine, specify the cluster shared volume path as the location to store the virtual machine. If you have an existing machine that you want to make highly available, you can move the virtual machine to this path. As an alternative, you also have the option to specify a SMB 3.0 file share as the storage location for the highly available virtual machine. Whether to select a cluster shared volume or an SMB 3.0 file share depends on your organization's storage configuration.

After the virtual machine is created, you can control it by using the Failover Cluster Manager console. The move option in the Actions pane allows you to select the cluster node that you want to move the virtual machine to.

In production environments, you should ensure that each Hyper-V host has an identical hardware configuration. In development environments however, this is not always possible. If different processor types are used, for example an Intel processor on one node and an AMD processor on another, you might have to perform a quick migration. Quick migration allows migration between nodes, but does cause a disruption in client connectivity. You can allow migration between Hyper-V nodes with different processor types or versions by enabling the processor compatibility setting on the virtual machine.

VM load balancing

VM load balancing is a new feature of Windows Server 2016 that identifies nodes in a Hyper-V cluster where CPU and memory resources are under pressure and redistributes workloads to other nodes that have lower CPU and/or memory utilization. VM load balancing is enabled by default and automatically moves VMs to a new node after you add that node to an existing Windows Server 2016 Hyper-V cluster.

You can configure VM load balancing so that workload redistribution happens automatically when a specific threshold is reached or you can configure load balancing to occur on a periodic basis. VMs are moved between Hyper-V cluster nodes using live migration without incurring downtime. You configure VM load balancing aggressiveness by using the following Windows PowerShell command:

```
(Get-Cluster).AutoBalancerLevel = <value>
```

The values listed in Table 11-1 determine automatic load balancer thresholds:

Table 11-1. Auto VM load balancer aggressiveness

AutoBalancerLevel	Aggressiveness	Action
1 (default)	Low	Move workloads when the node reaches 80 percent memory or processor utilization
2	Medium	Move workloads when the node reaches 70 percent memory or processor utilization
3	High	Move workloads when the node reaches 60 percent memory or processor utilization

You configure how the balancer functions by using the following Windows PowerShell command:

```
(Get-Cluster).AutoBalancerMode = <value>
```

CHAPTER 11

The values listed in Table 11-2 determine automatic load balancer mode.

Table 11-2. Auto VM load balancer mode

AutoBalancerMODE	Aggressiveness
0	Disables VM load balancing
1	Load balances each time a new node joins the Hyper-V cluster
2 (default)	Load balances each time a new node joins the Hyper-V cluster and every 30 minutes

Rolling upgrades

Cluster OS Rolling Upgrade allows you to upgrade a Windows Server 2012 R2 cluster hosting Hyper-V or Scale-Out file server workloads without taking those workloads offline. Other cluster hosted workloads, such as SQL Server, are only offline during failover from an original cluster node running Windows Server 2012 R2 to a new or upgraded cluster node running Windows Server 2016.

Upgrading a cluster involves either adding new nodes running Windows Server 2016 to an existing cluster running Windows Server 2012 R2 or upgrading existing nodes running Windows Server 2012 R2 to Windows Server 2016. The cluster can function normally with both Windows Server 2012 R2 and Windows Server 2016 nodes.

The nodes that you can add to a cluster depend on the cluster functional level. A cluster that only has nodes running Windows Server 2012 R2 is running at cluster functional level 8. Cluster functional level 8 supports nodes that run both Windows Server 2012 R2 and Windows Server 2016. You can also introduce cluster nodes that run either operating system to the cluster as long as the cluster is still configured to use cluster functional level 8. It's even possible to roll back to Windows Server 2012 R2 when all nodes are running Windows Server 2016 as long as you haven't upgraded the cluster functional level from level 8.

A cluster running at functional level 9 only supports nodes running Windows Server 2016. You should only upgrade the cluster functional level to level 9 when you are absolutely certain that you don't want to roll back the cluster upgrade and that all nodes have been upgraded.

You can determine which functional level a cluster is running at by running the following Windows PowerShell command:

```
Get-Cluster | Select ClusterFunctionalLevel
```

You can upgrade the cluster functional level by using the Update-ClusterFunctionalLevel cmdlet.

Cluster OS Rolling Upgrade has the following conditions:

- You can only upgrade a Hyper-V cluster if the CPUs support Second-Level Addressing Table (SLAT). Windows Server 2016 Hyper-V is only supported on processors that support SLAT.

- You need to use a Windows Server 2016 node to add nodes to the cluster.

- All cluster management tasks should be performed from a Windows Server 2016 node rather than from a Windows Server 2012 R2 node.

- Cluster rolling upgrade cannot be used to upgrade VM guest clusters that use a shared virtual hard disk as shared storage. VM guest clusters are clusters where each node is a virtual machine. A VM guest cluster that uses a shared virtual hard disk for shared storage cannot be upgraded, but a VM guest cluster that uses another form of shared storage, such as iSCSI, can be upgraded by using a rolling cluster upgrade.

- Before upgrading a Windows Server 2012 R2 node to Windows Server 2016, drain the node of workloads and evict the node from the cluster. After you've upgraded the node's operating system to Windows Server 2016, you can join it to the cluster again.

- Prior to commencing Cluster OS Rolling Upgrade, ensure that all elements of the cluster and its workloads are backed up.

- You can't lower the cluster functional level after it has been raised.

- Cluster OS Rolling Upgrade only works when the original cluster is running Windows Server 2012 R2. Cluster OS Rolling Upgrade does not work with Windows Server 2012, Windows Server 2008 R2, or Windows Server 2008.

Managing Failover clustering with PowerShell

You can use cmdlets in the FailoverClusters module, as described in Table 11-3, to manage failover clusters on Windows Server 2016.

CHAPTER 11

Table 11-3. Failover cluster PowerShell cmdlets

Noun	Verbs	Function
Cluster	Get, Test, Stop, New, Start, Remove	Manage failover clusters
ClusterAccess	Block, Get, Remove, Grant	Manage permissions to control access to a failover cluster
ClusterAvailableDisk	Get	View disks that support failover clustering that are visible to all nodes but are not yet clustered disks
ClusterCheckpoint	Add, Remove, Get	Manage cryptographic key or registry checkpoints for a cluster resource
ClusterDiagnosticInfo	Get	Get cluster diagnostic information
ClusterDisk	Add	Add a disk to a cluster
ClusterDiskReservation	Clear	Clears persistent reservation on a disk in a failover cluster
ClusterFaultDomain	Get, Set, Remove, New	Manage cluster fault domains
ClusterFaultDomainXML	Set, Get	Configure cluster fault domains using XML
ClusterFileServerRole	Add	Add the file server role to a cluster
ClusterFunctionalLevel	Update	Upgrade the cluster functional level
ClusterGeneric ApplicationRole	Add	Configure high availability for an application that was not originally designed to run in a failover cluster
ClusterGenericScriptRole	Add	Configure an application controlled by a script that runs in Windows Script host on a failover cluster
ClusterGenericServiceRole	Add	Configure high availability for a service that was not originally designed to run in a failover cluster

ClusterGroup	Remove, Start, Stop, Add, Get, Move	Manage cluster roles/ resource groups in a failover cluster
ClusterGroupFromSet	Remove	Remove a group from a cluster group set
ClusterGroupSet	Remove, Get, New, Set	Manage cluster group sets
ClusterGroupSet Dependency	Add, Get, Remove	Manage cluster group set dependencies
ClusterGroupToSet	Add	Add a group to a cluster group set
ClusterIPResource	Update	Renew or release DHCP lease for IP address resource used by a failover cluster
ClusteriSCSITarget ServerRole	Add	Create a highly available iSCSI Target server
ClusterLog	Get, Set	Manage cluster log settings
ClusterNameAccount	New	Create a cluster name account in Active Directory
ClusterNetwork	Get	View cluster network properties
ClusterNetworkInterface	Get	View cluster network interface properties
ClusterNetworkNameResource	Update	Register cluster resource names in DNS
ClusterNode	Get, Resume, Stop, Start, Remove, Add, Clear, Suspend	Manage specific cluster nodes
ClusterOwnerNode	Set, Get	Configure which nodes can own a resource
ClusterParameter	Set, Get	View and configure information about an object in a failover cluster
ClusterQuorum	Get, Set	Manage cluster quorum
ClusterResource	Remove, Move, Start, Suspend, Add, Get, Stop, Resume	Manage cluster resources
ClusterResourceDependency	Get, Set, Add, Remove	Manage cluster resource dependencies
ClusterResourceDependencyRe-port	Get	Generate a cluster resource dependency report

CHAPTER 11

ClusterResourceFailure	Test	Test failure of a cluster resource
ClusterResourceType	Add, Get, Remove	Manage cluster resource type
ClusterScaleOutFileServerRole	Add	Add a cluster scale out file server role
ClusterServerRole	Add	Add a cluster server role
ClusterSharedVolume	Get, Add, Remove, Move	Manage cluster shared volumes
ClusterSharedVolumeState	Get	View the state of cluster shared volumes
ClusterStorageSpacesDirect	Repair, Set, Disable, Enable, Get	Manage cluster storage spaces direct
ClusterStorageSpacesDirectDisk	Set	Configure cluster storage spaces direct disks
ClusterVirtualMachineConfiguration	Update	Update the configuration of a clustered virtual machine hosted on a failover cluster
ClusterVirtualMachineRole	Add, Move	Manage clustered virtual machine live migration
ClusterVMMonitoredItem	Add, Remove, Get	Manage clustered virtual machine monitored items
ClusterVMMonitoredState	Reset	Reset clustered virtual machine monitoring state

Network Load Balancing

Network Load Balancing (NLB) distributes traffic across multiple hosts in a balanced manner. NLB directs new traffic to cluster nodes under the least load. NLB works as a high availability solution because it detects node failures and automatically redistributes traffic to available nodes. NLB is also scalable, which means that you can start with a two node NLB cluster and keep adding nodes until you reach a maximum of 32 nodes. A node is a computer running the Windows Server operating system that participates in the NLB cluster. A computer can only be a member of one Windows NLB cluster.

NLB functions through the creation of a virtual IP and a virtual network adapter with an associated Media Access Control (MAC) address. Traffic to this address is distributed to the cluster nodes. In the default configuration, traffic is distributed to the least utilized node. You can also configure NLB so that specific nodes are preferred and process more traffic than other nodes in the cluster.

NLB is a high availability solution that is suitable for stateless applications. Imagine that you have a two tier web application where you have four servers running IIS as the web tier and two servers running SQL Server as the database tier. In this scenario, you add Web Server 1, Web Server 2, Web Server 3, and Web Server 4 to an NLB cluster as web servers host stateless applications. To make the database servers highly available, you would configure a failover cluster or AlwaysOn Availability Group, but you wouldn't configure NLB because SQL Server is a stateful application.

NLB is failure aware as long as the failure occurs on the node. For example, if you have a two node NLB cluster that you use with a web application and the network card fails on one of the nodes, NLB is aware of the failure and stops directing traffic to the node. If, instead of a network card failure, the web application fails but everything else remains operational, NLB remains unaware of the failure and continues to direct requests to the node that hosts the failed web application. In a real-world environment, you'd set up more sophisticated monitoring that allows you to detect the failure of the application, not just the failure of the node. Some hardware based NLB solutions are sophisticated enough to detect application failures rather than just host failures.

Network Load Balancing prerequisites

In terms of setup, NLB is straightforward and only requires you to install the feature. Although you can install the feature on a node, you must ensure that it meets some prerequisites before you can add it to a cluster. Before you add a host to an NLB cluster, you must ensure the following:

- All nodes in the NLB cluster must reside on the same subnet. While you can configure a subnet to span multiple geographic locations, the cluster is unlikely to converge successfully if the latency between nodes exceeds 250 milliseconds.

- All network adapters must either be configured as unicast or multicast. You can't use Windows NLB to create an NLB cluster that has a mixture of unicast and multicast addresses assigned to network adapters.

- If you choose to use the unicast cluster configuration mode, the network adapter needs to support changing its MAC address.

- The network adapter must be configured with a static IP address.

- Only TCP/IP is supported on the network adapter that is used for NLB. You are not able to bind other protocols, such as IPX or Banyan Vines, on the adapter.

There is no restriction on the number of network adapters in each host. You can have one host with three network adapters in a team and another host with five separate adapters participate in the same NLB cluster. You can run nodes on different editions of Windows Server, although considering that the only difference between the standard and datacenter edition is virtual machine licensing, you are unlikely to be running NLB on the datacenter edition. While it is possible to have working NLB clusters if you are running different versions of Windows Server, such as Windows Server 2012 R2 and Windows Server 2016, you should upgrade all nodes as soon as possible to the same operating system. You should also attempt to ensure that nodes have similar hardware capacity or are running on similarly provisioned virtual machines so that a client doesn't get a radically different experience when connecting to different nodes.

NLB cluster operation modes

When configuring an NLB cluster, you can choose between one of three separate cluster operation modes. The mode that you select depends on the configuration of the cluster nodes and the type of network switch that the cluster nodes are connected to. You can configure the cluster operation mode when creating the cluster. The operation modes are as follows:

- **Unicast mode.** If you configure an NLB cluster to use the unicast cluster operation mode, all nodes in the cluster will use the same unicast MAC address. Outbound traffic from node members uses a modified MAC address that is determined by the cluster host's priority settings. The drawback to using unicast mode with nodes that have a single adapter is that you are only able to perform management tasks from computers located on the same TCP/IP subnet as the cluster nodes. This restriction doesn't apply however when the cluster nodes have multiple network adapters that are not NIC team members. When you use unicast with multiple network adapters, one adapter is dedicated to cluster communication and you can connect to any other adapters to perform management tasks. You can improve cluster operation by placing the adapters that you use for cluster communication and the adapters that you use for management tasks on separate VLANs.

- **Multicast Mode.** This mode is suitable when each node only has one network adapter. When you configure multicast mode, each cluster host keeps its original network adapter's MAC address, but is also assigned a multicast MAC address. All nodes in the cluster use the same multicast MAC address. You can only use multicast mode if your organization's switches and routers support it. Unless you've got bargain basement network equipment, it's likely that your current network hardware supports multicast mode for NLB.

- **IGMP Multicast.** Internet Group Management Protocol (IGMP) multicast mode is an advanced form of multicast mode that reduces the chances of the network switch being flooded with traffic. It works by only forwarding traffic through the ports that are connected to hosts that participate in the NLB cluster, but it also requires a switch that supports this functionality.

Managing cluster hosts

You manage NLB clusters through the Network Load Balancing Manager console. The NLB console is available as part of the RSAT tools, meaning that you can manage one or more NLB clusters from a computer that is not a member of the cluster. You do however, need to manage clusters by using an account that is a member of the local Administrators group on each cluster node. You can use this console to create and manage clusters and cluster nodes.

After the cluster is set up and functioning, most maintenance operations, such as applying software updates, are performed on cluster nodes. When performing maintenance tasks, you should perform the task on one node at a time so the application that the cluster provides to users continues to remain available. Prior to performing maintenance tasks on a node, you should first stop incoming connections and allow existing connections to be completed naturally. When there are no connections to the node, you can then stop the node, apply the updates, and restart the node. You have the following options for managing cluster nodes:

- **Drainstop.** Blocks new connections to the cluster node, but doesn't terminate existing connections. Use this prior to planned maintenance to gracefully evacuate the cluster of connections.

- **Stop.** Stops the cluster node. All connections to the cluster node from clients are stopped. Use Stop after you use Drainstop so that you can then perform maintenance tasks, such as applying updates.

- **Start.** Starts a cluster node that is in a stopped state.

- **Suspend.** Pauses the cluster node until you issue the Resume command. Using Suspend does not shut down the cluster service, but it does terminate current connections as well as block new connections.

- **Resume.** Resumes a suspended cluster node.

Port rules

An NLB port rule allows you to configure how the NLB cluster responds to incoming traffic on a specific port and protocol, such as TCP port 80 (HTTP) or UDP port 69 (Trivial FTP). Each host in an NLB cluster must use the same port rules. While it is possible to configure port rules on a per-node basis, it's safer to configure them at the cluster level to ensure that they are consistent. The default port rule redirects traffic on any TCP or UDP port to each node in the cluster in a balanced way. If you want to create specific rules, delete the default rule.

CHAPTER 11

Filtering and Affinity

When you create a port rule, you also choose a filtering mode, which might require you to configure affinity. Filtering allows you to determine whether incoming traffic is handled by one, some, or all nodes in the NLB cluster. If you choose to allow multiple nodes to accept incoming traffic, you need to configure affinity. The affinity setting determines whether one node handles all subsequent requests from the same client, or if subsequent requests from the same client are redistributed across other nodes. Affinity is often important with web applications where a consistent session must exist between the client and one web server after the session is established. You can configure the following filtering modes:

- **Multiple Host.** This is the default filtering mode. This mode allows traffic to be directed to any node in the NLB cluster. You also need to specify one of the following affinity settings:

    - **Single.** When you configure this option, the incoming request is distributed to one of the cluster nodes. All subsequent traffic from the originating host is directed to that same node for the duration of the session. This is the default multiple host affinity. Don't confuse Multiple Host, Single Affinity with Single Host filtering.

    - **None.** Incoming traffic is distributed to the cluster node under the least load even if there is an existing session. This means that multiple nodes may handle traffic from a single session.

    - **Network.** This option directs clients to cluster nodes based on the requesting client's network address.

- **Single Host.** A single node handles all traffic sent to the cluster on this port rule. In this case, no load balancing occurs. For example, if you have a four node cluster, but you want node three to be the only one that handles traffic on TCP port 25, you would configure a port rule with the filtering mode set to Single Host.

- **Disable The Port Range.** When you configure this setting, the NLB cluster drops traffic sent to the cluster that matches the port rule.

Managing NLB with PowerShell

You can use the Windows PowerShell cmdlets listed in Table 11-4 to manage NLB clusters on Windows Server 2016.

Table 11-4. NLB PowerShell cmdlets

Noun	Verbs	Function
NlbClusterNode	Add, Get, Remove, Resume, Set, Start, Stop, Suspend	Configure and manage a cluster node
NlbClusterNodeDip	Add, Get, Remove, Set	Configure the cluster node's dedicated management IP address
NlbClusterPortRule	Add, Disable, Enable, Get, Remove, Set	Create and manage port rules
NlbClusterVip	Add, Get, Remove, Set	Configure the cluster's virtual IP address
NlbCluster	Get, New, Remove, Resume, Set, Start, Stop, Suspend	Configure and manage the cluster
NlbClusterDriverInfo	Get	Provides information about the cluster driver
NlbCluster-NodeNetworkIn-terface	Get	Provides information about the node's network interface driver
NlbClusterIpv6Ad-dress	New	Configure the cluster's IPv6 address
NlbClusterPortRu-leNodeHandling-Priority	Set	Manage priority on a per-port rule basis
NlbClusterPortRule-NodeWeight	Set	Configure the node weight on a per-port rule basis

Active Directory Certificate Services

Active Directory Certificate Services is the infrastructure service that most administrators don't pay much attention to until they need to perform a task, such as to generate certificates for an internal application or to support a specific type of server deployment.

You can install Certificate Services on both Server Core and Server with a GUI system, with Server Core being the more secure option because of its reduced attack surface. Because Certificate Services is an important security role, you should consider deploying it on a computer separate from other roles. You should also limit access to the server hosting Certificate Services so that only those directly responsible for performing administration tasks have access.

CA types

Windows Server Certificate Authorities (CAs) come in four basic types: Enterprise root, enterprise subordinate, standalone root and standalone subordinate. The type that you deploy depends on your certificate needs. Unless you are performing a new deployment, it's also likely it depends on the particular CA hierarchy that you want to use.

Before you can understand what type of CA you need to deploy, you need to understand how CA hierarchies work. The CA at the top of a hierarchy is known as the Root CA. A Root CA can have any number of subordinate CAs. Subordinate CAs can in turn function as the parent CAs of child CAs, which are also called subordinate CAs.

Each CA has a special certificate known as the CA certificate. The Root CA signs its own certificate. A subordinate CA has its CA certificate signed by a parent CA. For example:

- A Root CA named APEX_CA signs its own CA certificate

- APEX_CA signs the CA certificate of a subordinate CA named CHILD_CA

- CHILD_CA signs the CA certificate of a subordinate CA named GRANDCHILD_CA

CHAPTER 12

The way that certificate trust works is that if a client trusts the Root CA's CA certificate, it trusts all certificates issued by CAs that are directly or indirectly subordinates of that CA. For example, if a client trusts the ROOT_CA CA certificate, it automatically trusts the certificates issued by GRANDCHILD_CA.

You can use the pkiview console (pkiview.msc) to view your current organization's Certificate Services configuration. Figure 12-1 shows an enterprise PKI that has a root CA and a subordinate CA.

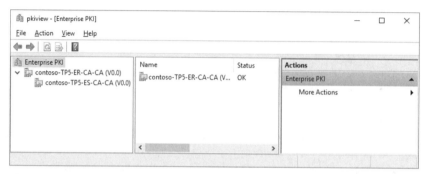

Figure 12-1 PKIview

Another concept that it is important to understand in the context of CA hierarchies is certificate revocation. A parent CA can revoke a child CA's CA certificate. When this happens, all certificates issued by the child CA are also invalidated. For example, if the administrator of APEX_CA from the earlier example revoked the CA certificate of CHILD_CA, all of the certificates issued by CHILD_CA would no longer function. This includes the CA certificate of GRANDCHILD_CA, which in turn invalidates all of the certificates issued by GRANDCHILD_CA. Needless to say, you only revoke the CA certificate of a subordinate CA in dire circumstances, such as when the child CA has been compromised by malware or hackers. If a child CA has been compromised, it might have issued certificates that you don't know about and the most secure response is to revoke all certificates issued from the CA and to start over from scratch.

Some other things to keep in mind before we delve more into the types of CAs that you can configure with Windows Server 2016 are:

- You can't convert a root CA to a subordinate CA

- You can't convert a subordinate CA to function as a root CA; however, a subordinate CA can function as the parent CA of another subordinate CA

- A subordinate CA's CA certificate cannot have a lifetime that extends beyond the current lifetime of the parent CA's certificate

Inside OUT
Remember to renew CA certificates

Remember that a CA's server certificate needs to be renewed. A CA can't issue certificates that have a lifespan beyond that of its CA certificate. If a CA's certificate has expired, so have all of the certificates issued by the CA.

Enterprise CA

An Enterprise CA is fully integrated with Active Directory. This has the following benefits:

- The Enterprise CA is automatically trusted by any computer that is a member of the same Active Directory forest

- All certificates published by the CA are automatically trusted by members of the same forest

- Certificate requests can be performed automatically and don't require the use of a request file

- Certificates requests can be approved automatically and certificates are automatically distributed and installed on domain clients

- Certificate revocation information is published to Active Directory

- Enterprise CAs can use certificate templates

- Enterprise CAs can issue certificates to devices that have domain membership and also to devices that are not members of an Active Directory domain

- An Enterprise subordinate CA can have a standalone CA as a parent CA

- A standalone subordinate CA can have an Enterprise CA as a parent CA

One of the primary drawbacks of an Enterprise CA is that it always needs to be online. If an Enterprise CA goes offline, certificate services in the domain don't function properly. Temporary shutdowns due to maintenance are fine, but shutting down or having an enterprise CA offline for a couple of weeks is likely to lead to headaches. Enterprise CAs must also always be installed on computers that are members of an Active Directory domain.

Enterprise Root

An Enterprise Root CA is an enterprise CA that signs its own signing certificate. As mentioned earlier, an Enterprise Root CA can only be installed on a computer that is a domain member and that computer should always be online. Because the Enterprise Root CA publishes certificate information to all domains in a forest, you need to configure it using an account that is a member of the Enterprise Admins group.

Inside OUT

Single CA deployments

Many smaller organizations, such as those with less than 300 users, have a single Enterprise Root CA as their only CA. While it's not the most secure way that you can do things, a single Enterprise Root CA is a pragmatic solution for organizations that have basic certificate services requirements. The best practice is to use an Offline Root CA, which is discussed later in this chapter.

After you've installed the binary files for a CA, you are then able to configure it. You do this by running the AD CS Configuration Wizard. You can run this wizard using the signed-on user's credentials, or by using separate credentials, which you specify on the Credentials page of the wizard shown in Figure 12-2. In the next few pages we'll go through the process of installing an Enterprise Root CA. The process of installing an Enterprise Root CA is similar to the process of installing other CA types.

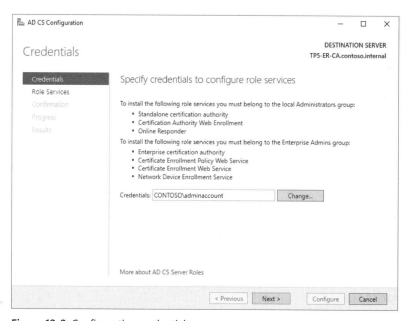

Figure 12-2 Configuration credentials

The next step in the wizard involves specifying which roles to configure. While it is possible to configure multiple roles at once, it's usually better to get the Certification Authority role functioning properly before adding and configuring additional role services, such as Certification Authority Web Enrollment. The other role services are discussed later in this chapter. Figure 12-3 shows the Certification Authority role selected.

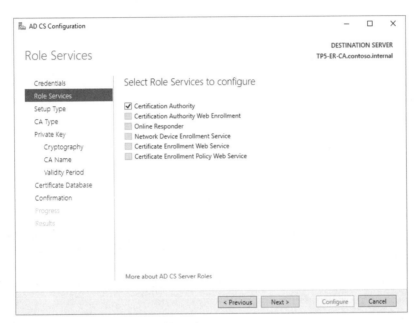

Figure 12-3 Certification Authority role

If the computer is a member of an AD DS domain, you get the option to install an Enterprise CA or a Standalone CA, as shown in Figure 12-4. If the computer is not a member of an AD DS domain, you are not able to select the Enterprise CA option. If you're sure that the computer is a member of the domain, but you can't select the Enterprise CA option, make sure that you are using an account that has Enterprise Admin privileges.

CHAPTER 12

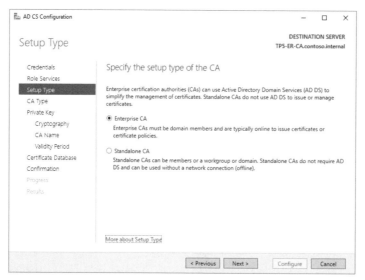

Figure 12-4 Enterprise CA

After you've chosen between Enterprise and Standalone CA, you need to choose between Root and Subordinate CA, as shown in Figure 12-5. Microsoft doesn't recommend having multiple enterprise root CAs in a forest. Unless you are deploying a single CA, the recommendation is to have no enterprise root CAs and to use a combination of an offline standalone root CA and enterprise subordinate CAs.

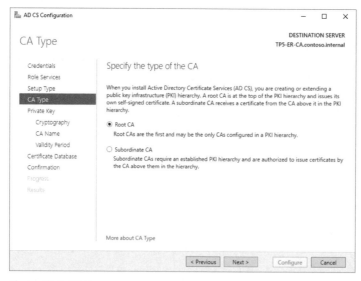

Figure 12-5 CA Type

On the Private Key page, shown in Figure 12-6, specify whether you want to create a new private key or use an existing private key. If you're deploying a new CA, create a new private key. If you are replacing a failed CA or migrating from an earlier version of Windows Server to a new Windows Server 2016 CA, use an existing private key. The trick with CA migration is to ensure that the destination server has the same name as the source server.

➤ You can find out more about CA migration at *https://technet.microsoft.com/en-us/library/ ee126140(v=ws.10).aspx*.

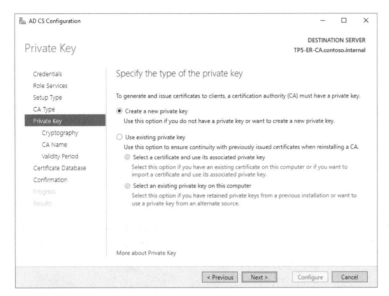

Figure 12-6 New private key

If you choose to create a new private key, you need to specify the cryptographic options for that key. In most circumstances the default options, shown in Figure 12-7, are fine. In some cases however, you might want to configure stronger cryptographic options. The important thing to remember is that the more advanced and stronger the cryptography you use, the more you limit yourself as to which clients are able to interact with the key. Table 12-1 provides a list of available cryptographic options.

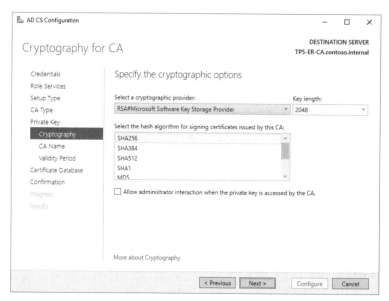

Figure 12-7 Cryptography

Table 12-1 CA Private Key cryptography options

Cryptographic providers	Available hash algorithms	Available key lengths
Microsoft Base Smart Card Crypto Provider	SHA1 MD2 MD4 MD5	1024 2048 4096
Microsoft Enhanced Cryptographic Provider v1.0	SHA1 MD2 MD4 MD5	512 1024 2048 4096
ECDSA_P256#Microsoft Smart Card Key Storage Provider	SHA256 SHA384 SHA512 SHA1	256
ECDSA_P521#Microsoft Smart Card Key Storage Provider	SHA256 SHA384 SHA512 SHA1	521

RSA#Microsoft Software Key Storage Provider (Default)	SHA256 SHA384 SHA512 SHA1 MD5 MD4 MD2	512 1024 2048 4096
Microsoft Base Cryptographic Provider v1.0	Sha1 Md2 Md4 Md5	512 1024 2048 4096
ECDSA_P521#Microsoft Software Key Storage Provider	SHA256 SHA384 SHA512 SHA1	521
ECDSA_P256#Microsoft Software Key Storage Provider	SHA256 SHA384 SHA512 SHA1	256
Microsoft Strong Cryptographic Provider	SHA1 MD2 MD4 MD5	512 1024 2048 4096
ECDSA_P384#Microsoft Software Key Storage Provider	SHA256 SHA384 SHA512 SHA1	384
Microsoft Base DSS Cryptographic Provider	SHA1	512 1024
RSA#Microsoft Smart Card Key Storage Provider	SHA256 SHA384 SHA512 SHA1 MD5 MD4 MD2	1024 2048 4096
DSA#Microsoft Software Key Storage Provider	SHA1	512 1024 2048
ECDSA_P384#Microsoft Smart Card Key Storage Provider	SHA256 SHA384 SHA512 SHA1	384

The CA name, shown in Figure 12-8, is automatically populated based on the computer's identity information. This name is important because it is present on each certificate issued by the CA. The distinguished name suffix is automatically generated. Unless you are issuing certificates to outside third parties, the default names provided here are likely to suffice.

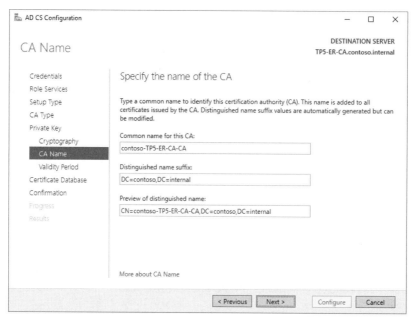

Figure 12-8 CA Name

On the Validity Period page, shown in Figure 12-9, specify the validity of the CA's certificate. When configuring this for a root CA, remember that no certificate issued by the CA or a subordinate CA can have a lifetime that exceeds the value of the CA's certificate. This is an important consideration when it comes to subordinate CAs. For example, you are installing a subordinate CA and you request a 5-year CA certificate from a root CA. If the root CA issuing the subordinate CA certificate only has 4 years of validity left on its CA certificate, the expiration date of the subordinate CA certificate is 4 years, not 5 years.

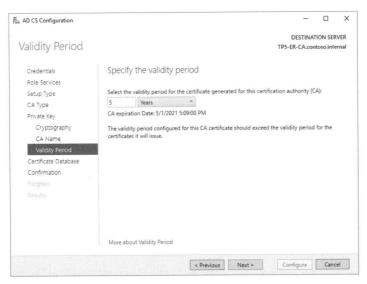

Figure 12-9 Validity Period

The final configuration step for an Enterprise Root CA is the location of the certificate database and the database log, as shown in Figure 12-10. These locations are important primarily from the perspective of backing up and recovering the database. If you enable key archiving, which is covered later in this chapter, the private keys of certificates issued by the CA are also written to this database in encrypted form.

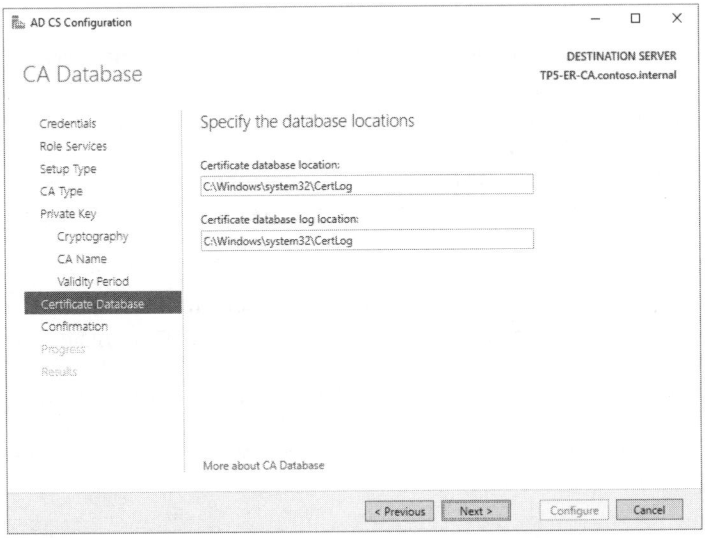

Figure 12-10 Certificate Database

CHAPTER 12

Enterprise subordinate

An enterprise subordinate CA is a CA that is integrated into Active Directory, but has another CA as the apex of the certificate trust chain. Similar to enterprise root CAs, enterprise subordinate CAs must remain online and must be a member of an Active Directory domain. Domain membership means computers that are members of the same forest as the enterprise subordinate automatically trust certificates issued by the CA. As is the case with enterprise root CAs, certificate revocation data is also published to Active Directory. Enterprise subordinate CAs can use certificate templates independently of where their CA certificate comes from.

You can acquire a signing certificate for an enterprise subordinate CA from an enterprise CA or from a standalone CA. Microsoft recommends using enterprise subordinate CAs with an offline root CA. You'll learn about offline root CAs later in this chapter.

If you are using a standalone CA, the installation wizard automatically generates a certificate request file and places it in the root directory on volume C: when the wizard completes. You can then submit this file to the CA to generate the subordinate CA's certificate. Until you install the subordinate CA certificate, the CA is not operational.

To install the CA certificate issued by the parent CA, perform the following steps:

1. Open the Certification Authority console.

2. Select the CA. In the Action menu, click All Tasks and then click Install CA Certificate.

3. In the Install CA Certificate dialog box, locate and open the certificate issued by the parent CA.

4. Ensure the CA is selected. In the Action menu, click All Tasks and then click Start Service.

Standalone CAs

Standalone CAs differ from enterprise CAs primarily in that one is highly integrated into Active Directory and the other is not. Additional differences between standalone CAs and enterprise CAs include:

- An enterprise CA must be installed on a domain member. You can install a standalone CA on a computer that isn't domain joined or on a computer that is domain joined.

- Standalone CA certificates are not automatically published to Active Directory.

- You can't use certificate templates with standalone CAs. The properties of the certificate are dependent on the certificate request.

- Standalone CAs cannot authenticate or use the identity of Active Directory users as part of the certificate request process even when installed on computers that are members of the domain.

- By default, all certificate requests to a standalone CA must be approved before a certificate is issued. With an enterprise CA, you can configure whether a certificate is automatically approved by configuring template properties.

While you can use standalone CAs to issue certificates to domain clients, they are not directly integrated into Active Directory in the way that an enterprise CA is. This means that domain members don't automatically trust certificates issued by a standalone CA and aren't automatically able to determine certificate revocation information by performing a query against Active Directory.

While you can deploy a standalone CA on a computer that is a domain member, standalone CAs are almost always deployed on computers that are not members of an Active Directory domain. Benefits of standalone CAs include:

- As the CA is not a member of the domain, it can be deployed on a perimeter network or in Azure.

- The CA can be shut down for extended periods.

- Members of Active Directory security groups, such as members of the Domain Admins group don't have access to the CA if it is deployed on a computer that does not have domain membership.

You can configure a client to trust a CA by importing the CA's certificate into the client's Trusted Root Certification Authority store. To do this, perform the following steps:

5. Open the Certificates snap-in of the Microsoft Management Console and set the snap-in to use the Computer account, as shown in Figure 12-11.

CHAPTER 12

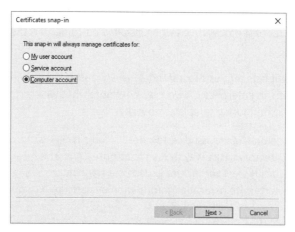

Figure 12-11 Computer account

6. Select the Certificates node under the Trusted Root Certification Authorities node as shown in Figure 12-2. On the Action menu, click All Tasks and then click Import.

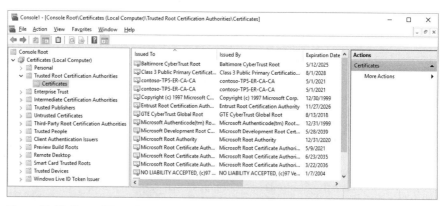

Figure 12-12 Trusted Root CAs

7. After you import the CA certificate, the client computer trusts all certificates issued by that CA. It also trusts all certificates issued by CAs that are subordinate to that CA in the trust chain.

In the event that you want to have all clients in a domain trust the certificates issued by a standalone root CA, you can use the certutil.exe command to publish the root CA's certificate to Active Directory. To do this, you need to run the certutil.exe command. Do this using an account that has Domain Admin privileges, and substitute the root CA certificate filename for the filename SA_ROOT_CA.crt used in the example command:

```
Certutil.exe -dspublish -f ROOT-CA.crt
```

Inside OUT

Deploy root certificates

You can use Microsoft Intune or System Center Configuration Manager to deploy root certificates to domain joined clients, non-domain joined clients, and managed mobile devices.

Standalone root

Standalone root CAs sign their own certificates, but aren't directly integrated into AD DS. A standalone root CA can be offline, but this causes problems if an online certificate revocation list distribution point is not present. Standalone root CAs often have the Certification Authority Web Enrollment service installed as a method of allowing people to submit certificate requests to the CA. After a request is submitted to the CA, you can approve or deny the request using the Certification Authority console. If the request is in the form of a .req file, you can use the certreq.exe utility to manage the request. You'll learn more about managing certificate requests later in this chapter.

Standalone subordinate

A standalone subordinate CA can be the child CA of an Enterprise CA or a standalone CA. Standalone subordinates are often deployed on perimeter networks when it is necessary to issue certificates to people outside the organization. Don't use an Enterprise CA in this scenario, as enterprise CAs can only be installed on domain joined computers and you should avoid deploying domain joined computers on perimeter networks. As is the case with standalone root CAs, standalone subordinate CAs often have the Certification Authority Web Enrollment service installed as a method of allowing people to submit certificate requests to the CA and as a method of retrieving certificates after they are issued.

Offline root

An offline root CA is a CA that is secured by being turned off and is only brought online when specific tasks occur, such as revoking an existing signing certificate, issuing a new signing certificate, or publishing a new certificate revocation list (CRL). Because the CA is offline, it is much less likely to be compromised.

The trick with deploying an offline root CA is that you need to configure the Certificate Revocation List and Authority Information Access distribution points so they are hosted on a computer that remains online when the offline root CA is offline. You also need to export the CA certificate and place it in a location accessible to clients performing revocation checks. You should renew the CA certificate for the offline root CA after updating the CRL and Authority Information Access (AIA) information because this way it is included with the offline root CA CA certificate. You'll learn more about configuring CRLs and AIA distribution points later in this chapter.

➤ You can find out more about offline root CAs at *http://social.technet.microsoft.com/wiki/contents/articles/2900.offline-root-certification-authority-ca.aspx.*

CHAPTER 12

Certificate revocation lists

A certificate revocation list (CRL) is a list of certificates a CA has issued that are no longer considered valid. A delta-CRL is a list of all certificates that have been revoked since the publication of the last CRL. By default, a CA publishes a new CRL every week and a delta-CRL every day. Both the CRL and the delta-CRL are stored on a CRL distribution point, also known as a CDP.

CRL distribution points

A CA can have multiple CDPs. CRL and CDP information is included with a certificate when the certificate is issued. Clients perform a check of certificate validity each time they encounter a new certificate and perform additional checks based on the CRL and delta-CRL publication intervals. Clients also check CDP locations in the order that they are configured on the CA.

You configure the CRL distribution point on the Extensions tab of the CA's properties, as shown in Figure 12-13. If you are publishing certificates that need to be used by people outside your organization, ensure that you have a CRL hosted in a publicly available location, such as on a web server on your perimeter network or in Microsoft Azure. Remember that any changes you make to CDP settings are only applied to certificates issued after the changes are made. If you make a change and then remove existing CDPs, clients encountering existing certificates are unable to perform revocation checks and the certificates are deemed invalid.

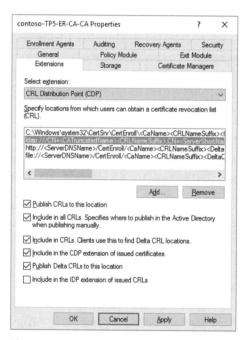

Figure 12-13 CRL DPs

Authority Information Access

The Authority Information Access (AIA) point settings specify where a client can retrieve the CA certificate of the CA that issued the certificate that the client has encountered. As with the CRL DP information, changes to the AIA information are only present in certificates issued subsequent to the change. This means that you need to keep existing AIA points in place until currently issued certificates either expire or are renewed. You configure AIA extensions on the Extensions tab of the CA properties, as shown in Figure 12-14. The AIA extensions are visible when you set the extension drop down to Authority Information Access.

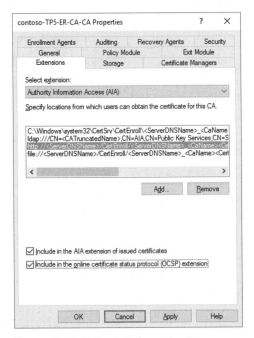

Figure 12-14 Authority Information Access

Revoking a certificate

Revoking a certificate makes it invalid and also involves several steps. The first step is to revoke the certificate itself, something you do from the CA management console. The second step is to update the CRL or delta-CRL and then publish the updates to the appropriate location. Revoking a certificate requires that you know the identity of the certificate you are revoking.

To revoke a certificate, perform the following steps:

1. Locate the certificate in the list of issued certificates on the CA that you issued the certificate from. Certificate serial numbers are in hexadecimal, but are listed sequentially in the console. Figure 12-15 shows a Basic EFS certificate selected.

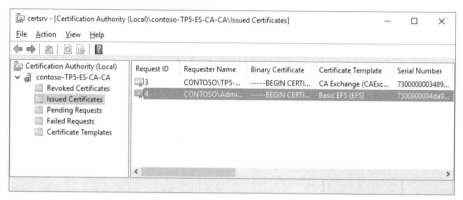

Figure 12-15 Issued certificates

2. On the Action menu, click All Tasks and then click Revoke Certificate.

3. On the Certificate Revocation dialog box, shown in Figure 12-16, select the reason for the certificate revocation and click Yes. You are asked to confirm the revocation. The revoked certificate is then listed in the Revoked Certificates node in the Certification Authority console.

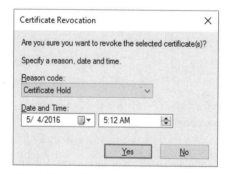

Figure 12-16 Certificate revocation

When you revoke a certificate, you need to specify a reason code. The following reason codes are available:

- Unspecified

- Key Compromise

- CA Compromise

- Change of Affiliation

- Superseded

- Cease of Operation

- Certificate Hold

The reason you specify is important if your organization is required to document why a specific certificate has been revoked. All reasons except Certificate Hold are irreversible. If you choose the Certificate Hold reason, you can undo the certificate revocation at a later point in time. Depending on the reason for performing the revocation and its severity, such as finding a subordinate CA compromised by remote access Trojan malware, you might want to publish a CRL or delta-CRL.

Publishing CRLs and delta-CRLs

CRLs and delta-CRLs are published automatically by CA. A new CRL is published by default once a week and a new delta-CRL is published once a day. You can configure the publication schedule using the Revoked Certificates Properties dialog box, shown in Figure 12-17. To access the dialog box, click the Revoked Certificates node of the Certification Authority console and then select Properties from the Action menu.

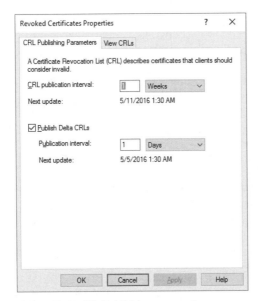

Figure 12-17 CRL Publishing parameters

For most organizations the default schedule is fine. If an organization issues certificates where revocation needs to propagate quickly, a shorter delta CRL publication interval would be more appropriate. This is because clients that have already accepted the certificate as valid have also learned about the CRL and delta CRL publication frequency. If you revoke a certificate and you have a delta CRL publication frequency of once a week and a CRL publication frequency of once a month, it could take up to a week before all clients encountering that certificate recognize it as invalid.

You can view the last time a CRL was published on the View CRLs tab of the Revoked Certificates Properties dialog box, shown in Figure 12-18.

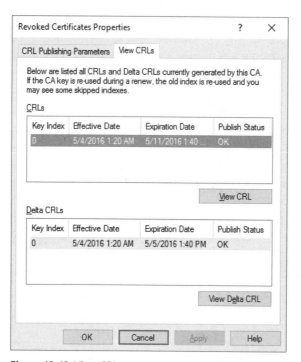

Figure 12-18 View CRLs

You can manually trigger publication of a CRL or delta-CRL by right-clicking the Revoked Certificates node, clicking All Tasks, and then clicking Publish. Select whether you want to publish a new CRL or a delta CRL as shown in Figure 12-19.

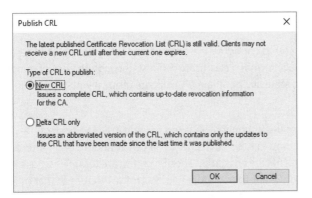

Figure 12-19 Publish CRL

Certificate services role services

The primary function of AD CS is the CA. In addition to the CA role, there are several ancillary roles that can be used for certificate requests, enrollment, and to handle revocation traffic. These roles are as follows:

- **Certificate Enrollment Policy Web Service.** Allows computers that are not members of the domain to obtain certificate enrollment policy information.

- **Certificate Enrollment Web Service.** Enables users in the same forest as the CA to interact with the CA through a web browser to request certificates, renew certificates, and retrieve CRLs.

- **Certification Authority Web Enrollment.** This role service allows people to navigate to a webpage and perform a certificate request. This can be either by filling out a web form with all the necessary details, or by pasting the contents of a certificate request file into the form. When the certificate is issued, people can revisit this webpage to retrieve their issued certificate.

- **Network Device Enrollment Service.** The Network Device Enrollment Service is a special service that you can configure to allow network devices like routers, switches, firewalls, and hardware based VPN gateways to obtain certificates from the CA.

- **Online Responder.** Online responders function in the same manner as CRL distribution points in that they provide a location where a client consuming a certificate can check whether a certificate is valid. The benefit of an online responder over a traditional CRL distribution point is that instead of downloading the entire revocation list, the client queries the online responder with a specific certificate ID.

CHAPTER 12

Certificate Templates

Certificate Templates allow you to configure the properties of different types of certificates. While it is possible to manually format a certificate request, through the use of templates, an enterprise CA is able to automatically populate a certificate request with relevant information stored in Active Directory.

By default, Certificate Authorities are only configured to issue a subset of all of the pre-configured certificate templates stored in Active Directory. You can configure each enterprise CA in your environment to issue certificates based on specific certificate templates. For example, as a security precaution, you might want to configure your PKI infrastructure so that only one CA is able to issue Data Recovery Agent certificates.

Deleting a template from the list of templates that can be issued in the Certification Authority console does not delete the certificate template from Active Directory. You can't remove any of the default certificate templates included with Windows Server 2016 from Active Directory using either the Certification Authority console or the Certificate Templates console. You can, however, remove custom certificate templates from Active Directory. Removing a certificate template just means that no new certificates can be issued from that template. It doesn't revoke any certificates issued from the template that are already in circulation.

To configure a CA to issue a specific certificate template, perform the following steps:

1. Select the Certificate Templates node under the CA in the Certification Authority console as shown in Figure 12-20. This shows you which certificate templates the CA is already configured to issue.

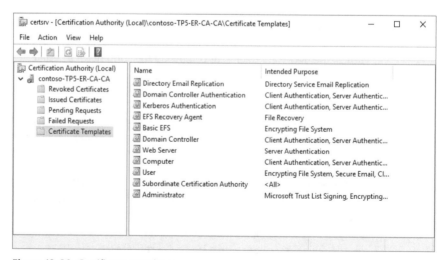

Figure 12-20 Certificate templates

2. If you want to have the CA issue certificates from a template not listed, you need to add the template. To do this, select the Certificate Templates node and click New from the Action menu. Next, click Certificate Template to Issue. This brings up the Enable Certificate Templates dialog box, shown in Figure 12-21. Select the certificate template that you want to issue and then click OK.

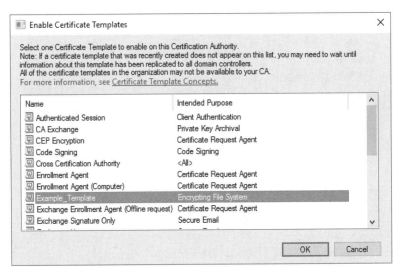

Figure 12-21 Enable templates

Template properties

You manage certificate templates from the Certificate Templates console. Each certificate template has properties that you configure to determine how certificates issued from the template function. The properties that are available in a template depend on the compatibility settings of the template. There are two compatibility settings, one for the CA and another for the certificate recipient. Figure 12-22 shows the CA setting configured for Windows Server Technical Preview and the certificate recipient set to Windows Technical Preview / Windows 10. This means that this template can only be used with a Windows Server 2016 CA. Over the next few pages you'll learn about some of the important areas of a certificate template's properties.

CHAPTER 12

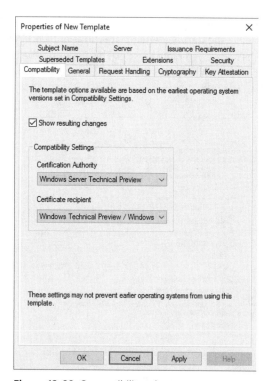

Figure 12-22 Compatibility tab

The General tab of a template, shown in Figure 12-23, allows you to configure both the template name and the template display name. You also configure the certificate validity period and the renewal period in this tab. You can also choose whether the certificate is published in Active Directory. Publication to Active Directory is useful when other people in the organization might need to access a public certificate. If it's published in Active Directory, the public certificate doesn't have to be manually shared or retrieved. The private key is not published to Active Directory when this option is enabled.

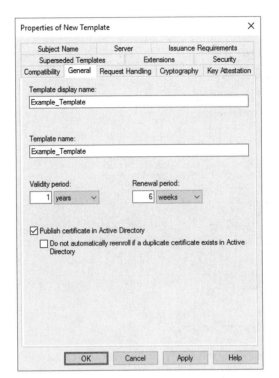

Figure 12-23 General tab

The Request Handling tab of the certificate template properties dialog box, shown in Figure 12-24, allows you to specify the certificate's purpose, which can be one of the following:

- Encryption

- Signature

- Signature and encryption

- Signature and smartcard logon

You can also use this tab to specify whether the subject's encryption private key is archived in the CA database, whether the private key can be exported, and whether the user is prompted during enrollment and when the private key is used.

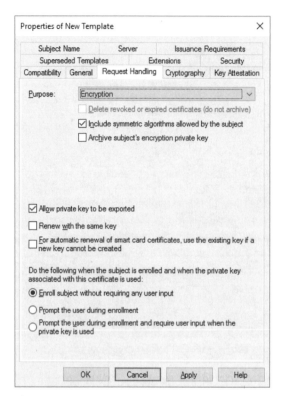

Figure 12-24 Request handling tab

The Cryptography tab of a certificate's properties, shown in Figure 12-25, allows you to specify the cryptographic properties of the certificate issued from the template. This includes specifying a minimum key size. You also use this tab to specify the properties of the cryptographic providers used for the certificate request. You do this to ensure that the certificate request meets a specific cryptographic benchmark. This setting is useful in environments that have very specific security requirements.

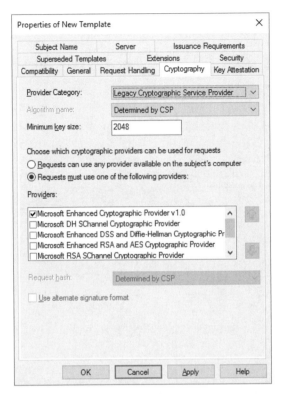

Figure 12-25 Cryptography tab

The Superseded Templates tab, shown in Figure 12-26, allows you to configure existing certificate templates that a newer template supersedes. For example, you might create a more advanced EFS certificate template that uses stronger cryptography and then specify the existing Basic EFS template as a template that the new template supersedes. When you configure autoenrollment correctly, a certificate from the new template automatically replaces the certificate from the superseded template.

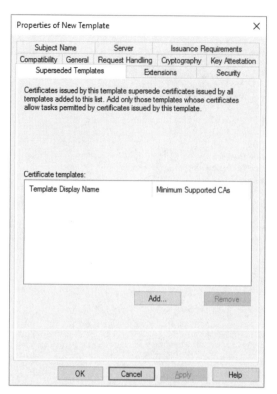

Figure 12-26 Superseded Templates tab

The Security tab, shown in Figure 12-27, allows you to configure which users and groups have permission to enroll and autoenroll in the certificate. A user that has permission to enroll in the certificate can request the certificate. Autoenrollment means that the certificate request is performed automatically. You configure autoenrollment through group policy. This process is described in more detail later in this chapter.

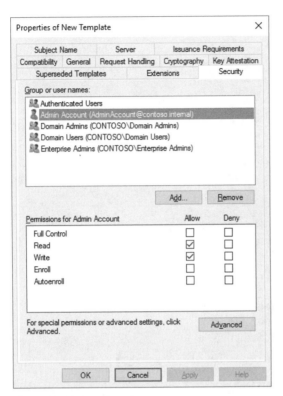

Figure 12-27 Security tab

You use the Issuance Requirements tab, shown in Figure 12-28, to specify whether requests against the template require certificate manager approval. You can also configure a certificate to require approval from more than one manager, which is useful for certificates issued from sensitive templates, such as the Key Recovery Agent template.

CHAPTER 12

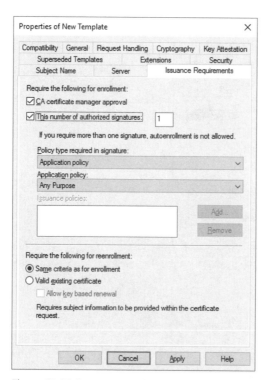

Figure 12-28 Issuance Requirements tab

Adding and editing templates

Windows Server 2016 includes 33 built-in templates. While you can edit some of the default templates should you want to make modifications, best practice is to create a duplicate of the default template and edit the duplicate. In the event that something goes wrong, you've still got the original. When your new certificate template is ready, you can add the new template to a CA and delete the old one from the CA. To create a duplicate template, right-click the template that you want to duplicate and click Duplicate Template.

Certificate autoenrollment and renewal

An advantage of enterprise CAs is that they allow for automatic certificate enrollment and automatic certificate renewal. This means that certificates can be issued automatically to users, services, or devices without requiring them to perform any explicit action. Autoenrollment substantially reduces the amount of administrative effort required to deploy and update certificates.

To configure Autoenrollment, you need to perform the following configuration steps for the certificate template associated with the certificate that you want to autoenroll:

- Ensure the certificate template for the certificate you want to allow autoenrollment for is configured for a Windows Server 2008 or higher level of compatibility. You configure this on the Compatibility tab of the certificate template's properties.

- Configure the Autoenroll permission for the certificate on the Security tab of the certificate template's properties, as shown in Figure 12-29. You should configure this permission for the security group that you want to automatically enroll.

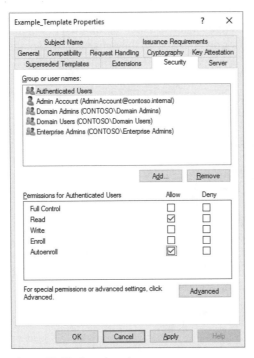

Figure 12-29 Security tab

The other half of configuring Autoenrollment is configuring the Certificate Services Client policy in the Default Domain GPO. Depending on whether you want to configure Autoenrollment for users or computers, this policy is found in one of the following nodes:

- Policies\User Configuration\Windows Settings\Security Settings\Public Key Policies

- Policies\Computer Configuration\Windows Settings\Security Settings\Public Key Policies

You can configure the following settings for this policy, as shown in Figure 12-30:

- **Configuration Model.** You can set this to Enabled, Disabled, or Not Configured. Setting this to Enabled allows certificate Autoenrollment.

- **Renew expired certificates, update pending certificates, and remove revoked certificates.** When you configure this setting, certificates that are configured for autoenrollment are automatically renewed before they expire.

- **Update certificates that use certificate templates.** This policy triggers autoenrollment in certificates that use new templates configured to supersede certificates issued from an existing template. Supersede settings are configured within the new certificate's template. The new certificate also needs to be configured with an appropriate autoenrollment permission.

- **Expiration notification.** When enabled, a user is prompted to trigger the reenrollment process. Notifications are triggered based on the remaining percentage of the certificate's lifetime.

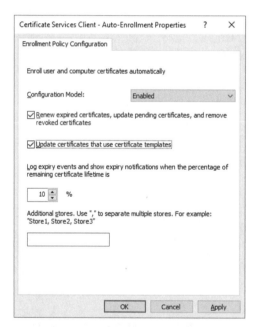

Figure 12-30 Enrollment Policy Configuration

CA management

You assign roles on a CA by assigning one of the following permissions, as shown in Figure 12-31:

- **Issue and Manage Certificates.** You assign this permission when you want to allow someone to issue and revoke certificates.

- **Manage CA.** You assign this permission when you want to allow someone to edit the properties of the CA. This includes the ability to assign CA permissions. You can't directly block someone that you have assigned the Manage CA permission to from granting themselves the Issue and Manage Certificates permission. Only by configuring auditing and alerts are you able to restrict this action. By default, members of the Enterprise Admins, Domain Admins, and local Administrators groups have the Manage CA permission on a computer that is a member of a domain.

- **Request Certificates.** You use this permission to control who is able to request certificates from the CA. Should you have a CA that you've configured to only issue certificates from especially sensitive templates, such as Key Recovery, you might choose to alter this setting.

- **Read.** You use this permission to allow someone to view CA information.

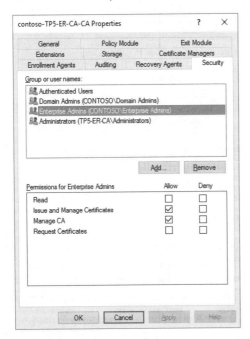

Figure 12-31 Security permissions

You can go further when configuring the ability to issue and manage certificates by configuring this ability on the basis of certificate templates. To configure a security group so they can issue certificates based on a specific template, you first need to assign the group the Issue and Manage Certificates permission on the Security tab of the CA properties dialog box. Then on the Certificate Managers tab, you need to choose the Restrict Certificate Managers option. After you've done that, you edit the list of certificate templates that each group is able to manage certificates for. Figure 12-32 shows the local KRA_Cert_Managers group configured to manage certificates based off of the Key Recovery Agent certificate template.

Figure 12-32 Certificate Managers

Handling certificate requests

All certificates on a standalone CA require approval by default. An enterprise CA uses the properties configured in the CA template. To approve a certificate, navigate to the Pending Requests node of the Certification Authority console, select the Pending Requests node, select the certificate that you want to approve or deny, click All Tasks from the Action Menu, and then click Issue or Deny.

You can alter whether an enterprise CA uses the template to determine whether approval is required, so that all certificates require approval, by editing the properties of the CA. To do so, click the Properties button on the Policy Module tab. This opens the Properties dialog box, shown in Figure 12-33, where you can configure this setting.

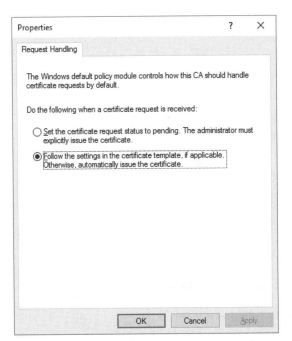

Figure 12-33 Request Handling

CA backup and recovery

You can back up and recover a CA, including the private key, CA certificate, CA database, and CA log from the Certification Authority console. To back up a CA, perform the following steps:

1. In the Certification Authority console, select the CA that you want to back up. On the Action menu, click All Tasks and click Back Up CA.

2. On the Welcome to The Certification Authority Backup page of the Certification Authority Backup Wizard, click Next.

3. On the Items to Backup page, choose from the following options, as shown in Figure 12-34:

    - **Private Key and CA Certificate.** Backs up the CA's private and public keys. Enables you to restore the CA on a different computer in the event that the CA fails.

    - **Certificate Database and Certificate Database Log.** Enables you to recover the public keys of the certificates that the CA has issued. If key archiving is enabled, this option enables you to recover private keys of these certificates.

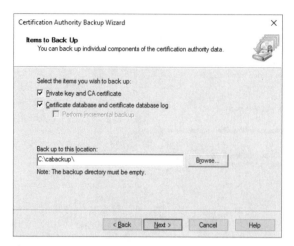

Figure 12-34 CA Backup

4. Provide a password to encrypt the backup data.

To recover a backup, perform the following steps:

1. In the Certification Authority console, right-click the CA, click All Tasks, and then click Restore CA.

2. On the warning about needing to stop Active Directory Certificate services, click OK.

3. On the Items to Restore page, shown in Figure 12-35, select the folder that holds the CA backup data and click Next.

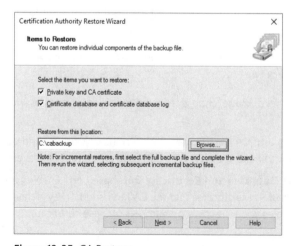

Figure 12-35 CA Restore

4. Provide the password used to protect the backup data and then complete the wizard. When the restoration is complete, you are prompted to restart Active Directory Certificate Services.

One thing that CA backup does not back up is the list of certificate templates that a specific enterprise CA has been configured to issue. If you have configured a CA to issue additional templates beyond the default templates, you need to configure a recovered CA to use the same templates. One method to keep track of which certificate templates a CA is configured to use is to use the Get-CATemplate PowerShell cmdlet. You can pipe the output of this cmdlet to a text file, which you can use as a record of which templates a specific CA has been configured to issue.

Key archiving and recovery

A key recovery agent allows an entity holding a properly configured key recovery agent certificate to recover a private key that has been archived in the AD CS database. To perform key recovery on a private certificate, the template the certificate is generated from needs to be configured so that private keys are archived to the AD CS database. This is done on the Request Handling tab of the template's properties, as shown in Figure 12-36.

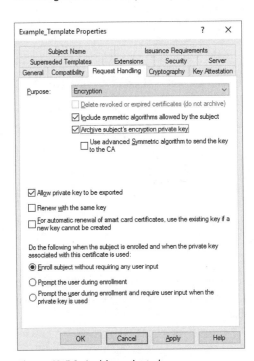

Figure 12-36 Archive private key

The CA also needs to be configured with one or more Recovery Agents. To configure a recovery agent, perform the following steps:

1. Create an account to be used by the recovery agent. While you can use the built-in administrator account, from a security perspective you're much better off having a separate account for this role. In an ideal environment, the individual using this account is separate from the individuals who manage the CA. Requiring separate individuals ensures that private keys are only recovered in authorized circumstances. You want to avoid allowing just anyone to recover private keys without oversight, especially in scenarios that involve encryption.

2. Configure a CA to issue Key Recovery certificates. To do this, open the Certification Authority console, right-click Certificate Templates, click New, and then click Certificate Template to Issue. On the Enable Certificate Templates dialog box, select Key Recovery Agent as shown in Figure 12-37 and click OK.

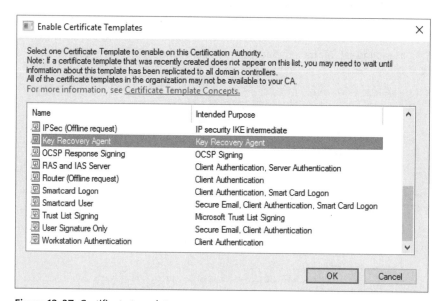

Figure 12-37 Certificate templates

3. The account you use for key recovery needs to then request a certificate based off of this template. They can do this using the Certificates snap-in of a Microsoft Management console, as shown in Figure 12-38.

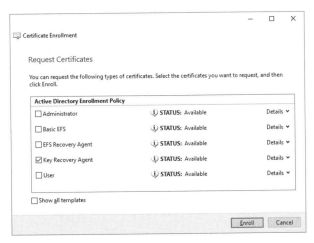

Figure 12-38 Certificate request

4. In the Certification Authority console, you need to approve the certificate request because the default template is configured to require approval and not have the certificate be issued automatically.

5. After the certificate is issued, export it from the Certificate Enrollment Requests node of the Certificates snap-in, including the private key as shown in Figure 12-39. After you've exported the private key to a .pfx file, you should then export the public key to a .cer file. Import this public certificate to the CA to enable key recovery.

Figure 12-39 Export private key

6. To configure the CA to archive private keys, on the Recovery Agents tab, select Archive the key, click Add, and on the Key Recovery Agent Selection dialog, shown in Figure 12-40, click the certificate then click OK. Note in Figure 12-40 that the name of the user account is Key Recovery. If your key recovery account has a different name, it is listed in this dialog box.

Figure 12-40 KRA selection

7. You need to restart the CA before the changes take place. When you've restarted the CA, the key recovery agent certificate is listed as Valid on the Recovery Agents tab, as shown in Figure 12-41.

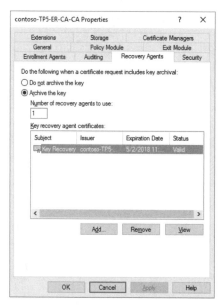

Figure 12-41 Recovery Agents

To recover an archived certificate using a KRA key, you need to perform the following steps:

1.   The first step is that a user who has CA Manager permissions needs to extract a blob that contains the private key. To do this, you need the serial number of the certificate that you want to recover. You do this by using the certutil command line utility with the -getkey option. For example:

     ```
     Certutil -getkey <certificate_serial_number> outputblob
     ```

2.   The user that has the key recovery agent certificate in the certificate store then needs to recover the private key. This task is also performed using the certutil command line utility.

     ```
     Certutil -recoverkey outputblob recoveredkey.pfx
     ```

CAPolicy.inf

The CAPolicy.inf file, located in the %systemroot% (usually C:\Windows) folder, allows you to customize CA settings. This file is not mandatory and is not present by default, but does allow you to provide a collection of settings to automatically configure the CA. You would use this primarily when providing certificates used outside your organization. If you have an internal CA that is only being used by organizational clients and the certificates aren't consumed by anyone outside the organization, you likely don't have to worry about using a CAPolicy.inf file.

The file is a text file. For example, the following CAPolicy.inf file could be used for a root CA:

```
[Version]
Signature= "$Windows NT$"
[Certsrv_Server]
RenewalKeyLength=4096
RenewalValidityPeriod=Years
RenewalValidityPeriodUnits=10
LoadDefaultTemplates=0
```

An enterprise CA could use the following CAPolicy.inf file:

```
[Version]
Signature= "$Windows NT$"
[PolicyStatementExtension]
Policies = LegalPolicy, LimitedUsePolicy
[LegalPolicy]
OID = 1.1.1.1.1.1.1.1.1
URL = "http://www.contoso.com/Policy/LegalPolicy.asp"
URL = "ftp://ftp.contoso.com/Policy/LegalPolicy.txt"
[LimitedUsePolicy]
OID = 2.2.2.2.2.2.2.2.2
URL = "http://www.contoso.com/Policy/LimitedUsePolicy.asp"
URL = "ftp://ftp.contoso.com/Policy/LimitedUsePolicy.txt"
LoadDefaultTemplates=0
```

The OIDs listed above are just for examples. In a real CAPolicy.inf file, you would use OIDs that you obtained from the ISO Name Registration Authority.

> ➤ You can find out more about the syntax of CAPolicy.inf files at *http://blogs.technet.com/b/ askds/archive/2009/10/15/windows-server-2008-r2-capolicy-inf-syntax.aspx.*

Managing Certificate Services using PowerShell

There are a number of PowerShell cmdlets that you can use to install and configure Certificate Services. These cmdlets are included in the ADCSAdministration and ADCSDeployment modules and are listed in Table 12-2 and Table 12-3.

Table 12-2. ADCSAdministration PowerShell Module cmdlets

CMDLET	Function
Add-CAAuthorityInformationAccess	Add a Uniform Resource Identifier (URI) for the Authority Information Access (AIA) or Online Responder OCSP address for a CA
Add-CACrlDistributionPoint	Add a CRL distribution point to all subsequently issued certificates
Add-CATemplate	Add a certificate template stored in Active Directory to the CA so that the CA can issue certificates from that template
Backup-CARoleService	Backs up both the CA database and the CA private key
Confirm-CAAttestationIdentityKeyInfo	Checks whether a CA trusts the attestation identity key for specific secure hardware
Confirm-CAEndorsementKeyInfo	Checks whether a CA trusts specific secure hardware for key attestation
Get-CAAuthorityInformationAccess	View the AIA and OCSP URI information configured for the CA
Get-CACrlDistributionPoint	View the CRL distribution point information configured for the CA
Get-CATemplate	View the list of templates that the CA is configured to issue. This is not the entire list of templates stored within AD DS
Remove-CAAuthorityInformationAc-cess	Remove a Uniform Resource Identifier (URI) for the Authority Information Access (AIA) or Online Responder OCSP address for a CA
Remove-CACrlDistributionPoint	Remove a CRL distribution point. This applies only to all subsequently issued certificates. Existing certificates still retain distribution point information that was valid at the time the certificate was issued
Remove-CATemplate	Removes a certificate template from a CA
Restore-CARoleService	Restore a CA database and private key from an existing backup

Table 12-3. ADCSDeployment PowerShell Module

Cmdlet	Function
Install-AdcsCertificationAuthority	Configures a CA. Cmdlet does not install the binaries, which need to be added separately using Install-WindowsFeature cmdlet
Install-AdcsEnrollmentPolicyWebService	Configures the Enrollment Policy Web Service on a computer where the binaries are already present
Install-AdcsEnrollmentWebService	Configures the Enrollment Web Service on a computer where the binaries are already present. Can also be used to add additional instances of the service on the computer
Install-AdcsNetworkDeviceEnrollmentService	Configure the Network Device Enrollment Service on a computer where the binaries are already present
Install-AdcsOnlineResponder	Configures the Online Responder role service on a computer where the binaries are already present
Install-AdcsWebEnrollment	Configures the Web Enrollment role service on a computer where the binaries are already present
Uninstall-AdcsCertificationAuthority	Removes the CA role service and deletes associated configuration information
Uninstall-AdcsEnrollmentPolicyWebService	Removes the Certificate Enrollment Policy Web Service
Uninstall-AdcsEnrollmentWebService	Removes the Certificate Enrollment Web Service, or specific instances of the service if more than one is present
Uninstall-AdcsNetworkDeviceEnrollmentSer-vice	Removes the Network Device Enrollment service from a computer it has been deployed on
Uninstall-AdcsOnlineResponder	Removes the Online Responder service from a computer it has been deployed on
Uninstall-AdcsWebEnrollment	Removes the Web Enrollment role service from a computer it has been deployed on

Managing certificate services using Certutil.exe and Certreq.exe

Not all certificate services functionality is available through PowerShell in Windows Server 2016. There are still several tasks that you need to use the certutil.exe and certreq.exe command line tools to perform.

Certutil.exe

Certutil.exe allows you to manipulate local certificates as well as to configure and manage certificate services. Some certutil.exe functionality is present in available PowerShell cmdlets. It is likely that, over time, all functionality that is present in certutil.exe will be available through PowerShell.

Important certutil.exe options are listed in Table 12-4.

Table 12-4. Certutil.exe options

Option	Function
-deny	Use this to deny a pending certificate request
-resubmit	Resubmit a pending certificate request
-revoke	Revoke a certificate
-CRL	Publish a new CRL
-renewCert	Renew the CA certificate
-backup	Backup the AD CS
-backupDB	Backup the AD CS database
-backupKey	Backup the CA certificate and private key
-restore	Restore AD CS from a backup
-restoreDB	Restore the AD CS database from a backup
-restoreKey	Restore the CA certificate and private key from a backup
-dsPublish	Publish a certificate or CRL to AD
-ADTemplate	List templates stored in AD
-TemplateCAs	List CAs configured to issue a template

> ➤ You can find out more about the certutil.exe command at *https://technet.microsoft.com/library/cc732443.aspx.*

Certreq.exe

You can use Certreq.exe to import a certificate request file and submit it to a CA. If the user running certreq.exe has the appropriate permissions on the CA, they are able to save the issued certificate. Important certreq.exe options are listed in Table 12-5.

Table 12-5. Certreq.exe options

Option	Function
-Submit	Submits a request to a CA
-Retrieve	Retrieves a response from a CA
-Enroll	Enrolls for a new certificate or renews a certificate
-Accept	Accepts and installs a certificate request response

➤ You can find out more about the certreq.exe command at *https://technet.microsoft.com/en-us/library/dn296456.aspx.s*

Active Directory Federation Services

Active Directory Federation Services (AD FS) is Microsoft's identity federation solution. Identity federation allows identification, authorization, and authentication to occur across organizational boundaries. When a federated trust is established, users can use their local credentials to access resources hosted by another organization. When configured properly, federation also enables users to access resources hosted in the cloud. Although it is possible to configure full forest or domain trust relationships when users in one organization need to use their credentials to access resources in another organization, these trust relationships are often more comprehensive than is necessary. AD FS makes it possible to configure highly restricted access to information and resources between partner organizations while still allowing each partner to authenticate using its own credentials.

AD FS components

AD FS deployments in Windows Server 2016 consist of two components:

- **Federation Server**. The computer that hosts the federation server role manages requests involving identity claims. There must be at least one federation server in an Active Directory forest when deploying AD FS.

- **Web Application Proxy**. When you want to provide AD FS functionality to clients on untrusted networks, such as on the Internet, you deploy the computer that functions as a web application proxy on a perimeter network. This server relays connections to the Federation Server on the internal network and this role can also be installed on a stand-alone computer. In Windows Server 2012 and earlier versions of AD FS, this role was known as the Federation Proxy.

Claims, claim rules, and attribute stores

AD FS provides claims-based authentication. Claims-based authentication works on the basis of a claim about the user, such as "allow access to this web application if this user is a full-time employee of the partner organization." AD FS uses the following when building tokens that contain claim data:

- **Claim**. Claims are descriptions made about an object based on the object's attributes. For example, a user account name, employee type, or a security group membership can constitute a claim. Claims are also used with Dynamic Access Control, which is covered in Chapter 14, "Active Directory Rights Management Services."

- **Claim rules**. Claim rules determine how a federation server processes a claim. You can have a simple rule, such as treating a user's email address as a valid claim. Claim rules can also be more complex where an attribute, such as job title from one organization, is translated into a security group membership in the partner organization.

- **Attribute store**. An attribute store holds the values used in claims. AD FS generally uses Active Directory as an attribute store. For example, a lookup of a user's Managed By attribute returns a value that lists the user account assigned as that user's manager.

Figure 13-1 shows how to create a claim rule where Active Directory functions as the attribute store and the Employee-Type attribute is mapped to an outgoing claim.

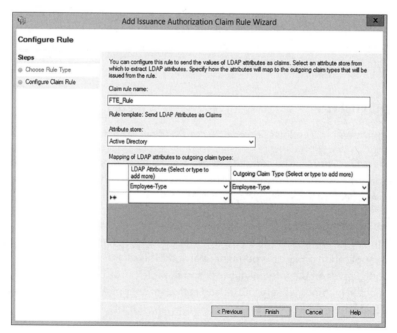

FIGURE 13-1 Claim rule

Claims provider

A claims provider is a federation server that provides users with claims. These claims are stored within digitally encrypted and signed tokens. When a user needs a token, the claims provider server contacts the Active Directory deployment in its native forest to determine if the user has authenticated. If the user is properly authenticated against the local Active Directory deployment, the claims provider then builds a user claim by using attributes located within Active Directory and within other attribute stores. The attributes that are added to the claim are dependent on the attributes required by the partner.

Relying party

The relying party server is a member of the Active Directory forest that hosts the resources that the user in the partner organization wants to access. The relying party server accepts and validates the claims contained in the token that the claims provider issued. The relying party server then issues a new token that the resource uses to determine what access to grant the user from the partner organization.

> ## Inside OUT
> ### Non-exclusive roles
> It is possible for a single AD FS server to function as both a claims provider server and a relying party server. This enables users in each partner organization to access resources in the other organization through a federation trust.

Relying party trust

You configure the relying party trust on the AD FS server that functions as the claims provider server. Although this might initially seem counterintuitive, it makes sense when you consider it as a statement: "A relying party trust means that a claims provider trusts a specific relying party." Figure 13-2 shows the Add Relying Party Trust Wizard where the address of the relying party server to be trusted is adl-dc.wingtiptoys.internal.

CHAPTER 13

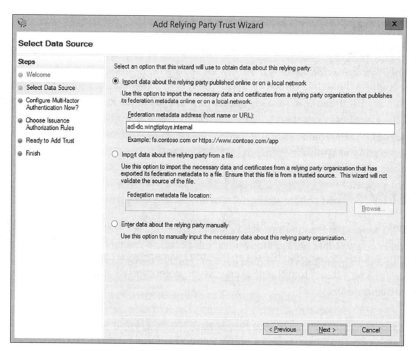

FIGURE 13-2 Select data source

Claims provider trust

You configure the claims provider trust on the Federation Server that functions as the relying party. This also seems counterintuitive until you consider the claims provider trust as a statement: "A claims provider trust means that a relying party trusts a specific claims provider." Figure 13-3 shows how to set up a claims provider trust where the address of the claims provider to be trusted is cbr-dc.contoso.com

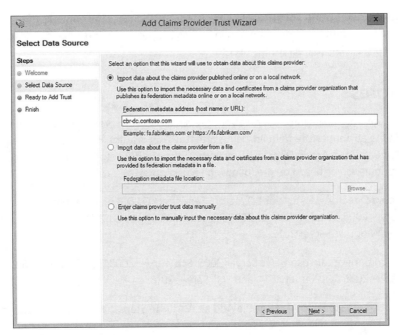

FIGURE 13-3 Select data source

Configuring certificate relationship

You need to configure partners so that the certificates issued by the opposite partner are trusted. You can accomplish this by using a trusted third-party CA or by configuring CA trusts between partners. To configure a CA trust, you need to import the CA certificate of the partner organization's CA into the Trusted Root CA store. You can do this either directly on the AD FS server, or you can configure Group Policy so that all computers within the policy's scope trust the partner organization's CA.

You can use a certificate issued from the computer certificate template, which is available through an Active Directory Certificate Services enterprise CA, to secure the federation server endpoint. When using a trusted third-party CA, you can also use a typical Secure Sockets Layer (SSL) certificate.

AD FS uses the following certificates:

- **Token-signing certificates.** The federation server uses the token-signing certificate to sign all the tokens that it issues. The server that functions as the claims provider uses the token-signing certificate to verify its identity. The relying party uses the token-signing certificate when verifying that the token was issued by a trusted federation partner.

- **Token-decrypting certificates.** The claims provider uses the public key from this certificate to encrypt the user token. When the relying party server receives the token, it uses the private key to decrypt the user token.

Attribute stores

The attribute store holds information about users. The AD FS server uses the information contained in the attribute store to build claims after the user is authenticated. In the majority of AD FS implementations, Active Directory functions as the attribute store. You can configure additional attribute stores based on the following technologies:

- Active Directory Lightweight Directory Services (AD LDS) on computers running Windows Server 2008, Windows Server 2008 R2, Windows Server 2012, Windows Server 2012 R2, and Windows Server 2016.

- All editions of Microsoft SQL Server 2005, SQL Server 2008, SQL Server 2008 R2, SQL Server 2012, SQL Server 2014, and SQL Server 2016.

You add attribute stores to AD FS in the Add an Attribute Store dialog box, as shown in Figure 13-4.

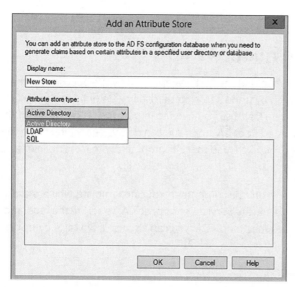

FIGURE 13-4 Attribute stores

Claim rules

Claim rules determine how AD FS servers send and consume claims. AD FS supports two different types of claim rules: relying party trust claim rules and claims provider trust claim rules.

Relying party trust claim rules

Relying party trust claim rules determine how the claims about a user are forwarded to the relying party. You can configure these rules by editing the relying party trust's claim rules on the AD FS server that functions as the claims provider. There are three types of relying party trust claim rules:

- **Issuance transform rules.** Determine how claims are sent to the relying party.

- **Issuance authorization rules.** Determine which users have access to the relying party. An issuance authorization claim rule is shown in Figure 13-5.

- **Delegation authorization rules.** Determine if users can act on behalf of other users when accessing the relying party.

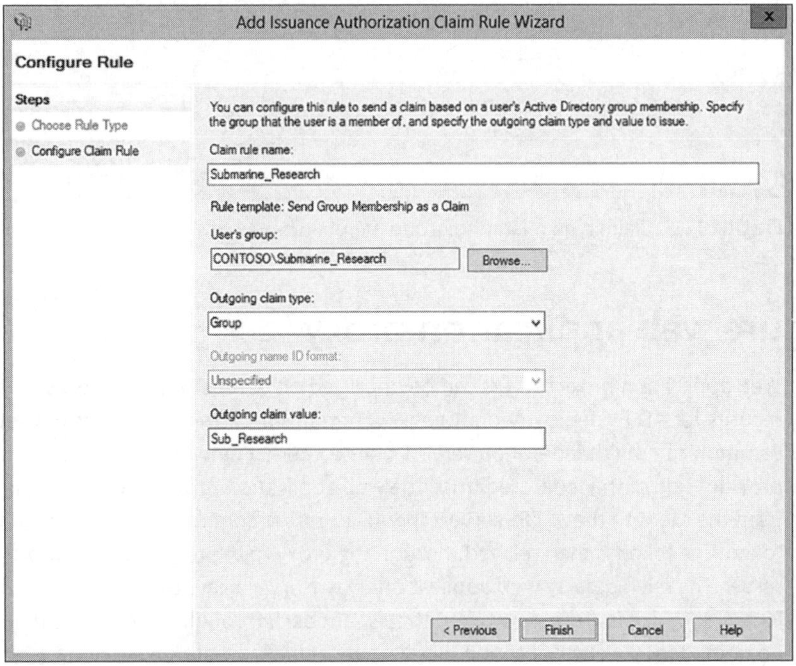

FIGURE 13-5 Choose a rule type

Claims provider trust claim rules

Claims provider trust rules determine how the relying party filters incoming claims. You can configure these rules by editing the claims provider trust's claim rules. All claims provider trust claim rules are acceptance transform rules. Figure 13-6 shows an incoming claim type related to group membership.

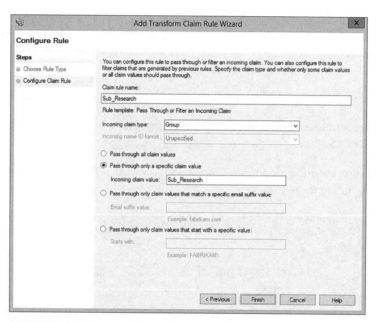

FIGURE 13-6 Claim type related to group membership

Configure web application proxy

Web application proxy servers can be deployed on perimeter networks as a way to increase security for AD FS deployments. Clients communicate with the AD FS proxy server, which then communicates with federation servers on the internal network. For example, on the claims provider side of the federated trust, the web application proxy forwards authentication data from the client to the AD FS server. The AD FS server confirms the authentication and issues the token. The token is then relayed through the proxy to the relying party web application proxy server. The relying party web application proxy server relays the token to the relying party AD FS server, which issues a new token that is sent back through the proxy to the original client. At no point does a web application proxy server actually create claims or generate tokens. All communication between a web application proxy server and a federation server occurs using the HTTPS protocol.

In Windows Server 2012 and earlier versions of AD FS, the web application proxy server role was performed by an AD FS proxy server. A web application proxy server in Windows Server 2016 differs from the AD FS proxy role service available in Windows Server 2012 because it has the following features:

- Is deployed as a Remote Access role service

- Provides secure remote access to web-based applications hosted on the internal network

- Functions as a reverse proxy for web-based applications

- Can be used to publish access to Work Folders

When deploying a web application proxy server, you need to ensure that the following certificates are present in the server's certificate store:

- A certificate that includes the federation service name. If the web application proxy server must support Workplace Join, the certificate must also support the following subject alternative names:
    - <federation servicename>.<domain name>
    - Enterpriseregistration.<domainname>

- A wildcard certificate, a subject alternative name certificate, or individual certificates to cover each web application that is accessible through the web application proxy.

- A copy of the certificate that external servers use if you are supporting client certificate pre-authentication.

The server hosting the web application proxy role must also trust the certificate authority that issues these certificates. After deploying the web application proxy role service, run the Web Application Proxy Configuration Wizard. Running the wizard involves specifying the federation service name and the credentials of an account that has AD FS administrative privileges, as shown in Figure 13-7.

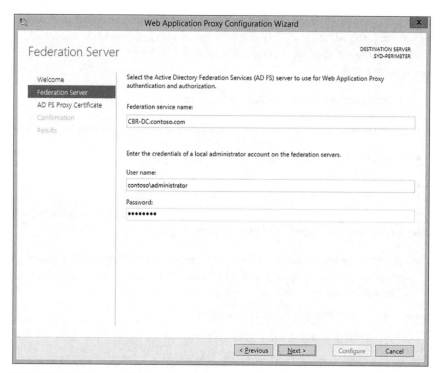

FIGURE 13-7 Web application proxy configuration

You also need to specify the certificate that the AD FS proxy component of the web application proxy uses, as shown in Figure 13-8. You need to have access to the certificate's private key as well as the public key when configuring the web application proxy's AD FS proxy component.

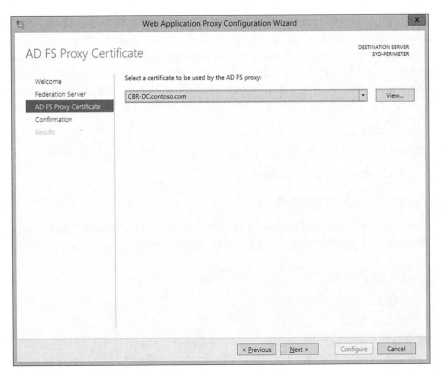

FIGURE 13-8 AD FS Proxy Certificate

Workplace Join

Workplace Join is a feature available in Windows Server 2016 and Windows Server 2012 R2 that you can use to allow non-domain joined devices and computers to access domain resources and claims-enabled applications in a secure manner. When a non-domain joined device or computer performs a Workplace Join, a special object representing the device is created in AD DS. The object stores attributes that describe the device that you can use when configuring access rules.

Workplace Join requires the following components:

- Windows 8.1, Windows 10, Android, or iOS 7 or later devices

- Claims aware application

- AD FS deployment on internal network

- Web application proxy deployed on the perimeter network

- Device registration service

Workplace Join also supports single sign-on (SSO). When a user authenticates to access one claims aware application, that authentication carries over to other claims-aware applications hosted by the organization as well. When supporting Workplace Join, consider acquiring certificates from trusted third-party CAs because the majority of the devices performing Workplace Join are managed by their owners rather than centrally by the IT department, which means that getting those devices to trust certificates from an internal CA requires extra administrative effort.

Enable Workplace Join by running the following Windows PowerShell cmdlets:

```
Initialize-ADFSDeviceRegistration
```

```
Enable-ADFSDeviceRegistration
```

After you've enabled Workplace join, you can enable device authentication by editing the Global Authentication Policy through the AD FS console, as shown in Figure 13-9.

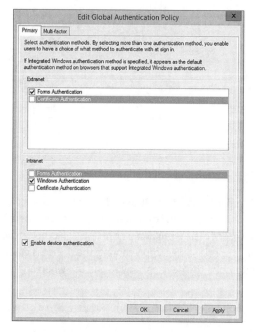

FIGURE 13-9 Enabling device authentication

Users authenticate by using their UPNs. When configuring Workplace Join, ensure that you configure your organization's external DNS zone with a record that maps enterpriseregistration. upndomainname.com (where upndomainname.com is the UPN suffix) to the Web Application Proxy server's IP address or the AD FS server that you've configured to support Workplace Join.

Multi-factor authentication

AD FS supports multi-factor authentication. When you implement multi-factor authentication, more than one form of authentication is required. For example, a username, password, and a code from an authenticator application running on a mobile device might be required. You can either configure multi-factor authentication in AD FS globally, as shown in Figure 13-10, or on a per-relying party trust basis.

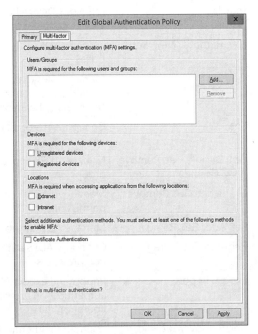

FIGURE 13-10 Multi-factor authentication

You can configure multi-factor authentication by using a third-party vendor's product or you can integrate Microsoft's Windows Azure Multi-Factor authentication service. Windows Azure Multi-Factor authentication allows the following authentication methods:

- **Telephone call.** An automated telephone call is made to the user's registered telephone number. The user enters the data provided in the call when authenticating.

- **Text message.** A text message is sent to the user's registered mobile telephone. The user enters the data provided in the text message when authenticating.

- **Mobile app.** The user installs a mobile authentication app on their mobile device that generates a periodically changing code. The user enters this code when authenticating.

CHAPTER 13

Managing AD FS with PowerShell

You can use the Windows PowerShell cmdlets from the ADFS module, listed in Table 13-1, to manage AD FS on Windows Server 2016.

Table 13-1. AD FS PowerShell cmdlets

Noun	Verbs	Function
ADDeviceRegistration	Initialize	Initializes Device Registration service config in the forest
AdfsAccessControlPolicy	Get, Remove, New, Set	Manage ADFS access control policy
AdfsAdditionalAuthenticationRule	Get, Set	Manage rules that trigger additional authentication providers to be invoked
AdfsAlternateTlsClientBinding	Set	Configure TLS certificate client binding
AdfsApplicationGroup	Get, Disable, Set, Remove, New, Enable	Manage ADFS application groups
AdfsApplicationPermission	Grant, Set, Get, Remove	Manage ADFS application permissions
AdfsAttributeStore	Set, Add, Get, Remove	Manage ADFS attribute store
AdfsAuthenticationProvider	Register, Get, Unregister	Configure ADFS authentication providers
AdfsAuthenticationProvider ConfigurationData	Export, Import	Import and export ADFS authentication provider configuration data
AdfsAuthenticationProviderWeb-Content	Get, Remove, Set	Configure authentication provider for web content
AdfsAzureMfaConfigured	Get	Get the Azure multi-factor authentication configuration
AdfsAzureMfaTenant	Set	Configure an existing Azure multi-factor authentication tenant
AdfsAzureMfaTenantCertificate	New	Configure a new ADFS azure multi-factor authentication tenant certificate
AdfsCertificate	Get, Update, Remove, Set, Add	Configure an ADFS certificate
AdfsCertificateAuthority	Disable, Get, Set	Configure an ADFS certificate authority
AdfsCertSharingContainer	Set	Configure an ADFS certificate sharing container

AdfsClaimDescription	Remove, Add, Get, Set	Manage claim descriptions
AdfsClaimRuleSet	New	Create a new ADFS claim rule set
AdfsClaimsProviderTrust	Set, Get, Update, Disable, Enable, Remove, Add	Configure an ADFS claims provider trust
AdfsClaimsProviderTrustsGroup	Remove, Get, Add	Configure an ADFS claims provider trusts group
AdfsClient	Remove, Set, Disable, Add, Get, Enable	Configure an ADFS client
AdfsContactPerson	New	Configure a new ADFS contact person
AdfsDeploymentSQLScript	Export	Export an SQL script for ADFS deployment
AdfsDeviceRegistration	Enable, Set, Disable, Get	Configure ADFS device registration
AdfsDeviceRegistrationUpnSuffix	Get, Set, Remove, Add	Configure an ADFS device registration UPN suffix
AdfsEndpoint	Disable, Set, Get, Enable	Manage an ADFS endpoint
AdfsFarm	Install	Install an ADFS farm
AdfsFarmBehaviorLevel	Restore	Restore a farm behavior level to a previous level
AdfsFarmBehaviorLevelRaise	Test, Invoke	Test or perform a farm behavior level raise
AdfsFarmBehaviorLevelRestore	Test	Check whether prerequisites have been met to restore the existing ADFS farm behavior level
AdfsFarmInformation	Set, Get	View and configure information about the ADFS farm
AdfsFarmInstallation	Test	Performs checks to test whether you can install a new federation server farm
AdfsFarmJoin	Test	Performs checks required before you run the Add-AdfsFarmNode cmdlet to add a computer to a farm
AdfsFarmNode	Remove, Add	Manage ADFS farm nodes
AdfsGlobalAuthenticationPolicy	Set, Get	Configure ADFS global authentication policy
AdfsGlobalWebContent	Get, Set, Remove	Configure ADFS global web content

AdfsLdapAttributeToClaimMap-ping	New	Configure ADFS attribute claim mapping
AdfsLdapServerConnection	New	Create a connection to an LDAP server for ADFS
AdfsLocalClaimsProviderTrust	Get, Enable, Disable, Add, Set, Remove	Configure ADFS Local Claims Provider Trust
AdfsNativeClientApplication	Remove, Get, Add, Set	Configure ADFS client application
AdfsNonClaimsAwareRelyingPar-tyTrust	Set, Enable, Disable, Add, Remove, Get	Configure non-claims aware relying party trust
AdfsOrganization	New	Create a new ADFS organization
AdfsProperties	Set, Get	Configure ADFS properties
AdfsProxyTrust	Revoke	Remove the proxy trust
AdfsRegistrationHosts	Get, Set	Configure ADFS registration hosts
AdfsRelyingPartyTrust	Set, Add, Enable, Update, Disable, Get, Remove	Configure relying party trusts
AdfsRelyingPartyTrustsGroup	Remove, Add, Get	Configure relying party trust group
AdfsRelyingPartyWebContent	Set, Remove, Get	Manage web content for the relying party
AdfsRelyingPartyWebTheme	Get, Set, Remove	Configure the web theme for the relying party
AdfsSamlEndpoint	New	Create a new ADFS SAML endpoint
AdfsScopeDescription	Add, Remove, Set, Get	Manage ADFS scope description
AdfsServerApplication	Remove, Set, Get, Add	Manage ADFS server applications
AdfsSslCertificate	Set, Get	Configure ADFS TLS certificates
AdfsSyncProperties	Set, Get	Manage ADFS sync properties
AdfsTrustedFederationPartner	Get, Remove, Add, Set	Manage ADFS trusted federation partners
AdfsWebApiApplication	Get, Remove, Set, Add	Manage ADFS web api applications
AdfsWebApplicationProxy RelyingPartyTrust	Add, Set, Disable, Get, Remove, Enable	Manage relying party trust for web application proxy

AdfsWebConfig	Get, Set	Configure AD FS web customization configuration settings
AdfsWebContent	Import, Export	Import and export properties of all web content objects
AdfsWebTheme	New, Get, Export, Set, Remove	Manage ADFS web themes

Managing Web Application Proxy with PowerShell

You can use the Windows PowerShell cmdlets from the WebApplicationProxy module, listed in Table 13-2, to manage AD FS on Windows Server 2016.

Table 13-2. Web Application Proxy PowerShell cmdlets

Noun	Verbs	Function
WebApplicationProxy	Install	Install the Web Application Proxy role
WebApplicationProxy Application	Remove, Set, Add, Get	Configure Web Application Proxy applications
WebApplicationProxy AvailableADFSRelyingParty	Get	View Web Application Proxy available ADFS relying party configuration information
WebApplicationProxy Configuration	Get, Set	View and configure Web Application Proxy configuration information
WebApplicationProxy DeviceRegistration	Update	Configure ADFS SSL endpoint listeners that correspond to UPN suffixes
WebApplicationProxy Health	Get	View health status of the Web Application Proxy
WebApplicationProxy SslCertificate	Get, Set	Configure the AD FS TLS certificate for the federation server proxy component of the web application proxy

Dynamic Access Control and Active Directory Rights Management Services

Dynamic Access Control (DAC) provides a way to dynamically assign access permissions to content based on the content's properties and information about the user and device that are attempting to access the content. Active Directory Rights Management Services (AD RMS) provides a way of securing content through encryption and through rules that are applied to the operating system and applications on what actions the user can perform with that content. Both technologies, if correctly implemented, can minimize the chance of information that should stay within organizational boundaries, finding its way outside of those boundaries.

Dynamic Access Control

If you've worked with NTFS permissions for a while, you are most likely aware that they are rarely properly implemented. At first glance, the system seems logical. You create a collection of groups that represent ways of describing a user or computer's place in the organization. You then use those groups to apply permissions to restrict access to files and folders. This is great in theory, but it requires that security groups are kept up to date and that the permissions themselves are accurately configured. In many organizations, the process of ensuring group membership is erratic and piecemeal, with users only being added to groups after they lodge a service desk ticket.

Dynamic Access Control (DAC) allows you to configure security using the properties of a user account or a computer account and the properties of the file. For example, you can configure DAC so that only people who have Don Funk as a manager are able to open files that contain the word Cake. You can do this by setting up classification rules and claims so that every file is checked to see if it contains the word Cake, and if it does, a custom attribute is configured to reflect that status. Another rule can be configured to set permissions on the file so that anyone whose Active Directory user account has the Managed By attribute set to Don Funk has access to open the file. Access is still mediated by NTFS permissions, but those NTFS permissions are configured based on the properties of the file and the accessing user, not using the traditional method of right-clicking the file or parent folder and setting them manually.

DAC has the following requirements:

- Windows Server 2016, Windows Server 2012 R2, or Windows Server 2012 with the File Server Resource Manager (FSRM) role service installed on the file servers that host files protected through DAC. DAC is not supported on Windows Server 2008 R2 and earlier file servers.

- Windows 10, Windows 8.1, or Windows 8 client computers to support device claims. Clients using Windows 7 to access files that have security applied through DAC are still able to access files, but device claims are ignored.

- A domain controller running Windows Server 2012, Windows Server 2012 R2, or Windows Server 2016 in the domain. It's also possible to apply an update to the Active Directory Schema if no Windows Server 2012 domain controllers are present, and all domain controllers are running Windows Server 2008 R2.

Configuring Group Policy to support DAC

Configuring Active Directory to support DAC requires that you configure a Group Policy that applies to all domain controllers in the domain. You can do this in a policy that applies to the domain or just to domain controllers. To enable support for DAC, enable the KDC Support For Claims, Compound Authentication And Kerberos Armoring policy. You can find this policy in the Computer Configuration\Policies\Administrative Templates\System\KDC node.

Configuring User and Device Claims

Before you can configure access rules, you need to configure claims. Claims are bits of information about users and computers and are usually derived from Active Directory attributes. You can edit Active Directory attributes by using Active Directory Administrative Center as well as by using other tools. DAC supports the following types of claims:

- **User Claim.** This is information about the user and can be based on a user account's attributes, such as EmployeeType. You can also use claims related to group membership.

- **Device Claim.** This is information about the computer that the user is accessing the file from. For example, you could edit the computer account's Location attribute and set it to secure. This allows you to configure DAC so a user can access a file from a computer that has the Location attribute set to secure, but cannot access the same file from another computer that does not have the Location attribute set to secure.

You create claims in Active Directory Administrative Center by navigating to the Claim Types section under the Dynamic Access Control section. When creating a claim type, select an existing Active Directory attribute as the basis for the claim. In Figure 14-1, you can see that the Department attribute forms the basis of a claim type. When you configure a claim, select whether the claim relates to Users or Computers. You can also specify suggested values to associate with the claim. In the case of a claim related to the Department attribute, this might be a list of departments within your organization.

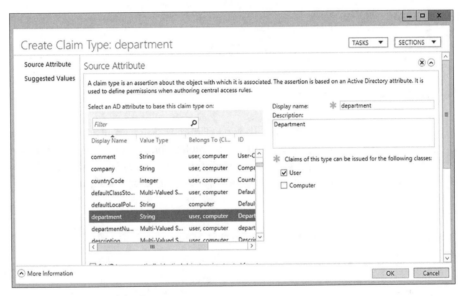

FIGURE 14-1 Create Claim Department

Configuring Resource Properties

Resource Properties determine the resource attributes that you can use when configuring central access rules. Windows Server 2016 ships with a collection of default resource properties, but you can also add extra resource properties based on available attributes. Figure 14-2 shows a custom resource property named Project and two value options, Hovercraft or Submarine. Resource Properties can be assigned to files either manually or automatically by configuring File Server Resource Manager File Classification Rules.

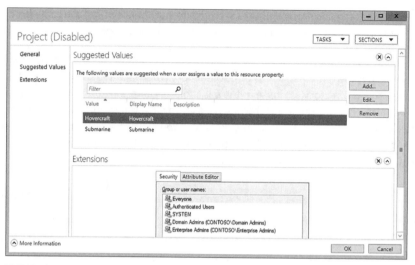

FIGURE 14-2 Hovercraft project

The Global Resource Property List, shown in Figure 14-3, is a list of all resource properties that you can use when configuring Central Access Rules. You can add and remove these properties as necessary. When you publish a property list through Active Directory, you can then assign these properties to files and folders either manually or automatically using File Server Resource Manager.

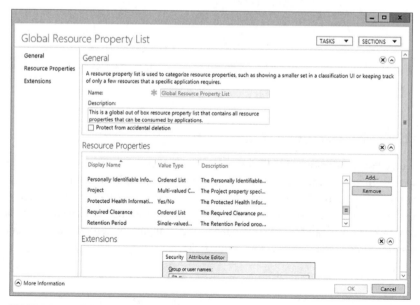

FIGURE 14-3 Global Resource Property List

You use File Server Resource Manager to apply properties to files through File Classification Rules. You can configure a classification rule to look for a particular string of text in a file and then to assign a particular property to that file based on the string. The example in Figure 14-4 shows that the Submarine value is assigned to the Project property for files that meet the classification requirements, the classification requirements in this case being any file that contains the text string "submarine."

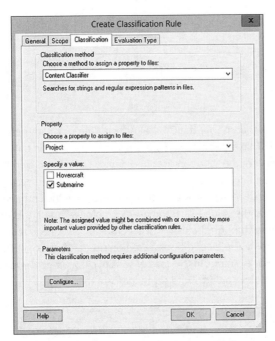

FIGURE 14-4 Create Classification rule dialog box

Central Access Rules

Central Access Rules include a set of permissions and the conditions under which those permissions are applied. For example, in Figure 14-5, the rule applying the permissions spelled out in the permissions entry is applied to the file or folder if the file or folder has the Project resource property set to Hovercraft. You can have multiple conditions in a central access rule. You can, for example, require that the Project resource property be set to Hovercraft and the Confidentiality resource property be set to High for the permissions configured in the permissions entry to be applied.

FIGURE 14-5 Central Access rule

After you configure the conditions that trigger the Central Access Rule, you can then specify the set of permissions that is applied. Unlike standard NTFS permissions, permission entries allow you to apply permissions that are conditional upon user and device claims. For example, the permissions entry shown in Figure 14-6 is conditional upon the user attempting access to not only be a member of the Hovercraft_Project security group, but also have the EmployeeType attribute in their user account set to the value FTE. If the user's EmployeeType attribute isn't set to FTE, the permissions assigned through the user's Hovercraft_Project group membership are not granted. You can configure multiple conditions based on user and device claims when configuring a permissions entry. For example, in the case of sensitive documents you might also require that the computer account have an attribute set to indicate that it is a secure computer.

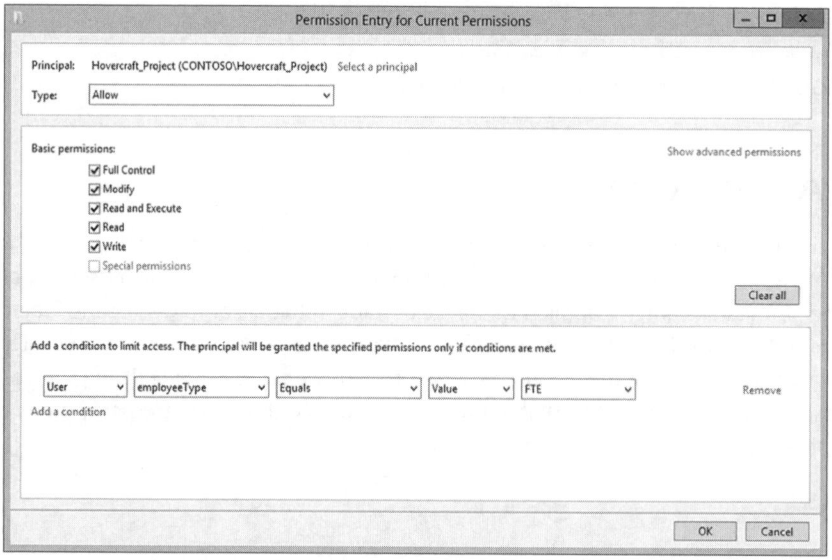

FIGURE 14-6 Permission Entry for Current Permissions

Central Access Policies

A Central Access Policy is a collection of central access rules. For example, the Contoso Policy Central Access Policy, shown in Figure 14-7, publishes two central access rules: Research_Projects and Secret_Projects. Only file servers running Windows Server 2012, Windows Server 2012 R2, or Windows Server 2016 that are within the scope of the Central Access Policy apply the rules that are contained within the policy.

FIGURE 14-7 Create Central Access Policy: Contoso Policy

You distribute central access policies through Group Policy. You do this by configuring the Manage Central Access Policies policy, which is located in the Computer Configuration\Policies\Windows Settings\Security Settings\File System node. This policy is shown in Figure 14-8.

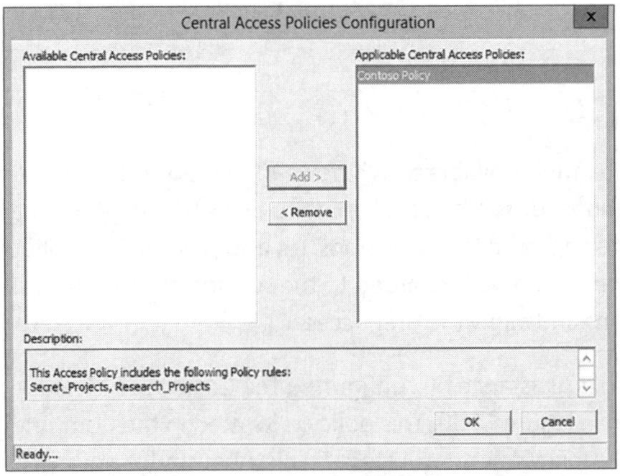

FIGURE 14-8 Central Access Policies Configuration

Staging

Staging allows you to configure a set of proposed rather than applied permissions. You use auditing to determine the results of these staged permissions before implementing them. You must enable auditing through Group Policy to determine the results of staged permissions. The policy you need to enable is the Audit Central Access Policy Staging Properties policy, which is located in the Computer Configuration\Policies\Windows Settings\Security Settings\Advanced Audit Policy Configuration\Audit Policies\Object Access node of a Group Policy Object (GPO).

You configure staged permissions in the Proposed area of a Central Access Rule by selecting the Enable Permission Staging Configuration option, as shown in Figure 14-9. You can verify the functionality of the proposed permissions by checking the Security event log. To do this, sign on the file server that hosts the files and by searching for events with event ID 4818.

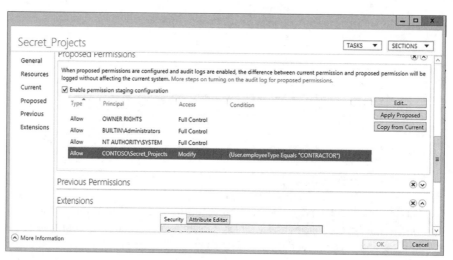

FIGURE 14-9 Secret Projects

Access Denied Assistance

Access Denied Assistance is a feature available to Windows 10, Windows 8.1, and Windows 8 clients that provides an informational dialog box explaining to users that they are unable to access a file because they do not have appropriate permissions. It's also possible to configure Access Denied Assistance so that an email can be forwarded to the support desk if their assistance is needed to untangle permissions and allow the user access.

You configure the Access Denied Assistance by configuring the Customize Message For Access Denied Errors policy, as shown in Figure 14-10. This policy is located in the Computer Configuration\Policies\Administrative Templates\System\Access-Denied Assistance node of a GPO.

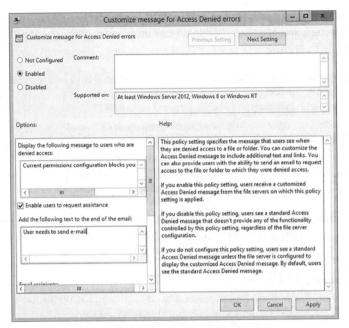

FIGURE 14-10 Customized message for Access Denied errors

Installing AD RMS

AD RMS uses the term "cluster" to describe an AD RMS deployment, even though it has nothing to do with failover clustering or network load balancing. When you deploy AD RMS, you first deploy a root cluster. An AD RMS root cluster is responsible for managing all of the AD RMS licensing and certificate traffic for the forest that it is installed in. You should only have one AD RMS root cluster per forest. Organizations that have multiple forests should deploy multiple AD RMS root clusters. After you have deployed a root cluster, you can configure additional licensing only clusters. Licensing only clusters distribute licenses that clients use to consume and publish content.

Installing AD RMS involves performing the following steps:

- **Specifying the database that AD RMS uses to store configuration information.** You can use a Microsoft SQL Server instance to perform this role or deploy the Windows Internal Database. You should only use Microsoft SQL Server in large AD RMS deployments. AD RMS can use SQL Server 2008 or later.

- **Specifying a service account**. This account needs to be a domain account and best practice is to use a specially configured group managed service account for this role.

Using a group managed service account ensures that the account password is managed by Active Directory and does not need to be manually updated on a periodic basis by an administrator.

- **Choose a cryptographic mode**. Mode 2 uses RSA 2048-bit keys and SHA-256 hashes. Mode 1 uses RSA 1024-bit keys and SHA-1 hashes. Mode 2 is more secure than mode 1 and is therefore the recommended choice.

- **Specify Cluster Key Storage**. This determines where the cluster key is stored. The default is to have the key stored within AD RMS, although you can also use a cryptographic service provider (CSP) if one is available. When you use a CSP, you have to perform manual key distribution when adding additional AD RMS servers.

- **Specify a cluster key password**. This password is used to encrypt the cluster key. You need to provide this password when joining additional AD RMS servers to the cluster and when recovering an AD RMS cluster from backup.

- **Input the cluster address**. This is a website address in FQDN format that is usually hosted on the AD RMS server. Best practice is to configure an SSL certificate with the FQDN of the AD RMS server. Although it is possible to specify a non-SSL protected address, doing so removes the ability to use AD RMS with identity federation. The cluster address and port cannot be altered after you deploy AD RMS.

- **Specify a Licensor certificate name**. This is the name used with the licensor certificate and should represent the certificate's functionality.

- **Determine whether to register the service connection point (SCP) in Active Directory**. The SCP allows domain members to locate the AD RMS cluster automatically. A user account must be a member of the Enterprise Admins security group to register an SCP. SCP registration can occur after AD RMS is deployed if the account used to deploy AD RMS is not a member of this security group.

AD RMS certificates and licenses

AD RMS uses four specific types of certificates. These certificates have the following functions:

- **Server licensor certificate (SLC).** This certificate is created when you install the AD RMS role on the first server in the AD RMS cluster. This certificate is valid for 7150 days and is used to issue the following certificates and licenses:
  - SLCs to additional servers that join the cluster
  - Rights Account Certificates
  - Client licensor certificates

- Publishing licenses
- Use licenses
- Rights policy templates

- **AD RMS Machine Certificate.** This certificate identifies a trusted device. The machine certificate public encrypts Rights Account Certificate private keys and the machine certificate private key decrypts Rights Account Certificates.

- **Rights Account Certificate (RAC).** This certificate identifies a user. AD RMS can only issue RACs to AD DS users whose user accounts are configured with an email address. By default, a RAC has a validity of 365 days. Temporary RACs are issued when a user accesses content from a device that is not a member of a trusted forest and has a validity of 15 minutes.

- **Client Licensor Certificate.** This certificate allows AD RMS protected content to be published to computers that are not able to connect directly to the AD RMS cluster. These certificates are tied to a user RAC. Other computer users are unable to publish AD RMS protected documents until a new connection to the AD RMS cluster is established from the computer.

In addition to the four certificate types, AD RMS uses two license types:

- **Publishing License.** A publishing license determines the rights that apply to AD RMS content. This license contains the content key and the URL and digital signature of the AD RMS server.

- **End-User License.** The end-user license allows a user to access AD RMS protected content. An end-user license is issued per user per document. End-user licenses are cached by default, although it's possible to disable caching so that an end-user license must be obtained each time the user attempts to access protected content.

AD RMS Templates

Rights Policy Templates allow you to apply rights policies to documents. When an author creates a document or sends an email message, the author can apply a template to that document. It's also possible to use File Server Resource Manager to automatically apply templates to documents based on the properties of those documents, such as the document having a particular resource property or containing a specific text string.

Rights Policy Templates are created by using the AD RMS Management Console. When creating a template, you can enable the following rights on a per user group or per user basis, with any right not granted unavailable to the user:

CHAPTER 14

- **Full Control.** The user has full control over the AD RMS protected content.

- **View.** Gives the user the ability to view the AD RMS protected content.

- **Edit.** Allows the user to modify the AD RMS protected content.

- **Save.** Allows the user to save the AD RMS protected content.

- **Export.** Allows the user to use the save as function with the AD RMS protected content.

- **Print.** Allows the user to print the AD RMS protected content.

- **Forward.** Used with Microsoft Exchange, allows the user to forward a protected message.

- **Reply.** Used with Microsoft Exchange, allows the user to reply to a protected message.

- **Reply All.**   Used with Microsoft Exchange, allows the recipient of a protected message to use the Reply All function.

- **Extract.** Allows a user to copy data from the AD RMS protected content.

- **Allow Macros.** Allows the user to use macros with the AD RMS protected content.

- **View Rights.** Allows the user to view rights assigned to the AD RMS protected content.

- **Edit Rights.** Allows the user to modify rights assigned to the AD RMS protected content.

Figure 14-11 shows the rights assigned to the submarine_project@contoso.com group. You can assign different rights to multiple groups. If a user is a member of more than one group, the rights are cumulative.

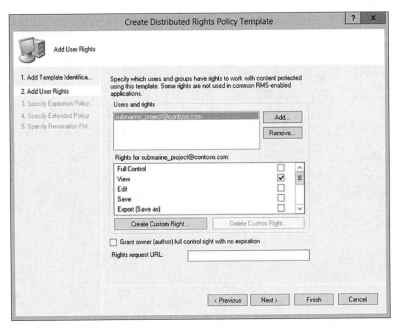

FIGURE 14-11 Create Distributed Rights Policy Template

When configuring an AD RMS Template, you can configure content expiration settings. Content expiration settings allow you to have content expire either on a certain date or after a certain number of days. The example in Figure 14-12 shows content expiration configured to expire 14 days after content publication. An additional setting allows you to configure use license expiration, which allows you to configure how often a user must connect to the AD RMS cluster to obtain a new license to access the content.

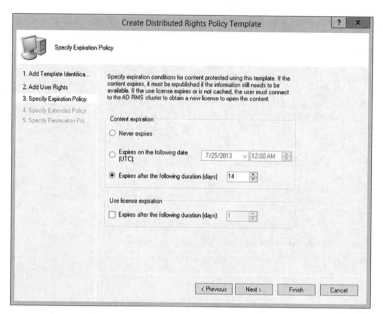

FIGURE 14-12 Create Distributed Rights Policy Template

The Extended Policy settings, as shown in Figure 14-13, allow you to configure whether AD RMS content can be viewed using a browser add-on and whether a new license must be obtained each time content is consumed.

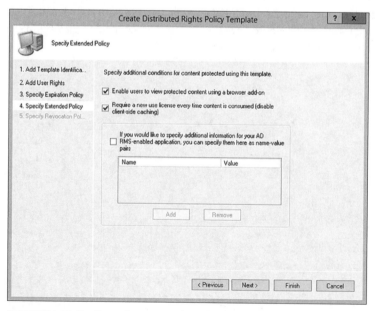

FIGURE 14-13 Configure browser and content settings

AD RMS administrators and super users

There are three separate local groups on an AD RMS server that you can add users to when you want to assign them privileges within AD RMS. These groups are as follows:

- **AD RMS Enterprise Administrators.** Members of this group can perform any task within AD RMS, including enabling the AD RMS Super Users group.

- **AD RMS Template Administrators.** Users that are members of this group can configure and manage AD RMS templates.

- **AD RMS Auditors.** Users that are members of this group are not able to make modifications to AD RMS server settings and templates, but are able to view the properties of the server and templates.

The AD RMS Super Users group is a special group that you can configure and enable on the AD RMS server. Members of the AD RMS Super Users group have full owner rights over all use licenses issued by the AD RMS cluster. Members of the Super Users group are able to:

- Recover expired content

- Recover content when a template is deleted

- Recover content without requiring author credentials

Because members of this group have access to all content, you should have strict policies about managing and auditing this group's membership. A Super Users group is not configured by default and the group that you configure as the Super Users group must have an associated email address, as shown in Figure 14-14.

CHAPTER 14

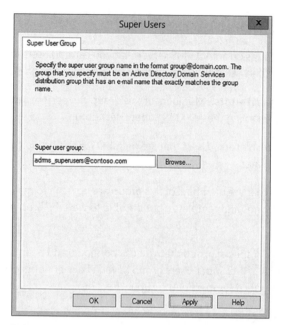

FIGURE 14-14 Super User Group

Trusted User and Publishing Domains

Trusted User Domains (TUDs) allow you to configure an AD RMS cluster to manage requests for CLCs for users that have been issued RACs from a different AD RMS cluster. For example, if an organization has two separate Active Directory forests and each forest has its own AD RMS deployment, you'd configure Trusted User Domains so that clients from one forest are able to issue CLCs to clients with RACs issued from the other forest. TUDs can be one-way or bi-directional. When configuring TUDs, you must export the TUD from the partner before importing the TUD locally.

Trusted Publishing Domains (TPDs) allow the AD RMS cluster in one forest to issue end-user licenses to content published with licenses issued from an AD RMS cluster in another forest. You must export the TPD file and have it imported by the partner AD RMS cluster before the AD RMS cluster in the partner forest can issue end-user licenses to local AD RMS clients.

Exclusion policies

Exclusion policies allow you to deny specific entities the ability to interact with AD RMS. You can configure exclusions on the basis of application, user, and lockbox version. Exclusion works in the following ways:

- **User Exclusion.** You can exclude a user based on email address or based on the public key assigned to the user's RAC. Use email based exclusions for users in the forest and public key based exclusions for external users.

- **Lockbox Exclusion.** Lockbox exclusion allows you to exclude specific client operating systems. Each version of the Windows operating system has a specific lockbox identity. If you want to block clients running Windows Vista or Windows 7 from interacting with AD RMS, configure an exclusion where the minimum lockbox version to the version available is Windows 8.

- **Application Exclusion.** This allows you to exclude specific applications from interacting with AD RMS. You must specify the application file name, the minimum version, and the maximum version.

When you configure an exclusion, the exclusion only applies to new certificate or licensing requests. Licenses and certificates that were issued during the exclusion period still exclude the application, user, or lockbox version. If you remove an exclusion, the removal only applies to new licenses or certificates.

Apply AD RMS templates automatically

You can use File Server Resource Manager to automatically apply AD RMS templates to files. You do this by performing the following general steps:

- Creating a new file management task with an appropriate name related to the template.

- On the Scope tab, set the scope of the task to the folders that host the files that you want to apply the AD RMS template to.

- On the Condition tab, specify the condition that allows the rule to recognize the files that you want to apply the AD RMS template to. For example, you can create a rule that is triggered if the file contains the text "SECRET."

- On the Action tab of the Create File Management Task dialog box, shown in Figure 14-15, specify RMS Encryption as the action type and the AD RMS template that you want to apply to the file.

- On the Schedule tab, configure how often the file management task should run and whether it should classify only new files or periodically attempt to reclassify existing files.

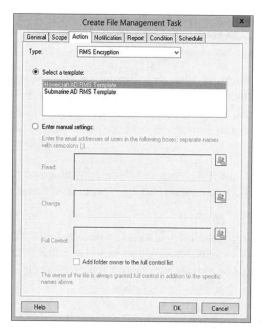

FIGURE 14-15   Create File Management Task

Managing AD RMS with Windows PowerShell

AD RMS PowerShell cmdlets are available in the ADRMS and ADRMSADMIN Windows Power-Shell module. The functionality of these cmdlets is described in Table 14-1.

Table 14-1. AD RMS PowerShell cmdlets

Noun	Verbs	Function
ADRMS	Install, Uninstall, Update	Install, remove, and update AD RMS after the binaries have been installed on the target server
RmsCertChain	Get	Generates a report detailing information on the certificate chain of a specific user request on the AD RMS server
RmsCertInfo	Get	Generates a report about a specific certificate used in a user request for the AD RMS cluster
RmsChildCert	Get	Returns all child certificates from a parent certificate used in a user request to an AD RMS cluster

RmsCluster	Update	Updates RMS cluster information
RmsCryptoMode2	Initialize	Configure an RMS cluster to transition to cryptographic mode 2
RmsEncryptedIL	Get	Determine use-license information from an issuance license associated with a user request
RmsMfgEnrollment	Install, Update, Uninstall	Configure Microsoft Federation Gateway service enrollment
RmsMfgSupport	Install, Uninstall	Install or remove Microsoft Federation Gateway configuration
RmsReportDefinitionLan-guage	Export	Export AD RMS report definition files
RmsRequestInfo	Get	Generate a report on a specific user request
RmsSvcAccount	Set, Get	Configure RMS service account
RmsSystemHealthReport	Get	View RMS system health
RmsTPD	Export, Import	Import and export trusted publishing domain information
RmsTUD	Import, Export	Import and export trusted user domain
RmsUserRequestReport	Get	View information about an RMS user request

Network Policy and Access Services

Today, we expect to be able to access work resources whether we're in the office, in an airline lounge, in a coffee shop, or at home on the couch. Remote access technologies allow authorized users to make a connection from their laptops and tablet computers to resources on their organization's internal network from any location on the public Internet.

In this chapter, you learn about Windows Server 2016 remote access technologies and how you can leverage those technologies to enable remote access to your organization's internal network. You learn how each technology is appropriate for a specific use case and why you might want to use several technologies to support all of the clients in your organization.

Remote Desktop Gateway

Remote Desktop (RD) Gateway allows users to make a connection from a host on the Internet to a host on the local area network using the Remote Desktop Connection (RDC) Client software. Remote Desktop Client software is included in all currently supported versions of Windows and is also available for Mac OS X computers, as well as iOS and Android devices. Although RD Gateway is typically used to connect to Remote Desktop Session Host servers or VDI virtual machines, you can also configure it to connect to desktop workstations. This allows a user to use an RD Gateway server to connect to her work PC from her laptop computer without having to connect through a VPN.

RD Gateway servers, like any other remote access servers, need to be placed on perimeter networks and need to have at least one public IP address. Connections to RD Gateway servers occur by using the Remote Desktop Protocol (RDP) over HTTPS protocol. When configuring the external firewall, network administrators need to allow access on port 443 from hosts on the Internet to the RD Gateway server. Connections from the RD Gateway server to RDP hosts on the internal network occur on port 3389.

RD Gateway servers don't need to be members of an Active Directory domain, but it is substantially more difficult to configure the RD Resource Authorization Policy (RAP) to limit connections to specific hosts without such membership. You can accomplish something similar through firewall rules. The drawback to domain membership however, is the risk involved in placing a domain-joined computer on a perimeter network and configuring the internal firewall to support the configuration.

RD Gateway connection and resource policies

RD Gateway connection and resource policies allow you to specify under what conditions users are able to connect to an RD Gateway server. RD Connection Authorization Policies (CAPs) can be stored on the RD Gateway server or in a Central RD CAP Store. Some of the benefits of using a Central CAP Store are that the same CAPs can apply to multiple RD Gateway servers without having to reproduce them on each server and that they can also be centrally updated as needed. If your organization only has a single RD Gateway server however, there is no need to use a central RD CAP Store.

On an RD Gateway server that is not a member of a domain, you might have to create a separate local user group with local user accounts to allow users to authenticate against the RD Gateway server prior to authenticating against the session target.

To create an RD Gateway CAP, perform the following general steps:

1. In the RD Gateway Manager console, right-click Connection Authorization Policies, click Create New Policy, and then click Custom.

2. On the New RD CAP dialog box, enter a policy name on the General tab.

3. On the Requirements tab, select Password or, if your organization supports it, Smart Card. Next, click Add Group to specify the User Group to which you want to grant access to RD servers through the RD Gateway server. You should create a separate security group for users you want to grant access to, which makes granting and revoking access just a matter of removing the user's account from this group.

4. On the Device Redirection tab, choose whether you want to enable device redirection for all client devices or disable it for specific types, such as volumes, clipboards, and plug-and-play devices. You also have the ability to restrict connections to only clients that enforce RD Gateway device redirection policies. You might do this if you want to block access to clients running non-Microsoft operating systems.

5. On the Timeouts tab you can enable an idle timeout, which disconnects users who aren't interacting with their session, and a session timeout, which limits all sessions including active sessions. Click OK to finish creating the policy.

After you have configured an RD CAP, you need to configure an RD Resource Authorization Policy (RAP). An incoming connection must meet the conditions specified in one RD CAP and one RD RAP before it can be successfully established. To create an RD RAP, perform the following steps:

1. In the RD Gateway Manager console, right-click Resource Authorization Policies, click Create New Policy, and then click Custom.

2. On the New RD RAP page, enter the policy name.

3. On the User Groups page, click Add to add the user groups that the policy applies to.

4. On the Network Resource page, choose between the following options:

   - Select an Active Directory Domain Services group

   - Select an existing RD Gateway managed group

   - Allow users to connect to any network resource

5. On the Allowed Ports page, choose to restrict connections from the RD Gateway server to port 3389, which is the default, to another specific port, or through any port. Unless the RD servers use alternate ports, the default is appropriate.

Configuring server settings

RD Gateway servers need a TLS certificate to encrypt and authenticate the RDP over an HTTPS connection. As is always the case with TLS certificates, obtaining a certificate from a trusted, third-party certification authority (CA) costs money, but this investment means that any client can use the RD Gateway without problems. Using an internal certificate is cheaper because it is not necessary to purchase a certificate, but it does require you to configure RD Gateway clients to trust the issuing authority. Given the organizational cost to support the distribution of an internal or self-signed certificate, it is usually just easier to obtain a certificate from a trusted, third-party CA.

Configuring clients to use RD Gateway

You can configure clients to use an RD Gateway server either by manually configuring the server's address by editing the advanced properties of Remote Desktop Connection, as shown in Figure 15-1, or by configuring the server's address through Group Policy.

Figure 15-1 RD Gateway Settings

There are three RD Gateway-related Group Policy items that can be configured to simplify the process of ensuring that clients connect to the correct server. These policy items are located in the User Configuration\Policies\Administrative Templates\Windows Components\Remote Desktop Services\RD Gateway node of a standard GPO. These policies can be used to configure the following:

- **Set RD Gateway Authentication Method.** This policy allows you to force a user to use a particular authentication method, but it also allows you to set a default authentication method that the user can override. The options are:

    - Ask For Credentials; Use NTLM Protocol.

    - Ask For Credentials; Use Basic Protocol.

    - Use Locally Logged-In Credentials.

    - Use Smart Card.

- **Enable Connection through RD Gateway.** When this policy is enabled, the client attempts to connect through the configured RD Gateway server in the event that it is unable to establish a connection to the specified target of the RD Connection. Set this policy and the RD Gateway Address Policy to ensure that domain clients connect through RD Gateway when they are not connected to the internal network.

- **Set RD Gateway Server Address.** This policy allows you to configure the RD Gateway server address, either on the basis of IP address or fully qualified domain name (FQDN). This policy should be set in conjunction with the Enable Connection Through RD Gateway policy to ensure that remote domain clients transparently connect through the RD Gateway server without having to configure anything themselves.

Virtual Private Networks

Windows Server 2016 supports four separate virtual private network (VPN) technologies: PPTP, L2TP/IPsec, SSTP, and IKEv2. PPTP is the simplest of these technologies to set up because it does not require integration with certificate services. The drawback of PPTP is that it is an older protocol, has known vulnerabilities, and is not as secure as the other VPN protocols available on Windows Server 2016. Some organizations use SSTP or IKEv2, but most use L2TP/IPsec.

Inside OUT

VPN Certificates

If you are using VPN protocols that rely on certificates generated by an internal enterprise CA, ensure that a Certificate Revocation List (CRL) Distribution Point (CDP) or Online Responder is accessible to clients on the Internet. Remember that clients need to be able to check the revocation status of certificates, which is difficult if the CDP is only accessible to clients on the internal network. You can deploy a CRL DP on the perimeter network or host it in the cloud, which is more common today.

IKEv2 VPN protocol

The IPsec Tunnel Mode with Internet Key Exchange version 2 (IKEv2) VPN protocol was introduced with the release of the Windows Server 2008 R2 and Windows 7 operating systems. The main benefit of IKEv2 is its capability to allow automatic reconnection without requiring re-authentication when the connection is disrupted. Automatic reconnection can occur even if the client's connection address changes and reconnection is possible for up to eight hours. For example, imagine that a user is connected to the internal network using an IKEv2 connection through a laptop computer's cellular modem and then boards an airplane and connects to the airplane's Wi-Fi. Under an IKEv2 scenario, the connection is automatically reestablished without requiring the user to manually re-authenticate, even though the connection method, from cellular network to airplane Wi-Fi, has changed. Connections only have to be reestablished when a user puts the computer into hibernation mode.

IKEv2 has the following features:

- Supports IPv6

- Enables VPN reconnect

- Supports EAP and Computer certificates for client authentication

- Does not support PAP or CHAP

- Only supports MS-CHAPv2 with EAP

- Supports data origin authentication, data integrity, replay protection, and data confidentiality

- Uses UDP port 500

To configure IKEv2 as an access protocol on a VPN server running Windows Server 2016, you need to do the following:

1. Deploy an enterprise CA.

2. Create a new certificate template based on the IPsec template. You need to modify the application policies of this template to ensure that it supports the IP security IKE intermediate policy and Server Authentication certificate.

3. Install a certificate generated from this template on the VPN server.

4. Ensure that at least one Certificate Revocation List Distribution Point is accessible to clients on the Internet. You can place this CRL DP on the perimeter network or host it in the cloud.

5. Ensure that all clients trust the enterprise CA that issued the VPN server's certificate.

Windows clients running the Windows 7 operating system or later attempt to establish an IKEv2 session before they try SSTP or L2TP/IPsec. If those options are unsuccessful, the client falls back to PPTP.

SSTP VPN protocol

Some locations block the ports that some VPN protocols use. The advantage of the SSTP VPN protocol is that it allows computers that might not normally be able to establish a remote access connection to do so through TCP port 443, which is usually used for TLS connections to websites. While it doesn't have the performance of other protocols, SSTP almost always works, even if it has to traverse NAT, firewalls, and proxy servers. SSTP doesn't work however, if there is a web proxy in place that requires manual authentication. For example, if you are in a hotel and you have to sign on to the Wi-Fi network through a browser, you need to perform this action before you attempt to establish an SSTP connection.

SSTP has the following requirements:

- You need to install a TLS certificate on the VPN server.

- All clients need to trust the CA that issued the TLS certificate.

- You need to configure the TLS certificate with a name that matches the FQDN that maps to an IP address associated with the external network interface of the VPN server.

- The Certificate Revocation List Distribution Point of the CA that issued the TLS certificate needs to be accessible to clients on the Internet.

L2TP/IPsec protocols

Layer Two Tunneling Protocol with IPsec (L2TP/IPsec) is a VPN protocol that has been used with Windows Server operating systems and clients since the release of Windows 2000. It works with almost every Windows and third-party operating system.

When configuring L2TP/IPsec you need to ensure that you have configured a CA that is able to automatically issue certificates to connecting clients. As is the case with other VPN protocols, the CA needs to be trusted by the client and the CDP must be accessible to clients making connections from the Internet. You would primarily deploy L2TP/IPsec as a way of providing secure access to clients that are not able to leverage the simpler to implement the Secure Socket Tunneling Protocol (SSTP) VPN protocol. Although L2TP/IPsec usually requires you to deploy digital certificates, it is possible, with special configuration, to get L2TP/IPsec to work with pre-shared keys.

PPTP VPN protocol

PPTP is the oldest VPN protocol supported by Windows Server 2016 and is also the least secure. It is most often used when organizations need to support clients running unsupported operating systems, such as Windows XP, or in situations where it isn't possible to deploy the certificate infrastructure required to implement L2TP/IPsec. PPTP connections provide data confidentiality, but do not provide data integrity or data origin protection. This means that captured data can't be read, but you also can't be sure that the transmitted data was the same data sent by the client.

Inside OUT

PPTP

PPTP requires no additional configuration beyond setting up the VPN server and ensuring that port 1723 is open for clients from the Internet. Just remember, PPTP has been around for a long time and isn't a secure VPN protocol.

VPN authentication

Although Windows Server 2016 supports many protocols that have been in use for some time, these protocols are often less secure than more recently developed protocols. Windows Server 2016 supports the following protocols, listed from most secure to least secure:

- **Extensible Authentication Protocol-Transport Level Security (EAP-TLS).** Use this protocol with Smart Cards or digital certificates. You can only use this protocol if you are using RADIUS authentication or if the remote access server performing authentication is domain-joined.

- **Microsoft Challenge Handshake Authentication Protocol version 2 (MS-CHAPv2).** Provides mutual authentication, which means that not only is the user authenticated, but the service that the user is connecting to is also authenticated. Allows for the encryption of the authentication process and the session.

- **Challenge Handshake Authentication Protocol (CHAP).** Authentication data is encrypted through MD5 hashing. The data is not encrypted.

- **Password Authentication Protocol (PAP).** This protocol does not encrypt authentication data, meaning that if the authentication is captured,

Deploying a VPN server

To configure a Windows Server 2016 server that has one network card connected to the perimeter network, which is accessible to clients on the Internet, and a second network card that is connected to the internal network to support VPNs, perform the following general steps:

1. Ensure that the prospective VPN server is connected to the Active Directory domain and log in with an account that is a Domain Admins group member.

2. Open an elevated PowerShell prompt and enter the following commands:

```
Install-WindowsFeature -IncludeAllSubfeature RemoteAccess
```

1. Open the Routing and Remote Access console, right-click the server name, and click Configure and Enable Routing and Remote Access. This opens the Routing and Remote Access Server Setup Wizard. Click Next.

2. On the Configuration page, select Remote access (dial-up or VPN) and then click Next.

3. On the Remote Access page, select VPN and then click Next.

4. On the VPN Connection page, select the network connection that is connected to the Internet and then click Next.

5. On the IP Address Assignment page, choose between assigning IP addresses automatically from an existing scope or from a specified range of addresses.

6. On the Manage Multiple Remote Access Servers page, select No, Use Routing and Remote Access to Authenticate Connection Requests, click Next, and then click Finish.

Disable VPN protocols

By default Windows Server 2016 server supports SSTP, PPTP, L2TP, and IKEv2 remote access connections. If you want to limit incoming connections to a specific protocol or disable an existing protocol, you need to edit the port properties related to that protocol. If you don't disable a specific protocol, clients might use that protocol to connect to the VPN server. For instance, if you've gone to the effort of configuring IKEv2, you don't want to find out a few weeks later that all of your clients are still falling back to using PPTP! To configure which VPN protocols are available, perform the following general steps:

1. Open the Routing and Remote Access console, right-click the Ports node under the VPN server, and then click Properties.

2. On the Ports Properties dialog box, select the VPN protocol that you want to limit connections for and then click Configure.

3. On the Configure Device dialog box, set the Maximum Ports to 1 and ensure that the Remote Access Connections (inbound only) item is not selected. Click OK.

Granting Access to a VPN server

If you only have a small number of users, you can grant access to those users on an individual basis by editing their user account properties in Active Directory Users and Computers. To grant access to an individual user, choose Allow access under Network Access Permission on the Dial-in tab of the user's account properties.

The default setting for network access for access to a Windows Server 2016 VPN server is for it to be controlled through a Network Policy Server (NPS) network policy. To be granted access, a user must meet the conditions of a connection request policy and a network policy. A connection request policy includes type of access, time of access, and which authentication protocols are available. A network policy can be as simple as specifying that a particular user group has access.

When you install a VPN server, a default connection request policy called Microsoft Routing and Remote Access Service Policy is created. You can view the policy's properties under the Policies\Connection Request Policies node of the Network Policy Server console on the VPN server. To configure this policy, perform the following steps:

1. Open the Network Policy Server console on the VPN server.

2. Expand the Policies\Connection Request Policies node. Right-click Microsoft Routing and Remote Access Service Policy and then click Properties.

3. On the Conditions tab, verify that the day and time restrictions match those that you want to enforce for the remote access policy. You can also use this tab to add conditions to the policy. Clients must meet all specified conditions, so keep in mind that the more conditions you add, the fewer clients the policy applies to. Conditions that you can add include the following:

- **User Name:** Specifies a specific HCAP user name.

- **Access Client IPv4 Address:** Specifies the RADIUS client IPv4 address.

- **Access Client IPv6 Address:** Specifies the RADIUS client IPv6 address.

- **Framed Protocol:** Specifies the protocol used for framing incoming packets, such as Point-to-Point Protocol (PPP) or Serial Line Internet Protocol (SLIP).

- **Service Type:** Limits clients to a specific service, such as Point-to-Point protocols.

- **Tunnel Type:** Restricts clients to a specific tunnel type, such as PPTP, L2TP, and SSTP.

- **Day and Time Restrictions:** Specifies when connections can be active.

- **Calling Station ID:** Specifies the Network Access Server telephone number.

- **Client Friendly Name:** Specifies the RADIUS client name.

- **Client IPv4 Address:** Specifies the RADIUS client IPv4 address.

- **Client IPv6 Address:** Specifies the RADIUS client IPv6 address.

- **Client Vendor:** Specifies the RADIUS client vendor.

- **Called Station ID:** Specifies the NAS identification string or telephone number.

- **NAS Identifier:** Specifies the NAS identification string.

- **NAS IPv4 Address:** Specifies the IPv4 address of NAS.

- **NAS IPv6 Address:** Specifies the IPv6 address of NAS.

- **NAS Port Type:** Specifies the RADIUS client access type, such as ISDN, VPN, IEEE 802.11 wireless, etc.

4. Settings are a set of categories that are required. You can select from the following:

- **Authentication Methods:** This setting enables you to specify which protocols clients can use to connect to the VPN server. The VPN server attempts to use the most secure protocol first and then, in order of most to least secure, attempts less secure protocols until it reaches the least secure protocol supported by the policy.

- **Authentication:** This setting determines whether the VPN server performs authentication or whether authentication credentials are passed to another server.

- **Accounting:** This setting enables you to record authentication information to a log file or SQL server database. Recording this information gives you a record of which people have gained access through VPN connections.

- **Attribute, RADIUS Attributes Standard & Vendor Specific:** These settings are only necessary if you are placing the VPN server into an existing RADIUS infrastructure.

Inside OUT
Default conditions and settings

In most situations, the default conditions and settings are likely to be adequate. Most administrators are just worried about ensuring that clients have remote access and are less concerned about whether a client is coming from a particular IPv6 address. Many of the available conditions are really only appropriate for site-to-site links rather than client VPN links. As most organizations use dedicated hardware devices for site-to-site VPN links, this topic is not covered in this book.

CHAPTER 15

After you ensure that the details of the connection request policies meet your needs, you can configure a network policy. Network policies are useful when you want to give a large number of users remote access, but do not want to configure access on a per-account basis. To create a new network policy that allows this access, perform the following general steps:

1. Open the Network Policy Server console. Right-click the Policies\Network Policies node and then click New. The Specify Network Policy Name and Connection Type opens.

2. Enter a name for the policy and set the Type of Network Access Server drop-down menu to Remote Access Server (VPN-Dial Up) and then click Next.

3. On the Conditions page, click Add and then add conditions. The conditions that you can add are as follows:

- **Windows Groups:** Limits access to user or computer groups.

- **Machine Groups:** Limits access to members of the specified computer group.

- **User Groups:** Limits access to members of the specified user group.

- **Day and Time Restrictions:** Restricts when the policy can be used for access.

- **Access Client IPv4 Address:** Specifies the network address of the client.

- **Access Client IPv6 Address:** Specifies the network address of the client.

- **Authentication Type:** Defines acceptable authentication protocols.

- **Allowed EAP Types:** Defines allowed EAP authentication protocols.

- **Framed Protocol:** Specifies the protocol used for framing incoming packets, such as Point-to-Point Protocol (PPP) or Serial Line Internet Protocol (SLIP).

- **Service Type:** Limits clients to a specific service, such as Point-to-Point protocols.

- **Tunnel Type:** Restricts clients to a specific tunnel type, such as PPTP, L2TP, and SSTP.

- **Calling Station ID:** Specifies the Network Access Server telephone number.

- **Client Friendly Name:** Specifies the RADIUS client name.

- **Client IPv4 Address:** Specifies the RADIUS client IPv4 address.

- **Client IPv6 Address:** Specifies the RADIUS client IPv6 address.

- **Client Vendor:** Specifies the RADIUS client vendor.

- **MS-RAS Vendor:** Specifies the Network Access Server (NAS) vendor.

- **Called Station ID:** Specifies the NAS identification string or telephone number.

- **NAS Identifier:** Specifies the NAS identification string.

- **NAS IPv4 Address:** Specifies the IPv4 address of NAS.

- **NAS IPv6 Address:** Specifies the IPv6 address of NAS.

- **NAS Port Type:** Specifies RADIUS client access type, such as ISDN, VPN, IEEE 802.11 wireless, etc.

After you have configured the network policy, it should be possible to establish a VPN connection.

LAN routing

You can configure Windows Server 2016 to function as a network router in the same way that you configure traditional hardware devices to perform this role. LAN routing is often used with virtual machines to connect private or internal virtual machine networks with an external network. To perform the LAN routing function, Windows Server 2016 must have two or more network adapters. Windows Server 2016 supports using Key Routing Information Protocol v2 (RIP) for route discovery. You can also use the Routing And Remote Access console to configure static routes.

To configure Windows Server 2016 to function as a router, perform the following steps:

1. From the Tools menu of Server Manager, click Routing And Remote Access.

2. In the Routing And Remote Access console, click the server you want to configure. In the Action menu, click Configure And Enable Routing And Remote Access.

3. On the Welcome page of the Routing And Remote Access Server Setup Wizard, click Next.

4. On the Configuration page, select Custom Configuration and click Next.

5. On the Custom Configuration page, select LAN Routing and click Next.

6. Click Finish. In the Routing And Remote Access dialog box, click Start Service.

If you want to enable IPv6 routing, perform the following additional steps:

1. In the Routing And Remote Access console, right-click the server and click Properties.

2. On the General tab of the server properties dialog box, select IPv6 Router to enable the server to also route IPv6 traffic.

Network Address Translation (NAT)

Network Address Translation (NAT) enables you to share an Internet connection with computers on an internal network. In a typical NAT configuration, the NAT server has two network interfaces, where one network interface is connected to the Internet and the second network interface connects to a network with a private IP address range. Computers on the private IP address range can then establish communication with computers on the Internet. It is also possible to configure port forwarding so all traffic that is sent to a particular port on the NAT server's public interface is directed to a specific IP address/port combination on a host on the private IP address range.

To configure a computer running the Windows Server 2016 operating system with two network adapters to function as a NAT device, ensure one adapter has connectivity to the Internet and perform the following steps:

1. Open the Routing And Remote Access console from the Tools menu in Server Manager.

2. Select the server you want to configure. On the Action menu, click Configure And Enable Routing And Remote Access.

3. On the Welcome To The Routing And Remote Access Server Setup Wizard, click Next.

4. On the Configuration page, select Network Address Translation (NAT) and click Next.

5. On the NAT Internet Connection page, select the network interface that connects to the Internet and click Next.

6. Click Finish to close the Routing And Remote Access Server Setup Wizard.

You can configure NAT properties by right-clicking the NAT node in the Routing And Remote Access console and by clicking Properties. Using the properties dialog box, you can configure address assignments for hosts on the private network, as shown in Figure 15-2. You can use the Name Resolution tab to determine how name resolution works on the private network. It enables clients to communicate using single names or FQDNs rather than IP addresses.

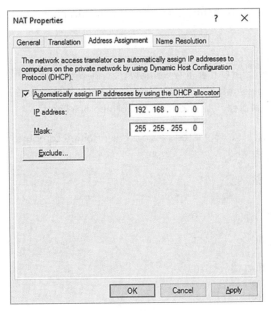

Figure 15-2 NAT address assignment

DirectAccess

DirectAccess is an always-on remote access solution, which means that if a client computer is configured with DirectAccess and connects to the Internet, a persistent connection is established between that computer and the organization's internal network. One big advantage of DirectAccess is that it does not require users to directly authenticate. The client computer determines that it is connected to the Internet by attempting to connect to a website that is only accessible from the internal network. If the client determines that it is on a network other than the internal network, it automatically initiates a connection to the internal network.

When determining its network connection status, the client first attempts to determine whether it is connected to a native IPv6 network. If the client has been assigned a public IPv6 address, it can make a direct connection to the organization's internal DirectAccess servers. If the client determines that it is not connected to a native IPv6 network, it attempts to create an IPv6 over IPv4 tunnel using the 6to4 and then Teredo technologies. If connections cannot be established using these technologies, it attempts to use IP-HTTPS, which is similar to the SSTP protocol discussed earlier, except that it encapsulates IPv6 traffic within the HTTPS protocol.

When a connection is established, authentication occurs using computer certificates. These computer certificates must be pre-installed on the client, but the benefit of this requirement is that user intervention is not required. Authentication occurs automatically and the connection occurs seamlessly.

Another big advantage of DirectAccess is that it supports remote client management through a feature named Manage Out. Manage Out enables remote management functionality for DirectAccess clients, allowing administrative tasks, including tasks that in the past could only be performed on computers on a local area network, to be performed on clients.

The primary drawback of DirectAccess is that it requires a domain-joined computer that runs one of the following operating systems:

- Windows 7 Enterprise edition

- Windows 7 Ultimate edition

- Windows 8 Enterprise edition

- Windows 8.1 Enterprise edition

- Windows 10 Enterprise edition

DirectAccess clients are configured through GPOs. The configuration GPO is automatically created through the DirectAccess setup process. This GPO is filtered so it only applies to the security group that you've designated to host the DirectAccess clients.

Unlike the version of DirectAccess that shipped with Windows Server 2008 R2, DirectAccess in Server 2012 and later does not require two consecutive public IPv4 addresses, nor is it necessary to have an Active Directory Certificate Services server deployed on the internal network.

DirectAccess topologies

DirectAccess supports multiple deployment topologies. You don't have to deploy the DirectAccess server with a network adapter directly connected to the Internet. Instead, you can integrate the DirectAccess server with your organization's existing edge topology. During your DirectAccess server deployment, the Remote Access Server Wizard asks you which of the topologies reflects your server configuration. The difference between them is as follows:

- **Edge.** This is the traditional DirectAccess deployment method. The computer hosting the server has two network adapters. The first network adapter is connected directly to the Internet and has been assigned one or more public IPv4 addresses. The second network adapter connects directly to the internal trusted network.

- **Behind An Edge Device (With Two Network Adapters).** In this type of deployment, the DirectAccess server is located behind a dedicated edge firewall. This configuration includes two network adapters. One of the network adapters on the DirectAccess server is connected to the perimeter network behind the edge firewall. The second network adapter connects directly to the internal trusted network.

- **Behind An Edge Device (With A Single Network Adapter).** In this type of deployment, the DirectAccess server has a single network adapter connected to the internal network. The edge firewall passes traffic to the DirectAccess server.

DirectAccess server

The DirectAccess server is a domain-joined computer running Windows Server 2012 or later that accepts connections from DirectAccess clients on untrusted networks, such as the Internet, and provides access to resources on trusted networks. The DirectAccess server performs the following roles:

- Authenticates DirectAccess clients connecting from untrusted networks

- Functions as an IPsec tunnel mode endpoint for DirectAccess traffic from untrusted networks

Before you can configure a computer running Windows Server 2012 or later to function as a DirectAccess server, you must ensure that it meets the following requirements:

- The server must be a member of an Active Directory Directory Services domain.

- If the server is connected directly to the Internet, it must have two network adapters: one that has a public IP address and one that is connected to the trusted internal network.

- The DirectAccess server can be deployed behind a NAT device, which limits DirectAccess to use IP over HTTPS (IP-HTTPS).

- A server connected to the Internet only requires a single public IPv4 address. Two-Factor Authentication, using either Smart Card or One-Time Password (OTP) however, requires two consecutive public IPv4 addresses.

- The DirectAccess server can also host a VPN server. This functionality was not present in the Windows Server 2008 R2 version of DirectAccess.

- You can configure DirectAccess in a network load-balanced configuration of up to eight nodes.

- The TLS certificate installed on the DirectAccess server must contain an FQDN that resolves through DNS servers on the Internet to the public IP address assigned to the DirectAccess server or to the gateway through which the DirectAccess server is published.

- The TLS certificate installed on the DirectAccess server must have a Certificate Revocation List (CRL) distribution point that is accessible to clients on the Internet.

Inside OUT

DirectAccess TLS Certificate

You should strongly consider obtaining the SSL certificate for your organization's DirectAccess server from a public CA. If you obtain the certificate this way, you don't have to worry about publishing the CRL from your internal certificate services deployment to a location that is accessible to the Internet. Using a trusted third-party CA ensures that the CRL is available to clients on the Internet. Although purchasing a certificate costs money, the financial cost is likely to be less than the organizational cost of having to install and configure a CRL distribution point in a location that is accessible to clients on the Internet.

A DirectAccess implementation also relies on the following infrastructure being present:

- **Active Directory domain controller.** DirectAccess clients and servers must be members of an Active Directory domain. By necessity, when you deploy a domain controller, you also deploy a DNS server. Active Directory, due to its basic nature, also makes Group Policy available.

- **Group Policy.** When you configure DirectAccess, the setup wizard creates a set of Group Policy Objects (GPOs) that are configured with settings you choose in the wizard. They apply to DirectAccess clients, DirectAccess servers, and servers that you use to manage DirectAccess.

Prepare DNS servers by removing the ISATAP name from the global query block list. You must take this step on all DNS servers that are hosted on computers running Windows Server operating systems. To complete this step, remove ISATAP from the GlobalQueryBlockList value on the Computer\HKEY_LOCAL_MACHINE\SYSTEM\CurrentControlSet\Services\DNS\Parameters hive of the registry so that it contains only the wpad entry, as shown in Figure 15-3. After making this configuration change, you must restart the DNS server.

Figure 15-3 GlobalQueryBlockList registry entry

As an alternative to editing the registry, you can also remove ISATAP from the DNS global query block list by issuing the following command on each DNS server and restarting the DNS Server service:

```
Dnscmd /config /globalqueryblocklist wpad
```

Network Location Server

The Network Location Server (NLS) is a specially configured server that enables clients to determine whether they are on a trusted network or an untrusted network. The NLS server's only function is to respond to specially crafted HTTPS requests. When the client determines that it has a connection to any network, it sends this specially crafted HTTPS request. If there is a response to this request, the client determines that it is on a trusted network and disables the DirectAccess components. If there is no response to this request, the client assumes that it is connected to an untrusted network and initiates a DirectAccess connection.

DirectAccess clients are informed of the NLS's location through Group Policy. You don't have to configure these policies manually because they are created automatically when you use the DirectAccess Setup Wizard. Any server that hosts a website and has an SSL certificate installed can function as the NLS. You should ensure that the NLS is highly available because if this server fails, it causes all clients that are configured for DirectAccess on the trusted network to assume that they are on an untrusted network.

CHAPTER 15

Configuring DirectAccess

After you understand the infrastructure requirements, configuring DirectAccess is straightforward. To configure DirectAccess, perform the following steps:

1. Create a security group in Active Directory and add all of the computer accounts for computers that are DirectAccess clients. This security group can have any name, but a name such as DirectAccess_Clients makes it easy to remember why you created it.

2. Ensure that you configure DNS with the following information:

- The externally resolvable DNS zone needs to have a record mapping the FQDN of the DirectAccess server's external interface to the public IPv4 address of the DirectAccess server.

- If you use a certificate issued by your organization's CA, ensure that a DNS record exists for the CRL location.

- The internal DNS zone needs a record mapping the name of the NLS to an IP address.

- Remove ISATAP from the global query block list on all DNS servers in the organization.

3. If you use your organization's CA, you have to configure an appropriate certificate template, as well as deploy a CRL distribution point in a location that can be accessed by clients on the Internet. The certificate template can be a duplicate of the Web Server Certificate Template. You can use this certificate for both the NLS's TLS certificate and the IP-HTTPS certificate for the DirectAccess server. If you don't use your organization's CA to issue certificates, you can use certificates from a public CA for the NLS and the DirectAccess server.

4. Configure firewall rules for all hosts on the trusted network that should be accessible to DirectAccess clients so they enable inbound and outbound ICMPv6 echo requests. You can configure these rules in a GPO that applies to hosts that DirectAccess clients can access. The rules should have the following properties:

- Rule Type: Custom

- Protocol Type: ICMPv6

- Specific ICMP Types: Echo Request

5. Install the Remote Access role on the computer that functions as the DirectAccess server.

6. Open the Remote Access console and then choose between running the Getting Started Wizard and the Remote Access Setup Wizard. The Getting Started Wizard enables administrators to quickly deploy DirectAccess by only requiring a minimal amount of information. The Remote Access Setup Wizard requires more detailed responses, but

enables administrators to customize their deployment. The rest of this procedure deals with the Remote Access Setup Wizard.

7. The Configure Remote Access page of the Configure Remote Access Wizard enables you to choose between deploying DirectAccess and VPN, deploying DirectAccess only, or deploying VPN only.

8. If you select Deploy DirectAccess Only, you are provided with the Remote Access Setup diagram. This diagram involves a series of steps that enable you to configure the DirectAccess server, clients, and infrastructure. There are four steps, including:

- Step 1: Remote Clients

- Step 2: Remote Access Server

- Step 3: Infrastructure Servers

- Step 4: Application Servers

Step 1: Remote Clients

The Step 1: Remote Clients section of Remote Access Setup enables you to configure which computers function as DirectAccess clients. When you click the Configure button in the Step 1 area, a three page wizard appears that enables you to configure the following settings:

1. Choose Deploy Full DirectAccess For Client Access And Remote Management or Deploy DirectAccess For Remote Management Only. If you choose the first option, the people using DirectAccess clients can access internal network resources when they have an active Internet connection. If you choose the second option, you can perform management tasks on the computer when it's connected on the Internet, but the user can't access internal resources.

2. Select which security groups containing computer accounts you want to enable for DirectAccess. On this page, you can choose Enable DirectAccess For Mobile Computers Only and Use Force Tunneling. When you enable force tunneling, computers designated as DirectAccess clients connect through the remote access server when they connect to both the Internet and the internal trusted network.

3. On the Network Connectivity Assistant (NCA) page you can configure connectivity information for clients, such as providing the DirectAccess connection name, the helpdesk's email address, and whether DirectAccess clients use local name resolution.

Step 2: Remote Access Server

The Step 2: Remote Access Server section of the Remote Access Setup diagram has a three-page wizard that enables you to do the following:

1. Configure the network topology and specify the public name or IPv4 address that clients use to connect to DirectAccess. The topology options are Edge, Behind Edge (Two Network Adapters), and Behind Edge (Single Network Adapter), which were discussed in the DirectAccess topology section of this chapter.

2. On the Network Adapters page, verify the network adapter configuration. You can also choose which certificate to use to authenticate IP-HTTPS connections. The certificate you choose should be a typical SSL certificate that uses an FQDN that clients use for connections. You can choose to use a self-signed certificate, although this is not recommended except on test deployments.

3. On the authentication page, choose whether you want to use Active Directory or Two-Factor Authentication. You can also configure authentication to use computer certificates, but when you do this, you must specify the CA that the computer certificates must be issued from.

Step 3: Infrastructure servers

After you have configured the remote access clients and the remote access server, the next step is to configure infrastructure servers. The Infrastructure Server Setup Wizard takes you through the following steps:

1. On the first page, specify the location of the NLS by using the server's URL and if you are specifying a separate server, remember to use https rather than http in the address. You also have the option to configure the DirectAccess server as the remote access server and use a self-signed certificate; however, self-signed certificates are more appropriate for tests rather than production deployments.

2. The DNS page enables you to specify the DNS suffixes that should be used with the name resolution and the address of the internal DNS server. On this page, you can also configure how clients should use the DNS server of their local Internet connection, by choosing one of the following options:

   - Use the DNS server of the local connection if the name isn't resolvable using the DNS server on the trusted network.

   - Use the DNS server of the local connection if the name isn't resolvable using the DNS server on the trusted network or if the DNS server on the trusted network cannot be contacted.

   - Use the DNS server of the local connection if any DNS error occurs.

3. The DNS Suffix Search List enables you to configure any DNS suffixes that should be used by the client for any unqualified names. The default settings add the domain name suffix.

4. The Management Servers page enables you to configure the servers used for DirectAccess client management. You can also configure NAP remediation servers if you are using NAP with DirectAccess.

Step 4: Application Servers

Step 4 of the Remote Access Management Console setup enables you to configure the addresses of application servers that require end-to-end authentication when interacting with DirectAccess clients. Unlike the other steps, this step involves configuring only one dialog box, where you specify the security group containing the computer accounts that you want to require end-to-end authentication and encryption for. You can also use this dialog box to limit DirectAccess clients so they can only connect to servers in the listed groups and can't connect to other servers on the trusted network. Use this option in environments with stringent security requirements.

Managing Remote Access using PowerShell

The RemoteAccess PowerShell module contains a large number of cmdlets that you can use to manage all aspects of Routing and Remote Access on Windows Server 2016. These cmdlets are described in Table 15-1

Table 15-1. Remote Access PowerShell cmdlets

Noun	Verbs	Function
BgpCustomRoute	Add, Remove, Get	View and manage BGP (Border Gateway Protocol) route information
BgpPeer	Get, Remove, Set, Start, Add, Stop	View and manage BGP peer configuration
BgpRouteAggregate	Get, Set, Add, Remove	View and manage aggregate BGP routes
BgpRouteFlapDampening	Clear, Enable, Get, Set, Disable	Manage the configuration of a BGP route dampening engine
BgpRouteInformation	Get	View BGP route information
BgpRouter	Get, Add, Remove, Set	Manage configuration information for BGP routers
BgpRoutingPolicy	Set, Add, Remove, Get	Manage BGP routing policies
BgpRoutingPolicyForPeer	Set, Remove, Add	Manage BGP peer routing policies

BgpStatistics	Get	Retrieves BGP peering-related message and route advertisement statistics
DAAppServer	Remove, Get, Add	Manage DirectAccess application server security groups
DAAppServerConnection	Set	Configures the properties of the connection to application servers and the IPsec security traffic protection policies for the connection
DAClient	Get, Set, Remove, Add	Manage the client security groups used for DirectAccess client configuration
DAClientDnsConfiguration	Get, Remove, Set, Add	Manage Name Resolution Policy Table (NRPT) entries and local name resolution properties
DAEntryPoint	Add, Get, Set, Remove	Manage DirectAccess entry point settings
DAEntryPointDC	Set, Get	Configure DirectAccess entry point domain controller settings
DAMgmtServer	Update, Add, Remove, Get	Manage DirectAccess management servers
DAMultiSite	Disable, Enable, Get, Set	Manage global settings applied to all DirectAccess entry points in a multi-site deployment
DANetworkLocationServer	Get, Set	Manage DirectAccess NLS settings
DAOtpAuthentication	Disable, Set, Enable, Get	Manage DirectAccess one-time password settings
DAServer	Get, Set	Manage DirectAccess Server Settings
RemoteAccess	Get, Install, Uninstall, Set	Manage DirectAccess and VPN configuration
RemoteAccessAccounting	Get, Set	Configure remote access accounting
RemoteAccessConfiguration	Get, Set	Manage remote access configuration
RemoteAccessConnectionStatistics	Get	View information about DirectAccess and VPN connections
RemoteAccessConnectionStatisticsSummary	Get	View summary information about DirectAccess and VPN connections

RemoteAccessHealth	Get	View the current health of a RemoteAccess (RA) deployment
RemoteAccessInboxAccounting-Store	Set, Clear	Manage the inbox of the remote access accounting store
RemoteAccessIpFilter	Add, Remove, Set, Get	Manage remote access IP filters
RemoteAccessLoadBalancer	Get, Set	Manage remote access load balancer settings
RemoteAccessLoadBalancerNode	Remove, Add	Add and remove remote access load balancer nodes
RemoteAccessRadius	Add, Get, Set	Manage RADIUS servers
RemoteAccessRoutingDomain	Get, Set, Disable, Enable	Manage remote access routing domains
RemoteAccessUserActivity	Get	Displays the resources accessed over the active DirectAccess and VPN connections and the resources accessed over historical DirectAccess and VPN connections
RoutingProtocolPreference	Set, Get	Manage routing protocol preferences
VpnAuthProtocol	Set, Get	Manage VPN server authentication parameters
VpnAuthType	Set	Configure VPN server authentication types
VpnIPAddressAssignment	Set	Manage VPN server IPv4 address assignment
VpnIPAddressRange	Remove, Add	Manage VPN server address range
VpnS2SInterface	Set, Add, Connect, Remove, Disconnect, Get	Manage site to site VPN interfaces
VpnS2SInterfaceStatistics	Clear, Get	View site to site VPN interface statistics
VpnServerConfiguration	Get, Set	Manage VPN server configuration
VpnSstpProxyRule	Add, Get, New, Set, Remove	Manage Tenant ID to gateway mappings
VpnTrafficSelector	New	Creates a VPN Traffic selector object that configures the IKE traffic selector
VpnUser	Disconnect	Disconnects a VPN connection originated by a specific user or originating from a specific client computer

CHAPTER 15

CHAPTER 16

Remote Desktop Services

Remote Desktop Services (RDS) allows an application to run on one computer with the graphical output of that computer displayed on another computer. The benefit of RDS include allowing relatively resource-poor clients to run resource-intensive applications remotely, or to run applications that are unable to run on one operating system to be accessed by users of another operating system.

There are several ways that you can leverage RDS in Windows Server 2016. The first is using Remote Desktop Session Host. In this form of RDS, people connect to remote desktop sessions that run on a server in a special isolated environment. In versions of Windows Server prior to Windows Server 2008 R2, Remote Desktop Session Host was called Terminal Services. The other primary way to leverage RDS in Windows Server 2016 is through Remote Desktop Virtualization Host. In this form of RDS, users connect to virtual machines to use their desktop environment to run their applications. Remote Desktop Virtualization Host is a form of Virtual Desktop Infrastructure, or VDI.

Deployment

Remote Desktop Services deployment differs from other Roles and Features deployment. With all other roles and features, you select the Role-based or feature-based installation option when running the Add Roles and Features Wizard. With Remote Desktop Services, you instead select the Remote Desktop Services installation option as shown in Figure 16-1.

CHAPTER 16

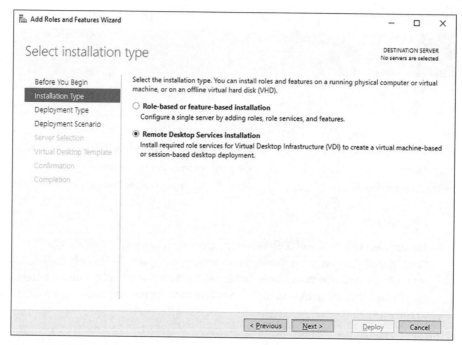

Figure 16-1 Installation type options

Once you've selected Remote Desktop Services installation, the next page in the wizard allows you to choose between the following options:

- **Standard deployment.** Choose this when you are deploying Remote Desktop Services across multiple servers.

- **Quick Start.** Use this option if you are deploying a single Remote Desktop Services server.

- **MultiPoint Services.** Use this option if you are creating a multipoint server deployment. Multipoint server allows you to run multiple client terminals connected to a single multipoint server. Multipoint services is commonly used in classroom environments.

When you choose the Standard deployment or Quick Start options, you then get to select the deployment scenario as shown in Figure 16-2.

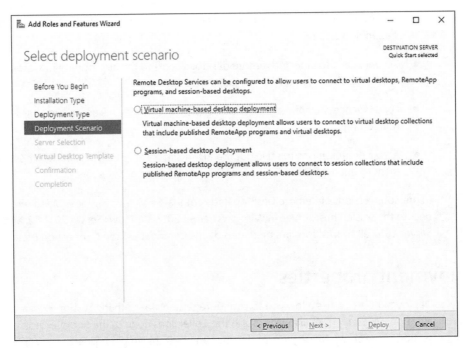

Figure 16-2 Deployment scenario

Session-Based deployments are generally less resource intensive than virtualization host deployments because they don't require that the session host server host full virtual machines for each session. Virtualization host deployments are more likely to provide better application compatibility because there are some applications that don't support being deployed in a Session host based environment.

Depending on your selection, completing the wizard involves selecting the server that the deployment will occur on, selecting a virtualization template for a virtualization host deployment, installing the roles and then rebooting the server to complete installation.

Remote Desktop Connection Broker

When initiating a connection, either through Remote Desktop Connection client software or RD Web Access interface, users connect to a session on a Remote Desktop Session Host server or a VDI virtual machine on a Remote Desktop Virtualization Host server through the Remote Desktop Connection Broker. The remote desktop connection broker role service provides the following functionality:

CHAPTER 16

- Connects incoming remote desktop clients to the appropriate RD session host or virtualization host server.

- Reconnects disconnected remote desktop clients to the appropriate RD session host session or RD virtualization host virtual machine.

- Load balances incoming remote desktop client connections according to session collection settings.

- Allows organizations to scale out the RD session host or RD virtualization host deployment by adding RD session host or RD virtualization host servers.

In previous versions of Remote Desktop and Terminal Services it was possible to directly connect to the session host server. In Windows Server 2012, Windows Server 2012 R2, and Windows Server 2016, all connections are mediated by the Remote Desktop Connection Broker.

Deployment properties

Deployment properties allow you to configure settings for both RD Session Host and RD Virtualization Host servers. Available through the Collections node of the Remote Desktop Services section of the Server Manager console, you can use Deployment Properties to configure the following settings:

- **RD Gateway.** This allows you to specify RD Gateway settings for your deployment. This includes whether the RD Gateway server is automatically determined, whether one is assigned, or whether to block the use of an RD Gateway server and the sign on method when using an RD Gateway server.

- **RD Licensing.** It allows you to configure the licensing mode and licensing servers. You can configure multiple RD license servers and the order in which they will be queried to obtain a license for a Remote Desktop Services client.

- **RD Web Access.** The address of the RD Web Access server. Clients can use this to connect to RemoteApp and Remote Desktop sessions using a browser, instead of through the Remote Desktop Connection client.

- **Certificates.** Shown in Figure 16-3, use this section to configure certificates for the Remote Desktop Services deployment.

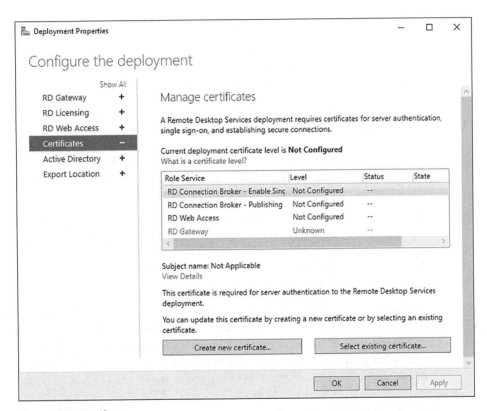

Figure 16-3 Certificates

- **Active Directory.** This is for RD Virtualization Host servers, and allows you to configure the domain and organizational unit that computer accounts for VDI virtual machines will be added to once they are joined to the AD DS domain.

- **Export Location.** The location where the virtual desktop template is copied to once selected for use when generating further RD virtualization host virtual machines.

Remote Desktop Session Host

Remote Desktop (RD) Session Host provides a full desktop environment to a user. Users connect to the RD Session Host server from a thin client, such as a Windows Thin PC or the Remote Desktop Connection client, which ships with Windows operating systems. An RD Session Host provides a full screen or window that reproduces a Windows desktop, including taskbar, Start menu, and desktop icons.

The benefits of using RD Session Host include:

- You can deploy an application to many users by installing it on a small number of RD Session Host servers. Users can run applications on RD Session Host servers that might be incompatible with their operating systems.

- Application updates are simplified. You update an application on the RD Session Host server rather than having to push the patch down to individual operating systems.

- It allows you to grant access to a standardized corporate desktop experience for users who have chosen to use their own computer at work in BYOD (Bring Your Own Device) scenarios.

- It allows you to grant access, through a VPN, to a standardized corporate desktop for users at remote locations or for those whom telecommute.

- It allows you to grant access to applications for operating systems that do not support RD Web Access or RD RemoteApp.

The drawbacks to RD Session Host servers is that they require applications that are compatible with the RD Session Host environment. These applications must be installed after the session host role is deployed. You should ensure that applications are installed on all servers that are available to a specific session collection because you won't know which RD session host server a user connecting to a session collection will be connected to.

Session collection settings

Session collections determine the properties of RD Session Host servers. You can configure the following RD Session Host settings on a per session collection basis:

- **User Groups.** This determines which user groups are associated with a specific session collection. If a user is a member of the user group, they can connect to session host servers that are members of the collection. They can also access RemoteApp applications published to the collection.

- **Sessions.** Shown in Figure 16-4, these settings determine the amount of time after which a session that is disconnected is automatically ended. The default value is Never. You can be configure the value to be as short as one minute. You can also configure active session limits, how long before an idle session is disconnected, and then determine what happens when a disconnection occurs. Should the session be automatically terminated or should reconnection be allowed. You can also use the settings contained in this area to configure whether to use temporary folders and whether those folders are deleted when the session ends.

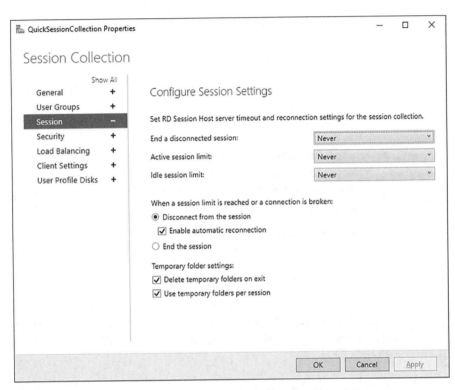

Figure 16-4 Session settings

- **Security settings.** They allow you to configure whether Remote Desktop Connections require RDP Security or TLS 1.0 security. Encryption options include Low, Client Compatible, High and FIPS Compliant. You should generally select High unless you are required to use FIPS Compliant. The drawback of doing so is that some older 3rd party remote desktop clients may not support this level of encryption.

- **Load balancing.** This section allows you configure the load balancing settings for a session collection, including the relative weight the server is assigned when multiple session host servers are available to the session collection and the limit to the number of sessions each session host server can host.

- **Client settings.** The Client Settings section allows you to configure which redirection options to enable. You can configure redirection for the following:

    - Audio and video playback
    - Audio recording
    - Smart cards

- Plug and play devices

- Drives

- Clipboard

- Printers, including using the default client printing device and the Remote Desktop easy print driver

- Monitor redirection

- **User profile disks.** User profile disks allow users to store settings and folders in a central location. This is useful to allow users to persist data and settings across different session host settings on multiple servers. You can choose the following user profile disk settings:

  - User profile disk location

  - Maximum size

  - Store all user settings and data on the profile disk, with specified folders excluded

  - Store only certain folders on the user profile disk

You can also use Session Collection settings to configure which remote app programs will be available to the Session Collection. You can also add and remove session host servers from the session collection. These servers should already have the RD Session Host role installed prior to performing this task.

Personal session desktops

Personal session desktops are new to Windows Server 2016 and allow you to create a special type of Session Collection where each user has access to their own personal session host where they enjoy administrative rights. Personal session desktops can be useful for developers who might need administrative rights without giving them those rights over a remote desktop session host server.

RemoteApp

Rather than open a full session, including a desktop, Start menu, and a task bar, RemoteApp allows a user to run one or more applications directly. The application runs in such a way that it appears as if it is executing on the local computer. When a client invokes multiple applications from the same host server, the server transmits the applications to the client using the same session.

RemoteApp includes the following benefits:

- Any application that can be run on the RD Session Host server can be run as a RemoteApp application.

- You can associate RemoteApp applications with local file extensions. This means that the RemoteApp application starts when the user attempts to open an associated document.

- Users are often unaware that an application is running remotely.

- RemoteApp applications can be used with RD Gateway, allowing access to clients on remote networks such as the Internet.

You publish a RemoteApp program to a Session Collection once you've installed it on a RD Session Host server through the session collection area of the Server Manager console.

Group Policy configuration

The Computer Configuration\Policies\Administrative Templates\Windows Components\Remote Desktop Services\RD Session Host server node of Group Policy contains several policies that you can use to configure Session Host servers. There are many settings that can only be configured through group policy and PowerShell that are not available in the Remote Desktop Services area of the Server Manager Console. The coverage here is brief, as there are a vast number of policies, and you've already learned about the functionality that most of them implement.

- **Application Compatibility.** Through the Application Compatibility node, you can access the Turn off Windows Installer RDS Compatibility, Turn on Remote Desktop IP Virtualization, Select the network adapter to be used for Remote Desktop IP Virtualization and Do not use Remote Desktop Session Host server IP address when virtual IP address is not available.

- **Connections.** Through the Connections node, you can access the following policies: Automatic Reconnection, Allow Users to Connect Remotely Using Remote Desktop Services, Deny Logoff of an Administrator Logged In to the Console Session, Configure Keep-Alive Connection Interval, Limit Number of Connections, Suspend user sign-in to complete app registration, Set Rules for Remote Control of Remote Desktop Services User Sessions, Select RDP transport protocols, Select Network Detection on the Server, Restrict Remote Desktop Services Users to a Single Remote Desktop Services Session, Allow Remote Start of Unlisted Programs, and Turn Off Fair Share CPU Scheduling.

- **Device and Resource Redirection.** Through the Device and Resource Redirection node, you can configure the following policies: Allow Audio And Video Playback Redirection, Allow Audio Recording Redirection, Limit Audio Playback Quality, Do Not Allow Clipboard Redirection, Do Not Allow COM Port Redirection, Do Not Allow Drive Redirection, Do Not Allow LPT Port Redirection, Do Not Allow Supported Plug And Play Device Redirection, Do Not Allow Smart Card Device Redirection, and Allow Time Zone Redirection.

- **Licensing.** You can access the Licensing node to configure the following policies: Use The Specified Remote Desktop License Servers, Hide Notifications About RD Licensing Problems That Affect the RD Session Host Server, and Set the Remote Desktop Services Licensing Mode.

- **Printer Redirection.** Through the Printer Redirection node, you can configure the following policies: Do Not Set Default Client Printer To Be Default Printer in a Session, Do Not Allow Client Printer Redirection, Use Remote Desktop Easy Print Printer Driver first, Specify RD Session Host Server Fallback Printer Driver Behavior, and Redirect Only the Default Client Printer.

- **Profiles.** You can find the following policies in the Profiles node: Limit The Size Of Tthe Entire Roaming User Profile Cache, Set Remote Desktop Services User Home Directory, Use Mandatory Profiles On The RD Session Host Server, and Set Path For Remote Desktop Services Roaming User Profile.

- **RD Connection Broker.** You can find the following policies in the RD Connection Broker node: Join RD Connection Broker, Configure RD Connection Broker Farm Name, Use IP Address Redirection, Configure RD Connection Broker Server Name, and Use RD Connection Broker Load Balancing.

- **Remote Session Environment.** You can use the Remote Session Environment node to locate the following policies: Limit Maximum Color Depth, Enforce Removal Of Remote Desktop Wallpaper, Use the Hardware Default Graphics Adapter For All Remote Desktop Services sessions, Limit Maximum Display Resolution, Limit Number of Monitors, Remove Disconnect Option from the Shut Down Dialog, Remove Windows Security Item from the Start Menu, Use Advanced RemoteFX Graphics For RemoteApp, Prioritize H2.64/AVC 444 graphics mode for Remote Desktop Connections, Configure H.264/AVC hardware encoding for Remote Desktop Connections, configure compression for RemoteFX data, configure image quality for RemoteFX Adaptive Graphics, enable RemoteFX encoding for RemoteFX clients designed for Windows Server 2008 R2 SP1, Configure RemoteFX Adaptive Graphics, Start a Program on Connection, Always Show Desktop On Connection, Allow desktop composition for Remote Desktop sessions, and Do Not Allow Font Smoothing.

- **RemoteFX for Windows Server 2008 R2.** This node contains the following policies: Configure Remote FX, Optimize Visual Experience when using RemoteFX, and Optimize Visual Experience for Remote Desktop Service Sessions.

- **Security.** The Security node contains the following policies: Server Authentication Certificate Template, Set Client Connection Encryption Level, Always Prompt for Password

Upon Connection, Require Secure RPC Communication, Require Use of Specific Security Layer for Remote (RDP) Connections, Do Not Allow Local Administrators to Customize Permissions, and Require User Authentication for Remote Connections by Using Network Level Authentication.

- **Session Time Limits.** You can find the following policies in the Session Time Limits node: Set Time Limit for Disconnected Sessions, Set Time Limit for Active but Idle Remote Desktop Services Sessions, Set Time Limit for Active Remote Desktop Services Sessions, End Session When Time Limits Are Reached, and Set Time Limit for Logoff of RemoteApp Sessions.

- **Temporary Folders.** The Temporary Folders node contains the following policies: Do Not Delete Temp Folder Upon Exit, and Do Not Use Temporary Folders Per Session.

Inside OUT
Useful policies

The most useful policy groups are in the Connections and Session Time Limits nodes. These contain policies that control how many clients are connected to each RD Session Host server and how long they remain connected, affecting the RD Session Host server's capacity.

Remote Desktop Virtualization Host

The Remote Desktop Virtualization Host allows you to configure Remote Desktop technologies to support Virtual Desktop Infrastructure (VDI). You can use RD Virtualization Host to allow clients to connect using Remote Desktop to personal virtual machines running on Hyper-V hosts. You can configure RD Virtualization Host to assign users to a specific unique virtual machine or you can configure RD Virtualization Host to direct users to a pool of shared virtual machines. The RD Virtualization Host role service needs to be installed on a computer that hosts the Hyper-V role and the client virtual machines.

This type of virtualization takes substantially more resources than RD Session Host sessions, but also allows greater customization of the user experience. Virtual machines can be treated just like desktop machines, with users using a thin client to access the RD Virtualization Host virtual machines. RD Virtualization Host integrates with RD Session Broker to ensure that users are redirected to their existing virtual machine in the event that their session is disconnected.

RD Virtualization Host computers have the following requirements:

- Must be available remotely via Windows PowerShell.

- Must be domain joined.

- Must be running Hyper-V.

- For Windows Server 2016 RD Virtualization Host deployments, must be running Windows Server 2016 or later.

- Server must support hardware-assisted virtualization. This means that you cannot run an RD Virtualization Host server within Hyper-V nested virtualization.

- Server must have a network adapter that supports the creation of a Hyper-V virtual switch.

- RD Connection Broker server must have the right to join virtual desktops to the AD DS domain.

- If performing a quick start deployment, use a prepared template computer desktop computer virtual hard disk as shown in Figure 16-5.

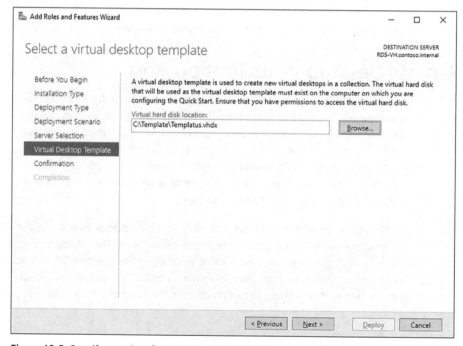

Figure 16-5 Specify template for RD Virtualization Host server

Virtual machine preparation

To prepare a virtual machine for use as a template in an RD Virtualization Host deployment, you should perform the following tasks:

- Deploy the virtual machine and install all of the applications that will be available to users of the RD virtualization host VMs. Perform this deployment on one of the Hyper-V servers that will function as an RD virtualization host. You can build this virtual machine on another computer and then import it on the RD virtualization host. Although not required, you should configure this virtual machine as a Generation 2 VM because this will give you the greatest flexibility in terms of virtual machine configuration.

- Once the applications are installed, sysprep the virtual machine, generalize and set it to boot using the Out Of Box Experience setting. Once sysprepped, the virtual machine will be shut down.

Virtual desktop collections

Virtual desktop collections function in a manner similar to a session collection. You configure who can connect. and select the resources they have access to on a per-collection basis. When creating the virtual desktop collection, you need to provide the following information:

- **Collection Name.** Name of the virtual desktop collection.

- **Collection Type.** This can be a pooled virtual desktop collection or a personal virtual desktop collection.

- **Virtual Desktop Template.** The prepared template virtual machine.

- **Virtual Desktop Settings.** You can specify a Sysprep answer file, or provide unattended installation settings. This information is used to join the virtual machine to the domain. This requires that the computer account of the host computer has permission to perform the AD DS domain join.

- **Unattended Settings.** Provide the time zone, AD DS domain, and organizational unit used in the domain join operation.

- **Users and user groups.** Shown in Figure 16-6, it allows you to specify which users and groups have access to the collection. It also allows you to configure the number of virtual desktops to be created in the collection, and the name prefix and suffix for the computer accounts of RDS VDI virtual machines.

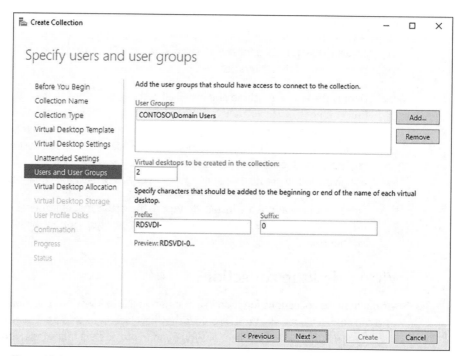

Figure 16-6 RDS VDI User and user group settings

- **Virtual Desktop Allocation.** Allows you to specify the allocation of VDI virtual machines in the collection to RD virtualization host servers. For example, you can have 10 virtual machines on one host server, and 20 on another.

- **Virtual Desktop Storage.** Allows you to configure the type of storage used for the virtual desktops.

- **User Profile Disks.** Allows you to configure and enable user profile disk settings and the location.

Once the virtual desktop collection is created, you can also configure client settings for the collection. This determines whether functionality such as audio and video playback, audio recording, smart cards, plug and play devices, drives, the clipboard, and printers are redirected from the Remote Desktop client to the RD virtual machine.

Pooled virtual desktops

Pooled virtual desktops are collections of identically configured virtual machines that users connecting a Remote Desktop virtualization host through a remote desktop connection broker are assigned. A user will be connected to the first available pooled virtual desktop on first sign on, and only redirected to the same pooled virtual desktop in the event their connection is disrupted and they haven't signed off. If they sign off and reconnect, they may be assigned to a new virtual desktop within the pool. Pooled virtual desktops do not retain session information. When a user signs off from a pooled virtual desktop, the virtual machine reverts to its original pre sign on state.

Personal virtual desktops

You use personal virtual desktops when you want to assign users persistent VDI virtual machines. This means that users can make customizations and store data on the virtual machines that persist across sessions. The virtual machines are associated with the user and they are automatically connected to that virtual machine when they initiate a session through the Remote Desktop connection broker. Personal virtual desktops retain session information across connections and are not reverted to their original pre sign on state when the session ends.

RemoteFX

RemoteFX allows virtual machines in a VDI deployment to leverage the graphical processing power of compatible graphics cards. This in turns allows workloads that need to leverage substantive graphical processing power, such as those used in Computer Aided Design (CAD). These graphics cards must be installed on the Remote Desktop Virtualization Host, and special graphics adapter drivers will need to be configured for each virtual machine that takes advantage of RemoteFX.

Remote Desktop Web Access

You can use Remote Desktop (RD) Web Access to allow clients to connect to an RD Session Host or Virtualization Host session through a web page link rather than through Remote Desktop Connection client software or by running a RemoteApp application. To use RD Web Access, clients need to run a supported version of the Windows Client or Windows Server operating system. You can also use Remote Desktop Web Access to publish applications directly to the Start menu of computers running the Windows 8.1 and Windows 10 operating systems.

Remote Desktop Licensing

Each client or user that accesses a Remote Desktop server, either through an RD Session Host session, a RemoteApp application, or an RD Web Access application needs to have a license. This special type of license is not included with the licenses you get when you purchase Windows Server or Windows client operating system such as Windows 10. This license is called a Remote Desktop Services Client Access License (RDS CAL). You install RDS CALs on an RD license server. When a user, computer, or thin client initiates a session to a Remote Desktop Services server, the server performs a check to verify that a valid license has been issued or is available.

You configure licensing settings for a Remote Desktop server through Deployment Properties as shown in Figure 16-7.

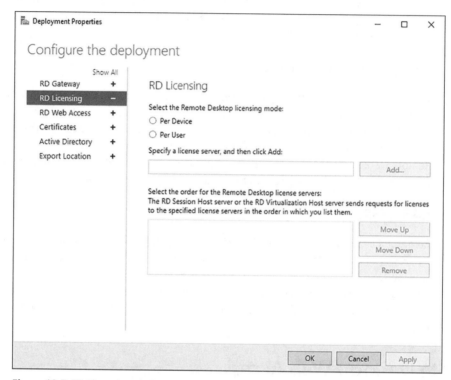

Figure 16-7 RD Licensing settings

Installing RDS CALs

You can install several types of licenses on an RD license server. The different license types are as follows:

- **RDS Per User CAL.** An RDS Per User CAL gives a specific user account the ability to access any RD Session Host server in an organization from any computer or device. This type of CAL is a good idea when you have the same person accessing Remote Desktop from different devices.

- **RDS Per Device CAL.** The RDS Per Device CAL licenses a specific device, such as a normal computer or thin client, with the ability to connect to an RD Session Host server. RDS Per Device CALs are reset automatically by the RD license server after a random period between 52 and 89 days. This means that if a computer or thin client is decommissioned, the license assigned to it is reclaimed automatically and can be used again. If you are decommissioning a large number of computers, you can revoke 20% of the RDS Per Device CALs.

- **RDS External Connector.** Use this license type to allow people that are external to your organization to access a single Remote Desktop Server. A separate RDS External Connector license must be purchased for each remote desktop server accessible to external users.

- **Service Providers License Agreement.** This is a special type of license agreement for service providers. It is useful when providing Remote Desktop Services to multiple organizations.

You can mix and match RDS Per User CALs and RDS Per Device CALS as necessary. When using Remote Desktop Virtualization Hosts, you also need to purchase a Virtual Enterprise Centralized Desktop licensing agreement for the VDI operating system. You can use the Manage RDS CALs Wizard in the RD Licensing Manager console to:

- Migrate RDS Cals to different RD Licensing Servers

- Rebuild the RD Licensing Server database

Inside OUT

Licensing is complicated

Unless you are certain, ensure that you check in with a Microsoft licensing specialist about your licensing configuration.

Activating a license server

You must activate an RD license server before it is able to issue CALs. The activation process is reasonably similar to the one that you need to go through when you perform product activation for a Windows operating system or for an application such as Microsoft Office. The method you use depends on whether the RD license server has a connection to the internet. If the server does have a connection to the internet, you can perform automatic activation. If the server does not have a direct connection to the internet, you can perform an activation using a telephone, or you can navigate to a website on a computer or mobile device that does have a connection to the internet and perform activation by filling out a form and entering the activation code on the RD license server.

Managing Remote Desktop Services Using PowerShell

The Remote Desktop PowerShell module contains a large number of cmdlets that you can use to manage all aspects of Remote Desktop Services on Windows Server 2016. These cmdlets are described in Table 16-1.

Table 16-1. Remote Access PowerShell cmdlets

Noun	Verbs	Function
RDActiveManagementServer	Set	Configure active RD Connection Broker server
RDAvailableApp	Get	View applications that can be published from a collection
RDCertificate	Get, New, Set	Manage Remote Desktop Services certificate configuration
RDClientAccessName	Set	Manage DNS name that clients use to connect to RDS deployment
RDConnectionBrokerHighAvailability	Get, Set	Configure connection broker high availability
RDDatabaseConnectionString	Remove, Set	Configure RD database connection strings
RDDeploymentGatewayConfiguration	Get, Set	Manage RD deployment gateway configuration
RDFileTypeAssociation	Get, Set	Manage RD filetype associations
RDLicenseConfiguration	Get, Set	Configure RD licensing
RDPersonalSessionDesktopAssignment	Export, Get, Import, Remove, Set	Manage association between personal session and a user
RDPersonalVirtualDesktopAssignment	Export, Get, Import, Remove, Set	Manage association between virtual desktop and a user
RDPersonalVirtualDesktopPatchSchedule	Get, New, Remove, Set	Configure personal virtual desktop patch schedule
RDRemoteApp	Get, New, Remove, Set	Manage RD RemoteApp
RDRemoteDesktop	Get, Set	Publish a remote desktop to a collection
RDServer	Add, Get, Remove	Manage server membership of a Remote Desktop deployment

CHAPTER 16

RDSessionCollection	Get, New, Remove	Manage RD session collections
RDSessionCollectionConfiguration	Get, Set	Manage RD session collection configurations
RDSessionDeployment	New	Create new RD session deployment
RDSessionHost	Add, Get, Remove, Set	Manage RD Session Host session collection server membership
RDUser	Disconnect	Disconnect a connected RD user
RDUserLogoff	Invoke	Sign off a connected RD user
RDUserSession	Get	View RD user session information
RDUserMessage	Send	Send a message to an RD user
RDVirtualDesktop	Get, Move	Manage RD virtual desktops
RDVirtualDesktopADMachineAccountReuse	Disable, Enable, Test	Manage whether RD Connection Broker server reuses existing AD computer accounts for pooled virtual desktops created using a template in a managed collection
RDVirtualDesktopCollection	Add, Get, New, Remove, Set, Update	Manage virtual desktop membership of virtual desktop collections
RDVirtualDesktopFromCollection	Remove	Remove a virtual desktop from a collection
RDVirtualDesktopCollectionConfiguration	Get	View virtual desktop collection configuration
RDVirtualDesktopCollectionJob	Stop	End a virtual desktop collection job
RDVirtualDesktopCollectionJobStatus	Get	View virtual desktop connection job status
RDVirtualDesktopConcurrency	Get, Set	Manage virtual desktop concurrency
RDVirtualDesktopDeployment	New	Create a new virtual desktop deployment
RDVirtualDesktopIdleCount	Get, Set	Manage virtual desktop idle settings

CHAPTER 16

RDVirtualDesktopTemplateExportPath	Get, Set	Configure virtual desktop template paths
RDWorkspace	Get, Set	Manage workspace name settings for Remote Desktop deployment
RDOUAccess	Grant, Test	Configures OU access for the RD Connection Broker server

Windows Server 2016 and Azure IaaS

Azure IaaS (Infrastructure as a Service) provides you with the ability to run virtual machine instances in the cloud. You can use Azure IaaS to run a variety of operating systems, including Windows Server 2016, but also Windows Server 2012 R2, Windows Server 2012, Windows Server 2008 R2, and a variety of supported Linux distributions.

In this chapter you'll learn what you need to know about deploying and managing Windows Server 2016 in Microsoft Azure.

Understanding IaaS

IaaS allows you to host your IT infrastructure in the cloud. Rather than deploy the virtual machine in an on-premises hypervisor, which you must pay for and maintain yourself, IaaS allows you to run your virtual machines in a cloud-provider's infrastructure, which the cloud providers are responsible for maintaining.

There are several benefits to running Windows Server 2016 in an Azure virtual machine over running a Windows Server 2016 VM on-premises. These include:

- **Efficient costing**. You will be charged on a per-minute basis for the hosted virtual machine. You aren't charged for deallocated virtual machines. In certain circumstances, this may be cheaper than paying for the infrastructure to host the virtual machine in your own datacenter.

- **Efficient use of licensing**. When you deploy Windows Server 2016 on IaaS, the operating system license is included in your charges. If you have an existing license, you can use "Bring your own license" functionality.

- **Up to date deployment images**. When deployed, the operating system will be fully patched with the latest software updates. This means that the operating system will be secure at deployment. When you maintain your own images, you need to either make sure that they are up-to-date, or spend time after deployment ensuring that they are up-to-date.

Resource groups

A resource group stores resources that are administratively related to one another. In the case of IaaS virtual machines, the network, the virtual machine's storage, and the virtual machine itself may be located in the same resource group or in separate resource groups. It's common to keep them in a single resource group because that simplifies the process of managing all of the resources associated with the virtual machine. For example, you can simply delete the resource group and all of its contents, rather than going through and deleting each individual element. Resource groups can contain resources from multiple regions, though it's important to remember that when thinking about IaaS VMs, that the network, storage, and VM itself must be in the same region.

To create a new Resource Group, perform the following steps:

1. In the Azure console, click Resource Groups and then click Add.

2. In the Resource Group blade, shown in Figure 17-1, provide the following information and click Create:

- **Resource Group N`ame**. This needs to be unique for the subscription.

- **Subscription**. If you have multiple subscriptions, choose the subscription to associate with the resource group.

- **Resource Group Location**. This is the location of the resource group. Resources placed in the resource group do not have to be located in the same location as the resource group.

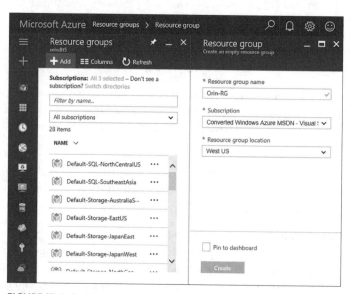

FIGURE 17-1 Create resource group

Storage accounts

You can configure a storage account to host virtual hard disks before deploying a virtual machine. Storage accounts can also be created automatically as part of the IaaS VM provisioning process. The main thing to remember is that the virtual machine and the storage account need to be in the same location, for example, such as US West or Australia South East. This makes sense if you remember that you probably don't want to have the disks for a virtual machine to be located in West US when the processor and RAM are located in Australia South East.

To create a new storage account, perform the following steps:

1. In the Azure console, click New, click Storage and then click Storage account.

2. In the Create Storage Account blade, provide the following information as shown in Figure 17-2.

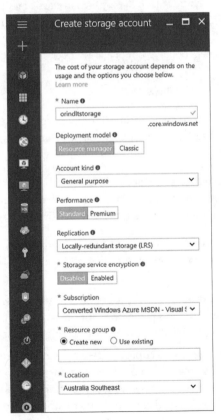

FIGURE 17-2 Storage account

- **Storage Account Name**. This name must be unique across all of Azure. It must also contain only lowercase letters and numbers and be between 3 and 24 characters long.

- **Deployment Model**. Choose between Classic and Resource Manager. You should choose Resource Manager because this is Microsoft's preferred option going forward.

Inside OUT

Classic versus ARM deployment

You can deploy Azure IaaS VMs using two methods. Today, the preferred method is to use the new ARM portal available at https://portal.azure.com. You can also deploy VMs using the classic portal at https://manage.windowsazure.com, or in classic mode from the new ARM portal. Classic mode is primarily available for backward compatibility, and at some point you won't be able to deploy VMs in classic mode, only to manage existing VMs that were deployed in classic mode. It's possible to migrate from classic to ARM mode. ARM mode is Microsoft's preferred option because it allows you to completely automate deployment of all resources, including VMs, network and storage settings, using JSON templates.

- **Account Kind**. You have the option of choosing General purpose or Blob. General purpose storage is suited for workloads such as virtual machine disks. Blob is suitable for unstructured data.

- **Performance**. You can choose between Standard and Premium. Standard storage provides high performance storage for IaaS VM virtual hard disks, but only allows locally-redundant storage. Premium storage is more expensive than standard storage.

- **Replication**. This determines how the storage is replicated for redundancy purposes. The more redundant the storage, the more you will be charged for it. The following options are available:

  - **Locally-Redundant Storage**. Three copies of data are stored within a single datacenter in a single region. This is the only option available if premium storage is chosen. It is also available if standard storage is chosen.

  - **Zone-Redundant Storage**. Three copies of data are stored across two or three facilities, either within a single region or across regions where a region has fewer than three datacenters. It is only available for standard tier storage and only available for block blobs. And zone-redundant storage is not suitable for virtual hard disks.

- **Geo-Redundant Storage**. Contains six copies of your data, with three replicas in the primary region and three in a secondary region.

- **Read-Access Geo-Redundant Storage**. Six copies of the data are kept, with the copies in the second location available for read access should the primary location become unavailable.

- **Storage Service Encryption**. Determines whether the storage is in an encrypted at rest state, or not in an encrypted state.

- **Subscription**. The Azure subscription that the storage account will be associated with.

- **Location**. The location that the storage account is associated with.

Azure virtual networks

Azure IaaS VMs can only use virtual networks that are in the same location as the IaaS virtual machine. For example, if you are deploying an IaaS VM to Australia South East, you'll only be able to connect the IaaS VM directly to a virtual network in Australia South East.

To create a new network, perform the following steps:

1. In the Azure console, click on New, click on Networking, and then click Virtual Network.

2. Select the deployment model. You can choose between Classic and Resource Manager. You should choose Resource Manager because this is Microsoft's preferred option going forward.

3. On the Create Virtual Network blade, shown in Figure 17-3, provide the following information:

- **Name**: Name of the virtual network, which needs to be unique to the subscription.

- **Address Space**: This is IPv4 address space that will be used by hosts on the virtual network.

- **Subnet Name**: This is the first subnet within the address space.

- **Subnet Address Range**: This is the address range of the first subnet within the address space. This range can consume the entire address space.

- **Subscription**. Choose which Azure subscription the virtual network will be associated with.

- **Resource Group**. Choose an existing resource group within the subscription or create a new resource group. The virtual network can be placed in a resource group that is in a different location. For example, you can create a virtual network in the Australia South-east region that is hosted in a resource group in the West US region.

FIGURE 17-3 Create virtual network

Once you have deployed the virtual network, you can configure the following properties for the virtual network using the Azure console:

- **Address Space**. This allows you to add additional address spaces to the Azure virtual net-work. You partition these address spaces using subnets.

- **Connected Devices**. Lists the current devices that are connected to the Azure virtual network. They include a list of VM network adapters and the internal IP address those adapters are assigned.

- **Subnets**. These are subnets that you create within the address space, allowing you to put different Azure virtual machines on separate subnets within the same virtual network.

- **DNS Servers**. Allows you to configure the IP address of the DNS servers assigned by the DHCP server used by the Azure virtual network. Use this to configure DNS settings when you deploy a domain controller on an Azure IaaS VM or when you deploy Azure AD DS for an Azure virtual network.

- **Properties**. Allows you to change which subscription the Azure virtual network is associated with.

- **Locks**. Allows you to apply configuration locks. This blocks changes being made to the settings of the resource unless the lock is first removed.

- **Automation Script**. Allows you to access the JSON template file that you can use to reproduce and redeploy virtual networks with similar settings.

VM types

When you deploy a VM on IaaS, you get to choose from a set of available types. The types available to you will depend on which operating system disk storage type you choose and will, to an extent, depend on the region you are in as some regions get new VM types, such as the ones with access to powerful GPU cards, before other regions.

The available VM types are always changing, with new options being introduced and old options eventually being retired. The more powerful and more capable the VM, the more you will be charged for using it. VMs are charged on a per-minute basis when they are allocated and you will pay additional charges depending on how storage is used.

TheVM types are as follows:

- **D, Dv2 series**. These VMs are designed for applications that require substantial processing power and high performance temporary disks. The OS disk is traditional HDD. The Dv2 series have more powerful processors than the D series.

- **DS, DSv2 series**. Similar to the D and Dv2 series, these VMs differ because they use SSD for the operating system drive, rather than traditional HDD.

- **F series**. These VMs provide similar computational power to the Dv2 VMs, but with a cheaper price than the Dv2 VMs. The F series will use Azure's new numbering system for VM sizes, with the number after the name describing the number of CPU cores. Choose this type if you need a substantial amount of processor resources, but not much memory.

- **G series**. This provides the greatest amount of VM RAM of any VM series available in Azure. Use this for memory intensive applications.

- **A8-A11 and H-series**. They are suitable for compute-intensive instances used in high performance computing applications.

Within a series, you get a choice of the number of processor cores, the amount of RAM, the number of available data disks, the maximum available IOPs, the size and type of the operating system disk, and whether the VM supports load balancing. You'll be provided with an estimate of the running costs on a monthly basis of each VM type.

CHAPTER 17

Deploying an IaaS VM

To deploy a new Windows Server 2016 on an Azure IaaS instance, perform the following steps:

1. In the Azure portal, click New, click Compute, and then click Windows Server 2016 Datacenter as shown in Figure 17-4.

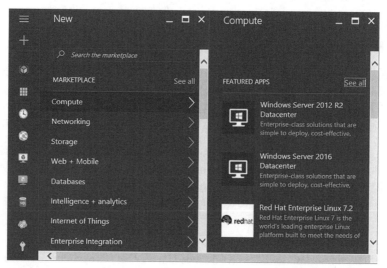

FIGURE 17-4 Select compute image

2. Review the legal disclaimer and then choose between Resource Manager (ARM) and the Classic deployment model and click Create. As Classic will eventually be deprecated and discontinued, you should choose Resource Manager.

3. On the Basics page, provide the following information:

- **Name**. Must be unique within the resource group.

- **VM Disk Type**. Choose between traditional HDD and SSD. HDD is cheaper and slower, and SSD will give the VM better storage performance, but it will incur higher charges.

- **User Name**. This is the name assigned to the local administrator account. You should choose a memorable name, but you will be unable to use common administrator names such as 'administrator' or 'root.'

- **Password**. The password assigned to the local administrator account. It must be at least 12 characters and include upper case letters, lower case letters, numbers and symbols. Avoid commonly used passwords, because Microsoft increasingly blocks passwords found in account data breaches from being used in its services.

- **Subscription**. If you have multiple Azure subscriptions, you can choose which one you want the virtual machine assigned to. If you want to deploy a virtual machine to an existing resource group, choose the subscription associated with that resource group.

- **Resource Group**. You can choose to create a new resource group or use an existing resource group. Place a VM in a new resource group if it's the first or only VM that you want to use. Place a VM in an existing resource group if you want it to interact directly with other VMs that you've already deployed in a manner similar to if you had them on the same subnet.

- **Location**. Which Azure region you want to deploy the virtual machine to. If you choose to create a resource group, this is the region the resource group will be located in. Generally speaking you should choose the region that's closest to you geographically.

4. Select the virtual machine size as shown in Figure 17-5. The available types will depend on whether you selected HDD for the primary OS disk, or SSD.

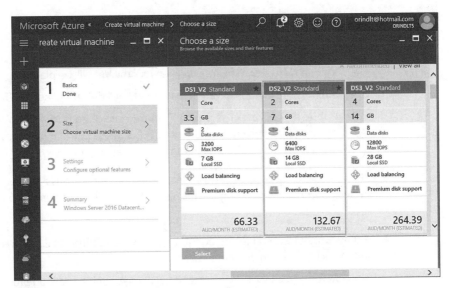

FIGURE 17-5 Choose the VM size

5. On the Settings page, configure the following optional features as shown in Figure 17-6.

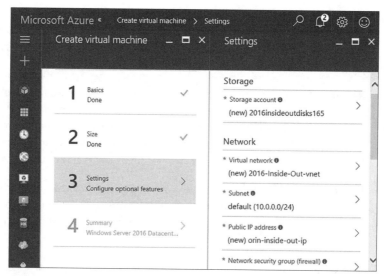

FIGURE 17-6 Settings

- **Storage Account**. Which storage account will be used to host the VM's disks.

- **Network**. Contains the following settings:

    - **Virtual Network**. Which virtual network the VM will be placed on.

    - **Subnet**. The IP address range that the VM will draw its IP address from.

    - **Public IP Address**. The public IP address assigned to the VM. You can also choose for VMs to not have a public IP address and only be accessible to clients that connect through a VPN to their virtual network.

- **Network Security Group**. Network security groups function as firewalls. You can apply network security groups at the virtual network, virtual machine, and network adapter level.

- **Extensions**. Allows you to add agents and software to the virtual machine. Available agents include, but are not limited to:

    - **Acronis Backup**. Provides the VM with an Acronis backup agent.

    - **Microsoft Anti-Malware**. Deploys Microsoft's anti-mawlare solution into the VM.

    - **PowerShell Desired State Configuration**. Allows you to apply desired state configuration to the VM after deployment.

    - **Puppet Agent**. Allows you to manage the configuration of the VM using Puppet.

    - **Windows Chef Extension**. Allows you to manage the configuration of the VM using Chef.

6. **High Availability**. Allows you to configure whether the VM will participate in a high-availability set. You can use an existing high availability set or create a new one. High availability is covered later in this chapter.

7. **Boot Diagnostics**. Allows you to view diagnostic screenshots of the IaaS virtual machine as it boots. You can then determine what may have gone wrong if an IaaS virtual machine is unable to boot.

8. **Guest OS Diagnostics**. Allows Azure to gather performance metrics on the running IaaS virtual machine. Guest OS diagnostics are covered later in the chapter.

9. **Diagnostics Storage Account**. Allows you to specify the storage account where diagnostic data will be stored.

Once you have completed specifying the IaaS virtual machine deployment parameters, you'll be provided with the option of downloading a template in JSON format or saving it to your library. Figure 17-7 shows a deployment template generated from a Windows Server 2016 IaaS VM deployment.

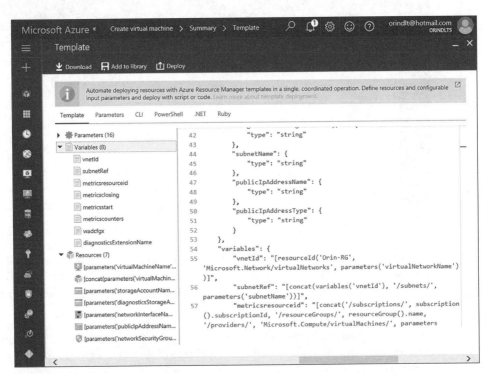

FIGURE 17-7 Template configuration

Saving a template to your library allows you to use it to deploy future IaaS VMs without having to configure the same settings. This is very useful when you are building out high-availability sets and need virtual machines that have identical configurations as nodes within the availability sets. You can also edit the properties of the template to make modifications as necessary, rather than going through the deployment wizard.

IP addressing

A virtual machine on an Azure network will have an internally assigned IP address in the range specified by the virtual network it is associated with. It may also have a public IP address. You can determine which IP addresses are assigned to an Azure virtual machine on the Network Interfaces blade of the VM's properties as shown in Figure 17-8. You can also use these settings to apply a region specific DNS name to the network interface so that you can connect to the VM using a FQDN rather than IP address. If you have a DNS server, you can then create a CNAME record that points to the region specific DNS name for future connections.

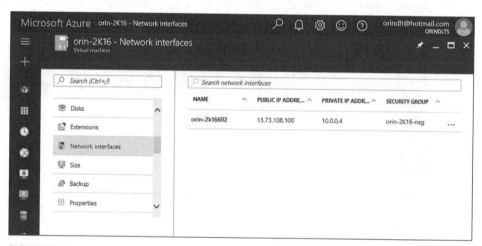

FIGURE 17-8 Network interfaces

The private IP address is assigned through a DHCP server running on the Azure virtual network. You cannot currently configure DHCP reservations on this network, and you can't run your own DHCP server on an Azure virtual network. Private IP addresses are distributed on a first come, first serve basis.

You can configure DNS server settings on a per-virtual network basis. You can also configure a set of custom DNS servers on the DNS Servers blade of the virtual network interface's properties as shown in Figure 17-9.

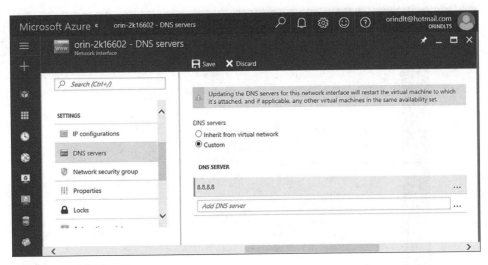

FIGURE 17-9 DNS Servers

If you want to retain the same public IP address for an Azure workload, including a virtual machine, you can organize for an IP address reservation. You'll be charged extra, but the workload will always have the same public IP address. If you don't use a reserved public IP address, it's possible that the IP address assigned to the workload will change during normal Azure maintenance operations, such as when the Azure host infrastructure has software updates applied.

Network security groups

Network security groups allow you to apply traffic control policies in the form of inbound and outbound security rules. Network security groups can be applied at the virtual network, virtual machine, and network adapter level. When you create an Azure IaaS VM, a network security group that has an inbound rule allowing RDP traffic will be assigned to the VM by default as shown in Figure 17-10.

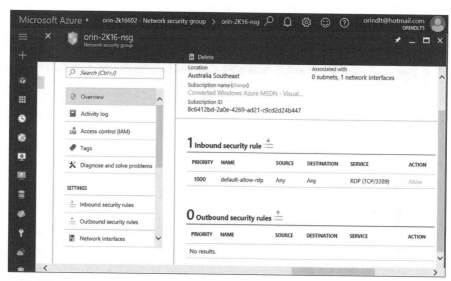

FIGURE 17-10 Network security groups

You can add Inbound our Outbound security rules by clicking on the Inbound security rules or Outbound security rules section of a network security group's properties. When creating a security rule, you need to specify the following settings as shown in Figure 17-11.

FIGURE 17-11 Inbound security rule

- **Name**. The name of the rule, which can contain letters, numbers, underscores, hyphens, and periods.

- **Priority**. Determines the order in which the rule applies. Rules assigned a lower numerical value will apply before rules are assigned a higher numerical value.

- **Source**. Can be set to Any, a specific IP address range in CIDR notation, or to a resource group tag.

- **Protocol**. This can be set to TCP, UDP, or Any.

- **Source Port Range**. Specifies which source port the traffic originates on.

- **Destination**. Can be set to Any, a specific IP address range in CIDR notation, or to a resource group tag.

- **Destination Port Range**. Specifies which port the traffic is trying to address. For example: port 80 for HTTP traffic, or port 443 for HTTPS traffic.

- **Action**. This setting allows traffic to be allowed or denied.

You can save network security groups as JSON templates, and to your subscription's library. This simplifies the process of deploying a complex set of security rules contained in a network security group to additional VMs, networks, or network interfaces in the future.

Remote Desktop

Remote Desktop is the primary method of administering an individual Windows Server IaaS VM. Once a Windows Server 2016 Azure IaaS VM is deployed you can also connect to it to enable remote PowerShell and perform management in that way.

When you click Connect on the virtual machine's Azure Portal page, a Remote Desktop connection shortcut that is pre-configured with the virtual machine's IP address or fully qualified domain name, if you have configured one, will be made available.

Inside OUT

Shutdown and deallocate

When you shut down an Azure IaaS virtual machine, but don't deallocate it, you'll still get charged for the reservation that the VM holds on resources including processor cores, networking resources such as IP addresses, and fast storage. This is okay if you need to spin the VM up rapidly, but incurs unnecessary costs should you just want the VM to be offline until you next need it. If you don't need the VM to spin up quickly, you should deallocate the VM. You can still deploy the VM, it will just take a little longer to start up than it would if it was just shut down. The advantage, though, is that while it's deallocated, you won't be getting charged for it.

Azure AD Domain Join

Just like on-premises virtual machines, Windows Server 2016 IaaS virtual machines can be joined to an Active Directory domain. There are three general options when it comes to using Active Directory with Windows Server 2016 IaaS virtual machines:

- Deploying a Windows Server 2016 IaaS virtual machine and then promoting it to become a domain controller. You can then join other Windows IaaS virtual machines on the same virtual network to the domain hosted by the IaaS VM domain controller. The trick to joining other VMs to Active Directory hosted on an IaaS VM is to configure the DNS servers for the virtual network, which points to the VM hosting the Active Directory instance.

- Use virtual private network or express route connections to configure the Azure virtual network as a branch office network. You can then either domain join Azure IaaS VMs to the on-premises network, or deploy a domain controller in a virtual machine and configure the Azure virtual network as a separate Active Directory site.

- Join an Azure AD domain. You can configure Azure Active Directory to project into a specific Azure Virtual Network. When you do this, you're able to join your Azure IaaS Windows operating system to the Azure AD domain. This Active Directory environment isn't currently as fully functional as joining a traditional Active Directory domain, but you can configure two existing group policy objects. While you can use the Active Directory users and computers console, you will need to perform most user management tasks, such as password reset, using the Azure portal, rather than Windows Server user management tools.

Encrypted VMs

You can use an Azure Key Vault to store an encryption key for an Azure IaaS VM in the same way that you would use a Trusted Platform Module (TPM) chip to store an encryption key for a BitLocker encrypted operating system deployed on bare metal or within a shielded virtual machine fabric. When you configure encryption for an Azure IaaS VM running Windows Server 2016, the contents of the VM's storage is encrypted while the VM is running and at rest.

Encrypting the contents of an Azure IaaS VM brings the following benefits:

- The VM storage will be in an encrypted state in the Azure datacenter. This is often necessary to meet specific compliance requirements around the storage of sensitive data. It's extremely improbable that an unauthorized third party will get access to the virtual hard disk files.

- While it's possible for an authorized person to export the VM from Azure, they won't be able to access the contents of the VM unless they have access to the recovery key stored in the key vault, or a separate copy of the BitLocker recovery key.

You should ensure that you store a copy of the BitLocker recovery key in a safe place as a part of your disaster recovery strategy.

High Availability

When deploying a VM, you can configure the VM to be a member of a high availability set. When deploying a high availability set, you configure the number of Update Domains and Fault Domains that the availability set will have, as shown in Figure 17-12.

- **Fault Domains**. Fault domains represent any part of an Azure deployment that share a common point of failure. You should deploy highly available workloads so that they are in separate fault domains. The maximum number of fault domains is three.

- **Update Domains**. Any virtual machine that shares an update domain could have the Azure host operating system updated at the same time. To ensure that VMs don't go offline during regular update cycles, ensure that highly available VMs are in separate update domains. The maximum number of update domains is 20.

FIGURE 17-12 Choose VM size

Inside OUT

Updating IaaS VMs

When you deploy a Windows Server 2016 VM, it will be up-to-date with all the most recent software updates. Once the IaaS VM is deployed you are responsible for keeping it up-to-date. This means coming up with some way to ensure that the regular monthly updates are applied to the machine, either automatically by configuring the appropriate update settings, or using a managed solution such as Operations Management Suite, a service available in Azure, or even an IaaS VM running WSUS.

Monitoring and diagnostics

You can enable diagnostic settings and metrics in the Monitoring section of an IaaS virtual machine's properties as shown in Figure 17-13. You can also configure alerts to be generated if certain performance counter values are exceeded.

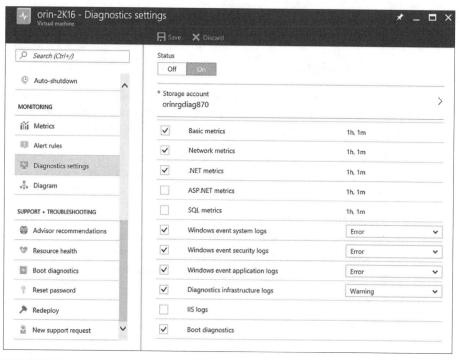

FIGURE 17-13 Diagnostic settings

Boot Diagnostics allow you to see a screen shot of the VM as it appears in the virtual machine's display window on the hypervisor. In the event that a boot error has occurred, you'll be able to view any error message displayed to this window. You can't interact with this image, but you can use it for informational purposes.

You can use the Reset Password functionality to reset the local administrator password, or reset the remote desktop service configuration, as long as you haven't enabled VM encryption.

VPN and ExpressRoute

While each VM can be assigned a public IP address, and you can configure network security groups to allow access to that VM over the public internet, you can also configure Azure virtual networks so that they can be accessed through a VPN connection, or a special connection known as ExpressRoute. You can configure a virtual network to support either site-to-site or point-to site, but not both. ExpressRoute connections can coexist with either the site-to-site or point-to-site VPN types.

Azure site-to-site VPN

Azure virtual networks support two basic types of VPN: site-to-site and point-to-site. A site-to-site VPN allows you to connect the IPv4 subnet hosted on an Azure virtual network to the subnets hosted on your on-premises network in a manner similar to how you'd connect a branch office IPv4 subnet to a head office subnet using a VPN across the public internet. Clients on your internal network using an Azure site-to-site VPN don't need any special configuration. Once the site-to-site connection is configured, they connect to resources on the Azure virtual network in the same way that they'd connect to resources on a remote branch office network. Some organizations configure an Azure site-to-site VPN between their on-premises network and an Azure virtual network, then deploy a writable or read-only domain controller on the Azure virtual network. They then treat the Azure virtual network as just another Active Directory site.

Azure point-to-site VPN

Point-to-site VPNs allow you to configure connections from individual clients through to an Azure virtual network. Point-to-site VPNs are a great solution if you have individual client computers in separate locations that you need to connect to an Azure virtual network, as opposed to a group of clients on the same network needing to connect to an Azure virtual network. If you have a number of clients spread across the internet and separate branch offices, choose to deploy an Azure point-to-site VPN.

Azure point-to-site VPNs authenticate using certificate based authentication, rather than username or password. This means that you need to install the VPN client on each computer to which you wish to grant access to the Azure virtual network. The drawback of this method is that you can't mediate access to an Azure virtual network based on identity.

ExpressRoute

An ExpressRoute connection is a dedicated high-speed connection between an on-premises network and an Azure virtual network. Unlike a site-to-site VPN, an ExpressRoute connection does not use the public internet. ExpressRoute connections are often used by organizations that want to run workloads in Azure, but for compliance or security reasons they are unable or unwilling to have traffic pass across the public internet even if encrypted through a VPN.

Organizations might also choose ExpressRoute because they need to have a specific dedicated high speed connection to Azure and be unable to get the necessary connection bandwidth and reliability out of a site-to-site VPN connection across the public internet. ExpressRoute availability is highly dependent on where you are in the world and whether Microsoft has an agreement with a local provider.

Importing virtual machine images

The primary way that people deploy new virtual machines to Azure is to take an image that is present in the gallery and to deploy it to a resource group. It is also possible to take a virtual machine image that you've prepared in your on-premises Hyper-V environment, and to deploy it to Azure, as long as you've taken the following steps:

- Azure doesn't currently support the importation of virtual hard disks in .vhdx format. Convert the virtual hard disk from .vhdx format to .vhd format using the Hyper-V tools or the Convert-VHD PowerShell cmdlet.

- Once you've ensured that the virtual hard disk is in .vhd format, you'll need to sysprep the virtual machine. When sysprepping, use the generalize option and then shut down the virtual machine.

- Create a storage account and then create a container within the storage account.

Once you have the sysprepped virtual hard disk in VHD format, you can upload that virtual hard disk to the container within the storage account. Once the VHD is uploaded, you can add the image to your list of custom images using the Add-AzureVMImage cmdlet. Once the VM is added to your list of custom images, you'll be able to deploy it to Azure as you would any other virtual machine image from the gallery.

CHAPTER 17

Azure Site Recovery

Azure Site Recovery (ASR) allows you to replicate on-premises workloads to Azure. This includes not only virtualized workloads running on Hyper-V, but compatible physical workloads, as well as workloads running on supported third party virtualization platforms including VMware.

ASR requires you to deploy servers on-premises to manage replication up to Azure. VMs replicated to Azure aren't activated until you perform failover. Until you perform failover, the VMs replicated to Azure are in a deallocated state and are not incurring charges.

The idea with Azure Site Recovery is that in the event a disaster strikes your on-premises deployment, you can perform failover and have those replicated workloads run in Azure until such time as you are ready to fail them back to your on-premises location. You can use Azure Site Recovery as a migration tool because it allows you to keep replicated workloads that you've failed over in Azure permanently. Rather than using it as a site recovery tool, you can use Azure Site Recovery as a tool allowing you to migrate current workloads to Azure with minimal downtime.

CHAPTER 17

Windows Server 2016 includes a variety of new and existing technologies that you can use to secure the operating system. While implementing each of these technologies increases the security of your Windows Server 2016 deployment, it's important to understand implementing no single technology or set of technologies guarantees that your deployment can't be compromised by the most determined of attackers. What you can do is make it substantially more difficult for an attacker to compromise the computers you are responsible for managing by configuring Windows Server 2016 in the ways described in this chapter.

Inside OUT

Assume breach

Assume breach is a security philosophy where you design a security implementation around the hypothesis that an attacker already has compromised and has privileged access to at least some of your organization's protected resources. You should not rely upon the assumptions that hostile actors only exist outside the perimeter network and that critical protected systems have not already been compromised. You should design your organization's security to mitigate the risk of a privileged insider acting maliciously, either deliberately or because their credentials have been compromised by a nefarious external third party.

Least privilege

Least privilege is the practice of assigning the minimum required privileges to an account that are required for the account to perform its assigned tasks. Put another way, accounts should not be assigned rights and privileges in excess of those required to perform the specific tasks that the account is used for.

The benefit of using least privilege is that in the event that an attacker in some way compromises an account, that attacker is limited to being only able to act with the privileges assigned to that account. Least privilege also reduces the chance that damage might inadvertently be done to a system. For example, an account used for backup and recovery can't be used to add or remove software from the server if that account doesn't have permission to do anything beyond backup and recovery.

When it comes to assigning privileges, a very bad habit of many IT professionals is to simply add an account to the local Administrators group on the computer where the privilege is required. This is especially true with service accounts where proper procedure is to edit the local security group policies and assign very specific rights, but many administrators take a quick shortcut and assign all necessary rights by adding the service account to the local Administrators group. This is one of the reasons that attackers go after service accounts, accounts which in many environments use a single unchanging organization-wide password, and which are also members of the local Administrator groups on which they are installed.

Inside OUT

Day-to-day accounts

IT operations staff and developers in your organization should have separate accounts for performing day-to-day activities such as reading email, browsing the Internet, and filling in TPS reports. The day-to-day accounts of IT operations staff and developers should not have local administrative privileges. Should a change in the configuration of IT staff workstations need to occur, a specific privileged account that exists to perform that task should be used. In highly secure well-resourced organizations, privileged accounts can only used on special privileged access workstations (PAWs). These workstations are locked down using technologies such as device and credential guard that makes them especially resistant to malware and credential theft and reuse attacks.

MORE INFO   LEAST PRIVILEGE

You can learn more about least privilege administrative models at *https://technet. microsoft.com/windows-server-docs/identity/ad-ds/plan/security-best-practices/ implementing-least-privilege-administrative-models.*

Role Based Access Control

Role Based Access Control (RBAC) operationalizes the principle of least privilege. The idea is instead of having all-powerful administrator accounts that can perform any task on any system, you instead parcel out administrative privileges limiting what an account can do, and where an account can do it.

For example, rather than giving help desk support staff the ability to reset the passwords of any user in the domain, you instead delegate them the right to only be able to reset the passwords of user accounts in a specific organizational unit. This way you allow the support staff to reset the passwords of a specific class of user account, for example those that are used by people in the Philosophy department, without giving support staff the ability to reset the passwords of domain administrator accounts.

You delegate privileges in Active Directory over organizational units using the Delegation Of Control Wizard, as shown in Figure 18-1.

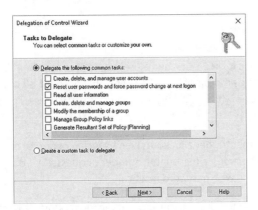

FIGURE 18-1 Delegating the reset password right

Password policies

Account policies include both password policies and account lockout policies. You configure the domain password and lockout policies by configuring the default domain GPO. You can override the domain policies for specific security groups or user accounts using fine-grained password policies. You configure fine-grained password policies using the Active Directory Administrative Center console.

Default password policy settings include:

- **Number of remembered passwords**. A user cannot change their password to a password remembered by the system. By default, Active Directory remembers the previous 24 passwords that have been used by an account.

- **Maximum password age.** This is the maximum amount of time in days that a password can remain the same before it needs to be changed. Default value is 42 days.

- **Minimum password age.** The minimum amount of time in days that a newly changed password must be kept. This policy stops users cycling through password changes to exceed the password history setting so that they can return to using the same password.

- **Minimum password length.** Minimum number of characters that are required for a password. The default is 7. Services such as Azure now require a minimum of 12 characters for administrator account passwords on IaaS virtual machines.

- **Password complexity requirement.** Determines whether password must include three of the four following characteristics: Upper case letters, lower case letters, numbers, and symbols. Enabled by default.

Lockout policy determines:

- The period of time an account is locked out when a user enters a specific number of incorrect passwords in a specific amount of time. Default is that account is not locked out and that an attacker or someone who is just forgetful, can brute force guess passwords without any lockout occurring.

- Number incorrect passwords that trigger a lockout over a specific period of time. When configuring this policy, allow a person a reasonable number of guesses. If you don't, you'll end up flooding the service desk with password reset calls.

- The amount of time that must elapse before the account lockout counter is reset. A correctly entered password also resets the lockout counter.

User rights

Rather than adding a user or service account to the local Administrators group, you should use Group Policy to assign the specific rights that a user account needs to perform the tasks it needs to perform. Assign rights as close to the object as possible. For example, don't give a user account the ability to log on through Remote Desktop Services to all computers in an OU if the user account only needs remote desktop access to one or two computers. You can use Group Policy to configure the rights outlined in Table 18-1.

Table 18-1 User Rights Assignment Policy

User rights assignment policy	Function
Access Credential Manager as a trusted caller	Used by Credential Manager during backup and restore. Do not assign this privilege to user accounts
Access this computer from the network	Specifies which accounts and groups may connect to the computer from the network. Does not affect Remote Desktop Services
Act as part of the operating system	Allow a process to impersonate an account without requiring authentication. Processes that require this privilege are often assigned the LocalSystem account
Add workstations to domain	Grants the ability to join workstations to the domain
Adjust memory quotas for a process	Configures which security principals can adjust the maximum amount of memory assigned to a process
Allow log on locally	Specify which accounts can sign in locally to a computer. Alter this policy on Privileged Access Workstations to remove members of the Users group. This limits which accounts can sign in to a computer. By default, any authenticated user can sign in to any workstation or server except for a Domain Controller
Allow log on through Remote Desktop Services	Determines which accounts and groups can sign in remotely to the computer using Remote Desktop. Configure this policy to allow users to access enhanced session mode for Hyper-V VMs
Back up files and directories	Grant permission to backup files, directories, registry, and other objects that the user account wouldn't normally have permission to. Assigning this right gives indirect access to all data on a computer. A person that holds the right can back that data up and then recover it in an environment over which they have complete control
Bypass traverse checking	Gives users with this right the ability to traverse directories on which they don't have permission. Does not allow the user to list the contents of that directory
Change the system time	Accounts with this right can alter the system time. System time is separate from the computer's time zone
Change the time zone	Account with this right can alter the time zone, but not the system time
Create a pagefile	Allows the account assigned this right the ability to create and modify the page file

CHAPTER 18

Create a token object	Specifies which accounts can be used by processes to create tokens that allow accesses to local resources. You should not assign this right to any user who you do not want to give complete control of the system. This privilege it can be used to elevate to local Administrator privileges
Create global objects	Determines which accounts can create global objects that are available to all sessions. You should not assign this right to any user who you do not want to give complete control of the system. This privilege it can be used to elevate to local Administrator privileges
Create permanent shared objects	Specify which accounts can create directory objects by using the object manager
Create symbolic links	Specify which accounts can create symbolic links from the computer they are signed in to. Assign this right only to trusted users because symbolic links can expose security vulnerabilities in apps that aren't configured to support them
Debug programs	Specify which accounts can attach a debugger to processes within the operating system kernel. Only required by developers writing new system components. Rarely, if ever, necessary for developers writing applications
Deny access to this computer from the network	Blocks specified accounts and groups from accessing the computer from the network. This setting overrides the policy that allows access from the network
Deny log on as a batch job	Blocks specified accounts and groups from signing in as a batch job. Overrides the Log on as a batch job policy
Deny log on as a service	When assigned, blocks service accounts from registering a process as a service. Overrides the Log on as a service policy. Does not apply to Local System, Local Service, or Network Service accounts
Deny log on locally	When assigned, blocks accounts from signing on locally. This policy overrides the allow log on locally policy
Deny log on through Remote Desktop Services	When assigned, blocks accounts from signing in by using Remote Desktop Services. This policy overrides the allow sign on through Remote Desktop Services policy
Enable computer and user accounts to be trusted for delegation	Determines whether you can configure the Trusted For Delegation setting on a user or a computer object
Force shutdown from a remote system	Accounts assigned this right are allowed to shut down computers from remote locations on the network
Generate security audits	Determines which accounts can use processes to add items to the security log. Because this right allows interaction with the security log, it presents a security risk when you assign this to a user account

Impersonate a client after authentication	Allows apps running on behalf of a user to impersonate a client. This right can be a security risk and you should assign it only to trusted users
Increase a process working set	Accounts assigned this right can increase or decrease the number of memory pages visible to the process in RAM
Increase scheduling priority	Accounts assigned this right can change the scheduling priority of a process
Load and unload device drivers	Accounts assigned this right can dynamically load and unload device drivers into kernel mode. This right is separate from the right to load and unload Plug and Play drivers. Assigning this right is a security risk because it grants access to the kernel mode
Lock pages in memory	Accounts assigned this right can use a process to keep data stored in physical memory, blocking that data from being paged to virtual memory
Log on as a batch job	Accounts assigned this right can be signed in to the computer by means of a batch-queue facility. This right is only relevant to older versions of the Windows operating system, and you should not use it with newer versions, such as Windows 10 and Windows Server 2016
Log on as a service	Allows a security principal to sign in as a service. You need to assign this right to any service that is configured to use a user account, rather than one of the built-in service accounts
Manage auditing and security log	Users assigned this right can configure object access auditing options for resources such as files and AD DS objects. Users assigned this right can also view events in the security log and clear the security log. Because attackers are likely to clear the security log as a way of hiding their tracks, you should not assign this right to user accounts that would not normally be assigned local Administrator permissions on a computer
Modify an object label	Users assigned this right can modify the integrity level of objects, including files, registry keys, or processes owned by other users
Modify firmware environment values	Determines which users can modify firmware environment variables. This policy is used primarily for modifying the boot configuration settings of Itanium-based computers
Perform volume maintenance tasks	Determines which accounts can perform maintenance tasks on a volume. Assigning this right is a security risk as it might allow access to data stored on the volume
Profile single process	Determines which accounts can leverage performance monitoring tools to monitor non-system processes
Profile system performance	Determines which accounts can leverage performance monitoring tools to monitor system processes
Remove computer from docking station	When assigned, user account can undock a portable computer from a docking station without signing in

Replace a process level token	When assigned, account can call the CreateProcessAsUser API so that one service can trigger another
Restore files and directories	Allows users assigned this right the ability to bypass permissions on files, directories, and the registry so that they can overwrite these objects with restored data. This right represents a security risk as a user account assigned this right can overwrite registry settings, and replacing existing permissions
Shut down the system	Assigns the ability for a locally signed in user to shut down the operating system
Synchronize directory service data	Assigns the ability to synchronize AD DS data
Take ownership of files or other objects	When assigned, account can take ownership of any securable object, including AD DS objects, files, folders, registry keys, processes, and threads. Represents a security risk because it allows assigned user the ability to take control of any securable object

Account security options

There are additional security options that you should consider configuring for highly privileged accounts. These include configuring the following settings:

- **Logon Hours**. Use this setting to configure when users can use an account. AD DS does not authenticate someone attempting to sign in outside of these hours. By default, accounts are configured so that users can sign in at all times. Consider configuring privileged accounts so that users can use them only at specific times. This stops someone signing in after hours, either specifically or with a compromised account, to get up to no good when they assume that no one is watching. Organizations that do need to use a privileged account to perform after hour maintenance tasks can create special accounts for that task, or temporarily modify an existing account.

- **Logon Workstations**. Use this setting to limit the computers that a particular account can sign in to. By default, users can use an account to sign in to any computer in the domain. Use this setting to ensure that users can use privileged accounts only on specific, specially configured administrative workstations, or certain servers. Limiting which computers' users can use an account reduces the scope of where that account can be used.

- **Password Never Expires**. Use this setting reluctantly to configure this option for privileged accounts because it absolves the account from the domain password policy. You can use products such as Microsoft Identity Manager to assist with password management for privileged accounts.

- **Smart Card Is Required For Interactive Logon**. Use this setting to ensure that a smart card must be present for the account sign-in to occur. In high security environments, you should deploy smart cards and enable this option to ensure that only an authorized person, who has both the smart card and the account credentials, can use the privileged account.

- **Account Is Sensitive And Cannot Be Delegated**. Use this setting to ensure that trusted applications cannot forward the account credentials to other services or computers on the network. Enable this setting for highly privileged accounts.

- **This Account Supports Kerberos AES 256 Bit Encryption**. Use this setting to allow Kerberos AES 256-bit encryption. Where possible, you would configure this option for privileged accounts and have them use this form of Kerberos encryption over the AES 128-bit encryption option.

- **Account Expires**. Use this setting to configure an expiration date for an account. Configuring privileged accounts with expiration dates ensures that privileged accounts do not remain in AD DS after they are no longer in use.

When you join a computer to a domain for the first time, it creates a computer account in the Computers container. If you want to create an account in a specific container, you'll need to pre-stage the computer account and place it in the appropriate OU. A pre-staged computer account must have a name that matches that of the computer that is joining the domain.

Computer accounts can be made members of the domain security group. This group membership influences how the Local System and Network Service accounts on the computer function. This is because, by default, these services use the computer's credentials when interacting with resources on the network. This gives the computer account the rights and privileges assigned to any security group that the computer is a member of.

Computer accounts have automatically assigned passwords that are updated every 30 days. If a computer doesn't connect to a domain within 30 days, a new password is assigned the next time a connection is established. If you disable a computer account, the computer cannot connect to the domain and domain users are unable to sign onto the computer until the account is re-enabled.

Resetting a computer account removes the relationship between the computer and the domain. To fix this, you'll need to either join the computer back to the domain, or reestablish the broken trust relationship using the following PowerShell command, specifying the credentials of a member of the Domain Administrator group:

```
Test-ComputerSecureChannel -credential <domain>\<admin> -Repair
```

If you delete a computer account, it's necessary to rejoin the computer to the domain manually. When you delete a computer account, all information associated with the account is removed from Active Directory. You should only ever delete computer accounts once a computer has been decommissioned.

CHAPTER 18

Service accounts

Service accounts allow services running on a computer to interact with the operating system as well as resources on the network. Windows Server 2016 uses three types of built-in service accounts, each of which is suitable for a specific set of circumstances. These accounts are as follows:

- The Local System (NT AUTHORITY\SYSTEM) account has privileges that are equivalent to those assigned to a user account that is a member of the local Administrators group on the computer. A service that uses this account can act by using the computer account's credentials when interacting with other resources on the network.

- The Local Service (NT AUTHORITY\LocalService) account has privileges that are equivalent to those assigned to a user account that is a member of the local Users group on the computer. A service that uses this account can access resources on the network without credentials. You use this account when a service does not need to interact with resources on the network and does not need local Administrator privileges on the computer on which it is running.

- The Network Service (NT AUTHORITY\NetworkService) account has privileges that are equivalent to those assigned to a user account that is a member of the local Users group on the computer. A service that uses this account accesses resources on the network by using the computer account's credentials.

In the past when you've needed to create a custom service account, you've probably created a user account and then assigned it an appropriate set of permissions. The challenge with this type of account is password management. Many organizations configuring custom service accounts with passwords that never expire.

A Group Managed Service Account (gMSA) is a special type of account that has AD DS manage its password. The password of a gMSA is updated every 30 days. You don't need to know the password of a gMSA, even when configuring a service to use that password because gMSA accounts provide you with a domain based service account identity without all the hassle of service account password management.

You can only use a gMSA if the forest is running at the Windows Server 2012 functional level or higher. Y0ou also have to have deployed the master root key for AD DS. You can deploy the master root key by running the following command using an account that is a member of the Enterprise Admins group:

```
Add-KdsRootKey -EffectiveTime ((get-date).addhours(-10))
```

You create the gMSA using the New-ADServiceAccount cmdlet. When creating the account you specify a hostname as well as service principle names. These should be associated with the purpose for which you are creating the gMSA. For example, to create a new gMSA with the name called SYD-SVC1 that is associated with the hostname SYD-SVC1.adatum.com, run the command:

```
New-ADServiceAccount SYD-SVC1 -DNSHOSTNAME SYD-SVC1.adatum.com
```

gMSAs are stored in the Managed Service Accounts container, which you can view using Active Directory Administrative Center, as shown in Figure 18-2.

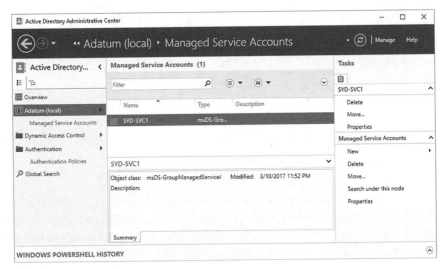

FIGURE 18-2 Managed Service Accounts container

Once the gMSA is created, you need to configure permissions for specific computers to be able to install and use the account. The simplest way to do this is to create a security group, and then use the Set-ADSeviceAccount cmdlet to assign the group permissions to the account. You then add computers to the group. For example, to allow computers in the group SYD-SVRS to use the gMSA SYD-SVC1, run the command:

```
Set-ADServiceAccount -Identity SYD-SVC1 -PrincipalsAllowedToRetrieveManagedPassword
SYD-SVRS
```

Once you've added a computer to the group that you've given permission to retrieve the account, you can install the account on the computer using the Install-ADServiceAccount cmdlet. Once the account is installed, you can assign it to a service by setting the log on as service, as shown in Figure 18-3. You only need to specify the account name, and can browse to the account. You don't need to specify the password setting because the password is managed by Active Directory.

CHAPTER 18

FIGURE 18-3 Protected Users group

A virtual account is the computer local equivalent of a group Managed Service Account. You can create a virtual account by editing the properties of a service and setting the account name to NT SERVICE\<ServiceName>. As with a gMSA, you don't need to specify a password because this is managed automatically by the operating system.

MORE INFO   GROUP MANAGED SERVICE ACCOUNTS

You can learn more about Group Managed Service Accounts at *https://technet.microsoft. com/en-us/library/jj128431(v=ws.11).aspx.*

Protected accounts

The Protected Users group, shown in Figure 18-4, provides you with a method of protecting highly privileged user accounts from being compromised. It does this by blocking the use of less secure security and authentication options.

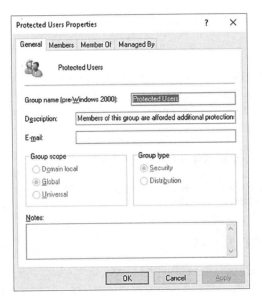

FIGURE 18-4 Protected Users group

For example, credentials are not cached if an account that is a member of this group signs on to a computer running Windows 8.1, Windows 10, Windows Server 2012 R2, or Windows Server 2016. Additionally, accounts that are members of this group cannot use the following security options:

- Default credential delegation (CredSSP)

- Windows Digest

- NTLM – NTOWF

- Kerberos long term keys

- Sign-on offline

If the domain functional level is Windows Server 2012 R2 or higher, user accounts that are members of the Protected Users group cannot:

- Use NT LAN Manager (NTLM) for authentication.

- Use DES for Kerberos pre-authentication.

- Use RC4 cipher suites for Kerberos pre-authentication.

- Be delegated using constrained delegation.

CHAPTER 18

- Be delegated using unconstrained delegation.

- Renew user tickets (TGTs) past the initial 240-minute lifetime.

Only user accounts should be added to the Protected Users group. You should not add computer accounts or service accounts to this group. In secure environments, all privileged accounts should be members of this group, with exceptions only occurring when specific incompatibilities arise that cannot be resolved in another way.

MORE INFO   PROTECTED USERS SECURITY GROUP

You can learn more about the Protected Users Security group at *https://technet.micro-soft.com/en-us/library/dn466518(v=ws.11).aspx*.

Authentication policies and silos

Authentication policy silos allow you to define relationships between the user, computer, and managed service accounts. A user, computer, and managed service account can only belong to a single authentication policy silo. This provides a more robust method, beyond configuring logon restrictions, and restricting which accounts can access specific servers in your environment.

Accounts in an authentication policy silo are associated with a silo claim. You can use this silo claim to control access to claims-aware resources. For example, you can configure accounts so that only accounts that are associated with a specific silo claim are able to access particularly sensitive servers. With this, only accounts that are associated with a Certificate Services silo claim are able to sign on to a computer that has the Active Directory Certificate Services role installed.

Authentication policies allow you to configure settings, such as TGT lifetime and access control conditions, which specify conditions that must be met before a user can sign in to a computer. For example, you might configure an authentication policy that specifies a TGT lifetime of 120 minutes and limit a user account so that users can only use it with specific devices, such as privileged access workstations. You can only use Authentication policies if you have configured the domain functional level at the Windows Server 2012 R2 or higher functional level.

You configure Authentication Policies and Authentication Policy Silos using Active Directory Administrative Center, as shown in Figure 18-5.

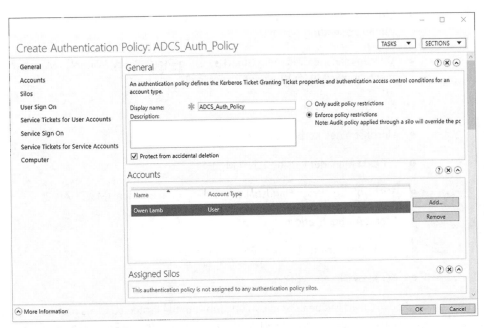

FIGURE 18-5 Authentication policies

> **MORE INFO   AUTHENTICATION POLICIES AND SILOS**
>
> You can learn more about authentication policies and silos at *https://technet.microsoft. com/en-us/library/dn486813(v=ws.11).aspx.*

Credential Guard

Credential Guard is a feature new to Windows Server 2016 and Windows 10 that allows you to leverage virtualization-based security to isolate secrets, such as cached user credentials, in a special separate virtualized operating system. The special separate virtualized operating system is configured so that only specific processes and memory in the host operating system can access this secret data. The processes running in the separate virtualized operating system are termed trustlets.

Credential Guard is primarily a response to pass-the-hash or pass-the-ticket attacks. Should a host that has credential guard be compromised by an attacker, that attacker won't be able to successfully run a pass-the-hash attack tool to extract cached credentials and then use them to access other computers on the network.

Credential guard includes the following features and solutions:

- Stores derived domain credentials in a virtualized environment that is protected from the running operating system.

- You can manage Credential Guard by using Group Policy, Windows Management Instrumentation (WMI), or Windows PowerShell.

Credential Guard does not allow:

- Unconstrained Kerberos delegation

- NT LAN Manager version 1 (NTLMv1)

- Microsoft Challenge Handshake Authentication Protocol (MS-CHAPv2)

- Digest Authentication

- Credential Security Support Provider (CredSSP)

- Kerberos DES encryption

Credential Guard can be used in conjunction with the Protected Users group in a layered approach to the protection of highly privileged accounts. The Protected Users group remains useful because your organization may not have computers that support Credential Guard. You can deploy Credential Guard only on computers that meet certain hardware requirements. Credential Guard is primarily useful for Privileged Access Workstations, but you should implement it eventually on any computer where IT operations personnel use privileged domain accounts.

Credential Guard has the following requirements:

- Windows Server 2016 or Windows 10 Enterprise

- UEFI firmware version 2.3.1 or higher

- Secure Boot

- Intel VT-x or AMD-V virtualization extensions

- Second Level Address Translation

- x64 processor architecture

- A VT-d or AMD-Vi IOMMU input/output memory management unit

- TPM 1.2 or 2.0

- Secure firmware update process

- Firmware updated to support Secure MOR implementation

To enable Credential Guard on an appropriately configured computer, you need to configure the Turn On Virtualization Based Security policy, which is located in the Computer Configuration\Administrative Templates\System\Device Guard node of a GPO. This is the same policy that you also use to configure Device Guard, which you learn about later in this chapter.

While configuring this policy, you must first set the policy to Enabled, and then you must set the platform security level to either Secure Boot or to Secure Boot and DMA Protection. Secure Boot with DMA Protection ensures that Credential Guard is used with Direct Memory Access protection.

Once this is done, you need to then set the Credential Guard Configuration option to Enabled with UEFI lock, or Enabled without lock. If you set the Enabled with UEFI lock, credential guard cannot be remotely disabled and can only be disabled by having someone with local Administrator privileges sign on and disable credential guard configuration locally. The Enabled Without Lock option allows Credential Guard to be remotely disabled.

MORE INFO   CREDENTIAL GUARD

You can learn more about Credential Guard at *https://blogs.technet.microsoft.com/ash/2016/03/02/windows-10-device-guard-and-credential-guard-demystified/*.

Just Enough Administration

Just Enough Administration (JEA) allows you to implement Role Based Access Control (RBAC) functionality through Windows PowerShell remoting. JEA allows you to specify which Power-Shell cmdlets and functions can be used when connected to a specific endpoint. You can go further and specify which parameters within those cmdlets and functions are authorized and even specify which values can be used with those parameters.

For example, you could create a JEA endpoint where a user is able to run the Restart-Service command, but only where the Name parameter is set to DHCPServer. This would allow the user to restart the DHCPServer on the computer they connected to, but not restart any other service on the computer.

You can also configure a JEA endpoint to allow other command line commands to be run, such as whoami.exe, though the drawback of this is that you don't have the same level of control when restricting how that command can be run.

JEA endpoints can leverage virtual accounts. This means that activities performed on the computer through the endpoint use a special temporary virtual account rather than the user's account. This temporary virtual account has local Administrator privileges, but is constrained to only using the cmdlets, functions, parameters, and values defined by JEA. The benefits of this include:

- The user's credentials are not stored on the remote system. If the remote system is compromised, the user's credentials are not subject to credential theft and cannot be used to traverse the network to gain access to other hosts.

- The user account used to connect to the endpoint does not need to be privileged. The endpoint simply needs to be configured to allow connections from specified user accounts.

- The virtual account is limited to the system on which it is hosted. The virtual account cannot be used to connect to remote systems. Attackers cannot use a compromised virtual account to access other protected servers.

- The virtual account has local administrator privileges, but is limited to performing only the activities defined by JEA. You have the option of configuring the virtual account with the membership of a group other than the local administrators group, to further reduce privileges.

JEA works on Windows Server 2016 and Windows 10, version 1511 or later directly. It also functions on previous versions of Windows client and server as long as Windows Management 5.0 is installed. Virtual accounts are not available when using JEA on Windows 7 or Windows 2008 R2 and all activities are performed using the privileges assigned to the account connecting to the JEA endpoint.

Inside OUT

JEA drawbacks

The biggest drawback to JEA is the amount of time that it takes to configure. You'll need to customize each JEA endpoint, which requires that you understand exactly which cmdlets, functions, parameters, and values are required to perform specific tasks. The other drawback of JEA is that it relies upon administrative tasks being performed using the command line. While most Windows Server administrators are comfortable performing tasks using PowerShell, some may be reluctant to be placed in a position where they can only use PowerShell for specific tasks rather than falling back on the RSAT consoles.

Role-capability files

A role-capability file is a special file that allows you to specify what tasks can be performed when connected to a JEA endpoint. Only tasks that are explicitly allowed in the role-capability file can be performed.

You can create a new blank role-capability file by using the New-PSRoleCapabilityFile cmdlet. Role-capability files use the .psrc extension. For example, to create a new role capability file for a role that allows someone to manage a DNS server, run the command:

```
New-PSRoleCapabilityFile -Path .\DNSOps.psrc
```

Inside OUT

Authoring JEA

When creating JEA configurations, it usually makes sense to put them in their own folders. For example, creating a DNSOps folder to store all the files related to configuring the DNSOps JEA configuration.

Once the .psrc file is created, you edit the role capability file and add the cmdlets, functions, and external commands that are available when a user is connected to the endpoint. You can allow entire Windows PowerShell cmdlets or functions, or list which parameters and parameter values can be used.

You can edit a role capability file in PowerShell ISE as shown in Figure 18-6. Editing the file involves commenting out the appropriate sections and filling them in with the configuration items that you want to set.

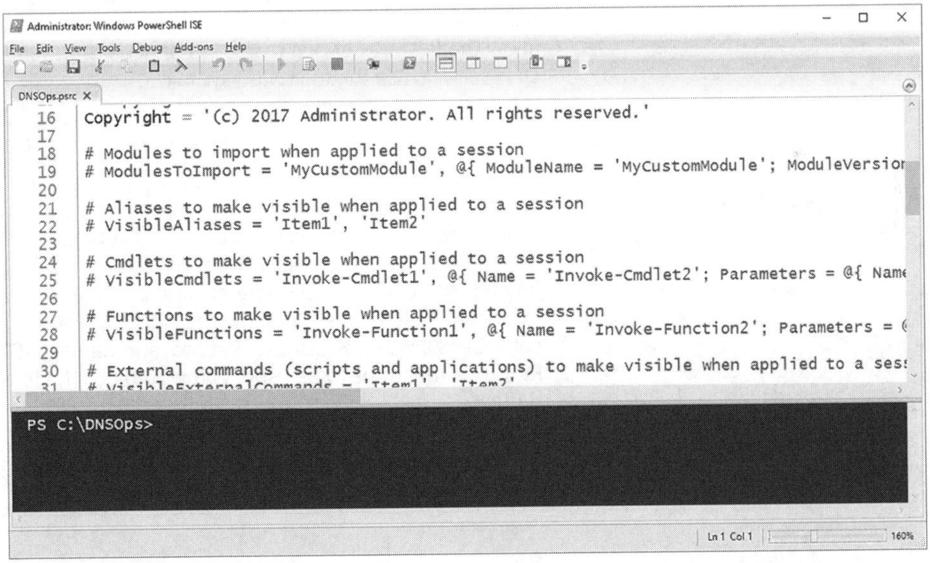

FIGURE 18-6 JEA role capability file

Inside OUT

Cmdlets, functions, and aliases

Authoring role capability files is one of those few times when you need to know whether something in PowerShell is a cmdlet or is a function. Mostly people refer to commands in PowerShell as cmdlets, but some are actually functions and others are aliases. You need to know the appropriate type when configuring a role capability file because if you put a function in as an allowed cmdlet, you won't get the expected result. You can figure out which designation is appropriate using the Get-Command cmdlet.

Table 18-2 describes the different options that you can configure in a role capability file.

Table 18-2 Role capability files

Capability	Description
ModulesToImport	JEA auto-loads standard modules, so you probably don't need to use this unless you need to import custom modules
VisibleAliases	Specify which aliases to make available in the JEA session. Even if an aliased cmdlet is available, the alias won't be unless it's here

VisibleCmdlets	Lists which Windows PowerShell cmdlets are available in the session. You can extend this by allowing all parameters and parameter values to be used or you can limit cmdlets to particular parameters and parameter values. For example, if you wanted to allow the Restart-Service cmdlet to only be used to restart the DNS service, use the following syntax:
	
	`VisibleCmdlets = @{ Name = 'Restart-Service';`
	`Parameters = @{ Name='Name'; ValidateSet =`
	`'DNS'}}`

VisibleFunctions	This field lists which Windows PowerShell functions are available in the session. You can choose to list functions, allowing all parameters and parameter values to be used, or you can limit functions to particular parameters and parameter values. For example, if you wanted to allow the Add-DNSServerResourceRecord, Get-DNSServerResourceRecord, and Remove-DNSServer-Resource functions to be used, you would use the following syntax:
	
	`VisibleFunctions = 'Add-DNSServerResourceRe-`
	`cord', 'Get-DNSServerResourceRecord','Remove-`
	`DNSServerResourceRecord'`

VisibleExternalCommands	This field allows users who are connected to the session to run external commands. For example, you can use this field to allow access to c:\windows\system32\whoami.exe so that users connected to the JEA session can identify their security context by using the following syntax:
	
	`VisibleExternalCommands = 'C:\Windows\System32\`
	`whoami.exe'`

VisibleProviders	This field lists Windows PowerShell providers that are visible to the session
ScriptsToProcess	This field allows you to configure Windows PowerShell scripts to run automatically when the session is started
AliasDefinitions	This field allows you to define Windows PowerShell aliases for the JEA session
FunctionDefinitions	This field allows you to define Windows PowerShell functions for the JEA session
VariableDefinitions	This field allows you to define Windows PowerShell variables for the JEA session
EnvironmentVariables	This field allows you to specify environment variables for the JEA session
TypesToProcess	This field allows you to configure Windows PowerShell type files to load for the JEA session
FormatsToProcess	This field allows you to configure Windows PowerShell formats to load for the JEA session
AssembliesToLoad	This field allows you to specify which assemblies to load for the JEA session

Session-configuration files

Session-configuration files determine which role capabilities are mapped to specific security groups. For example, if you wanted to allow only members of the CONTOS\DNSOps security group to connect to the JEA endpoint that is defined by the DNSOps role capability file, you would configure this in the session configuration file.

You use the New-PSSessionConfigurationFile cmdlet to create a session configuration file. These files use the .pssc extension. For example, to create a new session configuration file for the DNSOps role, run the following command:

```
New-PSSessionConfigurationFile -Path .\DNSOps.pssc -Full
```

Session configuration files have elements described in Table 18-3:

CHAPTER 18

Table 18-3 Session configuration files

Field	Explanation
SessionType	This field allows you to configure the session's default settings. If you set this to RestrictedRemoteServer, you can use the Get-Command, Get-FormatData, Select-Object, Get-Help, Measure-Object, Exit-PSSession, Clear-Host, and Out-Default cmdlets. The session execution policy is set to RemoteSigned. Example: `SessionType = 'RestrictedRemoteServer'`

RoleDefinitions	You use the RoleDefinitions entry to assign role capabilities to specific security groups. These groups do not need to have any privileges and can be standard security groups.
	Example:
	
	`RoleDefinitions =@{'CONTOSO\DNSOps' = @`
	`{RoleCapabilities='DNSOps'}}`

RunAsVirtualAc-count	When enabled, this field allows JEA to use a privileged virtual account created just for the JEA session. This virtual account has local Administrators privileges on member servers, and is member of the Domain Admins group on a Domain Controller. Use this option to ensure that credentials are not cached on the server that hosts the endpoint. Remember that you can configure the virtual account to be a member of groups other than the local Administrators group
TranscriptDirec-tory	This field allows you to specify the location where JEA activity transcripts are stored
RunAsVirtualAc-countGroups	If you do not want the virtual account to be a member of the local Administrators group (or Domain Admins on a domain controller) you can instead use this field to specify the groups in which the virtual account is a member

JEA endpoints

A JEA endpoint is a Windows PowerShell endpoint that you configure so that only specific authenticated users can connect to it. When those users do connect, they only have access to the Windows PowerShell cmdlets, parameters, and values defined by the appropriate session-configuration file that links security groups and role capabilities. When you use endpoints with virtual accounts, the actual activity that a user performs on the server that hosts the endpoint occurs using the virtual account. This means that no domain-based administrative credentials are stored on the server that hosts the endpoint.

A server can have multiple JEA endpoints, and each JEA endpoint can be used for a different administrative task. For example, a DNSOps endpoint to perform DNS administrative tasks and an IISOps endpoint to perform Internet Information Server related administrative tasks. Users do not have to have privileged accounts that are members of groups such as the local Adminis-trators group to connect to an endpoint. Once connected, users have the privileges assigned to the virtual account configured in the session-configuration file.

Inside OUT

Non-privileged groups

JEA lets you provide IT Ops staff with administrative privileges on specific computers without adding them to traditional privileged groups such as the Domain Admins or Enterprise Admins group.

You create JEA endpoints by using the Register-PSSessionConfiguration cmdlet. When using this cmdlet, you specify an endpoint name and a session-configuration file hosted on the local machine.

For example, to create the endpoint DNSOps using the DNSOps.pssc session-configuration file, enact the following command and then restart the WinRM service:

```
Register-PSSessionConfiguration -Name DNSOps -Path .\DNSOps.pssc
```

You can use the Get-PSSessionConfigurationFile to determine which endpoints are present on a computer. A user wanting to connect to a JEA session endpoint uses the Enter-PSSession cmdlet with the ConfigurationName parameter. For example, to connect to the DNSOps JEA endpoint on server MEL-DNS1, you would use the command:

```
Enter-PSSession -ComputerName MEL-DNS1 -ConfigurationName DNSOps
```

Once you've verified that JEA works, you'll need to lock down the default PowerShell endpoint. By default, only members of the local Administrators group can connect to this default end-point, and if you've implemented JEA properly, this group shouldn't need to have very many members anyway.

MORE INFO   JUST ENOUGH ADMINISTRATION

You can learn more about JEA *at https://aka.ms/JEA.*

CHAPTER 18

Enhanced Security Administrative Environment forest

Enhanced Security Administrative Environment (ESAE) forests are an approach to Active Directory privileged access design in which you deploy a dedicated administrative Active Directory forest to host privileged accounts, privileged groups, and privileged access workstations for a production forest. In this design, the ESAE forest is configured with a one-way trust relationship with a production forest. A one-way trust relationship means that accounts from the ESAE forest can be used in the production forest, but that accounts in the production forest cannot be used in the ESAE forest.

The production forest is the Active Directory forest in which an organization's day-to-day activities occur. You configure the production forest so that administrative tasks in the production forest can only be performed by using accounts that the ESAE forest hosts.

The ESAE forest design provides the following benefits:

- **Locked-down accounts**. A standard non-privileged user account in the ESAE forest can be configured as highly privileged user account in the production forest. For example, you make a standard user account in the ESAE forest a member of the Domain Admins group in a domain in the production forest. You can lock down the standard user account hosted in the ESAE forest so that it cannot sign on to hosts in the ESAE forest and can only be used to sign on to hosts in the production forest. Should the account be compromised, the attacker cannot use that account to perform administrative tasks in the ESAE forest.

- **Selective authentication**. ESAE forest design allows you to leverage a trust relationship's selective authentication feature. For example, you can configure sign-ins from the ESAE forest so that they can only occur on specific hosts in the production forest. One strategy is to configure selective authentication so that privileged accounts can only be used on privileged access workstations or jump servers in the production forest.

- **Simple way to improve security**. ESAE forest design provides substantive improvement in the security of existing production forests without requiring complete rebuilding of the production environment. The ESAE forest approach has a small hardware/software footprint and only affects IT Operations team users. In this design, standard user accounts remain hosted in the production forest. Only privileged administrative accounts are hosted in the ESAE forest. As part of the transition to the ESAE forest model, you eventually remove almost all privileged accounts that are native to the production forest. Because they are hosted in a separate forest, privileged administrative accounts can be subject to more stringent security requirements than standard user accounts in the production forest.

Inside OUT

Failsafe admin account

With an ESAE forest design, you should remove almost all privileged accounts from the production forest as possible. You should leave a failsafe admin account in the production forest that allows you to fix things should everything go pear shaped, but this admin account should be given an insanely long and complex password that's stored securely in a safe that someone who is not a member of the IT operations staff has access to and only be used as a last resort.

An ESAE forest design should have the following properties:

- Limit the function of the ESAE forest to hosting accounts of administrative users for the production forest.

- Do not deploy applications or additional resources in the ESAE forest. An exception to this is when you deploy technologies such as MIM, which is used to increase security when implementing PAM.

- The ESAE forest should be a single-domain Active Directory forest. The ESAE forest only hosts a small number of accounts that need to have strict security policies applied.

- Only use one-way trusts. You should only configure a one-way trust where the production forest trusts the ESAE forest. This means that accounts from the ESAE forest can be used in the production forest, but that accounts from the production forest cannot be used in the ESAE forest. Accounts used for administrative tasks in the production forest should be standard user accounts in the ESAE forest. If an account is compromised in the production forest, it cannot be used to elevate privileges in the ESAE forest.

Configure ESAE forest servers in the following ways:

- Validate installation media. Use the available checksums to validate that the media hasn't been modified.

- All servers should run the most recent version of the Windows Server operating system.

- Servers should be updated automatically with security updates.

- Security compliance manager baselines should be used as the starting point for server configuration.

- Servers should be configured with secure boot, BitLocker volume encryption, credential guard, and device guide.

- Servers should be configured to block access to USB storage.

- Servers should be on isolated networks. Inbound and outbound Internet connections should be blocked.

MORE INFO   SECURING PRIVILEGED ACCESS

You can learn more about securing privileged access at *https://technet.micro-soft.com/en-us/windows-server-docs/security/securing-privileged-access/securing-privileged-access-reference-material.*

Privileged Access Management

Privileged Access Management (PAM), also known as Just In Time (JIT) Administration, works on the concept that users can be granted permission for a finite amount of time rather than per-manently. It uses temporary membership of a security group that has been delegated privileges, rather than permanent membership of a security group that has been delegated privileges, to accomplish this goal.

For example, a user named Rooslan requires that his password be reset and submits a ticket to Oksana, who works at the service desk, to have Oksana perform this task. In a traditional environment, Oksana would use an account that is a member of a security group that has been delegated the reset-password privilege. In a PAM environment, Oksana requests the privilege to change Rooslan's user account password. The PAM process adds Oksana's user account temporarily to a group that has been delegated the reset password privilege on Rooslan's user account. Oksana then reset's Rooslan's user account password. After a certain period of time has elapsed, the PAM process removes Oksana's account from this group, removing the reset-password privilege for Rooslan's user account from Oksana's user account.

Privileges are assigned temporarily rather than permanently. Rather than assigning the IT Operations team privileged accounts, the IT Operations team members have standard accounts that are assigned privileges only when those privileges are required. PAM can be configured so that privileges are assigned when requested, assigned only after approval has been sought and granted, or a mixture of these methods depending on which privilege is being requested. For example, requesting permission to reset the password of a non-privileged user account might occur automatically whereas permission to add a domain controller to the domain might require approval.

PAM benefits

When properly implemented, PAM can provide the following security improvements:

- You can configure your environment so that all accounts that the IT Operations team use are standard user accounts. Privileges are only granted to these accounts after being requested and approved and are temporary. If a user account used by a member of the IT Operations team becomes compromised, the attacker gains no additional privileges beyond those assigned to a standard user account because any privileges that the account might hold are only ever assigned on a temporary basis.

- All requests for privileges are logged. In high-security environments, privilege use can be further tracked, with the activities of a user account granted temporary privileges written to a log file.

Once privileges are granted, a user needs to establish a new session, by opening a new Windows PowerShell session, or by signing out and signing in again to leverage the new group memberships configured for their account.

PAM components

A PAM deployment consists of the following elements:

- **Administrative forest**. An ESAE forest in which you have deployed Microsoft Identity Manager (MIM) 2016. Accounts from this forest are used to perform administrative tasks.

- **A production forest**. This is the forest that hosts the resources used on a daily basis by the organization.

- **Shadow principals**. A shadow principal is a copy of an account or group that exists in the production or source forest. Shadow security groups that are used in PAM use a process called SID History mirroring. SID History mirroring allows the shadow security group in the administrative forest to have the security identifier of the security group in the production or source forest. When a user is added to a PAM role, MIM adds the user's shadow account in the administrative forest to the shadow group in the administrative forest. When the user logs in by using this account, their Kerberos token then includes a security identifier that matches the security identifier of the original group from the production forest. This functionally makes the user a member of the group that the shadow group is mirroring.

- **PAM Client**. This client includes a collection of Windows PowerShell cmdlets or a custom solution that interacts with the PAM REST API to allow a PAM user to query and interact with the MIM PAM functionality. The PAM client is only required on computers where it is necessary to request access to a PAM role.

- **MIM Service**. The MIM server manages the privileged account management process, including adding and removing shadow principals from shadow groups when a PAM role is granted and when it expires.

- **MIM Portal**. The MIM Portal is a SharePoint site. It provides management and configuration functionality. For example, IT Operations users can sign on to this site to request privileges.

- **MIM Service Database**. The MIM service database can be hosted on SQL Server 2012, SQL Server 2014, or SQL Server 2016. This database holds configuration and identity information that the MIM Service uses.

- **PAM Component Service**. Manages the role-expiration process, removing the shadow account from the shadow group in the administrative forest.

- **PAM Monitoring Service**. Monitors the production forest and duplicates changes to the administrative forest or the MIM service.

- **PAM REST API**. Can be used to enable a custom client to interact with PAM.

PAM users and groups

You use the New-PAMUser cmdlet, available when you install Microsoft Identity Manager, to create a shadow user. When doing this, an existing PAM created trust relationship between the ESAE forest and the production must exist. You must also specify the source domain and source account name. For example, to create a new shadow user based on the Oksana account in the Adatum.com domain, you would use the following command:

```
New-PAMUser -SourceDomain adatum.com -SourceAccountName Oksana
```

You use the New-PAMGroup cmdlet, available when you install Microsoft Identity Manager, to create a shadow group. When creating a shadow group, you need to specify the source group name, the source domain, and a source domain controller in the source domain. For example, to create a new shadow group for the CorpAdmins group in the Adatum.com domain by using the mel-dc1.adatum.com domain controller, issue the following command:

```
New-PAMGroup -SourceGroupName "CorpAdmins" -SourceDomain adatum.com -SourceDC mel-dc1.
adatum.com
```

PAM roles

A PAM role represents the privileged role to be requested. For example, you might configure a specific PAM role for performing password resets or another for configuring Active Directory Certificate Services. You can configure PAM role settings by viewing the properties of the PAM role in the MIM web interface. A PAM role consists of the following options:

- **Display Name**. This is the name of the PAM role.

- **PAM Privileges**. This is a list of security groups that a user that is granted access to the role is temporarily added to. This does not list the privileges actually assigned to this group. For example, if you delegate the Reset User Password privilege to the CorpAdmins group, this dialog box does not indicate that this privilege has been delegated. This dialog box also lists the name of the shadow principal rather than the group in the original domain.

- **PAM Tole TTL(sec)**. This is the maximum amount of time that the member can be granted this role. The default is 3600 seconds (1 hour). You should configure the maximum lifetime for a Kerberos user ticket in line with the Time to Live (TTL) value to ensure that a user's ticket is updated to reflect the change in group membership after the PAM Role TTL expires.

- **MFA Enabled**. MIM's PAM functionality can be integrated with Azure Multi-Factor Authentication. When you enable this option, requests for a PAM role require two forms of authentication. This second form of authentication can include a text message or a telephone call to a registered number. When a text message is sent, the requesting user must enter the code sent to them. When a telephone call is made, the user must enter a PIN that they have previously configured.

- **Approval Required**. PAM roles can be configured so that PAM role membership is only granted if a PAM administrator approves the request. You configure PAM administrators by adding a user to the PAM Admins set. This can be done through the Sets section under Management Policy Rules in the MIM web console.

- **Availability Window Enabled**. When you configure an availability window for a role, the PAM role can only be used during certain hours. This provides an additional layer of security for a PAM role. For example, you might configure a role that allows modification to sensitive groups to only be used during business hours.

- **Description**. Use this option to provide a description of the PAM role.

Inside OUT

PAM and JEA

With JEA, you limit who can access a JEA endpoint on the basis of security group membership. With PAM you add user accounts to security groups on a temporary rather than an ongoing basis. You can combine PAM with JEA to allow users to only connect to JEA endpoints for a limited amount of time and to only be able to do so after they have explicitly requested access to a specific JEA endpoint.

MORE INFO   PRIVILEGED ACCESS MANAGEMENT

You can learn more about this subject at
https://docs.microsoft.com/en-us/microsoft-identity-manager/pam/
privileged-identity-management-for-active-directory-domain-services.

Local Administrator Password Solution

Local Administrator Password Solution (LAPS) is a tool that you can use to manage the passwords of local administrator accounts of each domain joined computer in your environment. LAPS allows you to avoid the problem present in many environments of there being a default local Administrator account password that never expires and is common to every computer in the domain. LAPS provides the following benefits:

- Local administrator passwords are unique on each computer managed by LAPS.

- Local administrator passwords are randomized and changed on a regular basis.

- LAPS stores local administrator passwords and secrets securely within AD DS.

- Access to passwords and secrets is controlled by configurable permissions.

- Passwords retrieved by LAPS are transmitted to the client in a secure encrypted manner.

You install the LAPS agent on each computer that you wish to manage. The LAPS agent is then managed through a Group Policy Client Side Extension. Installing LAPS requires an update to the Active Directory schema. You perform this update by running the Update-AdmPwdAD-Schema cmdlet, which is included in a PowerShell module made available when you install LAPS on a computer. To run this update, the account running the cmdlet must be a member of the Schema Admins group and this cmdlet should be run on a computer that is in the same Active Directory site as the computer that holds the Schema Master role for the forest.

When a group policy refresh occurs, LAPS does the following:

- LAPS checks if the password of the local Administrator account has expired.

- If the password hasn't expired, LAPS does nothing.

- If the password has expired, LAPS performs the following steps:
  - Changes the local Administrator password to a new random value based on the configured parameters for local Administrator passwords.
  - Transmits the new password to AD DS, where it is stored in a special confidential attribute associated with the computer account of the computer that has had its local Administrator Account password updated.

- ▪ Transmits the new password expiration date to AD DS, where it is stored in a special confidential attribute associated with the computer account of the computer that has had its local Administrator account password updated.

By default, accounts in the Domain and Enterprise Administrators group are able to retrieve local Administrator accounts. Domain and Enterprise Administrators are also able to trigger a local Administrator password change on a specific computer.

To configure computers so that their passwords are managed by LAPS, perform the following steps:

- Moving computer accounts of computers that you want to have use LAPS to manage passwords to an OU.

- Install LAPS on the computers that you want to manage the local administrator password for. You'll also need to install LAPS on an administrative computer that you can use to install the necessary template on.

- Install the GPO templates into AD DS. You can do this by running the installer and selecting the PowerShell module and GPO Editor templates installation option.

- Use the Set-AdmPwdComputerSelfPermission cmdlet to assign computers in an OU the ability to update the password of their local Administrator account when it expires. For example, for computers in the Adelaid OU, run the command:

```
Set-AdmPwdComputerSelfPermission -Identity "Adelaide"
```

Once installed, you'll be able to configure the following policies:

- **Enable local admin password management**. This policy enables LAPS and allows you to manage the local Administrator account password centrally.

- **Password settings**. This policy allows you to configure the complexity, length, and maximum age of the local Administrator password. The default is that upper and lower case letters, numbers, and special characters are used. The default password length is 14 characters, and the default password maximum age is 30 days.

- **Do not allow password expiration time longer than required**. When enabled, the password is updated according to domain password expiration policy.

- **Name of administrator account to manage**. Use this policy to identify custom local Administrator accounts.

To view local administrator passwords, you can either use the client that comes with the LAPS installer, the Get-AdmPwdPassword cmdlet, or view a computer's ms-Mcs-AdmPwd attribute.

CHAPTER 18

> **MORE INFO   LOCAL ADMINISTRATOR PASSWORD SOLUTION**
>
> You can learn more about LAPS at *https://technet.microsoft.com/en-us/mt227395.aspx.*

WSUS

You can install WSUS as a role on Windows Server 2016 in both the Server Core and GUI configurations. Although WSUS does include Windows PowerShell support, not all WSUS functionality has been replicated in Windows PowerShell, and you'll likely need to manage a WSUS server deployed on Server Core using the RSAT tools.

When you install WSUS, you can choose between using a local Windows Internal Database (WID) or a SQL Server instance. The advantage of using a SQL Server instance is that it's easier to back up and you can run more complex reports. The majority of WSUS deployments use the built-in WID database. When you install WSUS on Windows Server 2016, all prerequisite components are also installed.

Products, security classifications, and languages

During setup, you are asked to choose which update you want to download based on product name, security classification, and languages. Although you can choose to download updates for all product categories for all classifications in all languages, you'll minimize the amount of configuration required later if you download updates only for products used on your organizational network.

When WSUS synchronizes, it may update the list of available product names to reflect newly released software. If your organization deploys a new product, if it retires an old product, or if you simply want to alter which updates are synchronized, you can modify which products are updated using the Products And Classifications dialog box, available through Options in the Update Services console, and shown in Figure 18-7.

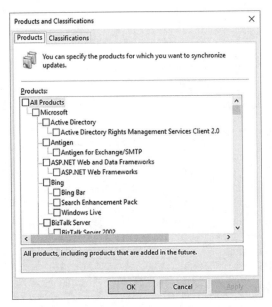

FIGURE 18-7 WSUS Products

Autonomous and replica modes

A single WSUS server can support approximately 25,000 clients. Large organizations often have multiple WSUS servers because it's better to have a local WSUS server at each large site, rather than having clients pull updates and approvals across wide area network (WAN) links. Instead of administrators performing the same approvals on each WSUS server in the organization, you can configure a WSUS server as a replica of another server. When you configure a WSUS server as a replica, the downstream server copies all update approvals, settings, computers, and groups from its parent. You can configure the Update Source settings, as well as specify information that enables WSUS to use a proxy server, through the Update Source And Proxy Server item in Options, in the Update Services console, and shown in Figure 18-8.

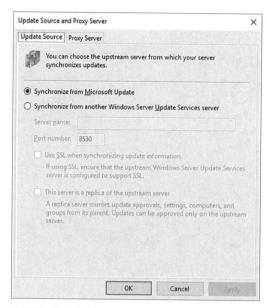

FIGURE 18-8 Update Source

Update files

One of the benefits of deploying WSUS is that clients on the local network download their updates from the WSUS server rather than downloading updates from the Microsoft Update servers on the Internet. You can configure update storage location settings using the Update Files And Languages item in the Options area of the Update Services console. You can configure the following options, as shown in Figure 18-9:

- **Store Update Files Locally On This Server**. When you choose this option, you can choose whether to download files only after they have been approved; download express installation files, which install quicker on clients; or download files from Microsoft Update. With the last option, you can configure a server as a replica server, but have update files downloaded from Microsoft Update rather than the upstream replica server.

- **Don't Store Update Files Locally; Computers Install From Microsoft Update.** When you configure this option, clients use WSUS for update approvals, but retrieve the updates from the Microsoft Update servers on the Internet. This option is most appropriate when you are providing update approvals to clients located outside of the organizational network.

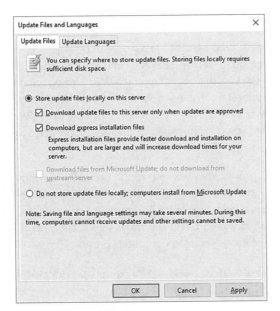

FIGURE 18-9 Update Files

WSUS security roles

In large organizations, you are more likely to separate the roles of server administrator and update administrator. When you install WSUS, two local security groups are created. By adding users to these groups, you grant users the permission to perform the tasks assigned with these roles. The roles are as follows:

- **WSUS Administrators**. Users who are added to the local WSUS Administrators group can perform any WSUS administration task. These tasks include approving updates, managing computer groups, configuring automatic approval rules, and modifying the WSUS server's update source.

- **WSUS Reporters**. Users who are members of this role can run reports on the WSUS server. These reports detail the update compliance status on the basis of update and computer. For example, a user who is a member of this group can run a WSUS report and determine which computers are missing a specific critical update.

WSUS groups

You can use WSUS groups to organize computers for the purpose of deploying updates. For example, you might have a WSUS group for servers in Sydney and another WSUS group for servers in Melbourne. A computer can be a member of multiple WSUS groups, and WSUS groups can exist in parent-child relationships. For example, the Australia WSUS group might have both the Melbourne and Sydney WSUS groups as members. Updates approved for the Australia group are automatically approved for members of the Melbourne and Sydney groups unless overridden.

You can assign computers to WSUS groups manually or through Group Policy. Computers can be assigned to WSUS groups through Group Policy only if the computer groups already exist on the WSUS server. To assign a computer manually, the computer must have already reported to the WSUS server. Computers that have reported to the WSUS server, but have not been assigned to a group, are members of the Unassigned Computers group.

An administrator must create WSUS groups. To create a WSUS group, perform the following steps:

1. Open the Update Services console.

2. Click the group you want to have as the parent group. The Computers/All Computers group is the parent group for all groups.

3. From the Action menu, click Add Computer Group.

4. Specify the computer group name, and click Add.

WSUS policies

You can configure most WSUS client options through Group Policy. Many of these policies are related to the experience that users of client operating systems have when updates are installed and are not directly applicable to updating server operating systems. Windows Update policies are located in the Computer Configuration\Policies\Administrative Templates\Windows Components\Windows Update node of a standard GPO, as shown in Figure 18-10.

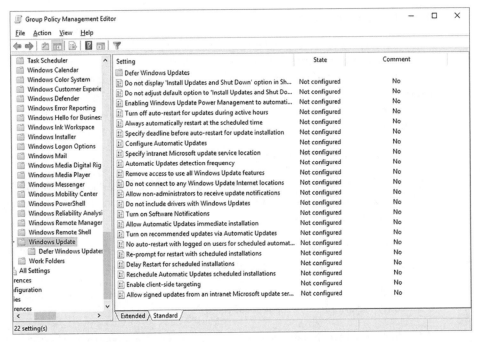

FIGURE 18-10 Update Policies

The most important policies from the perspective of the server administrator are as follows:

- **Configure Automatic Updates**. You can enable automatic updating, specify a day for update installations, and a time for update installation to occur. It's usually not a good idea to have this one policy to apply to all servers in your organization. Having all servers install and reboot at the same time can cause substantial disruptions.

- **Specify Intranet Microsoft Update Service Location**. You can specify the location of the WSUS server and the statistics server. (The statistics server receives information on successful update installation and is usually the same as the WSUS server.)

- **Automatic Update Detection Frequency**. Determines how often the computer checks for updates.

- **Enable Client-Side Targeting**. Use this policy to specify which WSUS groups computers should be a member of. If names do not match, computers end up in the Unassigned Computers group.

Deploying updates

When you deploy updates, you decide whether to deploy the update, to which computer groups you deploy the update, and what deadline should apply to the deployment. You can deploy an update multiple times to different groups, so you can deploy an update to a test group and then, if no issues arise with the update, deploy the update more generally. Prior to deploying updates, you should perform a synchronization, which ensures that the WSUS server is to be up to date before choosing whether to deploy updates.

To deploy an update, perform the following steps:

1. Open the Update Services console and select the Updates\All Updates node. You can also choose to select a child node, such as Critical Updates, if you want to view only available critical updates.

2. Set the Approval setting to Unapproved and the Status to Any, and click Refresh. All unapproved updates are then listed.

3. Click an update, or click multiple updates, if you want to select more than one update; then, click Approve in the Actions pane.

4. In the Approve Updates dialog box, select which computer groups the update is approved for. You can choose between the following settings:

   - **Approved For Install.** Approves the update.
   - **Approved For Removal.** Removes a previously deployed update.
   - **Not Approved.** Does not approve the update.
   - **Keep Existing Approvals.** Inherits the approval from the parent group.
   - **Deadline.** Specifies an update deployment deadline.

Automatic approval rules

Automatic approval rules enable specifically categorized updates to be automatically approved. For example, you might choose to automatically approve critical updates for the Sydney-Development-Servers WSUS group, as shown in Figure 18-11.

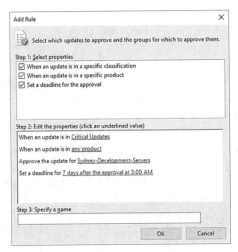

FIGURE 18-11 Automatic approval rules

To configure an automatic approval rule, perform the following steps:

1. Open the Update Services console. You can do this from the Tools menu of Server Manager, or by right-clicking the server in a server group and clicking Windows Server Update Services.

2. In the Update Services console, click Options, and then click Automatic Approvals.

3. In the Automatic Approvals dialog box, click New Rule.

4. In the Add Rule dialog box, choose the following rule options:

   - **When An Update Is In A Specific Classification**. You can choose that the rule applies when an update matches a specific classification or number of classifications. Update classifications include Critical Updates, Definition Updates, Drivers, Feature Packs, Security Updates, Service Packs, Tools, Update Rollups, and Updates. Microsoft includes classifications for each software update when it publishes the update.

   - **When An Update Is For A Specific Product**. You can specify products, either by category, such as Exchange, or by specific product, such as Exchange Server 2013.

   - **Approve The Update For A Specific Computer Group**. The update can be approved for selected computer groups.

   - **Set An Approval Deadline**. Sets an installation deadline for the update based on the time and date the update was first approved.

CHAPTER 18

Inside OUT

Canary users

Automatic approval rules aren't suitable for production servers hosting important workloads because it is possible that an update will be installed without being properly tested. Automatic approval rules are suitable for test groups. You should populate your test group with users who are more likely to "offer feedback" if something goes wrong. Just as a canary in a coal mine was used by miners to detect dangerous gas, "canary users" are likely to raise an alarm when a software update causes problems that indicate it shouldn't be deployed in a production environment. Users who complain are much more valuable as deployment targets for update testing than users who ignore problems and do not provide feedback.

MORE INFO   WSUS

You can learn more about WSUS at *https://technet.microsoft.com/en-us/windows-server-docs/management/windows-server-update-services/deploy/deploy-windows-server-update-services.*

Device Guard

Device Guard is a hardware and software based security system that restricts the execution of applications to those that are explicitly trusted. Device Guard uses virtualization-based security to isolate a special service named the code integrity service from the Windows kernel. Because the code integrity service is running as a trustlet in a special virtualized location, compromising the service is difficult, if not impossible, even if an attacker has complete control of the operating system.

Device Guard comprises the following features:

- **Virtual Secure Mode**. This is a special virtual container that isolates the ISASS.exe process from the operating system.

- **Configurable Code Integrity**. This is the rules engine that, in conjunction with Virtual Secure Mode Protected Code Integrity validates code that Windows Server attempts to enact.

- **Virtual Secure Mode Protected Code Integrity**. Uses two components to enforce Configurable Code Integrity policy. User mode code integrity manages whether or not user mode code can execute. Kernel mode code integrity manages whether or not kernel mode code can execute.

- **Platform and UEFI Secure Boot**. Ensures that the boot loader code and firmware are validated. Protects against malware modifying the boot environment.

To enable virtual secure mode, perform the following steps:

1. Enable Secure Boot and Trusted Platform Module (TPM)

2. Enable Hyper-V.

3. Enable Isolated User Mode.

4. Configure the Turn On Virtualization Based Security policy, located in the Computer Configuration\Administrative Templates\System\Device Guard\ node.

5. Configure the BCD store to start Virtual Secure mode. You do this by running the following command:

```
bcdedit /set vsmlaunchtype auto
```

By default, Device Guard runs in audit mode. This allows you to tune a policy to ensure that the software that you want to run can run and won't be blocked. You have several options when it comes to controlling which software can run on a computer protected by device guard. These are as follows:

- Only allow software that is digitally signed by a trusted publisher to run on the server. If you are using internally written code, you can use your organization's code signing certificate to digitally sign code. You use the New-CIPolicy cmdlet to create an XML file with all relevant details about signed files on a system, and then use the ConvertFrom-CIPolicy cmdlet to convert this XML file into a binary file that is placed in the C:\Windows\System32\CodeIntegrity folder and can be used by Device Guard to determine which software can run on the protected system.

- Use Package Inspector to create a catalog of all deployed and executed binary files for applications that you trust. You can use this when you need to deal with third-party applications that you do trust, but which are not digitally signed. Package Inspector is included with the operating system and is located in the C:\Windows\System32 directory. Package Inspector creates a catalog of hash files for each binary executable. Once the catalog file is created, you can digitally sign the catalog using signtool.exe, which is available in the Windows Software Development Kit (SDK) that you can download from Microsoft's website. Ensure that the signing certificate is added to the code integrity policy. Device Guard blocks any software that is not in the signed catalog from running. You can use Group Policy and Configuration Manger to deploy code integrity policies and catalog files.

You can deploy Device Guard on a test machine using the Device Guard Readiness Tool. This assesses a computer's readiness to be configured for Device Guard and allows you to perform a test deployment. Test deployments are important because you don't want to deploy Device Guard and then find that business critical software can no longer execute.

Once you've verified that a computer is ready for Device Guard, you configure the Turn On Virtualization Based Security policy, located in the Computer Configuration\Policies\Administrative Templates\System\Device Guard section of a GPO and configure the policy so that the Virtualization Based Protection of Code Integrity is set to either Enabled with UEFI lock, or Enabled without lock. The difference is that if you use the Enabled with UEFI lock, as shown in Figure 18-12, the policy can only be disabled by signing directly onto the server.

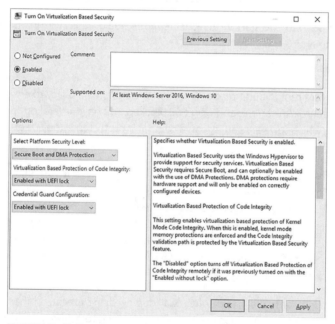

FIGURE 18-12 Turn On Virtualization Based Security

MORE INFO   DEVICE GUARD DEPLOYMENT GUIDE

You can learn more about deploying Device Guard at *https://technet.microsoft.com/ en-us/itpro/windows/keep-secure/device-guard-deployment-guide.*

Shielded VMs

Shielded VMs are a special type of virtual machine configuration that are protected against attacks against originating from the virtualization fabric. A virtualization fabric attack is one that comes from the infrastructure that hosts the virtual machine itself. Attacks that come from the virtualization infrastructure include:

- **Virtual Machine export attacks**. Rather than compromise a running virtual machine, an authorized administrator can simply use Hyper-V's built in export functionality to export a virtual machine. Once exported, the administrator can then examine the contents of the exported virtual machine at their leisure without any evidence existing of their access. Anything that can be done by an authorized administrator can also be done by a nefarious third party who has gained access to the administrator's account or has local administrator access on Hyper-V host. For example, someone with the appropriate privileges can export a virtualized domain controller, extract the ntds.dit Active Directory file, and then run an offline brute force analysis of that file to extract username and password data. They could then use that username and password data to gain administrative privileges and access that domain and its resources in a manner that seemed completely legitimate.

- **Virtual Machine movement attacks**. Rather than exporting a virtual machine, an attacker might attempt to move a shielded VM to an untrusted host. The intention in doing so would be to remove the protection associated with the VM. However, with shielded VMS, if the new host is not recognized as trusted based on an identifier related to the host's TPM, the shielded VM does not function and the contents of the VM remain protected.

Inside OUT

Exfiltrate all the things

In the past you could ensure the physical security of a server by putting it in a locked cage in a highly secure datacenter that was also protected by security guards and might even be surrounded by a piranha filled moat. Someone trying to steal the server had to be able to get past the piranhas, the security guard, and the locked cage. Today the vast majority of servers are virtualized and are functionally just a bunch of very large files. Rather than getting past the piranhas, stealing a server is mostly a case of uploading the files that comprise the virtual machine to a location you control somewhere on the Internet. Shielded VMs provide a way of protecting against this type of attack.

When you are thinking about shielded VMs, you separate the owner and operator of the VM, termed the tenant, from the owner and operator of the virtualization fabric, which in most cases is you as the Hyper-V virtualization administrator. Shielded VMs allow the VM operator to run their workload without the concern that anyone with local administrator privileges on the Hyper-V host server can access the data and applications stored on that virtual machine.

Shielded VMs include the following security features and requirements:

- **Secure Boot must be present and enabled**. This protects the boot environment of the VM from attacks that might modify the environment to introduce malware. This malware could be leveraged to gain access to the virtual machine.

- **Virtual TPM must be present and enabled**. Virtual TPMs function in a manner similar to a hardware-based TPMs in that they provide a secure location for the storage of cryptographic keys and secrets.

- **VM must have BitLocker enabled**. BitLocker protects the integrity of the boot environment as well as ensures that the VM's virtual hard disks are encrypted. If the virtual hard disk file was copied, it would be inaccessible unless the person attempting to access it had the necessary BitLocker recovery keys.

- **Only certain integration components are allowed**. Tools such as PowerShell Direct and Data Exchange are blocked. Blocking these integration services components blocks a Hyper-V administrator from indirectly accessing data stored in the virtual machine.

- **Virtual Machine Connection (console) cannot be enabled for the VM**. Access must be through remote access methods enabled within the VM operating system, such as PowerShell remote sessions or Remote Desktop. The only way to access the content of the VM is where the VM operating system has granted access to that content.

- **Restricted keyboard and mouse access**. Human Interface Devices, such as keyboard and mice, are disabled for the VM and can't be used to interact with it. For example, this means that an administrator couldn't interrupt the VM's boot process or use another attack to inject code into the VM in the way they might do so when attacking a physically deployed computer.

- **COM/serial ports**. Access through other virtual ports to the VM is disabled. This blocks a nefarious administrator using out of band management tools to access the VM.

- **Debugger access**. Debugger cannot be attached to the VM process on a shielded VM.

The following operating systems support being run as Shielded VMs:

- Windows Server 2016, Windows Server 2012 R2, and Windows Server 2012

- Windows 10, Windows 8, and Windows 8.1

Shielded VMs can only be hosted on specially configured Windows Server 2016 Hyper-V servers that are part of a shielded fabric. Shielded VMs must use virtual hard disks in VHDX format that have the following properties:

- Configured as GPT disks.

- Must be basic rather than dynamic disks.

- Disk that hosts operating systems must be configured with two partitions. One partition stores the Windows operating system, the other stores the active partition which includes the bootloader.

- Volumes on the disk must be formatted as NTFS.

While it's possible to convert an existing VM to become a shielded VM, Microsoft recommends that shielded VMs be deployed from scratch from trusted installation media, or digitally signed VM templates.

MORE INFO   SHIELDED VMS

You can learn more about shielded virtual machines at *https://technet.micro-soft.com/en-us/windows-server-docs/security/guarded-fabric-shielded-vm/guarded-fabric-configuration-scenarios-for-shielded-vms-overview*.

Guarded fabric

Before you can deploy a shielded VM, you need to configure a guarded fabric on which to deploy the VM. A guarded fabric is a special cryptographically secure virtualization host environment. A guarded fabric is made up of one Host Guardian Service (HGS), usually a cluster of three nodes, a number of guarded virtualization hosts, and the shielded VMs that run on those hosts.

Host Guardian Service

The Host Guardian Service (HGS) is a Windows Server 2016 role that manages attestation and the Key Protection Service (KPS). The KPS stores and is responsible for securely releasing keys to shielded VMs. One of the keys that the KPS stores is the transport key. The transport key is used to encrypt a shielded VM's virtual TPM. Microsoft recommends that you deploy the HGS role on a physically secure physical server running the Server Core operating system.

Validating a Hyper-V host involves verifying both its identity and configuration. Once the attestation service verifies both its identity and configuration, the KPS provides the transport key to that host that is required to unlock and run shielded VMs on that host.

Configuring a HGS server involves the deployment of a dedicated single domain AD DS forest. A HGS cluster comprises at least three nodes and each HGS cluster node is a domain controller for the root domain of this dedicated AD DS forest. Deploying a HGS cluster is different from a traditional domain controller deployment, and you don't go through the traditional AD DS promotion process, instead you take a standalone server, install the HGS role on that server, and then run the Initialize-HgsServer PowerShell cmdlet.

Running the Initialize-HgsServer PowerShell cmdlet triggers the process of configuring the server as a domain controller for the newly created single domain AD DS forest. The trusted Hyper-V hosts need to either be a member of the HGS forest, or members of a domain that has a one way trust relationship with the forest, with this second configuration being even more secure because a compromised virtualization host won't be able to make any modifications to the HGS forest because the trust relationship goes only in the opposite direction.

TPM and admin trusted attestation

Trusted attestation allows a shielded VM to verify that it is running on a virtualization host that participates in a guarded fabric. There are two methods that you can use to provide trusted attestation. The method that you provide depends on the hardware that you have available. Table 18-4 lists the different trusted attestation types.

Table 18-4 Attestation types

Attestation type	Functionality and benefits
TPM trusted	Provides strongest protection. Requires TPM 2.0 and UEFI 2.3.1 with secure boot. Guarded hosts are approved based on TPM ID, measured boot sequence and code integrity policies. Each guarded fabric virtualization host's TPM must be registered with the guardian service. To do this use Get-PlatformIdentifier cmdlet to generate a special file containing the TPM endorsement key's public and private keys, and then use the Add-HgsAttestationTpmHost cmdlet in registering the TPM with the guardian service. It's necessary to generate a baseline code-integrity policy for each virtualization host hardware SKU. This policy allows validation of the integrity of the software and hardware environment of each guardian fabric virtualization host. Best practice is to use Hardware Security Module to store HSM-backed certificates, though this is not mandatory
Admin trusted	Doesn't require TPM 2.0.Compatible with common server hardware. Guarded hosts approved by Host Guardian Service based on membership of specific AD DS security group. Guarded host forwards request to the HGS using an encrypted REST API. Use the Add-HgsAttestationHostGroup cmdlet to authorize the specific security group's SID with the attestation service. Guarded fabric virtualization hosts need to have a one-way trust relationship to HGS domain

MORE INFO   GUARDED FABRIC

You can learn more about guarded fabric at *https://technet.microsoft. com/en-us/windows-server-docs/security/guarded-fabric-shielded-vm/ guarded-fabric-configure-hgs-with-authorized-hyper-v-hosts.*

Encryption supported VMs

An encryption supported VM is a VM that can run in a semi-protected manner on a guarded fabric, but which doesn't have the stringent security requirements of a shielded VM. A virtualization administrator has a greater level of access to an encryption supported VM. This makes the deployment less secure than a shielded VM. Encryption supported VMs may be more appropriate for organizations where the VM administrator would normally have access to the VMs anyway, but where, for compliance reasons, VMs need to be run in a manner where the contents of virtual hard disks are encrypted.

The ways that encryption supported VMs differ from shielded VMs is outlined in table 18-5:

Table 18-5 Differences between encryption supported and shielded VMs

Security setting	Encryption Supported VM	Shielded VM
Secure Boot	Required, but configurable	Require and enforced
vTPM	Required, but configurable	Required and enforced
Encrypted VM state	Required, but configurable	Required and enforced
Live migration traffic encryption	Required, but configurable	Required and enforced
Integration components including PowerShell Direct	Configurable by fabric administrator, with PowerShell Direct and Data Exchange allowed	Data Exchange and PowerShell Direct blocked
Virtual Machine Connection	Allowed	Disabled
Keyboard, mouse, HID devices	Allowed	Disabled
COM/Serial ports	Supported	Disabled
Attach debugger to VM process	Supported	Disabled

Shielding data file

The shielding data file (also termed the provisioning data file or PDK file) is a special encrypted file that stores the following secrets:

- Administrator credentials.

- Answer file (unattend.xml).

- Security policy that determines whether VMs created using this shielded data file will be full shielded VMs or encryption supported VMs.

- An RDP certificate. This allows secure RDP communication with the VM.

- A volume signature catalog. This contains a list of trusted signed template-disk signatures that a VM can be created from. A shielded template disk is a template virtual hard disk that has a digital signature. This ensures that the template hard disk from which a new VM is deployed is trustworthy. During provisioning, the signature of the disk is computed and checked against a list of trusted shielded template disk signatures stored in the catalog. If the signatures match, deployment continues. If the signatures do not match, indicating that the shielded template disk has been modified, the deployment fails.

- A Key Protector that specifies which guarded fabrics a shielded VM generated based on this shielding data file is authorized to run on.

Tenant keys protect this file and the tenant uploads the shielding data file to the secure fabric. Because tenant keys protect the file, the virtualization administrator doesn't have access to the contents of the shielding data file. This means that the virtualization administrator does not have access to the local administrator password used with virtual machines deployed on the fabric that they manage.

The shielding data file ensures that any VMs are explicitly created with the parameters speci-fied by the tenant. The virtualization administrator can't swap in their own template hard disk, answer file, or administrator password. Should a template hard disk be swapped out or modi-fied by the virtualization administrator, it won't match the cryptographic signature of any authorized template hard disk listed in the shielding data file.

> MORE INFO   SHIELDED VM DEEP DIVE
>
> You can learn more about shielded VMs by watching the following deep dive video at *https://channel9.msdn.com/events/ignite/2016/brk3124.*

Windows Defender

Windows Server 2016 includes Windows Defender, the Microsoft anti-malware solution. Windows Defender is enabled by default when you deploy Windows Server 2016. To disable Windows Defender, you must remove it, either by using the Add Roles And Features Wizard, or by using the following Uninstall-WindowsFeature command:

```
Uninstall-WindowsFeature -Name Windows-Server-Antimalware
```

You can use the following PowerShell cmdlets to manage Windows Defender on computers running the GUI, or the Server Core version of Windows Server 2016:

- Add-MpPreference. Modifies Windows Defender settings.

- Get-MpComputerStatus. View the status of antimalware software on the server.

- Get-MpPreference. View the Windows Defender preferences for scans and updates.

- Get-MpThreat. View the history of malware detected on the computer.

- Get-MpThreatCatalog. Get known threats from the definitions catalog. You can use this list to determine if a specific threat is known to Windows Defender.

- Get-MpThreatDetection. Lists active and past threats that Windows Defender has detected on the computer.

- Remove-MpPreference. Removes an exclusion or default action.

- Remove-MPThreat. Removes an active threat from the computer.

- Set-MpPreference. Allows you to configure scan and update preferences.

- Start-MpScan. Starts an anti-malware scan on a server.

- Start-MpWDOScan. Triggers a Windows Defender offline scan.

- Update-MpSignature. Triggers an update for antimalware definitions.

MORE INFO   WINDOWS DEFENDER

You can learn more about Windows Defender at *https://technet.micro-soft.com/en-us/windows-server-docs/security/windows-defender/windows-defender-overview-windows-server.*

Windows Firewall with Advanced Security

Windows Firewall with Advanced Security (WFAS) is a bi-directional, host-level firewall. This means, not only can you set it to protect a host from incoming traffic, you can also have it block all or specific outgoing traffic. Generally, you can control outbound traffic only on very sensitive hosts. Controlling outbound traffic minimizes the chance of malware infecting the server phoning home. On sensitive hosts, you should allow outbound traffic on a per-application rule. For example, you should create a rule to allow a specific browser to communicate with the Internet rather than just allowing outbound traffic on port 80.

WFAS allows for the creation of rules based on program, port, or predefined rules. There are 45 predefined rules, which include categories such as Remote Desktop, Windows Firewall Remote Management, File and Printer Sharing, and Core Networking. One of the useful things about WFAS is that it generally enables the appropriate firewall rules when you enable a specific role, role service, or feature. These default rules are appropriate most of the time, but you may wish to edit the properties of these rules to make them more secure.

Firewall profiles

Firewall profiles allow you to treat traffic differently depending on the network to which the computer is connected. For example, the same server might be connected to the following:

- A remote site through a VPN connection that has the private profile applied

- A perimeter network by a network adapter, where the connection has the public profile applied

- To the organization's internal network through a second adapter that has the domain profile applied

The advantage of separate profiles is that each one allows you to have separate sets of firewall rules applied. You might allow Distributed File System (DFS) traffic on one profile, web traffic on another, and SMTP traffic on a third.

Profiles are independent of each other; the settings that you configure for one profile do not apply to other profiles. You can configure the following properties for each profile:

- **Firewall State**. You can set this to On (default) or Off.

- **Inbound Connections**. You can set this to Block (default), Block All, or Allow. The Block All setting means firewall rules that allow connections are ignored.

- **Outbound Connections**. You can set this to Block or Allow (default).

- **Settings**. This allows you to configure whether notifications are displayed, whether unicast responses are transmitted to multicast or broadcast traffic, and whether to merge rules when rules apply both locally and through Group Policy.

- **Logging**. This allows you to specify logging settings.

Firewall logs are written to the %systemroot%\system32\LogFilres\Firewall\pfirewall.log file. The default settings do not log dropped packets or successful connections, which means that, unless you change the defaults, nothing is logged. Firewall logging is most useful when you've determined that a particular service is unavailable to the network because of the firewall.

You can turn on firewall logging on a per profile basis by clicking the Customize button next to Logging on each profile's properties page. This displays the Customize Logging Settings dialog box shown in Figure 18-13. You can then enable logging for dropped packets and successful connections. If you are having trouble with a newly installed service on a server, enable the logging of dropped packets to determine the properties of the packets dropped, so that you can create a firewall rule that allows your service to be accessed from the network.

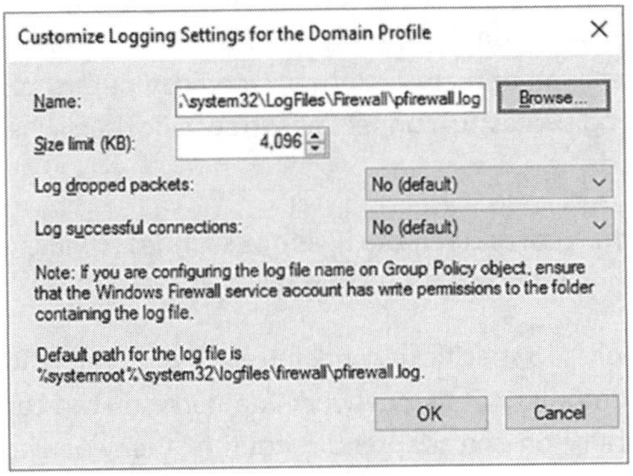

FIGURE 18-13 Custom logging settings

Inbound rules

Inbound rules are based on program, port, or one of 45 predefined categories, such as Branch-Cache Content Retrieval, or Network Policy Server. You can also create custom rules that include a mixture of these, where you specify a program and a port as well as rule scope. For example, you can use a custom rule to block all incoming traffic on port 80 to a particular application, but not block port 80 traffic to other applications on the server. The basic aspects of creating a firewall rule involve:

- **Specifying a program or port**. When you specify a port, you must choose whether the rule applies to TCP or UDP traffic.

- **Specify what action should be taken**. You can allow the connection, in which case all traffic that matches the rule is allowed by the firewall. You can allow the connection if it is authenticated, in which case traffic that meets the IPsec authentication requirements and the connection security rules is allowed, but traffic that is not properly authenticated according to these conditions is dropped.

- **Specify the network profiles in which the rule applies**. In general, rules should apply in all profiles, but there might be circumstances where you want to allow traffic from an interface connected to a domain network, but block the same traffic if it comes from an interface connected to a public network.

After you have created the rule, you can then edit the rule's properties. Editing the rule's properties allows you to configure more advanced options than are present in the Rule Creation Wizard. By editing a rule's properties, you can:

- Configure a rule to apply to a service rather than just a program.

- Limit the computers that can make authenticated connections. By default, if you configure the Allow Traffic If The Connection Is Authenticated option, any computer that can authenticate is able to successfully transmit traffic. By editing a firewall's rules, you can limit traffic to specific computers, rather than all authenticated computers. You can do the same with user accounts, limiting successful connections to specific users when authentication has successfully occurred.

- Edit the rule's scope, which is the local and remote IP address ranges to which the rule applies. You can also do this when you create a custom rule.

- Configure whether the rule applies to specific network interfaces, instead of just network profiles. For example, if your computer has two network adapters, you can configure a rule to apply so that it allows traffic on one adapter but not the other when both adapters have the same profile set.

- Configure whether or not to allow packets that have passed across a Network Address Translation (NAT) device.

Creating outbound rules

Default settings for Windows Firewall with Advanced Security do not block outbound traffic. In high-security environments, you should consider using outbound rules to block all but authorized outbound traffic.

The process for creating an outbound rule is almost identical to the process for creating an inbound rule. You specify the rule type on the New Outbound Rule Wizard, whether the connection is blocked, allowed, or allowed only if authenticated, and specify the network profiles in which the rule is active. By editing the properties of the rule after the rule is created, you can configure all of the advanced options configurable for inbound rules, such as rule scope, specific network interfaces, and which computers or users the rule allows outbound connections to.

Configuring IPsec

The IPsec Settings tab of Firewall Properties allows you to configure how IPsec is used when applied in connection security rules. On the tab itself, shown in Figure 18-14, you can configure whether or not you want to customize the IPsec defaults, exempt Internet Control Message Protocol (ICMP) traffic from IPsec, and whether you want to configure IPsec tunnel authorization.

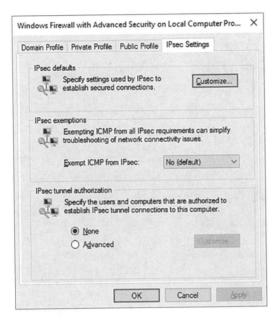

FIGURE 18-14 IPsec settings

Exempting ICMP traffic can be useful for diagnostic purposes because many administrators use the ping utility to diagnose whether a host has network connectivity. If connection security rules are enabled, the default IPsec settings mean that a successful IPsec negotiation must occur prior to an ICMP response being sent. If the IPsec negotiation is the problem, enabling ICMP response allows you to verify that there is network connectivity and that the problem just lies a bit further up the network stack.

If you click Customize next to IPsec defaults, you can change the Key Exchange, Data Protection, and Authentication Method. This dialog is shown in Figure 18-15. The default key exchange uses Diffie-Hellman Group 2 key exchange algorithm with a key lifetime of 480 minutes. You can modify these settings so that they use more secure methods, but this may reduce the ability to interact with some third-party devices.

CHAPTER 18

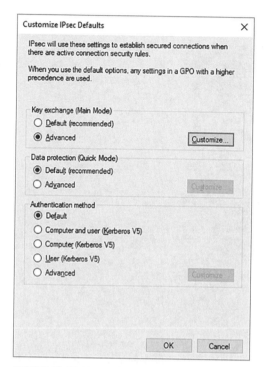

FIGURE 18-15 Customize IPsec defaults

The data protection settings allow you to configure the algorithms used for data integrity and encryption. Normally there isn't much reason to change this; however, if you feel you need the strongest encryption possible to protect your organization's network traffic, you can use a different algorithm, such as AES-CBC with a 256-bit key length. In general, the stronger the encryption, the greater the resources needed to support that encryption. Although you can make the protection a lot stronger, the benefit of doing so might be only marginal given the value of the data being protected.

The default authentication method used for IPsec connections is Computer (Kerberos V5). This means that a domain controller must be present to verify the identity of each computer before an IPsec session can be established. You can also use Computer (NTLMv2), a computer certificate from this certification authority (CA), or a pre-shared key to authenticate IPsec connections. A preshared key is not a recommended method of authentication, but might be necessary where there is not a certificate services infrastructure and computers aren't members of a domain.

Connection security rules

Connection security rules are a more intelligent type of firewall rule than a simple port-based rule. An interesting adaption to firewalls has been an increase of traffic through ports traditionally used for common applications. Connection security rules are about trusting incoming connections based on the identity of the remote host, rather than the remote host's network address or the communication port it uses.

Authentication exemptions

Authentication exemptions allow you to create very specific holes in connection security rules. These are useful in the event that you want to remotely manage a server, but all of the servers that would normally authenticate your connection, such as certificate servers or domain controllers, are for some reason unavailable. Authentication exemptions override existing connection security rules.

When you create an authentication exemption, you define the exemption on the basis of the source computer's IP address. As Figure 18-16 shows, you do this using a single IPv4 or IPv6 address, an IP address range, or a pre-defined set of computers. For security reasons, you should limit the number of IP addresses for which you create authentication exemptions to one or two specific privileged access workstations.

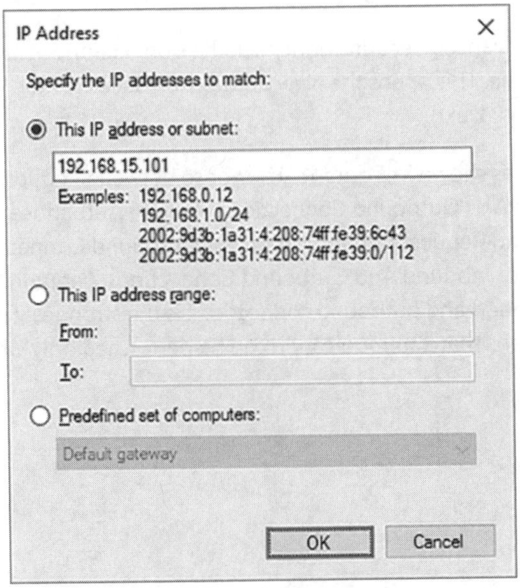

FIGURE 18-16 Authentication exemption

CHAPTER 18

To create an authentication exemption, perform the following steps:

1. In Windows Firewall With Advanced Security, right-click the Connection Security Rules node, and then click New Rule. This opens the New Connection Security Rule Wizard. Select Authentication Exemption.

2. On the Exempt Computers dialog, click Add. In the IP Address dialog, enter the IP address, subnet, or IP address range of the computers that you wish to exempt from connection security rules. You can also choose from a list of predefined addresses including the Default Gateway, DHCP servers, the local subnet, or DNS servers.

3. Select the profile to which you want the rule to apply, and specify a rule name.

Isolation rules

Isolation rules allow you to limit communication so that a server or computer communicates only with computers that have authenticated with it. Sometimes these are called domain isolation policies because they limit hosts to only communicating with other servers that are members of the same Active Directory forest. When you configure an isolation rule, it applies to all traffic from all hosts, unlike tunnel or server-to-server rules, which apply to traffic to and from specific hosts.

To create an isolation rule, perform the following steps:

1. In Windows Firewall With Advanced Security, right-click the Connection Security Rules node, and then click New Rule. This opens the New Connection Security Rule Wizard. Select Isolation, and then click Next.

2. On the Requirements page, as shown in Figure 18-17, choose between Request Authentication For Inbound And Outbound Connections, Require Authentication For Inbound Connections And Request Authentication For Outbound Connections, or Require Authentication For Inbound And Outbound Connections. Requiring authentication on both inbound and outbound connections is the strongest form of protection because it means that communication can be performed only with authenticated hosts.

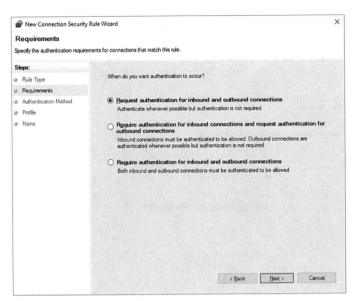

FIGURE 18-17 Connection security rule

3. Choose the authentication method. The default is to use the authentication method specified on the IPsec Settings tab of Firewall Properties. You can also choose between computer and user leveraging Kerberos version 5, or configure advanced authentication options, which include certificate-based authentication. It is also possible, though not recommended, to use a preshared key for authentication, which is useful when you need to communicate with computers running third-party operating systems.

4. The final step in setting up a connection security rule is to configure the profiles in which the rule applies. Unless there is a good reason otherwise, you should apply connection security rules in all profiles.

Server-to-server rules

Server-to-server rules are used to authenticate communication between two groups of computers. This can be a rule authenticating and encrypting a single, computer-to-computer connection, such as between a web server and a database server, or between computers on two separate subnets. Server-to-server rules differ from isolation rules, as isolation rules apply to communication from all hosts, whereas server-to-server rules apply to specific hosts.

To create a server-to-server rule, perform the following steps:

1. In Windows Firewall With Advanced Security, right-click the Connection Security Rules node, and then click New Rule. This opens the New Connection Security Rule Wizard. Select the Server-To-Server rule.

2.   In the Endpoints dialog, enter the IP addresses of the computers that are at one end of the connection, and the IP addresses of the computers that are at the other end of the connection. Figure 18-18 shows a rule defining one endpoint as the subnet 192.168.15.0/24, and the other endpoint as subnet 192.168.16.0/24.

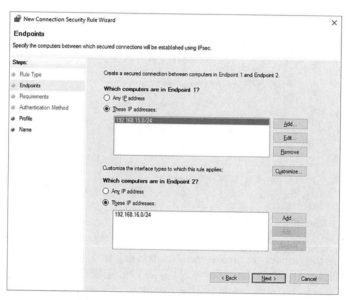

FIGURE 18-18 Connection security rule endpoints

3.   On the Requirements page, specify how you want authentication to occur. If you want only this computer to communicate on the profile using encrypted and authenticated connections, select Require Authentication For Inbound And Outbound Connections.

4.   Specify the authentication method. The default is to use a computer certificate issued by a designated CA. You can also specify computer-based Kerberos, NTLMv2, or a pre-shared key.

5.   Specify the firewall profiles in which this connection security rule applies, and a name for the rule.

Tunnel rules

Tunnel rules allow client computers to communicate with computers on a secure network behind a remote gateway. For example, if you have a single server located at a branch office that you want to connect to an internal network at another office, using a tunnel rule, you specify the location of a host that functions as a gateway to that secure network. This allows you to create an IPsec tunnel through which secure communication can occur.

To create a tunnel rule, perform the following steps:

1. In Windows Firewall With Advanced Security, right-click the Connection Security Rules node, and then click New Rule. This opens the New Connection Security Rule Wizard. Select Tunnel Rule.

2. On the Tunnel Type page, as shown in Figure 18-19, determine the type of tunnel that you want to create. To create the type of rule outlined above, select Client-To-Gateway.

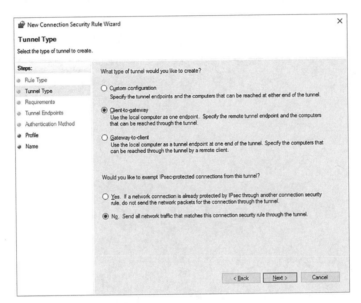

FIGURE 18-19 Tunnel Type

3. Choose whether you wish to require authentication for inbound and outbound connections.

4. Specify the address of the computer that functions as the gateway to the secure network.

5. Specify the authentication method. The default is to use a computer certificate issued by a designated CA. You can also specify computer-based Kerberos, NTLMv2, or pre-shared key.

6. Specify the firewall profiles in which this connection security rule applies, and a name for the rule.

MORE INFO   WINDOWS FIREWALL WITH ADVANCED SECURITY

You can learn more about deploying and managing Windows Firewall with Advanced Security, even though it deals with a previous version of Windows Server, at *https://tech-net.microsoft.com/en-us/library/jj721516(v=ws.11).aspx.*

CHAPTER 19

Monitoring and maintenance

Just like any other form of precision equipment, servers need to be monitored and maintained over their operational lifespans to ensure that they continue to function as well as they possibly can. Monitoring and maintenance not only involves regularly checking performance and event logs, but also ensuring that servers and the data that those servers host are backed up in such a way that all important data and settings can be recovered in the event of a catastrophic failure. In this chapter, you learn how to monitor Windows Server performance, manage event logs, configure advanced auditing, as well as use the built-in backup and recovery tools.

Data collector sets

Data collector sets enable you to gather performance data, system configuration information, and statistics into a single file. You can use Performance Monitor or other third-party tools to analyze this information to determine how well a server is functioning against an assigned workload.

You can configure data collector sets to include the following:

- **Performance counter data**. The data collector set not only includes specific perfor-mance counters, but also the data generated by those counters.

- **Event trace data**. Enables you to track events and system activities. Event trace data can be useful when you need to troubleshoot misbehaving applications or services.

- **System configuration information**. Enables you to track the state of registry keys and record any modifications made to those keys.

Windows Server 2016 includes the following built-in data collector sets:

- **Active Directory diagnostics**. Available if you have installed the computer as a domain controller and provides data on Active Directory health and reliability.

- **System diagnostics**. Enables you to troubleshoot problems with hardware, drivers, and STOP errors.

- **System performance**. Enables you to diagnose problems with sluggish system performance. You can determine which processes, services, or hardware components might be causing performance bottlenecks.

To create a data collector set, perform the following steps:

1. Open Performance Monitor from the Tools menu of the Server Manager console.

2. Expand Data Collector Sets.

3. Click User Defined. On the Action menu, click New and then click Data Collector Set.

4. You are given the option to create the data collector set from a template, which enables you to choose from an existing data collector set, or to create a data collector set manually. If you choose to create a data collector set manually, you have the option to create a data log, which can include a performance counter, event trace data, and system configuration information, or to create a performance counter alert.

5. If you select Performance Counter, next choose which performance counters to add to the data collector set. You also specify how often Windows should collect data from the performance counters.

6. If you choose to include event trace data, you need to enable event trace providers. A large number of event trace providers are available with Windows Server 2016. You use event trace providers when troubleshooting a specific problem. For example, the Microsoft Windows-AppLocker event trace provider helps you diagnose and troubleshoot issues related to AppLocker.

7. If you choose to monitor system configuration information, you can select registry keys to monitor. Selecting a parent key enables you to monitor all registry changes that occur under that key while the data collector set is running.

8. Next, specify where you want data collected by the data collector set to be stored. The default location is the %systemdrive%\PerfLogs\Admin folder. If you intend to run the data collector set for an extended period of time, you should store the data on a volume that is separate from the one hosting the operating system because this ensures that you don't fill up your system drive by mistake.

9. The final step in setting up a data collector set is to specify the account under which the data collector set runs. The default is Local System, but you can configure the data collector set to use any account that you have the credentials for.

You can schedule when a data collector set runs by configuring the Schedule tab of a data collector set's properties.

Alerts

Performance counter alerts enable you to configure a task to run when a performance counter, such as available disk space or memory, falls under or exceeds a specific value. To configure a performance counter alert, you create a new data collector set, choose the Create Manually option, and select the Performance Counter Alert option.

You add the performance counter, threshold value, and whether the alert should be triggered if the value exceeds or falls below the set value. When you create an alert by default, it only adds an event to the event log when it is triggered. This is useful if you have tools that allow you to extract this information from the event log and use the information as a way of tracking when alerts occur. You can also configure an alert to run a scheduled task when it is triggered. You can do this by editing the properties of the alert and by specifying the name of the scheduled task on the Task tab.

Event Viewer

Event Viewer enables you to access recorded event information. Windows Server 2016 not only offers the application, security, setup, and system logs, but it also contains separate application and service logs. These logs are designed to provide information on a per role or per application basis, rather than having all application and role service-related events funneled into the application log. When searching for events related to a specific role service, feature, or application, check to see whether that role service, feature, or application has its own application log.

Event log filters

Filters and event logs enable you to view only those events that have specific characteristics. Filters only apply to the current Event Viewer session. If you constantly use a specific filter or set of filters to manage event logs, you should instead create a custom view. Filters only apply to a single event log. You can create log filters based on the following properties:

- **Logged**. Enables you to specify the time range for the filter.

- **Event Level**. Enables you to specify event levels. You can choose the following options: Critical, Warning, Verbose, Error, and Information.

- **Event Sources**. Enables you to choose the source of the event.

- **Event IDs**. Enables you to filter based on event ID. You can also exclude specific event IDs.

- **Keywords**. Enables you to specify keywords based on the contents of events.

- **User**. Enables you to limit events based on user.

- **Computer**. Enables you to limit events based on the computer.

To create a filter, perform the following steps:

1. Open Event Viewer and select the log that you want to filter.

2. Determine the properties of the event that you want to filter.

3. On the Actions pane, click Filter Current Log.

4. In the Filter Current Log dialog box, specify the filter properties.

Event log views

Event log views enable you to create customized views of events across any event log stored on a server, including events in the forwarded event log. Rather than looking through each event log for specific items of interest, you can create event log views that target only those specific items. For example, if there are certain events that you always want to look for, create a view and use the view rather than comb through the event logs another way. By default, Event Viewer includes a custom view named Administrative Events. This view displays critical, warning, and error events from a variety of important event logs such as the application, security, and system logs.

Views differ from filters in the following ways:

- **Persistent**. You can use a view across multiple Event Viewer sessions. If you configure a filter on a log, it is not available the next time you open the Event Viewer.

- **Include multiple logs**. A custom view can display events from separate logs. Filters are limited to displaying events from one log.

- **Exportable**. You can import and export event log views between computers.

The process for creating an event log view is similar to the process for creating a filter. The primary difference is that you can select events from multiple logs and you give the event log view a name and choose a place to save it. To create an event log view, perform the following steps:

1. Open Event Viewer.

2. Click the Custom Views node and then click Create Custom View from the Actions menu.

3. In the Create Custom View dialog box select the properties of the view, including:

- When the events are logged

- The event level

- Which event log to draw events from

- Event source

- Task category

- Keywords

- User

- Computer

4. In the Save Filter To Custom View dialog box, enter a name for the custom view and a location to save the view in. Click OK.

5. Verify that the new view is listed as its own separate node in the Event Viewer.

You can export a custom event log view by selecting the event log view and clicking Export Custom View. Exported views can be imported on other computers running Windows Server 2016.

Event subscriptions

Event log forwarding enables you to centralize the collection and management of events from multiple computers. Rather than having to examine each computer's event log by remotely connecting to that computer, event log forwarding enables you to do one of the following:

- Configure a central computer to collect specific events from source computers. Use this option in environments where you need to consolidate events from only a small number of computers.

- Configure source computers to forward specific events to a collector computer. Use this option when you have a large number of computers that you want to consolidate events from. You configure this method by using Group Policy.

Event log forwarding enables you to configure the specific events that are forwarded to the central computer. This enables the computer to forward important events. It isn't necessary however to forward all events from the source computer. If you discover something from the forwarded traffic that warrants further investigation, you can log on to the original source computer and view all the events from that computer in a normal manner.

Event log forwarding uses Windows Remote Management (WinRM) and the Windows Event Collector (wecsvc). You need to enable these services on computers that function as event forwarders and event collectors. You configure WinRM by using the winrm quickconfig command and you configure wecsvc by using the wecutil qc command. If you want to configure subscriptions from the security event log, you need to add the computer account of the collector computer to the local Administrators group on the source computer.

To configure a collector-initiated event subscription, configure WinRM and Windows Event Collector on the source and collector computers. In the Event Viewer, configure the Subscription Properties dialog box with the following information:

- **Subscription Name**. The name of the subscription.

- **Destination Log**. The log where collected events are stored.

- **Subscription Type And Source Computers: Collector Initiated**. Use the Select Computers dialog box to add the computers that the collector retrieves events from. The collector must be a member of the local Administrators group or the Event Log Readers group on each source computer, depending on whether access to the security log is required.

- **Events To Collect**. Create a custom view to specify which events are retrieved from each of the source computers.

If you want to instead configure a source computer-initiated subscription, you need to configure the following Group Policies on the computers that act as the event forwarders:

- **Configure Forwarder Resource Usage**. This policy determines the maximum event forwarding rate in events per second. If this policy is not configured, events are transmitted as soon as they are recorded.

- **Configure Target Subscription Manager**. This policy enables you to set the location of the collector computer.

Both of these policies are located in the Computer Configuration\Policies\Administrative Templates\Windows Components\Event Forwarding node. When configuring the subscription, you must also specify the computer groups that hold the computer accounts of the computers that are forwarding events to the collector.

Inside OUT

OMS and Operations Manager

This chapter focuses on the tools that are built into Windows Server 2016. Organizations that are monitoring large numbers of Windows Server 2016 servers use tools such as System Center Operations Manager or the cloud based Operations Management Suite.

Event-driven tasks

Event Viewer enables you to attach tasks to specific events. A drawback to the process of creating event-driven tasks is that you need to have an example of the event that triggers the task already present in the event log. Events are triggered based on an event having the same log, source, and event ID.

To attach a task to a specific event, perform the following steps:

1. Open Event Viewer. Locate and select the event that you want to base the new task on.

2. On the Event Viewer Actions pane, click Attach Task To This Event. The Create Basic Task Wizard opens.

3. On the Create A Basic Task page, review the name of the task that you want to create. By default, the task is named after the event. Click Next.

4. On the When An Event is Logged page, review the information about the event. This lists the log that the event originates from, the source of the event, and the event ID. Click Next.

5. On the Action page, you can choose the task to perform. The Send An E-Mail and Display A Message tasks are deprecated, and you receive an error if you try to create a task using these actions. Click Next

6. On the Start A Program page, specify the program or script that should be automatically triggered as well as additional arguments.

7. After you create the task, you can modify the task to specify the security context under which the task executes. By default, event tasks only run when the user is signed on, but you can also choose to configure the task to run whether the user is signed on or not.

Network monitoring

Network monitoring enables you to track how a computer interacts with the network. Through network monitoring, you can determine which services and applications are using specific network interfaces, which services are listening on specific ports, and the volume of traffic that exists. There are two primary tools that you can use to perform network monitoring on computers running Windows Server 2016:

- Resource Monitor

- Message Analyzer

Resource Monitor

Resource Monitor enables you to monitor how a computer running the Windows Server 2016 operating system uses CPU, memory, disk, and network resources. Resource Monitor provides real time information. You can't use Resource Monitor to perform a traffic capture and review activity that occurred in the past, but you can use Resource Monitor to view activity that is currently occurring.

Resource Monitor provides the following information that is relevant to network monitoring:

- **Processes With Network Activity**. This view lists processes by name and ID and provides information on bits sent per second, bits received per second, and total bits per second.

- **Network Activity**. Lists network activity on a per-process basis, but also lists the destination address, sent bits per second, received bits per second, and total bits per second.

- **TCP Connections**. Provides information on connections based on local address, port, and remote address and port.

- **Listening Ports**. Lists the ports and addresses that services and applications are listening on. This option also provides information about the firewall status for these roles and services.

Message Analyzer

Microsoft Message Analyzer is the successor to Network Monitor. You can use Message Analyzer to perform network traffic capture and analysis. Message Analyzer also functions as a replacement for LogParser, which enables you to manage system messages, events, and log files. When performing a capture, select the scenario that best represents the type of event that you are interested in capturing traffic for. For example, the LAN scenario enables you to capture traffic on local area network (LAN) interfaces.

When performing certain types of network traffic captures, you need to run Message Analyzer using an account that is a member of the local Administrators group. After the capture is performed, you can analyze the content of each message. By applying appropriate filters, you can locate network traffic that has specific characteristics, such as traffic that uses a particular TCP port, source, or destination address.

Advanced auditing

There are two sets of audit policies in a Group Policy Object (GPO): traditional audit policies and advanced audit policies. The traditional audit policies are located in the Computer Configuration\Policies\Windows Settings\Security Settings\Local Policies\Audit Policies node. These are the audit policies that have been available with the Windows Server operating system since Windows 2000. The drawback of these policies is that they are general and you can't be specific in the way you configure auditing. When you use these policies, you not only audit the events that you're interested in, but you also end up auditing many events that you don't need to know about.

The advanced audit policies enable you to be more specific in the types of activity you audit. The advanced audit policies are located under the Computer Configuration\Policies\Windows Settings\Security Settings\Advanced Audit Policy Configuration node.

There are 10 groups of audit policy settings and 58 individual audit policies available through Advanced Audit Policy Configuration. The audit policy groups contain the following settings:

- **Account Logon**. You can audit credential validation and Kerberos-specific operations.

- **Account Management**. You can audit account management operations, such as changes to computer accounts, user accounts, and group accounts.

- **Detailed Tracking**. You can audit encryption events, process creation, process termination, and RPC events.

- **DS Access**. You can audit Active Directory access and functionality.

- **Logon/Logoff**. You can audit logon, logoff, and other account activity events, including IPsec and Network Policy Server (NPS) events.

- **Object Access**. You can audit access to objects including files, folders, applications, and the registry.

- **Policy Change**. You can audit changes to audit policy.

- **Privilege Use**. You can audit the use of privileges.

- **System**. You can audit changes to the security subsystem.

- **Global Object Access Auditing**. You can configure expression-based audit policies for files and the registry.

Expression-based audit policies

Traditional object audit policies involve specifying a group and configuring the type of activities that trigger an event to be written to the security log. For example, you can specify that an audit event is written each time a member of the Managers group accesses a file in a specific folder.

Expression-based audit policies enable you to go further. These policies enable you to set conditions for when auditing might occur. For example, you might want to configure auditing so that tracking only occurs for members of the Managers group who have access to sensitive files when they access those files from computers that aren't part of the Managers_Computers group. This way, you don't bother tracking access when members of this group access sensitive files from within the office, but you do track all access to those sensitive files when members of this group are accessing them from an unusual location.

You can integrate expression-based audit policies with Dynamic Access Control (DAC) to create targeted audit policies that are based on user, computer, and resource claims. Instead of just adding claims based on user or device group membership, the claim can be based on document metadata, such as confidentiality settings and site location. You can configure expression-based audit policies at the file or folder level or apply them through Group Policy by using policies in the Global Object Access Auditing node of Advanced Audit Policy Configuration.

File and folder auditing

After you configure object access auditing either through traditional or advanced audit policies, you can configure auditing at the file and folder level. The simplest way to configure auditing is at the folder level because you can configure all folders and subfolders to inherit those auditing settings. If you change the auditing settings at the folder level, you can use the Replace All Child Object Auditing Entries option to apply the new auditing settings to the folder's child files and folders.

You can configure auditing for a specific file and folder through the Advanced button on the Security tab of the object's properties. You can configure basic success and failure auditing. You can also configure expression-based auditing so that a specific security group member's activity is audited only if other conditions, such as membership of other security groups, are also met.

The advantage of using Global Object Access Auditing is that when you configure it, you can use file classification to apply metadata to files and then automatically have auditing enabled for those files. For example, by using file classification and DAC, you can configure a Windows Server 2016 file server so that all files containing the phrase "code secret" are marked as Sensitive. You can then configure Global Object Access Auditing so that all attempts to access files marked as Sensitive are automatically audited. Instead of having an administrator track down all the files that are sensitive and configuring auditing on those files, the process is automatic. All that needs to happen to trigger the audit is that the phrase "code secret" is included in the file.

Using auditpol with auditing

Auditpol.exe is a command line utility that you can use to configure and manage audit policy settings from an elevated command prompt. You can use auditpol.exe to perform the following tasks:

- View the current audit policy settings with the /Get subcommand.

- Set audit policy settings with the /Set subcommand.

- Display selectable policy elements with the /List subcommand.

- Back up and restore audit policies using the /Backup and /Restore subcommands.

- Delete all per user audit policy settings and reset the system policy settings using the / Clear subcommand.

- Remove all per user audit policy settings and disable all system policy settings using the / Remove subcommand.

For example, to enable success and failure auditing for the File System subcategory of Object Access, execute the following command:

```
Auditpol.exe /set /subcategory:"File System" /success:Enable /failure:Enable
```

To view the current audit policy settings for all audit policies, issue the following command:

```
Auditpol.exe /get /category:*
```

To view the current audit policy settings for a specific category, such as Object Access, issue the following command:

```
Auditpol.exe /get /category:"Object Access"
```

Windows Server Backup

Windows Server Backup is the default backup application included with Windows Server 2016. Windows Server Backup is a basic backup solution and it only enables you to back up to disk or network share. Tasks for long-term retention, like export to tape, require a more sophisticated solution, such as System Center Data Protection Manager. Windows Server Backup has a minimal level of reporting functionality and has no native functionality that makes it possible to send alerts to an administrator through email if a backup fails.

Windows Server Backup enables you to back up and recover the following:

- Full server (all volumes)

- Specific volumes

- Specific folders

- System State data

- Individual Hyper-V hosted virtual machines

- Volumes exceeding 2 terabytes (TB) in size

- Volumes with 4 kilobyte (K) sector size

- Cluster Shared Volumes

Although you can connect from the Windows Server Backup console to other computers to remotely manage Windows Server Backup, you can only use an instance of Windows Server Backup to back up the local computer. For example, whereas you can back up network shared folders that the computer is able to access, such as a mapped network drive, you can't configure Windows Server Backup on one computer to do a full volume or System State backup of another computer.

You can configure exclusions for backup jobs run on Windows Server Backup. Exclusions are specific file types that you want to exempt from the backup process. You can configure exclusions based on file type, or you can choose to exclude the contents of entire folders and their subfolders. For example, you can configure an exclusion that stops files with the .tmp extension in the c:\shared-docs folder and its subfolders from being written to backup.

Users who are local Administrators or members of the Backup Operators group are able to use Windows Server Backup to back up the entire computer, volumes, files or folders, and the System State. You can grant other security principals this right by editing the Back Up Files and Directories Group Policy item. Windows Server Backup does not encrypt backups by default, which means that the data stored in those backups might be read if the backup media falls into the wrong hands. When you are backing up data, you can configure access control so that only users with specific credentials can access the backup, but this still does not encrypt the backup.

Inside OUT

Backup security

The security of backups is important. Anyone who has access to backed up data can restore it to a separate location where they have complete access to that data. The security of backed up data is just as important as the security of the servers being backed up.

Backup locations

Windows Server Backup enables you to back up to any locally attached disk, to a volume, to the storage area network (SAN), or to any network folder. When configuring a scheduled backup, you should specify a destination volume or disk that is empty. If the disk is local or connected to the SAN, Windows Server Backup performs a full backup at least once every 14 days and incremental backups on subsequent backups. Incremental backups in Windows Server 2016 use block-level backups rather than file-level backups, meaning that the incremental backups are much smaller. Rather than backing up all the files that have changed since the last backup, only the data blocks that have changed on the hard disk are backed up. For example, if you change one image in a 25-megabyte (MB) PowerPoint file after it is backed up, only the data blocks associated with that image are backed up next time, not the whole 25-MB file.

Inside OUT

Backup location

Although you can write backup data to a different volume on the same disk, you should back up data to a different disk so that if your disk fails, you don't lose both the data being protected and the backup itself.

There is exception to the rule about how data is written during scheduled automatic full and incremental backups. This exception occurs when the backup data is written to a network folder. When you back up to a network folder, as opposed to a SAN-connected disk, which appears as local to Windows Server, each backup is a full backup and the previous full backup that was stored on the network share is erased. Because only one backup at a time can be stored on a network share, if you choose to back up to this location you can't recover data from any backup other than the most recently performed one.

You can modify the performance of full system and full volume backups by using the Optimize Backup Performance dialog box and you can increase backup performance by using the Faster

Backup Performance option. The drawback of selecting this option is that it reduces disk performance on the disks that host the volumes you are backing up.

Backing up data

You can back up data using a variety of methods with Windows Server Backup. You can configure a scheduled backup, which means a backup occurs on a scheduled basis. You can also perform a one-off backup. When you perform a one-off backup, you can either use the existing scheduled backup settings or you can configure a separate set of settings for one-off backups. For example, you can configure Windows Server Backup to perform a full server backup twice a day to a locally attached disk. You can connect at any time and perform a one-off backup where you select only specific files and folders and have them written to a location on the network.

Role- and application-specific backups

The majority of Windows Server 2016 roles and features store data in locations that are backed up when you perform a System State backup. System State data is automatically backed up when you perform a full server backup or select it for backup. Depending on the roles and features installed on the computer running Windows Server 2016, the System State can contain the following data:

- Registry

- Local users and groups

- COM+ Class Registration database

- Boot files

- Active Directory Certificate Services (AD CS) database

- Active Directory database (Ntds.dit)

- SYSVOL directory

- Cluster service information

- System files under Windows Resource Protection

- Internet Information Services (IIS) settings

Some applications also register themselves with Windows Server Backup. This means that when you perform a full server backup, you are able to recover data that is only relevant to the application without having to perform a full system restore. Support for application registration depends on the application. You can't select a specific application for back up using Windows

Server Backup, but you can restore applications that have registered themselves with Windows Server Backup as long as you've previously performed a full server backup.

Restore from backups

Windows Server Backup enables you to restore data that has been backed up on the local computer, or data that was backed up on another computer using Windows Server Backup that is accessible to the local computer. You can use Windows Server Backup to do the following:

- You can use Windows Server Backup to restore files and folders as well as applications.

- You can use Windows Server Backup to restore the System State data. After the System State data is restored, you need to restart the computer.

- You can use Windows Server Backup to restore any volume except the one that hosts the operating system. If you want to restore the volume that hosts the operating system, you need to boot into the Windows Recovery Environment.

- You can use the Windows Recovery Environment to perform a full server restore, also known as a bare metal recovery. When you do this, all existing data and volumes on the server are overwritten with the backed up data.

If multiple backups of the data you want to restore exist, you need to select which version to restore. If you are unsure which date holds the data you want to restore, you should restore to multiple alternative locations and then perform the comparison. This process saves you from restoring, figuring out you've restored the wrong data, performing another restore, and then figuring out that restore isn't right either.

Windows Server Backup writes backups to .vhdx files, the same type of file that is used with Hyper-V and when creating disks for Internet Small Computer System Interface (iSCSI) targets and disks in storage pools. Windows Server 2016 also allows you to mount the contents of a virtual hard disk (VHD), which allows you to examine those contents without having to perform a full restoration using Windows Server Backup.

Restore to an alternative location

When you are performing data restoration, you can choose to restore data to the original location or to an alternative location. It is not uncommon when restoring data to the original location for backup administrators to unintentionally overwrite good, live data with older, restored data. If you restore to an alternative location, it's possible to compare the restored data against the current data. It's also important when restoring data that you retain permissions associated with data.

If you choose to restore to the original location, you can configure Windows Server Backup to perform one of the following tasks:

- Automatically create copies if an original exists.

- Overwrite existing versions.

- Do not recover any item that exists in the recovery destination.

Azure Backup Agent

Azure Backup Agent is a client that allows you to back up data directly to the Microsoft cloud-based subscription backup service. You run the client on the Internet-connected computer server that you want to back up, and the backup data is stored on the Azure servers in the cloud. Azure Backup Agent functions as an off-site data storage and recovery location and can be used in conjunction with Windows Server Backup. In the event that a site is lost, you are still able to recover this important data from Azure. Azure Backup uses a recovery services vault in Azure to store backup data.

You can run both the Windows Server Backup and Azure Backup Agent services in parallel. This approach enables you to perform local backups and backups to Windows Azure on the same server. You can then do frequent full server backups locally, with infrequent critical data back-ups to Windows Azure. When you employ this strategy, you mostly restore data from your local backups. It's only when something goes drastically wrong that you need to restore data from Windows Azure.

The key to understanding what data to back up to Windows Azure is looking at what types of information your organization might lose if a site has some type of disaster. You can always rein-stall operating systems and applications from media that you can easily obtain again. The data stored on your servers however, such as documents and settings, is something that you can't generate from installation media. By storing data in the cloud, you are able to recover it in the event of a disaster after you've rebuilt your server infrastructure.

Preparing for Azure Backup Agent

Before you can start using Azure Backup Agent to back up data from a server running Windows Server 2016, you need to take several preliminary steps. These include performing the following steps:

- Create an Azure Recovery vault. You create the Azure Recovery vault within Azure. Azure Recovery vaults are the storage locations hosted within Azure that store your backup data. Azure enables you to select a recovery vault in an appropriate geographic location.

- Upload a specially configured public certificate that identifies the server to the public vault. This certificate can be self-signed using the Makecert.exe utility, can be obtained from an internal certificate authority (CA), or can be obtained from a trusted third-party CA. This certificate is used to identify the server and to secure the backup process.

Download and install the Azure Backup agent to the server that you want to protect. After you've installed the agent, you need to register the server with Azure Backup. This requires that the private key for the certificate you uploaded to Azure be located in the private certificate store of the computer you are registering. You also need to configure Azure Backup to use a specific recovery vault. To do this, select the recovery vault on the Vault Identification page of the Register Server Wizard. The final step is to configure an encryption passphrase. This passphrase is used to encrypt the data stored in the recovery vault. You are not able to restore the data to another location without providing the encryption passphrase, even if you have access to the recovery vault. The passphrase must be a minimum of 16 characters long and you can save it to an external location, such as a USB storage device.

Backing up data to Azure Backup Agent

Scheduling a backup to Azure Backup involves running a wizard that is very similar to the Schedule Backup Wizard in Windows Server Backup. When running this wizard, complete the following:

- **Select which items to back up.** Item selection is file and folder based. Although you can select a volume to back up, you don't use Azure Backup to perform full volume recovery in the same way you would use Windows Server Backup. At the time of writing, Azure Backup has a limit of 850 gigabytes (GB) per volume of data per backup operation. When selecting items to backup, you can configure exclusions for file types, folders, or folder trees.

- **Select a backup schedule.** This option determines how often a synchronization occurs. You can configure Azure Backup to synchronize up to three times per day. You can also configure bandwidth throttling. Throttling enables you to limit the utilization of bandwidth and ensures that your organization's Internet connection isn't choked with backup traffic replicating to the recovery vault on Azure during business hours.

- **Configure backup retention.** The retention setting, which you configure on the Specify Retention Setting page, determines how long backup data is stored in Azure before it is deleted. You can configure retention for Windows Server Backup when creating a policy in Windows PowerShell.

Restore from Azure Backup

Azure Backup enables you to restore files and folders that are stored in your Windows Azure recovery vault. You can't perform a full server recovery, System State recovery, or volume recovery using Azure Backup, you can only restore files and folders. Of course if you've backed up all the files and folders on a volume, you can either restore all of them individually or all at one time. Azure Backup also enables you to restore data from another server that you've backed up to Azure. Recovering data using Azure Backup involves performing the following steps:

- Select the server that you want to recover data from.

- Select whether you want to browse or search for files to recover.

- Select the volume that hosts the data you want to recover and the specific backup date and time that you want to recover data from.

- Select the items that you want to recover. You can recover files, folders, and folder trees.

- Select Recovery Options, including whether to restore to the original location, to an alternative location, or to create copies or overwrite original files. You can also use this page of the wizard to choose whether to restore the original permissions.

Vssadmin

Volume Shadow Copy Services (VSS) is a technology that provides a point-in-time snapshot of data on a volume as it existed at a specific point in time. VSS enables you to make a consistent backup of a file that is in use, such as a mailbox database or SQL Server database. Prior to the introduction of VSS, you might have needed to take such a database offline to ensure that the database's backup was consistent. Consistency issues arise when it takes so long to back up a large file or system that the configuration of the system or the contents of the file change during the backup. Windows Server Backup, Azure Backup Agent, and other backup products, such as Data Protection Manager, use VSS to ensure that the data backed up is consistent and represents the state of the backed up data as it was at the point when the backup started without having to take files in use offline.

Vssadmin is a command line utility that enables you to manage volume shadow copy snapshots. You can use VSS admin to perform the following tasks:

- Configure the location of shadow copy storage.

- Create a shadow copy.

- Delete a shadow copy.

- Delete shadow copy storage.

- View existing shadow copies.

- View existing shadow copy storage.

- View volumes that are configured with shadow copies.

- View subscribed shadow copy writers and providers (special software that creates and manages shadow copies).

- Resize shadow copy storage.

You can also view shadow copy status on a per volume basis through the Previous Versions tab. When used with file shares, the VSS snapshots exposed through the Previous Versions function- ality enable users to recover previous versions of files and folders without having to restore from backup. To do this, right-click the parent folder or volume and click Restore Previous Versions. You are then able to select previous versions of files that correspond to existing VSS snapshots.

Although Vssadmin allows you to create and manage VSS snapshots, you can't use Vssadmin to configure a schedule to automatically create VSS snapshots. You can configure a schedule to create VSS snapshots on a per-volume basis by right-clicking a volume and by clicking Configure Shadow Copies. After you enable shadow copies, you can configure a schedule in the Settings dialog box. By default, when you enable Shadow Copies, a shadow copy is created at 07:00 and noon every weekday, but you can modify the schedule so that copies are created more often. When doing this remember that after the initial allocated space used to store shadow copies is consumed, older shadow copies are removed to make space to store new versions. The amount of space needed to store shadow copies and the reten- tion period depends on the properties of the data stored on the volume.

Safe Mode and Last Known Good Configuration

Safe Mode is a boot option that you can access by pressing F8 when you start your computer, or you can enable it through the System Configuration (Msconfig.exe) utility. Safe mode enables you to start Windows Server 2016 with a minimal set of device drivers and services. You can use Safe Mode to disable drivers or services that are stopping a server from starting normally. There are three types of safe mode:

- **Safe mode.** Boots the computer to a desktop running a minimal number of services and drivers and enables you to access administrative tools. You need to use an account that has administrative privileges, which can be a local Administrator account or a Domain Administrator account that has cached credentials on the server.

- **Safe mode with networking.** Boots the computer to a desktop running a minimal num- ber of services and drivers, but includes network connectivity.

- **Safe mode with command prompt.** Boots the computer to a special mode where a command prompt is available, but the Windows Desktop is not. You can access both the command prompt and Windows PowerShell from this environment, although you have to type **Powershell.exe** from the command prompt to do this. It appears similar to Server Core, except that not all services configured to automatically start will have started.

Last Known Good Configuration is also accessible through the boot options menu that is available when you start the computer and press the F8 key. The Last Known Good Configuration is the most recent set of driver and registry settings that allowed a successful startup and user sign on. Each time a user successfully signs on to a computer after it first starts up, a new Last Known Good Configuration is written. If the server is unable to start and it is not possible to sign on, you can use Last Known Good Configuration. Last Known Good Configuration might allow you to access the desktop to perform troubleshooting tasks if you cannot perform these tasks in Safe Mode.

Configure the Boot Configuration Data store

The Boot Configuration Data (BCD) store hosts information that describes boot applications and boot application settings. You can modify the BCD store by using the BCDEdit command line utility. BCDEdit serves a similar function to the Bootcfg.exe utility that was available in previous versions of the Windows Server operating system. You can address entries in the BCD store by using the identifier GUID. When working with the currently loaded operating system, you can use {current} in commands instead of the GUID. For example, to create a duplicate BCD store entry of the currently loaded operating system entry, issue the following command:

```
Bcdedit /copy {current} /d "Duplicate Entry"
```

Monitoring and maintenance related PowerShell cmdlets

There are a variety of PowerShell cmdlets that you can use for monitoring and maintenance tasks. These cmdlets are described in Table 19-1.

Table 19-1. Cmdlets used for Event Logs and Windows Server Backup

Noun	Verbs	Function
EventLog	Clear, Get, Limit, New, Remove, Show, Write	Manage Windows Event logs, including viewing events, creating events, and clearing logs
WinEvent	Get, New	View and create events from traditional event logs as well as files generated by Event Tracing for Windows
WBApplicationRecovery	Start	Start application recovery
WBBackup	Start, Resume	Start or resume an existing backup

WBBackupSet	Get, Remove	Manage backups
WBBackupTarget	Get, Remove, Add, New	Manage backup targets
WBBackupVolumeBrowsePath	Get	View backup volumes
WBBareMetalRecovery	Remove, Get, Add	Configure bare metal recovery
WBCatalog	Restore, Remove	Manage Windows Server Backup catalog
WBDisk	Get	View disks online on the local computer
WBFileSpec	Get, New, Remove, Add	Manage items to include or exclude from a backup
WBHyperVRecovery	Start	Start Hyper-V VM recovery
WBJob	Stop, Get	Manage Windows Backup jobs
WBPerformanceConfiguration	Set, Get	Configure performance options
WBPolicy	Get, Remove, Set, New	Configure Windows Backup policies
WBSchedule	Set, Get	Configure Windows Backup schedule
WBSummary	Get	View backup summary information
WBSystemState	Add, Get, Remove	Manage backup of system state data
WBVirtualMachine	Add, Remove, Get	Manage the backup of virtual machines
WBVolume	Add, Remove, Get	Configure Windows Backup volumes
WBVolumeRecovery	Resume, Start	Manage volume recovery
WBVssBackupOption	Get, Set	Configure VSS backup options

CHAPTER 19

Upgrade and Migration

In the vast majority of cases, organizations that are deploying Windows Server 2016 will be deploying the operating system into an existing Windows Server environment. While initial prototype and proof-of-concept deployments are likely to involve a small number of servers, at some point organizations are going to want to upgrade or migrate their existing Windows Servers and the workloads hosted on those servers to Windows Server 2016.

While some organizations deploy a new server operating system and upgrade existing servers as soon as possible, and other organizations wait until their current servers reach end of extended support before planning a move, most organizations take a middle ground approach. New workloads are deployed on the newest version of the operating system, while existing workloads are left on the platform they were deployed to unless there is a pressing reason to upgrade.

In this chapter, you'll learn about upgrading or migrating several core Windows Server roles and features from previous supported versions of the Windows Server operating system to Windows Server 2016.

Supported Upgrade and Migration paths

A general rule about supported upgrade and migration paths is that you need to ensure that the product that you are upgrading from is still within Microsoft's extended support window and that you've applied all released service packs and software updates to the workload before attempting migration or upgrade. The difference between migration and upgrade is as follows:

- **Migration.** More common than an upgrade, a migration involves moving roles and data from an existing server running a supported version of Windows Server to a freshly deployed server running Windows Server 2016. Migration is Microsoft's preferred option and fits better with the "treat servers as cattle not and not as pets" philosophy of systems administration. This philosophy dictates that installation and configuration be as automated as possible, so instead of painstakingly crafting the configuration of an individual server, administrators can apply complex configurations quickly so that server upgrade or replacement is considered an uncomplicated routine operation rather than one that requires painstaking attention to arcane and not entirely understood processes.

- **Upgrade.** Sometimes called an in-place upgrade, this usually involves running the Windows Server 2016 setup routine from within an existing Windows Server 2012 or Windows Server 2012 R2 deployment. You cannot perform a direct upgrade to Windows Server 2016 from Windows Server 2008 R2 or Windows Server 2008. You perform upgrades when you need the new OS to use the same hardware as the source OS and you want to keep the roles and data that are on the source instance for the upgraded instance. Upgrades are only supported for certain roles. Upgrades are most often used in smaller organizations where the small number of servers means that the time required to build automated deployment and configuration tools and processes exceeds the time needed to deploy the organization's infrastructure manually.

Inside OUT

Do you need to migrate?

When Windows Server 2003 reached the end of support, there were still millions of servers running the operating system. Even though organizations had ample warning of the approaching deadline, many simply were unable to assign the resources to transition from the now-unsupported operating system. Hopefully IT departments are going to be better prepared for the end of support deadline for Windows Server 2008 with Service Pack 2 and Windows Server 2008 R2 with Service Pack 1, which is the 14th of January 2020. If your organization still has servers running these operating systems it's time to start planning, if not executing, a migration to a newer version of the Windows Server operating system, preferably Windows Server 2016. Windows Server 2016 is preferable because Windows Server 2012 and Windows Server 2012 R2 are going to reach their end of support date on the 1st of October 2023. Windows Server 2016 reaches its end of extended support on the 1st of November 2027. You should migrate to Windows Server 2016 as, when you migrate a workload, you might as well migrate to the platform that will be in extended support until November 2027 rather than October 2023.

An in-place upgrade is supported for certain editions of Windows Server 2012 and Windows Server 2012 R2 to Windows Server 2016. When you perform an in-place upgrade, all of the applications, data, roles and features that were present on the source server remain available on the upgraded server. While the applications, data, roles, and features will remain present, that doesn't mean that they will all be functional. Prior to attempting an in-place upgrade you should check whether applications that are hosted on the source operating system are compatible with Windows Server 2016.

Whether you can perform an upgrade depends upon the edition of Windows Server that is the source and the target of the upgrade. Upgrading the operating system is supported in the cases listed in Table 20-1:

Table 20-1 Supported edition upgrades

Source Edition	Can be upgraded to
Windows Server 2012 Standard	Windows Server 2016 Standard or Datacenter
Windows Server 2012 Datacenter	Windows Server 2016 Datacenter
Windows Server 2012 R2 Standard	Windows Server 2016 Standard or Datacenter
Windows Server 2012 R2 Datacenter	Windows Server 2016 Datacenter
Windows Server 2012 R2 Essentials	Windows Server 2016 Essentials

Upgrading Roles and Features

Table 20-2 lists which server roles and features can be directly upgraded and which server roles and features, if migrated, require the role or feature be taken offline for a period of time.

Table 20-2 Upgrades and migration

Role	Direct upgrade from Windows Server 2012 or Windows Server 2012 R2	Migration involves downtime?
AD CS	Yes	Yes
AD DS	Yes	No
AD FS	No	Yes
AD LDS	Yes	No
AD RMS	Yes	Yes
DHCP	Yes	No
DNS	Yes	No
Failover Clusters	Cluster rolling upgrade supported for Windows Server 2012 R2, but not for Windows Server 2012	No for Server 2012 R2, yes for Server 2012
File and Storage Servers	Yes	No

Hyper-V	When member of Windows Server 2012 R2 failover cluster	No for Server 2012 R2 with Scale-out file server role
Print and Fax Services	No	Yes
Web Server (IIS)	Yes	Yes
WSUS	Yes	Yes
Work Folders	Yes	No

Upgrades are constrained by the following additional limitations:

- Upgrades from one language to another are not supported. For example, you can't upgrade a French edition of Windows Server 2012 R2 to a German edition of Windows Server 2016.

- You can't upgrade from technical preview versions of Windows Server 2016 to RTM versions of Windows Server 2016.

- You cannot upgrade a Server Core installation to a Server with a Desktop installation. If the source operating system is running Windows Server 2012 or Windows Server 2012 R2, you can get around this by changing from Server Core to Server with a Desktop prior to performing the upgrade.

- You cannot upgrade a Server with a Desktop installation to a Server Core installation. If the source operating system is running Windows Server 2012 or Windows Server 2012 R2, you can get around this by converting to Server Core prior to performing the deployment.

- You cannot upgrade from a licensed version of a Windows Server operating system to an evaluation edition. Microsoft recommends that you only install evaluation editions as clean installations.

Converting evaluation version to licensed version

Although it is far from best practice, many organizations that deploy the 180 day evaluation version of Windows Server as part of a project prototype find, several months later, that the prototype has morphed into a critical component in the organization's workflow. Rather than reinstall Windows Server and migrate the prototype deployment to a properly licensed long term production platform, it is instead possible to convert an evaluation version of Windows Server 2016 to a properly licensed version by performing the following steps:

1. From an elevated command prompt, run the command *slmgr.vbs /dlv*. This will display the current computer's licensing information as shown in Figure 20-1.

FIGURE 20-1 Software Licensing information

2. Determine the current edition by running the command DISM /online /Get-CurrentEdition. This will display the edition ID, such as ServerStandard, or ServerStandardCore. You will need this edition ID for the next step.

3. Once you've determined the edition, run the command DISM /online /Set-Edition:<editionID> /ProductKey:xxxxx-xxxxx-xxxxx-xxxxx-xxxxx /AcceptEula.

Inside OUT

Evaluation Domain Controllers

You can't switch a computer that is running as a domain controller on an evaluation version of Windows Server 2016 to a retail version of the operating system. Microsoft's recommendation if you do have a domain controller running on an evaluation version that you wish to convert is to install an additional Windows Server 2016 domain controller running a non-evaluation licensed version of Windows Server 2016, then remove AD DS from the server running the evaluation version, perform the switch, and then reinstall AD DS.

Upgrading editions

You can also use DISM to upgrade from one edition of Windows Server 2016 to another. For example, if you want to upgrade from the Standard edition of Windows Server 2016 to the DataCenter edition, specify the ServerDatacenter or ServerDatacenterCore product edition and enter the appropriate product key using the DISM /online /Set-Edition:<editionID> /Product-Key: command.

You can use *slmgr.vbs* to switch between a retail license and a volume-license. To do this from an elevated prompt use the command slmgr.vbs /ipk <key> where <key> is the volume license key. If you are trying to convert an evaluation version of Windows Server 2016 to a volume licensed version, you must switch to a retail version as described earlier.

Windows Server Migration Tools

The Windows Server Migration Tools (WSMT) is a Windows Server 2016 feature that you can use to migrate a specific set of server roles, features, shared folders, operating system settings and data from a source computer running the Windows Server 2008, Windows Server 2008 R2, Windows Server 2012, Windows Server 2012 R2, and Windows Server 2016 operating system to a computer running Windows Server 2016.

You can use the WSMT to migrate the following roles and features:

- Active Directory Certificate Services

- Active Directory Federation Services

- Active Directory Rights Management Services

- File and storage services

- Hyper-V

- Network Policy Server

- Remote Desktop Services

- Windows Server Update Services

- Cluster Roles

- DHCP Server

- Web Server (IIS)

Inside OUT

2003 long out of support

Unless your organization had a custom support agreement with Microsoft, Windows Server 2003 and Windows Server 2003 R2 was not supported by Microsoft when Windows Server 2016 released. This means that there is no official upgrade path between Windows Server 2003 or Windows Server 2003 R2 and Windows Server 2016. It also means that tools designed for Windows Server 2016 are unlikely to work with Windows Server 2003. If you find yourself in a situation where you still have Windows Server 2003 deployed, one option you have is to migrate workloads to Windows Server 2012 R2. The Windows Server 2012 R2 version of the WSMT do support migration from Windows Server 2003. You can then choose if you want to migrate the workload from Windows Server 2012 R2 to Windows Server 2016, or leave the workload on Windows Server 2012 R2 and migrate from that operating system at some point in the future.

The WSMT supports:

- Migration from physically deployed operating systems to virtually deployed operating systems.

- Server Core and Server with a GUI installation option on Windows Server 2008 R2, Windows Server 2012, Windows Server 2012 R2, and Windows Server 2016 as the source operating system.

- Server Core and Server are supported with a GUI installation option for Windows Server 2016 as the destination operating system.

- You can't use WSMT with Server Core on Windows Server 2008. This is because the .NET framework is not available on the Server Core installation option of Windows Server 2008.

- USMT can only be used if the source and destination operating system are using the same UI language. The system UI language is the one used when setting up the operating system.

Inside OUT

Where possible, Server Core

The Server Core installation option is the Windows Server 2016 default. When migrating to Windows Server 2016, strongly consider shifting as many workloads to hosts running the Server Core installation option rather than the Desktop Experience installation option. Unless you are in an environment with a small number of servers, it's likely that you already use remote consoles and PowerShell to manage servers and rarely RDP to the server desktop. You won't be able to do it with all servers, especially those running applications that require desktop components, but you will be able to do it with a good number of servers such as those hosting boring roles such and functioning as file servers, DHCP servers, DNS servers, and Domain Controllers.

The WSMT have the following requirements:

- Must be deployed using an account that has local Administrator privileges on the source and destination server.

- The source server must have at least 23 MB of free space to store the WSMT deployment folder.

- The source server must have the .NET Framework 3.51 installed.

- Windows PowerShell must be present on the source server. PowerShell is included by default with Windows Server 2008 R2, Windows Server 2012, Windows Server 2012 R2, and Windows Server 2016. PowerShell is not included by default on servers running the Windows Server 2008 operating system, though it's likely that it has been installed at some point prior to the deployment of that operating system in your environment.

- You should always use the most recent version of the WSMT.

Installing the WSMT

You can install the WSMT on the destination server using the Install-WindowsFeature Migration PowerShell command or by installing the role using the Add Roles and Features Wizard as shown in Figure 20-2. When you do this, the WSMT are deployed in the %WinDir%\System32\ServerMigrationTools folder on the destination server.

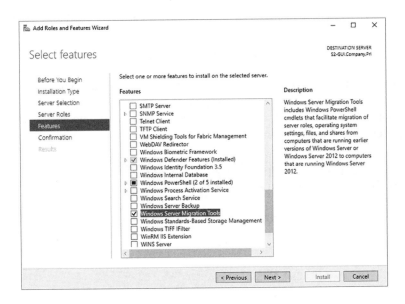

FIGURE 20-2 Windows Server Migration Tools

Once you've installed the WSMT, you need to configure a deployment folder from which you will deploy the appropriate version of the WSMT. Rather than deploy a generic version of the tools, deploy a version tailored for the source operating system. For example, to create a set of tools for a source computer running Windows Server 2012 R2, issue the command as shown in Figure 20-3:

```
Smigdeploy.exe /package /architecture amd64 /os WS12R2 /path <path to share>
```

```
Administrator: Command Prompt                                          —  □  ×

C:\Windows\System32\ServerMigrationTools>smigdeploy /package /architecture amd64 /os WS12R2 /path c:\deploy
SmigDeploy.exe is checking for prerequisites.
---------------------------------------------------------------------------
SmigDeploy.exe is copying Windows Server Migration Tools files to c:\deploy\SMT_ws12R2_amd64.
---------------------------------------------------------------------------

C:\Windows\System32\ServerMigrationTools>
```

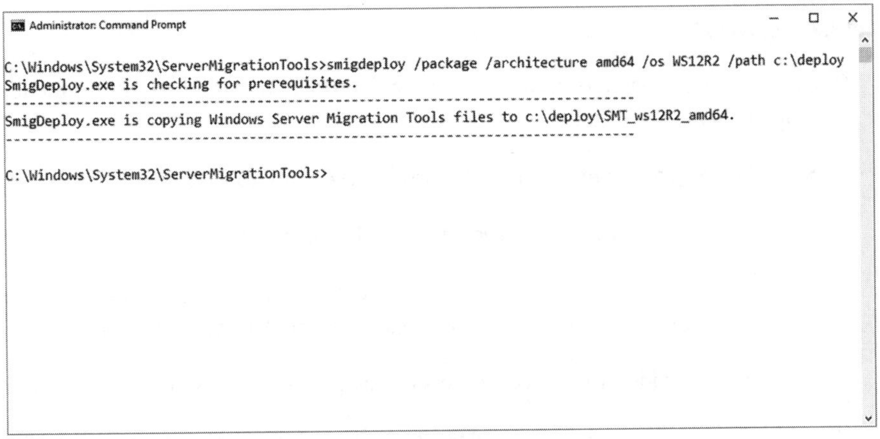

FIGURE 20-3 Create migration tools package

CHAPTER 20

To create a set of tools for a source computer running Windows Server 2008 R2, use this command:

```
Smigdeploy.exe /package /architecture amd64 /os WS08R2 /path <path to share>
```

You can either copy the contents of the deployment folder to the source computer, or enact the tools remotely over a network connection by running smigdeploy.exe from an elevated command prompt. Installing the tools on a source server running the GUI option will give you a special migration tools PowerShell session as shown in Figure 20-4.

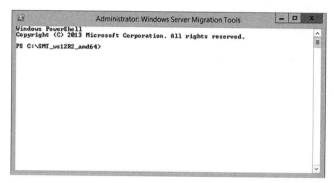

FIGURE 20-4 Server Migration tools running on Windows Server 2012 R2

If you are running the tools on a computer that is configured with the Server Core installation option, open an elevated PowerShell session and run the following command to add the WSMT cmdlets:

```
Add-PSSnapin Microsoft.Windows.ServerManager.Migration
```

Active Directory

Microsoft's recommended strategy for upgrading domain controllers in a domain or forest to Windows Server 2016 is to:

- Add member servers running Windows Server 2016 to a domain

- , Promote those member servers to domain controller

- Transfer FSMO roles across to the domain controllers running Windows Server 2016 from the domain controllers running previous versions of the Windows Server operating system

- Demoting those domain controllers running the older version of the operating system.

In some circumstances you may need to perform an upgrade of a domain controller rather than using the recommended strategy. Prior to attempting the upgrade, manually adprep /

forestprep and adprep /domainprep from the \support\adprep folder of the Windows Server 2016 installation media.

You should upgrade the domain controllers in the forest root domain and then upgrade domain controllers in any child domains. Once you've upgraded all of the domain controllers in your organization, you can then raise the domain functional level of each domain in the forest to Windows Server 2016 using the Active Directory Domains and Trust console as shown in Figure 20-5.

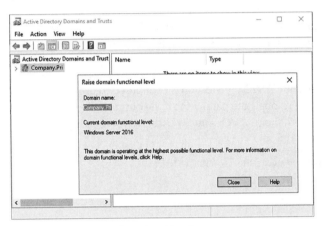

FIGURE 20-5 Domain functional level

Once you have raised the domain functional level of each domain in the forest to Windows Server 2016, you can raise the forest functional level to Windows Server 2016 using the Active Directory Domains and Trusts console as shown in Figure 20-6.

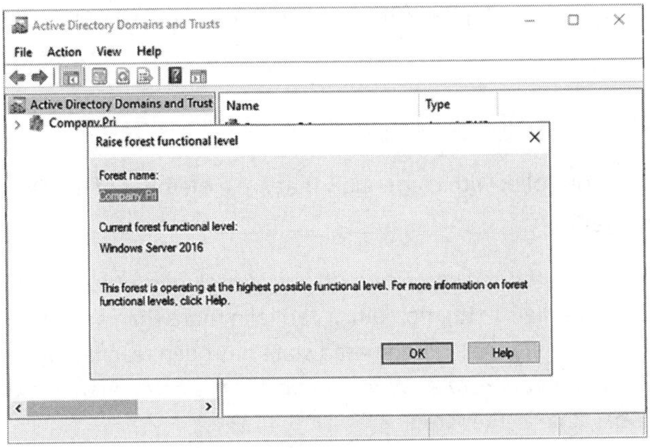

FIGURE 20-6 Forest functional level

> **MORE INFO   UPGRADING DOMAIN CONTROLLERS**
>
> You can learn more about upgrading domain controllers to Windows Server 2016 at: *https://technet.microsoft.com/windows-server-docs/identity/ad-ds/deploy/ upgrade-domain-controllers-to-windows-server-2012-r2-and-windows-server-2012.*

FRS to DFSR migration

Depending on the age of your organization's Active Directory deployment, especially if at any time a domain functioned at the Windows Server 2003 functional level, and how diligently Active Directory upgrades were performed, it's possible that SYSVOL replication is configured to use the older inefficient File Replication Service rather than the more efficient Distributed File System.

You can check whether or not SYSVOL replication is configured to use FRS of DFS using the dfsrmig.exe utility with the /globalstate parameter. If the output state of the command shows Eliminated, as in Figure 20-7, then SYSVOL already uses DFS for replication.

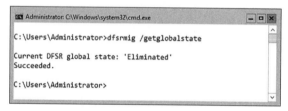

FIGURE 20-7 SYSVOL migration state

If the output of dfsrmig.exe instead shows that migration has yet to be initialized, you should update the SYSVOL replication. You should only use FSR for SYSVOL replication if your organization still has domain controllers running the Windows Server 2003 or Windows Server 2003 R2 operating systems.

To upgrade SYSVOL replication to DFS from FRS, perform the following steps:

1. Sign on to a domain controller with credentials that are a member of the Domain Admin or Enterprise Admin groups.

2. Start PowerShell and then run the command *dfsrmig /setglobalstate 1*. Depending on the number of domain controllers in the domain, it can take more than an hour to reach the prepared state. You can verify that the prepared state has been reached by running the command *dfsrmig /getmigrationstate*. When preparation is completed, the utility will report that the global state is 'Prepared.'

3. The next step to take is to place the DFSR state to Redirected. You do this using the command *dfsrmig /setglobalstate 2*. You use *dfsrmig /getmigraitonstate* to verify that the DFSR state is set to Redirected.

4. Once the DFSR state is set to Redirected, run the command *dfsrmig /setglobalstate 3*. This will finalize the transition of SYSVOL to the Eliminated state and DFS will be used for replication instead of FRS.

Migrating to a new forest

Many organizations have had their current Active Directory environment for more than a decade. The older an Active Directory environment is, the more likely it is to have an inefficient domain and OU structure, derelict user and computer accounts, unutilized sites, and forgotten group policy objects and groups. Just as Microsoft recommends performing fresh installations rather than in-place upgrades for individual computers, it may make more sense to migrate to a new forest than it does to remain with an existing Active Directory forest. This is especially true if an organization is considering moving toward a secure administrative model where the privileged accounts in a production forest are unprivileged standard accounts in the secure administrative forest.

The Active Directory Migration Tool (ADMT) is a special tool that you can use to migrate Active Directory objects to and from any Active Directory environments, from moving accounts within a forest, to migrating accounts to a new Active Directory forest.

You can use ADMT to perform an interforest restructure or an intraforest restructure. An intra-forest restructure allows you to modify your current domain and forest structure to reduce complexity. An interforest restructure involves creating a brand new simplified forest structure using Active Directory objects from your existing forest.

Table 20-3 lists the difference between each restructure type.

Table 20-3 Migration differences

Consideration	Interforest restructure	Intraforest restructure
Object preservation	Objects, such as accounts, will be cloned. The original object remains in the source forest	User and group objects are migrated and are no-longer present in the source location. Computer and managed service account objects are copied and remain in the source location
SID history maintenance	SID history maintenance is optional	SID history is mandatory for user, group, and computer accounts. It is not required for managed service accounts

Password retention	Password retention is optional	Passwords are always retained
Profile migration	Local profiles can be migrated using ADMT	Local profiles automatically migrated and account GUID is preserved

The Active Directory Migration Tool requires that you have access to a SQL Server instance. This can be a full SQL Server deployment, or a local SQL Server express instance. The ADMT includes the following wizards, shown in Figure 20-8.

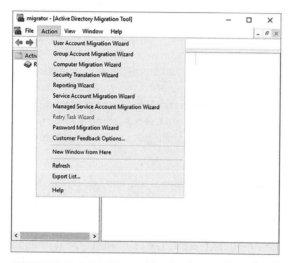

FIGURE 20-8 Active Directory Migration Tool

- **User Account Migration Wizard.** Allows you to perform an intra or inter-forest migration of user account objects.

- **Group Account Migration Wizard.** Allows you to perform an intra or inter-forest migration of group account objects, including group membership information.

- **Computer Migration Wizard.** Allows you to perform an intra or inter-forest migration of computer account objects.

- **Security Translation Wizard.** Wizard that allows you to transfer security permissions during object migration.

- **Reporting Wizard.** Generate the following reports:

  - **Migrated Users, Groups and Managed Service Accounts report.** Summarizes result of the migration of user, group and managed service accounts.

- **Expired Computers Report.** List of computers found that have expired computer account passwords.

- **Account References Report.** List of accounts that have been assigned permissions for resources on a specific computer.

- **Name Conflicts Report.** A list of user accounts and groups that are present in both the source and target domains.

- **Service Account Migration Wizard.** Allows you to perform intra or inter-forest service account migration.

- **Managed Service Account Migration Wizard.** Allows you to perform intra or inter-forest managed service account migration.

- **Password Migration Wizard.** Allows you to perform intra or inter-forest password migration.

MORE INFO   ACTIVE DIRECTORY MIGRATION TOOL

You can learn more about the Active Directory Migration Tool at: *https://technet.micro-soft.com/en-us/library/cc974332(v=ws.10).aspx.*

Active Directory Certificate Services

You can use WSMT to migrate an AD CS deployment from one server to another. The WSMT method works best when you are migrating a standalone root or subordinate CA. Prior to performing AD CS migration, you need to be aware of the following:

- It will be necessary to either turn off the source CA or stop the source server's certificate services service.

- The destination CA must have the same name as the source CA. The CA name is separate from the computer name.

- While the computer name of the destination CA does not need to match that of the source CA, the destination CA name must not be identical to the name assigned to the destination computer. For example, ContosoRootCA is the name of the source CA which is hosted on a computer named MEL-CA. When migrated, the destination CA will be called ContosoRootCA and might be hosted on a computer named MEL-NEW-CA. The destination computer just cannot be named ContosoRootCA.

- During migration the CA will be unable to issue certificates or publish CRLs.

- To ensure that revocation status checking can occur, ensure that a CRL is published prior to migration that will remain valid to a point in time after the expected completion of the migration.

- Ensure that at least one of the CRL distribution points specified for existing certificates remains available during migration. Enterprise CAs publish to Active Directory, but stand-alone CAs may only publish to the local server. If the CRL distribution point is unavailable, clients will be unable to perform revocation checks.

- The Authority Information Access (AIA) and CRL distribution point extensions of previously issued certificates may reference the name of the source CA. This is the default setting and will only be different if you explicitly changed it.

- If migrating an enterprise CA or standalone CA on a computer that is a member of a domain, the account used to perform the migration must be a member of the Enterprise Admins or Domain Admins group.

Inside OUT

AD CS Upgrades

You can directly upgrade a computer running Windows Server 2012 or Windows Server 2012 R2 that hosts the AD CS role to Windows Server 2016. If you've got a complex configuration that includes and enterprise CA, CA web enrollment, online responders, network device enrollment, and the certificate enrollment web services all on the same host, it's substantially easier to do it this way. Given the amount of work involved, if you are hosting this role and the role service on Windows Server 2008 or Windows Server 2008 R2, it may even be worth considering a hop-upgrade where you upgrade from Server 2008 or Server 2008 R2 to Windows Server 2012 R2 and then to Windows Server 2016. When it comes to AD CS, especially since AD integrated CAs, servers are definitely far more in the category of "pets" rather than "cattle".

CA migration can be carried out in three general phases:

- Preparation

- Migration

- Verification and post migration tasks

Preparation

To preparing the source server, perform the following steps:

- Export the CA templates list. This is the list of templates that the CA is configured to issue. The master list of templates is stored within Active Directory. You can export this list from the Certificate Services console by right clicking on the Certificate Templates node and selecting export. You can also do this using the command *certutil.exe -catemplates > catemplates.txt command.*

- Make a note of the CA's Cryptographic Service Provider (CSP) and which signature algorithm is used. This is visible on the CA's properties dialog box as shown in Figure 20-9. You can also do this using the command *certutil.exe -getreg ca\csp* > csp.txt.*

FIGURE 20-9 CSP and signature algorithm

- Backup the source server CA, including the private key, CA certificate, Certificate Database and Certificate Database Log. You can do this using the Certification Authority Backup Wizard as shown in Figure 20-10. Copy the contents of the backup folder to a location that will be accessible to the destination server.

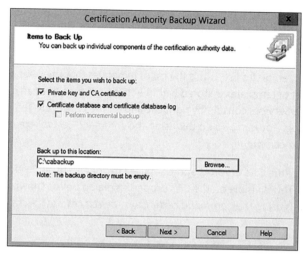

FIGURE 20-10 CA Backup Wizard

- Stop the Certificate Services service. You can do this using the Services console as shown in Figure 20-11 or by using the Stop-Service certsvc Windows PowerShell command. This will block the current certificate server from issuing any additional certificates.

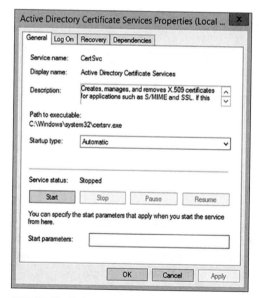

FIGURE 20-11 Stop certificate services service

- Backup the registry settings of the CA using the following command and place it in a location that is accessible to the destination server:

```
reg export HKLM\SYSTEM\CurrentControlSet\Services\CertSvc\Configuration <output file>.reg
```

- If the source CA uses a custom CAPolicy.inf file, you should copy this file to a location that is accessible to the destination server.

Migration

Once you have performed the necessary preparation steps, you should perform the following steps to complete the migration of the CA:

- Remove the CA role service from the source server once you have backed up the source CA and its registry settings. This is important because removing the role service from the server will also clean up data stored in Active Directory associated with the CA. If you don't perform this cleanup, you will encounter problems when introducing the migrated CA that shares the original CA's name.

- Removing the role service from the CA does not delete the CA database, private key, or CA certificate. This means that if the migration fails, you will be able to restore the CA by reinstalling the certificate services role on the server.

- Microsoft also recommends manually removing the source server from the domain prior to deploying the destination server. This is especially important if the source and destination server share the same computer name.

- Change the name of the destination server to match the name of the source server.

- Join the destination server to the domain.

- Import the CA certificates into the local computer's Personal certificate store.

- Once the computer is domain joined, add the CA role service to the destination server. Ensure that you install the server in the same manner, such as installing an Enterprise Root or Standalone Subordinate CA depending on the properties of the original source CA. During the installation routine on the Set Up Private Key page, utilize the Use Existing Private Key option, and select the existing private key. Complete the setup wizard.

- Use the Certification Authority snap-in to restore both the certificate database and the certificate database log from the backup taken on the source server. You will need to restart the certificate services server.

- Import the registry settings exported from the source CA. If the source CA and the destination CA share the same name and the same file paths, then this can be done without modification. If the source CA has a different name from the destination CA or uses different file paths, you'll need to manually alter these registry settings. Prior to importing the registry, stop the certificate services service. Use the command reg import backup.reg to import the registry file. Restart the certificate service.

- Import the list of CA templates that are issued from the CA using the command *certutil -setcatemplates* and then provide a list of templates that you backed up from the source server in comma separated format.

Verification and post migration tasks

To verify that the CA has migrated successfully, verify that you can successfully request and enroll a new certificate. You should also verify that you can successfully publish a CRL. How to perform these tasks is covered in Chapter 12, "Active Directory Certificate Services."

> ### MORE INFO   MIGRATE ACTIVE DIRECTORY CERTIFICATE SERVICES
>
> Even though the guide lists Windows Server 2012 R2, you can learn more about migrating Active Directory Certificate Services to Windows Server 2016 using the WSMT at: *https://technet.microsoft.com/en-us/library/cc974332(v=ws.10).aspx*.

DNS

The simplest way to migrate DNS is where DNS zones are Active Directory integrated. In that scenario, you add member servers running Windows Server 2016 to an existing domain, promote those servers to domain controllers, and make sure that you add the DNS role. Any existing AD integrated zones that are configured to replicate to other domain controllers in the domain will replicate to the newly promoted domain controller. Remember to add custom partitions if you have AD integrated zones that only replicate to specific domain controllers.

The trick to migrating primary zones from one DNS server to another is to first configure the destination server to host a secondary zone of the primary zone. Once the zone has replicated to the intended destination server, convert the zone from being a secondary zone to function as a primary zone. You can do this by performing the following steps:

1. On the General tab of the secondary zone properties, shown in Figure 20-12, click Change.

FIGURE 20-12 Zone general properties tab

2. On the Change Zone Type dialog box, shown in Figure 20-13, select Primary Zone and then click OK.

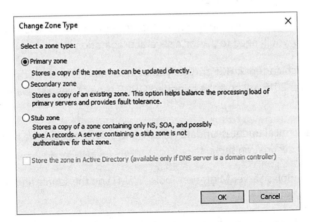

FIGURE 20-13 Change zone type

DHCP

You can use the WSMT to migrate a DHCP server, scopes, and settings from computers running both the server core and server with a GUI installation options of Windows Server 2008, Windows Server 2008 R2, Windows Server 2012, Windows Server 2012 R2, and Windows Server 2016 to Windows Server 2016.

To perform a migration of a DHCP server using WSMT, you need access to accounts with the following permissions:

- Permission to authorize the DHCP server in Active Directory.

- Membership of the local Administrator group on the computers that are both source and destination DHCP servers.

- Permission to write data to the WSMT migration store location.

DHCP migration follows the following general steps:

- Preparation

- Migration

- Verification and post migration tasks

Preparing to migrate DHCP

Before you start the process of migrating a DHCP server, its associated scopes and settings to Windows Server 2016, you'll need to perform several preparation steps.

- Determine which current DHCP servers you wish to migrate and which servers running Windows Server 2016 will host the migrated DHCP server roles, associated scopes, and settings.

- Ensure that all critical updates, update rollups, and service packs have been installed on the source and destination servers.

- Deploy the Windows Server Migration Tools (WSMT) on the source and destination servers.

- Install the DHCP role service on the destination server. This service must be present on the destination server prior to beginning the migration.

- Ensure that the source and destination servers have the same number of network adapters. Determine which subnet each network adapter is bound to on the source server and ensure that the destination server has network adapters bound to the same subnets. This will ensure that the migrated DHCP server can service the same subnets as the source DHCP server.

- Determine the IP address strategy for the destination server. DHCP servers should use static IP addresses on network interfaces that are used by the DHCP server service to manage DHCP traffic. Options include:

  - Assigning the destination server different static IP addresses that are on the same subnets as the static IP addresses assigned to network interfaces on the source server. Doing this will allow you to perform the migration with both the source and destination server online.

  - Assign the destination server the same IP addresses that are used for network interfaces for the source server. While this is possible, it will mean that the source and destination server cannot be online at the same time without causing IP address conflicts, or which would require extensive preparation of network virtualization. As existing clients will be able to renew their IP address information after migration from a destination server with a new IP address on the same subnet, only keep the same IP addresses on the source and destination server if there are substantive reasons for doing so.

- If the source server does not use the default path for the DHCP server database, such as having the database stored on a separate volume, the destination server will need to have a volume configuration that matches that of the source server. For example, if the DHCP database is stored on volume H: of the source server, the destination server will need a properly formatted volume H: for migration to be successful.

- Ensure that the migration store location is accessible to both the source and destination server.

- Ensure that both the source and destination server have network access to the AD DS environment.

- Perform a backup of the DHCP server from the DHCP console, rather than the Windows Server Backup, as shown in Figure 20-14. You can do this by just right-clicking on the DHCP server node, selecting backup, and specifying a location for the backup.

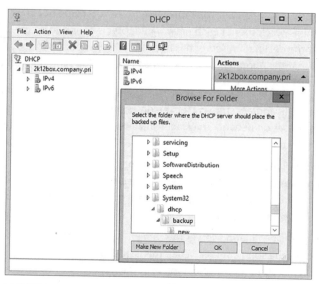

FIGURE 20-14 Backup DHCP database

- Once the backup is complete, stop the DHCP service on the source and the destination server, either by using the Services console as shown in Figure 20-15, or by running the Stop-Service DHCPserver Windows PowerShell cmdlet.

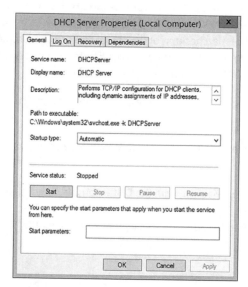

FIGURE 20-15 Stop DHCP Server service

Migration

Once the source and destination servers are prepared, the next step is to open the Windows Server Migration Tools PowerShell session. You perform the migration using the Export-SmigServerSetting PowerShell cmdlet. Specific parameters of the Export-SmigServerSetting cmdlet that are relevant to DHCP server migration include:

- Use the FeatureID DHCP to specify that it is the DHCP server role that you want to migrate.

- Use the Users parameter if the DHCP Administrators group includes local user accounts. Use the Group parameter to migrate all members of the DHCP administrators group that don't include local users, but do include domain users and groups.

- You can use the IPConfig parameter if you want to export the IP address configuration of the source server to the destination server.

- Use the Path parameter to specify the location of the svrmig.mig file. If you don't specify a network location, you'll need to manually transfer this file to a location that is accessible to the destination server.

Considerations around using the Import-SmigServerSetting cmdlet on the destination server include:

- Use the FeatureID DHCP to specify that it is the DHCP server role that you are importing. While the Import-SmigServerSetting cmdlet will install the DHCP server role if it is not already present on the destination server, Microsoft recommends installing the service and then placing it in a stopped state before importing data using the WSMT.

- Use the Users parameter if the DHCP Administrators group on the destination server will include local users. Use the Group parameter if the DHCP Administrators group contains domain users and groups.

- Use the Path parameter to specify the location of the svrmig.mig file. This file can be stored on an accessible network share or stored locally.

- Once migration is complete, start the DHCP server service using the Start-Service DHCPServer cmdlet.

- If you haven't already, you'll need to authorize the DHCP server in Active Directory before it will function.

Verification and Post Migration Tasks

Once the migration has occurred, ensure that the DHCP server service on the source server remains in a stopped state, as well as on a client release, and then renew an IP address to verify that the DHCP server service on the destination server is functioning properly. You should also manually check that the scopes and settings that were present on the source server are also present on the destination server. Once you have verified that the migration has completed successfully, remove the DHCP server service from the source computer.

MORE INFO   DHCP MIGRATION

Though the guide mentions Server 2012 R2, you can learn about migrating DHCP to *Windows Server 2016 at: https://technet.microsoft.com/library/dn495425.aspx.*

File and Storage Servers

You can use the WSMT to migrate the following file and storage services information from a computer running Windows Server 2008, Windows Server 2008 R2, Windows Server 2012, Windows Server 2012 R2, and Windows Server 2016 to Windows Server 2016:

- Server identity information

- Local users and groups

- Data and shared folders

- Shadow copies of Shared Folders

- Data Deduplication

- DFS Namespaces

- DFS Replication

- File Server Resource Manager (FSRM)

- Group Policy Settings related to SMB

- Group Policy settings for Offline Files

- iSCSI Software Target settings

- Network File System (NFS) shares

- Remote Volume Shadow Copy Service

The following migration scenarios are supported for file and storage services:

- The file server is a member of a domain

- The file server is a member of a workgroup

- File server data and shares are located on an external storage location such as a SAN or on direct attached storage as long as either storage medium preserves data permissions and file share permissions.

It is important to note that file migration using the WSMT is aimed at moving data sets smaller than 100GB, because only one file at a time is copied over a HTTPS connection. When moving larger data sets, Microsoft recommends using the robocopy.exe utility included with Windows Server 2016.

Migration permissions

Depending on the type of migration that you want to perform, a variety of permissions are necessary. If you are going to migrate data and shared folders, you must use an account that has local administrator permissions on the destination server.

Migration of DFS can be performed if an account is a member of a Domain Admins group. Alternatively, if there is more than one namespace server, the account used doesn't have to be a member of the Domain Admins group as long as it has permission to administer all namespaces on the source server, and is a member of the local Administrators group on the source and destination server.

Users that trigger migration of DFS replicas must either be members of the Domain Admins group, or must have been delegated permission to the appropriate replication groups and replication members. If the user account used to perform this action, it must be a member of the local Administrators group on the source and destination servers.

Preparing to migrate

To prepare to migrate the file and storage services role and data from a source server to a destination server, perform the following steps:

- Ensure that the source and destination server have their time correctly set. If the clocks on the source and destination server are out of synchronization, the migration will fail.

- Ensure that the same File Services role services are present on both the source server and the destination server.

- Ensure that Windows Server Migration Tools are deployed on both the source server and the destination server.

- Configure a firewall rule to allow traffic on TCP and UDP port 7000 between the source server and the destination server on both the source and destination server. TCP and UDP port 7000 is used by the Send-SmigServerData and Receive-SmigServerData cmdlets when establishing data migration connections.

- Ensure that the destination path has sufficient disk space to migrate data. If you have a configured NTFS quota or folder management, ensure that the quota limit will allow the migration of data.

- If migrating File Server Resource Manager data and settings, ensure that the destination server has the same volume configuration as the source server.

- While file and folder permissions are preserved during migration, remember that migrated files and folders inherit permission from parent folders. You should ensure that parent folders on the destination server have permissions that match those on the source server.

- If performing a DFS migration, ensure that the DFS Namespaces role service is installed and configured on the destination server. The DFS Namespace service must be running prior to commencing migration.

- If you are migrating DFS namespaces, back up the source server using a system state or full server backup. If the DFS namespaces are integrated into AD DS, it will be necessary to backup the system state on a domain controller to ensure that the AD DS configuration information for DFS namespaces is backed up.

- Ensure that the Server service on the destination computer is set to use the Automatic startup type as shown in Figure 20-16.

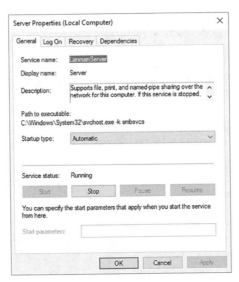

FIGURE 20-16 Server service settings

- You can backup the configuration information of a domain-based DFS namespace using the following command:

```
dfsutil.exe root export <\\<DomainName>\NameSpace> <BackupFileName>
```

Migrating File and Storage Services

Once you have completed the migration preparation steps, use the Export-SmigServerSetting cmdlet to capture the following settings on the source server so that you can import them on the destination server using the Import-SmigServerSetting cmdlet:

- SMB (Server Message Block) settings

- Offline Files settings

- DFS Namespaces configuration

- File Server Resource Manager settings

- Shadow Copies of Shared Folders

Running the cmdlet will generate the migration file svrmig.mig, which you'll need to then need to transfer to and import on the destination server. If you want to migrate local users and groups from the source server to the destination server, use the User All and Group parameters with the Export-SmigServerSetting cmdlet. Remember to specify the same parameters with the Import-SmigServerSetting cmdlet on the destination server.

Once settings have been transferred from source server to destination server, use the Send-SmigServerData and the Receive-SmigServerData cmdlets to transfer data between the source and destination servers.

For example, to send data to the computer named MEL-FS-2K16, of files that are located under the e:\fileshare folder on the source computer to the f:\fileshare folder on the destination computer, you would run the command:

```
Send-SmigServerData -ComputerName MEL-FS-2K16 -SourcePath e:\fileshare -DestinationPath
f:\fileshare -Recurse -Include All -Force
```

You must start the Receive-SmigServerData cmdlet in an elevated session on the destination server within five minutes of it being executed on the source server. Data transfer between the source and the destination server is encrypted.

> ### MORE INFO   FILE AND STORAGE SERVICES MIGRATION
>
> Though the guide mentions Server 2012 R2, you can learn about migrating file and storage services to Windows Server 2016 at: *https://technet.microsoft.com/en-us/library/dn479292(v=ws.11).aspx.*

Microsoft Server application compatibility

While any Microsoft server application released after the release of Windows Server 2016 will run on the platform, it can be challenging to determine which versions of server applications released prior to the release of Windows Server 2016, which include server applications with the year 2016 in the name, and are compatible with Windows Server 2016. The following Microsoft server applications are officially supported on Windows Server 2016:

- Microsoft SQL Server 2012

- Microsoft SQL Server 2014

- Microsoft SQL Server 2016

- Microsoft System Center Virtual Machine Manager 2016

- Microsoft System Center Operations Manager 2016

- Microsoft System Center Data Protection Manger 2016

- Microsoft System Center Configuration Manager (version 1606 and later)

- SharePoint Server 2016

- Project Server 2016

- Exchange Server 2016

- BizTalk Server 2016

- Host Integration Server 2016

- Visual Studio Team Foundation Server 2017

- Skype for Business Server 2015

While it can be possible, sometimes, by taking measures such as modifying registry settings, to install some Microsoft server applications such as Exchange Server 2013 and SharePoint Server 2013 on Windows Server 2016, organizations that are not running the most recent version of these server applications should continue to deploy them on the platforms that they were designed for.

MORE INFO   COMPATIBLE SERVER APPLICATIONS

You can find out up to date information about which Microsoft server applications are compatible with Windows Server 2016 at: *https://technet.microsoft.com/en-us/windows-server-docs/get-started/server-application-compatibility*.

CHAPTER 20

In this chapter you'll learn about troubleshooting methodologies for complex problems. This chapter provides general guidelines for solving problems above the simple "is it plugged into the network" or "did you switch it on and off again." In this chapter, you'll also learn about some of the Sysinternals tools which you can use to diagnose problems as well as the Azure Operations Management Suite Log Analytics product, which allows for machine learning analysis of data stored in event logs.

Troubleshooting methodology

There are a couple of tricks to troubleshooting problems. The first is to realize that you'll be far more effective about troubleshooting if you approach the problem systematically, rather than just trying random solutions.

The next is that, jokes aside, there is far more to IT troubleshooting than typing some problem characteristics into Google (or, this being a Microsoft Press Book, let's say Bing) and diligently applying any solution that turns up.

Some problems with the search engine approach include:

- Posts often provide an incomplete description of problem symptoms. This is often because the person asking for help in the post hasn't developed a full understanding of the nature of the problem they are trying to solve by posting a request for help.

- Unless you understand all of the symptoms it's possible that the post and the proposed solution aren't relevant to the problem that you are troubleshooting.

- Even when other posters in the same thread respond that the solution worked for them, you can't be certain that they had the same problem as you, or that they implemented the solutions proposed in responses to the post correctly.

This doesn't mean that you can't learn what the solution to a complex problem is by consulting online forums, it's just that you should treat solutions offered to other people's problems with an appropriate degree of confidence. Those solutions might work or they might not, but finding out through experimentation on your production environment probably isn't the best way to display your technical aptitude.

Inside OUT

Thinking, fast and slow

Nobel prize winner Daniel Kahneman discusses how we arrive at conclusions in his bestselling book "Thinking, Fast and Slow". Where this book is illuminating for people troubleshooting problems in IT is its ideas around intuitive and reasoned decision making. Kahneman suggests that our first response when tasked with solving a problem is to rely upon intuitive thinking. The problem with intuitive thinking is that it almost always involves jumping to conclusions with only minimal justification or evidence. As Kahneman explains, intuitive thinking is often no better than a random guess. Sometimes we justify these this guesswork by assuming that our own long prior experience in IT troubleshooting other problems must have given us superhuman intuition about the causes of technological problems. A good troubleshooting strategy involves reducing the amount of guesswork and intuitive thinking and preferences deductive reasoning. Good troubleshooters know to distrust their first assumptions about a complex problem and to spend some time investigating the problem further before becoming certain as to the cause and the resolution.

Redeployment

When I got started in IT, I'd often spend hours, if not days troubleshooting a problem with a server or desktop computer because each computer had a unique configuration, so deploying from scratch would take substantially longer. Not only would it be necessary to reinstall the operating system, but it would be necessary to locate the correct drivers, something that was a lot more challenging in the early days of the web when many hardware vendors weren't online, let alone providing websites with easy to locate driver downloads. With Windows NT 4.0, it was often necessary to keep boxes of disks around containing drivers to support each hardware configuration. The process of installing server applications was often similarly fraught. Vendor documentation was scarce, and other than the occasional helpful newsgroup post, there wasn't much help available online when it came to troubleshooting. Getting a server up and running in the 90's could be such an involved process that you would take the time to troubleshoot whatever problem you had as much as possible and only redeploy the workload when all other avenues were exhausted.

With Windows Server 2016, the vast majority of drivers utilized by the operating system are included, or are easily accessible on vendor websites. It's relatively straightforward to backup and reinstall applications and the web provides a cornucopia of documentation and advice on troubleshooting existing workloads.

If a workload with a known configuration has worked in the past and yet is experiencing errors now, one of the options that you have at your disposal is to redeploy rather than spend time troubleshooting. With tools such as desired state configuration, puppet, or chef, it's quite likely that you can redeploy in less time than it takes you to diagnose, research, and solve the problem you face.

The trick with all of this is that you need to have workload configuration and deployment highly automated. Building out that configuration automation will take a substantial amount of time and you will need to ensure that the configuration automation is updated each time you update the configuration of the workload in question. The argument for this approach is easy to make if you have a large number of servers that have similar configurations. In scenarios where you are only dealing with a small number of servers and where each workload is unique, you may end up spending more time automating configuration than you ever would deploying servers.

You'll also need to ensure that data is decoupled properly from the workload. A long term aspirational goal of any server administrator should be to automate the configuration of any workload that they manage, so that they can redeploy it quickly in another VM or on another physical chassis should something catastrophic happen with the original workload. It's likely that you are far from that goal at the moment in your own environment, but as you get closer to it, you'll find that redeployment as a troubleshooting step becomes a viable first response strategy to complex problems. Admittedly if it works, redeployment doesn't answer the tricky question of what might have caused the problem in the first place. However if it does work, you can ponder the question of what actually happened as an existential problem, rather than as a practical one.

In some cases redeploying the workload from what is believed to be a good configuration will not solve the issue. In that scenario, you'll need to perform a deeper investigation as to what is causing the problem.

Symptoms and diagnosis

Before you can solve a problem, you need to understand the nature of the problem. The first step in understanding the nature of a complex problem is having an understanding of the symptoms of that problem.

The easiest symptoms to document are the ones that caused you to notice that there was a problem in the first place. The thing that is important to realize is that there are likely to be other symptoms present. It's understanding all of these symptoms and their relationship with one another that will allow you to diagnose the cause and resolution of the problem. It might be that the first thing you notice about a problem is only tangential to that problem. By investigating further, you discover that far more problematic things are occurring than the thing that drew your attention to the problem in the first place.

> ## Inside OUT
>
> ### More than one cause
>
> Anyone who has diagnosed a complex problem knows that a single set of symptoms may have separate root causes. That's one reason why we might need to try multiple resolutions when troubleshooting. Generally though, the more evidence you can collect around problem symptoms, the better idea you can have about diagnosing the problem.

A diagnostic hypothesis is a hypothesis as to what might be causing the problem. It's what you suspect may be causing the problem before you have verification that what you suspect is causing the problem is actually causing the problem.

Rather than latching on to the first diagnostic hypothesis that occurs to you, try to list other things that might also be causing the problem. In thinking up other things, you're likely to gain more of an understanding about how you should be investigating the problem. You want to get as much evidence as possible about what's causing the problem before you try to solve it. As every experienced IT person knows, applying the wrong solution to a problem can often make the problem worse. By having as much information about the problem as possible, you reduce the chance that you'll apply an incorrect solution in attempting to solve the problem.

Ranking hypothetical solutions

A solution is hypothetical until it works. Before you apply a hypothetical solution in an attempt to solve a problem, you should rank them in order of how you should test whether the solution works. While simple problems often have obvious solutions, complex problems are likely to have a variety of apparent solutions and you generally won't know which is the appropriate solution until you've applied it and found that it works. Consider the following factors when ranking the order in which you should apply hypothetical solutions:

- Rank hypothetical solutions that are simple to implement and involve minimally changing the existing configuration higher than solutions that involve substantial changes to the existing configuration. This is because if the hypothetical solution turns out to be incorrect, you'll need to roll back the configuration changes before trying the next hypothetical solution. This is easier to do if the changes are less complicated than it is to do with a complex set of configuration changes. If a solution doesn't work, you need to go back to where you started rather than continuing on, making further configuration changes when a solution you tried didn't work.

- Rank hypothetical solutions for which you have more evidence higher than solutions where there isn't as much evidence. As mentioned earlier, try to figure out what other evidence you should see if your hypothesis about what is causing the problem is correct rather than just focusing on the symptoms the brought the problem to your attention in the first place. Try to think of ways to disprove a diagnostic hypothesis without taking invasive action. It's better to discard an incorrect solution before implementing it because you find evidence that indicates that it is impossible than to try the incorrect solution in your production environment and find out that it doesn't work.

- Rank hypothetical solutions that are low impact above solutions that are high impact. Always keep in the back of your mind that applying a solution could make things worse, so preference the solutions that will cause fewer problems should things go wrong than solutions that might require you to stay at work longer because a solution goes wrong?

- Rank hypothetical solutions that require a shorter amount of time to implement above solutions that take much longer to implement. When you don't know which solution is going to solve your problem, you are better off trying the one that takes a couple of minutes over the one that takes a couple of hours.

Applying solutions

As mentioned earlier, it's important that when you apply a hypothetical solution and it doesn't resolve the problem, you find a way to revert back to the configuration that existed prior to attempting the hypothetical solution. If you are diagnosing problems with a workload in a virtual machine, you should use snapshots or checkpoints to roll back to the "last known bad" configuration, which is much better than building a "completely undocumented worse" configuration.

What you want to avoid is trying a number of different hypothetical solutions that don't pan out that involve you making a large number of undocumented configuration changes to your production servers. In continually modifying the configuration of one server in an attempt to resolve one problem, you might end up causing a host of other problems.

So before applying any solution, ensure that you have a rollback strategy that will allow you to return to the current configuration. Put another way, always ensure that you have an escape route for when your meticulously crafted plans go wrong.

The other thing you should do before applying any solution is to have developed a set of criteria to determine what constitutes a resolution of the problem that you are trying to troubleshoot. You need to know what the problem resolution will look like. You should also test whether any of the characteristics of what you have decided constitute the resolution are present before you apply the resolution. If you don't do this it's entirely possible that part of your benchmark for declaring the problem solved may have been met before you attempted the solution. This can lead you to believe that you've solved a problem when the problem is still present. Alternatively, finding that one of your benchmarks for declaring the problem is solved prior to implementing a solution might provide further evidence that you don't understand all of the characteristics of the problem fully.

Operations Management Suite Log Analytics

Log analytics is a part of the Azure Operations Management Suite (OMS). Log analytics is able to analyze your Windows Server 2016 server's event logs and use what has been learned by analyzing millions of such logs to diagnose and report on issues that you may not be aware of. Log analytics uses the computing power available in Azure to perform analysis of log data.

When you configure Log Analytics, log data is forwarded from your on-premises data sources to an OMS repository hosted in Azure. Log Analytics isn't just limited to Windows Server event logs, but can collect data from other Windows logs such as IIS logs, SQL logs, Exchange Server logs, custom text logs and also collect log data from computers running Linux operating systems. Agents can be installed directly on computers, or you can forward data to Log Analytics from a System Center Operations Manager management group.

You interact with Log Analytics through the OMS portal in Azure, shown in Figure 21-1. The portal allows you to run queries to analyze data stored in the OMS repository. It's possible to customize the dashboard to suit your needs. For example, you add solutions to an OMS workspace and these allow you to configure Log Analytics to perform assessments of your environment based on the logs collected. For example, the Security and Audit solution will examine log data to determine if there are security related problems suggested by the logs that should be brought to your attention. The AD Assessment solution examines Active Directory related event log data and can provide you with recommendations to solve problems that you might not know you had.

FIGURE 21-1 Log Analytics dashboard

CHAPTER 21

> ### MORE INFO   LOG ANALYTICS
>
> You can learn more about the Log Analytics at: *https://docs.microsoft.com/en-us/azure/log-analytics/log-analytics-overview*.

Sysinternals tools

The Sysinternals tools are a collection utilities that you can use to diagnose and troubleshoot Windows Server 2016 as well as other Windows Server and client operating systems. The tools are hosted on Microsoft's website and can be used to interact not only with the GUI version of Windows Server 2016, but many of the tools can also be used with the Server Core and Nano Server versions, either directly or remotely. In the following pages you'll learn about several of the Sysinternals tools that you might find useful in troubleshooting and diagnosing your Windows Server 2016 deployment.

> ### MORE INFO   SYSINTERNALS TOOLS
>
> You can learn more about the Sysinternals tools as a whole at: *https://technet.microsoft.com/en-us/sysinternals/bb545021.aspx*.

Process Explorer

Process Explorer, shown in Figure 21-2, allows you to view real-time information about how processes are interacting with resources on a particular computer. Process Explorer can be thought of as a highly advanced version of the built in Task Manager tool. You can use Process Explorer to determine which processes have a specific file open. Process Explorer also allows you to determine which handles a specific process has open, as well as allowing you to see which DLLs and memory-mapped files have been loaded by a specific process.

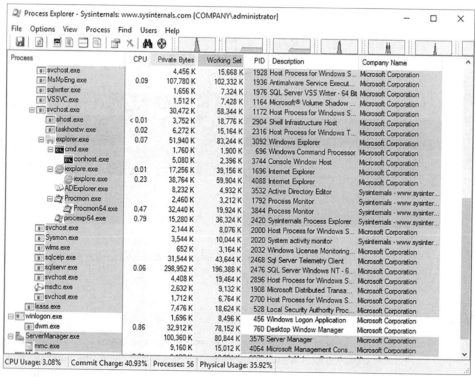

FIGURE 21-2 Process Explorer

Process Explorer includes the following functionality:

- Tree view. This allows you to see the parent/child relationships between processes.

- Color coding. Allows you to visually determine the process type and state, with services, .NET processes, suspended processes and processes running using the same credentials as the user running Process Explorer each being assigned a separate color code.

- Fractional CPU reporting. Shows where processes are consuming minimal amounts of CPU resources, rather than being rounded down to zero, which might imply that the processes were completely inactive.

- Suspicious process identification. Process Explorer will highlight processes that are flagged as suspicious by VirusTotal.com, an anti-malware service.

- Identification of all DLLs and mapped files loaded by a process.

- Identification of all handles to kernel objects opened by a process.

- Ability to determine which processes have open handles to kernel objects, including files and folders.

- Ability to determine which process have loaded a specific DLL.

- View process threads, including start addresses and stacks.

- Modify a process's priority, suspend the process, and terminate a process or a process tree.

- Create a process dump.

MORE INFO   PROCESS EXPLORER

You can learn more about Process Explorer at: *https://technet.microsoft.com/en-us/sysinternals/bb896653*.

Process Monitor

Process Monitor is a real time monitoring tool that you can use to view file system, registry and process/thread activity. You can configure Process Monitor to log data to a file for later analysis, and Process Monitor logging supports scaling to tens of millions of captured events and gigabytes of log data. Process Monitor also includes the ability to capture thread stacks for specific operation, allowing you to determine the root cause of an operation. You can also capture the details of processes including image path, command line, related user or service account, and session ID. Process Monitor is shown in Figure 21-3.

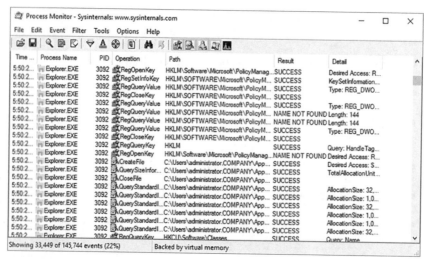

FIGURE 21-3 Process Monitor

> ### MORE INFO   PROCESS MONITOR
>
> You can learn more about Process Monitor at: *https://technet.microsoft.com/en-us/sysinternals/bb896645*.

ProcDump

ProcDump is a command line utility that you can use to monitor a specific application for CPU utilization spikes. You can then generate diagnostic dumps during the spike that allows a developer to determine what causes the spike. ProcDump includes hung window monitor, unhandled exception monitoring, and can be configured to trigger diagnostic dumps based on the values of specific system performance counters.

> ### MORE INFO   PROCDUMP
>
> You can learn more about ProcDump at: *https://technet.microsoft.com/en-us/sysinternals/dd996900*.

PsTools

The PS Tools Suite is a collection of tools named after the UNIX operating system PS utility rather than Microsoft's more recent PowerShell administrative scripting language. You can download the PS Tools Suite in its entirety off Microsoft's website, or download individual tools as you need them. Some tools that are in the PS Tools Suite have functionality that is mirrored by Windows Server 2016 command line utilities or PowerShell cmdlets. The PS Tools Suite has been around since the Sysinternals Tools were first released in the 1990's. The command line utilities and PowerShell cmdlets only became available more recently. Tools included in the PS Tools Suite are as follows:

- **PsExec.** Enact processes remotely.

- **PsFile.** View files that have been opened remotely.

- **PsGetSid.** View the SID of a user or computer.

- **PsInfo.** View system information.

- **PsPing.** Covered in detail later in the chapter, allows you to measure network performance.

- **PsKill.** Terminate processes on the basis of name or process ID.

- **PsList.** Determine detailed information about active processes on a system.

- **PsLoggedOn.** Determine which accounts are signed on locally and through resource sharing.

- **PsLogList.** Extract event log records.

- **PsPassword.** Change account passwords.

- **PsService.** View and manage services.

- **PsShutdown.** Shutdown or reboot a computer.

- **PsSuspend.** Suspends a running process.

Note that some anti-malware tools will flag utilities in the PS Tools Suite as malware. This is because some malware toolchains include and leverage utilities in the PS Tools Suite. If you are concerned that one of the utilities in the PS Tools Suite is malware, use the SigCheck utility, covered later in this chapter, to verify the integrity of the tool in question.

MORE INFO   PSTOOLS

You can learn more about the PsTools collection at: *https://technet.microsoft.com/en-us/ sysinternals/pstools.*

VMMap

VMMap allows you to analyze physical and virtual memory utilization. You can use VMMap to view a specific process's committed virtual memory types and the amount of physical memory (working set) that the operating system has allocated to the process. VMMap is useful when you

need to troubleshoot application memory utilization. Figure 21-4 shows VMMap used to analyze the application ADExplorer.exe.

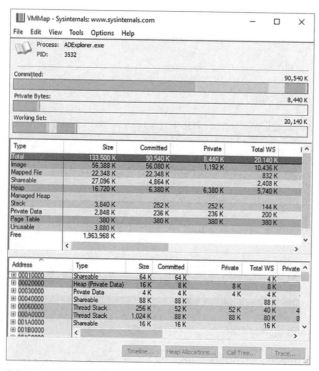

FIGURE 21-4 VMMap

> **MORE INFO   VMMAP**
>
> You can learn more about VMMap at: *https://technet.microsoft.com/en-us/sysinternals/ vmmap.*

SigCheck

Sigcheck is a command line utility that allows you to view the following information:

- File version number

- Time stamp

- Digitial signature details, including certificate chains

Sigcheck also allows you to check a file's status in VirusTotal, a database that scans against 40 separate antivirus engines. You can also use SigCheck to upload the file to be scanned by VirusTotal. Use SigCheck when you suspect a file may have been tampered with or may, for some other reason, not be legitimate. Figure 21-5 shows SigCheck used to check the signature of the file c:\Windows\notepad.exe.

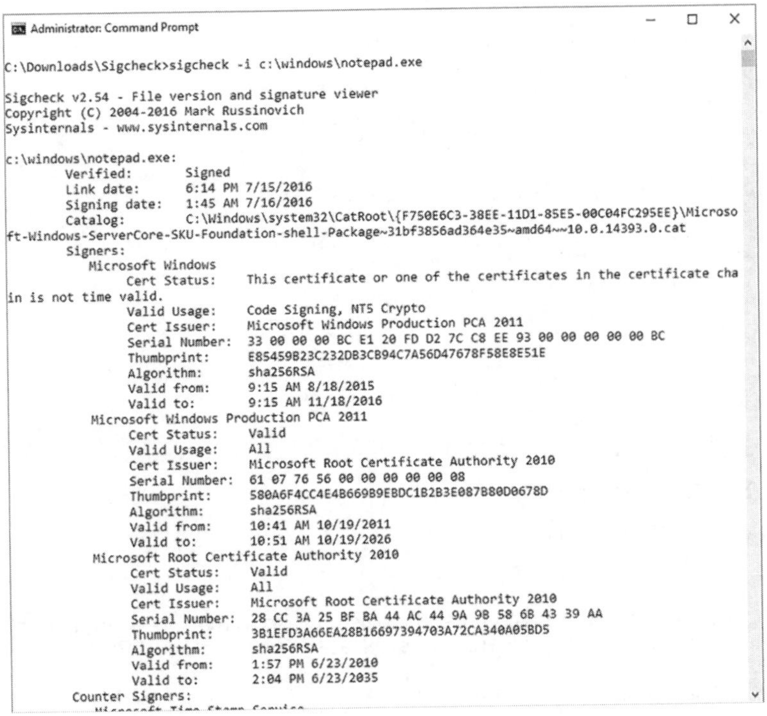

```
Administrator: Command Prompt

C:\Downloads\Sigcheck>sigcheck -i c:\windows\notepad.exe

Sigcheck v2.54 - File version and signature viewer
Copyright (C) 2004-2016 Mark Russinovich
Sysinternals - www.sysinternals.com

c:\windows\notepad.exe:
        Verified:       Signed
        Link date:      6:14 PM 7/15/2016
        Signing date:   1:45 AM 7/16/2016
        Catalog:        C:\Windows\system32\CatRoot\{F750E6C3-38EE-11D1-85E5-00C04FC295EE}\Microso
ft-Windows-ServerCore-SKU-Foundation-shell-Package~31bf3856ad364e35~amd64~~10.0.14393.0.cat
        Signers:
           Microsoft Windows
                Cert Status:    This certificate or one of the certificates in the certificate cha
in is not time valid.
                Valid Usage:    Code Signing, NT5 Crypto
                Cert Issuer:    Microsoft Windows Production PCA 2011
                Serial Number:  33 00 00 00 BC E1 20 FD D2 7C C8 EE 93 00 00 00 00 00 BC
                Thumbprint:     E85459B23C232DB3CB94C7A56D47678F58E8E51E
                Algorithm:      sha256RSA
                Valid from:     9:15 AM 8/18/2015
                Valid to:       9:15 AM 11/18/2016
           Microsoft Windows Production PCA 2011
                Cert Status:    Valid
                Valid Usage:    All
                Cert Issuer:    Microsoft Root Certificate Authority 2010
                Serial Number:  61 07 76 56 00 00 00 00 00 08
                Thumbprint:     580A6F4CC4E4B669B9EBDC1B2B3E087B80D0678D
                Algorithm:      sha256RSA
                Valid from:     10:41 AM 10/19/2011
                Valid to:       10:51 AM 10/19/2026
           Microsoft Root Certificate Authority 2010
                Cert Status:    Valid
                Valid Usage:    All
                Cert Issuer:    Microsoft Root Certificate Authority 2010
                Serial Number:  28 CC 3A 25 BF BA 44 AC 44 9A 9B 58 68 43 39 AA
                Thumbprint:     3B1EFD3A66EA28B16697394703A72CA340A05BD5
                Algorithm:      sha256RSA
                Valid from:     1:57 PM 6/23/2010
                Valid to:       2:04 PM 6/23/2035
        Counter Signers:
```

FIGURE 21-5 SigCheck

MORE INFO SIGCHECK

You can learn more about SigCheck at: ***https://technet.microsoft.com/en-us/sysinternals/bb897441.***

AccessChk

AccessChk is a command line utility that allows you to determine what access user, service, or group accounts have to specific files, folders, registry keys, or Windows services. Using the *Accesschk -?* command provides a list of all options that can be used as shown in Figure 21-6.

CHAPTER 21

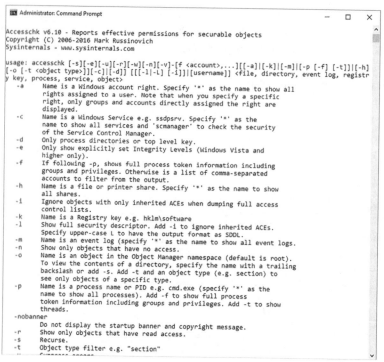

FIGURE 21-6 AccessChk options

For example, using the following command will list the access that the IT group in the Company domain has to the folder c:\downloads\accesschk as shown in Figure 21-7:

```
Accesschk "company\it" c:\downloads\accesschk
```

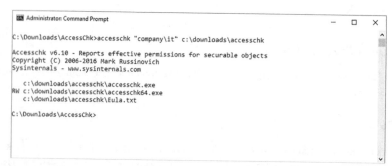

FIGURE 21-7 AccessChk

MORE INFO   ACCESSCHK

You can learn more about AccessChk at: *https://technet.microsoft.com/en-us/ sysinternals/accesschk*.

Sysmon

System Monitor (Sysmon) is a service and device driver that you can install on Windows Server 2016 that monitors and logs system activity to the event logs. Sysmon will remain installed and running across reboots. Sysmon allows you to identify anomalous or malicious activity. It is used by security experts to determine how malware and malicious actors operate when compromising a computer. It is important to understand that while Sysmon monitors and logs potentially hostile activity, it provides no method for you to analyze that activity. A competent attacker will be able to determine that Sysmon is present on a computer and will take appropriate countermeasures.

Sysmon includes the following functionality:

- Logs the creation of processes. This includes information about the command line for the currently created process as well as any parent process.

- Creates a hash of the process image file. The default is SHA1, but you can configure sysmon to use MD5, SHA256 or IMPHASH. You can have multiple hashes created for the same process image file.

- Logs the loading of drivers and DLLS. Records driver signatures and DLL hashes.

- Includes a GUID for each process. This allows you to track activity when Windows Server reuses process IDs for different processes over time.

- Includes a GUID related to each session. This allows you to correlate events to specific logon sessions.

- Logs opens when raw read access to disks and volumes occurs.

- Log network connections. Data written to the log includes connection source processes, IP addresses, port numbers, hostnames used, and port names.

- Detects modifications made to file creation time. Malware and intruders often modify file creation timestamps when cleaning up evidence of a breach.

- Reloads configuration if the configuration is modified in the registry.

- Supports rule filtering, allowing you to include or exclude specific events from being monitored and logged.

- Allows you to generate events during the system startup process. This allows you to capture activity caused by kernel-mode malware.

Sysmon events are stored in the "Applications and Services Logs\Microsoft\Windows\Sysmon\Operational" log folder shown in Figure 21-8.

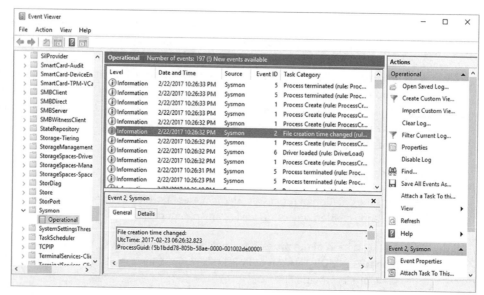

FIGURE 21-8 Sysmon events

Table 21-1 lists important event IDs generated by Sysmon.

Table 21-1 Important Sysmon Event IDs

Event ID	Description
1: Process creation	Includes detailed information about newly created processes. Includes the ProcessGUID field that uniquely identifies the process. Hash generated is a full hash of the associated file using the configured hashing algorithms
2: A process changed a file creation time	An event generated when file creation time is modified by a process. Use this even to track the accurate creation time of a file. Intruders often alter file creation times in an attempt to mask malware to make it look as though it was part of the original operating system installation. It is important to note that many standard processes alter file creation times and it will be necessary to investigate further to determine if the change was part of standard operating system behavior or malicious activity

3: Network connection	Logs TCP and UDP connections to the server. This option is disabled by default when you install Sysmon. When enabled, each connection is associated with a ProcessID an ProcessGUID. Event will record source, destination host names, IP addresses, and port numbers
4: Sysmon service state changed	Records when the Sysmon service starts or stops
5: Process terminated	Records when a process terminates
6: Driver loaded	Records when a driver has loaded. Provides hash and signature information for the driver. Signatures will be created asynchronously to minimize performance impact
7: Image loaded	Records when a process loads a specific module. It is disabled by default when Sysmon is installed and must be manually enabled. It generates hash and signature information asynchronously to minimize performance impact. Only enable with appropriate filtering, because enabling this process will cause a large number of events to be written to the monitoring log
8: CreateRemoteThread	Records when one process creates a thread in another process. This is one strategy used by malware when it injects code to hide it in the execution of another process. Event records both the source and target process. Provides information on the code that runs in the new thread, including StartAddress, StartModule, and StartFunction
9: RawAccessRead	Records when a process performs read operations from storage using the \\.\ denotation. This technique is tracked, because it is often used by malware when exfiltrating files locked for reading. It also avoids most file access auditing technologies. The event records the source process and target device
10: ProcessAccess	Records when one process opens another process, which may involve queries reading or writing data in the address space of the target process. This event ID often records hacking tools that copy the contents of memory used by processes such as the Local Security Authority (Lsass.exe) as part of a Pass-the-Hash attack. Enabling this type of auditing will generate a substantial number of events if diagnostic utilities that query the state of processes are being used on the server. In that case, create filters to remove this expected access
11: FileCreate	Records when a file is created or overwritten. Useful when investigating the status of autostart locations as well as temporary and download locations. These locations are often used by attackers when storing malware during initial server compromise events
12: RegistryEvent (Object create and delete)	Registry modification events, where keys and values are created or deleted, are mapped to this event. Use this event to determine if malware has made modifications to the registry
13: RegistryEvent (Value Set)	Registry modification events, where values are changed. The changes are written as event data

14: RegistryEvent (Key and Value rename)	Registry modification events, where keys and values are renamed. Name changes are written as event data
15: FileCreateStreamHash	Records when a named file stream is created. Creates a hash of the contents of the file. Useful to track malware variants that use browser downloads to drop executables or configuration settings. This problem is less likely to occur if you deploy Server Core or Nano Server as these operating systems don't have browsers built in
255: Error	Generated when Sysmon experiences an error. May occur if Sysmon is under extreme load

MORE INFO   SYSMON

You can learn more about Sysmon at: *https://technet.microsoft.com/en-us/sysinternals/sysmon*.

AccessEnum

AccessEnum allows you to determine where a file, directory, or registry key has separate permissions from its parent object. This allows you to view where permissions have been configured at the object level rather than where the object has inherited the permission from the parent level. This sort of configuration is almost always done manually, though won't be obvious unless surfaced by a tool such as AccessEnum. Figure 21-9 shows where one executable in a directory has different permissions applied to that of the parent directory.

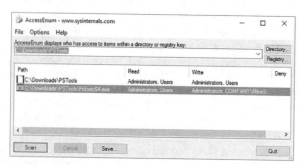

FIGURE 21-9 AccessEnum

MORE INFO   ACCESSENUM

You can learn more about AccessEnum at: *https://technet.microsoft.com/en-us/sysinternals/accessenum*.

ShellRunAs

ShellRunas provides you with the ability to quickly launch applications, including cmd.exe and PowerShell sessions, using the credentials of other users by right clicking and selecting Run as different user from the context menu. You must run shellrunas /reg from an elevated command prompt to register ShellRunas with the computer. Figure 21-10 shows ADExplorer.exe being configured to run with alternate credentials.

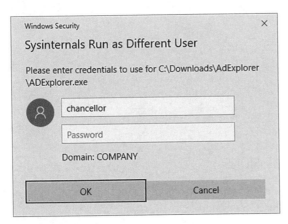

FIGURE 21-10 ShellRunAs

MORE INFO   SHELLRUNAS

You can learn more about ShellRunAs at: *https://technet.microsoft.com/en-us/sysinternals/cc300361*.

LogonSessions

LogonSessions is a command line utility that allows you to view the activity of all active sessions on a Windows Server 2016 system. When used with the *-p* option, as shown in Figure 21-11, you're also able to see which processes are running in each session. This tool can be also used when connected to a remote PowerShell session to determine which active sessions are present on a server.

```
Administrator: Command Prompt                                                — □ ×
  Logon time:     2/22/2017 5:35:52 PM
  Logon server:
  DNS Domain:     Company.Pri
  UPN:            S2-GUI$@Company.Pri
   2480: sqlceip.exe

[9] Logon session 00000000:000280cd:
  User name:      COMPANY\administrator
  Auth package:   Kerberos
  Logon type:     Interactive
  Session:        1
  Sid:            S-1-5-21-1209835909-451737803-142381162-500
  Logon time:     2/22/2017 5:36:36 PM
  Logon server:   DC1
  DNS Domain:     COMPANY.PRI
  UPN:            administrator@COMPANY.PRI
   2708: RuntimeBroker.exe
   2324: sihost.exe
   2312: svchost.exe
   2300: taskhostw.exe
   3084: explorer.exe
   3312: ShellExperienceHost.exe
   3392: SearchUI.exe
   3580: ServerManager.exe
   3744: Taskmgr.exe
   1748: iexplore.exe
   3304: iexplore.exe
   4416: ApplicationFrameHost.exe
   4272: cmd.exe
   3220: conhost.exe
```

FIGURE 21-11 Logon Sessions

MORE INFO   LOGONSESSIONS

You can learn more about LogonSessions at: *https://technet.microsoft.com/en-us/ sysinternals/logonsessions.*

Active Directory Explorer

Active Directory Explorer (AD Explorer) provides you with a detailed view of and ability to edit Active Directory objects. It's in some ways a more advanced and substantially more user friendly version of the ADSIEdit utility that is built into Windows Server 2016. You can use AD Explorer to view Active Directory object properties and attributes as shown in Figure 21-12.

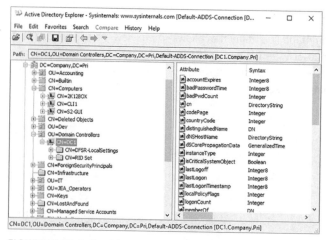

FIGURE 21-12 Active Directory Explorer

You can also use AD Explorer to save snapshots of the AD database for offline viewing. You can also use the tool to directly compare separate snapshots of the AD database, which can be very useful in recovery scenarios where you have several copies of the AD database and are unsure which version to restore to your production environment.

When connecting to a live AD instance, specify the domain name, user name and password as shown in Figure 21-13. You can also save connection properties, allowing you to reconnect to different domains as necessary.

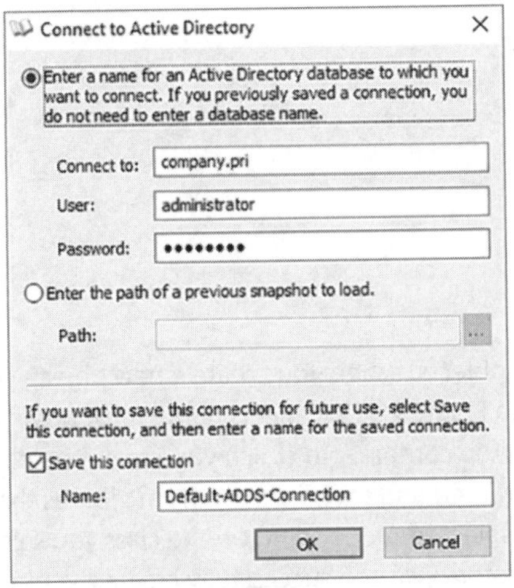

FIGURE 21-13 Connect to AD Database

When you specify the domain name, AD Explorer will connect to a domain controller in the same site. If you want to connect to a specific domain controller, you can specify the address of the domain controller using FQDN or the IP address. In addition to mounting existing snapshots of the Active Directory database, you can also use AD Explorer to connect to AD LDS instances.

You can use AD Explorer to rename or delete objects. You can also view and modify individual attributes of an object on the Attributes tab of the object's properties as shown in Figure 21-14.

FIGURE 21-14 Object properties

You can also use AD Explorer to create new objects. When you create a new object, you must specify which class is belongs to, as shown in Figure 21-15. Objects name must begin with the designator CN= and must be unique within the container in which you create the object. The object's attribute list will automatically be created and set based on the attributes that are mandatory for the class of object that you have selected. Depending on the class you select, you'll need to configure several of these objects before you can successfully create the object.

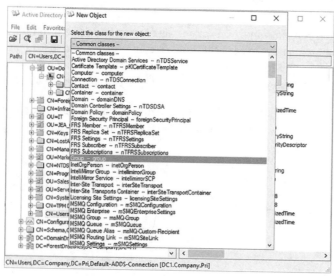

FIGURE 21-15 Create object

> **MORE INFO   ACTIVE DIRECTORY EXPLORER**
>
> You can learn more about ADExplorer at: *https://technet.microsoft.com/en-us/sysinternals/adexplorer*.

Insight for Active Directory

ADInsight (Insight for Active Directory) allows you to monitor LDAP traffic. You can use ADInsight to resolve problems with Windows authentication, DNS, and other applications and services that interact with Active Directory.

ADInsight allows you to troubleshoot LDAP traffic by intercepting calls that applications make to the wldap32.dll library. This library is the foundation used for Active Directory APIs including ADSI and ldap. ADInsight differs from traditional network monitoring tools in that it will intercept and interpret all Active Directory related client-side APIs. This includes those Active Directory related client-side APIs that do not directly transmit data to a domain controller. When used with administrator privileges, ADInsight allows you to monitor windows services and other system processes.

> **MORE INFO   INSIGHT FOR ACTIVE DIRECTORY**
>
> You can learn more about Insight for Active Directory at: *https://technet.microsoft.com/en-us/sysinternals/bb897539*.

PsPing

You can use PsPing as an advanced network diagnostic utility that has a superset of the ping. exe utility's functionality. PsPing allows you to measure TCP ping, network latency, and network bandwidth. PsPing is able to report information to within 0.01 milliseconds, which is 100 times more accurate than the standard Ping utility. Use the following commands to determine information about each mode:

- **Psping -? i.** Provides information on ICMP ping functionality.

- **Psping -? t.** Provides information on TCP ping functionality.

- **Psping -? l.** Provides information on TCP/UDP latency tests.

- **Psping -? b.** Shown in Figure 21-16, provides information on TCP/UDP bandwidth tests.

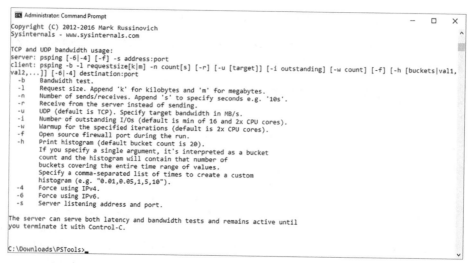

FIGURE 21-16 PsPing bandwidth check

MORE INFO   PSPING

You can learn more about PsPing at: *https://technet.microsoft.com/en-us/sysinternals/psping*.

RAMMap

RAMMap provides advanced information about how physical memory is used on computers running Windows operating systems. The separate tabs of RAMMap provide the following information:

- **Use Counts.** Shown in Figure 21-17, this tab provides summary information by type. Categories include Process Private, Mapped File, Sharable, Page Table, Paged Pool, Nonpaged Pool, System PTE, Session Private, Metafile, Address Windowing Extension (AWE), Driver Locked, Kernel Stack, Large Page and Unused.

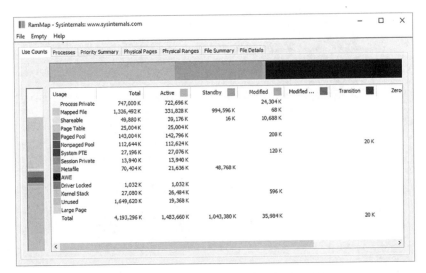

FIGURE 21-17 RAMMap

- **Processes.** Provides information about the size of process working sets. Includes information about PID, Private memory, Standby, Modified, Page Table and Total physical memory utilization.

- **Priority Summary.** Shows the size of prioritized standby lists. If items with priority 5 and higher show high repurpose counts, it's likely that the server is under memory pressure and would likely benefit from the addition of more physical memory.

- **Physical Pages.** Shows per page information of all physical memory in the computer. Provides physical page information including physical address, list membership, allocation type, priority, whether the page stores part of an image, offset within a page table, file name of mapped file, originating process, virtual address and any paged and non-paged memory pool tag.

- **Physical Ranges.** Lists the physical ranges used in terms of start address, end address, and overall size.

- **File Summary.** Provides details of files that are stored in physical memory.

File Details. Shown in Figure 21-18, displays memory pages in physical RAM on a per file basis.

CHAPTER 21

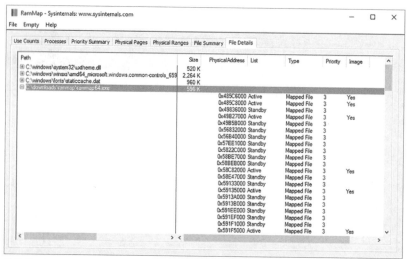

FIGURE 21-18 RAMMap File Details

You use RAMMap when you need to understand how Windows Server 2016 manages memory. For example, you can use it to determine how physical memory is allocated to a specific process or file. You can search memory for a specific file or process by using Ctrl+F. You can also RAM-Map to take snapshots of how physical memory is being allocated at a specific point in time for later analysis. You can also use RAMMap to purge portions of RAM when testing memory management scenarios.

MORE INFO   RAMMAP

You can learn more about RAMMap at: *https://technet.microsoft.com/en-us/sysinternals/rammap*.

Inside OUT

Support Calls

It's an old truism in IT that when all else fails, read the manual, and when that fails, call support. The trick to calling support is to have documented enough about the problem as possible that support doesn't need to spend time going back over pathways that you've already fruitlessly explored. The more information you can provide to support, the more quickly they can get down to investigating your issue and hopefully providing you with a resolution. You'll get a lot more out of your support experience if you go into it prepared rather than if you approach support without having done your homework and hoping that they can magically resolve everything for you.

Index

A